COST ACCOUNTING

A MANAGERIAL EMPHASIS

COST ACCOUNTING
a managerial emphasis

SECOND EDITION

CHARLES T. HORNGREN, Ph.D., C.P.A.
Stanford University

PRENTICE-HALL INC., ENGLEWOOD CLIFFS, N. J.

Library of Congress Catalog Card No.: 67-12604

Printed in the United States of America

Current Printing (last digit)
10

PRENTICE-HALL INTERNATIONAL, INC., London
PRENTICE-HALL OF AUSTRALIA, PTY. LTD., Sydney
PRENTICE-HALL OF CANADA, LTD., Toronto
PRENTICE-HALL OF INDIA (PRIVATE) LTD., New Delhi
PRENTICE-HALL OF JAPAN, INC. Tokoyo

TO PROFESSOR WILLIAM J. VATTER

preface

Cost Accounting: A Managerial Emphasis is a flexible textbook for cost accounting courses which presuppose at least one semester of basic accounting. Cost accounting provides data for three major purposes: (1) planning and controlling routine operations, (2) nonroutine decisions, policy-making and long-range planning, (3) inventory valuation and income determination. This volume gives abundant consideration to all three important purposes, but emphasis is placed on the first two.

This book's goal is to put cost accounting in focus as a highly developed quantitative device for helping managers select and reach their objectives. Ample attention is devoted to accounting systems and procedures for data accumulation, but stress is given to the concepts that make modern cost accounting dynamic and vital. In short, the major theme of this book is "different costs for different purposes."

Today the business world typically wants students with perspective, an ability to analyze, an ability to distinguish the important from the unimportant. Why then should the crucial and intriguing problems be withheld from the basic course in cost accounting? The time has come for a change in emphasis—a front and center spotlighting of costs for planning and control. The conventional emphasis on systems and procedures for data accumulation should be shifted either to the advanced cost accounting course or to the course on accounting systems. Too often, the accounting major learns procedures for data accumulation in the first cost accounting course and then again in a later course on accounting systems. This is wasteful because he is likely to obtain only a superficial exposure to the core of cost accounting. Furthermore, the student who can take only one course in cost accounting is being neglected if he has to settle for a course that dwells primarily on scorekeeping techniques.

The topics emphasized from the outset are those that jar the student and spur his curiosity. Because this book emphasizes costs for planning and control, the following topics of prime managerial significance are introduced early in the text: the role of the accountant in the organization; cost behavior and volume-profit relationships; responsibility accounting; standard costs; flexible budgets; cost structures for control and motivation; and relevant costs for nonroutine decisions.

The subjects that the student finds tedious are usually of second-ary importance from the viewpoint of the effective management account-ant. Consequently, the following topics appear either as appendices or as late chapters: factory ledgers, detailed payroll and material book-keeping, detailed process costing, routes of a multitude of business docu-ments, and alternate methods of overhead analysis. The favorable reaction to the format of the first edition of this book has demonstrated that the cost accounting course can be enriched, relieved of much drudgery, and broadened from a course in techniques alone to a full-fledged course in concepts, analysis, and techniques which pays more than lip-service to accounting as a managerial tool.

The overall coverage of subject matter is about the same as was contained in the first edition, except for the addition of a new chapter on sales mix and production mix and yield variances.

The major organizational changes in this revision are:

1.　Gathering the material on process costing in one place in Chapters 19 and 20, which can be considered in conjunction with Chapter 4 if desired;

2.　Switching the order of the old Chapters 5 and 6 so that the chapter on comprehensive budgeting precedes the first chapter on standard costs. In addition, this change permits a well-knit coverage of standard costs and flexible budgets in three successive chapters (6, 7, and 8);

3.　Switching the order of the old Chapters 8 and 9 so that the material on responsibility accounting and motivation may be studied after coverage of the techniques of standard costs and flexible budgets;

4.　Moving the old Chapter 20 (on divisional performance measurement) to Chapter 11 so that its fundamental importance in today's organizations is better recognized;

5.　Moving the old Chapter 18 (on nonmanufacturing costs) to Chap-ter 12 so that the student can readily see that cost accounting is not confined to manufacturing situations;

6.　Moving the old Chapter 21 (on advanced topics in capital budgeting) to Chapter 15 so that the material on capital budgeting is intact in two successive chapters.

This book is written to make the learning process as painless as possible. Four innovations in this regard have been introduced in this edition:

1.　Most chapters contain a Problem for Self-Study together with its solution.

2.　A glossary of cost accounting terms is available to ease the inevitable difficulties in the learning of terminology.

3.　A note at the beginning of the assignment material for each chapter points out those problems which may be of special importance.

4.　Many new problems have been added to stress key points. For instance, consider Problems 2-28, 3-24 through 3-26, 4-14, 4-16, 5-15, 6-23, and 6-29. Others are apparent for each chapter.

This book contains ample material for a two-semester or two-quarter course, especially if it is supplemented with outside readings in the second course. The first ten chapters plus Chapter 13 provide the essence of a one-term course. Instructors tend to disagree as to the proper sequence of teaching the chapters in almost any text. Hence the book has been organized and written to fit the desires of the individual instructor without breaking the smoothness of his presentation. For example, some instructors prefer to introduce process costing (Chapters 19 and 20) and payroll accounting (Chapter 24) immediately after the consideration of job order costing in Chapter 4. This can be easily done without destroying continuity.

Other instructors prefer to weave in the newer quantitative techniques as they relate to the introduction of particular topics. For instance, Chapter 26 (subjective probabilities) can be assigned along with Chapter 14 (capital budgeting); Chapter 27 (statistical methods) can be linked with Chapter 6 (standard costs). In sum, abundant cross-referencing throughout the book will help instructors tailor-make a cohesive course for particular groups of students.

The following listing may be a helpful guide to those instructors who may want to select certain late chapters for earlier treatment:

Chapter	Section 4	May be Assigned Anytime After Chapter
16	Inventory Planning, Control, and Valuation	13
17	Alternative Methods of Overhead Application and Reapportionment	8
18	Joint Product Costs and By-Product Costs	4
*19	Process Costing: A Type of Product Costing	4
*20	Spoilage, Waste, Defective Units, and Scrap	4
	Section 5	
22, 23	Any one of these chapters on accounting	
24	systems can be assigned anytime after Chapter 4.	
	Section 6	
25	Cost Accounting in the C.P.A. Examination	20
26	Decision-Making: Uncertainty, Subjective Probabilities, and the Accountant	13
27	Cost Accounting and Statistical Methods	6
28	Cost Accounting and Operations Research	13

*Excluding those sections on standard costing.

There is a full supply of the all-important homework material. The variety of problems allows wide choice both in subject matter and in range of difficulty. The need for pertinent, well-edited homework material has received extensive attention and has been regarded as a key phase of this book's preparation.

To summarize, this book approaches cost accounting from a multi-purpose viewpoint. Its organizational framework presents the important general topics near the front of the book. At the same time, special care has been taken in writing individual chapters to allow the utmost flexibility without sacrificing continuity.

I am indebted to many for ideas and assistance. The acknowledgments in the first edition contain a long list of my creditors. My primary obligation is to Professor William J. Vatter (now at the University of California, Berkeley), to whom this book is dedicated. For those who know him, no words are necessary; for those who do not know him, no words will suffice.

My former colleagues at the University of Chicago have my lasting gratitude.

Professor Samuel Laimon, University of Saskatchewan, has aided immeasurably with his detailed review of the manuscript of this edition. The reviews by Professors Gibbes Ulmer Miller, The Florida State University, and Alfred Rappaport, Tulane University, have also been significantly helpful.

Many students have read the manuscript and worked the new problems so that they are as error free as possible.

A special note of appreciation is extended to Raymonde Rousselot, for her cheerful, diligent, and skillful secretarial work.

Appreciation also goes to the American Institute of Certified Public Accountants, the National Association of Accountants, the Society of Industrial and Cost Accountants of Canada, the Certified General Accountants' Association of Canada, the Financial Executives Institute of America, and to many other publishers and companies for their generous permission to quote from their publications. Problems from the Uniform CPA Examinations are designated [C.P.A.]; problems from the Canadian examinations administered by the Society of Industrial and Cost Accountants are designated [S.I.C.A.]; problems from the Certified General Accountants' Association are designated [C.G.A.A.]. Many of these problems are adapted to highlight particular points.

Comments from users are welcome.

CHARLES T. HORNGREN

contents

COST ACCOUNTING
FUNDAMENTALS

Section 1

PLANNING AND CONTROLLING
ROUTINE OPERATIONS

Section 2

RETURN ON CAPITAL BY PLANTS, PRODUCTS, AND DIVISIONS: Allocations are needed; Rate-of-return targets are flexible; Harmony between goals; Over-emphasis on rate-of-return; The time period and managerial efficiency. TRANSFER PRICING: Intracompany transfers; Cost bases; Pricing at variable cost; Market price basis; Negotiated market prices; Fictitious profit centers; Coordination of objectives. ACCOUNTING ENTRIES FOR TRANSFERS. SUMMARY. SUGGESTED READINGS. PROBLEM FOR SELF-STUDY. QUESTIONS, PROBLEMS, AND CASES.

XII. nonmanufacturing costs 365

COMPARISON OF MARKETING AND MANUFACTURING COSTS. CON-TROLLING ORDER-FILLING AND ADMINISTRATIVE COSTS: Work measure-ment; Need for measurement; Budgeting of order-filling and administrative costs: two approaches; The variable cost approach: ideal standards; The dis-cretionary cost approach: currently attainable standards; Follow-up of dis-cretionary costs; Difficulties in applying work measurement; Budgets in practice: Combination of variable and fixed costs. ORDER-GETTING: General charac-teristics of order-getting costs; Need for experimentation; Concentration on profitable opportunities: planning is crucial; Budgeting order-getting costs: influential factors; Field selling; Example of control of salesmen; Standard costs and selling effort. THE ROBINSON-PATMAN ACT. CLASSIFICATION AND ALLOCATION: Allocation bases: weakness of sales dollars; Functional costing: allocate with care. EXAMPLES OF CONTRIBUTION APPROACH: Need for reports; Example 1: profitability of distribution channels; Example 2: profit contribution per unit of retail selling space. RESEARCH AND DEVELOPMENT: Definition; Accounting for research; Amount to be spent; Details of current con-trol; Allocating research costs to divisions; Disposition of research costs. SUM-MARY. SUGGESTED READINGS. PROBLEM FOR SELF-STUDY. QUESTIONS, PROBLEMS, AND CASES.

COST ANALYSIS FOR NONROUTINE DECISIONS
AND LONG-RANGE PLANNING

Section 3

XIII. relevant costs: a key concept in special decisions 405

THE ACCOUNTANT'S ROLE IN SPECIAL DECISIONS: Reporter of relevant data: relevance and accuracy; Qualitative and quantitative factors. MEANING OF RELEVANCE. ILLUSTRATIONS OF RELEVANCE: CHOOSING ACTIVITY LEVELS: The special order; Differential cost; Fixed expenses and unit costs; Short run and long run; Qualitative factors; Reports for decision making; Dropping a product line; Contribution per unit of constraining factor; Make

or buy and idle facilities; Essence of make or buy: opportunity cost; Policy making
for make or buy; Beware of unit costs. IRRELEVANCE OF PAST COSTS: Book
value of old equipment; Examining alternatives over the long run. THE PROB-
LEM OF UNCERTAINTY. SUMMARY. PROBLEM FOR SELF-STUDY. APPENDIX:
COST TERMS USED FOR DIFFERENT PURPOSES. QUESTIONS, PROBLEMS,
AND CASES.

XIV. introduction to capital budgeting (project selection)   439

CONTRASTS IN PURPOSES OF COST ANALYSIS.   DEFINITION OF
CAPITAL BUDGETING.   URGENCY AND PERSUASION.   DISCOUNTED
CASH FLOW: Time value of money; Time-adjusted rate of return; Explanation
of compound interest; Depreciation and discounted cash flow; Net present value
method.   COMPARISON OF NET PRESENT VALUE AND TIME-ADJUSTED
METHODS.   THE NET PRESENT VALUE COMPARISON OF TWO PROJECTS:
Incremental versus total project approach; Analysis of typical items under dis-
counted cash flow. PAYBACK: Uniform cash inflows; Nonuniform cash inflows;
The bail-out factor: a better approach to payback.   THE PAYBACK RECIP-
ROCAL: Annuity formula and payback reciprocal; Limitations of payback
reciprocal; Relationships of payback reciprocal to rate of return.   ADMINIS-
TRATION OF CAPITAL BUDGETS.   SUMMARY.   PROBLEM FOR SELF-STUDY.
APPENDIX A: ACCOUNTING METHOD OF RATE OF RETURN: Equations; The
denominator: investment base; Initial investment as a base; Current assets as a
part of investment base; Danger of understating investment; Accounting
method is an averaging technique; Conflict of concepts and purposes; Uneven
cash flows; Postaudit; Understandability; Problem for self-study for Appendix A.
APPENDIX B: NOTES ON COMPOUND INTEREST: Interest; Interest tables.
QUESTIONS, PROBLEMS, AND CASES.

XV. a closer look at capital budgeting   489

INCOME TAX FACTORS: Importance of income taxes; Timing and different
depreciation methods; The best depreciation method; Effects of income taxes
on cash flow; Income tax complications.   RATIONING CAPITAL AMONG
PROJECTS: Budget constraint; Different sizes of projects and budget constraints;
Mutually exclusive alternatives and budget constraints; Investment indivisibilities.
MULTIPLE ALTERNATIVES: Illustration of over-all versus incremental approach;
Incremental approach is best; Danger of using over-all approach.   RANKING
DIFFICULTIES AND UNEQUAL LIVES: Conflict of ranking techniques; Unequal
lives and reinvestment; Equipment replacement; Reinvestment outlook.   RE-
CAPITULATION. MINIMUM DESIRED RATE OF RETURN: COST OF CAPITAL:
Importance of concept; Complexity of measuring; Computation of cost of
capital; The problem of growth; Borrowing rate and lending rate; Degree of
risk or uncertainty; Using equity rate as cost of capital.   SUMMARY.   SUG-
GESTED READINGS.   PROBLEMS FOR SELF-STUDY.   APPENDIX: THE
FINANCIAL LEASE. QUESTIONS, PROBLEMS, AND CASES.

SPECIAL TOPICS FOR FURTHER STUDY

Section 4

ACCOUNTING SYSTEMS

Section

A REAPPRAISAL

Section 6

APPENDIXES

Section 7

COST ACCOUNTING
FUNDAMENTALS

SECTION 1

the accountant's role in the
organization

As this book goes to press, former accountants are the top executives in many large companies, including General Motors, General Electric, and Chrysler. Accounting duties played a key part in their rise to the managerial summit. The cost accountant's duties are entwined with executive planning and control.

The perceptive student soon discovers that the study of cost accounting yields insight and breadth regarding both the accountant's role and the manager's role in business. How are these two roles related? Where may they overlap? How can accounting help managers in running their companies? This book tries to answer these questions. In this chapter, we[1] shall try to get some notion of where the accountant should fit in modern business. Then we shall have a framework for the more technical discussions which begin in Chapter 2.

MANAGEMENT ACCOUNTING, FINANCIAL ACCOUNTING, AND COST ACCOUNTING

The accounting system is the major quantitative information system in almost every organization. It should provide information for three broad purposes:

1. Internal reporting to managers, for use in planning and controlling routine operations;

[1] Should an author use "I," "we," "the author," or "this writer," in contexts such as these? Each mode of expression has weaknesses, but I prefer "we." As used in this book, "we" denotes a mutual exploration of the subject by the author and the readers.

3

2. Internal reporting to managers, for use in making nonroutine decisions and in formulating major plans and policies; and
3. External reporting to stockholders, government, and other outside parties.

Both management and external parties share an interest in all three important purposes, but the emphases of financial accounting and management (internal) accounting differ. Financial accounting has been mainly concerned with the historical, custodial, and stewardship aspects of external reporting. The distinguishing feature of management accounting—of accounting for planning and control—is its emphasis on the first and second purposes.

Where does "cost accounting" fit within the above framework? In its broadest sense, cost accounting has three major purposes, which parallel the three purposes above. Its first and second purposes are identical to the first and second above. Its third purpose, costing products for inventory valuation and income determination, simultaneously fulfills the demands of outsiders and those of management for such information. So, when viewed in this way, cost accounting *is* management accounting plus a small part of financial accounting—to the extent that its product-costing function satisfies the requisites of external reporting. When the term *managerial cost accounting* is used in this book, it will denote an emphasis on the first two purposes. Clearly, managerial cost accounting is much more important than financial accounting in operating the firm itself.

"Managerial" cost accounting removes accounting from its bookkeeping straitjacket. The accumulation of figures—the costing of inventories—is only one aspect of the management accountant's duties. The modern emphasis is on the accountant's positive responsibility for objective analysis and interpretation. The management accountant deals primarily with the current period and the future instead of with the past. Managerial cost accounting is the most dynamic phase of the entire accounting field. As the scope of business extends beyond a one-man management operation, accounting serves management by supplying a quantitative means of wrestling with business problems. Managers are kept informed by accounting reports. The bigger the business, the greater the need becomes for useful reports.

Accounting is a service function. It helps management do a better job than can be done without it. Good accounting helps management; bad accounting hinders and misleads management. If accounting serves only to satisfy record-keeping laws or to compile historical reports for outsiders such as lending agencies, it serves primarily a financial purpose and its major usefulness to management is foregone.

Helping management to plan and control is the phase of accounting that offers the greatest challenges and the more intricate intellectual problems. It is the phase that overlaps many related areas—the behavioral sciences, engineering, economics, law, finance, statistics, and mathematics. Modern management, faced with a bewildering mass of decisions, realizes the need for a systematic, tailored approach to its problems at reasonable cost in terms of time, headaches, and money. Alert accountants can fulfill that need.

A CAPSULE LOOK AT MODERN MANAGEMENT

Information is needed for planning and control

Consider some fundamental ideas that are not new but that do need emphasis. Management's task is to plan and to control. *Planning* means selecting objectives and the means for their attainment. In other words, planning embraces the answers to two questions: What is desired? How and when is it to be done? *Controlling* means obtaining conformity to plans.

Both planning and controlling entail decision-making, which means choosing among alternative courses of action. Decisions tend to be more fruitful when they are based upon considered judgment rather than upon hunches or guessing. Considered judgment requires the gathering of *relevant* information in the right form at the right time. It requires the ability to distinguish the relevant from the irrelevant, the important from the unimportant. Such ability is the earmark of a good accountant and of a good manager.

Management by exception

Exhibit 1-1 shows the relationship between accounting and management planning and control. Note the management cycle: (1) plan; (2) act; (3) evaluate, with focus on exceptions for appraisal and corrective action.

EXHIBIT 1-1

ACCOUNTING FRAMEWORK FOR PLANNING AND CONTROL

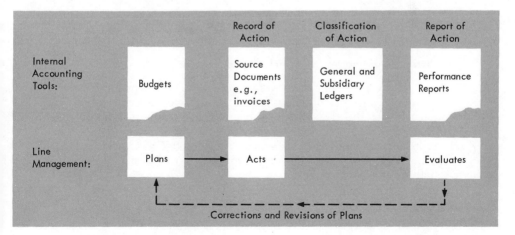

Accounting formalizes plans by expressing them in the language of figures as *budgets*. It formalizes control by *performance reports*, which compare results with plans and spotlight exceptions. These reports spur investigation of exceptions. Then operations are brought into conformity with the plans or the plans are revised. This is an example of *management by exception*, which means that the executive's attention and effort are concentrated on the important deviations from expected results. Such a system reflects the needs of managers, who want their attention directed to unusual situations and who do not want to be bothered about the smoothly running phases of operations.

As conceived here, managerial control means action and evaluation that keeps the company ship on course. Control action is taken primarily by individuals. Note that the definition of control implies that plans already existed. Thus the notion of control is necessarily interlocked with implicit or explicit managerial planning. Planning is really much more vital than control; that is, superior control is fruitless if faulty plans are being implemented. Planning and control are so intertwined that it seems artificial to draw rigid lines of separation between them. Still, at times we will find it useful to focus on one or the other phase of the planning-control cycle.

Well-conceived plans incorporate enough flexibility or discretion so that the manager may feel free to seize any unforeseen opportunities to improve efficiency or effectiveness. That is—and this is important—the definition of control as conformity with plans does not mean that managers should rigidly, blindly adhere to a pre-existing plan when unfolding events indicate the desirability of actions which were not encompassed specifically in the original plan.

Note that planning and controlling require good *organization*, which means that managers must know their limits and the requirements of their responsibility and authority. Good organization helps coordination and communications. A manager knows what is expected of him, and he also knows that those expectations will be compared with his performance. One of accounting's main tasks is to report these expectations and this performance in a clear, useful manner.

Example of budgets and performance reports

Assume that there is an assembly department for making chassis for television sets. A chassis is wired and tubes inserted, largely by hand operations. It is then inspected before it goes to the finishing department. The department assembles two basic types of chassis. In the light of the sales outlook, a production schedule for 1,000 Type A and 2,000 Type B chassis is planned for the coming month. Cost classifications include the following:

	Plan (Budget)
Material (detailed by type: tubes, wiring, solder, etc.)	$ 72,000
Assembly labor (detailed by job classifications, number of workers, etc.)	135,000
Other labor (inspectors, material handlers)	25,000
Utilities, repairs, etc.	5,000
Supplies (small tools, glue, sweeping compound, lubricants, etc.)	3,000
Total	$240,000

The operating plan (the department budget) for the coming month is prepared in conferences attended by the foreman, his supervisor, and an accountant. Each of the cost items subject to the foreman's control is scrutinized. Its average amount for the past few months often is used as a guide, especially where past performance has been reasonably efficient. However, the budget is a *forecast* of what costs should be. Each cost figure is projected, considering trends, price changes, alterations in product mix, specifications, and labor methods, and changes in production volume from month to month. The budget is then formulated; it becomes the foreman's target for the month.

As actual[2] factory costs are incurred during the month, the accounting department collects and classifies them by factory departments. At the end of the month (perhaps daily or weekly for key items such as materials or assembly labor), the accounting department prepares a *performance report* for the assembly department that might appear as follows:

ASSEMBLY DEPARTMENT
Performance Report*
For the Month Ending January 31, 19x1

	Budget	Actual	Variance[†]
Material	$ 72,000	$ 73,000	$1,000 U
Assembly labor	135,000	140,000	5,000 U
Other labor	25,000	24,000	1,000 F
Utilities, repairs, etc.	5,000	4,700	300 F
Supplies	3,000	3,400	400 U
	$240,000	$245,100	$5,100 U

U – Unfavorable
F – Favorable
* This report would be extremely detailed in practice.
† Explanations of reasons for variances should accompany this
  performance report.

The foreman and his superior(s) use this report to help appraise performance. The spotlight is cast on the *variances*—the deviations from the budget. It is through managerial investigation of these variances that improvements in operations are initiated. Whereas the budget aids planning, this *performance report* is the tool that aids controlling. Managerial effort is directed to exceptions (variances, deviations) with the help of the accounting system. Exhibit 1-1 shows that accounting does *not* do the controlling. Managers and their workmen do the controlling as action takes place. Accounting helps the managerial control function by providing a prompt record of the actions and by systematically pinpointing trouble spots. This management-by-exception approach frees managers from needless concern with those phases of operations that are functioning effectively.

[2] The word "actual" connotes a precision that is unattainable in practice. It is used here to distinguish sharply between incurred (actual) costs and budgeted costs.

Role of the accountant in organization: line and staff

Except for exerting line authority over his own department, the chief accounting executive generally fills a staff role in his company, as contrasted with the line roles of sales and production executives.   Most companies have the production and sale of goods as their basic objectives. Line managers are *directly* responsible for attaining these objectives as efficiently as possible.

Staff elements of organizations exist because the scope of the line manager's responsibility and duties enlarges to such a degree that he needs specialized help to operate effectively.   When a department's primary task is that of advice and service to other departments, it is a *staff* department.

However, many conflicting theories have arisen that blur the distinctions between "line" and "staff."   This is so because of the recent research in "organization theory," which has been accentuated by the telling effects of digital computers on organization structures.   But, despite the whirling confusion, we shall find that line-staff distinctions are useful in evaluating the accountant's role in the organization.

The accounting function is usually "staff" with responsibility for providing line managers, and also other staff managers, with specialized service.[3]   This includes advice and help in the areas of budgeting, controlling, pricing, and special decisions.   The accounting department does not exercise direct authority over line departments.   Uniformity of accounting and reporting is acquired through the top line management's delegation of authority on such matters to the controller.   Note carefully that when the controller prescribes the line department's role in supplying accounting information, he is speaking for top line management—not as the controller, a staff man.   The uniform accounting procedure is authorized by the president and is installed for him by the controller.

Theoretically, the controller's decisions regarding the best accounting procedures to be followed by line people are transmitted to the president.   In turn, the president communicates these procedures through a manual of instructions which comes down through the line chain of command to all people affected by the procedures.

Practically, the daily work of the controller is such that his face-to-face relationships with the production manager or foreman may call for his directing how production records should be kept or how work tickets should be completed.[4]   The controller usually holds delegated authority from top line management over such matters.

Exhibit 1-2 shows the general organizational relationships described above.   Exhibit 1-3 shows how a controller's own department may be organized.

---

[3] Management literature is hazy on these distinctions, and we shall not belabor them here. For example, some writers distinguish among three types of authority: line, staff, and functional. Line authority is exerted downward over subordinates. Staff authority is the authority to *advise* but not command others; it is exercised laterally or upward. Functional authority is the right to *command* action laterally and downward with regard to a specific function or specialty.

[4] According to some writers, this would be exercising the *functional authority* described in the previous footnote.

EXHIBIT 1-2

PARTIAL ORGANIZATION CHART OF A MANUFACTURING COMPANY

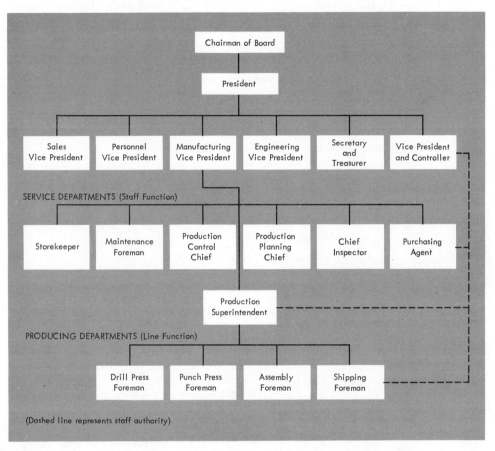

(Dashed line represents staff authority)

THE PERVADING DUTIES OF THE CONTROLLER: THE CHIEF MANAGEMENT ACCOUNTANT

Meaning of the word "controller"

The word *controller*[5] is applied to various accounting positions. The stature and duties of the controller vary from company to company. In some firms, he is little more than a glorified bookkeeper who compiles data primarily for conventional balance sheets and income statements. In other firms—for example, General Electric—he is a key executive who aids management planning and control in over 100 subdivisions. In most firms, he has a status somewhere between these two extremes. For example, his

---

[5] *Controller* is sometimes spelled *comptroller*, a French version of the same word. Both words should be pronounced kŏn trōl′ ẽr.

opinion on the tax implications of certain managerial decisions may be carefully weighed, yet his opinion on the other aspects of these decisions may not be sought. Whatever his title, he is viewed in this book as the chief management accounting executive. The point of terminology here is that the modern controller does not do any controlling in terms of line authority, except over his own department. Yet the modern concept of controllership maintains that the controller *does* control in a special sense. That is, by reporting and interpreting relevant data, the controller exerts a force or influence that impels management toward logical decisions consistent with objectives.

Distinctions between controller and treasurer

Many people confuse the offices of controller and treasurer. The Financial Executives Institute, an association of corporate treasurers and controllers, distinguishes their functions as follows:

Controllership	Treasurership
1. Planning for control	1. Provision of capital
2. Reporting and interpreting	2. Investor relations
3. Evaluating and consulting	3. Short-term financing
4. Tax administration	4. Banking and custody
5. Government reporting	5. Credits and collections
6. Protection of assets	6. Investments
7. Economic appraisal	7. Insurance

Note how managerial cost accounting is the controller's primary *means* of implementing the first three functions of controllership.

We shall not dwell at length on the treasurer's functions. As the seven points indicate, he is concerned mainly with financial, as distinguished from operating, problems. The exact division of various accounting and financial duties obviously varies from company to company.

The controller has been compared to the ship's navigator. The navigator, with the help of his specialized training, assists the captain. Without the navigator, the ship may flounder on reefs or miss its destination entirely, but the captain exerts his right to command. The navigator guides and informs the captain as to how well the ship is being steered. This navigator role is especially evident in Points (1) through (3) of the seven functions.

Point (2) of the functions emphasizes performance reports. Operating management has its tools for planning and control. Now it must use them. Peirce observes:

> *What happens when the measurement of performance has been made, reported and even interpreted? What action is taken and who takes it? The most typical case perhaps is the excess of actual expenditures over budget for a division of the business reporting to the president. Once this situation has been measured, analyzed, reported, interpreted, what is the controller's next move? First, if he is a sound controller, he will have given the same set of facts to both division head and president.*

It is then the job of the president, not the controller, to take whatever steps are in-
dicated. Neither good organization practice nor acceptable controllership would im-
pose on the controller the responsibility of approving or censuring the action of the
division head in exceeding his budget, or even of suggesting a higher budget. This
area is for the president and his subordinate to settle between them. The maximum
that can be said concerning the controller's influence in the matter is that the clarity
of his analysis and his insistence that the facts be understood may impel the proper
action.[6]

EXHIBIT 1-3

ORGANIZATION CHART OF A CONTROLLER'S DEPARTMENT IN A LARGE,
SINGLE-PRODUCT, SINGLE-PLANT COMPANY

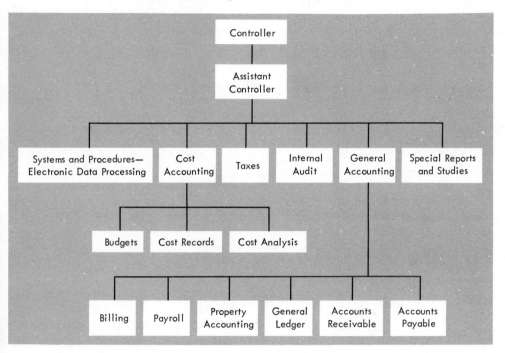

Difficulties of human relations

Line and staff relationships often result in friction because of a
lack of understanding of such relationships on the part of both line and
staff executives. Line executives complain that staff men are too distant to
understand their problems, want to seize line authority, lack perspective

[6] J. L. Peirce, "The Controllership Function: A Modern Concept," *The Controller*
(September, 1952), p. 422. Peirce has several thoughtful articles on various
aspects of controllership in the following issues of *The Controller:* September, 1953;
September, 1954; August, 1955; and August, 1956. Also see William J. Vatter,
"Control Function of Accountant in Management," *Journal of Accountancy* (June,
1952), pp. 705–710.

with regard to the interests of the entire organization, and always take credit but never bear the blame. Staff executives complain that line managers are too resistant to change, do not take advantage of staff help, and do not give staff enough authority.

As a staff man, the successful managerial cost accountant is alert to the sources of friction between line and staff. He avoids assuming line authority and losing the objectivity that he should possess. He foresees the ultimate impact of any change in accounting procedures on the line manager's attitudes and cooperation. *Management accounting records are only as accurate as their source documents (for example, requisitions and time cards).* Most source documents are initiated by line managers or their subordinates. Unless the line manager appreciates the necessity and benefit of the source documents that he originates, any accounting system, no matter how elaborate, will be nearly useless for purposes of management planning and control.[7]

Management accountant's future: new challenges

The function of the controller has always been to generate useful information for management. The 1950's and 1960's were marked by the application of operations research techniques and digital computers to business. These advances have made possible more sophisticated business information systems. Now the controller must know how to fuse operations research techniques, computer technology, and modern accounting for planning and control so that the quality of management will become better than ever. That is a tall order. It encompasses far more than the routine compilation of data for meeting payrolls and for preparing income statements. This text will concentrate on accounting per se, but where appropriate it will refer to related readings in other fields.

SUMMARY

The objectives of this chapter are to stimulate thinking about the interrelationship of accounting and management, to emphasize the breadth of the accounting field, to stress the human relations problems that evolve from the relationship of accountants and managers, and to underscore the importance of managerial cost accounting.

Managerial cost accounting is the most dynamic phase of the entire accounting field because it is interwoven with management itself. Accounting's main purpose is to help management plan and control operations. Accounting is a service function: accounting for management is not management as ordinarily conceived, but accounting aids management in doing a better job than can be done without it.

Managerial cost accounting emphasizes current and future data. Historical data are important only in so far as they help predict current

---

[7] The crucial problem of human relations is examined more carefully in Chapter 9.

and future performance or spur management investigation so that future control may be better maintained. Accounting uses (1) budgets to help planning and (2) performance reports to help controlling.

The chief management accountant is usually called the controller. His responsibilities typically embrace all phases of accounting, including income taxes and routine reporting to outside parties. But managerial cost accounting techniques are his main *means* of helping managers plan and control.

Management accountants are most effective if they avoid grasping or accepting line authority over any part of operations. They must be increasingly aware of the extreme importance of the human equation and its relationship to accounting. They should become as familiar as possible with all phases of their enterprise and problems and the viewpoints of all levels of management. In this way accountants maintain an over-all view that enhances their services to management. They should be familiar with facets of effective organizational structure and painstaking in keeping within the boundaries of that structure. As the main figure experts in the business, they must keep informed about statistical and mathematical techniques that may be pertinent to some aspects of their duties. Ideally the chief accounting executive and his staff should be general management wizards and technical masters. The final test of a management accountant's worth is how close he comes to these standards of business perfection.

QUESTIONS, PROBLEMS, AND CASES

Special note about the assignment material: No attempt has been made to distinguish among a question, a problem, or a case, because distinctions among them are so often artificial. Many problems are based on actual business situations. To aid selection, most problems have individual short titles which describe their subject matter. Although all assignment material has been carefully selected, a note at the beginning of the assignment material for each chapter will indicate those problems which are particularly helpful. Numbers 1-14 through 1-17 deserve special attention in this chapter.

1-1. Why do the controller and his staff have to understand the company organization structure?

1-2. As a new controller, answer this comment by a factory superintendent: "As I see it, our accountants may be needed to keep records for stockholders and Uncle Sam—but I don't want them sticking their nose in my day-to-day operations. I do the best I know how; no pencil-pusher knows enough about my responsibilities to be of any use to me."

1-3. "The way these modern controllers put themselves on a pedestal, you may as well give them the title of President and be done with it. Look at the first three points in their functions of controllership. With the change of a word or two, these points could be a job description for the company president." Discuss.

1-4. Define a *source document*. Why is it important? Name five source documents.

1-5. Define *planning*. Distinguish it from control.

1-6. "Planning is really much more vital than control." Do you agree? Why?

1-7. Define: *budget, performance report, variance.*

1-8. "The controller is both a line and a staff executive." Do you agree? Why?

1-9. "The modern concept of controllership maintains that the controller *does* control in a special sense." Explain.

1-10. What are some common causes of friction between line and staff executives?

1-11. How is cost accounting related to the concept of controllership?

1-12. Distinguish among line, staff, and functional authorities.

1-13. Prepare a Performance Report. The following is a summary of a month's performance by a machining department:

	Costs Incurred	Variance
Material handling labor	$ 2,000	$ 300 F
Depreciation—machinery and equipment	5,000	
Factory rent applicable to department	1,000	
Wages of machinery operators	20,000	2,000 U
Supplies (coolants, oils, polishing cloths)	400	50 U
Foreman's salary	800	
Materials	35,000	1,500 U
Power consumed	700	150 U
Other labor	1,000	100 F
Heat applicable to department	100	20 F
Small cutting tools, grinding wheels, etc., consumed	700	80 F

F = favorable; U = unfavorable.

REQUIRED:

Prepare a performance report with three columns: (1) budget, (2) actual, and (3) variance. At the bottom of your report, briefly indicate possible explanations for the variances. Why are there no variances for certain cost items?

1-14. Budgets and Control of Maintenance. A certain division of a telephone company has two major tasks: (a) construction of plant and equipment and (b) maintenance. The company uses a budget to help exert much closer control over maintenance. Each worker may be employed on some construction jobs and some maintenance jobs. The worker keeps a daily time sheet showing time spent on each construction job and each maintenance job.

Over a period of a few weeks, an independent observer noted the start and stop time of each maintenance and each construction job. He compared these times with the craftsmen's time sheet charges.

REQUIRED:

1. How do you think his records compared with those of the craftsmen?
2. What should be done, if anything, to correct the situation?

1-15. Draw an Organization Chart. Draw an organization chart for a company which has the following positions:

Vice president, controller and treasurer
Chief designer
Receiving and stores superintendent
Branch A sales manager
Production superindendent
Chief of finished stockroom
Shipping room head
Chief of cost accumulation
Maintenance superintendent
Employment manager
Building and grounds superintendent
Welding and assembly superintendent
Machining superindendent
Vice president, manufacturing
Finishing department superintendent

Vice president, chief engineer
Foundry superintendent
Head of job evaluation
Vice president, personnel
Head of general accounting
Budget director
Tool room superintendent
Chief purchasing agent
Head of cost analysis
Inspection superintendent
Stamping superintendent
Head of research
President
Head of production control
Vice president, sales

1-16. Responsibility for Analysis of Performance. John Phillipson is the new controller of a huge company which has just overhauled its organization structure. The company is now decentralized. Each division is under an operating vice president who, within wide limits, has responsibilities and authority to run his division like a separate company.

Phillipson has a number of bright staff members, one of whom, Bob Garrett, is in charge of a newly created performance analysis staff. Garrett and his fellow staff members prepare monthly divisional performance reports for the company president. These reports are divisional income statements, showing budgeted performance and actual performance, and are accompanied by detailed written explanations and appraisals of variances. Each of Garrett's staff members had a major responsibility for analyzing one division. Garrett's staff members consulted with divisional line and staff executives and became generally acquainted with the divisions's operations.

After a few months, Bill Whisler, vice president in charge of Division C, has stormed into the controller's office. The gist of his complaint follows:

"Your staff is trying to take over part of my responsibilities. They come in, snoop around, ask hundreds of questions, and take up plenty of our time. It's up to me, not you and your detectives, to analyze and explain my division's performance to central headquarters. If you don't stop trying to grab my responsibilities, I'll raise the whole issue with the president."

REQUIRED:

1. What events or relationships may have led to Whisler's outburst?
2. As Phillipson, how would you answer Whisler's contentions?
3. What are some alternative actions that Phillipson can take to improve future relationships?

1-17. Accountant's Role in Planning and Control. Dick Victor has been president of Sampson Company, a multi-division textile company, for ten months. The company has an industry reputation as being conservative and having average profitability. Previously, Victor was associated with a very successful company that had a heavily formalized accounting system with elaborate budgets and effective uses of performance reports.

Victor is contemplating the installation of a formal budgetary program. To signify its importance, he wants to hire a new vice president for planning and control. This fellow would report directly to Victor and would have complete responsibility for implementing a system for budgeting and reporting performance.

REQUIRED:

If you were controller of Sampson Company, how would you react to Victor's proposed move? What alternatives are available to Victor for installing his budgetary program? In general, should figure specialists all report to one master figure expert, who in turn is responsible to the president?

● **1-18. Organization of Accounting Department: Centralization or Decentralization.*** The following quotation is from an address made by an officer of Ford Motor Company:

"We can all, I think, take pride in the way cost accounting has kept pace with industrial development in this country. Tremendous strides have been made during the last quarter of a century, and I'm sure that much more progress will be made in the future. In fact, progress will *have* to be made if we are to keep the science of cost accounting abreast of the times. The whole of industry is now operating on a different level than we have known before—a higher plateau on which cost accounting appears in a new light, becomes more and more significant as a factor in business management.

"It is my experience that the function of cost determination is basic to every other function of a modern business. Cost factors thread their way through every phase of a business and to a large extent influence the make-up of the entire enterprise—its products, its markets, and its methods of operation.

"We must, of necessity, have rather complex and extensive costing organizations, but the principle according to which they work is the same—finding out what each of the operations costs before it is too late to avoid doing the wrong thing.

"I am sure you would be interested in knowing that the accounting office at Ford was formerly almost completely centralized and that we have begun to install a decentralized system . . . .

"It is planned that after the decentralized and the local organizations are prepared to assume the responsibilities involved, these accounting offices will be placed under the direct jurisdiction of the managers of the operations which they serve . . . .

"Under the decentralized system each division has its own complete accounting service . . . . Each separate activity, such as each assembly plant, has been provided with an accounting office to compile its own internal operating reports for its own use, and to forward the financial statements required by the central office."

REQUIRED:

1. Under the decentralized organization of the accounting work, would it be better for the controller of the Ford Motor Company to have direct authority or functional authority over the branch and divisional accounting offices? Discuss.

2. Will the decentralized system, in your opinion, make the cost accounting activities more significant in business management? In other words, is the change to a decentralized system in keeping with the trend that is outlined in the first three quoted paragraphs? Explain your answer, stating and illustrating advantages and disadvantages of the decentralized system in this case.

*N.A.C.A. *Bulletin*, Vol. 29, No. 7, Sec. II.

cost terminology and two major purposes
of cost accounting

CHAPTER

In this chapter we shall become acquainted with the twofold purpose of the day-to-day operations of the accounting system: (1) planing and control, hereafter for brevity's sake often called *control*, and (2) product costing. We shall also learn some basic terminology—the jargon that every technical subject seems to possess. Above all, we shall quickly realize that there are different costs for different purposes. In general, cost means sacrifice or foregoing, but there is no unique "correct" classification of cost that is applicable to all situations, that is pertinent for all purposes.

This chapter considers (1) unit costs and total costs, (2) variable costs and fixed costs, and (3) product costs and period costs. These types are sufficient to demonstrate the twofold purpose that will be stressed throughout this book. There are many, many other types of costs, but we shall not be swamped by them in this chapter. It will be more efficient if we ease into the subject matter of cost accounting. To do so, a discussion of the many ways and difficulties of classifying costs is being deliberately postponed until later. For example, the notion of controllable and uncontrollable costs will be covered at length in Chapter 9, and the idea of opportunity costs will be covered in Chapter 13.

Some form of cost accounting is applicable to manufacturing companies, retail stores, insurance companies, advertising agencies, and nearly all organizations. We shall consider both manufacturing and non-manufacturing companies throughout this book, but we shall begin with the manufacturing company because it provides the most general case— embracing production, marketing, and general administration functions. This will develop a completely general understanding of cost accounting which you can readily apply to any organization.

UNIT COSTS AND TOTAL COSTS

For now, let us think of costs as measures in the conventional accounting sense: dollars that must be paid for bundles of services. A unit cost is computed by dividing a total cost by the number of times that the total service will be utilized in terms of units of activity or volume. A unit cost is a useful communicative device because it often expresses costs as they are best understood. For example, the total bill for a fraternity party may be estimated at $200, but the bill is much more meaningful when it is expressed as an amount per couple or per person. If 200 people attend, the unit cost is $1.00 per person; if 40 attend, the unit costs becomes $5.00 per person. The unit cost will influence the fraternity's decision regarding a possible admission price and regarding whether to have the party at all. Unless it is unitized, the $200 total is difficult to interpret; it must be related to some useful base.

In management accounting, different measurement bases (denominators) may be used as units, depending on the circumstances. Generally, *unit costs should be expressed in terms most meaningful to the people who are responsible for incurring the costs*. The unit in question is not always a physical product; the unit (base) should be that objectively definable statistic of production which is most closely correlated with cost incurrence. Thus, the base may differ between departments: for example, it may be machine hours in a factory department, pounds handled in the shipping department, and number of invoices processed or lines billed in the billing department.

The unit cost of making a finished good is computed by accumulating manufacturing costs and then dividing the total by the number of units produced. Assume that 1,000 units of a finished product are produced for $380. The unit cost is $380 ÷ 1,000 units, or 38¢ per unit. If 200 units remain in ending inventory and 800 units are sold, cost of goods sold would be $304 (800 × 38¢) and ending inventory would be $76 (200 × 38¢). Thus, the "unit cost" notion facilitates the assignment of a total cost to different classifications. However, unit costs are averages, and they must be interpreted with care. This point is discussed more fully in Chapter 13.

VARIABLE COSTS AND FIXED COSTS

Costs and changes in activity

The unit cost approach is helpful not only in product costing but also in costing for planning and control. Although the notion of unit costs is basically simple, the behavior of certain items of cost in total and in relation to the base is often deceptive and is the cause of much misunderstanding among executives. Consider two examples:

1. If Massive Motors Company buys one type of battery at $5.00 each for its M-1 model car, then the total cost of batteries should be $5.00

times the number of cars produced. This is an example of a variable cost, a cost which is uniform *per unit* but which fluctuates in total in direct proportion to changes in the total activity (volume). Examples include most material and parts, many types of assembly labor, certain supplies and sales commissions.

Variable cost behavior may be plotted graphically. Exhibit 2-1 shows the relationship between total commissions and dollar sales, whereas Exhibit 2-2 shows the relationship between raw material costs and units produced.

EXHIBIT 2-1

SALES COMMISSIONS—10% OF SALES

EXHIBIT 2-2

RAW MATERIAL COSTS—$1.00 PER UNIT

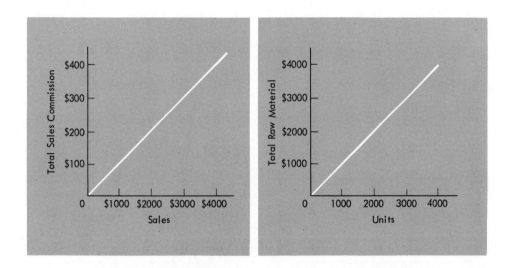

2. If Massive Motors buys special tools and dies at a cost of $100 million in order to produce its M-1 model car, then the unit cost of tools and dies applicable to each car produced will depend on the total produced. If 500,000 cars are made, the unit cost for tools and dies would be $100 million divided by 500,000, or $200. If one million cars are made, the unit cost would become $100. This is an example of a *fixed cost*, a cost which does not change in total over the life of the model but becomes progressively smaller on a *per unit* basis as production increases. Fixed costs are those that will not change in total over wide ranges of volume. Examples include property taxes, insurance, executive salaries, rent, and depreciation.

Fixed costs are usually necessary for mechanization and mass production. Mass production results in the spreading of fixed costs over more units, with a consequent decrease in costs per unit; therefore, selling prices fall and markets widen.

Fixed costs and shutdown costs

A fixed cost is fixed only in relationship to a given period of time and a given, though wide, range of activity, called the "relevant range." Thus, a company's fixed costs may be unchanged for a given year, although property tax rates and executive salaries may be higher the next year. In addition, the fixed-cost level may be applicable to, say, a range of 30,000 to 95,000 hours of activity per month. But a prolonged strike or economic recession may cause executive salary cuts, layoffs, or shutdowns. Therefore, fixed costs may be reduced substantially if activity levels fall drastically. In some cases, an entire plant may be shut down, virtually eliminating the need for executive and service personnel.

These relationships are shown in Exhibit 2-3. The likelihood of activity being outside the relevant range is usually slight, so $50,000 becomes the fixed-cost level. Exhibit 2-4 shows how this $50,000 figure may actually be plotted in practice. The three-level refinement in Exhibit 2-3 is not usually required, for the chances are very remote that activity will be less than 30,000 hours or more than 95,000 hours.

EXHIBIT 2-3

TOTAL MONTHLY FIXED COSTS—CONCEPTUAL ANALYSIS

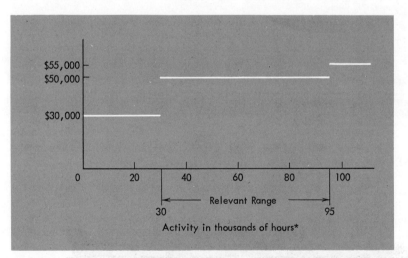

*$50,000 level between 30,000 and 95,000 hours.
$55,000 level in excess of 95,000 hours: hiring of additional supervision.
$30,000 level from shutdown (zero hours) to 30,000 hours: laying-off of supervision.

Nearly every business has costs which may be classified as either variable or fixed. Throughout this book we shall see why the accountant and the manager find this distinction helpful. For now the major point is that managers must have knowledge of their firm's cost behavior patterns

EXHIBIT 2-4

TOTAL MONTHLY FIXED COSTS AS PLOTTED IN PRACTICE

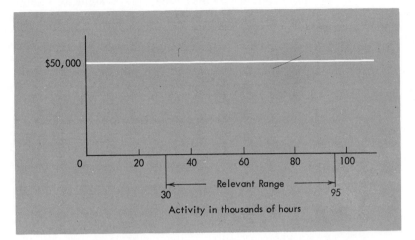

in order to predict the impact of their decisions on profits and in order to formulate means for controlling cost incurrence.

Such cost behavior is not confined solely to manufacturing costs; selling and administrative costs also have fixed and variable components. As will be seen later, some costs are difficult to categorize as being either strictly variable or strictly fixed. For the time being, however, we shall assume that costs may be placed in one of these two classifications. In practice, of course, the task of classification is exceedingly difficult and nearly always necessitates some simplifying assumptions.

PRODUCT COSTS AND PERIOD COSTS

Distinctions between manufacturing and nonmanufacturing activities

Historically, accounting techniques for planning and control arose in conjunction with manufacturing rather than nonmanufacturing because the measurement problems were less imposing and external factors such as economic conditions, customer reactions, and competitor activity were generally less influential. However, the basic concepts of planning and control are equally applicable to both manufacturing and nonmanufacturing activities. These distinctions are explored more deeply in Chapter 13. At the moment, we will examine manufacturing and nonmanufacturing from the viewpoint of inventory costing and income determination—the product-costing purpose.

Manufacturing is the transformation of raw materials into finished goods through the use of labor and factory facilities. Merchandising is the selling of goods without changing their basic form. For example, assume that Jack Nentlaw wants to make and sell hair dressing directly to re-tailers. He may buy certain oils and fancy containers, purchase a factory and equipment, hire some workers, and manufacture thousands of units of finished product. This is his manufacturing function. But in order to persuade retailers to buy his hair dressing, Nentlaw will have to convince the ultimate consumer that this product is desirable. This means adver-tising, including the development of a sales appeal, the selection of a brand name, the choice of media, and so forth. To maximize his success, Nentlaw must effectively manage both manufacturing and merchandising functions.

Three manufacturing cost elements

Compare the basic difference between the conventional income statements of Nentlaw's business and Crump's Department Store in Exhibit 2-5. In the cost of goods sold section, the Nentlaw statement has a "cost of goods manufactured" line instead of the "purchases" line found in the Crump statement. The details of the cost of goods manufactured appear in a separate supporting schedule.

There are three major elements in the cost of a manufactured product:

1. *Direct material.* All raw material which is an integral part of the finished good and which may be conveniently assigned to specific physical units: for example, sheet steel and subassemblies. Certain minor material, such as glue or nails, may be considered as either *supplies* or *in-direct material*, rather than direct material, because of the impracticality of tracing these items to specific physical units of product.

2. *Direct labor.* All labor which is obviously related to and ex-pediently traceable to specific products: for example, labor of machine operators and assemblers. Much labor, such as that of material handlers, janitors, and plant guards, is considered as *indirect labor* because of the difficulty or impracticality of tracing such items to specific physical units.

The word "direct," as it is used in product costing, largely em-braces all those cost items that can be conveniently identified with a batch of product. (The "batch" may be thousands of gallons of paint, or it may be a single, unique packaging machine.) For our purposes in this chapter, assume the latter. That is, a wide variety of products, each batch receiving varying attention and effort, is being manufactured. Examples include printing, aircraft, furniture, and machinery.

3. *Factory overhead.* All factory costs other than direct material and direct labor. Other terms to describe this category include *factory burden, indirect manufacturing costs, manufacturing overhead, and manufacturing expenses.* There are two major types of factory overhead:

a. *Variable factory overhead.* The two main examples are sup-plies and most indirect labor. Whether the cost of a specific subcategory of indirect labor is variable or fixed depends on its behavior pattern in a given company. In this book, unless we specify otherwise, indirect labor will be considered a variable rather than a fixed cost.

b. *Fixed factory overhead.* Examples are rent, insurance, prop-erty taxes, depreciation, and supervisory salaries.

EXHIBIT 2-5

COMPARISON OF INCOME STATEMENTS

NENTLAW (A manufacturer)	CRUMP'S (A retailer)
Income Statement	Income Statement
For the Year Ended December 31, 19x2	For the Year Ended December 31, 19x2

Sales		$210,000	Sales			$1,500,000
Less cost of goods sold:			Less cost of goods sold:			
Finished goods,			Merchandise			
December 31, 19x1	$ 22,000		inventory, December 31,			
Cost of goods manu-			19x1	$ 95,000		
factured (see			Purchases	1,100,000		
schedule)	104,000		Cost of goods			
Cost of goods avail-			available for			
able for sale	$126,000		sale	$1,195,000		
Finished goods,			Merchandise			
December 31, 19x2	18,000		inventory, December 31,			
Cost of goods sold		108,000	19x2	130,000		
Gross margin		$102,000	Cost of goods sold			1,065,000
Less selling and administrative			Gross margin			$ 435,000
expenses (detailed)		80,000	Less selling and administrative			
			expenses (detailed)			315,000
Net income		$ 22,000	Net income			$ 120,000

NENTLAW
Schedule of Cost of Goods Manufactured*

Direct materials:		
Inventory, December 31, 19x1	$11,000	
Purchases of direct materials	73,000	
Cost of direct materials available for use	$84,000	
Inventory, December 31, 19x2	8,000	
Direct materials used		$ 76,000
Direct labor		18,000
Factory overhead:		
Indirect labor	$ 4,000	
Supplies	1,000	
Heat, light and power	1,500	
Depreciation—Plant building	1,500	
Depreciation—Equipment	2,500	
Miscellaneous	500	11,000
Manufacturing costs incurred during 19x2		$105,000
Add work in process inventory, December 31, 19x1		6,000
Manufacturing costs to account for		$111,000
Less work in process inventory, December 31, 19x2		7,000
Cost of goods manufactured* (to Income Statement)		$104,000

*Note that the term cost of goods manufactured refers to the cost of goods fully completed (finished) during the year. Some of the manufacturing costs incurred are held back as costs of the ending work in process; similarly, the costs of the beginning work in process become a part of the cost of goods manufactured for 19x2. Note too that this schedule can become a Schedule of Cost of Goods Manufactured and Sold simply by including the opening and closing finished goods inventory figures in the supporting schedule rather than directly in the body of the income statement.

Two of the three major elements are sometimes combined in cost terminology as follows: *Prime cost* consists of (1) + (2), direct material plus direct labor. *Conversion cost* consists of (2) + (3), direct labor plus factory overhead.

Product costs (inventoriable costs) and income measurement

The scope of the term *cost* is extremely broad and general. When used, the word *cost* usually is linked with some adjective in order to avoid ambiguity. For example, costs may be *unexpired* or *expired*. Unexpired costs are carried forward to future periods as assets. Expired costs are those which should be released to the current period (period costs) as *expenses* or *losses*; they are costs which cannot be justifiably carried forward to future periods either because these costs do not represent future benefits or because the future benefits are so uncertain as to defy measurement.

A major objective of accounting is meaningful income measurement. In their efforts to refine the measure of income, accountants have developed certain practical classification techniques for distinguishing between assets and expenses. This is accomplished to a large extent by viewing manufacturing costs as inventoriable costs.

If costs can be looked upon as "attaching" or "clinging" to units produced, they are classified as *inventoriable costs*, also commonly called *product costs*. These costs are assets until the goods to which they relate are sold; then the costs are released as expenses and matched against sales. All costs in the schedule of cost of goods manufactured in Exhibit 2-5 are called product costs. Direct material, direct labor, and factory overhead items are inventoriable costs because they are costs of services utilized in forming the product. In general, the costs of operating the factory—the manufacturing costs—are classified as product costs.

Two decisions are made about costs with regard to income determination. Decision 1: Which costs apply to the current accounting period? Decision 2: Which of those under decision (1) are inventoriable? For example, a three-year $300 insurance premium may be charged originally to an asset account, *unexpired insurance*. The subsequent accounting for this cost will hinge on (1) the amount applicable to the current period— say, $100 for the first year—and (2) the purpose of the insurance coverage. Insurance on factory machinery is inventoriable and is therefore transferred from unexpired insurance to an inventory account. Insurance on a sales office is not inventoriable and is therefore transferred from unexpired insurance to an outright expense account.

Let us review the terminology. In manufacturing accounting many unexpired costs (assets) are transferred from one classification of unexpired costs to another before becoming expired costs (expense). Examples are factory insurance, depreciation on plant, and wages of production workers. These items are held back as product costs (inventory costs); they are released later to expense as part of cost of goods sold (an expense). The reader should distinguish sharply between the merchandising accounting and the manufacturing accounting for such costs as insur-

EXHIBIT 2-6

RELATIONSHIPS OF PRODUCT AND PERIOD COSTS

Merchandising Company

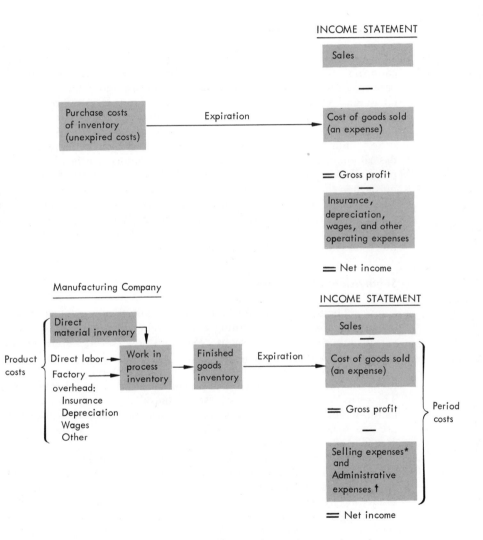

*Examples: insurance on salesmen's cars, depreciation on salesmen's cars, salesmen's salaries.

†Examples: insurance on corporate headquarters building, depreciation on office equipment, clerical salaries.

Note particularly that where insurance and depreciation relate to the manufacturing function, they are inventoriable; but where they relate to selling and administration, they are not inventoriable.

ance, depreciation, and wages. In merchandising accounting, such items are generally treated as expired costs (expenses), whereas in manufacturing accounting most of such items are related to production activities and thus are inventoriable costs—costs which do not expire (become expense) until the goods to which they relate are sold. These relationships are depicted in Exhibit 2-6.

Troublesome terminology

There are many terms that have very special meanings in accounting. The meanings often differ from company to company. Each organization seems to develop its own distinctive and extensive accounting language. This is why you will save much confusion and wasted time if you always find out the exact meanings of any strange jargon that you encounter.

For example, the term *manufacturing expenses*, which is often used to describe factory overhead, is a misnomer. Factory overhead is not an expense. It is a part of product cost and will funnel into the expense stream only when the product costs are released as cost of goods sold.

Also, *cost of goods sold* is a widely used term that is somewhat misleading when trying to pin down the meaning of cost. Cost of goods sold is an *expense* because it is an expired cost; cost of goods sold is every bit as much an expense as salesmen's commissions.

Subdivisions of labor costs

The terminology for labor costs usually is the most confusing because each organization seemingly has developed its own interpretation of various labor cost classifications. We shall now consider some commonly encountered labor terminology.

All factory labor costs other than direct labor are usually classified as *indirect labor*, a major component of indirect manufacturing costs. The term "indirect labor" usually has many subsidiary classifications to facilitate appraisal of these costs. Thus, wages of fork-lift truck operators are generally not commingled with janitors' salaries, although both are regarded as indirect labor.

Costs are classified in a detailed fashion primarily in the attempt to associate a specific cost with its specific cause or reason for incurrence. Two classes of indirect labor need special mention. *Overtime premium* paid to factory workers is usually considered a part of overhead. If a lathe operator gets $3.00 per hour for straight time and time and one-half for overtime, his *premium* would be $1.50 per overtime hour. If he works forty-four hours, including four overtime hours, in one week, his gross earnings would be classified as follows:

Direct labor:	44 hours × $3.00	$132.00
Overtime premium (factory overhead):		
	4 hours × $1.50	6.00
	Total earnings	$138.00

Another subsidiary classification of indirect labor is *idle time*. This typically represents wages paid for unproductive time caused by machine breakdowns, material shortages, sloppy production scheduling, and the like. For example, if the lathe operator's machine broke down for three hours, his earnings would be classified as follows:

Direct labor:	41 hours × $3.00	$123.00
Overtime premium (factory overhead):		
	4 hours × $1.50	6.00
Idle time (factory overhead):		
	3 hours × $3.00	9.00
	Total earnings	$138.00

Why is overtime premium usually considered an indirect cost rather than direct? After all, it can usually be traced to specific batches of work. It is usually not considered a direct charge because the scheduling of production jobs is generally random. For example, assume that Jobs Nos. 1 through 5 are scheduled for a specific work day of ten hours, including two overtime hours. Each job requires two hours. Should the job scheduled during hours 9 and 10 be assigned the overtime premium? Or should the premium be prorated over all the jobs? The latter approach does not penalize a particular batch of work solely because it happened to be worked on during the overtime hours. Instead, the overtime premium is considered to be attributable to the heavy over-all volume of work, and its cost is thus regarded as factory overhead, which is borne by all units produced.

Payroll fringe costs

The classification of factory payroll fringe costs such as employer contributions to Social Security, life insurance, health, pension, and miscellaneous other employee benefits differs from company to company. In most companies, these are classified as factory overhead. For instance, a direct laborer such as a lathe operator, whose gross pay check is computed on the basis of a $3.00 straight-time hourly rate, may enjoy payroll fringe benefits totaling, say, $.75 per hour. Most companies tend to classify the $3.00 as direct labor and the $.75 as factory overhead. In some companies, however, the fringe benefits related to direct labor are charged as an additional direct labor cost; these companies would classify the entire $3.75 as direct labor.

Balance sheet

Balance sheets of manufacturers and merchandisers differ with respect to inventories. The merchandise inventory account is supplanted in a manufacturing concern by three inventory classes: *materials and supplies inventory*; *work in process inventory* (cost of uncompleted goods still on the production line containing appropriate amounts of the three major manufacturing costs: direct material, direct labor, and factory overhead); and *finished goods* (fully completed goods). The only essential difference between the structure of the balance sheet of a manufacturer and that of the balance sheet of a retailer would appear in their respective current asset sections:

CURRENT ASSET SECTIONS OF BALANCE SHEETS

Manufacturer			Retailer	
Cash		$ 4,000	Cash	$ 30,000
Receivables		5,000	Receivables	70,000
Finished goods	$12,000			
Work in process	2,000			
Raw materials and supplies	3,000			
Total inventories		17,000	Merchandise inventories	100,000
Prepaid expenses		1,000	Prepaid expenses	3,000
Total current assets		$27,000	Total current assets	$203,000

Perpetual and periodic inventories

There are two fundamental ways of accounting for inventories: perpetual and periodic. The *perpetual inventory method* keeps a continuous record of additions to or reductions of raw materials, work in process, and cost of goods sold on a day-to-day basis. Such a record facilitates managerial control and preparation of interim financial statements. Physical inventory counts are taken at least once a year in order to check on the validity of the clerical records.

The *periodic inventory method* does not keep a day-to-day record of inventories. Instead, costs are recorded by natural classifications, such as Material Purchases, Freight In, and Purchase Discounts. Costs of material used or costs of goods sold cannot be computed accurately until ending inventories, determined by physical count, are subtracted from the sum of the opening inventory, purchases, and other operating costs. See Exhibit 2-7 for a comparison of perpetual and periodic inventory methods.

NUMEROUS CLASSIFICATIONS OF COST

This chapter has merely hinted at the vast number of classifications of cost which have proven useful for various purposes. Among others, classifications can be made by:

1. Degree of averaging
   a. Total cost
   b. Unit cost
2. Behavior in relation to volume changes
   a. Variable
   b. Fixed

  3. Function
     a. Manufacturing
     b. Selling
     c. Administrative
  4. Ease of traceability
     a. Direct
     b. Indirect

  Note: Whether a cost is direct or indirect depends on the purpose and difficulty of the computation. For instance, a department manager's salary is direct with respect to costs being classified by *departments* and indirect with respect to costs being classified by *products*.

  5. Timing of charges against revenue
     a. Product costs
     b. Period costs
  6. Time when computed
     a. Historical
     b. Budgeted or predetermined

EXHIBIT 2-7

SUMMARY COMPARISON OF PERIODIC AND PERPETUAL INVENTORY METHODS
(Figures from Exhibit 2-5)

Periodic Method		Perpetual Method	
Beginning inventories (by physical count)	$ 22,000	Cost of goods sold (kept on a day-to-day basis rather than being determined periodically)*	$108,000
Add: Manufacturing costs (direct material used, direct labor, factory overhead)	104,000		
Cost of goods available for sale	126,000		
Less ending inventories (by physical count)	18,000		
Cost of goods sold	$108,000		

*Such a condensed figure does not preclude the presentation of a supplementary schedule showing details of production costs similar to that in Exhibit 2-5.

SUMMARY

  Cost accounting systems provide data for: (1) *planning and control* and (2) *product costing*. Costs may be classified in many ways, depending on the purpose at hand.

  Unit costs are computed by dividing any total cost by some common denominator such as time (hours or minutes), physical measures (units of product, gallons, or tons), or sales dollars. Unit costs sometimes create a more meaningful understanding of cost behavior; they are also a means of assigning a total cost to different classifications.

The notions of variable and fixed costs are extremely important from the viewpoint of managerial planning and control. We shall see examples of this in Chapter 3.

Manufacturing costs are the costs of production. They may logically be treated as costs of *product* (*inventoriable costs*). This classification of *product costs* is important for purposes of income determination and balance sheet presentation.

This chapter has stressed only two methods of classifying costs: (1) variable or fixed costs, (2) product or period costs. There are many other means of classification. However, we have delayed discussing these for the time being, principally because our immediate aim is to emphasize the fact that different purposes and different classifications exist rather than to present too bewildering a variety of cost terms. When analyzing and evaluating cost reports, the accountant or manager should incessantly ask himself: "What is the purpose of this cost report? Product costing or planning and control?" This is a basic step toward intelligent evaluation and decision making. One of the first things you should fully recognize is that there is no sole cost classification which is pertinent for all purposes.

To recapitulate, the following itemization of costs is an example of how a given cost may be classified in more than one way:

	Manufacturing Costs	
	Direct (D) or Indirect (I)	Variable (V) or Fixed (F)
1. Cutting bits in a machinery department.	I	V
2. Workmen's compensation insurance in a factory.	I	V
3. Cement for a roadbuilder.	D	V
4. Steel scrap for a blast furnace.	D	V
5. Paper towels for a factory washroom.	I	V
6. Food for a factory cafeteria.	I	V
7. Factory rent.	I	F
8. Salary of a factory storeroom clerk.	I	F
9. Foreman training program.	I	F
10. Abrasives (sandpaper, etc.).	I	V

A glossary of cost terms is at the end of this book.

PROBLEM FOR SELF-STUDY

Consider the following data of the Laimon Company for the year 19x1:

Sandpaper	$ 2,000	Depreciation—Equipment	$ 40,000
Material handling	40,000	Factory rent	50,000
Lubricants and coolants	5,000	Property taxes on equipment	4,000
Overtime premium	20,000	Fire insurance on equipment	3,000
Idle time	10,000	Direct material purchased	400,000

Miscellaneous indirect labor	40,000	Direct material, 12/31/x1	50,000
Direct labor	300,000	Sales	1,200,000
Direct material, 12/31/x0	40,000	Sales commissions	60,000
Finished goods, 12/31/x1	150,000	Sales salaries	100,000
Finished goods, 12/31/x0	100,000	Shipping expenses	70,000
Work in process, 12/31/x0	10,000	Administrative expenses	100,000
Work in process, 12/31/x1	14,000		

REQUIRED:

Prepare an income statement with a separate supporting schedule of cost of goods manufactured. For all items except sales, purchases of direct material, and inventories, indicate by "V" or "F" whether each is basically a variable or fixed cost. If in doubt, decide on the basis of whether the total cost will fluctuate substantially over a wide range of volume. *Try to solve this problem before examining the solution that follows.*

Solution

LAIMON COMPANY
Income Statement
For the Year Ended December 31, 19x1

Sales			$1,200,000
Less cost of goods sold:			
Finished goods, December 31, 19x0	$ 100,000		
Cost of goods manufactured (see schedule below)	900,000		
Cost of goods available for sale	$1,000,000		
Finished goods, December 31, 19x1	150,000		
Cost of goods sold		850,000	
Gross margin		$ 350,000	
Less selling and administrative expenses:			
Sales commissions	$ 60,000 (V)		
Sales salaries	100,000 (F)		
Shipping expenses	70,000 (V)		
Administrative expenses	100,000*	330,000	
Net income		$ 20,000	

*Probably a mixture of fixed and variable items.

LAIMON COMPANY
Schedule of Cost of Goods Manufactured
For the Year Ended December 31, 19x1

Direct materials:	
Inventory, December 31, 19x0	$ 40,000
Purchases of direct materials	400,000
Cost of direct materials available for use	$440,000
Inventory, December 31, 19x1	50,000
Direct materials used	$390,000 (V)
Direct labor	300,000 (V)

Manufacturing overhead:

Sandpaper	$ 2,000	(V)
Lubricants and coolants	5,000	(V)
Material handling (example: wages of fork-lift truck operators)	40,000	(V)
Overtime premium	20,000	(V)
Idle time	10,000	(V)
Miscellaneous indirect labor	40,000	(V)
Factory rent	50,000	(F)
Depreciation—Equipment	40,000	(F)
Property taxes on equipment	4,000	(F)
Fire insurance on equipment	3,000	(F)

Fire insurance on equipment	214,000
Manufacturing costs incurred during 19x1	$904,000
Add work in process, December 31, 19x0	10,000
Manufacturing costs to account for	$914,000
Less work in process, December 31, 19x1	14,000
Cost of goods manufactured (to Income Statement)	$900,000

QUESTIONS, PROBLEMS, AND CASES

Note: Problems 2-23 through 2-28 are especially effective. Problems 2-26 and 2-27 provoke much (sometimes too much) class discussion because many of the answers are not clear-cut.

2-1. What two major purposes of cost accounting were stressed in this chapter?

2-2. Distinguish between *manufacturing* and *merchandising*.

2-3. What are the three major elements in the cost of a manufactured product?

2-4. Define the following: *direct material, direct labor, indirect material, indirect labor, factory overhead, prime cost, conversion cost.*

2-5. Give at least four terms which may be substituted for the term *factory overhead.*

2-6. Distinguish between *direct labor, indirect labor, overtime premium,* and *idle time.*

2-7. What is the major difference between the balance sheets of manufacturers and merchandisers?

2-8. Distinguish between *unexpired costs* and *expired costs.* How are manufacturing costs classified in relation to the problem of income measurement?

2-9. "For purposes of income determination, insurance, depreciation, and wages should always be treated alike." Comment.

2-10. Why is the term *manufacturing expenses* a misnomer?

2-11. "Cost of goods sold is an expense." Do you agree? Explain.

2-12. Why is the unit cost concept helpful in accounting?

2-13. Define: *variable cost, fixed cost, relevant range.*

2-14. Give three examples of variable factory overhead.

2-15. Distinguish between *costing for control* and *product costing*.

2-16. Give three examples of fixed factory overhead.

2-17. "Fixed costs are really variable. The more you produce, the less they become." Do you agree? Explain.

2-18. "An action once taken cannot be changed by subsequent events." What implications does this have for the cost accountant?

2-19. Why is overtime premium usually considered an indirect cost rather than direct?

2-20.   Periodic or Perpetual Inventory Methods. The terms *periodic* and *perpetual inventories* are referred to frequently in presenting the accounting procedures which are followed by businesses in recording their business transactions in any given period of their operations. Discuss the difference between periodic and perpetual inventory procedures and indicate the advantages and disadvantages of each method. [S.I.C.A.]

2-21.   Statement of Cost of Goods Manufactured and Sold. The following items pertain to Sorter Corporation (in dollars):

		For Year 19x2	
Work in process, Dec. 31, 19x2	2,000	Selling and administrative expenses	
Finished goods, Dec. 31, 19x1	40,000	(total)	70,000
Accounts receivable, Dec. 31, 19x2	30,000	Direct materials purchased	80,000
Accounts payable, Dec. 31, 19x1	40,000	Direct labor	70,000
Direct materials, Dec. 31, 19x1	30,000	Factory supplies	6,000
Work in process, Dec. 31, 19x1	10,000	Property taxes on factory	1,000
Direct materials, Dec. 31, 19x2	5,000	Factory utilities	5,000
Finished goods, Dec. 31, 19x2	12,000	Indirect labor	20,000
Accounts payable, Dec. 31, 19x2	20,000	Depreciation—Plant and equipment	9,000
Accounts receivable, Dec. 31, 19x1	50,000	Sales	350,000
Prepaid selling and administrative		Miscellaneous factory overhead	10,000
expenses:			
Dec. 31, 19x1	8,000		
Dec. 31, 19x2	2,000		

REQUIRED:

Prepare an income statement and a supporting schedule of cost of goods manufactured.

● **2-22.   Answers from Incomplete Data.** The following accounts of a manufacturing company appeared in the balance sheets of December 31, 19x1 and December 31, 19x2:

	December 31, 19x1	December 31, 19x2
Raw material inventory	$30,000	$46,000
Goods in process inventory	17,500	19,000
Finished goods inventory	23,000	18,200
Accrued factory payroll	3,100	2,400
Accrued interest on notes receivable	120	80

The following amounts appeared in the income statement for 19x2:

Raw material used	$300,000
Cost of goods sold	920,000
Factory labor	275,000
Interest income	400

REQUIRED:

1. Raw material purchased in 19x2.
2. Cost of goods manufactured for 19x2.
3. Factory labor paid in 19x2.
4. Interest received on notes in 19x2.

● **2-23. Statement of Cost of Goods Manufactured and Sold.** From the Eldred Manufacturing Company's adjusted trial balance of December 31, 19x1, the following account balances have been obtained:

Raw materials, January 1, 19x1	$ 75,000
Work in process, January 1, 19x1	21,200
Finished goods, January 1, 19x1	50,000
Purchases	185,000
Purchase returns and allowances	3,000
Direct labor	125,000
Indirect labor	40,000
Heat, light, and power	35,000
Insurance (75% of which is apportioned to factory)	8,000
Factory and machine maintenance	8,000
Factory supplies	6,000
Depreciation—Factory building	9,000
Depreciation—Equipment	23,000
Property taxes (90% of which are apportioned to factory)	4,000

In addition, raw materials costing $187,000 were used, the cost of goods manufactured for the year 19x1 was $440,000, and the cost of goods sold was $430,000.

REQUIRED:

A statement of cost of goods manufactured and sold for the year 19x1.

2-24. Finding Unknown Balances. For each of the following cases, find the unknowns, designated by letters:

	Case 1	Case 2	Case 3	Case 4
Finished goods inventory, 1/1	$ 5,000	$ 4,000	$ 7,800	$ G
Direct material used	8,000	6,000	3,600	5,000
Direct labor	13,000	11,000	8,000	6,000
Factory overhead	7,000	D	13,000	7,000
Purchases of direct material	9,000	7,000	8,000	8,000
Sales	42,000	31,800	E	40,000

	Case 1	Case 2	Case 3	Case 4
Accounts receivable, 1/1	2,000	1,400	3,000	400
Accounts receivable, 12/31	6,000	2,100	3,000	2,800
Cost of goods sold	A	22,000	28,000	15,000
Accounts payable, 1/1	3,000	1,700	1,600	300
Accounts payable, 12/31	1,800	1,500	1,800	1,200
Finished goods inventory, 12/31	B	5,300	F	7,600
Gross profit	11,300	C	10,000	25,000
Work in process, 1/1	–0–	800	1,300	2,000
Work in process, 12/31	–0–	3,000	300	2,500

2-25. Fire Loss; Computing Inventory Costs. A distraught employee, Fang W. Arson, put a torch to a factory on a blustery February 26. The resulting blaze completely destroyed the plant and its contents. Fortunately, certain accounting records were kept in another building. They revealed the following for the period December 31, 19x1–February 26, 19x2:

> Prime costs average 70 per cent of goods manufactured.
> Gross profit percentage based on net sales, 20 per cent.
> Cost of goods available for sale, $450,000.
> Direct material purchased, $160,000.
> Work in process, 12/31/x1, $34,000.
> Direct material, 12/31/x1, $16,000.
> Finished goods, 12/31/x1, $30,000.
> Factory overhead, 40 per cent of conversion costs.
> Sales, $500,000.
> Direct labor, $180,000.

The loss was fully covered by insurance. The insurance company wants to know the approximate cost of the inventories as a basis for negotiating a settlement, which is really to be based on replacement cost, not historical cost.

REQUIRED:

Calculate the cost of:
1. Finished goods inventory, 2/26/x2.
2. Work in process inventory, 2/26/x2.
3. Direct material inventory, 2/26/x2.

2-26. Different Cost Classifications for Different Purposes. A machining department has a number of cost accounts. Some accounts selected at random are reproduced below.

Use two columns to classify each account in two ways:

> Direct or Indirect Product Costs   D or I
> Variable or Fixed Costs*   V or F

*If in doubt, select on the basis of whether the item will vary over wide ranges of activity.

EXAMPLE: Foreman's salary I, F.

1. Cutting tools
2. Lubricants
3. Patterns
4. Nails, rivets, etc.

5. Factory rent
6. Repairs
7. Castings
8. Freight in on castings
9. Material handling
10. 25 per cent of superintendent's salary
11. Direct labor
12. Idle time
13. Overtime premium
14. Employer payroll taxes
15. Compensation insurance
16. Fire insurance on equipment
17. Depreciation—Equipment
18. Property taxes on equipment
19. Blueprints prepared by Drafting Department

2-27. Classification of Costs; Objective Answers. The following example is a guide for solving this problem. Five columns are to be used as choices for possible classification.

EXAMPLE:

	Selling Cost	General Administrative Cost	Manufacturing Cost		Variable or Fixed*	Other (Specify)
			Direct or Indirect			
Direct materials	_____	_____	D		V	_____
Bond interest expense	_____	_____	_____		F	Financial expense
Fire loss	_____	_____	_____		_____	Nonrecurring loss
President's salary	_____	√	_____		F	_____
Insurance on factory equipment	_____	_____	I		F	_____

*If in doubt, decide on the basis of whether the total cost will fluctuate substantially over a wide range of volume.

On a separate sheet, do the same for the following accounts, all of which are not necessarily for a single company. You may use numbers to list the accounts instead of recopying the account descriptions.

1. Salesmen's entertainment costs.
2. Public accounting fees.
3. Salary of factory stores clerk.
4. Overtime premium—Punch Press.
5. Idle time—Assembly.
6. Rework—Machining.
7. Salaries—Engineering department.
8. Sandpaper purchases for a furniture manufacturer.
9. Cost estimator's salary for a missile manufacturer.
10. Cleanup labor—Machining.
11. Material handling labor—Machining.

12. Factory power.
13. Shop patterns and forge dies.
14. Property taxes.
15. Freight in on materials used.
16. Shipping supplies.
17. Heat of factory.
18. Costs of developing patents—Factory engineering department.
19. Amortization of patents.
20. Freight out.
21. Salesmen's commissions.
22. Salesmen's salaries.
23. Fire insurance—Factory.
24. Executive training program—general.
25. Company picnic costs.
26. Salesmen's samples.
27. Bribes paid to public officials.
28. Perfume bottles of a perfume manufacturer.
29. Individual boxes for perfume.
30. Glue for labels on perfume bottles.
31. Packing cartons of various sizes used by shipping department.
32. Salaries—Production control.

2-28.   Comprehensive Problem on Unit Costs, Product Costs, Variable and Fixed Costs, and Budgeted Income Statement.   The Fancher Company makes a single product. Costs are as follows (V stands for variable; F, for fixed):

Production in units	100,000
Costs incurred:	
Direct material used	$100,000 V
Direct labor	70,000 V
Power	5,000 V
Indirect labor	10,000 V
Indirect labor	20,000 F
Other factory overhead	8,000 V
Other factory overhead	20,000 F
Selling expenses	30,000 V
Selling expenses	20,000 F
Administrative expenses	50,000 F
Work in process inventory, December 31, 19x1	—
Direct material inventory, December 31, 19x1	2,000 lbs.
Finished goods inventory, December 31, 19x1	$ 20,970

Dollar sales were $318,500 in 19x1. There were no beginning inventories in 19x1. The company's ending inventory of finished goods was carried at the average unit cost of production for 19x1. Direct material prices have been stable throughout the year. Two pounds of direct material are used to make a unit of finished product.

REQUIRED:

1. Direct material inventory, total cost, December 31, 19x1.
2. Finished goods inventory, total units, December 31, 19x1.
3. Unit sales price, 19x1.
4. Net income, 19x1. Show computations.
5. This part is more difficult than parts (1)–(4). Management has asked that you prepare a budgeted income statement for 19x2, assuming that all unit prices for sales and variable costs will not change. Assume that sales will be 102,000 units and that ending inventory of finished goods, December 31, 19x2, will be 12,000 units. Assume that fixed costs will remain the same. Show supporting computations, and include a schedule of cost of goods manufactured. The ending inventory of finished goods is to be carried at the average unit cost of production for 19x2.

cost-volume-profit relationships

CHAPTER

The previous chapter distinguished sharply between two major purposes of cost accounting: (1) planning and control and (2) product costing. This chapter and the next will examine, in turn, these two purposes in more depth. Cost-volume-profit analysis is an inherently appealing subject to most students of business because it gives a sweeping overview of the planning process and because it provides a concrete example of why an understanding of cost behavior is important. That is why we consider this subject now, even though it could just as easily be studied later.

THE BREAKEVEN POINT

We learn quickly that knowledge of cost behavior patterns—the response of costs to a variety of influences—is invaluable in guiding management decisions. First, we obtain an overview by examining the interrelationships of changes in costs, volume, and profits—sometimes too narrowly described as breakeven analysis. The breakeven point is often only incidental in these studies. Instead, the focus is on the impact upon net income of various decisions which affect sales and costs. The breakeven point is that point of activity (sales volume) where total revenues and total expenses are equal; it is the point of zero profits.

BASIC TECHNIQUE

EXAMPLE A. A person plans to sell a toy rocket at the state fair. He may purchase these rockets at 50¢ each with the privilege of returning all unsold rockets. The booth rental is $200, payable in advance.   The rockets will be sold at 90¢ each.   How many rockets must be sold to break even?

Equation technique

The first approach to a solution may be called the *equation technique.* Every income statement may be expressed in equation form as follows:

Sales = Variable Expenses + Fixed Expenses + Net Income

This equation may be adapted to any breakeven or profit-estimate situation. For Example A:

Let X = Number of units to be sold to break even
$\$.90X = \$.50X + \$200 + 0$
$\$.40X = \$200 + 0$

$$X = \frac{\$200 + 0}{\$.40}$$

$X = 500$ units

Contribution margin technique

A second solution method is the *contribution margin* or *marginal income* technique.   Contribution margin is the excess of sales over variable expenses. Sales and expenses are analyzed as follows:

1. *Unit contribution margin* to coverage of fixed expenses and desired net income

= Unit sales price − Unit variable expense = $\$.90 - \$.50 = \$.40$

2. *Breakeven point* in terms of units sold

$$\frac{\text{Fixed Expenses} + \text{Desired Net Income}}{\text{Unit Contribution Margin}} = \frac{\$200 + 0}{\$.40} = 500 \text{ units}$$

Stop a moment and relate this contribution margin technique to the equation technique. The key calculation was dividing $200 by $.40. Look at the third line in the equation solution. It reads:

$$\$.40X = \$200 + 0$$

$$X = \frac{\$200 + 0}{\$.40}, \text{ giving us a general formula:}$$

$$\text{Breakeven in Units} = \frac{\text{Fixed Expenses} + \text{Desired Net Income}}{\text{Contribution Margin per Unit}}$$

The *contribution margin* technique is merely a restatement of the *equation* in different form. Use either technique; the choice is a matter of personal preference.

The term *contribution margin* will be used frequently in this book. It may be expressed as a total, as an amount per unit, or as a percentage. In our example, the *total contribution margin* is 500 units × $.40, or $200;

the *unit contribution margin* is $.40; and the *contribution margin percentage or ratio* is $.40 ÷ $.90, or 44.44 per cent.

The contribution margin ratio is necessary for cost-volume-profit analysis where the information is expressed in terms of dollars instead of units. Most companies have more than one product, and the over-all breakeven point is often expressed in sales dollars because of the variety of product lines. For instance, although apples and oranges cannot be meaningfully added, their sales values provide a useful common denominator. In Example A, the breakeven point in dollars may be computed most easily by merely multiplying the 500 units by $.90 to obtain $450. However, the breakeven point may also be obtained by the following version of the contribution margin approach:

$$\text{Breakeven Point in Dollars} = \frac{\text{Fixed Expenses} + \text{Desired Net Income}}{\text{Contribution Margin Ratio}}$$

$$= \frac{\$200 + 0}{.4444} = \$450$$

The first problem for self-study in this chapter elaborates on the uses of the contribution margin ratio.

Graphic approach

The relationships in Example A may be graphed as shown in Exhibit 3-1.

EXHIBIT 3-1

COST-VOLUME-PROFIT CHART

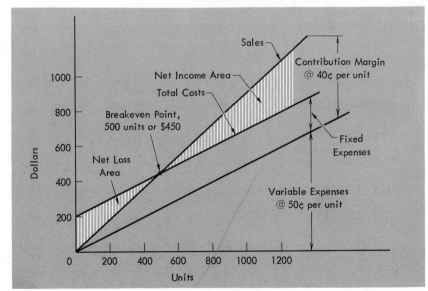

The graph in Exhibit 3-1 used the following building blocks:

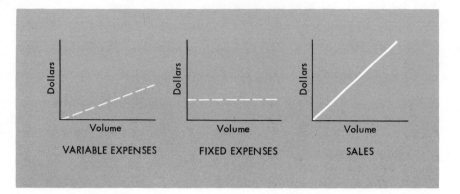

Note that total sales and total variable expenses fluctuate in direct proportion to changes in physical volume, whereas fixed expenses are the same in total over the entire volume range.

Now combine the fixed and variable expenses in a single graph:

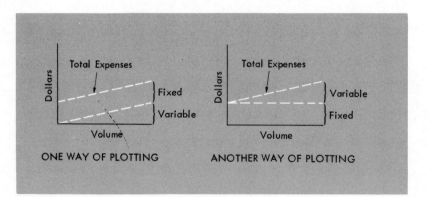

Note that the total expenses line is the same under either method. The graph which plots fixed expenses above the variable expenses is preferred by many accountants because it emphasizes the contribution margin notion. (See Exhibit 3-1.) When operations are below the breakeven point, the vertical distance between the sales line and the variable cost line measures the "contribution" that sales volume is making to fixed expenses.

Finally, introduce the sales line:

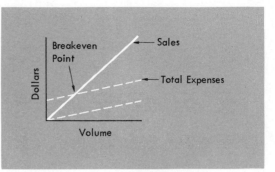

Exhibit 3-1 shows the complete breakeven chart. The *breakeven point* is the point where the total sales line and total expense line intersect. But note further that this graph shows the profit or loss outlook for a wide range of volume. The confidence which we place in any particular break-even chart is naturally a consequence of the relative accuracy of the cost-volume-profit relationships depicted.[1]

Target net income

Let us introduce a profit element by asking: *How many rockets must be sold to yield a 20 per cent operating margin?* The same basic approach may be used:

Equation technique

Let X = Number of units to be sold to yield desired profit.
Sales = Variable Expenses + Fixed Expenses + Desired Net Income
$\$.90X = \$.50X + \$200 + .20(\$.90X)$
$\$.90X = \$.50X + \$200 + \$.18X$
$\$.22X = \$200$
$\quad X = 910$ units

Proof:

Sales = 910 × \$.90		\$819	100.00%
Variable expenses = 910 × \$.50		455	55.56
Contribution margin		\$364	44.44%
Fixed expenses		200	24.42
Net income		\$164	20.02%

Find the 910-unit volume on the graph in Exhibit 3-1. The difference between sales and total expenses at that volume is the \$164 profit.

[1] For an exploration of the role of uncertainty in cost-volume-profit analysis, see Problem 26-21.

Contribution margin technique:

$$X = \frac{\text{Fixed Expenses} + \text{Desired Net Income}}{\text{Unit Contribution Margin}}$$

$$X = \frac{\$200 + \$.20\,(\$.90X)}{\$.40}$$

$$\$.40X = \$200 + \$.18X$$
$$\$.22X = \$200$$
$$X = 910 \text{ units}$$

Cost-volume-profit assumptions

The following assumptions usually underlie breakeven analysis:

1. The behavior of costs and revenues has been reliably determined and is linear over the relevant range.

2. Costs may be resolved into fixed and variable elements.

3. Fixed costs remain constant over the volume range on the breakeven chart.

4. Variable costs fluctuate proportionally with volume.

5. Selling prices are to be unchanged.

6. Prices of cost factors are to be unchanged.

7. Efficiency and productivity are to be unchanged.

8. The analysis either covers a single product or it assumes that a given sales mix will be maintained as volume changes. *Sales mix* may be defined as the relative combination of quantities of a variety of company products that compose total sales. If the mix changes, over-all sales targets may be achieved, but the effects on profits depend on whether low-margin or high-margin goods predominate in the sales mix. (See the appendix to this chapter for an illustration.)

9. Revenue and costs are being compared on a common activity base (for example, sales value of production or units produced).

10. Perhaps the most basic assumption of all is that volume is the only relevant factor affecting cost. Of course, other factors, such as wars, strikes, legislation, competition, and so forth, also affect costs and sales. Ordinary cost-volume-profit analysis is a crude oversimplification when these factors are unjustifiably ignored.

11. Changes in beginning and ending inventory levels are insignificant in amount. (The impact of inventory changes on cost-volume-profit analysis is discussed in Chapter 10.)

The reliability of cost-volume-profit analysis is dependent upon reasonably accurate portrayals of cost behavior. The first step in analyzing costs is to divide them into fixed and variable categories. The objective is to determine total fixed costs and the rate at which variable costs change with volume.

Cost behavior is affected by the interplay of a number of factors. Volume is only one of these factors; others include unit prices, sales mix, efficiency, changes in production methodology, wars, strikes, legislation, and so forth. Any breakeven analysis is based on assumptions made about the behavior of revenue, costs, and volume. A change in expected behavior will alter the breakeven point; in other words, profits are affected by changes in other factors besides volume. A breakeven chart must be interpreted in the light of the limitations of its underlying assumptions, especially with respect to the price and sales mix factors. *The real benefit of preparing breakeven charts is in the enrichment of understanding of the interrelationships of all factors affecting profits, especially cost behavior patterns over ranges of volume.*[2]

Relevant range

In a real-life company situation, the breakeven point may be drawn as shown in Exhibit 3-1. However, the many assumptions that underlie the chart are subject to change if actual volume falls outside the relevant range which was the basis for drawing the chart. It would be more realistic if the lines on these charts were not extended back to the origin, as follows:

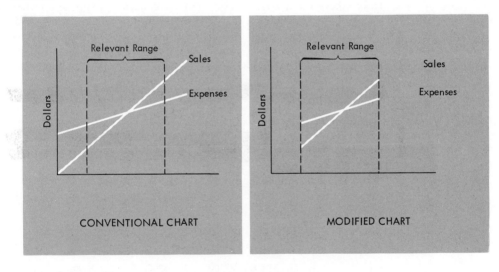

[2]The principal differences between the accountant's breakeven chart and the economist's are:

(a) The accountant usually assumes a constant unit variable cost instead of a unit variable cost that changes with the rate of production.

(b) The accountant's sales line is drawn under the assumption that price does not change with the rate of production or sale, but the economist assumes that price changes may be needed to spur sales volume. Therefore, the economist's chart is nonlinear.

(c) The accountant excludes the cost of equity capital, but the economist does not.

(d) The economist not only specifies the breakeven point; he also indicates the equilibrium condition.

The modified chart highlights the fact that tenuous, static assumptions underlie a graph of cost-volume-profit relationships. The sales and expense relationships may be valid within a band of activity called the *relevant range*. The relevant range is usually a range in which the firm has had some recent experience. But the same relationships are unlikely to persist if volume falls outside the limits of the relevant range. For example, as shown in the previous chapter, some fixed costs may be avoided at low volume levels.

Business is dynamic, not static. The user of cost-volume-profit analysis must constantly challenge and re-examine his assumptions in the light of changes in business conditions, prices, cost factors, sales mixes, cost mixes, and the like. Moreover, cost-volume-profit analysis need not adhere rigidly to the traditional linear assumptions.

INTERRELATIONSHIPS OF COST, VOLUME, AND PROFITS

Variable cost and contribution margin

In breakeven analysis, variable cost is generally expressed either as a percentage of the sales dollar, as an amount per unit, or as an absolute amount. When the variable cost ratio—the total variable costs divided by total sales—is known, the total variable costs at any level of activity are easily computed. But the variable cost ratio may be altered by changes in material prices, wage rates, efficiency, and selling price.

The *contribution margin ratio* is the complement of the *variable cost ratio*. It is the proportion of the sales dollar available for coverage of fixed costs and attainment of profit. It is computed by subtracting the variable cost ratio from 100 per cent. This relationship may be expressed in dollars as the *contribution margin*—the difference between total revenue and total variable costs at any volume.

If the contribution margin ratio is known, the change in profits forthcoming from a contemplated change in sales may be easily calculated. For example:

	Given Volume	Per Cent	Increase in Volume	Decrease in Volume
Sales	$1,000	100	$200	$300
Variable costs	700	70	140	210
Contribution margin	$ 300	30	$ 60	$ 90
Fixed costs	300		(Unchanged)	(Unchanged)
Net income	$ -0-		$ 60	$ 90

The application of the contribution margin ratio, 30 per cent, to the sales increment, $200, or the sales decline, $300, will easily yield the above answers of $60 and $90—*the changes* which would result. Because total fixed costs do not change over the contemplated volume range, they are not relevant in the computation of any change in profit arising from changes in volume.

The contribution margin ratio may provide management with some useful information. If a firm is operating at a loss, the contribution margin ratio indicates how much the net loss will either diminish or increase with each dollar change in sales. A high contribution margin ratio will cause greater profits than a smaller contribution margin ratio as volume in dollars increases above the breakeven point. The opposite holds when sales volume is below the breakeven point: the higher the contribution margin ratio, the greater the loss as the dollar volume of sales decreases. A low contribution margin ratio necessitates great increases in volume to obtain noticeable increases in profits. The larger the ratio, the larger the change in profit for a given change in volume (*N.A.A. Research Series No. 17, p. 533*):

> ... For example, a high marginal income ratio (contribution margin ratio) indicates that comparatively large additional expenditures for advertising and selling directed toward obtaining added sales volume may be profitable because the margin available from such sales is adequate to absorb the expenditures and still leave a contribution to profits. However, it should be recognized that additional expenditures for sales promotion may partly or wholly cancel the advantage gained. As an alternative, price reductions might be used if sales volume responds readily to price changes, although here again action should not be taken without considering the probable action of competitors. Reductions in price required by competition can also be absorbed more readily by a company having a high marginal income ratio. Since changes in variable cost also affect the marginal income ratio, this ratio indicates how readily the business can absorb cost increases without serious loss of profit.

Both the contribution margin and the breakeven point are altered by changes in unit variable costs. Thus, in the toy rocket example (Example A), if the cost of a toy rocket is raised from 50¢ to 70¢ and the sales price is unchanged, the unit contribution falls from 40¢ to 20¢, and the breakeven point increases from 500 to 1,000 units. A decrease in rocket cost from 50¢ to 30¢ would change the unit contribution from 40¢ to 60¢. The new breakeven point would become 334 units ($200 fixed expenses divided by 60¢).

A major task of management is to find the optimum combination of fixed and variable costs. Efficient management constantly strives for reductions of variable costs which are consistent with over-all company objectives.

Variable costs are subject to various degrees of control at different volumes because of psychological as well as other factors. When business is booming, management tends to be preoccupied with the generation of volume "at all costs." When business is slack, management tends to ride herd on costs. Decreases in volume are often accompanied by increases in selling expenses and lower selling prices; but at the same time labor turnover falls, labor productivity tends to increase, and raw material prices may drift down. This is another illustration of the limitations of a breakeven chart; conventional breakeven charts assume proportional fluctuations of variable costs with volume. This implies adequate and uniform control over costs. In practice, such control is often erratic.

Changes in fixed costs

Fixed costs are not static year after year. They may be deliberately increased in order to obtain more profitable combinations of production and distribution; these affect the three major profit determinants: revenue, variable costs, and fixed expenses. For example, a sales force may be established to reach markets directly instead of through wholesalers, thereby obtaining increased unit sales prices. More complicated machinery may be bought so as to reduce unit variable costs. Increases in labor rates are likely to make it desirable for a firm to invest in labor-saving equipment. In some cases, on the other hand, it may be wise to reduce fixed costs in order to obtain a more favorable combination. Thus, direct selling may be supplanted by the use of manufacturers' agents. A company producing stoves may find it desirable to dispose of its foundry if the resulting reduction in fixed costs would more than counterbalance increases in the variable costs of purchased castings over the expected volume range. When a major change in fixed cost is proposed, management needs forecasts of the effect on the breakeven point and the contribution margin as a guide toward a wise decision. The management accountant makes continuing analyses of cost behavior and redetermines breakeven points periodically. He keeps management informed of the cumulative effect of major and minor changes in the company's cost and revenue patterns.

Fixed costs are constant only over contemplated ranges of activity. The volume range rarely extends from shutdown levels to 100 per cent capacity. Thus, when a radical reduction in volume is foreseen, many fixed costs are "jarred loose" by managerial action. The slashing of fixed costs lowers the breakeven point and enables the firm to endure a greater decrease in volume before losses appear.

Example of importance of fixed costs

In November, 1950, some months after the Korean outbreak, a major automobile company applied to the federal price control agency for permission to raise car prices. A frequent reason for price increases is the increased cost of labor and materials. But this case was different; the company wanted to increase prices because of the fixed cost-volume relationship. The government's drastic curtailment of output for the consumer markets had resulted in the halving of the company's production. Although variable costs had remained fairly steady per car, the fixed costs had to be spread over 50 per cent fewer units. Thus, a price increase was granted in order that an equitable return on investment might be earned. For example (totals are in millions):

Before Korean War			After Korean War		
Sales, 100,000 units @ $2,000		$200	Sales, 50,000 units @ $2,000		$100
Variable expenses, 100,000 units @ $900	$90		Variable expenses, 50,000 units @ $900	$45	
Fixed expenses	30	120	Fixed expenses	30	75
Gross profit, 40% of sales		$ 80	Gross profit, 25% of sales		$ 25

The spreading of $30 million of fixed costs over 50,000 units instead of 100,000 units resulted in the application of $600 to each car instead of the former $300 amount. Note that the basis for the price increase was the mere drop in production, not an increase in unit prices of variable-cost factors. Fixed costs remained the same—$30 million; the reduced number of units sold had to carry higher price tags in order to get a large enough contribution margin per unit to recover the fixed costs and provide the same percentage gross profit on sales.

Margin of safety

The *margin of safety* is the excess of budgeted or actual sales over the breakeven sales volume. The margin of safety reveals the amount by which sales may decrease before losses occur. This concept may be expressed as a percentage through dividing the dollar margin of safety by budgeted or actual sales (M/S). The validity of such a margin depends on the accuracy of cost estimates at the contemplated breakeven point. Often any drastic decrease in sales is accompanied by severe slashes in costs; the margin of safety is an approximation which presupposes given cost relationships.

The combination of high fixed costs, a high contribution margin ratio, and a low margin of safety usually calls for managerial action to get reductions in fixed costs or to stimulate sales volume.

If both the margin of safety and the contribution margin ratio are low, management would tend to concentrate on possible upward revisions in selling prices or on ways and means of reducing variable expenses.

APPLICATIONS OF COST-VOLUME-PROFIT ANALYSIS

Breakeven analysis has wide applicability for managerial decision making. Cost-volume-profit analysis provides helpful information for decisions as to pricing, cost alternatives, sales mix, channels of distribution, possible sales promotion, addition or deletion of product lines, acceptance of special orders, entering foreign markets, and changing plant layout.

Cost-volume-profit analysis and budgets

The derivation of cost-volume-profit relationships, whether in connection with breakeven charts or budgets, permits a quick preview of potential profits over a wide range of volume. Many firms use preliminary budget figures as a basis for a breakeven chart. If the forecast does not satisfy management, changes are made before a final budget is drawn.

The breakeven chart is a convenient way of reporting on the overall business plan (the budget). The chart often has decided educational advantages in that it conveys the story to line executives more easily than do numerical exhibits. Thus, it creates a greater awareness of these relationships on the part of line executives.

In long-run capital budget situations, breakeven charts may be helpful in showing future operating conditions if certain expenditures are to be made. A form of breakeven chart is also helpful in showing the relative costs of borrowing and additional ownership capital.

Contribution margin and the short run

In the short run it is often helpful to offer numerical income statements which highlight the contribution margins of various products. As compared with the conventional income statements, where sharp distinctions between fixed costs and variable costs are not made, the contribution margin statement better explains basic cost-revenue-profit behavior. This type of statement reflects a useful management approach to decisions with respect to hiring a salesman, conducting a special advertising campaign, making or buying a part, bidding on a special order, and so on. The differences in costs are compared with the differences in revenue in order to obtain an accurate basis for decision. Further, this type of statement helps to direct management attention toward the high- or low-margin-producing power of its various products.

The decisions mentioned in the previous paragraph will be given more attention in later chapters, but an illustration may clarify the importance of volume in relation to total contribution margin and net profit.

A large brewery circulated a written explanation of breakeven analysis to its wholesalers. The explanation contained the following assumptions for a typical wholesaler:

		Per Unit
Sales price		$2.60
Variable expenses:		
Laid-in cost of beer	$2.00	
Variable selling expenses	.15	2.15
Contribution margin		$ .45

Fixed expenses, $30,000 per year.

	Breakeven Volume	Present Volume	Possible Changes	Possible Volume
Cases per year	66,667	100,000	25,000	125,000
Sales @ $2.60	$173,333	$260,000	$65,000	$325,000
Variable expenses @ $2.15	143,333	215,000	53,750	268,750
Contribution margin @ $.45	$ 30,000	$ 45,000	$11,250	$ 56,250
Fixed expenses	30,000	30,000	—	30,000
Net income	$ -0-	$ 15,000	$11,250	$ 26,250

The brewery used breakeven analysis to point out the sizable impact on profits of high-volume operations. In this situation, if a wholesaler could increase his volume by 25,000 cases, his income would rise by $11,250 (a change in revenue of $2.60 × 25,000 cases, or $65,000, minus change in expenses of $2.15 × 25,000 cases, or $53,750). Fixed expenses have already been recovered and are not affected by the volume change. The only additional outlays are the variable expenses. The brewery suggested that the wholesaler could achieve a dramatic change in net income (a 75 per cent change) with a mere 25 per cent increase in volume. The brewery also suggested that the wholesaler could easily incur a special promotional expense, say $5,000, because the increase in volume would still leave a $6,250 increase in income for the wholesaler.

The validity of this approach to a specific decision again depends on the facts in a case. If the wholesaler described above was working at peak capacity at a 100,000-case level, in order to increase volume he would have to buy more trucks, rent more storage space, raise more capital, and so forth. Then the facts change, and the analysis would depend not only on the extra contribution margin to be gained, but also on the additional fixed costs to be incurred.

The size of the contribution margin would also influence the decision. If the margin were only 12¢ a case instead of 45¢, the 25,000-case extra volume would not increase the total contribution margin enough (25,000 × 12¢, or $3,000) to warrant the risk of a large promotional outlay.

A word of caution is needed here. Costs must be related to time; that is, a cost which is fixed over a short period is variable over a longer period. Profits may increase momentarily by applying the contribution margin approach to decisions; but over the long run, profits may suffer by inordinate use of such an approach. For example (*N.A.A. Research Series No. 17*, p. 552):

> *One company stated that it solicits subcontract work for other manufacturers during periods when sales of its own products do not fully utilize the plant, but that such work cannot be carried on regularly without expansion of its plant. The profit margin on subcontracts is not sufficiently large to cover these additional costs and hence work is accepted only when other business is lacking. The same company sometimes meets a period of high volume by purchasing parts or having them made*

by subcontractors. While the cost of such parts is usually higher than the cost to make them in the company's own plant, the additional cost is less than it would be if they were made on equipment which could be used only part of the time.

Long-range planning

Knowledge of cost behavior patterns is helpful for long-run planning. The following description illustrates how a five-year plan is formulated by studying fixed costs and variable costs, relating costs to target sales, and then revising the plan as needed (*N.A.A. Accounting Practice Report No. 10*, p. 32):

> *We have established a five-year planned profit goal based on an equitable return on investment from a five-day, two-shift operation. With this as a starting point, we have planned our fixed charge budgets. The profit goal, plus fixed cost, equals the total contribution margin which must be generated to cover the fixed cost and the desired profit return. We compute our two-shift, five-day volume and arrive at the gross profit per unit. Since we then have only variable costs to consider, we use our experienced standard variables by product line and, adding this to the gross profit, we arrive at a net sales figure which must be attained if we are to meet our profit objective.*
>
> *If the sales figure so reached is not competitive, we reverse the procedure by starting with competitive prices and determining the number of units we would sell on a two-shift, five-day basis. From this, we deduct our variable costs and then fixed expense and compare the operating profit result with our goal. If we find our expected profit is less than the goal, we know that we must: (1) review and reduce fixed charges, (2) reduce variable cost, (3) increase the sales volume and extend operations above the normal level, and/or (4) develop new or improved products commanding a higher price in relation to variable costs.*
>
> *All of these approaches are investigated before top management reaches final agreement on the five-year goals, or goals for the immediate year ahead. This program is reviewed annually or more often if general economic conditions require it.*

Other instances of cost-volume-profit analysis and long-range planning are examined in Chapter 14.

SUMMARY

The modern multi-product company's performance is influenced by so many factors that the attempt to portray all of them on a breakeven chart by making assumptions is an ambitious one. The breakeven chart may be compared to the use of a meat-ax, not a scalpel. The chart is useful as a frame of reference for analysis, as a vehicle for expressing overall performance, and as a planning device.

The following points highlight the analytical usefulness of cost-volume-profit analysis as a tool for profit planning:

1. A change in either the selling price or the variable cost rates alters the breakeven point and the contribution margin ratio (marginal income ratio).

2. As sales exceed the breakeven point, a high contribution margin ratio will result in greater profits than a small contribution margin ratio.

3. A low contribution margin ratio necessitates great increases in volume to obtain noticeable increases in profits.

4. If other factors do not change, a percentage change in fixed costs alters the breakeven point by the same percentage and the net profit by the amount of the change.

5. A large margin of safety means that a large decrease in sales can occur before losses are suffered.

Whenever the underlying assumptions of cost-volume-profit analysis do not correspond to a given situation, the limitations of the analysis must be clearly recognized. A single breakeven graph is static because it is a picture of relationships which prevail only under one set of assumptions. If conditions change, a different set of cost-volume-profit relationships is likely to appear. The fluid nature of these relationships must be kept uppermost in the minds of the executives and accountants if the breakeven tool is to be useful and educational.

Properly used, cost-volume-profit analysis offers essential background for important management decisions regarding distribution channels, outside contracting, sales promotion expenditures, and pricing strategies. It offers an over-all view of costs and sales in relation to profit planning, and it provides clues to possible changes in management strategy. It is also the springboard for a different type of income statement which emphasizes cost behavior patterns. This is often called the "contribution" income statement; it is contrasted with the traditional income statement in Problem 2 of the Problems for Self-Study in this chapter.

SUGGESTED READINGS

The National Association of Accountants (N.A.A.) has published a vast number of research reports throughout the years. A complete list will be found at the rear of this book. The following reports are especially pertinent to cost-volume-profit analysis: Nos. 16, 17, 18, 23, and 37.

In subsequent chapters, additional references will be made to pertinent N.A.A. reports, not only for their own sake, but because they also usually contain helpful references to applicable literature.

PROBLEMS FOR SELF-STUDY

Problem 1. Here is the income statement of *C* Company:

Net sales		$ 500,000
Less expenses:		
Variable	$350,000	
Fixed	250,000	600,000
Net loss		$(100,000)

Assume that variable expenses will always remain the same percentage of sales.
  (a) If fixed expenses are increased by $100,000, what amount of sales will cause the firm to break even?

(b) With the proposed increase in fixed expenses, what amount of sales will yield a net income of $50,000?

Solution 1.   This problem differs from Example A because all data are expressed in dollars; no information on the number of units is given:

(a) Let S = Breakeven sales in dollars.

S = Variable Expenses + Fixed Expenses + Desired Net Income

$$S = \frac{\$350,000}{\$500,000} S + (\$250,000 + \$100,000)$$

S = .70 S + $350,000
.30 S = $350,000
S = $1,166,667

(b) Let S = Sales needed to earn $50,000.

S = .70 S + $350,000 + $50,000
.30 S = $400,000
S = $1,333,333

Note that 30 per cent of each sales dollar is available for the coverage of fixed expenses and the making of *net income*. *This contribution margin ratio (variable income ratio or contribution percentage)* is computed by subtracting the variable expense percentage, 70 per cent, from 100 per cent. This relationship is the foundation for the following commonly used formulas:

(a) B.E. $= \dfrac{\text{Fixed Expenses + Desired Net Income}}{1 - \dfrac{\text{Variable Expenses}}{\text{Sales}}}$

or $\dfrac{\text{Fixed Expenses + Desired Net Income}}{\text{Contribution Margin Ratio}}$

B.E. $= \dfrac{\$350,000}{1 - \dfrac{\$350,000}{\$500,000}}$ or $\dfrac{\$350,000}{.30}$

B.E. = $1,166,667

(b)   Required Sales $(RS) = \dfrac{\text{Fixed Expenses + Desired Net Income}}{\text{Contribution Margin Ratio}}$

$$RS = \frac{\$400,000}{.30}$$

$$RS = \$1,333,333$$

These examples demonstrate some very fundamental points about breakeven analysis. The most important point is the contribution-margin notion, the idea that every dollar of sales contains the same contribution toward the coverage of fixed costs and the earning of net income.

Problem 2.   Costing for planning and control emphasizes variable and fixed cost behavior patterns. In contrast, product costing emphasizes functional cost classifications. When cost behavior is the focus, financial statements are often based on a contribution approach rather than on the traditional functional approach that you learned in Chapter 2. Exhibit 3-2 shows the difference in outline form:

EXHIBIT 3-2

Contribution Approach		Traditional (Functional) Approach	
Sales	xxx	Sales	xxx
Less all variable expenses	xxx	Less manufacturing cost of goods sold	xxx
Contribution margin	xxx	Gross profit	xxx
Less fixed expenses	xxx	Less selling and administrative expenses	xxx
Net operating income	xxx	Net operating income	xxx

Using the following data (in millions) for 19x3 for the Sprouse Company, prepare a contribution income statement and a traditional income statement. Assume that there are no beginning or ending inventories. (The problem of changes in inventory levels and how they affect these statements is discussed in Chapter 10.)

Sales	$150	Variable factory overhead	$ 5
Variable selling expenses*	15	Direct labor	20
Variable administrative expenses	12	Direct material used	50
Fixed selling expenses	20	Fixed administrative expenses	5
Fixed factory overhead	10		

*These and other expenses would be detailed.

Solution 2

SPROUSE CO.
Contribution Income Statement
For the Year Ending Dec. 31, 19x3
(In millions of dollars)

Sales		$150
Less variable expenses:		
Direct material used	$50	
Direct labor	20	
Variable factory overhead	5	
Total variable manufacturing costs	$75	
Variable selling expenses	15	
Variable administrative expenses	12	
Total variable expenses		102
Contribution margin		$ 48
Less fixed expenses:		
Fixed factory overhead	$10	
Fixed selling expenses	20	
Fixed administrative expenses	5	
Total fixed expenses		35
Net operating income		$ 13

SPROUSE CO.
Traditional (Functional) Income Statement
For the Year Ending Dec. 31, 19x3
(In millions of dollars)

Sales			$150
Less manufacturing cost of goods sold:			
Direct material used		$50	
Direct labor		20	
Variable factory overhead		5	
Fixed factory overhead		10	85
Gross profit			$ 65
Selling expenses:			
Variable	$15		
Fixed	20	$35	
Administrative expenses:			
Variable	$12		
Fixed	5	17	
Total selling and administrative expenses			52
Net operating income			$ 13

APPENDIX: SALES MIX AND COST-VOLUME-PROFIT ANALYSIS

Sales mix may be defined as the relative combination of quantities of a variety of company products that compose total sales. Product lines may be analyzed by their contribution margin behavior; the problem of allocation of fixed costs to products does not arise in such an analysis. However, the determination of product-line breakeven points raises the problems of allocation of fixed costs to products. The validity of such allocations depends largely upon the relationship of the fixed costs to the product; the relationship is obvious where there are separate plants or separate sales organizations. Because the individual allocation of fixed costs to a variety of products is arbitrary in most companies, product analysis generally concentrates on the total contribution margins of product lines to over-all fixed costs.

Sales mix is an important factor in calculating an over-all company breakeven point. If the proportions of the mix change, the cost-volume-profit relationships also change. Over-all sales targets may be achieved, but profits may be much greater because of a higher-than-anticipated proportion of sales of high-margin goods; the opposite effect applies when low-margin goods predominate in the sales mix. A breakeven chart reflects a given sales mix. *When the sales mix changes, the breakeven point is altered.* Of course, if all other things are equal, companies continuously try to boost the proportion of high-margin goods. *N.A.A. Research Series No. 17* illustrated the effect of sales mix as follows:

EFFECT OF SHIFT IN SALES MIX
(000 omitted)

Assuming that the budgeted sales of $6,000 represents sales of four products which are expected to be sold in the mixture shown below, a profit of $630 and a breakeven point of $4,200 results.

	Product				
	A	B	C	D	Totals
Sales	$2,000	$2,500	$1,000	$500	$6,000
Percentage of total sales	33⅓ %	41⅔ %	16⅔ %	8⅓ %	100%
Variable cost	1,200	1,700	800	200	3,900
Contribution margin balance	$ 800	$ 800	$ 200	$300	$2,100
Contribution margin ratio	40%	32%	20%	60%	35%
Fixed costs					$1,470
Operating profit					$ 630

Breakeven point: $\dfrac{\$1,470}{0.35}$ is $4,200

If, however, sales should shift toward a larger proportion of the products carrying lower contribution margin ratios, the following figures illustrate the possible results:

	Product				
	A	B	C	D	Totals
Sales	$1,500	$2,200	$2,000	$300	$6,000
Percentage of total sales	25%	36⅔ %	33⅓ %	5%	100%
Variable cost	900	1,496	1,600	120	4,116
Contribution margin balance	$ 600	$ 704	$ 400	$180	$1,884
Contribution margin ratio	40%	32%	20%	60%	31.4%
Fixed costs					$1,470
Profit					$ 414

Breakeven point: $\dfrac{\$1,470}{0.314}$ is $4,681

A *mix variance* has arisen in this situation, calculated as follows:

	Budgeted	Actual	Variance
Contribution margin	$2,100	$1,884	$216 Unfavorable
	35.0%	31.4%	3.6%

The variance in this case may be termed a mix variance because it is explained solely by deviations from the budgeted mix. There are no subsequent changes in unit variable costs, in unit selling prices, or in total sales. Therefore, the difference between the original contribution margin percentage and the actual percentage, multiplied by the actual sales will yield the mix variance:

$$(35.0\% - 31.4\%) \times \$6,000 = \$216.$$

Chapter 21 investigates the mix variance in more detail.

QUESTIONS, PROBLEMS, AND CASES

Note: Problems 3-8 and 3-9 cover the essential techniques of cost-volume-profit analysis. Problem 3-25 introduces the contribution approach to the income statement. Problem 3-26 is an excellent review of Chapters 2 and 3.

3-1. Why is it more accurate to describe the subject matter of this chapter as *cost-volume-profit relationships* rather than as *breakeven analysis*?

3-2. Why is it often more desirable to plot variable costs above the fixed costs on a breakeven chart?

3-3. What are the principal differences between the accountant's and the economist's breakeven chart?

3-4. Define: *contribution margin, variable cost ratio, contribution margin ratio,* and *margin of safety.*

3-5. "This breakeven approach is great stuff. All you need to do is worry about variable costs. The fixed costs will take care of themselves." Discuss.

3-6. A lithographic company follows a policy of high pricing each month until it reaches its monthly breakeven point. After this point is reached, the company tends to quote low prices on jobs for the rest of the month. What is your opinion of this policy? As a regular customer, and suspecting this policy, what would you do?

3-7. Define *sales mix*. What relation does sales mix have to cost-volume-profit analysis?

3-8. Cost-Volume-Profits and Shoe Stores. Walk Rite Shoe Company operates a chain of rented shoe stores. The stores sell ten different styles of men's shoes, having identical purchase costs and selling prices. Walk Rite is trying to determine the desirability of opening another store which would have the following expense and revenue relationships:

Variable data:	Per Pair
Selling price	$5.00
Cost of shoes	$4.00
Salesmen's commissions	.25
Total variable expenses	$4.25
Annual Fixed expenses:	
Rent	$ 5,500
Wages	17,600
Utilities	2,100
Other fixed costs	4,800
	$30,000

REQUIRED:

Consider each question independently:

1. What is the annual breakeven point in dollar sales and in unit sales?

2. If 35,000 pairs of shoes are sold, what would be the store's net income (loss)?

3. If the store manager were paid 5¢ per pair as commission, what would be the annual breakeven point in dollar sales and in unit sales?

4. Refer to the original data. If sales commissions were discontinued in favor of an $8,000 increase in fixed salaries, what would be the annual breakeven point in dollars and in unit sales?

5. Refer to the original data. If the store manager were paid 10¢ per pair as commission on each pair sold in excess of the breakeven point, what would be the store's net margin if 50,000 pairs were sold?

3-9. Exercises in Cost-Volume-Profit Relationships. The Fresh Buy Grocers Corporation owns and operates twelve supermarkets in and around Chicago. You are given the following corporate budget data for next year:

Sales	$10,000,000
Fixed costs	1,650,000
Variable costs	8,200,000

REQUIRED:

Compute expected profit for each of the following deviations from budgeted data. (Consider each case independently.)

A. 10 per cent increase in total contribution margin.
B. 10 per cent decrease in total contribution margin.
C. 5 per cent increase in fixed costs.
D. 5 per cent decrease in fixed costs.
E. 8 per cent increase in sales volume.
F. 8 per cent decrease in sales volume.
G. 10 per cent increase in fixed costs and 10 per cent increase in sales volume.
H. 5 per cent increase in fixed costs and 5 per cent decrease in variable costs.

♦ **3-10. Effect of Price Changes.** 1. The Magna Company has just been formed. They have a patented process which will make them the sole distributors of product Y. Their first year, the capacity of their plant will be 9,000 units, and this is the amount they feel they will be able to sell.
   Their costs are:

> Direct labor, $1.50 per unit.
>
> Raw materials, $0.50 per unit.
>
> Other variable costs, $1.00 per unit.
>
> Fixed costs, $24,000.

If the company wishes to make a profit of $21,000 the first year, what should their selling price be? What is the contribution margin?
   2. At the end of the first year, they wish to increase their volume. An increase of $10,000 in annual fixed costs will increase their capacity to 50,000 units. They now want a profit of $76,000, and to achieve this end they also invest $50,000 in advertising. No other costs change. Under these new conditions, how many units will they have to sell to realize this profit, if their new selling price will be $7.00 per unit?

3-11. Effects of Size of Machines. The Dore Foods Company is planning to manufacture doughnuts for its chain of coffee shops throughout the city. Two alternatives have been proposed for the production of the doughnuts—by means of a semi-automatic machine, or with a fully automatic machine.
   The shops now purchase their doughnuts from an outside supplier at a cost of $.05 per doughnut.

	Semi-Automatic	Automatic
Annual fixed cost	$3,000	$5,000
Per-doughnut variable cost	$ .02	$ .015

REQUIRED:

The president has asked for the following information:

   1. For each machine, the minimum annual number of doughnuts which must be sold in order to have the total annual costs equal to outside purchase costs.

2. The most profitable alternative for 300,000 doughnuts annually.

3. The most profitable alternative for 600,000 doughnuts annually.

4. The volume level that would produce the same net income regardless of the type of machine owned.

3-12. Effects of Sales Forecast. The Frail Company has just been incorporated and plans to produce a product which will sell for $10.00 per unit. Preliminary market surveys show that demand will be less than 10,000 units per year, but it is not, as yet, clear how much less.

The company has the choice of buying one of two machines, each of which has a capacity of 10,000 units per year. Machine A would have fixed costs of $30,000 per year and would yield a profit of $30,000 per year if sales were 10,000 units. Machine B has a fixed cost per year of $16,000 and would yield a profit of $24,000 per year at sales of 10,000 units. Variable costs behave linearly for both machines.

REQUIRED:

1. Breakeven sales for each machine.

2. The sales level where both machines are equally profitable.

3. The range of sales where one machine is more profitable than the other.

3-13. Fill in Blanks. In the data presented below, fill in the information that belongs in the blank spaces.

Sales	Variable Expenses	Fixed Expenses	Total Costs	Net Profit	Contribution Margin Ratio
$1,000	$700	$____	$1,000	$____	____
1,500	____	300	____	____	.30
____	500	____	800	1,200	____
2,000	____	300	____	200	____

3-14. Cost-Volume-Profit Relationships. The Dowell Company makes and sells brooms.

Facts: Present sales volume, 500,000 units per year at a selling price of 50¢ per unit.
Fixed expenses, $80,000 per year. Variable expenses are 30¢ per unit.

REQUIRED (Consider each case separately):

1. (a) What is present total profit for a year?
   (b) What is the present breakeven point in dollars?

Compute the new profit for each of the following changes:

2. A 4¢-per-unit increase in variable expenses.

3. A 10 per cent increase in fixed expenses and a 10 per cent increase in sales volume.

4. A 20 per cent decrease in fixed expenses, a 20 per cent decrease in selling price, a 10 per cent decrease in variable expenses per unit, and a 40 per cent increase in units sold.

Compute the new breakeven point in units for each of the following changes:

5. A 10 per cent increase in fixed expenses.
6. A 10 per cent increase in selling price and a $20,000 increase in fixed expenses.

• 3-15. Choosing Most Profitable Volume Level.

1. Company B manufactures and sells dresses at a variable cost of $3.00 each and a fixed cost of x. It can sell 6,000 dresses at $5.00 and net $2,000 profit, or it can sell 3,500 at $6.00 and another 2,000 at $4.00 each. Which alternative should Company B choose?

2. Company C manufactures and sells a consumer item. It can produce and sell up to 3,000 units at a variable cost of $1.50 per unit and fixed costs of $5,000; from 3,001 to 6,000 units, at a variable cost of $1.00 per unit and fixed costs of $7,000; and from 6,001 to 10,000 units, at a variable cost of 50¢ per unit and fixed costs of $15,000. The president of Company C has discovered that 2,500 units can be sold at a price of $6.00 each or 5,000 at a price of $4.00 each. 8,000 units probably could be sold at $3.50 per unit if advertising were increased by $1,000 and selling costs by 10¢ per unit. The latter costs are in addition to those already stated for the 6,001-to-10,000-unit range. How many units should Company C plan to produce and sell—2,500, 5,000, or 8,000?

3-16. Target Net Incomes and Contribution Margins.

Clair Company has a maximum capacity of 200,000 units per year. Variable manufacturing costs are $12 per unit. Fixed factory overhead is $600,000 per year. Variable selling and administrative costs are $5.00 per unit, whereas fixed selling and administrative costs are $300,000 per year. Current sales price is $23 per unit.

REQUIRED (Consider each situation independently):

1. What is the breakeven point in (a) units, (b) dollar sales?
2. How many *units* must be sold to earn a target net income of $240,000 per year?
3. Assume that the company's sales for the year just ended totaled 185,000 units. A strike at a major supplier has caused a material shortage, so that the current year's sales will reach only 160,000 units. Top management is planning to slash fixed costs so that the total for the current year will be $59,000 less than last year. Management is also thinking of either increasing the selling price or reducing variable costs or both in order to earn a target net income that will be the same dollar amount as last year's. The company has already sold 30,000 units this year at a sales price of $23 per unit with variable costs per unit unchanged. What contribution margin per unit is needed on the remaining 130,000 units in order to reach the target net income?

3-17. Effect on Profits of Change in Price.

The Canadian Zinc Diecasting Company is one of several suppliers of part "X" to an automobile manufacturing firm. Orders are distributed to the various diecasting companies on a fairly even basis; however, the sales manager of Canadian Zinc believes that by a reduction in price he could secure another 30 per cent increase in units sold.

The general manager has asked you to analyze the sales manager's proposal and submit your recommendation.

The following data are available:

	Present	Proposed
Unit price	$2.50	$2.00
Unit sales volume	200,000 units	Plus 30%
Variable cost (total)	$350,000	Same unit variable cost
Fixed cost	$120,000	$120,000
Profit	$ 30,000	?

REQUIRED:

1. Net profit or loss based on the sales manager's proposal.
2. Unit sales under the proposed price required to make the original $30,000 profit. [S.I.C.A.]

3-18. Effect of Cost Behavior on Profits; Changing Channels of Distribution. Eastinghouse Co., an appliance manufacturer, has always sold its products through wholesalers. Last year its sales were $2,000,000 and its net profit 10 per cent of sales.

As a result of the increase in appliance sales in department stores and discount houses, Eastinghouse is considering eliminating its wholesalers and selling directly to retailers. It is estimated that this would result in a 40 per cent drop in sales, but net profit would be $180,000 as a result of elimination of the middleman. Fixed expenses would increase from the present figure of $200,000 to $300,000 owing to the additional warehouses and distribution facilities required.

REQUIRED:

1. Would the proposed change raise or lower the breakeven point in dollars? By how much?
2. What dollar sales volume must Eastinghouse obtain under the proposed plan to make as much profit as it made last year?

3-19. Influence of Relevant Range on Cost Behavior. The Charm Company's cost behavior is as follows:

Production Range in Units	Fixed Costs
0– 20,000	$160,000
20,001– 65,000	190,000
65,001– 90,000	210,000
90,001–100,000	250,000

At a normal capacity of 70,000 units per year, variable costs total $280,000. Full capacity is 100,000 units per year.

REQUIRED:

Note: Each case given below is independent of any other and should be considered individually.

1. Production is now set at 50,000 units per year with a sales price of $7.50 per unit. What is the minimum number of additional units needed to be sold in an unrelated market at $5.50 per unit to show a total net profit of $7,500 per year?

2. Production is now set at 60,000 units per year. By how much may sales promotion costs be increased to bring production up to 80,000 units and still earn a net profit of five per cent of total sales if the selling price is held at $7.50?

3. If net profit is currently $10,000, with fixed costs at $160,000, and a two per cent increase in price will leave units sold unchanged but increase profits by $5,000, what is the present volume in units?

3-20. Comparison of Two Companies. Black and White are the owners of the Modern Processing Company and the Oldway Manufacturing Company, respectively. These companies manufacture and sell the same product, and competition between the two owners has always been friendly. Cost and profit data have been freely exchanged. Uniform selling prices have been set by market conditions.

Black and White differ markedly in their management thinking. Operations at Modern are highly mechanized and the direct labor force is paid on a fixed salary basis. Oldway uses manual hourly paid labor for the most part and pays incentive bonuses. Modern's salesmen are paid a fixed salary, whereas Oldway's salesmen are paid small salaries plus commissions. Mr. White takes pride in his ability to adapt his costs to fluctuations in sales volume and has frequently chided Mr. Black on Modern's "inflexible overhead."

During 19x2, both firms reported the same profit on sales of $100,000. However, when comparing results at the end of 19x3, Mr. White was startled by the following results:

	Modern		Oldway	
	19x2	19x3	19x2	19x3
Sales revenue	$100,000	$120,000	$100,000	$150,000
Costs and expense	90,000	94,000	90,000	130,000
Net income	$ 10,000	$ 26,000	$ 10,000	$ 20,000
Per cent on sales	10%	$21\frac{2}{3}\%$	10%	$13\frac{1}{3}\%$

On the assumption that operating inefficiencies must have existed, White and his accountant made a thorough investigation of costs but could not uncover any evidence of costs that were out of line. At a loss to explain the lower increase in profits on a much higher increase in sales volume, they have asked you to prepare an explanation.

You find that fixed costs and expenses recorded over the two-year period were as follows:

| Modern | $70,000 each year |
| Oldway | $10,000 each year |

REQUIRED:

1. Prepare an explanation for Mr. White showing why Oldway's profits for 19x3 where lower than those reported by Modern despite the fact that Oldway's sales had been higher. Show relevant calculations to clarify the issue.

2. Indicate the volume of sales Oldway would have to have had in 19x3 to achieve the profit of $26,000 realized by Modern in 19x3.

3. Comment on the relative future positions of the two companies when there are reductions in sales volume.   [S.I.C.A. Adapted]

3-21. Comparison of Two Businesses.   Consider two businesses with the following unit prices and fixed and variable costs:

Business A:

Selling price per unit	$1.00
Variable cost per unit	$ .20
Fixed cost of operations per year	$5,000

Business B:

Selling price per unit	$1.00
Variable cost per unit	$ .60
Fixed cost of operations per year	$2,500

REQUIRED:

1. Calculate the breakeven point of each business in units.

2. Compute the profits of each business if sales in units are 10 per cent above the breakeven point.

3. Which business would fare better if sales dropped to 5,000 units? Why?

4. Which business would fare better if the market collapsed and the price per unit fell to 50¢? Why?

3-22. Components of Breakeven Chart.   A breakeven chart, as illustrated below, is a useful technique for showing relationships among costs, volume, and profits.

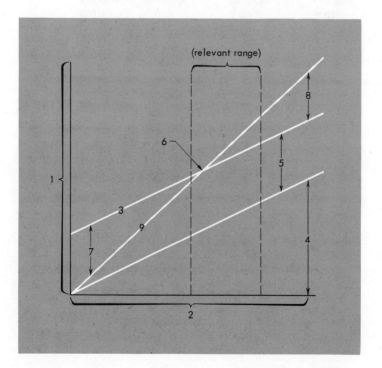

REQUIRED:

1. Identify the numbered components of the breakeven chart.
2. Discuss the significance of the concept of the "relevant range" to breakeven analyses.   [C.P.A. Adapted]

3-23. The P/V Chart. The following graph is called a P/V chart. It is a special version of the typical breakeven chart. The vertical axis indicates the total amount of profit or loss. The horizontal axis shows the total units produced (volume).

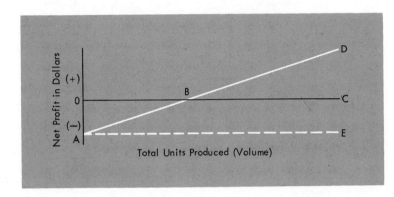

REQUIRED:

1. What is represented on the usual breakeven chart by OA?
2. What is represented on the usual breakeven chart by CD?
3. What is represented on the usual breakeven chart by B?
4. What does $DE \div AE$ represent?
5. What does $DC \div OC$ represent?

3-24. Cost-Volume-Profit and Demand Relationships. The Neumann Company is the sole supplier of a unique metal-treating compound. Its variable costs are $2.00 per pound, regardless of the level of output. Fixed expenses are $30,000 annually. The total pounds sold are influenced by the price. Market analysis indicates that the number of pounds which can be sold at a price of p dollars per pound is $40,000 \div p$.

REQUIRED:

1. At what price will the company break even?
2. What is the net income when the price is $5.00 per pound?
3. What price should be set to generate a net income of $5,000?

3-25. Miscellaneous Alternatives; Contribution Income Statement. The income statement of Hull Company appears on the next page. Commissions are based on sales dollars; all other variable expenses vary in terms of units sold.

The factory has a capacity of 150,000 units per year. The result for 19x1 have been disappointing. Top management is sifting among a number of possible ways to make operations profitable in 19x2. Consider the situations on the following page as independent of one another.

HULL COMPANY

Income Statement

For the Year Ended December 31, 19x1

Sales (90,000 units @ $4.00)			$360,000
Cost of goods sold:			
Direct materials		$90,000	
Direct labor		90,000	
Factory overhead:			
Variable	$18,000		
Fixed	80,000	98,000	278,000
Gross margin			$ 82,000
Selling expenses:			
Variable:			
Sales commissions*	$18,000		
Shipping	3,600	$21,600	
Fixed:			
Advertising, Salaries, etc.		40,000	$61,600
Administrative expenses:			
Variable		$ 4,500	
Fixed		20,400	24,900	86,500
Net loss			$ (4,500)

*Based on sales dollars, not physical units.

REQUIRED:

1. Recast the income statement into a contribution format. There will be three major sections: sales, variable expenses, fixed expenses. Show costs per unit in an adjacent column. Allow adjacent space for entering your answers to part (2).

  2. The sales manager is torn between two courses of action.
    (a) He has studied the market potential and believes that a 15 per cent slash in price would fill the plant to capacity.
    (b) He wants to increase prices by 25 per cent, to increase advertising by $120,000, and to boost commissions to 10 per cent of sales. Under these circumstances, he thinks that unit volume will increase by 50 per cent.

Prepare the budgeted income statements, using a contribution margin format and two columns. What would be the new net income or loss under each alternative? Assume that there are no changes in fixed costs other than advertising.

  3. The president does not want to tinker with the price. How much may advertising be increased to bring production and sales up to 130,000 units and still earn a target profit of 6 per cent of sales?

  4. A mail-order firm is willing to buy 60,000 units of product if the price is right. Assume that the present market of 90,000 units at $4.00 each will not be disturbed. Hull Company will not pay any sales commission. The mail-order firm will pick up the units directly at the Hull factory. However, Hull must refund $18,000 of the total sales price as a promotional and advertising allowance for the mail-order firm. In addition, special packaging will increase manufacturing costs

on these 60,000 units by 10¢ per unit. At what unit price must the mail-order chain business be quoted in order for Hull to break even in 19x2?

　　5. The president's mother-in-law thinks that a fancy new package will aid consumer sales and ultimately Hull's sales. Present packaging costs per unit are all variable and consist of 5¢ direct material and 4¢ direct labor; new packaging costs will be 30¢ and 13¢, respectively. Assuming no other changes in cost behavior, how many units must be sold to earn a net profit of $12,000?

3-26. Review of Manufacturing Accounts and Cost-Volume-Profit Relationships. For each of the following independent cases, find the unknowns, designated by letters.

	Case 1	Case 2	Case 3	Case 4
Sales	$100,000	$100,000	$ M	$100,000
Direct material used	29,000	H	55,000	40,000
Direct labor	10,000	30,000	25,000	15,000
Variable selling and administrative expenses	16,000	K	70,000	T
Fixed manufacturing overhead	30,000	I	Q	20,000
Fixed selling and administrative expenses	9,000	J	R	10,000
Gross profit	A	25,000	P	20,000
Finished goods inventory, 1/1	-0-	-0-	-0-	5,000
Finished goods inventory, 12/31	-0-	-0-	-0-	5,000
Contribution margin (dollars)	E	30,000	40,000	V
Direct material inventory, 1/1	1,000	12,000	N	50,000
Direct material inventory, 12/31	10,000	5,000	15,000	W
Variable manufacturing overhead	C	5,000	10,000	X
Work in process, 1/1	-0-	-0-	-0-	9,000
Work in process, 12/31	-0-	-0-	-0-	9,000
Purchases of direct material	D	15,000	60,000	10,000
Breakeven point (in dollars)	F	66,667	S	Y
Cost of goods manufactured	B	G	110,000	U
Net income (loss)	1,000	L	5,000	(5,000)

cost accumulation for product costing: job order accounting

This chapter examines some general problems of cost accumulation in their relationship to two prime purposes of a cost accounting system: for planning and control and for product costing. Here we must dwell heavily on techniques because they are an essential part of the accounting function. Equally important, there is an opportunity to become familiar with many terms and fundamental ledger relationships which will aid visualization and comprehension of the key subjects covered in Chapters 5 through 11.

If you have never worked in a factory, you will need to study this chapter and its appendix with care. The chapter was written to be understood by the student with little business background. If you have had some business experience, you will probably be able to skip the appendix to this chapter. If you want a more complete study of the bookkeeping aspects of cost accounting, refer to the appendix to Chapter 22 and to Chapter 24.

In any event, all students should study the section on overhead accounting very carefully.

JOB ORDER APPROACH TO COSTING PRODUCTS

Departments or cost centers—production and service departments

A factory's primary purpose is to produce goods. Thus, the major departments of a factory are the *producing* or *operating* departments—for example, drill press department, assembly department, and finishing department. In order to facilitate production, most plants also have *service* departments—for example, production control department, personnel department, and cafeteria. Service departments exist only to help producing departments with their major task, the efficient production of goods.

Management accounting concentrates on departments as the locus of cost planning, cost accumulation, and cost control. These departments are often called *cost centers*. A cost center is the smallest segment of activity or area of responsibility for which costs are accumulated. Typically, cost centers are departments, but in some instances a department may contain several cost centers. For example, although a machining department may be under one foreman, it may contain various groups of machines, such as lathes, punch presses, and milling machines. Each group of machines sometimes is regarded as a separate cost center with its own assistant foreman.

The individuals in charge of departments or cost centers should have the authority and the responsibility for efficient performance. An accounting system may accumulate costs by departments or cost centers to assist planning and control by pinpointing responsibility as much as possible.

A second major objective of the accounting system is product costing for purposes of inventory valuation and income determination. This product-costing purpose means that departmental costs must be applied (assigned) to the physical units which pass through the departments. Therefore, the accountant must satisfy two purposes: control and product costing.

Traditionally, accounting systems have been oriented toward product costing rather than planning and control. This chapter will examine the job order costing method as an example of a traditional and widespread accounting system that emphasizes product costing.

Distinction between job costing and process costing: a matter of averaging

The two polar extremes of product costing are usually labeled as *job order costing* and *process costing*. *Job order* (or *job cost* or *production order*) accounting methods are used by companies whose products are readily identified by individual units or batches each of which receives varying degrees of attention and skill. Industries which commonly use job order methods include construction, printing, aircraft, furniture, and machinery.

Process costing is most often found in such industries as chemicals, oil, textiles, plastics, paints, flour, canneries, rubber, lumber, food processors, glass, mining, cement, and meat packing. In these there is mass production of like units, which usually pass in continuous fashion through a series of uniform production steps called *operations* or *processes*. This is in contrast to the production of tailor-made or unique goods, such as special-purpose machinery or printing.

Where manufacturing is conducted by continuous operations, costs are accumulated by departments (sometimes called *operations* or *processes*). The center of attention is the total department costs for a given time period in relation to the units processed. Accumulated department costs are divided by quantities produced during a given period in order to get broad, average unit costs. Then unit costs are multiplied by units transferred to obtain total costs applied to those units. These details of *process costing* are discussed in Chapter 19, which may be studied immediately after Chapter 4, if preferred.

EXHIBIT 4-1

JOB COST SHEET

SAMPLE COMPANY   Job Order No._____

For stock_____ Customer_____

Product_____ Date started_____ Date completed_____

Department A

	Direct Material			Direct Labor			Overhead	
Date	Reference	Amount	Date	Reference	Amount	Date	Amount	
	(Stores requisition number)			(Work ticket number)			(Based on Predetermined overhead rate)	

Department B

	Direct Material			Direct Labor			Overhead	
Date	Reference	Amount	Date	Reference	Amount	Date	Amount	

Summary

Selling Price				xxx
	Dept. A	Dept. B	Total	
Costs: Direct Material	xx	xx	xxx	
Direct Labor	xx	xx	xxx	
Factory Overhead Applied	xx	xx	xxx	
	xxx	xxx		
Gross Profit				xxx
				xx

The distinction between the job cost and the process cost methods centers largely around how product costing is accomplished. Unlike process costing, which deals with broad averages and great masses of like units, the essential feature of the job cost method is the attempt to apply costs to specific jobs which may consist of either a single physical unit (like a custom sofa) or a few like units (such as a dozen tables) in a distinct batch or job lot. The most important point is that product costing is an averaging process. The unit cost used for inventory purposes is the result of taking some accumulated cost and dividing it by some measure of production. The basic distinction between job order costing and process costing is the breadth of the denominator: in job order costing, it is small (for example, one painting, 100 advertising circulars, or one special packaging machine); but in process costing, it is large (for example, thousands of pounds, gallons, or board feet).

Again one must distinguish between costs for control and product costs. Whether a process cost or a job cost approach is used, costs must be accumulated by cost centers or departments for control purposes. The typical job order approach uses one account for tracing product cost and another account or accounts for accumulating department costs.

The basic document used to accumulate product costs is called the *job order* or *job cost sheet.* The file of uncompleted job orders makes up the subsidiary ledger for Work in Process Control. Exhibit 4-1 illustrates a job cost sheet.

Job shops usually have several jobs passing through the plant simultaneously. Each job typically requires different kinds of material and departmental effort. Thus, jobs may have different routings, different operations, and different times required for completion. *Stores requisitions* (Exhibit 4-2) are used to charge job cost sheets for direct material used.

EXHIBIT 4-2

STORES REQUISITION

STORES REQUISITION			
Job No._____ Department_____ Debit Account_____ Authorized by_____		Date_____	
Description	Quantity	Unit Cost	Amount

Work tickets (Exhibit 4-3) are used to charge jobs for direct labor used. This work ticket (sometimes called *time ticket* or *time card*) indicates the time spent on a specific job. An employee who is paid an hourly wage and who operates a lathe will have one *clock card* (Exhibit 4-4), which is used as a basis for determining his individual earnings; but he will also fill out or punch several *work tickets* each day as he starts and stops work on particular jobs or operations.

EXHIBIT 4-3

WORK TICKET

WORK TICKET

Employee No. _741_   Date _2/22_   Job No. _41_

Operation _drill_   Account _Work in Process_   Dept. _A_

Stop _4:45 P.M._   Rate _$2.40_   Pieces:
Worked _15_
Rejected _—_

Start _4:00 P.M._   Amount _$1.50_   Completed _15_

EXHIBIT 4-4

CLOCK CARD

CLOCK CARD

Name _____   Employee Number _____

Department _____   Week ending _____

Date	AM		PM		Excess Hours		Total Hours
	In	Out	In	Out	In	Out	

Regular Time _____ hrs. @ _____   _____

Overtime Premium _____ hrs. @ _____   _____

Gross Earnings   _____

Responsibility and control

The departmental responsibility for usage of direct material and direct labor is very real. Copies of direct material requisitions and direct labor work tickets are used for two purposes. One copy is used to post to job cost sheets; another copy is used for fixing responsibility by departments. The department heads are usually kept informed of their direct material and direct labor performance by daily or weekly classified summaries of requisitions and work tickets charged to their departments.

In addition, the job cost sheets serve a control function. Comparisons are made between estimates of job costs and the costs finally applied to the job. Deviations are investigated so that their underlying causes may be discovered.

Illustration of job order accounting. Because each job order often contains different materials and gets a different routing through departments, the time, costs, and attention devoted by departments to any given job may vary considerably. It is desirable, therefore, to keep a separate account for inventory purposes and another account(s) for department responsibility purposes. In practice, a Work in Process account, supported by a subsidiary ledger of individual job orders, is widely used for product-costing purposes. However, practice differs greatly as to the general ledger accumulation of costs for department responsibility purposes.

Now let us turn to a specific example. Assume that a factory has two departments and uses the job cost system. Department A is the machining department; Department B is the assembly department. Exhibit 4-5 shows T-account relationships. Typical general journal entries for a job cost system follow. Special points are included in the explanation for each entry.

1. Stores control*	60,000	
Accounts (or vouchers) payable		60,000
To record purchases of materials and supplies.		

*The word "control," as used in journal entries and general ledger accounts, has a narrow bookkeeping meaning. As contrasted with "control" in the management sense, "control" here means that the control account in question is supported by an underlying subsidiary ledger. To illustrate, in financial accounting, Accounts Receivable—Control is supported by a subsidiary customers' ledger. The same meaning applies here.

All purchases of materials and supplies are charged to Stores as purchased because the storekeeper is accountable for them. The subsidiary records for Stores Control would be perpetual inventory records called *stores cards*. As a minimum, these cards would contain quantity columns for receipts, issues, and balance. Exhibit 4-6 is an illustration of a stores card.

2. Work in process control	48,000	
Factory department overhead control (supplies)	4,000	
Stores control		52,000
To record materials and supplies issued.		

EXHIBIT 4-5

JOB COST SYSTEM, DIAGRAM OF LEDGER RELATIONSHIPS

(Circled numbers refer to journal entries described more thoroughly in text.)

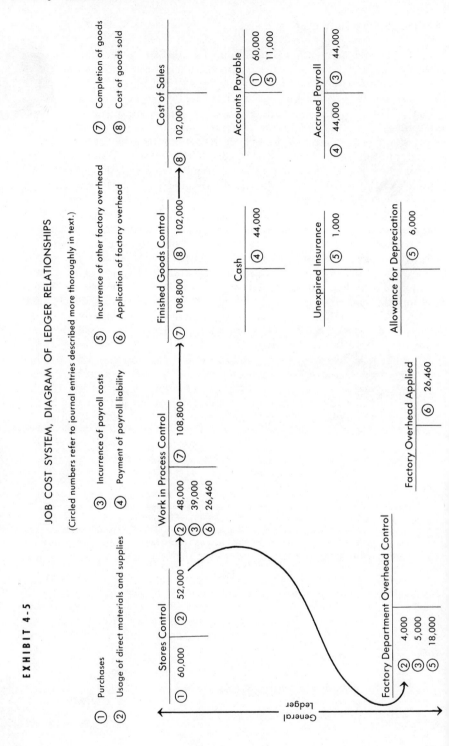

① Purchases
② Usage of direct materials and supplies
③ Incurrence of payroll costs
④ Payment of payroll liability
⑤ Incurrence of other factory overhead
⑥ Application of factory overhead
⑦ Completion of goods
⑧ Cost of goods sold

Stores Control

| ① 60,000 | ② 52,000 |

Work in Process Control

② 48,000	⑦ 108,800
③ 39,000	
⑥ 26,460	

Finished Goods Control

| ⑦ 108,800 | ⑧ 102,000 |

Cost of Sales

| ⑧ 102,000 | |

Factory Department Overhead Control

② 4,000	
③ 5,000	
⑤ 18,000	

Factory Overhead Applied

| | ⑥ 26,460 |

Cash

| | ④ 44,000 |

Accounts Payable

| | ① 60,000 |
| | ⑤ 11,000 |

Unexpired Insurance

| | ⑤ 1,000 |

Accrued Payroll

| ④ 44,000 | ③ 44,000 |

Allowance for Depreciation

| | ⑤ 6,000 |

General Ledger

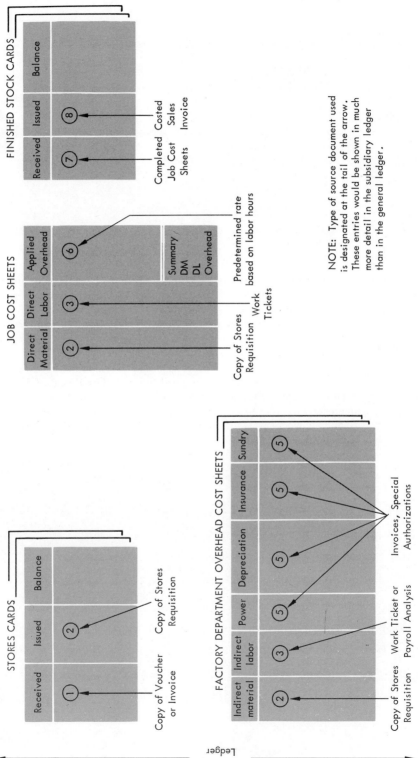

EXHIBIT 4-5 (Cont.)

EXHIBIT 4-6

		Received			Issued			Balance		
			Unit	Total		Unit	Total		Unit	Total
Date	Reference	Quantity	Cost	Cost	Quantity	Cost	Cost	Quantity	Cost	Cost

STORES CARD

Item_____

Responsibility is fixed by using *stores requisitions* (sometimes called *material requisitions*) as a basis for charging departments. A stores requisition was shown in Exhibit 4-2.

Direct materials are charged to job orders; indirect materials (supplies) are charged to individual department overhead cost sheets which form a subsidiary ledger for Factory Department Overhead Control. In job cost accounting, a single Factory Department Overhead Control account may be kept in the general ledger. The detail of factory overhead is charged to departments and recorded in departmental subsidiary overhead ledgers (department overhead cost sheets). (See Exhibit 4-7.) In turn, the overhead is applied to jobs, as will be described later.

EXHIBIT 4-7

FACTORY DEPARTMENT OVERHEAD COST SHEET

Date	Source Document	Lubricants	Other Supplies	Material Handling	Idle Time	Overtime Premium	Other Labor	Util-ities	Insur-ance	Depr.
	Requisitions	xx	xx							
	Labor Recap.			xx	xx	xx	xx			
	Invoices							xx		
	Special memos from chief accountant on accruals, pre- payments, etc.							xx	xx	xx

FACTORY DEPARTMENT OVERHEAD COST SHEET

3. Work in process control (direct labor)	39,000	
Factory department overhead control (indirect labor)	5,000	
Accrued payroll		44,000
To record incurrence of factory payroll costs.		

Withholdings are ignored in this example. Responsibility is fixed by using work tickets (Exhibit 4-3) or individual time summaries as a basis for tracing direct labor to jobs and direct and indirect labor to departments. Clock cards (Exhibit 4-4) are widely used as attendance records and as the basis for computation of payroll.

4. Accrued payroll	44,000	
Cash		44,000
To record payment of payroll.		

Actual payments and entries may be made weekly, even though entry (3) is made monthly. The reason for this is that paydays seldom coincide with the conventional accounting period (the month) for which costs are accumulated in the general ledger.[1] Thus, the Accrued Payroll account appears as follows:

Accrued Payroll

Payments	Gross Earnings
	Balance represents wages earned but unpaid.

5. Factory department overhead control	18,000	
Accounts payable		11,000
Unexpired insurance		1,000
Allowance for depreciation—Equipment		6,000
To record incurrence of other factory overhead costs:		
Utilities, repairs, etc.	$11,000	
Depreciation	6,000	
Insurance	1,000	
	$18,000	

The detail of these costs is distributed to the appropriate columns of the individual department overhead cost sheets which make up the subsidiary ledger for Factory Department Overhead Control. The basic documents for these distributions may be vouchers, invoices, or special memos from the responsible accounting officer.

6. Work in process control	26,460	
Factory overhead applied		26,460
To record application of factory overhead to		
job orders.		

[1] For a detailed treatment of the mechanics of payroll accounting, see Chapter 24.

The predetermined overhead rate used here is $2.70 per direct labor hour. Thus, the amount of overhead applied to a particular job is dependent on the amount of direct labor hours used on that job. It is assumed here that 9,800 direct labor hours were used for all jobs, resulting in a total overhead application of $26,460. This entry is explained further in a subsequent section of this chapter.

7. Finished goods control   108,800
      Work in process control   108,800
   To record completion of jobs Nos. 101–108.

As job orders are completed, the job cost sheets are totaled. Some companies use the completed job cost sheets as their subsidiary ledger for finished goods. Other companies use separate finished stock cards to form a subsidiary ledger.

8. Cost of sales   102,000
      Finished goods control   102,000
   To record cost of goods sold.

The eight summary entries are usually made monthly. The biggest share of clerical time is devoted to compiling the day-to-day details which are recorded in subsidiary ledgers. Students should try to visualize the mass of daily detail which finds its way to subsidiary ledgers, in contrast to the summaries of the detail which are posted monthly to the general ledger. Incidentally, these "ledgers" are increasingly being kept on magnetic tape rather than on looseleaf pages.

THE CONCEPTUAL APPROACH
TO ACCOUNTING FOR PRIME COSTS

The general ledger treatment of prime costs—direct material and direct labor—differs extensively between companies. The method illustrated in our example is probably the easiest to learn because it uses the fewest journal entries and accounts. However, the conceptual treatment ought to be examined so that the short-cut treatment may be viewed as a practical expedient rather than as the best theoretical design. See Exhibit 4-8 for a comparison of the conceptual notion with a treatment common in practice.

Exhibit 4-8 shows that direct material and direct labor conceptually are (a) charged to departments and (b) then applied to jobs. But note that the department account becomes a clearing account for direct material and direct labor. For example, the debit to Department Responsibility Cost Control in 2(a) is immediately offset by the credit in 2(b). A common practical treatment is to charge these items directly to the Work in Process account and not use the Department Responsibility account for either direct material or direct labor. This simplifies the general ledger and, as we shall see, highlights the intricate problem of overhead accounting. Make no mistake—accounting records are kept of department re-

EXHIBIT 4-8

JOURNAL ENTRIES FOR DIRECT MATERIAL AND DIRECT LABOR—JOB ORDER SYSTEM

Conceptual Treatment	Practical Treatment
Direct material and direct labor are (a) charged to the department and (b) applied to product.	Direct material and direct labor are charged directly to product. Accounting records are kept outside the general ledger to fix department responsibility for material and labor usage. Analysis sheets which summarize material usage and labor usage by departments are used for performance reports. These reports may be made weekly, daily, or sometimes even hourly. Furthermore, the direct material usage and labor usage may be reported separately.

Direct Material Usage

2(a). Department responsibility				2. Work in process control		xx	
cost control	xx			Stores control			xx
Stores control		xx					
2(b). Work in process							
control	xx						
Department responsibility cost control		xx					

Direct Labor Usage

3(a). Department responsibility				3. Work in process control		xx	
cost control	xx			Accrued payroll			xx
Accrued payroll		xx					
3(b). Work in process							
control	xx						
Department responsibility cost control		xx					

sponsibility for direct material and direct labor, but they are material and labor usage summaries and reports, which are kept outside the general ledger itself.

These reports, plus the report on departmental overhead costs, may easily have different timing. Depending on their relative importance, direct material usage may be reported daily; direct labor usage, weekly; and departmental overhead incurrence, monthly. In such cases, there is little need for keeping a subsidiary multi-columned, departmental cost sheet for direct material, direct labor, and overhead items. *Instead, the departmental cost sheet is usually kept only for overhead items, whereas direct material usage and direct labor usage reports are automatically produced in summaries of requisitions and work tickets. Thus, source documents for direct material and direct labor are used directly as a basis for control without necessarily having them formally summarized by department in either the subsidiary ledgers or the general ledger.*

LIMITATIONS OF GENERAL LEDGER

We cannot overemphasize the fact that many appropriate accumulations of costs for planning and control are too broad and too deep to be fitted into a general ledger. The scope of management accounting extends far beyond ledger bookkeeping. Because most general ledgers are traditionally oriented toward product costing, especially in accounting for material and labor, the reader must be on guard to avoid being preoccupied with the product-costing purpose while losing sight of the major purpose of management accounting: that of aiding planning and control. A practical compromise that we shall take is to have the general ledger emphasize the responsibility approach to cost accounting without allowing the entries to become impossibly voluminous. Put another way, the position here is that costing for control is a day-to-day task that is primarily accomplished by source documents and daily or weekly summaries. Although the control devices may be fully integrated into the general ledger, its resulting complexities are more cumbersome than the benefits derived.

OVERHEAD APPLICATION

Tracing overhead to product

Entry (6) [see page 77] in our master illustration used a predetermined overhead rate to apply factory overhead to product. Direct material and direct labor may be traced to physical units worked on with the help of requisitions and work tickets. But, by its very nature, factory overhead cannot be specifically identified with physical units. Yet the making of goods would be impossible without the incurrence of such overhead costs as depreciation, material handling, janitorial services, repairs, property taxes, heat, light, and so on.

Overhead is applied to products because of the managerial need for a close approximation of costs of different products prior to the end of a fiscal period. Essentially, this need is for pricing, income determination, and inventory valuation. If such product costs are to be helpful to management, they must be as accurate as possible.

Accountants have chosen an averaging process for identifying overhead with product. Overhead items are carefully classified into variable and fixed categories. The behavior of individual overhead items is forecast for the forthcoming year. The total forecasted overhead is related to some common denominator or base, such as expected total machine hours, direct labor hours, or direct labor dollars for the ensuing year. An overhead rate is obtained by dividing the expected overhead costs by the appropriate base. This rate is used to apply overhead to specific jobs.

To illustrate, a company may budget its factory overhead for a forthcoming year as shown in Exhibit 4-9.

In our illustration, assume that the forecast is based on a volume of activity expressed in direct labor hours. Then if detailed forecasts result in an estimate of total overhead of $324,000 for the forthcoming year at an anticipated 120,000-direct-labor-hour level of activity, the overhead rate would be: $324,000 divided by 120,000 hours, or $2.70 per direct labor hour. (This example assumes that the same overhead rate is appropriate for Departments A and B. This is an oversimplification. There are usually different overhead rates for different departments. These are illustrated and explained in Chapter 17, which can just as easily be studied now if desired.)

The $2.70 rate would be used for costing job orders. For example, during 19x1 a job cost sheet for Job 323 included the following information:

Direct material cost	$40
Direct labor cost	$60
Direct labor hours	40

The overhead to be applied to Job 323 would be: 40 hours times $2.70, or $108. The total cost of Job 323 would be: $40 plus $60 plus $108, or $208.

$$\text{Predetermined overhead rate} = \frac{\text{Total budgeted overhead}}{\text{Total budgeted volume expressed in direct labor hours}}$$

$$= \frac{\$324,000}{120,000} = \$2.70 \text{ per hour}$$

EXHIBIT 4-9

Budget of Factory Overhead For the Year Ending 19x1

	Department A	Department B	Total
Overhead expected:			
Variable items:			
Lubricants	$ 5,000	$ 3,000	$ 8,000
Other supplies	19,000	21,000	40,000
Material handling[1]	9,000	12,000	21,000
Idle time[2]	2,000	2,000	4,000
Overtime premium	3,000	5,000	8,000
Other labor	30,000	35,000	65,000
Utilities and other variable overhead	34,000	24,000	58,000
Total variable overhead	$102,000	$102,000	$204,000
Fixed items:			
Insurance	$ 2,000	$ 3,000	$ 5,000
Depreciation	30,000	35,000	65,000
Supervision	16,000	15,000	31,000
Other fixed overhead	12,000	7,000	19,000
Total fixed overhead	$ 60,000	$ 60,000	$120,000
Total budgeted overhead	$162,000	$162,000	$324,000
Divided by:			
Expected direct labor hours	60,000	60,000	120,000
Predetermined overhead rate per hour	$ 2.70	$ 2.70	$ 2.70

[1] Labor costs of moving materials and supplies.
[2] Labor costs incurred for employee time not devoted to production. Causes include equipment failure, poor scheduling, material shortages, and the like.

If actual results for the year conform to the forecast of the $324,000 overhead cost and the 120,000-direct-labor-hour level of activity, total overhead costs will be exactly applied to products worked on during the year. The basic idea of this approach is to use an annual average overhead cost per hour without changing this annual overhead rate in costing jobs from day to day and from month to month. The resultant product costs are more properly called *normal costs* rather than *actual costs* because they include an average or normalized chunk of overhead.

Annualized rates

Should overhead rates be set in the basis of weekly or monthly or yearly activity? There are two major conditions which have prompted the use of annualized predetermined rates:

1. To overcome distortions in computed unit costs that would result because of fluctuations in the volume of activity (the denominator reason) from month to month. This is the dominant reason.

2. To overcome the distortion in computed unit costs that would result because of seasonal, calendar, and other peculiar variations in the total level of overhead costs (the numerator reason) incurred each month.

1. The Denominator Reason: Fluctuations in Monthly Activity.

Some overhead costs are variable (for example, supplies and indirect labor) whereas others are fixed (for example, property taxes, rent, and depreciation). If production fluctuates from month to month, variable overhead cost incurrence will change in close proportion to variations in production, whereas total fixed overhead will remain unchanged. This means that overhead rates based on monthly activity will differ violently from month to month because of fluctuations in the unit charge for fixed overhead.

Exhibit 4-10 gives an example of a company that gears production of its single product to a highly seasonal sales pattern. Few people support the contention that an identical product should be inventoried with an $11.00 or $51.00 overhead cost at the end of July or August and only a $2.25 or $2.00 overhead cost at the end of March or April. These different overhead rates are not acceptable because they are not representative of typical, normal production conditions. Management has committed itself to a certain level of fixed costs in the light of foresseable needs far beyond a mere thirty days. Thus, where production fluctuates, monthly overhead rates are inadequate. An average, annualized rate based on the relationship of total annual overhead to total annual activity is more representative than a monthly rate. (In some cases, annual rates may also be inadequate and a three- to five-year average is more appropriate.)

2. The Numerator Reason: Peculiarities of Specific Overhead Items.

The fundamental idea underlying the annualized rate is that a business is a going concern, one which operates month after month without

EXHIBIT 4-10

MONTHLY VERSUS ANNUAL OVERHEAD RATES

Month	Total Factory Overhead Budgeted ($50,000 per month plus $1 per unit)	Units to Be Produced	Monthly Rate Per Unit	Annual Rate Per Unit*
January	$ 70,000	20,000	$ 3.50	$3.715
February	80,000	30,000	2.67	3.715
March	90,000	40,000	2.25	3.715
April	100,000	50,000	2.00	3.715
May	65,000	15,000	4.33	3.715
June	60,000	10,000	6.00	3.715
July	55,000	5,000	11.00	3.715
August	51,000	1,000	51.00	3.715
September	55,000	5,000	11.00	3.715
October	60,000	10,000	6.00	3.715
November	65,000	15,000	4.33	3.715
December	70,000	20,000	3.50	3.715
	$821,000	221,000	—	3.715

*Can be subdivided as follows:

$$\text{Variable overhead portion} = \frac{\$821,000 - (\$50,000 \times 12)}{221,000} = \$1.000$$

$$\text{Fixed overhead portion} = \frac{\$600,000}{221,000} = 2.715$$

$$\text{Combined overhead rate} = \underline{\$3.715}$$

interruption. If management is committed to continuous operation, the averaging of certain costs over a year's production becomes more acceptable.

Fluctuation in monthly volume rather than fluctuation in monthly costs incurred is the dominant reason for using an annualized overhead rate. Still, certain costs are incurred in different amounts at various times of the year. If a month's costs alone were considered, the heating cost, for example, would be charged only to winter production and the air-conditioning cost only to summer production.

Typical examples of erratic behavior include repairs, maintenance, and certain supplies requisitioned in one month which will last two or more months. These items may be charged to a department on the basis of monthly repair orders or requisitions. Yet the benefits of such charges may easily extend over a number of months' production. It would be illogical to load any single month with costs which benefit several months' operations.

The calendar itself has an unbusinesslike design; some months have twenty workdays while others have twenty four or more. Is it sensible to say that a product made in February should bear a greater share of overhead like depreciation and property taxes than it would if it were produced in March?

Other erratic items that distort monthly overhead rates are vacation and holiday pay, professional fees, and subscriptions that may fall due in one month, extra costs of learning, idle time connected with the installation of a new machine or product line, and the employer's share of Social Security taxes—which is lightest late in the year after employee wages exceed the taxable maximum.

All of the costs and peculiarities mentioned above are collected in the annual overhead pool along with the kinds of overhead that do have uniform behavior patterns (for example, supplies and indirect labor). In other words, the accountant throws up his hands and says, "We have to start somewhere, so let's pool the year's overhead and develop an annual overhead rate regardless of month-to-month peculiarities of specific overhead costs." Such an approach has a logical foundation because a *normal* product cost is more meaningful and representative for inventory purposes than a so-called "actual" product cost that is distorted by month-to-month fluctuations in production volume and by erratic or seasonal behavior of many overhead costs.

Ledger procedure for overhead

Let us see how the above notions affect general ledger procedure. For some reason, students have much trouble in understanding this phase of product costing; therefore, special study of this section is warranted.

As overhead costs are incurred by departments from month to month, these "actual" costs are charged in detail to department overhead cost sheets (the subsidiary ledger) and in summary to Factory Department Overhead Control. These costs are accumulated weekly or monthly without regard to how factory overhead is applied to specific jobs. This ledger procedure serves the purpose of managerial control of overhead. These actual costs are compared with budgeted amounts in performance reports.

Because a predetermined overhead rate (at $2.70 per direct labor hour) is an average used to apply costs to products, the daily, weekly, or monthly costing of *inventory* is independent of the incurrence of overhead costs by *departments*. For this reason, at any given time during the year, the balance in Factory Department Overhead Control is unlikely to coincide with the amount applied to product. In other words, managerial control is exercised by comparing, say, actual lubricants used with the budget for lubricants. The actual lubricants used are accumulated on the departmental overhead cost sheet. For product costing, all overhead items are lumped together, a predetermined overhead rate is computed, and this average rate is used on job orders for costing Work in Process. The use of an annual average results in inventories bearing a normalized share of factory overhead.

Most accountants stress this peculiarity of overhead accounting by confining Factory Department Overhead Control to the accumulation of "actual" overhead charges incurred and by setting up the credit side in a separate account called *Factory Overhead Applied* (sometimes called Factory Overhead *Absorbed*), much as Allowance for Depreciation is the separate credit side of, say, a Machinery account. To illustrate:

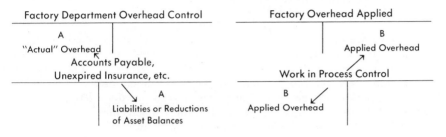

Under- or over-applied overhead

The workings of the ledger accounts for overhead may be more clearly understood if we pursue our master illustration. Let us assume that the month's entries are for January, the first month of the company's year. Postings would appear as follows:

Factory Department Overhead Control		Factory Overhead Applied	
Jan. 31(2) 4,000			Jan. 31(6) 26,460
Jan. 31(3) 5,000			
Jan. 31(5) 18,000			
Jan. 31			
Balance 27,000			

The monthly debits to Factory Department Overhead will never equal the monthly credits to Factory Overhead Applied except by coincidence. In January, for example, there is a $540 difference between the two balances. This $540 amount is commonly referred to as *under-applied* (or *under-absorbed*) *overhead*. Overhead is under-applied when the applied balance is less than the incurred (actual) balance; it is over-applied when the applied balance exceeds the incurred balance.

Although the month-end balances may not coincide, the final year-end balances should be nearly equal. Experienced budgetary accountants can predetermine rates with astounding accuracy (with one per cent error). Of course, the accuracy of predetermined overhead rates depends largely on the skill of those who do the predicting and on the nature of the business. Assume that the year's overhead costs incurred are $326,000 while only $324,000 has been applied to product. The year-end balances are closed out against one another; any insignificant difference between the final balances is generally carried to Cost of Sales as an adjustment of that figure. Several bookkeeping techniques may be used. One simple way is:

Cost of sales	2,000	
Factory overhead applied	324,000	
Factory department overhead control		326,000

To close and to charge under-applied overhead to
Cost of Sales. If overhead is over-applied, the
over-application would be credited to Cost of Sales.

Conceptually, the disposition of under- or over-applied overhead should entail correction of the costs of jobs worked on during the year. These jobs were costed by using a predetermined overhead rate instead of the actual overhead rate, which can be determined only at year-end. Ideally, a clerk would get all the job orders worked on during the year and would adjust their final costs. Thus, the most defensible way to convert job orders to "actual" costs would appear as in Exhibit 4-11.

Assume that the year-end analysis is as shown in Exhibit 4-11. Ideally, the $2,000 under-applied overhead should be spread over the three accounts that contain the job costs. This proration theoretically should be in proportion to the unadjusted overhead component in each account. The journal entry would appear as follows:

Cost of sales	1,700	
Finished goods	200	
Work in process	100	
Factory overhead applied	324,000	
Factory department overhead control		326,000

To close and to prorate under-applied overhead among
the three relevant accounts.

EXHIBIT 4-11

ANALYSIS FOR PRORATION OF UNDER-APPLIED OVERHEAD

		Ending Balance in Accounts				Correction for Under-Applied Overhead	
		Overhead	%	Total Product Cost	%	Account	Based on Overhead Applied (First choice)	Based on Total Costs in Accounts (Second choice)
Jobs worked on: 101 - 150								
Sold: 101 - 140	$275,400	85	$900,000	90	Cost of sales	$1,700	$1,800
Finished: 141 - 146	32,400	10	70,000	7	Finished goods	200	140
In process: 147 - 150	16,200	5	30,000	3	Work in process	100	60
	$324,000	100%	$1,000,000	100%		$2,000	$2,000

Some companies will prorate in proportion to total product costs. This method is theoretically valid only when the proportions of direct material, direct labor, and overhead costs are constant between jobs. To illustrate, if alligator leather is used for making 100 purses (Job A) whereas imitation alligator is used for making 100 identical purses (Job B), the respective total job costs will differ markedly; yet their overhead components are unlikely to differ because the labor hours on each job should be about the same. In this case, to adjust for under-applied overhead on the basis of total product costs would be distorting, because conceptually a different base is used for year-end adjustments from what was used for overhead application during the year. Despite these objections, many companies will prorate on the basis of total product costs because the difference in final results is not significant enough to warrant further refinements. For example, examine the small difference in the results of the two methods as shown in Exhibit 4-11.

Despite the theoretical superiority of the foregoing kinds of adjustments, *adjusting Cost of Sales for all the under- or over-applied overhead is the most expedient treatment.* It is valid as long as final results are not greatly distorted. Exhibit 4-11 shows that more refined calculations which result in proration may not affect final costs enough to be significant. However, if under- or over-applied overhead is large enough to indicate some significant error in the overhead rate, the under- or over-applied overhead should be spread over the three accounts that contain the jobs which bear the faulty rate.

Interim financial statements

The elaborate closing process for under- and over-applied overhead ordinarily takes place only at the end of the year. But what happens from month to month when interim financial statements must be prepared?[1]

We have already seen that month-to-month balances in the incurred and applied accounts do not agree. Look at these two accounts again:

Factory Department Overhead Control		Factory Overhead Applied	
Jan.	$27,000	Jan.	$26,460
Feb.	26,000	Feb.	26,810
Together	$53,000	Together	$53,270

Statements for January (not for the two months together) may be prepared on one of two options:

[1] For a thorough, provocative discussion of these problems, see David Green, Jr., "Towards a Theory of Interim Reports," *Journal of Accounting Research*, Spring, 1964, pp. 35–49. Also see Alfred Rappaport, "Towards a Theory of Interim Reports: A Modification and an Extension," *Journal of Accounting Research*, Spring, 1966, pp. 121–126.

OPTION ONE
Partial Income Statement

Sales (assumed)		$150,000
Cost of sales (per account)	$102,000	
Add:		
Under-applied factory overhead*	540	
Adjusted cost of sales		102,540
Gross margin		$ 47,460

Balance Sheet

(Prepared on usual basis)

*Difference between January 31 balances in Factory Department Overhead Control and Factory Overhead Applied.

OPTION TWO
Partial Income Statement

Sales	$150,000	
Cost of sales	102,000	
Gross margin	$ 48,000	

Balance Sheet

ASSETS			EQUITIES	
Current assets:				
Cash	$ xx		Liabilities	$ xx
Receivable	xx		Ownership	
Inventories	xx		equity	xx
Under-applied overhead	540	$ xx		
Other assets		xx		
Total		$ xx	Total	$ xx

Option One treats under-applied overhead as if it were immediately chargeable to the period. Option Two treats under-applied overhead as a cost that will benefit the rest of the year's production. Top-management preference would dictate which of the two options is to be used for reporting purposes. This author prefers Option Two because it allows Cost of Sales to be stated at average or representative amounts; it also recognizes the fact that overhead cost incurrence does not necessarily mean that such cost should be immediately written off to expense. For example, a repair will benefit the entire year's production, not just one month's. Further, the central idea of overhead application is the use of a predetermined annual average rate. There are bound to be random month-to-month under- or over-applications which should come near to offsetting one another by the end of the year. The most frequent causes of these month-to-month deviations are (a) operations at different levels of activity and (b) the presence of seasonal costs, such as heating, that are averaged in with other overhead items in setting an annual overhead rate.

January and February results taken together show a net over-applied balance of $270. Option One's approach would deduct this amount from Cost of Sales on the income statement for the two months ending February 28, 19x1. Option Two's approach would show the $270 either as a deferred credit on the right-hand side of the balance sheet or as an offset to inventory.

Analysis of reasons for under- or over-applied overhead

There can be a variety of reasons and explanations for the existence of under- or over-applied overhead. This complex subject is discussed fully in Chapters 9 and 17. At this stage, the reader should concentrate on terminology and ledger relationships.

SUMMARY

Score-keeping for the planning and control purpose consists largely of *accumulating* costs by departments; for the product-costing purpose, it consists largely of *applying* costs to products in order to obtain a representative indication of the relative attention and effort devoted to various physical units of product. As in most phases of accounting, the bulk of clerical time is spent on basic source documents and subsidiary ledgers rather than on the general ledger itself. However, the general ledger relationships of job costing offer a bird's-eye view of an entire system.

Industry uses a variety of general ledger designs, but nearly all general ledgers are concerned primarily with product costs rather than cost control. This does not necessarily mean that cost control is neglected. It is doubtful that the general ledger itself, with its emphasis on historical summaries, yields much insight into the problem of cost control. Control is an hour-to-hour, day-to-day task that is accomplished mainly via source documents and prompt summaries.

There are two widely used approaches to assigning costs to manufactured goods: job order costing and process costing. In practice, each company's approach is tailored to its needs and is usually some sort of hybrid. Job order costing was discussed at length in this chapter. Chapter 19 discusses process costing and compares it with job order costing.

Many companies apply overhead with predetermined rates. The resultant product cost consists of "actual" direct material, "actual" direct labor, and "predetermined" overhead. Thus, this total product cost should be called a *normal* cost rather than an *actual* cost. Therefore, a given product-costing system can properly be called an *actual cost* system (where no costs are predetermined), a *normal cost* system (where predetermined rates are used to apply overhead), or a *standard cost* system (where, as discussed in Chapters 6, 7, and 8, predetermined rates are used to apply material, labor, and overhead). Within a given system, either a job order costing approach or a process costing approach or some hybrid approach is tailored to needs.

Some thoughtful solving of homework at this stage will strengthen your understanding of basic relationships and terminology.

SUGGESTED READINGS

At this point, working out several homework problems is much more important than supplementary reading.

PROBLEM FOR SELF-STUDY

Restudy the illustration of job order accounting in this chapter. Then try to solve one or two straightforward job order problems such as Problems 4-8 and 4-11. Then try to solve the following problem, which requires consideration of most of this chapter's important points.

Problem

You are asked to bring the following incomplete accounts up to date through January 31, 19x2. Also consider data that appear after the T-accounts.

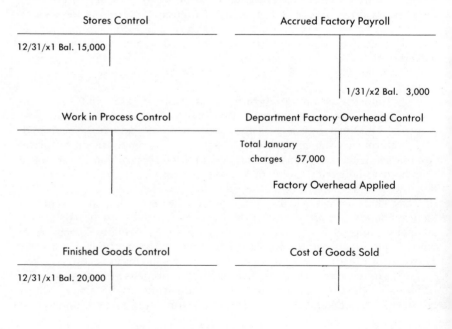

Stores Control		Accrued Factory Payroll	
12/31/x1 Bal. 15,000			1/31/x2 Bal. 3,000

Work in Process Control		Department Factory Overhead Control	
		Total January charges 57,000	

		Factory Overhead Applied	

Finished Goods Control		Cost of Goods Sold	
12/31/x1 Bal. 20,000			

Additional Information

1. The overhead is applied using a predetermined rate that is set every December by forecasting the following year's overhead and relating it to forecasted direct labor costs. The budget for 19x2 called for $400,000 of direct labor and $600,000 of factory overhead.

2. The only job unfinished on January 31, 19x2 was No. 419, on which total labor charges were $2,000 (1,000 direct labor hours) and total direct material charges were $8,000.

3. Total materials placed into production during January totaled $90,000.

4. Cost of goods completed during January was $180,000.

5. January 31 balances on stores cards totaled $20,000.

6. Finished goods inventory as of January 31 was $15,000.

7. All factory workers earn the same rate of pay. Direct man-hours for January totaled 20,000. Indirect labor and supervision totaled $10,000.

8. The gross factory payroll paid on January paydays totaled $52,000. Ignore withholdings.

9. All "actual" factory overhead incurred during January has already been posted.

1. Materials purchased during January.
2. Cost of goods sold during January.
3. Direct labor costs incurred during January.
4. Overhead applied during January.
5. Balance, Accrued Factory Payroll, December 31, 19x1.
6. Balance, Work in Process, December 31, 19x1.
7. Balance, Work in Process, January 31, 19x2.
8. Over- or under-applied overhead for January.

Solution

1. $95,000	3. $40,000	5. $5,000	7. $13,000
2. $185,000	4. $60,000	6. $3,000	8. $ 3,000
			over-applied

Entries in T-accounts are keyed in accordance with the "additional information" in the problem.

Stores Control

(given)	12/31/x1 Bal.	15,000		
	(5)	95,000	(3)	90,000
1/31/x2 Bal.	(5)	20,000		

Work in Process Control

12/31/x1 Bal. *		3,000	(4)		180,000
Direct materials	(3)	90,000			
Direct labor	(7)	40,000			
Overhead	(7) & (1)	60,000			
1/31/x2 Bal.	(2)	13,000			

Finished Goods Control

(given) 12/31/x1	Bal.	20,000			
(4)		180,000	(6)		185,000
1/31/x2 Bal.	(6)	15,000			

Accrued Factory Payroll

(8)	52,000	*		5,000
		(7)		$\begin{cases} 40,000 \\ 10,000 \end{cases}$
		1/31/x2 Bal.		3,000
		(given)		

Department Factory Overhead Control

January charges (given)	57,000

Factory Overhead Applied

	(7) & (1)	60,000

Cost of Goods Sold

(6)	185,000

Notes: (1) Overhead rate is 150% of direct labor cost.
(2) Ending work in process is $8,000 + $2,000 + 150% of $2,000.

*Can be computed only after all other postings in the account have been found.

APPENDIX: SUPPLEMENTARY DESCRIPTION OF LEDGER RELATIONSHIPS

This appendix explains some of the paper work that underlies the general ledger relationships described in this chapter. It also contains an exhibit that summarizes sample accounting entries for job costing.

Subsidiary ledgers and general ledger

The general ledger is a summary device. Postings are made to it from totals and subtotals of underlying transactions. For example, the Stores balance may be supported by a voluminous file of stores cards. Postings to the debit side of the Stores account may be made from the Stores column in a special journal, such as a purchases journal or a voucher register. But the specific stores card in the subsidiary ledger is posted from a copy of a voucher or an invoice.

The general ledger gives a bird's-eye view of cost accounting relationships; the subsidiary ledgers contain the underlying details—the worm's-eye view. In turn, source documents, such as voucher copies, stores requisitions, work tickets, clock cards, and other memoranda, are the primary means of recording business events. In a sense, the source documents are the everyday tools for systematically recording operating activities. They are vital because all subsequent accounting classifications and reports are dependent on source documents.

Direct material usage reports

A multi-copied stores requisition may be made out by a foreman. For example, separate copies may serve as follows:

Copy 1. Kept by storekeeper.
Copy 2. Used by job order cost clerk to post to job cost sheet.
Copy 3. Used by accounting department as a basis for a summary of requisitions.

This summary is the support for the general ledger entry;

Work in process	xx	
Stores		xx

This entry is usually made monthly, although it
  can be made more frequently if desired.

Copy 4. Used by departmental cost clerk as a basis for material usage reports to departments. If these reports are to prove useful for control, they typically must be prepared more often than once a month. Stale, month-old reports concerning major costs are not helpful. Daily or weekly reports are common. This is another reason why the general ledger is oriented toward product costing rather than toward costing for control. The reports for control are needed before formal postings can be made.
Copy 5. Retained by foreman. He can use these as a cross-check against the usage reports sent to him by the accounting department.

The accounting department may use punched cards as requisitions. These may be sorted in many ways. For example:

DIRECT MATERIAL REQUISITION SUMMARY					
Requisition Number	Job Order	Department	Amount	Job Order Subtotals	Department Subtotals
501	1415	26	$ 32.00		
502	1415	27	51.00	$83.00	
503	1408	26	204.00		
504	1414	26	19.00		$255.00
505	1409	28	101.00		

Machine accounting facilitates the accumulation and tabulation of data so that they may be classified, re-classified, summarized, and re-summarized to provide the specific information needed by management. Thus, a material usage report like the following may be submitted to the foreman of Department 26 on a daily, weekly, or monthly basis:

Department 26 DIRECT MATERIAL USAGE For the week ending_____		
Requisition Number	Job Order	Amount
501	1415	$ 32.00
503	1408	204.00
504	1414	19.00
510	1408	55.00
511	1412	122.00

Direct labor cost recapitulation

Similar analysis can be applied to the sorting of direct labor costs, using the work ticket as the source document. Producing departments may have their labor classified by operations as well as by jobs. For example, the machining department may perform one or more of the following operations: milling, cleaning, grinding, and facing. Thus, work tickets may be recapitulated as follows:

DIRECT LABOR COST RECAPITULATION								
Work Ticket Number	Employee Identification Number	Job Number	Department Number	Operation Number	Amount	Job Subtotals	Operation Subtotals	Department Subtotals
14	49	1410	26	6500	$20.00		$20.00	
15	49	1410	26	6501	6.00		6.00	$26.00
16	52	1410	27	7520	19.00		19.00	
17	53	1410	27	7522	16.00	$61.00		
19	30	1411	25	5298	30.00	30.00	30.00	30.00
19	61	1409	28	8414	24.60		24.60	24.60
20	52	1409	27	7522	9.75	34.35	25.75	44.75

This labor recapitulation can be used as a basis for the general ledger entry that charges direct labor to product:

Work in process	xx	
Accrued payroll		xx

This entry is usually made monthly, although it
can be made more frequently if desired.

The recapitulation also supplies the information for daily, weekly, or monthly usage reports to the departmental foreman. These reports may be broken down by jobs or operations to suit the wants and needs of the foreman.

Work tickets may also be used for idle time (for example, caused by machine breakdowns or shortages of material), overtime premium, material handling, and so forth. A clerk or timekeeper may have the duty of preparing a daily reconciliation of employee clock cards with individual work tickets to see that all clock-card time is accounted for as direct labor, idle time, overtime premium, and so forth.

Sample entries

Exhibit 4-12 summarizes the accounting entries for job costing.

QUESTIONS, PROBLEMS, AND CASES

Note: Problems 4-8, 4-11, 4-14, and 4-18 or 4-19 cover the essential points in this chapter. Problems 4-9, 4-23, and 4-24 probe the relationships between general ledgers, subsidiary ledgers, and source documents in depth.

4-1. Distinguish between producing departments and service departments.

4-2. Give two definitions of *control* as the word may be used by an accountant.

4-3. What is the purpose of a *department cost sheet?*

4-4. What is the principal difference between job cost and process cost accounting systems?

4-5. Distinguish between a *clock card* and a *work ticket.*

4-6. What are the limitations of the general ledger as a cost accounting device?

4-7. What is a *normal product cost?*

4-8. Journal Entries. The following data relate to operations of the Tuttle Manufacturing Co. for the year 19x4, its first year of operations:

1. Materials and supplies purchased on account	$150,000
2. Materials issued to the producing departments for production	120,000
3. Supplies issued to the producing departments	10,000
4. Materials returned to the storeroom from the factory	5,000

EXHIBIT 4-12

JOB ORDER SYSTEM SAMPLE ENTRIES

Transaction	General Ledger Effects	Subsidiary Ledgers	Source Documents	Explanatory Comments
1. Purchases of materials or supplies	Stores control Accounts payable	Dr. Stores card, "Received" column	Approved invoice	
2. Issuance of direct materials	Work in process control Stores control	Dr. Job order Cr. Stores card, "Issued" column	Stores requisition	Requisitions are summarized and classified by department for hourly, daily, weekly, or monthly direct material usage reports.
3. Issuance of supplies	Factory department overhead control Stores control	Dr. Department overhead cost sheets, appropriate columns Cr. Stores card, "Issued" column	Stores requisition	
4. Distribution of labor costs	Work in process control Factory department overhead control Accrued payroll	Dr. Job orders Dr. Department overhead cost sheets, appropriate columns for various classes of indirect labor	Summary of work tickets or daily time analyses. This summary is sometimes called a labor cost distribution summary or a payroll recapitulation	
5. Payment of payroll (For a complete description, see Chapter 23.)	Accrued payroll Withholdings payable Cash		Summary of clock cards and individual withholdings as shown on payroll sheets.	This entry is usually made weekly, while the cost distribution (the prior entry) is not necessarily made at the same time.
6. Payment of withholdings	Withholdings payable Cash			Withholdings are usually broken down by type rather than lumped in one account
7. Employer payroll taxes	Factory department overhead control Employer payroll taxes payable	Dr. Department overhead cost sheets, appropriate columns	Accrual memoranda from accounting officer	

(Continued on next page)

Transaction	General Ledger Effects	Subsidiary Ledgers	Source Documents	Explanatory Comments
8. Utilities	Factory department overhead control Accounts payable or Accrued utilities	Dr. Department overhead cost sheets, appropriate columns	Approved invoices or accrual memoranda	
9. Depreciation on factory equipment	Factory department overhead control Allowance for depreciation—Equipment	Dr. Department overhead cost sheets, appropriate columns	Depreciation schedule	
10. Factory insurance write-off	Factory department overhead control Unexpired insurance	Dr. Department overhead cost sheets, appropriate columns	Insurance register or memoranda from accounting officer	
11. Application of overhead to product	Work in process control Factory overhead applied	Dr. Job order	Predetermined overhead rate computed by using overhead budget	
12. Transfer completed goods to finished stock	Finished goods control Work in process control	Dr. Finished stock card, "Received" column Cr. Job order	Production report	Sometimes the completed job order serves as a finished stock card.
13. Sales	Accounts receivable control Sales	Dr. Customers' accounts	Copy of sales invoice	
14. Cost of sales	Cost of sales Finished goods control	Dr. Cost of sales record (optional) Cr. Finished stock cards	Copy of sales invoice plus costs as shown on finished stock cards	
15. Yearly closing of overhead accounts	Factory overhead applied Factory department overhead control Cost of sales (cr. if overhead is overapplied; dr. if overhead is under-applied)		General ledger balances	

97

5. Labor used directly on production	100,000
6. Indirect labor incurred	30,000
7. Depreciation—Plant and equipment	10,000
8. Miscellaneous factory overhead incurred (ordinarily would be detailed)	23,000
9. Overhead applied at a rate of 60 per cent of direct labor cost	?
10. Cost of production completed	250,000
11. Sales	200,000
12. Cost of goods sold	180,000
13. Returned sales—at selling prices, $5,000; at factory cost, $4,500.	

REQUIRED:

1. General journal entries. Number your entries.

2. Show the T-account for Factory Department Overhead Control. Sketch how this account's subsidiary ledger would appear, assuming that there are four factory departments. You need not show any numbers in the subsidiary ledger.

3. Show T-accounts and the closing balances for all inventories. Assume that over- or under-applied overhead is closed directly to cost of goods sold (show the journal entry).

4-9. Source Documents. Refer to Problem 4-8. For each entry, (a) indicate the most likely name of the source documents that would authorize the entry and (b) give a description of the entry into the subsidiary ledgers, if any, affected.

4-10. Journal Entries. The *GHI* Company uses a job order cost system. The following relate to the month of March:

1. Raw materials issued to production:

Order No. 301	$2,000	
Order No. 302	6,100	
Order No. 303	7,000	
Order No. 304	5,300	
Order No. 305	6,200	$26,600

2. Direct labor analysis:

Order No. 301	1,000 hrs.	$ 800	
Order No. 302	2,000 hrs.	4,500	
Order No. 303	5,000 hrs.	6,000	
Order No. 304	2,000 hrs.	3,000	
Order No. 305	3,000 hrs.	4,000	$18,300

3. Manufacturing overhead is applied to production on the basis of $2.00 per direct labor hour.

4. Total manufacturing overhead for the month was $27,000.

5. Production orders 301, 303, 304, and 305 were completed during the month.

6. Production orders 301 and 304 were shipped and invoiced to customers during the month at a profit of 15 per cent.

REQUIRED:

Prepare the general journal entries required to record this information. What is the ending balance of work in process? Prepare a job cost sheet for order No. 302. [S.I.C.A.]

4-11.　Accounting for Overhead; Predetermined Rates.

1. The Sain Company uses a predetermined overhead rate in applying overhead to production orders on a *labor cost* basis for Department A and on a machine-hour basis for Department B. At the beginning of 19x1, the company made the following *estimates:*

	Dept. A	Dept. B
Direct labor cost	$20,000	$10,000
Factory overhead	30,000	50,000
Direct labor hours	16,000	5,000
Machine hours	1,000	20,000

REQUIRED:

1. What is the predetermined overhead *rate* that should be used in Department A? In Department B?

During the month of January the cost sheet for production order No. 200 shows the following:

	Dept. A	Dept. B
Materials requisitioned	$2.00	$10.00
Direct labor cost	$5.00	$ 7.00
Direct labor hours	4	3
Machine hours	1	13

2. What is the *total overhead* cost of production order No. 200?

3. Assuming that Job No. 200 consisted of 20 units of product, what is the *unit cost* of Job No. 200?

4. At the *end* of 19x1 it was found that *actual* factory overhead costs amounted to $31,500 in Department A and $47,000 in Department B.

Give the over- or under-absorbed overhead amount for each department and for the factory as a whole. Assume that total actual direct labor costs and machine hours conformed with the original estimates.

4-12.　Incomplete Data; Journal Entries.

The following account balances were selected from the general ledger of the Aaron Manufacturing Company at the start of business on January 1, 19x1, and the close of business on December 31, 19x1. The company uses perpetual inventories.

	Balances, January 1, 19x1	Balances, December 31, 19x1
Stores	$ 5,000	$20,000
Manufacturing overhead	—	22,000
Manufacturing overhead applied (at a rate of $\frac{2}{3}$ of the direct labor cost)	—	20,000
Work in process	35,000	15,000
Finished goods	20,000	30,000
Cost of goods sold	—	100,000

REQUIRED:

Entries in general journal form summarizing the operating activities of the year 19x1, which were recorded in the above accounts. Present T-accounts also.

4-13. Incomplete Data; Find Unknowns. The Alou Company uses perpetual inventories. Following are selected balances taken from certain accounts:

	Balances December 31, 19x1	Balances December 31, 19x2
Stores	$20,000	$ 22,000
Cost of goods sold	—	130,000
Factory overhead applied (at 50% of direct labor cost)	—	30,000
Work in process	14,000	10,000
Factory overhead control	—	32,000
Finished goods	30,000	50,000

REQUIRED:

Before considering any year-end adjustments for over- or under-applied overhead:
1. What was the cost of goods completed during 19x2?
2. What was the cost of materials purchased during 19x2?

4-14. Overview of General Ledger Relationships. The Blakely Company uses a job order cost system. The total debits and credits in certain accounts at year end are:

	December 31, 19x6	
	Total Debits	Total Credits
Direct material control	$100,000	$ 70,000
Work in process control	320,000	305,000
Factory department overhead control	85,000	—
Finished goods control	325,000	300,000
Cost of goods sold	300,000	—
Factory department overhead applied	—	90,000

Note that "total debits" in the inventory accounts would include beginning inventory balances, if any.

The above accounts *do not* include the following:

(a) The labor cost recapitulation for the December 31 working day: direct labor, $5,000, and indirect labor, $1,000.
(b) Miscellaneous factory overhead incurred on December 30 and December 31: $1,000.

Additional Information

Factory overhead is applied as a percentage of direct labor.
Direct material purchases during 19x6 were $80,000.
There were no returns to suppliers.
Direct labor costs during 19x6 totaled $150,000, not including the December 31 working day described above.

REQUIRED:

1. Beginning inventories of direct material, work in process, and finished goods. Show T-accounts.
2. Prepare all adjusting and closing journal entries for the above accounts. Assume that all under- or over-applied overhead is closed directly to Cost of Goods Sold.
3. Ending inventories, after adjustments and closing, of direct material, work in process, and finished goods.

4-15.   Meaning of Over-Applied Overhead.   The Walgenbach Company had budgeted the following performance for 19x3:

Units	100,000
Sales	$110,000
Total variable expenses	65,000
Total fixed expenses	40,000
Net income	5,000
Factory overhead:	
Variable	5,000
Fixed	30,000
Beginning inventories	None

It is now the end of 19x3. A factory overhead rate of 35¢ per unit was used throughout the year for costing product. Total factory overhead incurred was $35,000. Over-applied factory overhead was $1,050. There is no work in process. How many units were produced during 19x3?

4-16.   Year-End Disposition of Overhead.   The Bower Company's overhead is applied to products using a predetermined rate that is set every December by forecasting the following year's overhead and relating it to forecasted direct labor *dollars*. The budget for 19x2 was $500,000 for direct labor and $250,000 for factory overhead.

The only job unfinished on December 31, 19x2 was No. 485, on which total direct labor charges were $50,000 (20,000 direct labor hours). Machine hours were 5,000, and total direct material charges were $25,000.

The total charges to Department Factory Overhead Control through December 31 were $270,000. Total direct labor costs for the year were $480,000, representing 200,000 direct labor hours.

There were no beginning inventories. In addition to the ending work in process described above, the ending finished goods showed a balance of $400,000. Cost of goods sold for the year totaled $500,000. These figures are *normal* costs; that is, no year-end adjustments have been made for under- or over-applied overhead.

REQUIRED:

1. Balance, Work in Process, December 31, 19x2 (at *normal cost*).
2. Over- or Under-applied Overhead for 19x2. Be certain to designate whether the dollar amount you show represents over- or under-applied overhead.
3. For this part, assume (ignore your answer to part 2) that overhead for 19x2 was under-applied by $50,000. The company usually charges or credits over- or under-applied overhead to Cost of Goods Sold at year end. If instead the com-

pany followed the alternative practice of prorating over- or under-applied overhead over the ending balances (at normal cost) of Work in Process, Finished Goods, and Cost of Goods Sold, by what amount would net income differ?

4-17.   Journal Entries, Year-End Disposition of Overhead.   Tuttle Company uses a job order cost system. Factory overhead is applied at a rate of $2.50 per direct labor hour. Both beginning and closing balances in work in process and finished goods are zero. You are given the following data for 19x4, and the fact that all goods manufactured are sold.

Direct labor hours used	50,000
Direct material used	$ 50,000
Direct labor used	100,000
Indirect labor used	25,000
Indirect supplies used	10,000
Rent—plant and equipment	50,000
Miscellaneous overhead	50,000
Cost of goods sold	275,000

All under- or over-applied overhead is allocated wholly to cost of goods sold at the end of the year.

REQUIRED:

1. Factory overhead applied.
2. Factory overhead incurred.
3. Prepare journal entries to record all of the above facts including all necessary entries to adjust for over- or under-applied overhead.

4-18.   Multiple Choice; Incomplete Data.   Some of the general ledger accounts of the Sharman Manufacturing Company appear as follows on January 31, 19x1.

The accounts are incomplete because the accountant had an emergency operation for ulcers after he ate lunch in the company cafeteria on January 31. The treasurer, an old friend of yours, supplied you with the following incomplete accounts and three bits of additional information.

Direct Material Stores Control	
Bal. Jan. 1 5,000	
40,000	

Work in Process Control	
Bal. Jan. 1 1,000	40,000
Direct mate-	
rials requi-	
sitioned 20,000	

Finished Goods Control	
Bal. Jan. 1 10,000	20,000

Cost of Goods Sold	

Accrued Factory Payroll	
	Bal. Jan. 1 1,000
	Gross earnings
	of all factory
	workers 40,000

Additional Information

(a) Factory Overhead Applied is credited for all indirect costs that are applied to production orders.

(b) Work tickets for the month totaled 22,000 direct man-hours. All factory workers received $1.50 per hour.

(c) Indirect costs are applied at a rate of $1.00 per direct man-hour.

After giving you a few minutes to look over the data given, your old friend asks you the following (Place all answers on an answer sheet. Indicate your answer by letter.):

1. The January 31 balance of Direct Material Stores Control should be:

(a) $45,000	(d) $15,000
(b) 25,000	(e) 40,000
(c) 20,000	(f) None of the above.

2. The amount of total direct labor cost that should have been charged to all the individual production orders worked on during January should be:

(a) $40,000	(d) $33,000
(b) 41,000	(e) 30,000
(c) 55,000	(f) None of the above.

3. The *total* factory labor cost for the month of January (ignoring employer's Social Security contributions) is:

(a) $40,000	(d) $33,000
(b) 41,000	(e) 56,000
(c) 55,000	(f) None of the above.

4. The total *indirect* cost that should have been applied to production is:

(a) $17,000	(d) $33,000
(b) 75,000	(e) 24,000
(c) 40,000	(f) None of the above.

5. The January 31 balance of Work in Process Control should be:

(a) $75,000	(d) $35,000
(b) 77,000	(e) 36,000
(c) 76,000	(f) None of the above.

6. The January 31 balance of Finished Goods Control should be:

(a) $30,000	(d) $25,000
(b) 10,000	(e) 5,000
(c) 20,000	(f) None of the above.

7. *Total* indirect costs actually incurred during the month amount to $24,000. The balance in Factory Overhead Control at the end of January should be:

(a) $17,000	(e) $22,000
(b) 24,000	(f) 2,000
(c) 26,000	(g) None of the above.
(d) 41,000	

8. The Cost of Goods Sold during January was:

(a) $40,000   (d) $30,000
(b) 20,000   (e) 50,000
(c) 10,000   (f) None of the above.

9. The January 31 balance of Factory Overhead Applied should be:

(a) $33,000   (e) $26,000
(b) 40,000   (f) 30,000
(c) 24,000   (g) None of the above.
(d) 22,000

10. The amount of under-absorbed (or over-absorbed) costs for January is:

(a) Under-absorbed by $1,000
(b) Under-absorbed by $2,000
(c) Over-absorbed by $1,000
(d) Over-absorbed by $2,000
(e) Over-absorbed by $3,000
(f) Neither over-absorbed nor under-absorbed.
(g) None of the above.

4-19. General Ledger Relationships; Incomplete Data. You are asked to bring the following incomplete accounts up to date through May, 19x1. Also consider the additional information which follows the T-accounts.

Stores Control	Accounts Payable
5/31/x1 Bal. 18,000	4/30/x1 Bal. 10,000

Work in Process Control	Department Factory Overhead Control
4/30/x1 Bal. 2,000	Total charges for May 15,000

	Factory Overhead Applied

Finished Goods Control	Cost of Goods Sold
4/30/x1 Bal. 25,000	

Additional Information

1. The overhead is applied by using a predetermined rate that is set at the beginning of each year by forecasting the year's overhead and relating it to forecasted direct labor hours. The budget for 19x1 called for a total of 150,000 hours of direct labor and $225,000 of factory overhead.

2. The accounts payable are for direct materials only. The balance on May 31 was $5,000. Payments of $35,000 were made during May.

3. The finished goods inventory as of May 31 was $22,000.

4. The cost of goods sold during the month was $65,000.

5. On May 31 there was only one unfinished job in the factory. Cost records show that $1,000 (400 hours) of direct labor and $2,000 of direct material had been charged to the job.

6. A total of 9,400 direct man-hours were worked during the month of May. All factory workers earn the same rate of pay.

7. All "actual" factory overhead incurred during May has already been posted.

REQUIRED:

1. Materials purchased during May.
2. Cost of goods completed during May.
3. Overhead applied during May.
4. Balance, Work in Process, May 31, 19x1.
5. Materials used during May.
6. Balance, Stores Control, April 30, 19x1.
7. Over- or under-applied overhead for May.

4-20. Under-Applied Overhead on Interim Income Statements.
The following data are available for *ABC* Company covering the month of January, 19x4.

Sales	$100,000
Cost of sales (per account)	75,000
Factory overhead incurred	25,500
Factory overhead applied	25,100
Selling and administrative expenses	10,000

REQUIRED:

You are to prepare interim income statements for the month of January:
1. Assuming under-applied overhead is immediately chargeable to the period.
2. Assuming under-applied overhead as a cost that will benefit the rest of the year's production.

4-21. Overhead Application and Interim Earnings. Taken from Nash-Hudson merger proxy statement:

> *"The final Hudson loss is greater than was reported in earlier accounting periods. The loss was caused primarily by external market conditions, the full impact of which was not evident until close to the end of the year. Heavy outlays for tooling for new models during 1953 did not result in the increased volume which had been expected. Sales prices had been established on the basis of amortizing costs over a volume of car shipments higher than was later actually realized, and the amortization of tooling, absorption of certain elements of inventory, and expensing of prepaid advertising at the unit rates originally established resulted in asset balances at December 31, 1953 greater than reasonably could be expected to be absorbed against future operations. Year-end adjustments have therefore been made as at December 31, 1953, and the portions considered applicable to the nine months ended September 30, 1953 have been included in the Statement of Consolidated Income for that period.*
>
> *"The adjustments applied to the nine months ended September 30, 1953 are summarized below.*

"Loss for the nine months ended September 30, 1953, before
    year-end adjustments, as published November 6, 1953 $ 838,100

"Adjustments:

Additional costs resulting from lower-than-expected volume:

Increased amortization of dies, jigs and fixtures largely acquired during 1953	$ 7,911,047
Obsolescence of inventory for 1953 models, resulting from early introduction of 1954 models	1,551,875
Reduction of the cost of inventories to estimated realizable market	1,198,000
Additional local-area advertising expense	578,000
	$11,238,922
Add, Price redetermination of a defense contract during December, 1953; portion applicable to nine months ended September 30, 1953	843,515
	$12,082,437
Deduct, other adjustments of accruals, etc., net credit	416,303
	$11,666,134
Deduct, increase in the amount of the federal income tax carry-back credit, resulting from the above adjustments	6,039,037
Net adjustments	$ 5,627,097
Loss for the nine months ended September 30, 1953, as published January 26, 1954 and as included in this Proxy Statement	$ 6,465,197

"The Company believes that operations for the fourth quarter of 1953 will show a loss of approximately $4,000,000, increasing the loss of $6,465,197 reported for the nine months ended September 30, 1953 to approximately $10,465,197 for the year ended December 31, 1953. The corresponding amounts before net federal income tax carry-back credits are $4,825,000, $13,041,634, and $17,866,634 respectively."

REQUIRED:

What criteria should be used in setting amortization rates for dies, jigs, and fixtures? What is your impression of the timing of managerial action with respect to interim financial reporting?

4-22. Federal Government Fixed-Price Incentive Contract. Graystone Electronics Corporation's sole activity in 19x4 was a federal government fixed-price incentive contract awarded in January 19x4. The Corporation's prior government contracts were cost-plus-fixed-fee or firm fixed-price contracts which were completed by December 19x3.

Provisions of the fixed-price incentive contract include the following:

1. Graystone is to construct eight identical digital computers, deliveries to be made between July 19x4 and June 19x5.

2. The total contract target price is $780,000, which includes a target cost of $700,000. The total adjusted price cannot exceed a ceiling of $810,000.

3. The incentive clause states:

"The total adjusted price (final contract price) shall be established by adding to the total adjusted cost (final negotiated cost) an allowance for profit determined as follows:

WHEN THE TOTAL ADJUSTED COST IS:	THE ALLOWANCE FOR PROFIT IS:
Equal to the total target cost	Total target profit.
Greater than the total target cost	Total target profit less 20% of the amount by which the total adjusted cost exceeds the total target cost.
Less than the total target cost	Total target profit plus 20% of the amount by which the total adjusted cost is less than the total target cost."

The following information is available at December 31, 19x4:

1. Costs accumulated on the contract:

Direct materials	$170,000
Direct labor	192,000
Overhead	240,000
Total.............................	$602,000

2. The estimated costs to complete the contract:

Direct materials	$ 30,000
Direct labor	48,000
Overhead	60,000
Total.............................	$138,000

3. Past experience indicates that 1 per cent of the gross amount of accumulated overhead charges will be disallowed by government auditors as contract costs. No provision has been made for this disallowance.

4. In addition to the estimated 1 per cent disallowance in "3," the following 19x4 costs will probably be disallowed:

  a. Depreciation on excess equipment, $1,000. The equipment was sold in January, 19x5.

  b. Special nonrecurring recruiting costs, $4,000.

5. The Corporation failed to take cash discounts totaling $2,000 in 19x4. Lost discounts are credited to costs when found by government auditors. The Corporation treats cash discounts, when taken, as a reduction of costs.

6. All costs that will probably be disallowed have been treated consistently as period costs by the Corporation. Estimated allowable costs have been consistently allocated equally to identical units being manufactured under a contract.

7. Five computers were delivered in 19x4 and billed at the target price. Progress payments of $75,000 were received for each computer delivered.

REQUIRED:

1. Prepare a schedule computing the estimated total adjusted price (estimated final contract price) for the fixed-price incentive contract.

2. Prepare a schedule computing the work in process inventory at estimated cost at December 31, 19x4.

3. Assume that the estimated total adjusted price determined in "1" was $800,000. Prepare a schedule computing the estimated total amount receivable

from the federal government at December 31, 19x4, for the computers that were delivered. [C.P.A.]

4-23. Analysis of General Ledger Accounts; Multiple Choice. The following is a partial list of the accounts appearing on the trial balance of the Stanky Manufacturing Company.

STANKY MANUFACTURING COMPANY
Partial General Ledger Trial Balance (Adjusted)
September 30, 19x0

	Dr.	Cr.
Materials and Supplies Stores Control	$ 17,500	
Work in Process Control	21,000	
Finished Goods Stock Control	39,400	
Sales, Net after Discounts		$275,000
Factory Costs of Goods Shipped	155,000	
Selling Cost Control	14,000	
Manufacturing Overhead Control	95,000	
Manufacturing Overhead Applied to Product		98,000
Administrative and General Cost Control	11,500	

For the following statements, in terms of inferences to be made from the partial data, indicate:

A — if the statement is a likely inference to be made;
B — if the statement is *not* a likely inference to be made;
C — if the statement is such that no reasonable inference can be made.

1. The Company owns its factory building.
2. Indirect Labor would be a debit in the completed trial balance.
3. Factory Cost of Goods Shipped is debited with the actual costs incurred.
4. Officers' Salaries would be a debit in the completed general ledger trial balance.
5. A perpetual inventory record is maintained, at least for materials and supplies.
6. Manufacturing Overhead control is an expense account.
7. There have been no losses on uncollectible accounts this period.
8. The difference between the Manufacturing Overhead Control account and the account Manufacturing Overhead Applied to Product is the amount by which the computation of "normal" product cost for the year to date differs from the actual costs of running the factory for the same period.
9. There is, at the time of this trial balance, an over absorption of factory cost.
10. Selling Cost Control is an expense account.
11. The Board of Directors should be able to declare a dividend when they meet on October 15.
12. The Manufacturing Overhead Applied to Product records total normal costs applicable to units of product worked upon, as determined by cost accountant's computations.

4-24. Comprehensive Review Problem—Job Order Costs. This problem is intended to provide a summary of general ledger and subsidiary ledger relationships for factory costs under a job order cost system. The facts are un-realistic because, to save student time, the tremendous detail and number of accounts in a real situation are not reproduced here. But the solving of this problem should provide the student with a comprehensive view of the basic ledger frame-work.

Assume that the Mafco Company has been in business for many years. It rents its factory building. Mafco uses a job order cost system because it has a wide variety of products which receive varying attention and effort in the two factory de-partments, Machining and Assembly.

Mafco has the following trial balance as of December 31, 19x0.

Cash	$ 15,000	
Accounts receivable	40,000	
Stores control	29,600	
Work in process control	4,000	
Finished goods control	20,000	
Unexpired insurance	12,000	
Office equipment	15,000	
Accumulated depreciation—		
Office equipment		$ 5,000
Factory equipment	950,000	
Accumulated depreciation—		
Factory equipment		220,000
Accounts payable		23,000
Accrued payroll		1,000
Accrued utilities		2,000
Accrued property taxes		3,000
Capital stock		100,000
Retained earnings		731,600
	$1,085,600	$1,085,600

Detail on Subsidiary Records as of December 31, 19x0

Stores:

Code	Quantity	Unit Cost	Amount
A	5,000	$2.00	$10,000
B	10,000	1.50	15,000
C	400	8.00	3,200
Supplies	Various	—	1,400
			$29,600

Work in process:

Job Order Number	Department	Direct Material	Direct Labor	Factory Overhead	Total
100	Machining	$1,800	$800	$900	$3,500
	Assembly	200	200	100	500
					$4,000

Finished goods:

Stock No.	Reference	Quantity	Unit Cost	Amount
X-1	Job 97	100	$80	$ 8,000
X-2	Job 99	1,000	$12	12,000
				$20,000

The following factory overhead budget has been prepared for the coming year 19x1.

Factory Overhead
Budget for Year Ending December 31, 19x1

	Machining	Assembly	Total
Factory overhead:			
Controllable:			
Supplies	$ 14,400	$ 5,400	$ 19,800
Indirect labor	22,800	16,800	39,600
Utilities	30,000	9,000	39,000
Repairs	24,000	6,000	30,000
Miscellaneous	22,800	12,000	34,800
	$114,000	$ 49,200	$163,200
Uncontrollable:			
Insurance	$ 7,200	$ 2,400	$ 9,600
Depreciation	114,000	14,400	128,400
Rent	24,000	16,800	40,800
Property taxes	4,200	1,200	5,400
Supervision	14,400	19,200	33,600
	$163,800	$ 54,000	$217,800
Total factory overhead	$277,800	$103,200	$381,000

This budget has been prepared after careful consideration of the sales outlook for the coming year. The production schedules are geared to the forecasted sales pattern.

In order to cost jobs as they are worked on, a predetermined overhead rate is computed as follows:

	Year 19x1	
	Machining	Assembly
Factory overhead	$277,800	$103,200
Machine hours	69,450	
Direct labor cost		$206,400
Rate per machine-hour	$ 4.00	
Rate per direct labor dollar		50%

These overhead rates will be used throughout the year to cost various jobs as they are worked on by each department. All overhead will be applied to all jobs worked on during the year in proportion to the machine-hour or direct labor cost factor devoted to each job. If management predictions are accurate, total overhead applied to the year's jobs through the use of predetermined rates should be equal to the total overhead costs actually incurred.

January data:

1. Purchases for stores (credit Accounts Payable)

	Quantity	Unit Cost	January
A	7,500	$2.00	$15,000
B	14,000	1.50	21,000
C	2,125	8.00	17,000
Supplies			2,000
			$55,000

2. Returns (debit Accounts Payable): 50 units of Material B.
3. The direct materials requisitions were summarized, and the following data were shown on a material usage report. These reports were submitted weekly to departmental foremen, although monthly data are shown here.

MACHINING DEPARTMENT
Direct Material Usage
For the Month ending January 31, 19x1

Requisition	Type	Job Order	Quantity	Unit Cost	Amount
M89	B	101	1,500	$1.50	$ 2,250
M90	A	102	3,000	2.00	6,000
M91	A	103	1,000	2.00	2,000
M92	B	103	1,000	1.50	1,500
M93	B	102	3,000	1.50	4,500
M94	B	101	200	1.50	300
M95	A	104	2,000	2.00	4,000
					$20,550

ASSEMBLY DEPARTMENT
Direct Material Usage
For the Month ending January 31, 19x1

Requisition	Type	Job Order	Quantity	Unit Cost	Amount
A301	C	100	5	$8.00	$ 40
A302	C	103	200	8.00	1,600
A303	C	101	800	8.00	6,400
A304	C	102	1,500	8.00	12,000
A305	C	103	20	8.00	160
					$20,200

4. A summary of payroll costs incurred follows. Compare with item 7 below. Payments (settlements) are independent of recognition of cost incurrence. In other words, costs may be summarized monthly while settlements are made weekly.

Work Ticket*	Job Order	Labor Hours		Cost		Total
		Machining	Assembly	Machining	Assembly	
ML480	101	20		$ 50	$	$ 50
ML481	101	1,500		3,750		3,750
ML482	103	1,000		2,500		2,500
ML483	102	1,200		3,000		3,000
ML484	104	500		1,250		1,250
ML485	103	100		250		250
AL 60	100		20		40	40
AL 61	102		7,000		14,000	14,000
AL 62	101		500		1,000	1,000
AL 63	103		1,000		2,000	2,000
AL 64	102		200		400	400
Total direct labor		4,320	8,720	$10,800	$17,440	$28,240
Indirect labor				2,000	1,500	3,500
Supervision				1,200	1,600	2,800
Total factory labor				$14,000	$20,540	$34,540
Selling and administrative wages						6,000
Total payroll costs						$40,540

*In practice, there would be many more of these. Often they are recapitulated daily and posted to each job in groups rather than as individual tickets.

5. Apply overhead to jobs. Rates as calculated when overhead budget was prepared: Machining, $4.00 per machine-hour; Assembly, 50 per cent of direct labor cost. See data for entry 6 to obtain machine-hours worked.
6. Production and sales data:

Job	Units Completed	Finished	Finished Stock No.	Units Sold	Sold for	January Machine-Hours Worked in Machining Dept.
97	100	19x0	X-1	100	$ 9,000	
98	—	—	—	—		
99	1000	19x0	X-2	1000	16,000	
100	50	Jan. 5, 19x1	X-1	20	1,800	
101	1750	Jan. 12, 19x1	X-2	900	14,400	3,000
102	1000	Jan. 19, 19x1	X-3	950	55,000	2,000
103	100	Jan. 30, 19x1	X-4	50	6,500	150
104	Unfinished					800
					$102,700	5,950

7. Gross payroll paid in cash during month, $39,000.
8. The following additional overhead costs were incurred during January:

Item	Total	Department Machining	Assembly	Selling and Administrative	General Ledger Account to Be Credited
Supplies requisitioned	$ 2,000	$ 1,500	$ 400	$ 100	?
Utilities (cost recognized on basis of usage estimates for month rather than on basis of invoices, which may cover other dates than a current calendar month)	4,000	2,700	800	500	Accrued Utilities Payable
Repairs by outsiders (parts and labor)	3,000	2,350	600	50	Accounts Payable
Miscellaneous	3,000	2,000	900	100	Accounts Payable
Insurance	1,000	600	200	200	?
Depreciation on equipment	11,000	9,500	1,200	300	?
Rent	4,000	2,000	1,400	600	Accounts Payable
Property taxes	500	350	100	50	Accrued Property Taxes
	$28,500	$21,000	$5,600	$1,900	

9. Utility bills received, $2,900 (dr. Accrued Utilities).
10. Utility bills paid, $2,525 (dr. Accounts Payable).
11. Other selling and administrative expenses, $15,000 (cr. Accounts Payable).
12. Payments on accounts payable, other than the $2,525 in (10), $65,300.
13. Collections on accounts receivable, $99,000.

REQUIRED:

1. Enter beginning balances in general ledger T-accounts.
2. Draw up stores cards, job cost sheets, and finished goods stock cards. Be sure to put in "reference" columns so that appropriate requisitions and work tickets, as well as dollar amounts, may be entered in the subsidiary ledger. A sample stores card and job cost sheet appear on page 114.

Finished stock cards would be similar in design to stores cards.

The factory overhead cost sheets have columns for: date, reference, supplies, indirect labor, utilities, repairs, miscellaneous, insurance, depreciation on equipment, rent, property taxes, and supervision.

Post beginning balances to subsidiary records.

3. Journalize and post entries for January.
4. Prepare a trial balance as of January 31, 19x1. Also prepare schedules of subsidiary ledger balances.

STORES CARD

Material A

Reference	Received			Issued			Balance			
	Quantity	Unit Cost	Amount	Quantity	Unit Cost	Amount	Date	Quantity	Unit Cost	Amount
Vouchers, Invoices, or Requisitions							$12/31/x0$	5,000	$2.00	$10,000

Job Order No. 100

MACHINING DEPARTMENT

Direct Material				Direct Labor				Overhead	
Reference	Quantity	Unit Cost	Amount	Reference	Quantity	Unit Cost	Amount	Machine Hours Worked	Amount
Req. #A88	900	$2.00	$1800	Work tickets	320 hrs	$2.50	$800	225	$900

ASSEMBLY DEPARTMENT

Direct material				Direct Labor				Overhead	
Reference	Quantity	Unit Cost	Amount	Reference	Quantity	Unit Cost	Amount	Reference	Amount
Req. #A300	25	$8.00	$200	Work tickets	100 hrs	$2.00	$200	50% of direct labor	$100

Summary		Machining	Assembly	Total
	Direct material	$ _____	$ _____	$ _____
	Direct labor	_____	_____	_____
	Factory overhead applied	_____	_____	_____
	Total cost	$ _____	$ _____	$ _____

5. Prepare an income statement for January and a balance sheet as of January 31, 19x1. Under-applied overhead is treated as a balance sheet item on interim financial statements.

6. Prepare factory overhead performance reports for January, one for Machining and one for Assembly. Show actual overhead, budgeted overhead, and variances. Assume arbitrarily that budget figures for January are $1/12$ of those shown in the annual overhead budget.

7. Assume that operations continue for the remainder of 19x1. Certain balances at December 31, 19x1 follow:

Stores	$ 30,000	
Work in process	10,000	
Finished goods	30,000	
Cost of sales	960,000	
Factory overhead control	400,000	
Factory overhead applied		$385,000

Prepare journal entries to close the factory overhead accounts, assuming that:

(a) Under-applied overhead is treated as a direct adjustment of Cost of Sales.

(b) Under-applied overhead is spread over appropriate accounts in proportion to their unadjusted ending balances.

PLANNING AND CONTROLLING ROUTINE OPERATIONS

SECTION

budgeting in general:
profit planning

CHAPTER V

A budget is a quantitative expression of a plan of action and an aid to coordination and control. Budgets may be formulated for the organization as a whole or for any subunit. Budgeting has come to full flower in the 1960's. For example, *Time* (February 18, 1966) reports: "Today, the President does not consider the budget just a report on spending or an accounting of his stewardship, as it once was, but a powerful tool for controlling the whole government and a potent instrument for manipulating the economy."

In this chapter we examine the planning and coordinating aspects of budgets. We take an over-all view, a look at a comprehensive master budget. In Chapters 6 and 7 we shall examine the control aspects.

Although this book emphasizes how accounting helps the *operating* performance of management (how effectively assets are acquired and utilized), we also need to recognize the importance of the *financing* function (how funds for investment in assets are obtained). That is why this chapter examines cash budgets as well as operating budgets. The leading corporations usually are marked by impressive operating management *and* financial management. Business failures are often attributable to management's shirking of the financial phases of its responsibilities.

MAJOR FEATURES OF BUDGETS

Mechanical and human aspects

Long-run profit maximization is the primary goal of management. Other objectives, such as power, growth, and social service, often rise to the forefront, but long-run profits are essential for survival. Budgeting helps plot the profit course. Budgets basically are forecasted financial statements—formal expressions of managerial plans. They are targets that encompass all phases of operations—sales, production, distribution, and financing.

Budgeting is too often looked upon from a purely mechanistic viewpoint, and yet the budget is an inanimate tool in the hands of administrators. The human factors in budgeting are more important than the accounting techniques. The success of a budgetary system depends upon its acceptance by the company members who are affected by the budgets. Attitudes ideally are sympathetic, cooperative, and cost-conscious.

Budgets place managers under the spotlight. The natural reaction to restriction, to criticism, and to control is resistance and self-defense. *The job of education and selling is overwhelmingly important here.* Too many department heads think that budgets represent a penny-pinching, negative brand of managerial pressure.[1] To them, the word *budget* is about as popular as, say, *layoff, strike,* or *pay decrease.* Ideally, company personnel should understand and accept the role of budgets as positive vehicles for company improvement, department improvement, and individual improvement. The budget is not a heinous means of squeezing the last drop of sweat out of employees. Properly used, it is simply a systematic tool for establishing standards of performance, for providing motivation, for gauging results, and for helping management advance toward its objectives. The budget technique in itself is free of emotion; its administration, however, is often packed with trouble. The budget's major role is to communicate the various motivations that basically already exist among the management personnel so that everybody sees, understands, and coordinates the goals, means, and drives of the organization.

The importance of these human aspects cannot be overemphasized. Without a thoroughly educated and cooperative management group at all levels of responsibility, budgets are a drain on the funds of the business and are a hindrance instead of a help to efficient operations. A budgetary program per se is not a remedy for weak managerial talent, faulty organization, or a poor information system.

Advantages and applicability of budgets

Budgetary systems are more common in larger companies, where formalized and sophisticated techniques are developed to serve management. Yet the usefulness of budgeting to very small concerns should not be overlooked. Many deaths (and unwarranted creations) of small businesses could have been circumvented by an early attempt to quantify the

---

[1] Pressure, in varying amounts, is a part of almost every job responsibility. Used with care, pressure motivates toward goals and is thus desirable. However, the word *pressure* has unappealing connotations and usually indicates unreasonable, unbearable stress.

dreams of headstrong but sloppy-thinking entrepreneurs who never faced the realities of their venture in terms of dollars and cents.

For example, a small business moved into a lush market for school equipment with hopes of flaming success. However, failure to quantify the long collection periods, to forecast a realistic sales potential, and to control costs from the outset resulted in disaster within a year. Budgets for small businesses need not be as elaborate as those outlined in budgeting textbooks, but some budgeting is useful to any-sized enterprise. In fact, many companies have implicit budgets without even realizing their existence; that is, every businessman considers the future as he makes decisions.

Many businessmen claim that the uncertainties which are peculiar to their business make budgets impractical for them. Yet one can nearly always find at least some companies in the same industry that use budgets. Such companies are usually among the industry leaders, and they regard budgets as indispensable aids. The point is that managers must grapple with uncertainties, either with a budget or without one. The advocates of budgeting maintain that budgets make the grappling more effective. The benefits from budgeting nearly always exceed the costs. At least some budget program will be helpful in almost every organization.

When administered wisely, budgets (1) compel management planning, (2) provide definite expectations that are the best framework for judging subsequent performance, and (3) promote communication and coordination among the various segments of the business.

1. Compelled Planning. "Plan ahead" are redundant watchwords for business managers and for any individual as well. Yet too often everyday problems interfere with such planning; operations drift along until the reality of time catches the firms or individuals in undesirable situations which should have been anticipated and avoided.

Budgets formulate expected performance; they express managerial targets. Without such targets, operations lack direction, problems are not foreseen, results lack meaning, and the implications for future policies are dwarfed by the pressure of the present. The planning role of all levels of management should be accentuated and enlarged by a budgetary system. Managers will be compelled to look ahead and will be ready for changing conditions. This forced planning is by far the greatest contribution of budgeting to management.

Budgets have direct or indirect influence on business policies. Policies are relatively general and permanent plans which change as conditions or objectives change. For example, new products are added, old products are dropped, organizations are revamped, and production methods are changed. Budgets definitely affect the formulation of over-all company policies and then help to implement such policies. These policy changes are often affected either directly by budgetary information or indirectly by the managerial thinking which evolved from dealing with budgets.

2. Expectations as a Framework for Judging Performance. Despite the existence of complex computers and automation, individuals still run businesses, from the president down to the foreman of the smallest department. Employees do not like to fumble along not really knowing what their superiors anticipate or to see such expectations vary depending upon, for example, the condition of the superior's sinus trouble. The budget helps meet this difficulty by letting employees know what is expected of them.

As a basis for judging actual results, budgeted performance is generally viewed as being a better index than past performance. The fact that sales are better than last year's, or that direct labor costs are lower than last year's, may be encouraging but it is by no means conclusive as a measure of performance. For example, the news that a company sold 100,000 units this year as compared with 90,000 units in the previous year may not necessarily be greeted with joy. Perhaps sales should have been 112,000 units this year. The major weakness of using historical data for judging performance is that inefficiencies may be buried in the past performance. Furthermore, the usefulness of comparisons with the past may be hampered by intervening changes in technology, personnel, products, competition, and general economic conditions.

3. Communication and Coordination.   Coordination is the meshing and balancing of all the factors of production and of all the departments and functions of the business so that the joint objectives are obtained —so that the interests of the individual managers are subordinated for the benefit of the business as a whole.

The concept of coordination implies, for example, that purchasing officers integrate their plans with production requirements, and that production officers use the sales budget as a basis for planning manpower needs and utilization of machinery.

Budgets help management to coordinate as follows:

1. The existence of a well-laid plan is the major step toward achieving coordination. Executives are forced to think of the relationship of individual operations, other operations, and the company as a whole.

2. Budgets help to restrain the empire-building efforts of executives. Budgets broaden individual thinking by helping to remove unconscious biases on the part of engineering, sales, and production officers.

3. Budgets help to search out weaknesses in the organizational structure. The administration of budgets isolates problems of communication, of fixing responsibility, and of working relationships.

The idea that budgets improve coordination and communication may look promising on paper, but it takes plenty of intelligent administration to achieve in practice. For instance, the use of budgets to judge performance may cause managers to wear blinders and concentrate more than ever on their individual worlds. We shall examine this problem in more detail in Chapter 9.

The cost-conscious, cooperative attitudes toward budgetary control must permeate all levels of management. A skeptical top-management attitude will trickle down to the detriment of the entire company. *Top management must understand and enthusiastically support the budget.*

Administration of budgets must not be rigid. Changed conditions call for changes in plans. The budget must have respect, but it does not have to be revered so that it prevents a manager from taking prudent action. A department head prepares and accepts his budget; he commits himself to the outlined performance. But if matters develop so that some special repairs or a special advertising outlay will best serve the interests of the firm, the manager should feel free to request permission for such outlays. Or the budget itself can provide enough flexibility to permit a manager reasonable discretion in deciding how best to get his job done.

TYPES OF BUDGETS

Time coverage

Budgets may span a period of one year or less and, in cases of capital budgeting for plant and product changes, up to ten or more years. More and more companies are using budgets as essential tools for long-range planning. The usual planning and control-budget period is one year. The annual budget is often broken down by months for the first quarter and by quarters for the remainder of the year. *Continuous budgets* are increasingly used, whereby a twelve-month forecast is always available by adding a month or quarter in the future as the month or quarter just ended is dropped. *Continuous budgets* are desirable because they force management constantly to think concretely about the forthcoming twelve months irrespective of whether the month at hand is May or October. The choice of budget periods largely flows from the objectives, uses, and dependability of the budget data.

Classification of budgets

Budgets are basically forecasted financial statements. They are sometimes called *pro forma* statements. Various descriptive terms for budgets have arisen. The difficulties of terminology are not insurmountable, but the reader should remember that terms vary among firms.

The following is a simplified classification of budgets. Many subsidiary budget schedules are necessary in actual practice.

MASTER BUDGET, CONSISTING OF

Operating Budget, Consisting of	Financial Budget, Consisting of
Budgeted income statement	Cash budget
Sales budget	Receipts
Production budget	Disbursements
Materials	Budgeted balance sheet
Direct labor	Budgeted statement of sources and
Factory overhead	applications of funds
Inventory levels	
Cost of goods sold budget	
Selling expense budget	
Administrative expense budget	

SPECIAL BUDGET REPORTS

Comparisons of planning budgets with actual performance

Reports for specific managerial needs, for example, breakeven projections

Long-term budgets, often called capital budgets or facilities budgets
(see Chapter 14)

Flexible overhead budget (see Chapter 7)

ILLUSTRATION OF MASTER BUDGET

Try to take the following basic data and prepare the required budgets before glancing at the solution. A basic approach to formulating a master budget is described after the basic data are given.

Basic Data and Requirements. The M Company uses a normal cost system. The company is ready to prepare its master budget for the year 19B. Having carefully examined all relevant factors, the executives expect the following for 19B:

Materials:

Material 111	$1.20 per unit
Material 112	$2.60 per unit
Direct labor	$2.05 per hour

Overhead is applied on the basis of direct labor hours.

	Product F, Special Widgets	Product G, De Luxe Widgets
Finished products (content of each unit):		
Material 111	12 units	12 units
Material 112	6 units	8 units
Direct labor	14 hours	20 hours

The balance sheet for the year just ended is given below:

M COMPANY
Balance Sheet
December 31, 19A

ASSETS

Current assets:		
Cash	$ 10,000	
Accounts receivable	25,000	
Materials	19,000	
Finished goods	14,480	
		$ 68,480
Fixed assets:		
Land	$ 50,000	
Building and equipment	380,000	
Accumulated depreciation	(75,000)	355,000
Total assets		$423,480

EQUITIES

Current liabilities:		
Accounts payable	$ 8,200	
Income taxes payable	5,000	$ 13,200
Stockholders' equity:		
Common stock, no-par—25,000 shares outstanding	$350,000	
Retained income	60,280	410,280
Total equities		$423,480

Additional information regarding the year 19B:

	Finished Product	
	F	G
Expected sales in units	5,000	1,000
Selling price per unit	$ 105.40	$ 164.00
Desired ending inventory in units	1,100	50
Beginning inventory in units	100	50

	Direct Material	
	111	112
Beginning inventory in units	5,000	5,000
Desired ending inventory in units	6,000	1,000

Work in process is negligible and may be ignored.
At anticipated volume levels, the following costs will be incurred:

Factory overhead:	
Supplies	$ 30,000
Indirect labor	70,000
Payroll fringe costs	25,000
Power—variable portion	8,000
Maintenance—variable portion	20,000
Depreciation	25,000
Property taxes	4,000
Property insurance	500
Supervision	20,000
Power—fixed portion	1,000
Maintenance—fixed portion	4,500
	$208,000

Selling and administrative expenses:	
Sales commissions	$ 20,000
Advertising	3,000
Sales salaries	10,000
Travel	5,000
Clerical wages	10,000
Supplies	1,000
Executive salaries	21,000
Miscellaneous	5,000
	$ 75,000

Budgeted cash flows are:

	Quarters			
	1	2	3	4
Collections from customers	$125,000	$150,000	$160,000	$221,000
Disbursements:				
For material	20,000	35,000	35,000	44,200
For other costs and expenses	25,000	20,000	20,000	27,000
For payroll	90,000	95,000	95,000	109,200
For income taxes	5,000	—	—	—
For machinery purchase	—	—	—	20,000

(The quarterly data are given for your convenience. The figures are based on the cash effects of the operations formulated in Schedules 1 through 8 in the solution.)

The company desires to maintain a $15,000 minimum cash balance at the end of each of the first three quarters, but increased working capital requirements at the end of the year 19B will necessitate a minimum ending cash balance of $40,000. Money can be borrowed or repaid in multiples of $500 at an interest rate of six per cent per annum. Management does not want to borrow any more cash than necessary and wants to repay as promptly as possible. In any event, all loans may not extend beyond four quarters. Interest is computed and paid when the principal is repaid. Assume that borrowings take place at the beginning and repayments at the end of the quarters in question. Compute interest to the nearest dollar.

REQUIRED:

Prepare a master budget for the year 19B. Include the following detailed schedules:

1. Sales budget
2. Production budget
2. Direct material purchases budget
4. Direct labor budget
5. Factory overhead budget
6. Ending inventory budget
7. Cost of goods sold budget
8. Selling and administrative expense budget

and

I. Budgeted income statement (Assume income taxes for 19B to be $20,000.)
II. Budgeted statement of cash receipts and disbursements by quarters, including details of borrowings, repayments, and interest
III. Budgeted balance sheet

Basic Approach to Formulating Master Budget. This chapter provides a review of the technical material covered in the previous chapters, because the master budget (the over-all business plan) is basically nothing more than the preparation of the familiar financial statements. The major technical difference is that the accountant is dealing with expected future data rather than with historical data.

The following techniques are basic to the study of budgeting. First, the steps in preparation are presented. Second, some condensed, illustrative budget reports are shown in the solution to the problem.

The basic steps in preparing budgeted financial statements follow:

1. *The sales forecast is the starting point for budgeting*, because inventory levels and production (and, hence, costs) generally are geared to the rate of sales activity.[2] (Schedule 1 in the solution)
2. After sales are budgeted, the production budget may be prepared. First, the units of budgeted production of finished products must be predetermined. This unit calculation may be expressed: Units to Be Produced equals Desired Ending Inventory of Finished Goods plus Planned Sales minus Beginning Inventory of Finished Goods. (Schedule 2)
3. When the level of production activity has been determined, the following budget schedules may be constructed:

   a. Material usage and purchases. Usage will depend upon the level of production activity determined in step 2 above. Purchases are affected as follows: Purchases in units equals Desired Ending Material Inventory Quantities plus Usage minus Beginning Inventory Quantities. (Schedule 3)
   b. Direct labor costs. These depend upon the type of products produced and the labor rates and the methods which must be used to obtain desired production. (Schedule 4)
   c. Factory overhead costs. These depend upon the behavior of costs of the individual overhead items in relation to the anticipated level of production. (Schedule 5)
   d. Inventory levels. These are the desired ending inventories. This information is required for the construction of budgeted financial statements. (Schedule 6)
4. Cost of goods sold budget. This budget depends upon the information gathered in step 3. (Schedule 7)
5. Budget of selling, administrative, and other expenses. (Schedule 8)
6. Budgeted income statement. (Exhibit I)
7. Cash budget. Estimate effects on cash position of the above level of operations. (Exhbit II) The illustrative cash budget is presented by quarters to show the impact of cash-flow tim-

[2]Occasionally, limits to productive capacity result in sales being geared to production rather than vice versa. Examples are shortages of machinery, manpower, or materials because of wars, strikes, or other imbalances in supply and demand.

ing on bank loan schedules. In practice, monthly, and sometimes weekly, cash budgets are very helpful for cash planning and control. Cash budgets aid in avoiding unnecessary idle cash and unnecessary cash deficiencies. The astute mapping of a financing program keeps cash balances in reasonable relation to needs. Ordinarily, the cash budget would be condensed and supported by a number of subsidiary schedules such as the following:

a. Cash receipts—depends on collections of receivables and other sources such as the sale of bonds. Behavior studies of collectivity of accounts receivable are needed in order to make accurate forecasts. Key factors include bad debt experience and average lag between sales and collections.

b. Cash disbursements:
   (1) Material purchases—depends on credit terms extended by suppliers and bill-paying habits of the buyer.
   (2) Direct labor and other wage outlays—depends on payroll dates.
   (3) Other costs and expenses—depends on timing and credit terms.
   (4) Other disbursements—purchases of fixed assets, long-term investments.

c. Determine cash excess or deficiency by subtracting (b) from (a).

d. Determine financing requirements, considering computed cash excesses or deficiencies and also any minimum or desired ending cash balances.

8. Budgeted balance sheet. Each item is projected in the light of the details of the business plan as expressed in the previous schedules. (Exhibit III)

Solution.

M COMPANY
Sales Budget
For the Year Ending December 31, 19B

Schedule 1

	Units	Selling Price	Total Sales
Product F (de luxe)	5,000	$105.40	$527,000
Product G (super de luxe)	1,000	164.00	164,000
			$691,000

M COMPANY
Production Budget,* in Units
For the Year Ending December 31, 19B

Schedule 2

	Products	
	F	G
Planned sales (Schedule 1)	5,000	1,000
Desired ending finished goods inventory	1,100	50
Total needs	6,100	1,050
Less beginning finished goods inventory	100	50
Units to be produced	6,000	1,000

*Work in process is negligible and is ignored.

M COMPANY
Direct Material Purchases Budget
For the Year Ending December 31, 19B

Schedule 3

	Material 111	Material 112	
Desired ending direct material inventory in units	6,000	1,000	
Units needed for production (Note A)	84,000	44,000	
Total needs	90,000	45,000	
Less beginning direct material inventory in units	5,000	5,000	
Units to be purchased	85,000	40,000	
Unit price	$ 1.20	$ 2.60	
Purchase cost	$102,000	$104,000	$206,000

Note A to Schedule 3—Usage of Direct Materials in Units and Dollars

	Production		Total		
			Direct	Material	Cost of
	Product F	Product G	Material	Unit	Materials
Direct Material	(6,000 units)	(1,000 units)	Usage	Cost	Used
111 (12 units per finished product)	72,000	12,000	84,000	$1.20	$100,800
112 (6 units per Product F, 8 units per Product G)	36,000	8,000	44,000	2.60	114,400
					$215,200

M COMPANY
Direct Labor Budget
For the Year Ending December 31, 19B

Schedule 4

	Units Produced	Direct Labor Hours Per Unit	Total Hours	Total Budget @ $2.05 per hour
Product F	6,000	14	84,000	$172,200
Product G	1,000	20	20,000	41,000
			104,000	$213,200

M COMPANY
Factory Overhead Budget
For the Year Ending December 31, 19B

Schedule 5

At anticipated activity of 104,000 direct labor hours:

Supplies	$ 30,000	
Indirect labor	70,000	
Payroll fringe costs	25,000	
Power—variable portion	8,000	
Maintenance—variable portion	20,000	
Total variable overhead		$153,000
Depreciation	$ 25,000	
Property taxes	4,000	
Property insurance	500	
Supervision	20,000	
Power—fixed portion	1,000	
Maintenance—fixed portion	4,500	
Total fixed overhead		55,000
Total factory overhead: ($208,000 ÷ 104,000 is $2.00 per direct labor hour)		$208,000

M COMPANY
Ending Inventory Budget
December 31, 19B

Schedule 6

	Units	Unit Cost	Total Amount	
Direct materials:				
111	6,000	$ 1.20	$ 7,200	
112	1,000	2.60	2,600	$ 9,800
Finished goods:				
F	1,100	$ 86.70*	95,370	
G	50	116.20*	5,810	101,180
Total				$110,980

*Computation of unit costs:

		Product F		Product G	
	Unit Cost	Units	Amount	Units	Amount
Material 111	$1.20	12	$14.40	12	$ 14.40
Material 112	2.60	6	15.60	8	20.80
Direct labor	2.05	14	28.70	20	41.00
Factory overhead	2.00	14	28.00	20	40.00
			$86.70		$116.20

M COMPANY
Cost of Goods Sold Budget
For the Year Ending December 31, 19B

Schedule 7

	From Schedule		
Direct materials used	3		$215,200
Direct labor	4		213,200
Factory overhead	5		208,000
Total manufacturing costs			$636,400
Add finished goods, December 31, 19A	Given	$ 14,480	
Less finished goods, December 31, 19B	6	101,180	
Inventory increase for year			(86,700)
			$549,700

M COMPANY

Selling and Administrative Expense Budget

For the Year Ending December 31, 19B

		Schedule 8
Sales commissions	$20,000	
Advertising	3,000	
Sales salaries	10,000	
Travel	5,000	
Total selling expenses		$38,000
Clerical wages	$10,000	
Supplies	1,000	
Executive salaries	21,000	
Miscellaneous	5,000	
Total administrative expenses		37,000
Total selling and administrative expenses		$75,000

M COMPANY

Budgeted Income Statement

For the Year Ending December 31, 19B

	From Schedule		Exhibit I
Sales	1		$691,000
Cost of goods sold	7		549,700
Gross margin			$141,300
Selling and administrative expenses	8	$75,000	
Interest expense ($1,058 + $233)	Exhibits II and III	1,291	76,291
Net income before income taxes			$65,009
Income taxes	Assumed		20,000
Net income after income taxes			$ 45,009

M COMPANY
Budgeted Statement of Cash Receipts and Disbursements
For the Year Ending December 31, 19B

Exhibit II

	Quarters				For the Year as a Whole
	1	2	3	4	
Cash balance, beginning	$ 10,000	$ 15,000	$ 15,000	$ 15,072	$ 10,000
Add receipts:					
Collections from customers	125,000	150,000	160,000	221,000	656,000
Total available before current financing	$135,000	$165,000	$175,000	$236,072	$666,000
Less disbursements:					
For material	$ 20,000	$ 35,000	$ 35,000	$ 44,200	$134,200
For other costs and expenses	25,000	20,000	20,000	27,000	92,000
For payroll	90,000	95,000	95,000	109,200	389,200
For income tax	5,000	—	—	—	5,000
For machinery purchase	—	—	—	20,000	20,000
Total	$140,000	$150,000	$150,000	$200,400	$640,400
Excess (deficiency)	$ (5,000)	15,000	$ 25,000	$ 35,672	$ 25,600
Financing:					
Borrowings (at beginning)	$ 20,000	$ —	$ —	$ 15,500	$ 35,500
Repayments (at end)	—	—	(9,500)	(10,500)	(20,000)
*Interest (at 6% per annum)	—	—	(428)	(630)	(1,058)
Total	$ 20,000	$ —	$ (9,928)	$ 4,370	$ 14,442
Cash balance, end	$ 15,000	$ 15,000	$ 15,072	$ 40,042	$ 40,042

*The interest payments pertain only to the amount of principal being repaid at the end of a given quarter. Note that the $20,000 loan must be completely repaid by the end of the fourth quarter.

M COMPANY
Budgeted Balance Sheet
December 31, 19B

Exhibit III

ASSETS

Current assets:

Cash	$ 40,042	
Accounts receivable (1)	60,000	
Materials (2)	9,800	
Finished goods (2)	101,180	$211,022

Fixed assets:

Land (3)		$ 50,000	
Building and equipment (4)	$400,000		
Accumulated depreciation (5)	100,000	300,000	350,000
Total assets			$561,022

EQUITIES

Current liabilities:

Accounts payable (6)	$ 70,000	
Income taxes payable (7)	20,000	
Notes payable (8)	15,500	
Accrued interest payable (9)	233	$105,733

Stockholders' equity:

Common stock, no-par, 25,000 shares outstanding (10)	$350,000	
Retained income (11)	105,289	455,289
Total equities		$561,022

Notes:

Beginning balances are used as a start for most of the following computations:

(1) $25,000 + $691,000 sales − $656,000 receipts = $60,000.
(2) From Schedule 6.
(3) From beginning balance sheet.
(4) $380,000 + 20,000 purchases.
(5) $75,000 + $25,000 depreciation.
(6) $8,200 + ($206,000 purchases, $213,200 direct labor, $183,000 factory overhead, $75,000 selling and administrative expenses) − $615,400 payments = $70,000.
(7) $5,000 + $20,000 current year − $5,000 payment.
(8) From Exhibit II, fourth quarter.
(9) $15,500 × .06 × ¼ = $233.
(10) From beginning balance sheet.
(11) $60,280 + $45,009 net income.

SALES FORECASTING—A DIFFICULT TASK

Factors in sales forecasting

Incurrence of cost is necessarily keyed to production activity. Activity, in turn, depends on estimated sales. The sales estimate is the foundation for the quantification of the entire business plan.[3]

The chief sales officer has direct responsibility for the preparation of the sales budget. The task of preparation forces him to crystallize his plans. He must have realistic perspective; he must decide on reasonably attainable, anticipated sales.

The sales forecast is made after consideration of the following factors:

1. Past sales volume.
2. General economic and industry conditions.
3. Relationship of sales to economic indicators such as gross national product, personal income, employment, prices, and industrial production.
4. Relative product profitability.
5. Market research studies.
6. Pricing policies.
7. Advertising and other promotion.
8. Quality of sales force.
9. Competition.
10. Seasonal variations.
11. Production capacity.
12. Long-term sales trends for various products.

Forecasting procedures

An effective aid to accurate forecasting is to approach the same goal by several methods; each forecast acts as a check on the others. The three methods described below are usually combined in some fashion which is suitable for a specific company.

1. Sales Staff Procedure. As for all budgets, those responsible should have an active role in sales budget formulation. If possible, the budget data should flow from individual salesmen or district sales managers upward to the chief sales officer. A valuable benefit from the budgeting process is the holding of discussions, which generally result in adjustments and which tend to broaden participants' thinking.

Previous sales volumes are usually the springboard for sales estimates. Sales executives examine historical sales behavior and relate it to

[3]The term sales *forecast* is sometimes distinguished from sales *budget* as follows: The forecast is the estimate, the prediction, which may or may not become the sales budget. The forecast becomes the budget only if management accepts it as an objective. Often, the forecast leads to adjustments of managerial plans, so that the final sales budget differs from the original sales forecast.

other historical data such as economic indicators, advertising, pricing policies, and competitive conditions. Current information is assembled, production capacity is considered, and then the outlook is derived for the ensuing months (years, in long-run sales budgets).

One of the common difficulties in budgeting sales is the widespread aversion of sales executives for figures. The usefulness of budgeting needs to be sold to salesmen. The best sales executives may not particularly enjoy working with figures, but they realize that prudent decisions cannot be made without concrete information. Market research is a sales executive's tool which helps to eliminate hunches and guessing.

2. Statistical Approaches.   Trend, cycle projection, and correlation analysis are useful supplementary techniques. Correlations between sales and economic indicators help make sales forecasts more reliable, especially if fluctuations in certain economic indicators precede fluctuations in company sales. No firm should rely on this approach. Too much reliance on statistical evidence is dangerous, because chance variations in statistical data may completely upset a program. As always, there is no substitute for acute executive judgment.

3. Group Executive Judgment.   All top officers, including production, purchasing, finance, and administrative officers, may use their experience and knowledge to project sales on the basis of group opinion. This quick method dispenses with intricate statistical accumulations; however, it muddles responsibility for sales estimates and ignores the need for a toughminded, scientific approach to this important task.

It is beyond the scope of this book to give a detailed description[4] of all phases of sales budget preparation, but its key importance should be kept in mind.

SUMMARY

Comprehensive budgeting is the expression of management's master operating plan—the formalized outlining of company objectives and their means of attainment. When administered wisely, budgets (1) compel management planning, (2) provide definite expectations that are the best framework for judging subsequent performance, and (3) promote communication and coordination among the various segments of the business.

The human factors in budgeting are more important than the technical intricacies. The job of education and selling is crucial. Otherwise, employees will resist and thwart the effectiveness of budgets as a helpful planning and control tool.

The foundation for budgeting is the sales forecast. Inventory,

---

[4]See Glenn A. Welsch, *Budgeting: Profit-Planning and Control* (2nd ed., Englewood Cliffs, N.J.: Prentice-Hall, Inc., 1964), Chapter 4. Also see D. Knight and E. Weinwurm, *Managerial Budgeting* (New York: The Macmillan Company, 1964), Chapters 4 and 5.

production, and cost incurrence generally are geared to the rate of sales activity.

PROBLEM FOR SELF-STUDY

Before trying to solve the homework problems, review the illustration in this chapter.

APPENDIX: INSTALLING AND ADMINISTERING THE BUDGET

Effective organization

Two essential requirements for budgeting are an effective organizational structure and well-informed personnel. Effective budgeting usually works best from the bottom to the top rather than from the top to the bottom; that is, the foreman and other departmental chiefs must be convinced of the usefulness of budgets. The foreman must regard his budget as the expression of an attainable and realistic plan. Consequently, he must have a firm voice in its preparation.

The imposition of budgets on a badly organized company which is peppered with managerial factions will hamper management, not aid it. Budgets are not panaceas for fundamental managerial ills. Although budgets may improve managerial effectiveness, they are not substitutes for management.

Budgeting and the accounting system

The accounting system and the budgetary system should be synchronized with the organizational structure. Although budgets may be used for *planning* without being integrated with the accounting system, they rarely may be used for comprehensive *control* without being so integrated. Progressive firms link a budget with an accounting system which accumulates homogeneous information from the lowest levels of responsibility to the highest.

Budget director

Although line management has the ultimate responsibility for the preparation of individual budgets, there is also an evident need for technical, unbiased help and over-all responsibility for the budget program. This need is usually satisfied by assigning responsibility to a budget director for establishing preparatory procedures, designing forms, *effective educating and selling*, collecting and coordinating data, verifying information, and reporting performance. The budget director is usually the controller or somebody who is responsible to the controller. He serves as the staff expert, the person upon whom line management depends for technical guidance. He also may be a valuable communications official between line and staff departments.

The able budget director typically has warm rapport with line management. He particularly avoids grabbing line authority—an easy trap to fall into because of his position as the company expert on budgetary matters.

Budget committee

A budget committee usually serves as a consulting body to the budget officer. Members usually include the budget director and the top-level line executives. However, very large businesses often exclude line executives other than the president from their budget committee; membership is confined to the budget director, the treasurer, the economist, and the president. Special budget committees are formed also, for example, sales budget committee and production budget committee.

The budget committee is concerned with the development and scrutiny of long-term operating and financial plans, offering advice, reconciling divergent views, and coordinating budgetary activities. The committee's very existence lends an aura of formality and prestige to the budget program.

The budget committee generally has an advisory role only; yet its advice is usually very influential. Initially, the committee would assemble, review, and transmit underlying economic conditions and assumptions in relation to the ensuing budget period. It would review departmental budgets and make recommendations. It would scrutinize periodic reports comparing actual performance with the budget. As a result, it would submit a variety of recommendations for top-management decision making.

Budget manual

It is usually desirable to have policies, organizational structure, and designations of responsibility and authority expressed in writing. The budget manual is a written set of instructions and pertinent information which serves as a rule book and a reference for the implementation of a budget program. It tells what to do, how to do it, when to do it, and which form to do it on. The effort and time needed for the manual's preparation are justified by its long-run usefulness, its tendency to crystallize all aspects of a budget program, and its documentation of procedures that otherwise are carried around in the heads of individuals who will not have the same job forever.

Follow-up is important

The investigation of budget deviations is the line manager's responsibility. The controller may assist to a very large extent, but the actual preparation of individual department budgets and decisions on deviations should be the responsibility of line management.

Ineffective budgetary systems are marked by failure to develop and use budgets to their fullest potential. That is, budgets are often used as tools for *planning* only. Great benefits from budgeting lie in the quick investigation of deviations and in the subsequent corrective action. Budgets should not be prepared in the first place if they are ignored, buried in files, or improperly interpreted. Abuses in this area of control probably outnumber the good uses. Again this points up the dire need for the education of company personnel.

QUESTIONS, PROBLEMS, AND CASES

Note: Problems 5-8, 5-11, and 5-15 cover the essential points of the chapter.

5-1. What are the two major features of a budgetary program? Which feature is more important? Why?

5-2. What are the elements of the budgetary cycle?

5-3. Define: *continuous budget, pro forma statements.*

5-4. "The sales forecast is the cornerstone for budgeting." Why?

5-5. Enumerate four common duties of a budget director.

5-6. What is the function of a *budget committee? A budget manual?*

5-7. "Budgets are half-used if they serve only as a planning device." Explain.

• **5-8. Budgeting Material Purchases.** The X Company has prepared a sales budget of 42,000 finished units for a three-month period. The company has an inventory of finished goods on hand at December 31 and desires a finished goods inventory at the end of the succeeding quarter as follows:

	Units	
	Dec. 31	March 31
Finished product	22,000	24,000

It takes three units of direct material to make one unit of finished product. The company has an inventory of units of raw material at December 31 and desires an ending raw material inventory as follows:

	Units	
	Dec. 31	March 31
Direct material	100,000	110,000

How many units of direct material should be purchased during the three months ending March 31?

• **5-9. Cash Budget.** The directors of the *TUV* Company Limited, of which you are accountant, decide that in the future a short-term cash budget should be prepared for each quarter. Your company sells directly to the public for cash and through trade outlets on credit terms of 2/10, n/30. The accounts receivable have been analyzed and show the following record of collection:

70 per cent of credit sales collected within the discount period.

20 per cent paid at the end of the 30-day period.

Balance paid at the end of a 60-day period.

At the end of any month, 25 per cent of sales on which the cash discounts will be taken are on the books as unpaid accounts receivable. Estimated sales for your first quarterly cash budget are as follows:

	19x1		
	January	February	March
Cash sales	$30,000	$38,000	$45,500
Credit sales	74,000	79,000	85,000

TUV Company Limited makes purchases of goods for resale by paying for goods as delivered. By so doing they obtain a cash discount of 3 per cent.

The mark-up on sales presently in effect provides a gross margin of 50 per cent on gross cost (before cash discounts).

The minimum inventory required for efficient operation is $100,000 at retail prices.

Expenses are estimated as follows:

	Selling	General
Fixed expenses	$6,000 per month	$10,000 per month
Variable expenses	10% of sales	5% of sales

Expenses are paid monthly as they arise.

Ten per cent of fixed expenses represents depreciation and amortization of deferred charges.

A piece of land priced at $30,000 is under option. Your cash budget will indicate to the directors whether or not they can purchase the land for cash on March 31, 19x1. Cash must be available to pay a quarterly dividend of $7,500 on preferred shares on March 31. The purchase of land must not affect the general current position of the company.

The following information is taken from the December 31, 19x0, Balance Sheet:

Cash	$29,000
Accounts receivable	20,000*
Inventory at gross cost	70,000

*Credit sales for December were $31,580, of which $15,000 are still outstanding. November sales still outstanding are $4,000. $1,000 is uncollectible.

REQUIRED:

1. Schedule of collections on accounts for each month of January, February, and March.

2. Schedule of cash required for purchases for each month of January, February, and March.

3. Cash budget for each of the three months ended January 31, February 28, and March 31, 19x1.

4. Brief comments for directors on the significance of the cash budget.

[S.I.C.A. Adapted]

5-10. Budget of Cash Requirements.   Based on a sales forecast for the season, the Planning Department of a manufacturing company has prepared the following production schedule for the coming month: 30,000 units of Product A and 20,000 units of Product B. The manufacturing specifications for the products are as follows:

Product A	Product B
2 lbs. material X @ $.30	3 lbs. material W @ $.80
1/2 lb. material Y @ $.20	3/4 lb. material Y @ $.20
2 hours direct labor @ $2.00	1.5 hours direct labor @ $2.00

To the direct labor hours, a 5 per cent allowance for idleness (accounted for as overhead) should be added. Indirect labor time is estimated to be 5 per cent of direct labor hours (excluding idleness), and the wage rate for indirect labor is $1.50. The overhead estimate (not shown above) is as follows:

Fixed Costs Per Month		Variable Costs
Depreciation	$ 6,900	$.80 per direct labor hour.
Expired insurance	800	NOTE: This rate includes the
Superintendence	3,000	costs of idle time
	$10,700	and indirect labor.

It is planned to increase the inventory of raw material X by 4,000 lbs., and to decrease the inventory of raw material W by 2,000 lbs. as of the beginning of the next month.

REQUIRED:

Prepare an estimate of the amount of cash necessary for the manufacturing operations of the coming month. Assume that materials and payroll costs are paid for in the month of purchase.   [C.G.A. Adapted]

5-11. Comprehensive Budget; Fill in Schedules. Following is certain information relative to the position and business of Newport Stores Company:

Current assets as of Sept. 30:	
Cash on deposit	$12,000
Inventory	63,600
Accounts receivable	10,000
Fixed assets—net	100,000
Current liabilities as of Sept. 30:	None
Recent and anticipated sales:	
September	$ 40,000
October	48,000
November	60,000
December	80,000
January	36,000

Credit sales. Sales are 75 per cent for cash, and 25 per cent on credit. Assume that credit accounts are all collected within 30 days from sale. The accounts receivable on Sept. 30 are the result of the credit sales for September (25 per cent of $40,000).

Gross profit averages 30 per cent of sales. Purchase discounts are treated on the income statement as "other income" by this company.

Expenses: Salaries and wages average 15 per cent of sales, rent 5 per cent, all other expenses, excluding depreciation, 4 per cent. Assume that these expenses are disbursed each month. Depreciation is $750 per month.

Purchases. There is a basic inventory of $30,000. The policy is to purchase each month additional inventory in the amount necessary to provide for the following month's sales. Terms on purchases are 2 per cent, 10 days; net 30 days. Assume that payments are made in the month of purchase, and that all discounts are taken.

Fixtures: In October $600 is spent for fixtures, and in November $400 is to be expended for this purpose.

Assume that a minimum cash balance of $8,000 is to be maintained. Assume that all borrowings are effective at the beginning of the month and all repayments are made at the end of the month of repayment. Interest is paid only at the time of repaying principal. Interest rate is 6 per cent per annum.

REQUIRED:

On the basis of the facts as given above:
1. Complete Schedule A.

SCHEDULE A—ESTIMATED MONTHLY DOLLAR RECEIPTS

Item	September	October	November	December
Total sales	$40,000	$48,000	$60,000	$80,000
Credit sales	10,000	12,000		
Receipts:				
Cash sales		$36,000		
Collections on accounts receivable		10,000		
Total		$46,000		

2. Complete Schedule B. Note that purchases are 70 per cent of next month's sales.

SCHEDULE B—ESTIMATED MONTHLY CASH DISBURSEMENTS FOR PURCHASES

Item	October	November	December	Total
Purchases	$42,000			
Less 2% cash discount	840			
Disbursements	$41,160			

3. Complete Schedule C.

SCHEDULE C—ESTIMATED MONTHLY CASH DISBURSEMENTS FOR OPERATING EXPENSES

Item	October	November	December	Total
Salaries and wages	$ 7,200			
Rent	2,400			
Other expenses	1,920			
Total	$11,520			

4. Complete Schedule D.

SCHEDULE D—ESTIMATED TOTAL MONTHLY DISBURSEMENTS

Item	October	November	December	Total
Purchases	$41,160			
Operating expenses	11,520			
Fixtures	600			
Total	$53,280			

5. Complete Schedule E.

SCHEDULE E—ESTIMATED CASH RECEIPTS AND DISBURSEMENTS

Item	October	November	December	Total
Receipts	$46,000			
Disbursements	53,280			
Net cash increase				
Net cash decrease	$ 7,280			

6. Complete Schedule F (Assume that borrowings must be made in multiples of $1,000).

SCHEDULE F—FINANCING REQUIRED BY NEWPORT STORES COMPANY

Item	October	November	December	Total
Opening cash	$12,000	$8,720		
Net cash increase				
Net cash decrease	7,280			
Cash position before financing	4,720			
Financing required	4,000			
Interest payments				
Financing retired				
Closing balance	$ 8,720			

7. What do you think is the most logical means of arranging the financing needed by Newport Stores Company?

8. Prepare a pro-forma income statement for the fourth quarter and a balance sheet as of December 31.

9. Certain simplifications have been introduced in this problem. What complicating factors would be met in a typical business situation?

5-12. Cash Budget. The *XY* Trading Company follows the practice of annually preparing a sales forecast. This forecast for the company's fiscal year ending June 30, 19x1 was that the company would sell 160,000 units, distributed monthly as follows:

July	9%	November	10%	March	6%
August	10%	December	15%	April	7%
September	12%	January	3%	May	6%
October	9%	February	5%	June	8%

The company's average rate of gross profit on gross costs is 33⅓ per cent (before considering cash discounts). Its terms for sales are 2 per cent 10 days, net 30 days, and it has been its experience that discounts on 80 per cent of billings have been allowed and that, of the remainder, one-half have been paid during the month following the billing and the balance in the succeeding month.

Regarding its purchases of merchandise, the company receives the terms of 2 per cent 10 days, net 60 days. However, it regularly takes discount on the tenth day after the invoice date.

Because the company stresses promptness of delivery in its advertising, to ensure the immediate filling of orders, the inventories at December 31 and January 31 are maintained at 6 per cent of the number of units estimated to be sold throughout the year; during the rest of the year, the inventories are maintained at 10 per cent of that number.

Total budgeted selling, administrative, and general expenses for the fiscal year ended June 30, 19x1, are estimated at $624,000, of which $240,000 are fixed expenses (inclusive of $48,000 annual depreciation). These fixed expenses are incurred uniformily throughout the year. The other selling, administrative, and general expenses, which amount to $384,000 or 12 per cent of total sales, vary proportionately with sales. Expenses are paid as incurred, without discounts.

Assume:

1. That one-third of the purchases of any month are due for discount and are paid for in the following month.

2. That the cash balance at January 1, 19x1 is $224,000.

3. That all discounted items are collected during the month of sale.

REQUIRED:

A budget of the cash receipts, disbursements, and balance for the three months ending March 31, 19x1. [S.I.C.A.]

5-13. Cash Budget. The Standard Mercantile Corporation is a wholesaler and ends its fiscal year on December 31. You have been requested in early January 19x4 to assist in the preparation of a cash forecast. The following information is available regarding the Company's operations:

1. Management believes the 19x3 sales pattern is a reasonable estimate of 19x4 sales. Sales in 19x3 were as follows:

January	$ 360,000
February	420,000
March	600,000
April	540,000
May	480,000
June	400,000
July	350,000
August	550,000
September	500,000

October	400,000
November	600,000
December	800,000
Total	$6,000,000

2. The accounts receivable at December 31 total $380,000. Sales collections are generally made as follows:

During month of sale	60%
In first subsequent month	30%
In second subsequent month	9%
Uncollectible	1%

3. The purchase cost of goods averages 60 per cent of selling price. The cost of the inventory on hand at December 31 is $840,000, of which $30,000 is obsolete. Arrangements have been made to sell the obsolete inventory in January at half of the normal selling price on a C.O.D. basis.

The Company wishes to maintain the inventory as of the first of each month at a level of three months' sales as determined by the sales forecast for the next three months. All purchases are paid for on the tenth of the following month. Accounts payable for purchases at December 31 total $370,000.

4. Recurring fixed expenses amount to $120,000 per month, including depreciation of $20,000. For accounting purposes the Company apportions the recurring fixed expenses to the various months in the same proportion as that month's estimated sales bears to the estimated total annual sales. Variable expenses amount to 10 per cent of sales.

Payments for expenses are made as follows:

	During Month Incurred	Following Month
Fixed expenses	55%	45%
Variable expenses	70%	30%

5. Annual property taxes amount to $50,000 and are paid in equal installments on December 31 and March 31. The property taxes are in addition to the expenses in item "4" above.

6. It is anticipated that cash dividends of $20,000 will be paid each quarter on the fifteenth day of the third month of the quarter.

7. During the winter unusual advertising costs will be incurred which will require cash payments of $10,000 in February and $15,000 in March. The advertising costs are in addition to the expenses in item "4" above.

8. Equipment replacements are made at the rate of $3,000 per month. The equipment has an average estimated life of six years.

9. A $60,000 installment of the Company's income tax for 19x3 is due on March 15, 19x4.

10. At December 31, 19x3 the Company had a bank loan with an unpaid balance of $280,000. The loan requires a principal payment of $20,000 on the last day of each month plus interest at $\frac{1}{2}$ per cent per month on the unpaid balance at the first of the month. The entire balance is due on March 31, 19x4.

11. The cash balance at December 31, 19x3 is $100,000.

REQUIRED:

Prepare a cash forecast statement by months for the first three months of 19x4 for The Standard Mercantile Corporation. The statement should show the amount of cash on hand (or deficiency of cash) at the end of each month. All computations and supporting schedules should be presented in good form.

[C.P.A., Adapted]

5-14. Production Budget. The Bigbee Company manufactures a single product. The basic characteristics of the company's operations and accounting are as follows:

1. Production is scheduled to maintain finished goods inventory at a constant ratio (10 per cent) to current sales.

2. Production is spaced evenly during each period.

3. Finished goods inventory at the end of the period is valued at the average cost of manufacture for the period.

4. Inventories of work in process and raw materials are small and may be ignored.

Production and sales data and the manufacturing cost of sales for the two preceding periods are as follows:

	Period	
Units	1	2
Beginning inventory	1,000	2,000
Production	21,000	31,000
	22,000	33,000
Sales	20,000	30,000
Ending inventory	2,000	3,000

	Period 1		Period 1	
	Amount	Per Unit	Amount	Per Unit
Sales	$361,520		$552,000	
Cost of sales:				
Direct materials	$ 44,078	$2.10	$ 68,508	$2.21
Direct labor	80,220	3.82	130,200	4.20
Factory overhead	49,713	2.37	62,213	2.01
Inventory variation	(7,510)		(8,680)	
Cost of sales	$166,501		$252,241	
Gross profit	$195,019		$299,759	

Other pertinent data are as follows:

1. The product is made by mixing materials A and B. The relative quantity of each of the two materials entering production and in finished units can be varied, but it was kept constant during periods 1 and 2. In period 3, the quantity of raw material A used in a unit of product will be decreased 8 per cent, and the quantity of raw material B used in a unit of product will be increased 12 per cent. The price of material A is expected to continue the trend of the past two periods and the price of material B is expected to increase 5 per cent in period 3.

The cost of each raw material used in production has been as follows:

Material	Period 1		Period 2	
	Amount	%	Amount	%
A	$23,141	52.5	$37,542	54.8
B	20,937	47.5	30,966	45.2
Total	$44,078	100.0	$68,508	100.0

2. Direct labor man-hours per unit have been approximately constant during periods 1 and 2 and are expected to remain at the same figure in period 3. Effective at the middle of each of periods 1 and 2, wage increases of 10 per cent per man-hour have been granted. A similar increase is expected at the middle of period 3.

3. The amount of fixed factory overhead was $23,463 during periods 1 and 2 and is expected to continue at the same amount during period 3. The variable portion of factory overhead is expected to remain at the same amount per unit of production as in periods 1 and 2.

4. Sales in period 3 are expected to be 25,000 units at $19 per unit.

Prepare a projected statement of sales, manufacturing cost of sales, and gross profit for period 3, based on the preceding data. Support this statement with schedules of your computations of (1) production data for period 3; (2) material costs; (3) direct labor costs; (4) factory overhead, showing the fixed and variable elements; and (5) inventory variation (increase or decrease).

Note: Round off all total costs to the nearest dollar and all unit costs to the nearest cent. For Schedule 2 (Material) it is necessary to obtain the unit costs for period 3. For periods 1 and 2, the unit cost for material A may be computed by dividing, for each period, the total cost of material A by the total units produced. Note the percentage increase in unit costs from period 1 to period 2. Increase period 2's unit cost by the same percentage to get period 3's unit cost. Follow the same procedure for material B. (Plenty of time can be wasted here on trying to get *physical* changes in mix of A and B from period to period; the answer to this mix question is indeterminable from the data given.)   [C.P.A.]

5-15. Cash Budgeting. On Dec. 1, 19x1, the *XYZ* Wholesale Co. is attempting to project cash receipts and disbursements through Jan. 31, 19x2. On this latter date, a note will be payable in the amount of $10,000. This amount was borrowed in September to carry the company through the seasonal peak in November and December.

The trial balance on Dec. 1 shows in part:

Cash	$ 1,000	
Accounts receivable	28,000	
Allowance for bad debts		$1,580
Inventory	8,750	
Accounts payable		9,200

Sales terms call for a 2 per cent discount if paid within the first ten days of the month after purchase, with the balance due by the end of the month after purchase. Experience has shown that 70 per cent of the billings will be collected within the discount period, 20 per cent by the end of the month after purchase, and 8 per cent in the following month, and that 2 per cent will be uncollectible.

The unit sales price of the company's one product is $10. Actual and projected sales are:

October actual	$ 18,000
November actual	25,000
December estimated	30,000
January estimated	15,000
February estimated	12,000
Total estimated for year ending June 30	150,000

All purchases are payable within fifteen days. Thus, approximately 50 per cent of the purchases in a month are due and payable in the next month. The unit purchase cost is $7.00. Target ending inventories are 500 units plus 25 per cent of the next month's unit sales.

Total budgeted selling and administrative expenses for the year are $40,000. Of this amount, $15,000 is considered fixed (includes depreciation of $3,000). The remainder varies with sales. Both fixed and variable selling and administrative expenses are paid as incurred.

REQUIRED:

Prepare a columnar statement of estimated cash receipts and disbursements for December and January.

introduction to standard costs:
direct material and direct labor

CHAPTER VI

We now turn to standard costs, the building blocks of a day-to-day operational control system. Standard costs can be used in a wide variety of industries and in conjunction with either process costing or job order costing.

STANDARD COSTS AS MANAGEMENT AIDS

Nature of standards

Standard costs are carefully predetermined costs; they are target costs, costs that *should be* attained under efficient operations. Standard costs provide a framework for gauging performance, for building useful budgets, for guiding pricing, for meaningful product costing, and for bookkeeping economy.

Cost control depends on a set of standards as a frame of reference which outlines how a task should be accomplished and how much it should cost. As work is done, actual costs incurred are compared with standard costs to reveal variances. The variances are investigated to discover better ways of adhering to standards, of altering standards, or of accomplishing objectives.

Consider the following example. If the standard cost of material for a garden tool is 50¢ per unit, then superior or inferior performance may be judged by comparing incurred costs with standard costs. If the incurred cost happens to be 60¢, then the 10¢ variance may be analyzed and investigated to discover reasons for the variation. As will be seen later, the difference may be due to price changes, shoddy materials, faulty workmanship, and so forth. The important point at this stage is that an evaluation of performance depends on a comparison of actual costs with some stable goal. Merely to compare this month's costs with last month's or with those of the corresponding month of last year is likely to provide less meaningful data because of the *inefficiencies which may already be reflected in prior costs.* Moreover, changes in technology, equipment, and methods also limit the usefulness of comparisons with the past.

Distinction between budgets and standards

The words "budget" and "standard" are so closely related that they are often used interchangeably. If standards are currently attainable, as they are assumed to be in this book, there is no conceptual difference between a budget amount and a standard amount. Sometimes it is helpful to think of the budget as a *total* concept, and of the standard as a *unit* concept. In this sense, a standard is a budget for a single unit. The standard cost for a pound of raw material may be $1.00; the budget for using 10,000 pounds would therefore be $10,000.

Literature and practice tend to be fuzzy in distinguishing between standards and budgets. The difficulty is that budgets may be used for planning or control or both. When standards do not represent attainable efficient performance because of management policy reflected in the use of outdated or unrealistic standards, the amount budgeted for financial (cash) planning purposes will differ from the amount budgeted for operating control purposes (using the standard as the building block).

In these instances, unrealistic or outdated standards may be used for compiling performance reports. However, *expected or budgeted variances* are brought into the master budget for financial planning, as a bridge between the performance budget and the master budget. For example, if unusually strict standards are used for direct labor, the standard allowance may be, say, $2.00 per finished unit even though top management realistically expects an "unfavorable" performance variance of, say, $.25 per unit. In the master budget, the labor costs would be totaled at a rate of $2.25 per unit: $2.00 plus a *budgeted variance* of $.25.

Analysis of variances

All variance analysis consists of a general approach wherein a total variance should be computed first. In turn, the total variance is subdivided into two component variances: (a) price or rate and (b) usage or efficiency as shown at the top of page 151.

Essentially, efficient operating control means getting the maximum possible good outputs for a given quantity of inputs; or, expressed another way, it means utilizing the minimum possible inputs for a given quantity of good outputs. The input-output distinction is helpful in retaining perspective on the analysis of variances.

Assume that a table manufacturer uses formica tops. Formica is

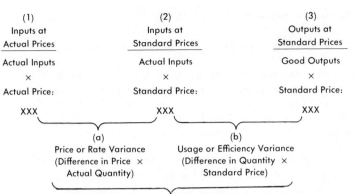

(1)	(2)	(3)
Inputs at	Inputs at	Outputs at
Actual Prices	Standard Prices	Standard Prices
Actual Inputs	Actual Inputs	Good Outputs
×	×	×
Actual Price:	Standard Price:	Standard Price:
XXX	XXX	XXX

(a)
Price or Rate Variance
(Difference in Price ×
Actual Quantity)

(b)
Usage or Efficiency Variance
(Difference in Quantity ×
Standard Price)

Total variance to be explained

purchased in large sizes and is cut down as needed and then glued to the tables. A given-sized table will require a specified amount of formica. If the amount of formica needed per Type F TV table is 4 square feet and the cost per square foot is 65¢, then the standard cost of formica for a single TV table would be $2.60. But a certain production run of 1,000 tables results in usage of 4,300 square feet at 68¢ per square foot, a total cost of $2,924. Total standard cost would be $2,600 (1,000 units @ $2.60, or 4,000 square feet @ 65¢). The total variance of $324 would be analyzed as follows:

(1)	(2)	(3)
Inputs at Actual Prices	Inputs at Standard Prices	Outputs at Standard Prices
Actual Inputs	Actual Inputs	Good Outputs
×	×	×
Actual Price:	Standard Price	Standard Price
(4,300 sq. ft. × $.68)	(4,300 sq. ft. × $.65)	(4,000 sq. ft. × $.65)
$2,924	$2,795	$2,600

Component analysis of variances

(a) Price Variance
(4,300 × $.03) or $129 U

(b) Quantity Variance
(4,300 − 4,000) × $.65, or $195 U

Total Variance

Total variance to be explained $324 U

U = Unfavorable (price exceeds standard price; or usage exceeds standard usage allowed).

A short-cut approach follows:

(a) *Price variances:*
(Difference in unit price) times (actual inputs used)
(68¢ − 65¢) × 4,300 square feet is $129 U

(b) *Quantity or usage variance:*
(Difference in inputs and outputs) times (standard unit price)
(4,300 − 4,000) × 65¢ is   195 U

Total variance $324 U

How output is expressed

The most difficult concept to grasp at this stage is how outputs are measured and expressed. Note under column (3) in our example that the outputs are measured and expressed, not as 1,000 tables, but as 4,000 square feet—the standard quantity of formica allowed to produce 1,000 tables. The point is that, to ease the input-output analysis, production is often expressed in terms of what inputs *should* have been utilized rather than what inputs actually were utilized. For instance, if it takes one quarter-hour to assemble a table, the analysis of direct labor input-output will be facilitated by expressing the output of 1,000 tables in terms of the standard number of hours allowed to produce the tables, $\frac{1}{4} \times 1,000$ or 250 hours. In these situations, output may be expressed as *250 standard hours allowed* (also called *standard hours allowed for work done* or *standard hours worked* or *standard hours earned*). This is a key concept in standard costs. Standard hours allowed is the number of hours that *should* have been used to produce a given output. This way of expressing output is particularly helpful when a factory produces a variety of products, each having a different standard time allowance. *Standard hours allowed* becomes the common denominator and the best way to express over-all production. (An example of the analysis of direct labor appears later in this chapter.)

Pinpointing responsibility

Cost control is aided by measuring variances in terms of responsibilities. Typically, usage is the major responsibility of one department head (a foreman), whereas price may be the major responsibility of a different department head (a purchasing officer). Therefore, the dollar measure of the quantity variance should not be influenced by changes in unit prices. Price is held constant at standard and the resultant quantity variance is attributable solely to off-standard usage by the foreman's department. In the case of the price variance, because the purchasing officer does not influence the quantity used, the difference in unit price is said to be applicable to all quantities used.

A chart of the relationship of price and quantity variances may be helpful. Exhibit 6-1 shows a graphic analysis which demonstrates variance computations in rectangular terms. Theoretically, as shown in the graph, the price variance should be subdivided into two variances:

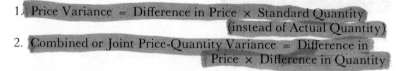

1. Price Variance = Difference in Price × Standard Quantity (instead of Actual Quantity)
2. Combined or Joint Price-Quantity Variance = Difference in Price × Difference in Quantity

The importance of this refinement depends on the significance and usefulness of isolating the joint variance. Where executive bonuses depend on variances, this refinement may be necessary. For example, an unfavorable total price variance, as ordinarily computed, could be partially attributable to inefficient usage. Thus $9.00 ($.03 × 300 sq. ft.) of the $129 price variance in our example would not have arisen if the quantities used did not exceed standard. In this book, we shall not refine our analysis this far; all of the $129 is called a price variance.

EXHIBIT 6-1

GRAPHIC ANALYSIS OF VARIANCES

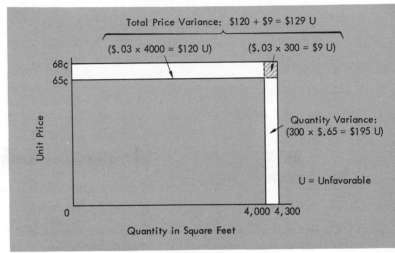

Analysis of variances may be further subdivided beyond price and quantity variances. For example, the quantity variance may be partially explained by inferior quality; by faulty workmanship, such as sloppy trimming or careless glueing; by substitute materials; by improper mix of materials; or for some other reason. The specific reasons are sought to pin down responsibility for control purposes.

The key questions in deciding how variances should be collected and analyzed are: *Why* do we wish to identify this particular variance? What will we *do* with it? If we cannot make practical use of the variance, then we should not bother to compute it.

Physical standards and improvement of operations

Elaborate standard cost accounting systems and fancy reports of variance analysis will be of little benefit if the managers responsible do not use the reports as clues for investigation of off-standard performance. The real benefits become evident when managers seize the system and the reports as the starting points for improving operations.

Physical standards are the foundation of a standard cost system. Ideally, they should represent reliable engineering or physical estimates which are expressed in tons or gallons produced, in operation methods, and in minutes or hours of labor. These standards are constructed from systematic observation, measurement, and controlled experiment, or are the result of merely careful planning. Analyses of the kinds and amounts of material, labor time and methods, and necessary overhead items lead to these so-called engineered standards. The entire productive process is divided into various operations or activities and the proper material and labor usage is rigorously estimated.

Textbooks generally give the impression that standard costs are always based on technical engineering studies and rigorous specifications. Accurate measurement is indeed the foundation for control. However, although a rigorous approach is desirable, it should be remembered that even less scientific standards provide a forceful way of presenting information in order to stimulate corrective action. An accounting system is effective when it automatically calls management's attention to the areas that most sorely need investigation.

Converting physical standards into dollars

Standard costs are developed by multiplying the physical standards by appropriate price factors. In other words, physical usage and prices are combined to obtain standard costs. In the formica example cited previously, the physical standard was 4 square feet per Type F table. The standard cost per table was secured by multiplying the standard square footage times the unit price of 65¢ to obtain $2.60 per table.

The use of price factors allows all standards in the company to be expressed in a common denominator—dollars. Furthermore, the pricing of physical standards calls attention to the expensive items that tend to deserve more managerial attention.

In many instances, the building of standard costs is not extraordinarily difficult, especially where operations are repetitive and extensive quantities of similar products are produced. But in other cases, the technical complexities are imposing because of the nonuniformity of products. In the latter cases, labor operations must be dissected into individual steps as far as possible, so that the individual steps, with their specific costs, may be regrouped to build standard costs for a variety of products which may require different sequences of labor operations. For example, a table manufacturer may apply formica tops to some types of tables and not to others. The standard labor cost of formica tables would naturally include the costs of applying formica, whereas such costs would be excluded from costing other types of tables. Note that costing for control concentrates on the *operation* in a *cost center*, whereas costing for inventory concentrates on the physical unit as the costing objective.

Responsibility for developing standards

Physical standards are usually developed by the engineering or operating employees. In order to be effective, the standards must be accepted by the people who are going to be subject to comparisons. These managers preferably should have an active role in setting standards. When a person accepts a goal as being fair, he will be more likely to cooperate in trying to reach that goal.

The job of the accounting department is (1) to price the physical standards, that is, to express the physical standards in the form of dollars and cents, and (2) to report operating performance in comparison with standards.

Types of standards

How demanding should standards be? Should they express perfection, or should they allow for the various factors that prevent perfect performance? Accounting writers have coined a variety of names for different kinds of standards. Standards are often classified into three types:

1. Basic cost standards are unchanging standards. They provide the base for comparing actual costs through the years with the same standard. Thus, the accounting reports spotlight trends. Price effects and changes in efficiency are gauged by comparison with the prices and efficiency that prevailed when standards were determined. Basic standard costs are seldom used because frequent changes in products and methods necessitate changes in standards.[1] Thus, the trends lose their significance because of the short time that elapses between changes in products and methods. Also, most managements have found other types of standards to be more meaningful, mainly because executives tend to think in terms of current and future performance rather than of their past performance.

2. Perfection, ideal, maximum efficiency, or theoretical standard costs reflect industrial engineers' dreams of a factory heaven. Ideal standard costs are the absolute minimum costs which are possible under the best conceivable operating conditions using existing specifications and equipment. Ideal standards, like other standards, are used where the management feels that they provide the best type of standard for motivation and cost control. Ideal standards, as Professor Sidney Davidson tells his students, are like a dream of Sophia Loren—distant, desirable, and rarely attainable. But their use is desirable where management believes them to be psychologically productive.

3. Currently attainable standard costs are the costs that should be incurred under forthcoming efficient operating conditions. They are difficult to reach but possible to achieve. Attainable standards are looser than ideal standards because of allowance for normal spoilage, ordinary machine breakdowns, and lost time. However, attainable standards are usually set tight enough to that the operating people will consider the

---

[1] In his unpublished workshop paper, "The Standard Cost Matrix," University of Chicago, April 29, 1965, Professor David Green, Jr., maintains that basic cost standards can be used effectively by using index numbers to reflect changes in the basic standards as they arise. These changes can be injected into the standard cost system on a continuous basis, not just once a year.

achievement of standard performance to be a satisfying accomplishment. In other words, variances are more likely to be slightly unfavorable rather than favorable—but favorable variances may be attained by a little more than expected efficiency.

Manufacturers ordinarily select a combination of the second and third types of standards described above. Instead of any one, a blend of the two types may be used, or management may use one type for control of materials and another for control of labor. As one may easily imagine, ideal standards are more likely to be used for material specifications than for labor control. At the same time, an ideal standard as to *quantity* of material used may be combined with an attainable standard for individual *prices* of material components.

Terminological difficulties should be kept in mind as well. Thus, an *ideal standard* may be a *currently attainable standard* in some cases. For example, the outside purchases of expensive subassemblies such as tires or picture tubes should result in no waste in the assembly of a finished product. The standard here would be both *ideal* and *currently attainable*.

Another benefit from using *currently attainable standards* is the multi-purpose use of the resultant standard costs. In this way, such standard costs may be directly useful for master budgeting and product costing. Note also that if currently attainable standards are not used, provision must be made for expected or budgeted variances, which become the bridge between the master budget and the performance control budget.

A paramount consideration is that standards for control must be patterned for a specific company's needs. Standards will change as companies alter their products, methods, equipment, and personnel through the years.

Tightness of standards—cost reduction or cost control

N.A.A. Research Series No. 11 (p. 705) states:

> *While it is sometimes said that an unattainably tight standard provides an incentive to reduce costs, it seems that this use of the standard confuses the objectives of cost reduction and cost control. Cost reduction proceeds by finding ways to achieve a given result through improved design, better methods, new layouts, incentive plans, etc. Hence cost reduction results in the establishment of new standards. On the other hand, cost control is a process of maintaining performance at as near existing standards as is possible. If standards are tighter than performance currently attainable, the lower cost will not necessarily follow unless the cost reduction program has first shown a practical method whereby the tighter standard can be attained. On the other hand, a standard which is set so loose that it can be met by poor performance buries the very inefficiencies that standard costs are intended to disclose.*

Control points

Sharp distinctions between controllable and uncontrollable costs are necessary both for appraising performance and for securing cooperation of operating managers. The problem of distinguishing between controllable and uncontrollable costs becomes more acute with overhead items than with direct materials and direct labor. Quantities used of the latter two items generally are considered controllable by a given department head. Price factors are considered uncontrollable by cost centers except where a supervisor uses types of material or labor which are not specified in the standards. For example, if standards specify the use of formica that costs 65¢ per square foot, and through carelessness formica costing 80¢ per square foot is used, the 15¢ "price" variance (better called a "substitution" variance) is not attributed to the purchasing agent.

Timing

Control cannot be exercised after the fact. Control is achieved while or before an act takes place. If managers depend on some form of performance report as a guide for control, then such reports must be timely. Thus, daily or even hourly reports are frequently used for major items such as labor usage, material usage, and scrap. The timeliness of issuance has a direct bearing on the effectiveness of reports. Appropriate questions on this point would be: Do operating managers anxiously await their control reports, or do they rely on individual, informal guides to control? Do their own hunches or little black books tell them the "real story"?

Costing for control versus product costing

Costing for control requires breaking down manufacturing elements so that they may be regulated at the source (the cost center) on an individual basis. Thus, the standards for usage of material *elements* and labor *elements* are more significant than over-all product cost standards.

For example, the standard cost of making a kitchen table may be $18. For control purposes, this cost is not as significant as its component parts because control must be exercised by regulating usage of the separate elements which make up the cost.

MATERIAL PRICE STANDARDS

Basis for material price standards

Material costs are affected by two major factors, price and quantity. Prices are not subject to as much control as quantity factors are, because significant outside influences such as general economic conditions, strikes, and scarce supplies are typically beyond the influence of management. But the isolation of price factors is helpful for a variety of reasons, one of the major ones being the isolation of the quantity variances which are subject to control. Thus, the separation of price factors from usage factors will remove price influences from quantity control reports.

Our formica illustration showed how the price and usage variances for materials were computed simultaneously as production took place. This approach is adequate where material prices are not too volatile, or where heavy raw material inventories are not carried, or where the purpose is solely to remove influences of price from usage reports. However, when current control of purchasing activities is also a major objective of isolating price variances, the approach should be modified, as we shall see.

Material price standards are usually based either on expected prices for the period in question (usually a year) or on prices prevailing at the time that standards are set. Price variances for purposes *of control* are computed at the time of *purchase* by taking the difference between actual and standard unit price times the actual quantity acquired. To delay the computation of the price variance until the time the quantity is *issued* usually defeats the usefulness of the information for control because corrective action is then seldom possible.

Ideally, where price variances are used for *control* purposes, they should be computed when the original purchase order is sent to the supplier. Practically, such variances are usually not computed until the invoice is received, because the latter event triggers entry into the formal accounting records, whereas the sending of the purchase order does not.

Who sets material price standards?

If any one person is responsible for material price variances, it is probably the purchasing officer. Therefore, he should have a strong role in setting price standards. Nevertheless, many companies have the accounting department and the purchasing department work out the task jointly.

Responsibility as to price standards is twofold:

1. Because prices are often set by external influences, setting price standards is mostly a task of accurate prediction. Thus, price variances are probably more a measure of forecasting ability than of failure to buy at predetermined standard prices.

2. Some control may be exerted over prices by getting numerous quotations, purchasing in optimum lots, hunting for bargains, selecting the most economical means of transportation, and taking advantage of cash discounts. Effective price standards help reduce the tendency of many purchasing people to play favorites among suppliers. Some check is desirable on the purchasing officer's setting of price standards. He should have to submit evidence in support of his standards to a standards committee or to the accounting department.

Failure to meet price standards often may be due to external factors mentioned previously or to departments other than the purchasing department. For example, sudden rush orders or unexpected volume changes in production may upset material price standards. In such cases, the major responsibility for variances may rest with the sales manager because of his faulty forecasting or with the head of production planning because of his sloppy production scheduling. The intelligent analysis of variances will help pinpoint responsibility in these situations.

Reporting material price variances

Most companies prepare monthly reports of material price variances for top management, for the purchasing department, and for use by the accounting department itself. These reports are designed for the needs of the recipients. As in most reports, top management will get less detail than will the members of the purchasing department. Some companies have special material price variance reports, whereas other companies have such variances included in a single over-all report which includes both price and quantity variances for all elements of costs.

Variance reports are useless if they are untimely or if they fail to serve as signals for management guidance. The reports of price variances often are the starting point for management's finding substitute materials, changing methods or specifications, and altering selling prices. Thus, the computation of material price variances can be a helpful managerial control tool.

Even when price factors are regarded as outside of company control, it is still desirable to pinpoint them and to keep them out of performance reports dealing with the efficient usage of the material or services in question. Only then will the executive responsible for *prices* and the executive responsible for *usage* each be appraised with measuring rods that are uncontaminated by factors beyond their control.

MATERIAL QUANTITY STANDARDS

Nature of quantity standards

Although material prices are frequently difficult to control, the quantity of direct materials used is subject to closer regulation.

Most companies rely on engineering studies as a basis for determining quantity standards for material. Blueprints, product specifications, normal spoilage, unavoidable waste, and production methods are considered in preparing the *standard bill of materials* (Exhibit 6-2), which is the formal expression of material quantity standards. Note that we are considering physical standards; price factors are not relevant from a quantity control standpoint, once the types and quantities of materials are determined. A quantity variance may be expressed in dollars by merely multiplying the standard unit price by the physical quantity variance.

In addition to formal engineering studies, sample runs under regulated conditions or historical studies of material usage in a specific product may be used in setting material quantity standards. Of course, care must be exercised when relying on past performance because it may have been off-standard. Depending on specific materials or plant conditions, companies may use engineering studies, sample runs, historical studies, or some combination thereof.

EXHIBIT 6-2

STANDARD BILL OF MATERIAL		
Assembly No. __b__	Description __TV Table__	
Part Number	Number Required	Description
A 1426	4 sq. ft.	Formica – Pearl grey
455	1/8 lb.	Adhesive
642	1	Table top
714	4	Steel legs
961	1	Nut and bolt kit

Setting

Quantity standards are usually set by the engineering department with the aid of the production departments and the cost accounting department. Although the production executive responsible for meeting the standards should participate, he should not have the final authority in setting the standards. But at least he should understand the standards and accept them as being realistic.

Control of usage

Control over usage of material is best exerted when the foreman has timely comparisons of actual results with standards. When very important, these comparisons may be made continuously, or at least hourly. The exact control procedure depends on several factors, such as the following (*N.A.A. Research Series No. 12*, p. 908):

1. *The nature and value of the materials.*
2. *The type of accounting plan used.*
3. *The methods used for detecting and measuring losses of material in production.*
4. *The extent to which cost reports are employed by management for purposes of cost control.*

1. Nature and Value of the Materials.   Usage of subassemblies and expensive parts can be predicted easily and can be accurately accounted for. Predictions of usage of bulk materials such as iron ore, alcohol, and coal are based on average consumption. Variances for these materials are assembled as totals for given periods.

2. The Type of Accounting Plan Used. Where process costing is used, quantity variances often are determined periodically. Where job order costing is used, quantity variances may be determined for each order if desired.

3. The Methods Used for Detecting and Measuring Losses of Material in Production. When a department is expected to turn out a given job, batch, or specified number of product units, *a standard bill of materials* or stores requisition may be submitted to stores for withdrawal of the standard amount of direct material needed. *As production takes place, any additional material needed may be obtained from stores only by submitting an excess materials requisition, which is usually of a distinct color.* Thus, the foreman is immediately informed of off-standard performance because he must sign the excess materials requisition. A periodic summary of these requisitions provides the total unfavorable quantity variance. If performance is better than standard, special returned materials forms are used to compute favorable quantity variances.

Other control methods are necessary when there is a varying amount of output from a given amount of input. A comparison of good production with input of direct materials is needed in order to judge performance, the key question being whether the standard amount of materials was used to obtain the given output. The difficulty here is that computation of variances is delayed until production is completed. To better achieve control in these cases, procedures have been developed to detect some variances prior to completion of work. These procedures include inspection at key operation points while work is in process so that spoilage and other losses may be measured before full completion of the product.

4. The Extent to Which Cost Reports Are Employed by Management for Purposes of Cost Control. Daily and weekly reports of variances are often expressed in physical terms only—gallons used, pounds consumed, and so on. The bases for these reports usually are the original source documents, such as excess material requisitions, scrap reports, inspection reports, and the like. To be useful, reports must fix responsibility. Systematic follow-up is necessary in order to obtain full benefit of the standard cost system.

GENERAL LEDGER ENTRIES FOR MATERIAL

Two ways of reflecting variances

There is a wide variety of general ledger treatments of accounting for direct materials in standard cost accounting. Just because standards are used for control does not necessarily mean that they have to be integrated into the general ledger. However, most standard cost systems are reflected in the general ledger. Usually, the general ledger relationships follow the timing of the isolation of detailed variances in day-to-day cost control. Keep in mind, however, that general ledger entries are usually monthly summaries of detailed variances which were isolated from day to day. Thus, the general ledger accounts do not provide any particular help for cost control purposes.

Consider the following data:

Standard price per square foot	$.65
Actual price per square foot	.62
Standard quantity allowed	4,000 square feet
Actual quantity used	4,300 square feet
Actual quantity purchased	5,000 square feet

Case 1. Our formica example demonstrated the simultaneous isolation of price and usage variances. This approach is easiest to see, but as was pointed out on page 158, its delay in segregating price variances is unsuitable if current control of *purchasing* activities is a major objective of the price variance computation. From this point on, then, we shall stress this control feature, which simply calls for the isolation of variances just as early as is feasible. When price variances are isolated as materials are purchased, the following general ledger entry is made:

1. Stores (5,000 sq. ft. @ 65¢) 3,250
   Material price variance (5,000 sq. ft. @ 3¢) (F) 150
   Accounts payable (5,000 sq. ft. @ 62¢) 3,100
   To record direct material purchases. The variance
   would be posted, as a debit if unfavorable (U), as
   a credit if favorable (F).

If quantity variances are isolated by use of excess material requisitions, the following general ledger entry is made:

2. Work in process (4,000 sq. ft. @ 65¢) 2,600
   Material quantity variance (300 sq. ft. @ 65¢) (U) 195
   Stores (4,300 sq. ft. @ 65¢) 2,795
   To record direct material used.

T-accounts would appear as follows:

Stores		Material Price Variance	
1. Actual quantity purchased × standard price, $3,250.	2. Actual quantity requisitioned × standard price, $2,795.		1. Actual quantity purchased × difference in price, $150.

Work in Process		Material Quantity Variance	
2. Standard quantity requisitioned × standard price, $2,600.		2. Difference in quantity used × standard price, $195.	

Case 2. (This is the method featured earlier in our formica example. It is less desirable for current control of purchasing activities,

but it is often found in practice. The reader should concentrate on Case 1.) Some companies prefer to carry materials in Stores at actual prices. The typical entry for a purchase would be:

1. Stores	3,100	
Accounts payable		3,100

Entry upon issuance:

2. Work in process (4,300 × 65¢)	2,795	
Material price variance (4,300 × 3¢) (F)		129
Stores (4,300 × 62¢)		2,666

As mentioned previously, because of continuous processing, some companies do not discover the material quantity variances until goods are completed. A typical entry for completion would be:

3. Finished goods (4,000 × 65¢)	2,600	
Material quantity variance (300 × 65¢) (U)	195	
Work in process (4,300 × 65¢)		2,795
To transfer completed goods and isolate quantity variance.		

or the above entry may be divided into two parts, each part perhaps being entered at different times:

3(a) Finished goods	2,600	
Work in process		2,600
To transfer.		

and

3(b) Material quantity variance (U)	195	
Work in process		195
To isolate quantity variances, which are not discovered until physical inventories of work in process are taken or approximated.		

T-accounts would appear as follows:

Stores		Material Price Variance	
1. Actual quantity purchased × actual price, $3,100.	2. Actual quantity requisitioned × actual price, $2,666.		2. Actual quantity requisitioned × difference in price, $129.

Work in Process		Material Quantity Variance	
2. Actual quantity requisitioned × standard price, $2,795.	3(a) Standard quantity finished × standard price, $2,600. 3(b) Difference in quantity needed to complete × standard price, $195.	3(b) Difference in quantity used × standard price, $195.	

Comparison of cases 1 and 2

The author favors the Case 1 approach, where practical, because it stresses the control aspects of standard costs; that is, timeliness of information is needed for control, and Case 1 isolates variances more quickly. For example, price variances are isolated when *purchases* are made rather than when materials are issued. Quantity variances are isolated as excess material requisitions are prepared while goods are in process rather than being isolated *after* goods are completed.

The Case 1 approach will be used in this book, *but the reader should be aware of other possible general ledger treatments.* Note, for example, that Work in Process is always carried at *standard* quantities and standard prices in the Case 1 approach, whereas Case 2 shows Work in Process being carried at *actual* quantities and standard prices until the variance is removed.

Carefully compare the approaches for Case 1 and Case 2. Note that they basically try to obtain two major types of variances: price and usage. Although everything dovetails neatly in Case 2, the approach in Case 1 is more useful for purposes of controlling purchasing activities because it isolates price variances at the point of purchase rather than at the point of usage. Which approach to measuring material price variance, Case 1 or Case 2, is better? There is no pat answer. Again and again we shall see that the "best" methods in cost analysis depend heavily on the purpose sought. In this instance, the Case 1 approach is better only if a serious attempt is made to use the resulting price variances for purposes of current control of purchasing activities, or if management prefers that materials inventories be carried at standard rather than actual prices. If instead the price variance is being computed primarily to remove the influences of price from usage reports, then the Case 2 approach is adequate for that *purpose.*

Note further that there is no difference in the usage variances between Cases 1 and 2. (The usage variance measures, for any given output, the difference between the actual input and the standard input allowed, multiplied by a standard price.) The difference in price variance between Cases 1 and 2 is explained by the delay in isolating such variances until the material is used. Therefore, the price variance is associated with the 4,300 square feet used instead of the 5,000 square feet purchased.

Columnar format: an important analytical technique

Although many short-cut techniques are available for analyzing variances, you will find the following columnar technique extremely valuable:

For Case 1 (the approach that will be used almost exclusively throughout this book):

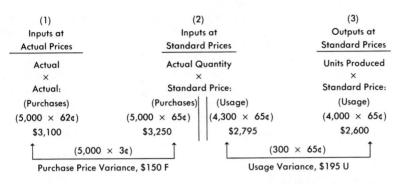

(1)	(2)	(3)
Inputs at	Inputs at	Outputs at
Actual Prices	Standard Prices	Standard Prices
Actual	Actual Quantity	Units Produced
×	×	×
Actual:	Standard Price:	Standard Price:
(Purchases)	(Purchases) (Usage)	(Usage)
(5,000 × 62¢)	(5,000 × 65¢) (4,300 × 65¢)	(4,000 × 65¢)
$3,100	$3,250 $2,795	$2,600

(5,000 × 3¢)   (300 × 65¢)

Purchase Price Variance, $150 F   Usage Variance, $195 U

For Case 2 (where the price variance refers only to the material used in production):

(1)	(2)	(3)
Inputs at	Inputs at	Outputs at
Actual Prices	Standard Prices	Standard Prices
Actual	Actual Inputs	Units Produced
×	×	×
Actual:	Standard Price:	Standard Price:
(4,300 × 62¢)	(4,300 × 65¢)	(4,000 × 65¢)
$2,666	$2,795	$2,600

(4,300 × 3¢)   (300 × 65¢)

Price Variance, $129 F   Usage Variance, $195 U

Total variance explained, $66 U

LABOR RATE STANDARDS

Price factors are usually not subject to as much control as are quantity factors. Department heads' control of labor rates is usually limited because the rates are the result of union negotiations or local conditions of labor supply and demand. The cost department computes standard costs by applying the rates to the physical labor standards. Most companies change labor rate standards as rates change. Therefore, the timing often follows labor contract changes.

If rate standards are kept up to date, the variances should be relatively small. Such variances are regarded as the responsibility of the foreman. He must match the men and the machines to the tasks at hand by using the proper grade of labor. Variances usually arise from (1) the use of a man with a wrong rate for a specific operation, (2) use of excess men per machine, or (3) paying expensive day rates because of low productivity instead of prescribed piece rates.

If rate standards are not kept in line with changes in actual labor rates, the resulting variances cannot be considered the foreman's responsibility.

To develop standard unit costs, a single average labor rate may be used for a given operation. The rates of individual workers performing this operation may vary slightly from the average rate because of seniority or inexperience.

Rate variances generally are not large and consequently do not get the managerial attention that time variances get. In companies where rate variances are small, little formal reporting of variances takes place. In companies where rate variances are important, variance reports are submitted to the executives responsible for the controllable variances.

LABOR EFFICIENCY STANDARDS

General characteristics

The human element makes the setting of labor quantity (also called *labor performance*, *labor time*, and *labor efficiency*) standards a complicated task. As may be expected, disputes over proper standards are much more likely to arise over labor efficiency standards than over material quantity standards.

Time and motion study is the most widely used method of setting operation time standards. To be effective it must consider the conditions prevailing around the labor operation as well as the operation itself. This means thorough consideration of such factors as equipment, material handling and availability, routing, and instructions for the worker. Properly trained and experienced methods engineers, acting in a staff capacity, usually set labor time standards. Time standards are typically set for each individual operation. In turn, *master operations lists*, such as the one in Exhibit 6-3, may be compiled for scheduling and routing a variety of individual products.

What factors are usually considered in setting time standards? Some allowance is usually made for fatigue, rest time, and faulty material. Because the purpose of time standards is to measure efficiency, factors not caused by variations in individual efficiency are isolated and often are treated as part of factory overhead. Examples are machine breakdowns, idle time spent awaiting materials, rework, and vacation time.

Time standards are usually set tight enough to provide incentives and yet not so tight as to be unattainable. Thus, time variances generally are unfavorable. Favorable variances are usually caused by exceptionally efficient performance or loose standards. The latter exist because of failure to have standards reflect changes in operating methods or failure to have uniform working conditions. For cost control purposes, time standards should be reviewed for change whenever operation methods have changed.

Foremen are held responsible for time variances under their control. Variance reports are regularly submitted to foremen, often on a daily or weekly basis. The source documents for such reports are usually some type of work ticket. These work tickets are analyzed and variances are coded and classified. These classifications are almost always by responsi-

EXHIBIT 6-3

OPERATIONS ROUTING SHEET

MASTER OPERATIONS LIST				

Part name _____ Fuel pump body with bushings _____   Part number _____ B-489 _____

Stock specifications _____ Grey iron casting _____   Standard quantity _____ 200 _____

Operation Number	Department Number	Standard Time Allowed in Minutes		Description of Operation
		Setup	Operation Per Unit	
20	27	90	10.2	Drill, bore, face, chamfer and ream
25	29	18	.7	Face and chamfer hub
30	29	12	1.5	Mill eng. fit pad
35	31	18	8.0	Drill and tap complete
40	29	12	1.5	Mill clearance
45	29	–	1.8	Clean and grind hose connection
50	29	12	2.3	Press in 2 bushings G-98 and face flange on mandrel
	13			Inspect
	21			To stockroom

bility (that is, by cost center), and often by operations, products, orders, and causes. Thus, a work ticket may have a number designating departmental responsibility and another number designating the cause of the variance. Causes may include machinery breakdowns, rework, faulty material, use of nonpreferred equipment, and so forth.

When variance reports are submitted, major variances are discussed by the interested executives. Investigations of possible operating improvements may be conducted by either line executives or staff experts on standards or both. Foremen generally have to explain off-standard performance to their superiors.

Setup time

Machines and accessory equipment often must be adjusted and "made ready" before a particular operation or job can commence. This setup time is easily traceable to an operation or a job, yet its total cost is seldom affected by whether 100 pieces or 2,000 pieces are subsequently processed. The question then is whether setup costs should be treated as direct labor or as a part of factory overhead. No categorical answer can be given. It seems clear that if production runs fluctuate wildly, setup costs should not ordinarily be regarded as direct labor, because the cost *per unit* of product would gyrate solely because of the length of production run.

For analytical purposes and for cost control follow-up, setup costs should not be commingled and averaged with the regular direct labor costs even if it seems desirable to trace setup costs to specific jobs or operations. Most standard cost systems have standard lot sizes for production runs. Often setup costs are allowed for in the standard direct labor cost per unit by allocating the setup labor for each operation over the quantity in the standard lot. This practice may be suitable for product-costing purposes. But it has drawbacks for cost control purposes, especially where standard lot sizes are seldom adhered to, because it mixes together two dissimilar elements which are subject to different control features. As a minimum, then, setup costs should always be coded so that they may be sharply distinguished from operating labor costs. In this book, we shall assume that setup costs are classified as a part of overhead.

GENERAL LEDGER ENTRIES FOR DIRECT LABOR

The handling of direct labor costs in the general ledger varies considerably. The objective is to charge products at standard cost (standard usage × standard rate) but to recognize actual liabilities as incurred.

Case 1. The basic treatment is as follows:

Facts:

Standard hours	20,000
Standard rate	$2.00 per hour
Actual hours	20,526
Actual rate	$1.90 per hour

Entry:

Work in process (20,000 × $2.00)	40,000.00	
Direct labor efficiency variance		
(526 × $2.00)	1,052.00	
Direct labor rate variance		
(20,526 × $.10)		2,052.60
Accrued payroll (20,526 × $1.90)		38,999.40

To record liability for and distribution of direct labor costs. Note again that unfavorable variances are debits and favorable variances are credits.

Note again that Work in Process is carried at *standard* hours allowed times standard rates. The basic format for analysis of labor variances follows:

(1) Inputs at Actual Prices	(2) Inputs at Standard Prices	(3) Outputs at Standard Prices
		Standard Hours
Inputs ×	Actual Inputs ×	Allowed × Standard
Actual Rate:	Standard Rate:	Rate:
(20,526 × $1.90)	(20,526 × $2.00)	(20,000 × $2.00)
$38,999.40	$41,052.00	$40,000.00

↑   Rate variance   ↑   Efficiency variance   ↑

(20,526 × $.10) or $2,052.60 F   (20,526 − 20,000) × $2.00, or $1,052.00 U

↑   Total variance   ↑

$1,000.60 F

F = Favorable   U = Unfavorable

Case 2. There are many other ways of handling direct labor. One method is to isolate (a) rate variances as payrolls are accrued or paid and (b) time variances as units are transferred from Work in Process to Finished Goods. Appropriate entries follow:

1. Work in process (actual quantity × standard rate)   41,052.00
   Direct labor rate variance (F)   2,052.60
   Accrued payroll   38,999.40
   To record payroll liability for and distribution
   of direct labor costs.

2. (a) Finished goods   40,000.00
   Work in process   40,000.00
   To transfer.

   (b) Direct labor efficiency variance (U)   1,052.00
   Work in process   1,052.00
   To isolate efficiency variance.

Note here that Work in Process is carried at *actual* hours times standard rate.

The timing of labor entries, number of labor accounts used, and isolation of labor variances depend on management preference and the feasibility of collecting time variances prior to completion of goods.

BOOKKEEPING ECONOMY

Some companies use standard costs primarily for bookkeeping economies rather than for control purposes. Clerical effort is saved mostly because subsidiary inventory records are not kept on the actual cost basis used in ordinary accounting systems. Thus, *stores records, job cost sheets, and finished stock cards may carry quantity data, but detailed pricing is avoided.* Material requisitions and work tickets are charged to departments but not to specific jobs. Goods may be costed out of Work in Process immediately upon completion instead of waiting for postings to job cost sheets; all that is necessary is to multiply quantities finished by standard unit cost. Reports to management are more timely and are more quickly interpreted because standards aid interpretation of actual costs. Budgets are more easily prepared because there is no need for time-consuming preoccupation with past costs.

ANALYSIS OF VARIANCES—ILLUSTRATIONS

Example of analysis of direct labor variances

N.A.A. Research Series No. 22, p. 1561, reports:

> *This company's operations consist of machining and assembly on a job order basis. The number of employees in all operations is approximately 3,800. Labor variances, expressed in man-hours only, are analyzed according to a predetermined list of causes.*
>
> *On completion of each operation, the foreman indicates the reason for labor hours over or under standard, using the code shown in Exhibit 6-4. Time-keepers record the information on time cards and summaries are produced by mechanical tabulation.*

EXHIBIT 6-4

DEPARTMENTAL MANUFACTURING EFFICIENCY IN COMPLETED OPERATIONS

Dept. No _____   Month of _____

Code	Reason for Variance (C means controllable, N non-controllable)		Actual Hours	Variance Hours	Cost
0	No reason, variances less than 10 per cent	C			
1	Estimated running time too high. Reported to Standards Dept.	N			
2	Estimated setup time too high. Reported to Standards Dept.	N			
3	Men's effort and/or ability above average	C			
4	New machine, standard has not been changed	N			
5	Change in methods, standard has not been changed	N			
6	New or improved tools, standard has not been changed	N			
7	Used setup from previous job	C			
8	Time set for man operating one machine, ran two	C			
9	Time clock registers to 0.1 hour only	N			
10	Work done under special supervision	C			

TOTAL GAINS

Code	Reason for Variance (C means controllable, N non-controllable)		Actual Hours	Variance Hours	Cost
0	No reason, variances less than 10 per cent	C			
51	Standard too low. Reported to Standards Department	N			
52	First time job was made	C			
53	Slow or obsolete machine used	N			
54	Planning not correct. Was changed. Standards Dept. notified	N			
55	Could not follow operation as planned. Delivery requirements	N			
56	Operations in previous departments not performed as planned	N			
57	Time set for man operating two machines. One available	N			
58	Quantity too small	N			
59	Extra setup result of machine breakdown	N			
60	Extra work	N			
61	Two men had to be assigned to job due to nature of job	N			
62	Learner, apprentice, or student	N			
63	Man inexperienced. Undergoing instruct.	N			
67	Operation not performed correctly. Added time required	C			
68	Parts spoiled. Had to make more parts	C			
72	Broke tool. Time lost redressing and sharpening	C			
73	Oversized material used	N			

	TOTAL LOSSES				
	TOTAL				

Efficiency % Controllable by Foreman	C
Efficiency % Non-controllable	N
Efficiency % Over-all	

When the variance is less than 10% of standard time, no explanation is required. If a given variance is due to two or more causes, the foreman apportions the variance hours between the causes. Variance data recorded by the time-keepers is summarized monthly by the accounting department to produce the report shown in Exhibit 6-4. In the report, individual variance causes are designated as controllable or noncontrollable according to whether or not the cause is controllable by the foremen. This classification of variances was developed jointly by accounting and top factory management. While the position of some items may be questionable, the classification is sufficiently reliable to have practical usefulness. Supervision over foremen is relied upon to overcome any tendency to designate controllable causes as non-controllable.

It was stated that supplementary explanations are seldom needed since the reports have been designed to answer most of the questions which arise in connection with labor variance causes.

A careful study of this example demonstrates how management uses a standard cost system to control by the principle of exception. The system supplies variances, but the total variances are not enough. It is through detailed analysis of the variances that better ways of getting things done are found. Exhibit 6-4 readily shows a *partial* list of the great variety of causes of direct labor efficiency variances.

Example of analysis of direct material variance

Unlike the previous example, this illustration (*N.A.A. Research Series No. 22*, p. 1563) demonstrates a less formalized approach to analysis:

> *Inasmuch as direct materials constitute approximately 80% of manufacturing cost for this company, the company has placed major emphasis upon control and reduction of direct material cost. The stated objective was to provide a simple and flexible program for investigating causes of material losses and to stimulate action to reduce costs · · · repetitive analysis following a predetermined pattern has been avoided.*
>
> *Quantity variances for direct materials are available by departments with breakdowns by kind of materials used. This makes it possible for the chief cost accountant to detect and localize major variances. Analysis of these variances are made by a staff of three cost analysts permanently assigned to such studies. On assignment to a project, one of these men goes into the department concerned and studies the usage of the materials in question under actual operating conditions. An individual study may cover a period of weeks or longer and may entail a balancing of materials coming in against materials going out. Accounting for materials going out includes determining the quantities of good material in products, scrap, waste, and all other possible dispositions of material until causes of the variances are discovered.*
>
> *The staff cost analyst then makes an informal report of his findings to the chief cost accountant and the latter takes the matter up with the production supervisor concerned to devise possible remedial actions. Production men have been trained to work with the cost department through company policy which emphasizes team work and oral communication. It was stated that savings directly traceable to cost analysis amply repay the costs of the analysis work.*

Personalizing variances

The reporting of variances is only one step in attaining effective cost control. The step that pays off is the rigorous analysis and follow-up of variances. This can be accomplished under various organizational arrangements; in any event, the focus of the technique is obtaining answers to the question: Who is primarily responsible for this variance? The mere accumulation and reporting of variances is useless unless the variances are assignable to various executives.

For example, a member of the controller's department, or perhaps a member of a separate "planning and control" department, may have the duty of assigning portions of variances so that all variances are accounted for. The machining foreman would be responsible for excess labor time; the purchasing chief or production scheduling executive would be responsible for lack of material; the sales department, for rush orders; and so forth. Unless these variances are broken down by responsibility, the familiar buck-passing game will thwart the objectives of the standard cost system. If the foreman of the assembly department realizes that he alone is going to be charged with excess labor costs, he is likely to be much more careful in the study of his labor performance reports and in the assignment and supervision of work.

The contribution of this responsibility accounting approach is also exemplified by the following:

> *The sales department requests a rush production. The plant scheduler argues that it will disrupt his production and cost a substantial though not clearly determined amount of money. The answer coming from sales is: "Do you want to take the responsibility of losing the X Company as a customer?" Of course the production scheduler does not want to take such a responsibility, and he gives up, but not before a heavy exchange of arguments and the accumulation of a substantial backlog of ill feeling.*
>
> *Analysis of the payroll in the assembly department, determining the costs involved in getting out rush orders, eliminated the cause of the argument. Henceforth, any rush order was accepted with a smile by the production scheduler, who made sure that the extra cost would be duly recorded and charged to the sales department—"no questions asked." As a result, the tension created by rush orders disappeared completely; and, somehow, the number of rush orders requested by the sales department was reduced to an insignificant level.[2]*

Analysis of variances and statistics

The heart of the managerial use of standard costs is the analysis of variances. Managerial judgment is the typical basis for deciding whether a given variance deserves investigation. For some items, any tiny variance may spark scrutiny. For other items, 5 per cent, 10 per cent, or 25 per cent variances from standard may call for follow-ups. Although these methods are essentially arbitrary, they generally grow from the experience and knowledge of the executives involved. Guesses or hunches or feelings for situations are fundamental parts of managerial behavior. Yet these subjective methods often engender management disagreements, barren investigations, and a sense of frustration.

Another difficulty is that the accounting system commonly compiles variances for a period of time. A cost-conscious management will follow up variances quickly—sometimes daily or even hourly. But delayed reports and everyday busy work often allow variances to accumulate, so that causal events are too old or too buried to merit investigation. Further, offsetting favorable and unfavorable variances are frequently bundled together so that significant variances may be submerged in accounts and in management reports. This combination of delayed reporting and cost accumulations that represent a conglomeration of different operations makes it difficult to find causes for variances and to trace causes for them below the foreman level to individual machines, men, and materials.

[2]Raymond Villers, "Control and Freedom in a Decentralized Company," *Harvard Business Review*, Vol. XXXII, No. 2, p. 95.

Certain statistical tools, especially the statistical control chart, use samples as a way of isolating operating situations that need investigation. The control chart helps separate chance variances from variances that need investigation. For a further discussion, see Chapter 27.

STANDARD COST VARIANCES AND THE INCOME STATEMENT

The advocates of currently attainable standard costs for product costing maintain that the results are conceptually superior to the results under "actual" or "normal" product-costing systems. They contend that variances are measures of inefficiency or abnormal efficiency. Therefore, variances are not inventoriable and should be completely charged or credited against revenue of the period instead of being prorated among inventories and cost of sales. In this way, inventory valuations will be more representative of desirable and attainable costs.

An example of the effects of these conflicting viewpoints follows:

STAN COMPANY PROBLEM

Stan Company has the following results for the year:

Purchases of direct material (charged to Stores at standard prices)	$100,000
Purchase price variance	10,000
Direct labor—applied at standard rate	40,000
Direct labor rate variance	1,000
Direct labor efficiency variance	4,000
Direct material usage variance	4,000
Direct material—applied at standard prices	80,000
Manufacturing overhead applied—at standard rate	40,000
Manufacturing overhead incurred	45,000
Sales	135,000
Selling and administrative expenses	20,000

Assume that there is no ending work in process. Assume that one uniform product is made and that 60 per cent of the production has been sold. There were no beginning inventories.

REQUIRED:

A comparative analysis of the effects on net income of the following assumptions:

1. Actual historical costing. That is, no predetermined costs are used.
2. Normal costing with proration of under-applied overhead.
3. Normal costing without proration of under-applied overhead.
4. Standard costing with proration of all variances.
5. Standard costing without proration of any variances.

Try to solve this example before examining the solution that is in Exhibit 6-5. The answers show that differences could become significant, particularly where inventories have increased or decreased substantially or where the variances are relatively large.

In practice the charging or crediting of variances directly to Cost of Sales is considered acceptable as long as the standards are deemed to be currently attainable or as long as the net income and inventory figures are not greatly distorted; otherwise, the complete proration of variances is desirable and necessary. Many accountants favor showing the variances as completely separate deductions after the gross margin on sales. The latter approach helps distinguish between product costing (Cost of Sales at Standard) and loss recognition (unfavorable variances are lost costs because inefficiencies are not inventoriable).

The most accurate proration of material price variances would be over five accounts—Direct Material Usage Variance, Stores, Work in Process, Finished Goods, and Cost of Sales—in proportion to the standard material charges in each account. As the next step, the adjusted Material Usage Variance should be prorated to Work in Process, Finished Goods, and Cost of Sales. Labor variances and overhead variances are usually prorated in the same manner as the material usage variance. Variations of these proration methods may be desirable under certain conditions. For instance, efficiency variances may be viewed as being currently avoidable and price variances as being unavoidable and therefore proratable. Conceptually, this is superior to the other methods because the costs of avoidable inefficiency are written off, whereas unavoidable costs are not. This is correct because the costs of avoidable inefficiency do not qualify as assets under any economic test.

The author believes that variances do not have to be inventoried as long as standards are currently attainable. However, if standards are not up to date, or if they reflect ideal performance rather than expected performance under reasonably efficient conditions, then conceptually the variances should be split between that portion which reflects departures from currently attainable standards and that which does not. The former should be written off as period charges; the latter should be prorated to inventories and cost of sales. For example, assume that an operation has an ideal standard time allowed of 50 minutes, which is reflected in a formal standard cost system. The currently attainable standard is 60 minutes. Now if it takes, say, 75 actual minutes to perform the operation, the conceptual adjustment would call for writing off 15 minutes of the 25-minute variance as a period cost and for treating the remaining 10-minute variance as a product cost.

SUMMARY

Standard costs are used for gauging performance, for building useful budgets, for guiding pricing, for meaningful product costing, and for bookkeeping economy.

---

[3] Overhead variances are not considered in detail until Chapter 8.

EXHIBIT 6-5

Solution to Stan Company Problem

Assumption	(1)	(2)	(3)	(4)	(5)
			Comparative Income Statements		
Sales	$135,000	$135,000	$135,000	$135,000	$135,000
Less cost of goods sold—at standard, .60 × ($80,000 + $40,000 + $40,000), or .60 × $160,000	96,000	96,000	96,000	96,000	96,000
Add proration of variances (see schedule):					
(1)	13,440				
(2)		13,440			
(3) $13,200 + $2,000 (see schedule)			15,440		
(4)				13,440	
(5)					24,000
Cost of goods sold—adjusted for variances	109,440	109,440	111,440	109,440	120,000
Selling and administrative expenses	20,000	20,000	20,000	20,000	20,000
Total charges to revenue	129,440	129,440	131,440	129,440	140,000
Net income (loss)	$ 5,560	$ 5,560	$ 3,560	$ 5,560	$ (5,000)

General Schedule of Proration of Variances (in dollars, all unfavorable)

	Total	Direct Material Usage	To Stores	To Finished Goods	To Cost of Goods Sold
Standard costs of materials	100,000	4,000	16,000	32,000	48,000
Prorations of variances:					
Purchase price	10,000	400	1,600	3,200	4,800
Direct material usage:					
Unadjusted balance	4,000	4,000			
Add prorated price variance (from above)		4,400			
Adjusted balance		4,400	—	1,760	2,640
Direct labor rate	1,000			400	600
Direct labor efficiency	4,000			1,600	2,400
Manufacturing overhead	5,000			2,000	3,000
	24,000		1,600	8,960	13,440

(1) Actual historical costing. Except for the purchase price variance, the schedule prorates 40 per cent of all variances to Finished Goods and 60 per cent to Cost of Goods Sold.

(2) Normal costing with proration of under-applied overhead. Final result is the same as under (1).

(3) Normal costing without proration of under-applied overhead. The $2,000 charged to Finished Goods under (1) and (2) would be charged to Cost of Goods Sold.

(4) Standard costing with proration of all variances. Final result is the same as under (1) and (2).

(5) Standard costing without proration of any variances. All variances are charged to Cost of Goods Sold.

Cost control needs a set of standards as a framework which outlines how a task should be achieved and how much it should cost as work is done. Actual costs incurred are compared with standard costs to obtain variances. The variances are investigated to discover better ways of adhering to standards or of accomplishing objectives.

Material and labor variances are primarily divided into two categories: (1) price or rate and (2) usage or efficiency. Price or rate variances are computed by multiplying differences in price times actual quantities. Usage or efficiency variances remove influences of price changes; they are computed by multiplying differences in quantities times a standard price.

General ledger treatments for standard costs vary considerably. The method advocated in this book stresses isolation of variances as quickly as possible.

It is extremely important to personalize variances so that each variance is assignable to the person primarily responsible. Otherwise, the investigative follow-ups of reported variances—where the real payoff lies—will be fruitless. There also is a need to have some objective way to decide when a given variance is significant enough to warrant investigation.

The advocates of currently attainable standard costs for product costing maintain that the results are conceptually superior to the results under "actual" or "normal" product-costing systems. They contend that the costs of inefficiency are not inventoriable.

SUGGESTED READINGS

Bennett, C., *Standard Costs: How They Serve Modern Management.* (Englewood Cliffs, N.J.: Prentice-Hall, Inc., 1957.)

Gillespie, C., *Standard and Direct Costing.* (Englewood Cliffs, N.J.: Prentice-Hall, Inc., 1962.)

Henrici, S., *Standard Costs for Manufacturing* (3rd ed.; New York: McGraw-Hill Book Company, Inc., 1960.)

N.A.A. Research Reports No. 11-15 and *No. 22* also thoroughly cover the subject.

PROBLEM FOR SELF-STUDY

The Scarni Company uses a standard costing system. Operations began on January 2, 19x1. A summary of results for the year follows:

Direct material purchased, 100,000 lbs. @ $1.10

Production in units, 80,000

Sales in units, 60,000

Pounds of direct material consumed, 90,000

Standard allowances per unit of finished output:

Direct material, 1 lb. @ $1.00	=	$1.00
Direct labor, 1 hour @ $3.00	=	3.00
Factory overhead, 1 hour @ $2.00	=	2.00
Total standard cost per unit		$6.00

Direct labor incurred, 85,000 hours @ $3.05, or $259,250

Factory overhead incurred, $161,000

REQUIRED:

1. In adjoining columns, prepare journal entries to record the above information under (a) standard costing, using the Case 1 approaches to isolating variances that were described in this chapter, and (b) normal costing, as described in Chapter 4. Note that Work in Process is charged on the basis of standard allowances under standard costing, in contrast to the basis of *inputs* under normal costing. In a sense, standard cost systems can be thought of as being *output*-oriented, whereas normal costing systems are *input*-oriented. For example, the factors of production are charged and credited to Work in Process at what they *should* cost for the good output, not at what they actually cost in terms of inputs.

2. Assume that sales were $500,000 and that selling and administrative expenses were $90,000. Prepare a comparative schedule showing net income computations under standard costing and normal costing. Assume that all variances, including under- or over-applied overhead, are written off at year end as adjustments to Cost of Goods Sold.

3. Prepare a detailed reconciliation explaining the difference between the net incomes computed in requirement (2). You will be aided if you set up a supporting schedule of all variances as follows:

	Total Variance	Applicable to		
		Finished Goods	Cost of Goods Sold	Stores
Example, direct labor efficiency (etc.)	$15,000	$3,750	$11,250	—

See Solution (1) on next page.

Solution (1)

JOURNAL ENTRIES

		Standard Costing		Normal Costing	
1.	Stores control	100,000		110,000	
	Direct material purchase price variance	10,000			
	Accounts payable		110,000		110,000
2.	Work in process (80,000 lbs. @ $1.00)	80,000		99,000	
	Direct material usage variance	10,000			
	Stores (90,000 lbs. @ $1.00)		90,000		
	Stores (90,000 lbs. @ $1.10)				99,000
3.	Work in process (80,000 hrs. @ $3.00)	240,000		259,250	
	Direct labor rate variance (85,000 hrs. @ $.05)	4,250			
	Direct labor efficiency variance (5,000 hrs. @ $3.00)	15,000			
	Accrued payroll		259,250		259,250
4.	Factory department overhead control	161,000		161,000	
	Miscellaneous accounts		161,000		161,000
5.	Work in process (80,000 hrs. @ $2.00)	160,000			
	Work in process (85,000 hrs. @ $2.00)			170,000	
	Factory overhead applied		160,000		170,000
6.	Finished goods (80,000 units @ $6.00)	480,000		528,250	
	Work in process		480,000		528,250
7.	Cost of goods sold (60,000 units @ $6.00)	360,000			
	Cost of goods sold (60,000 units @ $6.603125)			396,188	
	Finished goods		360,000		396,188

Solution (2)

NET INCOME COMPUTATIONS

Standard Costing		Normal Costing	
Sales	$500,000	Sales	$500,000
Cost of goods sold—at standard	360,000	Cost of goods sold—at normal	396,188
Add unfavorable variances (schedule)	40,250	Less over-applied overhead	9,000
Cost of goods sold—at "actual"	400,250	Cost of goods sold—at "actual"	387,188
Selling and administrative expenses	90,000	Selling and administrative expenses	90,000
Total expenses	490,250	Total expenses	477,188
Net income	$ 9,750	Net income	$ 22,812

Schedule of Variances

Direct material purchase price	$ 10,000
Direct material usage	10,000
Direct labor rate	4,250
Direct labor efficiency	15,000
Total overhead variance	1,000
Total variances	$ 40,250

Solution (3)

SCHEDULE EXPLAINING THE DIFFERENCE IN NET INCOME

Net income under normal costing	$ 22,812
Net income under standard costing	9,750
Difference to be explained	$ 13,062

Explained as follows:
Inventories are higher under normal costing:

	Normal	Standard	Difference
Stores	$ 11,000	$ 10,000	$ 1,000*
Finished goods	132,062	120,000	12,062[†]
	$143,062	$130,000	$ 13,062

*Consist of $1,000 price variance that was written off as current expense under standard costing.
[†]A more detailed analysis follows:

Solution 3 continued next page.

	Total	Direct Material Usage	To Finished Goods	To Cost of Goods Sold	To Stores
Standard costs of materials	$100,000	$10,000	$20,000	$60,000	$10,000
Prorations of variances:					
Purchase price	$10,000	$ 1,000	$ 2,000	$ 6,000	$ 1,000
Direct material usage:					
Unadjusted balance	10,000	10,000			
Add prorated price variance (from above)					
Adjusted balance		11,000	2,750	8,250	
Direct labor rate	4,250		1,062	3,188	
Direct labor efficiency	15,000		3,750	11,250	
Total overhead variance	1,000		250	750	
	$40,250		$ 9,812	$29,438	$ 1,000
Amount of over-applied overhead in finished goods inventory under normal costing, 25% of $9,000			2,250		
Difference explained			$12,062		

APPENDIX: LEARNING CURVES AND LABOR STANDARDS

Labor standards imply a uniform expected time for routine operations such as drilling holes or assembling parts. However, routine operations are being performed increasingly by automatic machines. Many companies, particularly in defense industries such as aircraft and missiles, are faced with complex, lengthy, highly skilled labor operations on a restricted quantity of production. What labor costs "should be" incurred on such operations? This is a very important practical question not only for controlling labor costs but also for preparing cost estimates on contemplated new products.

Many companies use the so-called *learning curve* to solve the problem of predicting changes in labor costs (and standards) as workers gradually become familiar with their tasks. Case studies have shown that labor time needed per unit of product should become progressively smaller at some constant percentage rate as the operator becomes better acquainted with his specific task. The applicable percentage rate varies from 60 per cent to 85 per cent, but 80 per cent seems to be most common. Thus, as cumulative quantities double, average time per unit should fall 20 per cent. These relationships are best seen graphically. Exhibit A demonstrates the 80 per cent learning curve, using the following data.[4]

[4]For an expanded discussion, see W. B. Hirschman, "Profit from the Learning Curve," *Harvard Business Review* (January–February, 1964). Also see N. Baloff,

Quantity		Time in Minutes	
Per Lot	Cumulative	Cumulative	Cumulative Average per Unit
10	10	300	30.0
10	20	480	24.0 (30.0 × 80%)
20	40	768	19.2 (24.0 × 80%)
40	80	1,232	15.4 (19.2 × 80%)
80	160	1,968	12.3 (15.4 × 80%)

As Exhibit A indicates, as production quantities increase, the average time per unit starts to level off; so if total production were large enough, the time per unit would become quite stable. Learning-curve analysis with respect to setting time standards is mainly applicable where there is a restricted quantity of production.

Learning curves are also used as a basis for pricing, subcontracting at fair prices, scheduling personnel needs, and other miscellaneous production-planning needs. Of course, any cost estimates based on learning curves should be confined to those costs that are affected by the learning process: mainly direct labor and a few other items such as power. However, many cost items are unaffected by the learning process. These typically include materials, supplies, packing, and selling costs.

EXHIBIT A

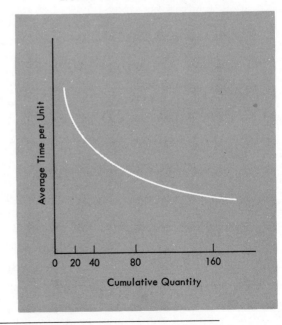

EIGHTY PER CENT LEARNING CURVE

"Startups in Machine-Intensive Production Systems," *Journal of Industrial Engineering* (January, 1966). In practice, these curves are plotted on log-log graph paper so that they appear as straight lines for ease of use.

QUESTIONS, PROBLEMS, AND CASES

Note: Problems 6-20, 6-22, 6-23 or 6-25, and 6-27 cover the basic points in this chapter.

6-1. What are standard costs? Why is their use superior to comparisons of actual data with past data?

6-2. What are the key questions in deciding how variances should be collected and analyzed?

6-3. List and briefly describe three different types of standards.

6-4. "Cost control means cost reduction." Do you agree? Why?

6-5. List four common causes of material price variances.

6-6. List the major factors which affect control procedures for material quantities.

6-7. Define: *standard bill of materials, excess materials, requisition, operations list.*

6-8. "Setup costs are easily traceable to specific jobs. Therefore, they should be classified as direct labor costs." Do you agree? Why?

6-9. "Standard costing is O.K. for big companies that can afford such an elaborate system. But our company relies on an 'actual' system because it saves clerical costs." Comment.

6-10. How does management decide when a variance is large enough to warrant investigation.

6-11. List five purposes of standard costs.

6-12. Who ordinarily should be responsible for the extra costs arising from rush sales orders? Why?

6-13. Define *learning curve*. Name four of its uses.

6-14. Who is responsible for developing standards?

6-15. Why do budgeted variances arise?

6-16. When will budgets differ from standards? When will they be the same.

6-17. Inefficiency and Product Costing. Discuss the following quotation from the standpoint of:

1. The places in the accounting procedure at which wastes may be most readily recognized, measured, and analyzed.
2. The accounting techniques available to aid in isolating these wastes.

> "*Gradually the older belief that every expense incurred in the factory must be considered a cost of the products of the factory is giving way to the more logical one which recognizes that some of the expenditures . . . are costs of goods and some are costs of idleness, of wasted time and material, and of general inefficiency . . . .*"
>
> [C.P.A.]

6-18. Choice of Material Specifications. Your company is in the furniture manufacturing business. It follows the policy, whenever possible, of using the lowest-grade lumber consistent with costs. The particular order under review involves a cutting of the following range of sizes: 35″, 27″, 21″, and 15″, the grade of the finished piece to be clear on one side.

Two grades of lumber are suitable for this order. If the cutting is made from No. 1 common lumber, the wastage is 34 per cent; if it is made from No. 2

common lumber, the wastage is 42 per cent. Percentages are based on input, not net yield.

The cost of lumber and of the direct labor involved in its conversion are as follows:

Lumber:

$165 per thousand feet kiln-dried for No. 1 common.

$115 per thousand feet kiln-dried for No. 2 common.

Lumber cut before allowing for wastage in an 8-hour day:

either 5,000 No. 1 common

or   4,000 No. 2 common

Labor:

Labor cost per hour on the basis of an 8-hour day: $13 per hour.

Labor overtime cost per hour: time and a half.

REQUIRED:

Assuming that there are sufficient orders to keep production running at normal capacity (no overtime) if the most efficient grade (minimum total cost) is always used, compute the saving on this particular order per thousand feet of net yield when the more efficient grade is used.   [S.I.C.A.]

• 6-19. Analysis of Variances.   Chemical, Inc., has set up the following standards for materials and direct labor.

	Per Finished Batch
Material: 10 lbs. @ $3.00	$30.00
Direct labor: 4 hours @ $2.50	10.00

10,000 finished units were budgeted for the period.   9810 units were actually produced.

Actual results were:

Materials: 98,073 lbs. used	
Direct labor: 39,300 hrs.	$98,240

During the month, purchases amounted to 100,000 lbs. at a total cost of $301,193.

REQUIRED:

1. Give journal entries to record the above data.
2. Show computations of all material and labor variances.
3. Comment on each of the variances.

• 6-20. Budgets and Expected Variances.   The Werelius Manufacturing Company uses standard costs and budgets for planning and controlling current production of its two products, F and G.   Schedules for the year ending December, 19x1, call for the production of 6,000 units of F and 1,000 units of G.

The standards set for direct labor call for 14 direct labor hours per unit for F and 20 direct labor hours for G.   However, these standards have been deliberately made tight so as to encourage better performance.   Management expects that direct labor performance will fall short of these goals by one direct labor hour per unit for each product.

The standard rate for direct labor is $1.90 per hour. However, negotiations are under way with the union for a new contract. Although the results of these negotiations are uncertain, management expects the rate for direct labor to rise to $2.05 per hour.

Develop the budget for direct labor showing both standard cost and expected cost, and show any expected or budgeted variances.

6-21. Learning Curve and Cost Estimation.   The Smyth Company is a subcontractor for the aircraft and missile industry. Smyth Company has been asked to bid on a prospective contract for 900 units of a precision missile part. Two months ago Smyth Company had produced 300 of these parts at the following total costs:

Direct materials	$12,000
Direct labor (6,000 hours @ $4.00)	24,000
Tooling cost*	3,000
Variable overhead[†]	3,000
Other overhead[‡]	6,000
Total costs	$48,000

*Tooling can be re-used even though all of its cost was assigned to the original order of 300 parts.
[†]Variable overhead incurrence is directly affected by direct labor hours.
[‡]Other overhead is assigned at a flat rate of 25 per cent of direct labor cost for purposes of bidding on contracts.

The Smyth Company has used an 80 per cent learning curve as a basis for forecasting what pertinent costs should be.

REQUIRED:

Prepare an estimate of the total expected costs for bidding on a contract of 900 units.

6-22. Comparison of General Ledger Entries for Direct Material and Direct Labor.   The Sweeney Co. has the following data for the month of March, when 1,100 finished units were produced:

Direct material used, 3,600 pounds. The standard allowance per finished unit is 3 pounds at $3.00 per pound. Five thousand pounds were purchased at $3.25 per pound, a total of $16,250.

Direct labor, actual hours, was 2,450 hours at a total cost of $9,800. The standard labor cost per finished unit was $7.60. Standard time allowed is 2 hours per unit.

REQUIRED:

1. Prepare journal entries for a "normal" cost system.
2. Prepare journal entries for a "standard" cost system. Support your entries with a detailed variance analysis, using the columnar analytical format illustrated in the chapter.

3. Show an alternate approach to the way you quantified the material price variance in (2). Which way is better, and why?

4. Generalize on the major differences between (1), (2), and (3). Which method produces the more "acceptable" inventory valuation? Why?

6-23. Journal Entries for Standard Costs. A machining department works on three varieties of a basic product. The product contains two raw materials and entails a sequence of from two to four operations, depending on the model type.

STANDARD USAGE PER FINISHED UNIT

Finished Product	Units of Raw Material		Standard Time Per Labor Operation in Hours			
	A	B	1	2	3	4
X	3	1	1	2	–	–
Y	3	2	1	–	3	–
Z	3	3	1	2	3	1

STANDARD PRICES AND LABOR RATES

Raw material A, $5 per unit.

Raw material B, $1 per unit.

Labor rates:

Operation	Per Hour
1	$2.40
2	3.00
3	3.20
4	4.00

OPERATING DATA

Purchases:

Material A	120,000 units	$612,000
Material B	65,000 units	61,750

Material requisitions:

Issued from stores:	A	B
Standard quantity	105,000	61,000
Over standard	5,000	3,000
Returned to stores		400

Direct labor:

Operation	Actual Hours	Total Actual Cost
1	36,000	$ 90,000
2	48,000	144,960
3	58,000	174,000
4	6,900	28,980
		$437,940

There are no beginning or ending work in process inventories. Units produced:

X	16,000
Y	12,000
Z	7,000

REQUIRED:

1. Journal entries, assuming that material price variances are isolated upon purchase.
Accompany each journal entry with a detailed analysis of variances as far as the data permit.
2. Prime standard costs per unit for Products X, Y, and Z.   Show computations.
3. What are some of the frequent causes for the variances computed in (1)?
4. What is the merit of isolating price variances as material is purchased rather than as it is issued?

● 6-24. **Revision of Standards.** Following is the previously computed standard prime cost of Product X, manufactured by the *XYZ* Manufacturing Company:

	Prime Cost
Material A	$10.00
Material B	5.00
Material C	2.00
Direct Labor—Cutting	8.00
Direct Labor—Shaping	4.00
Direct Labor—Assembling	2.00
Direct Labor—Boxing	1.00
Total	$32.00

The budget called for the manufacture of 10,000 units of Product X at a total prime cost of $320,000 for the period under review.
The following variance accounts relating to Product X appear on the books for the period:

	Debit	Credit
Material price variance:		
Due to a favorable purchase of total		
requirements of Material A		$19,500
Material usage variance:		
Excessive waste during period	$ 3,000	
Labor rate variance:		
5% wage increase to direct workers	7,500	
Labor productivity variance:		
Due to shutdown caused by strike	15,000	

The inventory at the end of the period is as follows:

100 units Material A	@	$10.00	$ 1,000
100 units Material B	@	5.00	500
100 units Material C	@	2.00	200
200 units Product X in process—cut	@	25.00	5,000
200 units Product X in process—shaped	@	29.00	5,800
200 units Product X in process—assembled	@	31.00	6,200
200 units Product X finished and boxed	@	32.00	6,400
Total			$25,100

REQUIRED:

1. A schedule of revised standard prime cost which will clearly indicate the cumulative standard for each successive operation.
2. A schedule applying the revised standard to the ending inventory.

[C.P.A.]

6-25. Journal Entries for Standard Costs. Here is a summary of certain September data for a job shop which uses standard costs for direct material and direct labor.

Material	Purchases	Purchase Cost	Standard Price Per Pound	Usage
A	2,000 lbs.	$10,200	$5.00	1,800 lbs.
B	4,000 lbs.	26,800	7.00	3,500 lbs.

The company produced a wide variety of job orders, two of which required all the A and B material used above. The standard quantities allowed for the output on which A and B were used were:

		Per Unit of Finished Product	
Finished Product	Job Nos.	Material A	Material B
800 widgets	101, 104, 109	1.1 lbs.	3 lbs.
200 gidgets	103, 105	5.0 lbs.	6 lbs.

Four basic operations were used in the shop, but not all operations are used uniformly on all jobs.

	Operation				Finished Units
	1	2	3	4	
Standard hours per unit	1	2	4	3	
Standard labor rate per hour	$1.50	$2	$4	$3	
Operations performed:					
Job No. 101	✓	✓	✓	✓	400
103	✓		✓	✓	150
104		✓	✓	✓	200
105	✓	✓	✓		50
109	✓	✓		✓	200

Summary of actual direct labor usage on the above jobs:

	Hours	Actual Direct Labor Costs Incurred
Operation 1	850	$ 1,190
Operation 2	1,670	3,340
Operation 3	3,300	13,860
Operation 4	2,800	8,540

REQUIRED:

1. Journal entries, assuming that material price variances are isolated upon purchase. Also assume that Stores Control is the general ledger account for all materials. Support all journal entries with detailed analyses of variance computations.

2. What are the relative merits of isolating material price variances upon purchase rather than upon withdrawal from the storeroom?

3. In terms of clerical costs, compare a standard cost system with a regular job order cost system.

6-26.   Proration of Variances.   The Du-Rite Corporation was established in 19x3 and manufactures a single product which passes through several departments. The Company has a standard cost system.

The Company's inventories at standard cost are as follows:

	December 31, 19x3
Raw material	–0–
Work in process:	
Material	$ 75,000
Labor	7,500
Overhead	15,000
Total	97,500
Finished goods:	
Material	60,000
Labor	20,000
Overhead	40,000
Total	120,000
Total inventories	$217,500

The Company's preliminary income statement for the year ended December 31, 19x3, prior to any year-end inventory adjustments, follows:

Sales		$900,000
Cost of goods sold:		
Standard cost of goods sold:		
Material	$300,000	
Labor	100,000	
Overhead	200,000	
Total	600,000	

Sales brought forward		$900,000
Variances:		
Material	25,400	
Labor	25,500	
Over-absorbed overhead	(16,500)	
Total	34,400	634,400
Gross profit		265,600
Selling expenses:		
Salaries	28,000	
Commissions	72,000	
Shipping expense	18,000	
Other	7,000	
Total	125,000	
General and administrative expenses	50,000	175,000
Profit from operations		90,600
Other income:		
Purchases discount	8,000	
Scrap sales	9,000	17,000
Net income before taxes		$107,600

All purchase discounts were earned on the purchase of raw materials. The Company has included a scrap allowance in the overhead cost standards; the scrap sold cannot be traced to any particular operation or department.

REQUIRED:

1. Prepare a schedule computing the "actual" cost of goods manufactured. The schedule should provide for a separation of costs into material, labor and overhead costs.

2. Prepare a schedule comparing the computation of ending inventories at standard cost and at actual cost. The schedule should provide for a separation of costs into material, labor, and overhead costs.   [C.P.A. Adapted]

6-27. Income Effects of Standard Costs and Normal Costs. The Drake Company began business on January 1, 19x1. A standard cost system has been in use. Balances in certain accounts at December 31, 19x1 are as follows:

At standard unit prices:	
Stores	$ 20,000
Work in process	10,000
Finished goods	30,000
Cost of goods sold	60,000
	$120,000

Variances (unfavorable):

Direct material usage	$ 10,000
Direct material purchase price	12,000
Direct labor rate	2,000
Direct labor efficiency	10,000
Under-applied overhead	5,000
	$ 39,000
Sales	$150,000

REQUIRED:

1. The executives have asked you to compute the gross margin (after deductions for variances, if any) had the company followed these assumptions:

A. Actual historical costing—that is, no predetermined costs are used.
B. Normal costing with proration of under-applied overhead.
C. Normal costing without proration of under-applied overhead.
D. Standard costing with proration of all variances.
E. Standard costing without proration of variances.

Assume that all variances which are not prorated are considered direct adjustments of standard cost of goods sold. Assume that prorations are based on the ending balances of the applicable accounts affected, even though more refined methods would be possible if additional data were available. There are not enough data about the direct material components in the various accounts to warrant the proration of some of the direct material purchase price variance to the direct material usage variance; therefore, prorate the price variance directly to Stores, Work in Process, Finished Goods, and Cost of Goods Sold.

2. Analyze the results in requirement (1). Which assumption writes costs off to expense most quickly? What other generalizations about the five assumptions can be made? Do you think Drake's standards were currently attainable? Why or why not?

3. What approach would you take if you had more data and wanted to obtain a more accurate proration of variances?

cost behavior, factory overhead, and flexible budgets

CHAPTER VII

Two basic questions must be answered in approaching the control of costs: (1) How do individual costs behave? (2) Who is responsible for their control? In this chapter we shall concentrate on cost behavior. In Chapter 9 we shall examine the question of responsibility more closely.

TYPES OF VARIABLE COSTS

Cost behavior—the response of cost to a variety of influences—is a key subject. The most important single aspect of intelligent cost planning and control is the knowledge of cost behavior patterns and influences. Here we examine the major factors which influence cost behavior and some techniques for estimating cost behavior. Although there are no hard-and-fast answers in this area, there are practical approaches to studying cost behavior that have proved useful.

The fundamental distinction between variable and fixed cost behavior was made earlier in this book. The power of cost-volume-profit analysis was also demonstrated. We are now ready to refine our distinctions between costs as strictly variable, step-variable, discretionary fixed, committed fixed, and mixed.

Strictly variable and step-variable costs

Variable costs are those which are expected to fluctuate, in total, directly in proportion to sales, production volume, or some other *measure of activity*. The last is stressed because some items may be variable but may

193

lead or lag in relation to production or sales. For example, the number of service calls on product warranties in a given period may have no relation to the sales or production of that period. Still the cost of service calls is regarded as variable.

Raw materials are examples of *strictly variable* costs. These items may be acquired in the exact quantities needed. Moreover, they may be stored for future use. They are strictly variable because they should fluctuate directly in proportion to changes in activity or volume.

Labor costs of all sorts—direct or indirect, manufacturing or administrative—often represent step-variable costs. These increase or decrease abruptly at intervals of activity because their acquisition comes in indivisible chunks. Labor services are more difficult to acquire in the exact quantities needed. Excess services cannot be stored for future use and are either utilized or lost as the workday ebbs away. They cannot be turned on or off like a faucet.

The graphs in Exhibit 7-1 show the difference between strict linear variability and step variability of costs. The ideal objective in the planning and control of step costs is to attain activity or utilization at the highest volume for any given step. This will maximize returns for each dollar spent because the services involved will be fully utilized and their unit cost will be least.

The problems of measurement are much more difficult for step-variable costs than for strictly variable costs. The need for a unit of raw material is easy to determine, but the measurement of direct labor, in-direct labor, administrative labor, and selling labor becomes progressively more difficult. In practice, secretaries, stock boys, file clerks, and others

EXHIBIT 7-1

VARIABLE COST BEHAVIOR

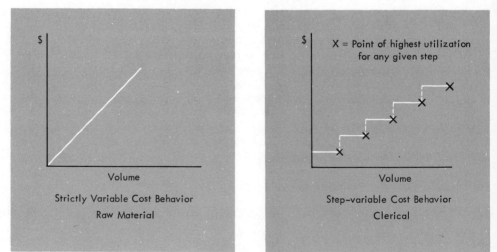

are frequently subject to uneven work pressures. They may be able to work intensively or leisurely for various spurts of time.

The width and height of the steps may vary among the types of labor services. For instance, the number of hours worked by each direct laborer may be closely geared to production. The use of overtime, part-time help, or short work weeks may cause the direct labor cost steps to be very narrow and very small so that they approximate a strictly variable cost behavior pattern. On the other hand, failures to use part-time help, to gear the work week to current needs, and to use overtime tend to widen and heighten the labor-cost steps.

Step costs and work measurement

To portray cost behavior as it responds to volume, we need to measure volume (the horizontal axis) as well as cost (the vertical axis). Industrial engineers and others concerned with cost control stoutly maintain that control is impossible without careful measures of work loads and capability. Work measurement began in the factory but has extended into selling and administrative clerical areas in recent years. It entails the careful analysis of a task, its size, the methods which are used in its performance, and the efficiency with which it is performed. The work load is expressed in *control factor units*, which are used in formulating the budget. For example, the control factor units in a payroll department might include operations performed on time cards, on notices of change in the labor rate, on notices of employee promotion, on new employment and termination reports, and on routine monthly reports. All of these would be weighted. The estimated work load, expressed in control factor units, would then be used for determining the required labor force and budgetary allowance.

Work measurement may be formal or informal. The latter is often achieved through a supervisor's regular observation so that he knows how efficiently work is being performed. Sometimes, more extreme action is taken. A controversial recommendation is short-interval scheduling,[1] where all clerical work is routed through a supervisor who batches the work in hourly lots. This develops standards of productivity, controls backlogs, and provides close follow-up of work. For an elaboration of work measurement as applied to clerical cost control, see Chapter 12.

Assumption of strict linearity

Economists tend to draw variable cost *curves*; accountants tend to draw variable cost *lines*. Economists correctly view variable costs as behaving differently at low and high volumes. The accountant usually takes a straight-line approach because he generally can assume that the curve is

[1] Vincent Melore, "Cutting Payroll Costs in Manufacturing Staffs," *Management Services* (July-August, 1964), p. 24.

straight within the relevant range of activity (see Exhibit 7-2) with only a small error.

EXHIBIT 7-2

VARIABLE COST BEHAVIOR, CURVILINEAR

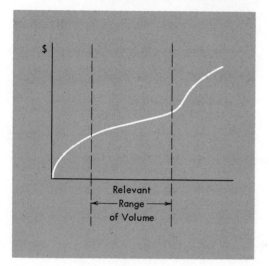

TYPES OF FIXED COSTS

Fixed costs provide capacity

Fixed costs are those which are not expected to change in total within the current budget year, regardless of fluctuations in the volume of activity. As companies become more obligated to stabilize employment, and as industry becomes more automated, the likelihood is great that most companies will contend with a higher proportion of fixed costs as compared with variable costs. Because all costs vary in the long run, fixed costs must always be analyzed in relation to given conditions or plans. In general, few day-to-day or month-to-month decisions affect fixed costs, so that a company's performance is somewhat locked in by far-reaching decisions concerning fixed costs. That is why the *planning* process is crucial.

Fixed costs, also called *capacity costs*, measure capacity for manufacturing, sales, administration, and research. They reflect the capability for sustaining a planned volume of activity. Once acquired, the capacity should be *utilized* as much as possible—provided, of course, that the increase in revenue exceeds the increase in variable costs as volume increases. In short, fixed costs have two major implications for management. First, planning is crucial. Second, full utilization of capacity is often desirable.

The size of fixed costs is influenced by long-run marketing conditions, by technology, and by the methods and strategies of management. Examples of the latter include sales salaries versus sales commissions and one-shift versus two-shift operations. Fixed costs often are the result of a trade-off decision whereby lower variable costs are attained in exchange for higher fixed costs. For example, automatic equipment may be acquired to reduce labor costs.

Generally, a heavier proportion of fixed to variable costs lessens management's ability to respond to short-run changes in economic conditions and opportunities. Still, unwillingness to incur fixed costs reveals an aversion to risk that may exclude a company from profitable ventures. For instance, the launching of new products often requires very large fixed costs for research, advertising, equipment, and working capital.

Committed costs

For planning and control, fixed costs may be usefully subdivided into committed and discretionary costs. *Committed costs* consist largely of those fixed costs which arise from the possession of plant, of equipment, and of a basic organization. Examples are depreciation, property taxes, rent, insurance, and the salaries of key personnel. These costs are affected primarily by long-run sales forecasts that, in turn, indicate the long-run capacity needs.

The behavior of committed costs may best be viewed by assuming a zero volume of activity in an enterprise which fully expects to resume normal activity (for example, during a strike or a shortage of material that forces a complete shutdown of activity). The committed costs are all those organization and plant costs which continue to be incurred and which cannot be reduced without injuring the organization's competence to meet long-range goals. Committed costs are the least responsive of the fixed costs, because they tend to be less affected by month-to-month and year-to-year decisions.

In planning, the focus is on the impact of these costs over a number of years. Such planning usually requires tailoring the capacity to future demand for the organization's products in the most economical manner. For example, should the store be 50,000 square feet, or 80,000, or 100,000? Should the gasoline station have one, or two, or more stalls for servicing automobiles? Such decisions usually involve selecting the point of optimal trade-off between present and future operating costs. That is, constructing excess capacity now may save costs in the long run, because construction costs per square foot may be much higher later. On the other hand, if the forecasted demand never develops, the organization may own facilities which are unnecessarily idle.

These decisions regarding capital expenditures are generally shown in an annual budget called the *capital budget* or *capital spending budget*. As you recall, the *master budget* is based primarily on the annual sales forecast, the cornerstone of budgeting. Similarly, all capital spending decisions are ultimately based on long-range sales forecasts. Capital budgeting is discussed in Chapter 14.

Once buildings are erected and equipment is installed, little can be done in day-to-day operations to affect the *total level* of committed costs. From a control standpoint, the objective is usually to increase current utilization of facilities because this will ordinarily increase net income.

There is another aspect to the control problem, however. A follow-up, or audit, is needed to find out how well the ensuing utilization harmonizes with the plan that authorized the facilities in the first place. The latter approach helps management to evaluate the wisdom of its past long-range plans and, in turn, should improve the quality of future plans.

Discretionary costs

Discretionary costs (sometimes called *managed* or *programmed costs*) are fixed costs which arise from periodic (usually yearly) appropriation decisions which directly reflect top-management policies. Discretionary costs may have no particular relation to volume of activity. Examples are research and development, advertising, sales promotion, donations, management consulting fees, and many employee training programs. Conceivably, these costs could be reduced almost entirely for a given year in dire times, whereas the committed costs would be much more difficult to reduce.

Discretionary costs are decided upon by management at the start of the budget period. Goals are selected, the means for their attainment are chosen, the maximum expense to be incurred is specified, and the total amount to be spent is appropriated. For example, a company may appropriate $5 million for an advertising campaign. The company's advertising agency is unlikely to exceed that amount, nor is it likely to spend much less than $5 million in trying to attain the company goals. In the give-and-take of the process of preparing the master budget, the discretionary costs are the most likely to be revised.

Discretionary costs represent an assortment of manufacturing, selling, administrative, and research items. Like committed costs, the resources acquired should be carefully planned and fully utilized if net income is to be maximized. Unlike committed costs, they can be influenced more easily from period to period. It is also harder to measure the utilization of resources acquired via discretionary costs, principally because the results of services like creative personnel, advertising, research, and training programs are much more difficult to isolate and quantify than the results of utilizing plant and equipment to make products.

The behavior of some discretionary costs is easy to delineate. Advertising, research, donations, and training programs, for example, are usually formulated with certain objectives in mind. The execution of such projects is measured by comparing total expenditures with the appropriation. Because the tendency is to spend the entire appropriation, the resulting dollar variances are generally trivial. But planning is far more important than this kind of day-to-day control. The perfect execution of an advertising program—in the sense that the full amount authorized was spent in the specified media at the predetermined times—will be fruitless if the advertisements are unimaginative and lifeless and if they reach the wrong audience.

MIXED COSTS

Nature of mixed costs

As the name implies, a mixed cost has both fixed and variable elements (see Exhibit 7-3). The fixed element represents the minimum cost of supplying a service. The variable element is that portion of the mixed cost which is influenced by changes in activity (for example, repairs, power, and some clerical costs).

EXHIBIT 7-3

MIXED COST

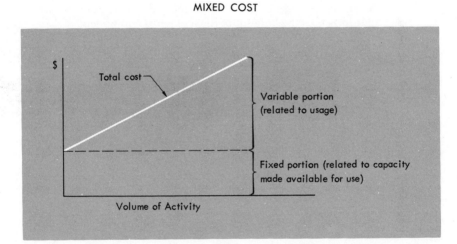

Ideally, there should be no accounts for mixed costs. All such costs should be subdivided into two accounts, one for the variable portion and one for the fixed portion. In practice, these distinctions are rarely made in the recording process because of the difficulty of analyzing day-to-day cost data into variable and fixed sections. Costs like power, indirect labor, repairs, and maintenance are generally accounted for in total. It is generally very difficult to decide, as such costs are incurred, whether a particular invoice or work ticket represents a variable or fixed item. Moreover, even if it were possible to make such distinctions, the advantages might not be worth the additional clerical effort and costs. Whenever cost classifications are too refined, the perpetual problem of getting accurate source documents is intensified.

In sum, mixed costs are merely a blend of two unlike cost behavior patterns; they do not entail new conceptual approaches. Anybody who obtains a working knowledge of the planning and controlling of variable and fixed costs, separately, can adapt to a mixed-cost situation when necessary.

Budgeting mixed costs

How should mixed costs be budgeted? Ideally, of course, their variable and fixed elements should be isolated and budgeted separately. One widely practiced method is a budget formula which contains both a fixed and a variable element. For example, repairs for delivery trucks might be budgeted at $15 per month plus 1¢ per mile.

The estimation of mixed-cost behavior patterns preferably should begin with a scatter chart of past cost levels, a graph on which dots are plotted to show various historical costs. A line is fitted to the points, either visually or by the statistical method of least squares (described in the Appendix to this chapter). The intersection of the line with the vertical axis indicates the amount of the fixed-cost component.

A simplified version of the scatter chart is the *high-low two-point method*. Although this method is not sufficiently accurate for wide use, it illustrates the utility of studying past cost behavior patterns.

The High-low Two-point Method of Estimating Mixed Costs (Exhibit 7-4) requires the plotting of two points, representing the highest cost and the lowest cost, respectively, *over the contemplated relevant range*.

A solid line is used to connect the high point and the low point. This line is extended back to intersect the vertical axis at the height at

EXHIBIT 7-4

HIGH-LOW TWO-POINT METHOD OF ESTIMATING MIXED COSTS

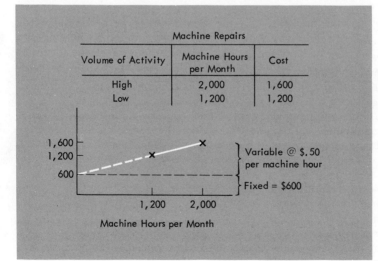

which the fixed portion of the cost has been plotted ($600 in Exhibit 7-4). The slope, or rate of change, of the line (50¢ per machine-hour) represents the variable portion of the mixed cost. Thus, the formula that depicts the behavior of this mixed cost is $600 per month plus 50¢ per machine-hour.

The same results could be computed by using the following algebraic technique:

$$\text{Variable rate} = \frac{\text{Change in mixed cost}}{\text{Change in machine-hours}}$$

$$= \frac{\$1,600 - \$1,200}{2,000 - 1,200} = \frac{\$400}{800} = \$.50 \text{ per machine-hour} \quad (1)$$

Fixed overhead component
$$= \text{Total mixed cost less variable component} \quad (2)$$

At 1,200-hour level of activity:
$$= \$1,200 - \$.50(1,200) = \$1,200 - \$600 = \$600$$

At 2,000-hour level of activity:
$$= \$1,600 - \$.50(2,000) = \$1,600 - \$1,000 = \$600$$

Cost formula = $600 per month plus $.50 per machine-hour. (3)

Such cost formulas are only the first step in the budgetary process. The budgeted figures are expected *future* data, so cost formulas must be altered to reflect anticipated changes in prices, efficiency, technology, and other influential factors.

FLEXIBLE BUDGETS FOR OVERHEAD

Major features of overhead cost control

Total factory overhead usually is a significant portion of all factory costs. Yet individual overhead items generally are not large in comparison with direct material and direct labor. The previous chapter emphasized the necessity of fixing responsibility, setting standards, and measuring performance against the standards. Special source documents, such as excess material requisitions and work tickets, were used as a basis for collecting variances for direct material and direct labor. The ideas underlying control of overhead are basically the same, but the techniques differ because (1) the size of individual overhead costs usually does not justify elaborate individual control systems; (2) the behavior of individual overhead items is either impossible or inconvenient to trace to specific lots or operations; (3) various overhead items are the responsibility of different people; and (4) the behavior of individual overhead items differs drastically. Make no mistake—overhead is controlled; but the complex nature of this class of cost has given rise to special budgetary control techniques.

In practice, direct material and direct labor are said to be controlled with the help of *standard costs*, whereas factory overhead is usually said to be controlled with the help of *departmental overhead budgets*. This distinction probably arises because the timing and the techniques for controlling direct material, direct labor, and overhead differ. For example, in a paper mill direct material usage may be closely watched on an hour-to-hour basis; direct labor efficiency may be followed on a day-to-day basis; and departmental overhead may be scrutinized on a month-to-month basis. Conceptually, however, *all* factory costs—direct material, direct labor, and overhead—can properly be included in a single factory department budget. The notion of a flexible budget may also be applied to administrative and selling functions. The key point is not what items are included or excluded from a particular flexible budget; instead, it is the flexibility which is incorporated in the technique.

As you saw in Chapter 5, budgets may be developed on a company-wide basis to cover all activities, from sales to direct material to sweeping compound, and from spending on new plant to expected drains on petty cash. A budget may be expressed on the accrual basis or on a cash-flow basis; it may be highly condensed or exceedingly detailed. All of the budgets discussed in Chapter 5 are *static* (inflexible). That is, a typical master planning budget is a single plan which is tailored to a target volume level of, say, 100,000 units. All results would be compared with the original plan, regardless of changes in ensuing conditions—even though, for example, volume turns out to be 90,000 units instead of the original 100,000.

In contrast, flexible budgets, also called variable budgets, have the following distinguishing features: (1) They are prepared for a range of activity instead of a single level. (2) They supply a dynamic basis for comparison because they are automatically geared to changes in volume. The flexible budget approach says, "You tell me what your activity level was during the past week or month, and I'll provide a budget that specifies what costs *should have been*. I'll tailor a budget to the particular volume— *after the fact*."

Comparison of static and flexible budgets

In a *static budget* (Exhibit 7-5), a set of figures is drawn for *one* level of activity. These figures are used for comparison with actual results.

Assume that January has ended. Only 9,300 standard direct labor hours of production were attained. Exhibit 7-6 is the performance report which would be prepared under a static budget approach.

How helpful is Exhibit 7-6 in judging the foreman's performance? He has two major responsibilities: (1) to meet his production schedules; and (2) to produce any given output efficiently. These two responsibilities can and should be separated in evaluating his performance. The fault of the static budget is that it does not distinguish between these two facets of a manager's performance.

The notion of comparing performance at a 9,300-hour activity level with a plan that was developed at a 10,000-hour level is nonsense from a *control* viewpoint—from the viewpoint of judging how efficiently a manager has manufactured any given output. However, such a comparison may bear on how well a manager has adhered to a single objective, the

EXHIBIT 7-5

M COMPANY
Static Budget, Factory Overhead
Department A
For the Month beginning January 1, 19x1

Standard direct labor hours	10,000
Indirect labor	$10,000
Maintenance	1,000
Lubricants	500
Cutting tools	800
Variable costs	$12,300
Property taxes	$ 300
Insurance	200
Depreciation—Machines	1,000
Fixed costs	$1,500
Total factory overhead	$13,800

meeting of a target production schedule. The foreman and his superiors may want to know about the top line in Exhibit 7-6, which disclosed that volume was 9,300, not 10,000 hours. The use of a static budget for this purpose provides helpful information. However, the use of a 10,000-hour budget for judging how efficiently (on the next four lines of the report) the given output of 9,300 hours was manufactured is an illustration of using a good tool for the wrong purpose. Note too, as we shall stress later, that the fixed cost portion of the budget and of the performance report yields little insight into the problems of planning and controlling *current* operations. These costs simply are not influenced by short-run fluctuations in volume.

EXHIBIT 7-6

PERFORMANCE REPORT

	Actual	Budget	Variance
Standard direct labor hours allowed	9,300	10,000	700 U
Indirect labor	$9,100	$10,000	$900 F
Maintenance	1,000	1,000	—
Lubricants	467	500	33 F
Cutting tools	784	800	16 F
Variable costs	$11,351	$12,300	$949 F
Property taxes	$ 300	$ 300	—
Insurance	200	200	—
Depreciation—Machines	1,000	1,000	—
Fixed costs	$ 1,500	$ 1,500	—
Total factory overhead	$12,851	$13,800	$949 F

The approach of the flexible budget

The flexible budget performance report (Exhibit 7-8) contains unfavorable variances, in contrast to the favorable variances in the performance report prepared under the static budget (Exhibit 7-6). Unfavorable variances do not always indicate inefficiency. Random influences will always affect variances to some extent. Also, there may be outside influences such as storms or strikes. However, it is evident that the flexible budget shows a more meaningful comparison of the foreman's day-to-day cost control because the level of activity underlying the comparison is the same. On the other hand, the flexible budget fails to report directly the foreman's ability to meet his production schedule. Moreover, there is serious doubt that the foreman can influence these fixed costs in either the short or the long run.

The flexible budget permits more meaningful comparisons, because the level of activity underlying the comparison is the same. The technique is essentially a means for constructing a budget tailored to *any* level of activity within the relevant range. Exhibit 7-7 shows how the flexible budget is a set of different budgets which is keyed to different levels of operations.

EXHIBIT 7-7

M COMPANY
Flexible Budget, Factory Overhead
Department A
For the Month beginning January 1, 19x1

	Various Levels of Activity			Budget Formula
Standard direct labor hours allowed	9,000	10,000	11,000	
Indirect labor	$ 9,000	$10,000	$11,000	$1.00 per SDLH
Maintenance	900	1,000	1,100	.10
Lubricants	450	500	550	.05
Cutting tools	720	800	880	.08
Variable costs	$11,070	$12,300	$13,530	$1.23 per SDLH
Property taxes	$ 300	$ 300	$ 300	$ 300 per month
Insurance	200	200	200	200
Depreciation—Machines	1,000	1,000	1,000	1,000
Fixed costs	$ 1,500	$ 1,500	$ 1,500	$1,500 per month
Total overhead	$12,570	$13,800	$15,030	$1,500 per mo. + $1.23 per SDLH

Note that the budget would not necessarily have to be compiled for the 9,000- through 11,000-hour levels. The basic ingredient is the budget formula, $1,500 per month plus $1.23 per standard direct labor hour allowed, which may be used in constructing a budget allowance for any particular cost for any given activity level within the relevant range. For example, the performance report in Exhibit 7-8, prepared at the *end* of January, shows the application of the budget formula to the 9,300-hour level.

EXHIBIT 7-8

M COMPANY
Performance Report, Factory Overhead
Department A
For the Month Ending January 31, 19x1

	Budget	Actual	Variance	Explanation
Standard direct labor hours allowed—9,300.			U = unfavorable F = favorable	
Indirect labor	$ 9,300	$ 9,100	$200 F	New material handling equipment
Maintenance	930	1,000	70 U	Major breakdown
Lubricants	465	467	2 U	— —
Cutting tools	744	784	40 U	Substitute cutting materials
Variable costs	$11,439	$11,351	$ 88 F	

The best combination, therefore, is a flexible budget for measuring efficient use of input factors, accompanied by information, perhaps expressed in units only, about the manager's ability to meet any single production schedule (or, in the case of a sales manager, any single sales target).

Fixed costs in flexible budgets and performance reports

Exhibit 7-8 may be contrasted with Exhibit 7-6 in other ways. First, note that the budgeted figures in Exhibit 7-8 were constructed *after the fact*, after the production for the month was known. It may seem strange that a budget is not compiled until the actual results are known, but this is done because a budget *formula* (prepared prior to this month's operations) is basically used to assemble the total budget. It is the variable cost portion of the formula that injects the flex into the flexible budget.

Second, the fixed cost portion of the flexible budget was excluded from Exhibit 7-8 to emphasize the modern idea that a foreman's performance report should contain only those items subject to his day-to-day control. The fixed costs are here regarded as uncontrollable by the foreman. (Avoid the conclusion that variable costs are always controllable and that fixed costs are always uncontrollable. Although this is a handy rule of thumb, there are many exceptions. See Chapter 9 for a discussion of controllability and uncontrollability.)

There is no uniformity of opinion on whether uncontrollable costs should be included in a performance report. In any event, most agree that, where included, uncontrollable costs should be sharply separated from controllable costs. Advocates of inclusion maintain that the reporting of all costs emphasizes the services rendered by other departments and the existence of necessary, sometimes heavy, fixed costs.

Third, the flexible budget is not as flexible as its title implies. It really consists of two parts. The part representing variable costs may be accurately referred to as flexible. *The part representing fixed costs is really a static budget*, as Exhibit 7-7 demonstrates. Therefore, when the flexible budget encompasses both variable and fixed items, its combined form is mixed, much like a *mixed cost*. The combined flexible budget (Exhibit 7-7) consists of a static fixed portion per month plus a dynamic variable portion geared to fluctuations in activity. Exhibit 7-9 shows these relationships.

EXHIBIT 7-9

STATIC AND DYNAMIC PORTIONS OF FLEXIBLE BUDGET

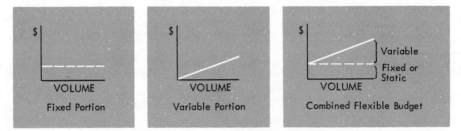

Fourth, although several diverse items may be arrayed in a flexible budget, and although over-all performance may be gauged by flexible budget *totals* and *summaries*, the heart of planning and controlling is a tough-minded evaluation of the *individual* items, one by one.

Trade-off and control

Sometimes budgets are too detailed and refined. The operating manager should have leeway, or else he may make imprudent decisions in order to adhere to the budget. For example, at Allis-Chalmers, Inc., maintenance and repair costs are budgeted in total and not subdivided. The manager may incur some repair costs in order to minimize replacement costs on small tools, which are also considered as current operating costs under the maintenance and repair category. In turn, he minimizes total repair and maintenance costs, which is the budget category for these two items.[2] Thus, the desirability of trade-off between these two costs is recognized in the budget.

[2]W. D. Knight, *Profit and Loss Budgeting* (Madison: Bureau of Business Research and Service, University of Wisconsin, 1954), p. 13, p. 60.

SUMMARY OF CONTROL OF VARIABLE COSTS

There is a general similarity in the control approach to *all* variable costs: material, labor, and variable manufacturing, selling, and administrative overhead. Let us apply the basic approach (see Exhibit 6-1 in Chapter 6) to variable factory overhead.

Spending and efficiency variances

Assume that a department is scheduled to produce 10,000 units of product in 10,000 standard direct labor hours. However, it has taken 12,000 actual direct labor hours to produce the 10,000 units. The variable overhead items are as follows:

	Budget Formula per Standard Direct Labor Hour	Actual Costs Incurred
Indirect	$1.00	$13,500
Maintenance	.10	1,400
Lubricants	.05	600
Cutting tools	.08	1,500
	$1.23	$17,000

The actual direct labor rate is $3.10 per hour; the standard rate is $3.00.

You are asked to:

1. Prepare a detailed performance report, with two major sections: direct labor and variable overhead.

2. Prepare a summary analysis of the direct labor rate variance, direct labor efficiency variance, variable overhead spending variance, and variable overhead efficiency variance.

3. Explain the similarities and differences between the direct labor and the variable overhead variances.

Try to prepare your answers to (1) and (2) before studying the solution in Exhibit 7-10. The format at the bottom of the exhibit is particularly helpful in variance analysis.

Solution

1 and 2. See Exhibit 7-10.

3. The subdivision (in Exhibit 7-10) of the budget variance for variable overhead into *spending variance* and *efficiency variance* is similar to the split of the total direct labor variance into *rate variance* and *efficiency variance*.

The efficiency variance for overhead is a measure of the extra overhead costs (or savings) incurred solely because direct labor usage exceeded (or was less than) the standard direct labor hours allowed. Because variable overhead is often most closely related to labor time, fluctuations in overhead costs should correspond with variances in labor time.

Overhead efficiency variance =
(Actual hours − Standard hours allowed) × Overhead rate

Note the similarity between the efficiency variances for direct labor and for variable overhead. Both are differences between actual hours and standard hours allowed multiplied by a standard rate.

The spending variance is similar to the labor rate variance, but its causal factors encompass more than price changes alone. Other causes include: poor budget estimates for one or more individual overhead items; variation in attention to and control of individual costs; and erratic behavior of individual overhead items that have been squeezed for convenience into a budget formula with only one base (that is, hours of labor). The cost of indirect labor for handling materials, for example, may be closely related to the number of units started during a period and have nothing directly to do with the standard direct labor hours worked. Also, the usage of cutting tools may be more closely related to machine-hours than to labor hours. In these days of automation, one laborer may operate several machines simultaneously.

Above all, the limitation of the analyses of variances should be underscored. The *only* way to discover why variable overhead performance did not agree with the budget is to investigate possible causes, item by item, from Indirect Labor to Maintenance to Lubricants to Cutting Tools. However, the summary analysis yields an over-all view which may be used as a springboard for a more rigorous analysis.

How should activity be measured?

So far we have been expressing measures of activity or volume in convenient terms. In practice, the measurement of volume is not so easy, except in the rare instance of a department which produces only one uniform product. When there are a variety of products or operations, the following criteria should be of help in selecting a measure of volume:

1. Cause of Cost Fluctuation. An individual cost should be related to some activity that causes that cost to vary. Common measures include hours of labor, machine-hours, weight of materials handled, miles traveled, number of calls made by salesmen, number of beds in a hospital, number of lines billed, number of credit investigations, and so forth.

2. Independence of Activity Unit. The activity unit should not be greatly affected by variable factors other than volume. For example, the use of a total direct labor dollars or total dollar sales, as a measure of volume, is subject to the basic weakness of being changeable by labor rate or price fluctuations. The use of machine-hours or labor hours eliminates the unwanted influence of fluctuations in the purchasing power of the dollar. Then, if physical volume does not change, a change in wage rates does not necessarily mean a change in other costs. The effects of price

EXHIBIT 7-10

M COMPANY
Analysis of Direct Labor and Variable Overhead Variances
Department Performance Report
Direct Labor and Variable Overhead

	Actual Costs Incurred	Budget Based on 10,000 Standard Direct Labor Hours Allowed for 10,000 Units (Standard × Standard)	Total Budget Variance to be Explained
Actual Hours Allowed	12,000		
Standard Hours Allowed	10,000		
Excess Hours	2,000		
Direct labor	$37,200	$30,000	$7,200U
Variable overhead:			
Indirect labor	$13,500	$10,000	$3,500U
Maintenance	1,400	1,000	400U
Lubricants	600	500	100U
Cutting tools	1,500	800	700U
Total variable overhead	$17,000	$12,300	$4,700U

Summary Explanation:

Direct Labor

(1) Inputs × Actual Rate	(2) Inputs × Standard Rate*	(3) Flexible Budget: Outputs × Standard Rate
(12,000 hrs. × $3.10)	(12,000 hrs. × $3.00)	(10,000 hrs. × $3.00)
$37,200	$36,000	$30,000

12,000 hrs. × ($3.10−$3.00) = Rate variance, $1,200U

(12,000 hrs. − 10,000 hrs.) × $3 = Efficiency variance, $6,000U

Total budget variance $7,200U

Variable Overhead

(12,000 hrs. × average rate of $1.4167†)	(12,000 hrs. × $1.23)	(10,000 hrs. × $1.23)
$17,000	$14,760	$12,300

12,000 hrs. × ($1.4167−$1.23) = Spending variance, $2,240U

(12,000 hrs. − 10,000 hrs.) × $1.23 = Efficiency variance, $2,460U

Total budget variance $4,700U

*Note that this can be thought of as the flexible budget allowance based on actual hours (input-oriented). In contrast, the flexible budget amount in column (3) is based on standard hours allowed (output-oriented).

†Actual rate = $17,000 ÷ 12,000 hrs. = $1.4167. This calculation is not essential to the solution.

changes should not affect the unit with which activity is measured; this is usually accomplished by using standard wage rates or uniform sales prices.

3. Ease of Understanding.   Units for the measurement of activity should be easily understandable and should be obtainable at minimum clerical expense. Complicated indexes are undesirable.

4. Adequacy of Control over Base.   The common denominator which serves as a measure of activity must be under adequate control. *Because it is not affected by variations in performance, the standard direct labor hours allowed (or machine-hours allowed) for units produced is a better measure of volume than actual direct labor hours.* A department head should not enjoy a more generous budget allowance because of his inefficiency, which would increase both the actual hours and his budget—if the budget were based on actual hours instead of standard hours allowed.

If standard allowances are developed for all the factors of production, one factor may be tied to the other so that all factors may be related to a common base. For example, if it takes one pound of direct material, one grinding wheel, one machine-hour, and one direct labor hour to produce one finished unit, usage may be related to the standard direct labor hour as follows: If 1,000 standard direct labor hours are used, the use of 1,000 units of each of the other factors may be anticipated. These relationships may be expedient and meaningful even though use of grinding wheels, repairs, and the like is most closely related to finished units produced or to an assortment of causal factors. It is because of the latter phenomenon that we have stressed the need for an item-by-item analysis of variances.

To summarize, an index of activity based on actual hours fluctuates with efficiency; it is not a uniform common denominator. The use of standard hours or of some base built on standard hours (for example, standard direct labor dollars) causes the cost variations due to inefficient usage of the budget base factor to appear as variances.

PROJECTIONS OF INDIVIDUAL COSTS

The first step in predicting cost behavior is the determination of the basic nature of the cost item. Has managerial action resulted in classifying the cost as variable, fixed, or mixed?

Next, a combination of the following approaches to the measurement of cost changes in relation to volume may be used:

1. Statistical analysis of past experience.
2. Direct estimates.
3. Industrial engineering studies to determine how costs should vary with volume.

Past experience

Past experience is used as a guide for predicting the future. Simple statistical or mathematical techniques are usually adequate analytical tools.

EXHIBIT 7-11

SCATTER CHARTS

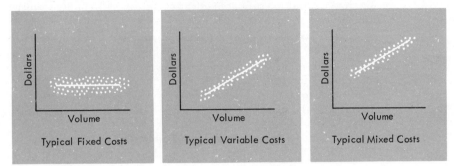

The scatter chart is often used to analyze cost variation.

Past monthly behavior of individual costs at different volumes is plotted on separate charts. Scrutiny of the scatter of points will indicate the degree of correlation between cost and volume. A clear pattern of behavior of the points is indicative of a high degree of correlation. A widely dispersed arrangement of points is indicative of low correlation.

If the position of the plotted points indicates that cost follows volume, a line is either visually located or is fitted to the points by the method of least squares, or multiple regression may be used in complex cases. This line indicates the specific dollar cost to be budgeted at different volumes. The slope of the line reflects the rate at which the particular cost has fluctuated with each unit change in volume. If cost behavior is irregular, so that it is difficult to fit the data to a formula, the graph is used as a basis for assigning costs at different activity levels directly to a departmental budget.

One of the dangers in over-reliance on the statistical analysis of past cost behavior is the tendency to ignore other important factors. *Concern with the past is justified only insofar as it helps prediction.* Management wants to plan what costs should be, not what costs have been.

Poor correlation

Many factors besides volume cause costs to vary. *N.A.A. Research Series No. 16*, p. 1229, points out that when costs show a poor correlation with volume, "it is necessary to assume that these nonvolume factors affecting costs will remain constant for the period during which the conclusions are to be applied." The combined effect on costs of the factors discussed below tend to becloud the fluctuations due to volume alone. Some adjustment or selection of data is usually needed before the rate at which cost should vary with volume can be formulated.

Non-volume factors include:

1. Changes in Plant and Equipment. Mechanization or reshuffling of plant and equipment may make it necessary to ignore certain prior cost behavior.

2. Changes in Products Made, Materials Used, or Methods of Manufacture.   Where such changes alter cost behavior, experience with prior changes and the probable effect of the current changes must be used as a basis for forecasting.

3. Changes in Organization, Personnel, Working Hours or Conditions, and Efficiency.   In particular, where variable costs have not been effectively controlled in relation to volume, a scatter chart is likely to show a poor correlation between cost and volume.

4. Changes in Prices Paid for Cost Factors.   Projected costs should reflect the expected price level of various factors for both variable and fixed costs.

5. Changes in Managerial Policy Toward Costs.   Changes in policy such as the following affect costs: layoffs, voluntary labor turnover, purchasing policies, research, and advertising.

6. Lag Between Cost Incurrence and Measurement of Volume.   When costs are incurred long before production emerges, great care must be taken in the selection of the measure of volume.   It is best to measure volume in these cases by input (labor hours), not output (finished units).

7. Random Fluctuation of Costs.   Costs sometimes deviate from their regular pattern during certain periods owing to wars, strikes, labor slowdowns, changes in supervisors, and so forth.   (See *N.A.A. Research Series No. 16*, pp. 1230–1233.)

8. Seasonal Costs.   Costs such as heating and air conditioning are often more closely related to the weather than to any other factor. Furthermore, efficiency may be influenced by general weather conditions like prolonged hot spells.

Direct estimate

Sometimes historical data are unavailable for use in projecting future costs, management decisions cause historical cost patterns to change, or specific cost estimates, such as new supervision and terminal wage payments, are nearly impossible to approach by other methods.   In these cases, estimates are usually prepared for each mixed cost at several volume levels within the anticipated activity range.   The executives concerned usually agree on amounts after discussion and the use of analytical studies made by the industrial engineering and budget staffs.

Sometimes the entire flexible budget for a department is prepared on a direct estimate basis.   A leading equipment manufacturer uses the following procedure:

> *Operating departmental budgets are prepared by cost centers in conferences attended by the foreman and supervisor involved, as well as by representatives of the works manager and the budget department.   For each of the detailed items in the departmental budget the average monthly expenditure for a representative recent period is recorded.   This figure is adjusted to account for trends and plans expected to affect the item in the coming year . . . .   The operating managers are also asked to estimate the expenditure on each item for a level of operations 133% of the anticipated level and 67% of that level . . . .   The principal merit of this procedure lies in realistic plan-*

ning by each cost-center foreman or supervisor as to how each expenditure item would be managed at each of the three operating levels. Such planning involves careful consideration of the number of shifts to be operated and sub-contracting to be done, and of personnel, equipment and supplies needed at each of the three levels, and finally the preparation of a consistent, coordinated plan of operation for each level. [3]

Industrial engineering approach

The engineering approach involves a study to find the most efficient means of achieving wanted production. It entails a systematic review of material, labor, services, and facilities needed to accomplish objectives. Time and motion studies and evaluation of men and materials are essentials. The industrial engineering staff works in conjunction with those people responsible for budgets. Engineers express requirements in terms of physical measures—hours of labor, tons of material, number of supervisors, and so forth. Then the physical measures are transformed into dollar budgets by the application of appropriate unit prices.

Standard costs are usually determined for direct material and direct labor. If they reflect current price levels, these standard costs are usually used in building the budget for materials and labor. Other costs are studied separately. To illustrate, indirect labor is usually divided into its components, such as janitorial, clerical, supervisory, inspection, and so forth. Each individual labor duty is reviewed in the setting of the budget. The duty is examined with respect to its characteristics and objectives. The number of employees needed for each duty at two or more volumes is then determined. When converted into dollar cost, these data compose the basis for the flexible budget. Similar procedures are used in budgeting other costs.

SUMMARY

In practice, most costs are classified as either variable or fixed. But there are many subcategories of these costs: strictly variable, step-variable, discretionary, and committed. There are also mixed costs, which generally may be subdivided into variable and fixed components for analytical purposes. A manager must understand the assorted characteristics of these costs to control them effectively.

Although direct materials and direct labor are said to be controlled with the help of standard costs, factory overhead is usually said to be controlled with the help of department flexible overhead budgets. However, in many companies direct material and direct labor are included in one over-all flexible budget document.

So-called flexible overhead budgets are flexible only insofar as the nonfixed overhead portion is concerned. Fixed overhead items do not change over wide ranges of activity. Thus, flexible budgets really consist of

[3]Knight, *op. cit.*, p. 3.

two parts. The part representing nonfixed costs may be accurately referred to as flexible. The part representing fixed costs really is a static budget.

The selection of a measure of activity is extremely important. Criteria include:

(1) There must be a logical relationship between each specific cost item and the activity factor which causes the cost to vary.

(2) The activity measure used should not be greatly affected by factors other than volume. Price or rate factors should not influence the activity measure.

(3) Management must have control over the activity base. Because it is not affected by variations in performance, the standard hour is superior to the actual hour as the activity measure.

The budget variance for variable overhead may be subdivided into *spending* and *efficiency* variances, a subdivision that is similar to the split of the total direct labor variance into a *rate variance* and an *efficiency variance*.

In this book, standards are attainable goals that coincide with expectations, so that budgeted totals are compilations of individual standard costs for direct material, direct labor, and variable overhead. To be specific, the total standard cost applied to work in process for a given period will coincide with the total allowed in a flexible budget for direct material, direct labor, and variable overhead. Fixed overhead, which really requires a static budget, presents some special control problems that will be discussed in the next chapter.

The job of cost analysis is quickly complicated in the real world by a variety of causal factors which underlie any particular result. Modern cost accounting offers useful techniques, although they sometimes seem too crude for the task at hand. Measurement frequently seems to be performed with a yardstick rather than with a micrometer. But a yardstick is sufficient for many measurement problems where a micrometer is either unnecessary or impractical.

SUGGESTED READINGS

Beyer, Robert, *Profitability Accounting for Planning and Control.* (New York: The Ronald Press Company, 1963.)

Beyer's book is particularly strong in the area of flexible budgeting. *N.A.A. Research Reports No. 16–18* and *N.A.A. Practice Report No. 10* explore the subject thoroughly.

PROBLEMS FOR SELF-STUDY

Problem 1 (C.P.A., Adapted). On a lined sheet of paper number the first ten lines from 1 through 10. Select the graph which matches the numbered factory cost or expense data and write the letter identifying the graph on the appropriate numbered line.

The vertical axes of the graphs represent *total* dollars of expense and the horizontal axes represent production. In each case the zero point is at the intersection of the two axes. The graphs may be used more than once.

1. Depreciation of equipment, where the amount of depreciation charged is computed by the machine-hours method.
2. Electricity bill—a flat fixed charge, plus a variable cost after a certain number of kilowatt hours are used.
3. City water bill, which is computed as follows:

First 1,000,000 gallons or less	$1,000 flat fee
Next 10,000 gallons	.003 per gallon used
Next 10,000 gallons	.006 per gallon used
Next 10,000 gallons	.009 per gallon used
etc.	etc.

4. Cost of lubricant for machines, where cost per unit decreases with each pound of lubricant used (for example, if one pound is used, the cost is $10.00; if two pounds are used, the cost is $19.98; if three pounds are used, the cost is $29.94; with a minimum cost per pound of $9.25).
5. Depreciation of equipment, where the amount is computed by the straight-line method. When the depreciation rate was established, it was anticipated that the obsolescence factor would be greater than the wear-and-tear factor.

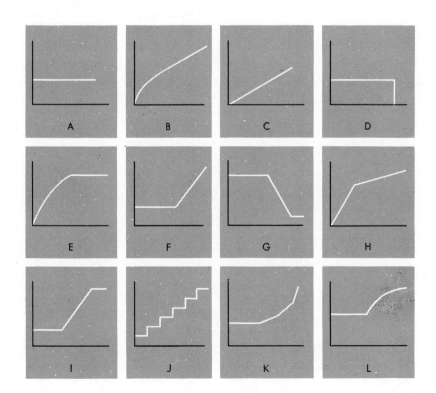

6. Rent on a factory building donated by the city, where the agreement calls for a fixed-fee payment unless 200,000 man-hours are worked, in which case no rent need be paid.
7. Salaries of repairmen, where one repairman is needed for every 1,000 machine-hours or less (that is, 0 to 1,000 hours requires one repairman, 1,001 to 2,000 hours requires two repairmen, and so forth).
8. Federal unemployment compensation taxes for the year, where labor force is constant in number throughout the year (average annual salary is $6,000 per worker). Maximum salary subject to tax is $3,000 per employee.
9. Cost of raw material used.
10. Rent on a factory building donated by county, where agreement calls for rent of $100,000 less $1 for each direct labor hour worked in excess of 200,000 hours, but minimum rental payment of $20,000 must be paid.

Solution to Problem 1. There is often a tendency to oversimplify portrayals of cost behavior. This problem demonstrates the variety of cost behavior that may appear in practice.

1. C
2. F
3. K
4. B
5. A Note that the total cost will be the same regardless of the activity level.
6. D
7. J This is a classic step cost.
8. H Note that, although the labor force is constant in *number*, different people could be employed. Therefore the wages of a person hired in December would be subject to unemployment tax. That is why H is probably the most realistic choice.
9. C
10. G

Problem 2. The Rank Company had scheduled production of 1,000 units of product in 1,000 hours. However, it has taken 1,100 hours to manufacture the 1,000 units. The variable overhead items are:

	Expected Cost Behavior [Per Standard Direct Labor] Hour	Costs Incurred
Rework and inspection	$ .60	$ 720
Cleanup time	.20	250
Oilers and cleaners	.10	120
Maintenance	.10	130
	$1.00	$1,220

REQUIRED:

1. Prepare a detailed performance report for the foreman showing:

(1) Incurred	(2) Budget Based on 1,100 Actual Hours	(3) Budget Based on 1,000 Standard Hours Allowed	(4) (1) - (3) Total Budget Variance	Analysis of (4)	
				(1) - (2) Spending Variance	(2) - (3) Efficiency Variance

2. Prepare a summary analysis of the total variance for total variable overhead.

3. The analysis in parts (1) and (2) basically assumed that the budget allowances were based on the standard hours allowed for good *output*. Repeat parts (1) and (2), but assume that budget allowances are based solely on actual hours worked (*inputs*). What would be the total budget variance? Could it be subdivided for further analysis?

Solution to Problem 2.

1.

	(1) Inputs: Incurred	(2) Inputs: Budget Based on 1,100 Actual Hours of Work Done	(3) Outputs: Budget Based on 1,000 Standard Hours of Work Allowed for Units Produced	(4) (1) - (3) Total Budget Variance	Analysis of (4) (1) - (2) Spending Variance	(2) - (3) Efficiency Variance
Rework and inspection	$ 720	$ 660	$ 600	$120 U	$ 60 U	$ 60 U
Cleanup time	250	220	200	50	30	20
Oilers and cleaners	120	110	100	20	10	10
Maintenance	130	110	100	30	20	10
Total variable overhead	$1,220	$1,100	$1,000	$220 U	$120 U	$100 U

2.

(1) Inputs × Actual Rates	(2) Inputs × Standard Rates	(3) Outputs × Standard Rates*
(1,100 hours × $1.1091)	(1,100 hours × $1.00)	(1,000 hours × $1.00)
$1,220	$1,100	$1,000

↑————— Spending variance —————↑————— Efficiency variance —————↑

1,100 hours × ($1.1091 − $1.00) = $120 U   (1,100 hours − 1,000 hours) × $1.00 = $100 U

↑————————————————— Total (budget) variance, $220 U —————————————————↑

U = Unfavorable.
*This coincides with the flexible budget allowance based on standard hours allowed for good output.

3. A performance report based solely on actual hours worked would have three columns. The first two would coincide with columns (1) and (2) in requirement 1. The third would coincide with the spending variance column in requirement 1, but now it would be labeled as the total budget variance, $120. As a total budget variance, this variance could not be subdivided for further analysis in a manner similar to requirements 1 and 2.

Think carefully about the differences in approach. Restudy the section in the chapter entitled "Summary of Control of Variable Costs." Ideally, a performance report based on *both* bases, such as the one in requirements 1 and 2, would be most informative. If one base is to be used, standard hours is the better base because the overhead budget will not be influenced by the variations in usage of the labor hours (inputs) that formulate the base. In other words, an unchanging yardstick based on good output is used to judge cost incurrence. The amount of overhead that a department head should incur is not increased because the usage (input) of direct labor has been excessive. Furthermore, the use of standard hours (*output-oriented*) as a budget base generates two subvariances: *efficiency* and *spending*. On the other hand, the use of actual hours as the budget base generates only the *spending* variance.

APPENDIX: METHOD OF LEAST SQUARES

The method of least squares is the most accurate device[4] for formulating the past cost behavior of a mixed cost. A scatter diagram is prepared to see whether a straight-line relationship exists between the mixed cost and the activity measure. The line itself is not plotted visually, however; it is located by means of two simultaneous linear equations:

$$\Sigma Y = na + b\Sigma X$$
$$\Sigma XY = a\Sigma X + b\Sigma X^2$$

where a is the fixed component; b is the variable cost rate; X is the activity measure; Y is the mixed cost; n is the number of observations; and Σ means summation.

For example, assume that nine monthly observations of power costs are to be used as a basis for developing a budget formula. A scatter diagram indicates a mixed cost behavior in the form $Y = a + bX$. Computation of the budget formula by the method of least squares is shown in Exhibit A. The answer is: Total cost equals $9.82 per month + 60.9¢ per machine-hour.

[4]Costs are often influenced by more than one factor. In such cases, multiple regression techniques are applicable. See George J. Benston, "Multiple Regression Analysis of Cost Behavior," *Accounting Review* (October, 1966) and Eugene E. Comiskey, "Cost Control by Regression Analysis," *Accounting Review* (April, 1966).

EXHIBIT A

LEAST-SQUARES COMPUTATION OF BUDGET
FORMULA FOR MIXED COST[5]

Month	Machine Hours X	Total Mixed Cost Y	XY	X^2
1	22	$ 23	$ 506	484
2	23	25	575	529
3	19	20	380	361
4	12	20	240	144
5	12	20	240	144
6	9	15	135	81
7	7	14	98	49
8	11	14	154	121
9	14	16	224	196
	129	$167	$2,552	2,109

[5] Adapted from *Separating and Using Costs As Fixed and
Variable*, N.A.A., *Bulletin*, Accounting Practice Report No.
10 (June, 1960), p. 13. For a more thorough explanation,
see any basic text in statistics.

(1) $\Sigma XY = a\Sigma X + b\Sigma X^2$
(2) $\Sigma Y = na + b\Sigma X$
(1) $\$2552 = 129a + 2109b$
(2) $\$ 167 = \quad 9a + \quad 129b$
(1) Multiply by 3: $\$7656 = 387a + 6327b$
(2) Multiply by 43: $\$7181 = 387a + 5547b$
  Subtract: $\$ 475 = \qquad\qquad 780b$
           $b = \$.609$
(2) Substitute $.609 for b in (2): $\$167 = 9a + 129(\$.609)$
           $a = \$9.82$

Therefore, fixed cost is $9.82 and variable cost is 60.9 cents per machine
hour.

QUESTIONS, PROBLEMS, AND CASES

Note: Problems 7-14, 7-15, 7-17, and 7-19 cover the basic points.

7-1. Why do techniques for overhead control differ from techniques for
control of direct material and direct labor?

7-2. When can't the terms *budgeted performance* and *standard performance*
be used interchangeably?

7-3. What two basic questions must be asked in approaching the control of overhead?

7-4. Define: *step cost, mixed cost.*

7-5. "For practical purposes, curvilinear variable costs almost always may be treated as if they had straight-line behavior." Why?

7-6. What factors must management consider in the year-to-year planning of fixed costs?

7-7. "There are different types of fixed costs." Explain.

7-8. "The idea of comparing performance at one activity level with a plan that was developed at some other activity level must be pertinent in judging the effectiveness of planning and control." Comment.

7-9. Why is the title "flexible budget" a misnomer?

7-10. "If only one budget base is to be used for appraising performance, *standard* direct labor hours is a better base than *actual* direct labor hours." Do you agree? Why?

7-11. List four criteria for selecting a volume base.

7-12. List six factors besides volume which cause costs to vary.

7-13. Effects on Profits of Changes in Selling Prices, Costs, and Capacity. The president of Beth Corporation, which manufactures tape decks and sells them to producers of sound reproduction systems, anticipates a 10 per cent wage increase on January 1 of next year to the manufacturing employees (variable labor). He expects no other changes in costs. Overhead will not change as a result of the wage increase. The president has asked you to assist him in developing the information he needs to formulate a reasonable product strategy for next year.

You are satisfied by regression analysis that volume is the primary factor affecting costs and have separated the semivariable costs into their fixed and variable segments by means of the least-squares criterion. You also observe that the beginning and ending inventories are never materially different.

Below are the current-year data assembled for your analysis:

Current selling price per unit.	$ 80.00
Variable cost per unit:	
Material	$ 30.00
Labor	12.00
Overhead.	6.00
Total.	$ 48.00
Annual volume of sales	5,000 units
Fixed costs	$51,000

REQUIRED:

Provide the following information for the president, using cost-volume-profit analysis:

1. What increase in the selling price is necessary to cover the 10 per cent wage increase and still maintain the current contribution margin ratio?

2. How many tape decks must be sold to maintain the current net income if the sales price remains at $80.00 and the 10 per cent wage increase goes into effect?

3. The president believes that an additional $190,000 of machinery (to be depreciated at 10 per cent annually) will increase present capacity (5,300 units) by 30 per cent. If all tape decks produced can be sold at the present price and the wage increase goes into effect, how would the estimated net income before capacity is

increased compare with the estimated net income after capacity is increased? Prepare computations of estimated net income *before* and *after* the expansion.

[C.P.A. Adapted]

• **7-14. Fundamentals of Flexible Budgets.** The Barry Company produces one uniform product. The assembly department encounters wide fluctuations in activity levels from month to month. However, the following departmental overhead budget depicts expectations of currently attainable efficiency for an "average" or "normal" level of activity of 20,000 units of production per month:

	Budget— Normal Month	Incurred "Actual" Costs in June
Indirect labor—variable	$20,000	$19,540
Supplies—variable	1,000	1,000
Power—variable	1,000	980
Repairs—variable	1,000	880
Other variable overhead	2,000	1,800
Depreciation—fixed	10,000	10,000
Other fixed overhead	5,000	5,000
	$40,000	$39,200

REQUIRED:

1. Prepare a columnar flexible budget at 16,000-, 20,000-, and 24,000-unit levels of activity.

2. Express (1) in formula form.

3. In June the department operated at a 17,600-unit level of activity. Prepare two performance reports comparing actual performance with (a) budget at normal activity and (b) budget at a 17,600-unit level of activity.

4. Which comparison, 3(a) or 3(b), would be more helpful in judging the foreman's effectiveness? Why?

5. Sketch a graph (not necessarily to exact scale) of how the flexible budget total behaves over the 16,000- to 24,000-unit range of activity. Sketch a graph of how the variable overhead items behave and of how the fixed overhead items behave. Why is the "flex" in the flexible budget confined to variable overhead?

7-15. Flexible Budget, Selection of Appropriate Activity Base, and Analysis of Variable Overhead Variances. The Selkirk Company has produced 10,000 units of product. The *standard direct labor hours allowed* (also called *standard hours earned* or *standard hours worked*) were 2 hours per unit, or a total of 20,000 hours. The actual direct labor hours worked were 21,000. The standard direct labor rate is $3.00 per hour. Actual direct labor costs totaled $65,100. Variable overhead was divided into the following categories:

Incurred	Type of Overhead Item	Standard Cost Behavior Pattern*
$14,700	Indirect labor—variable	$ .70
2,000	Supplies—variable	.10
2,200	Repairs—variable	.10
2,100	Power—variable	.10
$21,000	Total variable overhead	$1.00

*Per standard direct labor hour.

REQUIRED:

1. Standard costs applied to production have sometimes been referred to as a function of *outputs*, whereas actual costs incurred have sometimes been called a function of *inputs*. Analyze the variances for direct labor and then comment on your analysis in relation to the outputs-inputs distinction and to the terminology distinction between *standard hours worked* and *actual hours worked*.

2. Prepare a detailed performance report for the foreman showing:

(1) Incurred	(2) Budget Based on 21,000 Hours	(3) Budget Based on 20,000 Hours	(4) (1) - (3) Total Budget Variance	Analysis of (4)	
				(1) - (2) Spending Variance	(2) - (3) Efficiency Variance

3. Prepare a summary analysis of the total variance for total variable overhead.

4. The analysis in parts (2) and (3) basically assumed that the budget allowances were based on the standard hours allowed for good *output*. Repeat parts (2) and (3), but assume that budget allowances are based solely on actual hours worked (inputs). What would be the total budget variance? Could it be subdivided for further analysis?

5. Compare and contrast the rate and efficiency variances of direct labor with the spending and efficiency variances of variable overhead.

7-16.. Flexible Budget; Selection of Volume Base. The variable overhead components of a machining cost center include:

Costs Incurred this Week		Cost Behavior Pattern for Weekly Budget Per Direct Labor Hour
	Indirect labor:	
$ 225	Inspectors	$ .15
30	Rework	.05
175	Idle time	None allowed for
425	Material handling	.30
340	Set up time	.20
90	Oilers and cleaners	.05
	Overtime premium	.10
	Supplies:	
200	Grinding and polishing wheels	.15
70	Paints and lubricants	.05
90	Miscellaneous	.05
420	Maintenance and repairs	.20
165	Power	.10
$2,230	Total per direct labor hour	$1.40

The cost center was scheduled to work 2,000 standard direct labor hours for a given week.

A severe thunderstorm in midweek forced a temporary curtailment of power and cut production to 1,500 standard hours of work done.[6] Actual time devoted to the work accomplished was 1,600 hours.

REQUIRED:

1. Prepare a performance report for the foreman showing:

(1) Incurred	(2) Budget Based on 1,600 Hours	(1) - (2) Variance	(3) Budget Based on 1,500 Hours	(1) - (3) Variance

2. From the point of view of control budgets, should management base budget allowances on actual hours worked or on standard hours worked? Why?

3. How can such overhead items as inspection labor, setup time, and grinding wheels be related to direct labor hours as an activity base? What other possible bases seem more sensible?

● **7-17. Division of Mixed Costs Into Variable and Fixed Components.** The controller of the Ijiri Co. wants you to approximate the fundamental variable and fixed cost behavior of an account called Maintenance from the following:

Monthly Activity in Machine-Hours	Monthly Maintenance Costs Incurred
4,000	$1,000
7,000	1,600

7-18. Flexible Budget and the Special Order. Although the company had planned for production and sales of 60,000 units per month, results for the first month of this fiscal year showed production of 50,000 units and sales of only 40,000 units. The outlook for the near future makes it doubtful whether additional sales can be made at present prices; indeed, the level of 40,000 units per month seems to be a maximum at the present price of $3.50 per unit. Operating charges for the first month (which agree precisely with the flexible budget figures) and the budget for 60,000 units of production and sales are given below:

	Manufacturing Costs Last Month	Original Budget
Units produced	50,000	60,000
Costs of manufacturing:		
Direct materials	$60,000	$72,000
Direct labor	45,000	54,000
Other payroll costs (Indirect labor, Supervision, Payroll taxes, etc.)	12,000	13,200
Power	8,000	9,600
Depreciation and maintenance	2,000	2,000
Miscellaneous	5,000	5,000

[6] An example of the distinction between actual hours worked and standard hours worked is: A lathe operation may require a standard of ten pieces to be turned per hour. If the necessary operation is performed on 100 pieces in 11 hours, the actual hours worked would be 11 but the standard hours worked (sometimes called *standard hours earned* or *standard hours allowed*) would be 100 ÷ 10, or only 10 hours.

	Selling and Other Costs Last Month	Original Budget
Units sold	40,000	60,000
Costs of selling and administration:		
Salesmen's commissions	$ 6,000	$ 9,000
Packing costs	9,000	12,000
Shipping costs	4,000	6,000
Advertising	1,000	1,200
Miscellaneous payrolls (office)	2,000	2,400
Other miscellaneous costs	3,000	3,000

The management of this company is considering an offer from a well-known chain to contract for 10,000 units of this product per month at a price of $3.00 each, terms net, f.o.b. the company's plant. This contract would have no effect upon the company's other sales, although commissions will have to be paid at regular rates (per cent of sales dollar) to the company's salesmen on deliveries to the chain. The firm's policy is to carry no finished goods inventory beyond the 10,000 units now on hand; it schedules its production to fit customer demand. All cost behaviors are continuous and linear.

REQUIRED:

From the data given, show your calculations to support or refute the desirability of accepting the offer.

● **7-19. Prepare Scatter Diagram to Determine Cost Behavior.*** You are the factory accountant of Rex Products, Inc., and you are a member of the plant budget committee. The other members are the works manager, the methods and standards engineer, and the plant superintendent. The committee is engaged in establishing departmental budget allowances for the coming year. One of the problems of the committee is to establish budget standards for in-plant trucking. Formerly the cost of this service was borne by the various processing departments, but in the future it will be charged to a newly formed department to be called Internal Transportation Department. You have volunteered to make a study of the labor cost, which has in the past been charged to the natural classification Trucking Labor, and you have tabulated plant totals of this cost and of direct hours and direct labor cost, as shown in the accompanying table.

		Trucking Labor	Direct Man-Hours	Direct Labor Cost
19x1	Nov.	$ 9,600	200,000	$320,000
	Dec.	10,000	200,000	320,000
19x2	Jan.	10,000	210,000	336,000
	Feb.	9,600	190,000	304,000
	Mar.	9,800	210,000	336,000
	Apr.	10,000	220,000	352,000
	May	10,400	220,000	352,000
	June	11,000	230,000	368,000
	July	11,000	240,000	384,000

*Adapted from a problem prepared by Professor James H. March.

		Trucking Labor	Direct Man-Hours	Direct Labor Cost
	Aug.	10,800	230,000	368,000
	Sept.	11,000	200,000	320,000
	Oct.	11,200	210,000	378,000
	Nov.	10,000	190,000	342,000
	Dec.	9,000	150,000	270,000
19x3	Jan.	9,200	160,000	288,000
	Feb.	8,400	140,000	252,000
	Mar.	8,600	150,000	270,000
	Apr.	8,200	140,000	252,000
	May	8,800	150,000	270,000
	June	8,400	150,000	270,000
	July	6,400	100,000	180,000
	Aug.	7,600	130,000	234,000
	Sept.	7,600	120,000	216,000
	Oct.	7,800	120,000	240,000
	Nov.	7,600	110,000	220,000
	Dec.	7,400	100,000	200,000
19x4	Jan.	8,200	120,000	240,000
	Feb.	8,000	120,000	240,000
	Mar.	8,400	130,000	262,000
	Apr.	8,600	130,000	262,000
	May	9,000	140,000	282,000
	June	9,200	140,000	282,000
	July	7,200	100,000	200,000
	Aug.	8,400	120,000	242,000
	Sept.	8,800	130,000	262,000
	Oct.	8,600	140,000	284,000

REQUIRED:

1. Prepare a scatter diagram to show the relationship of in-plant trucking labor and direct man-hours.

2. Prepare a scatter diagram to show the relationship of in-plant trucking labor and direct labor cost.

3. Inspect the two scatter diagrams and select the one that comes the closer to a straight-line pattern. By inspection fit a straight line to the plotted points on the scatter diagram that you have selected. Determine the equation of the line.

4. Answer the following questions:

   a. When wage rates have been subject to marked fluctuation, would you expect the monthly variations in trucking labor cost to conform more closely to variations in direct hours or to variations in direct labor dollars?

   b. Which of the two variables (direct hours or direct labor cost) would be a better measure of the physical volume of internal trucking?

   c. What adjustment should be made in the budgets of the processing departments owing to the establishment of the Internal Transportation Department?

d. In your opinion, is it an accounting function to determine the budget allowances? Discuss.

7-20. Least-Squares Method of Determining Cost Behavior. By the method of least squares compute the equation of linear relationship between the trucking cost and the direct labor cost of Rex Products, Inc., on the basis of the data given in Problem 7-19. Compare.

7-21. Least Squares and Sales Forecast. The Progressive Co., Ltd., has recorded the following sales since its inception in 19m2:

19m2	$ 10,000
19m3	20,000
19m4	30,000
19m5	45,000
19m6	70,000
19m7	90,000
19m8	125,000
19m9	150,000
19m0	180,000
19n1	220,000
19n2	270,000

REQUIRED:

(a) By the method of least squares calculate 19n3 sales.
(b) If the directors have determined from an outside consultant that the cyclical factor in 19n4 will cause sales to be 10 per cent above the forecast trend, what will they amount to?

[S.I.C.A.]

7-22. Matching Graphs with Descriptions of Cost Behavior.* Given below are a number of charts, each indicating some relationship between cost and another variable. No attempt has been made to draw these charts to any particular scale; the absolute numbers on each axis may be closely or widely spaced.

You are to indicate by number which of the charts best fits each of the situations or items described. Each situation or item is independent of all the others; all factors not stated are assumed to be irrelevant. Only one answer will be counted for any item. Some charts will be used more than once; some may not apply to any of the situations. Note that category 14, "No relationship," is not the same as 15, "Some other pattern."

A. Taking the horizontal axis as rate of activity over the year and the vertical axis as *total cost* or *revenue*, indicate the pattern or relationship for each of the following items:

1. Direct materials cost.
2. Federal Social Security tax, as legally assessed, per worker, with workers earning over $7,800 per year, which is the maximum subject to tax.
3. Foremen's salaries.
4. A breakeven chart.

*Prepared by Professor David Green, Jr.

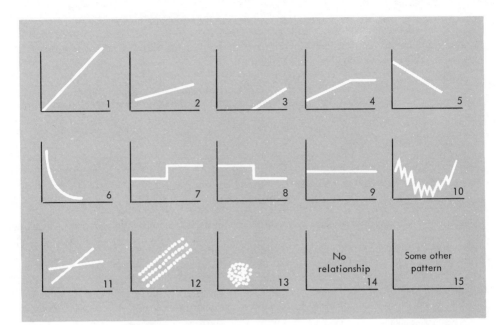

5. Total average unit cost.

6. Mixed costs—for example, electric power *demand charge* plus usage rate.

7. Average versus marginal cost.

8. Depreciation of plant, computed on a straight-line, time basis.

9. Data supporting the use of a variable cost rate, such as $2 per direct man-hour.

10. Vacation pay accrued for all workers in a department or plant.

11. Data indicating that an indirect cost rate based on the given activity measure is spurious.

12. Variable costs *per unit* of output.

13. Incentive bonus plan, operating only above some level of activity.

14. Interest charges on money borrowed to finance acquisition of plant, before any payments on principal.

B. Taking the horizontal axis to represent a time series of weeks during a year and the vertical axis as representing *total cost per week*, match the following items with the relationship shown by the charts:

15. Direct labor cost under stable production.

16. Direct materials purchased in small quantities during a period of widely fluctuating prices (inventory held at zero).

17. Effect of declining production volume over the year.

18. Result of a shutdown because of vacations, a serious casualty, or complete failure of demand. The shutdown continues to the end of the year.

19. Under- or over-absorbed factory overhead, taken weekly over the year, when volume varies widely and the cost rate is assumed to be correct.

20. Seasonal fluctuation in the use of fuel for heating the plant building over the year.

C. Taking the horizontal axis to represent a time series of weeks or months during a year, but the vertical axis to represent *unit-product cost* as determined by conventional methods, that is, by using indirect cost rates, match the charts with each of the following items:

21. Upward revision during the year of the variable indirect cost rate, because of changes in price, or other factors, expected to be permanent.

22. Indirect materials acquired for immediate use in small quantities at fluctuating prices.

23. Unusual repair charges caused by careless operation of the machinery.

24. A downward revision of the fixed indirect cost rate because of greater volume than was anticipated; the higher volume is expected to continue over the rest of the year.

7-23. Budgeting Indirect Labor; Mixed Cost. A certain unionized company hires indirect laborers to support direct laborers by performing a variety of unskilled tasks such as machine cleanup and material handling and trucking. The direct laborers usually run two machines simultaneously. The relationships that have prevailed in the past three years are as follows:

	19x6			19x7		
	Direct Labor	Machine-Hours	Auxiliary Labor	Direct Labor	Machine-Hours	Auxiliary Labor
First quarter	$150,000	100,000	$20,000	$162,000	90,000	$22,800
Second quarter	182,000	120,000	22,000	183,000	100,000	24,000
Third quarter	163,000	110,000	21,000	200,000	110,000	25,200
Fourth quarter	158,000	105,000	20,500	205,000	115,000	25,800

	19x8		
	Direct Labor	Machine-Hours	Auxiliary Labor
First quarter	$238,000	120,000	$29,040
Second quarter	199,000	100,000	26,400
Third quarter	206,000	105,000	27,060
Fourth quarter	189,000	95,000	25,740

The company is installing a budgetary system. You have been asked to prepare an estimate of the quarterly costs of auxiliary labor for 19x9, given the above data and the following. The union contract for auxiliary labor has not been negotiated for 19x9 as yet.

	19x9	
	Direct Labor	Machine-Hours
First quarter	$231,000	110,000
Second quarter	189,000	90,000
Third quarter	199,500	95,000
Fourth quarter	210,000	100,000

Thoroughly justify your estimate with computations and words that can be understood by the president, a nasty sort who despises technical jargon but admires clear reasoning.

standard costs and product costing:
analysis of overhead variances

CHAPTER VIII

This chapter is very important because it integrates, contrasts, and compares the control and product-costing purposes of cost accounting. It also gives you a chance to consolidate and crystallize your study of the previous two chapters. You will then have a solid grasp of flexible budgets and standard costs.

The objective of this chapter is to examine the relationships of overhead control and overhead application, with particular emphasis on the variances between incurrence and application. Although the ideas presented here are simple, the analysis of overhead variances becomes confusing if the two purposes of overhead accounting—control and product costing—are overlooked or misunderstood.

Chapter 4 contained a discussion of the necessity for using pre-determined overhead rates in applying overhead to products.[1] Now we shall consider this problem in more detail.

Because of the differences in behavior and controllability of costs, management has found that the distinction between variable costs and fixed costs is useful in budgeting and in product costing. Where feasible, it is desirable to classify overhead items into variable and fixed categories.

---

[1] Predeterminations of overhead behavior are an integral part of overhead accounting for control. For example, the entire framework of flexible overhead budgets is predetermined.

Several important intricacies of overhead accounting are being skipped temporarily. They include: (a) factors to be considered in selecting the appropriate base for product costing, (b) department versus plant-wide overhead rates, and (c) reapportionment of service department costs to producing departments before setting rates. These issues are discussed in Chapter 17.

Two overhead rates are established: a variable overhead rate and a fixed overhead rate. First, we shall consider the variable overhead rate.

VARIABLE OVERHEAD RATE

Developing the rate

As we saw in Chapter 7, the budget usually covers a range of anticipated activity expressed in terms of the base for overhead allocation. On a monthly basis, the flexible budget may appear as in Exhibit 8-1.

EXHIBIT 8-1

M COMPANY
Machining Department
Simplified Flexible Factory Overhead Budget
for Anticipated Monthly Activity Range

Standard direct labor hours allowed	8,000	9,000	10,000	11,000
Variable factory overhead:				
Material handling	$ 8,000	$ 9,000	$10,000	$11,000
Idle time	800	900	1,000	1,100
Rework	800	900	1,000	1,100
Overtime premium	400	450	500	550
Supplies	3,600	4,050	4,500	4,950
Total	$13,600	$15,300	$17,000	$18,700

Variable overhead rate,
$1.70 per DLH.

Fixed factory overhead: (To be considered in Exhibit 8-4)

For purposes of computing standard unit costs of products, detailed studies of usage of direct material and direct labor are made to trace these costs to the physical units produced. If overhead costs have been properly classified, variable overhead may be assigned to products with assurance because the hourly or product rate used is valid at any level of production over wide ranges. Thus, a standard cost sheet may contain the following:

M COMPANY
Standard Cost Sheet
Product X (Per Unit)

Direct material, 40 pounds @ 20¢	$8.00
Direct labor, 3 hours @ $2.00	6.00
Variable overhead, 3 hours @ $1.70	5.10
Fixed overhead, 3 hours @ ? (to be discussed later)	?
Total standard cost per unit	$?

By definition, total variable overhead costs fluctuate in proportion to changes in activity levels. A variable overhead rate is often developed with labor hours as the base. This rate is merely multiplied by the number of standard hours necessary to produce a product; the result is the variable overhead component of the total standard cost per unit of product (3 hours × $1.70, in the example).

Consider these additional facts concerning one month's operations:

Variable overhead incurred for 7,900 actual direct labor hours worked	$14,250
Variable overhead rate, $1.70 per hour or $5.10 per unit of product	

Good output expressed in:

Standard hours allowed, 8,000 × $1.70 or Units produced, 2,666-2/3 × $5.10	13,600
Variable overhead variance	$ 650 Unfavorable

General ledger entries

The summary general ledger treatment of the above facts would be:

Variable factory overhead control	14,250	
Accounts payable, Accrued Payroll, etc.		14,250

To record actual variable overhead incurred. Detailed postings of variable overhead items, such as material handling, supplies, and idle time, would be made to the departmental overhead sheets in the subsidiary ledger for Variable Factory Overhead Control.

Work in process (at standard)	13,600	
Variable factory overhead applied		13,600

To apply overhead at the predetermined rate times work done as expressed in standard hours allowed (often called standard hours worked or standard hours earned). This would be $1.70 × 8,000 standard hours. Note that this calculation coincides with the flexible budget total for this level of activity expressed in standard hours. The budget total would be $1.70 × 8,000 hours, or $13,600.

The only change in general ledger procedure in this chapter is the replacement of a single Department Factory Overhead Control account with two new accounts, one for variable overhead and another for fixed overhead. Also, there will be two Applied accounts instead of the single Applied account used previously.

At this point, note that the total variable overhead variance is not in a separate variance account, whereas direct material and direct labor variances are com-

monly isolated in separate accounts as general ledger entries are made. However, the total variable overhead variance may be readily computed by taking the difference between the Variable Factory Overhead Control balance and the Variable Factory Overhead Applied balance.

The general ledger treatment practiced in standard cost systems is not at all uniform. The reader who really understands the features of standard costs can easily adapt himself to any given bookkeeping system. Differences in general ledger treatment usually center around (a) the number of detailed variance accounts desired and (b) the timing of isolation of variances in the ledger.

Analysis of variable overhead variances

The previous chapter (specifically, Exhibit 7-10) demonstrated how variances in variable overhead were analyzed, so there is no need for repetition here. However, there are a few points that deserve emphasis:

1. As Exhibit 8-2 shows, the variable overhead applied to product in the general ledger ($13,600) coincides *exactly* with the amount provided in the flexible budget. Therefore, there is no conflict between the information generated for product-costing purposes and that developed for control purposes.

2. The total variance to be explained, $650, is often called the *budget* or *controllable* variance because it is the difference between the amount incurred and the amount of variable cost provided for in the flexible budget.

EXHIBIT 8-2

M COMPANY
Machining Department
Summary Analysis of Variable Overhead
For the Month Ending March 31, 19x1

(1) Inputs × Actual Rate	(2) Inputs × Standard Rate*	(3) Outputs × Standard Rate
	(7,900 × $1.70)	(8,000 × $1.70)
$14,250	$13,430	$13,600

Spending variance, $820 U   Efficiency variance, $170 F

(8,000 − 7,900 hours) × $1.70 = $170

Total (budget) variance, $650 U

*This is akin to preparing a flexible budget based on actual hours of input rather than one based on standard hours allowed.

3. Many companies refrain from subdividing the variable overhead variance beyond the *budget variance* stage. This simplifies reports, but

it does not yield as much information. Such an approach would yield an itemized report as follows:

Detailed Analysis	Actual	Budget— 8,000 Standard Hours Allowed	Variance	Explanation
Variable factory overhead:				
Material handling	$ 8,325	$ 8,000	$325 U	High-rate workers used
Idle time	850	800	50 U	Machine #1 breakdown
(and so forth)		(and so forth)		
Total variable overhead	$14,250	$13,600	$650 U	

FIXED OVERHEAD AND STANDARD COSTS OF PRODUCT

Selecting a rate of activity

By definition, *total* fixed overhead costs do not change over wide ranges of activity. However, unit costs do change; the higher the level of activity, the lower the unit cost. A costing difficulty arises here because management desires a single representative standard cost for a *product* despite month-to-month changes in production volume. What level of activity should be used in developing a single application rate for applying fixed overhead to product? Consider this illustration:

M COMPANY
Standard Cost Sheet
Product X (Per Unit)

Direct material, 40 pounds @ 20¢	$8.00
Direct labor, 3 hours @ $2.00	6.00
Variable overhead, 3 hours @ $1.70	5.10
Fixed overhead, 3 hours @ ?	?
Total standard cost per unit	$?

Now consider the budget for fixed overhead (the bottom half of the flexible budget in Exhibit 8-3).

Total fixed overhead is $10,000. Although Exhibit 8-3 indicates an 8,000- to 11,000-hour range, monthly volume expressed in standard labor hours might gyrate even more widely, from 5,000 up to a maximum of 15,000. Thus, the hourly cost of fixed overhead could fluctuate from $2.00 down to $66\frac{2}{3}$¢, with a consequent effect on standard product costs. This problem does not arise with variable overhead, because by definition anticipated total variable overhead would be $8,500 at a 5,000-hour level of capacity and $25,500 at a 15,000-hour level of capacity—a constant hourly rate of $1.70 no matter what the volume.

EXHIBIT 8-3

M COMPANY
Machining Department
Simplified Flexible Factory Overhead Budget
For Anticipated Monthly Activity Range

			Normal Activity	
Standard direct labor hours allowed	8,000	9,000	10,000	11,000
Variable factory overhead:				
Material handling	$ 8,000	$ 9,000	$10,000	$11,000
Idle time	800	900	1,000	1,100
Rework	800	900	1,000	1,100
Overtime premium	400	450	500	550
Supplies	3,600	4,050	4,500	4,950
Total	$13,600	$15,300	$17,000	$18,700
Variable overhead rate		$1.70 per DLH		
Fixed factory overhead:				
Supervision	$ 1,700	$ 1,700	$ 1,700	$ 1,700
Depreciation—Plant	2,000	2,000	2,000	2,000
Depreciation—Equipment	5,000	5,000	5,000	5,000
Property taxes	1,000	1,000	1,000	1,000
Insurance—Factory	300	300	300	300
Total	$10,000	$10,000	$10,000	$10,000
Fixed overhead rate based on normal activity of 10,000 hours		$1.00 per DLH		

Normal activity

To obtain a single standard product cost for pricing and inventory uses, a selection of an appropriate activity (often called volume) level is necessary to develop a predetermined rate for applying fixed overhead. One widely used basis for developing fixed overhead rates is *normal activity* (also called *normal volume, standard volume,* and *standard activity*).

Normal activity is the level of capacity utilization that will satisfy average consumer demand over a span of time long enough to include seasonal, cyclical, and trend factors. Consideration of market potential and production capabilities will influence the selection of normal activity. The use of normal activity for applying fixed overhead avoids fluctuations in unit costs for product costing because the same unit rate is used despite short-run changes in activity. Normal activity is the expected average utilization of available production capability or capacity over a span of years rather than over just one year.

Expected annual activity

Another frequently used basis for determining a fixed overhead rate is the expected activity for the coming year. Proponents of this method maintain that each year should be considered alone; the objective is to apply the year's total fixed overhead to the year's production. In addition, this method is considered more workable when company or industry conditions prevent a reliable forecast of volume beyond the ensuing year.

The notion of *normal activity* is more likely to be used than *expected annual activity* where a hefty portion of fixed commitments are for plant facilities and for supervisory and technical organizations.[2] Although these factors will not be completely utilized constantly, facilities and organizations exist in order to satisfy peak demands to the extent that it is profitable to do so. Thus, it is expected that these outlays will ultimately be recovered, although not necessarily in one or even two years.

In practice, *normal activity* has two meanings: (1) for most companies, it is the average rate of activity needed to meet average sales demand over a business cycle; (2) for other companies, it is the term used to describe *expected annual activity*.

In this book, the term *normal activity* will denote the long-run utilization idea as opposed to *expected annual activity*. Of course, in highly stable companies, these ideas coincide. For an amplified discussion, see Chapter 17.

Practical capacity

Practical capacity is the maximum activity (production potential) that can be reached in regularly scheduled hours. It is the engineered capacity which allows for normal down time. It reflects the best volume attainable under efficient conditions in a given situation (either one, two, or three shifts). Practical capacity may be used as a basis for determining fixed overhead rates when operations are near maximum utilization. Because plants rarely operate at practical capacity for extended periods, fixed overhead rates based on practical capacity are not widely used.

Choosing the activity base

The selection of an appropriate activity level for the predetermination of fixed overhead rates is a matter of judgment. For instance, a dozen

---

[2] It is difficult to make sweeping generalizations about how companies apply overhead to product. Studies of practice show conflicting results about whether actual or predetermined rates are used. In the latter cases, there are no clear patterns as to how normal activity, expected annual activity, or some other basis for application is selected in a particular company. See Charles R. Purdy, "Industry Patterns of Capacity or Volume Choice: Their Existence and Rationale," *Journal of Accounting Research* (Autumn, 1965), pp. 228–241.

independent accountants or engineers would probably decide on a dozen versions of normal activity based on the same set of available facts. Thus, the standard product cost would differ, depending on who sets the rate for fixed overhead.

Ideally, separate criteria may be used in selecting a base for a variable overhead rate, as opposed to those used in selecting a different base for a fixed overhead rate. The variable overhead rate would be related to that activity base which is most logically linked to fluctuations in variable overhead costs. On the other hand, fixed overhead does not vary in relation to any base; therefore, the preferred base for applying fixed overhead is that which best expresses the production capability of the plant. One of the purposes of fixed overhead application is to obtain some measurement of the utilization of capacity. Where there are a variety of products, this capacity measure is often fundamentally expressed as labor hours or machine-hours.

Although fixed overhead rates are important for product costing and long-run pricing, such rates *have limited significance for control purposes*. At the lower levels of supervision, almost all fixed costs are not under direct control; even at higher levels of supervision, few fixed costs are controllable within wide ranges of anticipated activity.

General ledger entries

Consider the following facts as an example of the general ledger treatment of fixed overhead:

Fixed overhead budgeted (this total is the same over wide ranges of activity)	$10,000
Normal monthly activity, expressed in standard hours allowed for good output	10,000
Predetermined overhead rate per hour	$ 1.00
Fixed overhead incurred	$10,200
Fixed overhead applied:	
Good output expressed in standard hours allowed, 8,000 × $1.00	$ 8,000
Total fixed overhead variance, $10,200 − $8,000	$ 2,200
Actual hours worked	7,900

The summary general ledger treatment of the above facts would be:

Fixed factory overhead control	10,200	
Accrued payroll, Allowance for depreciation, etc.		10,200

To record actual fixed overhead incurred. Detailed postings of fixed overhead items, such as salaries, depreciation, property taxes, and insurance, would be made to the departmental overhead sheets in the subsidiary ledger for Fixed Factory Overhead Control.

Work in process (at standard)	8,000	
Fixed factory overhead applied		8,000

To apply overhead at the predetermined rate times work done as expressed in standard hours allowed. Note that this total differs from the fixed overhead budget for this level of activity. The budget total for fixed overhead is $10,000 at any level of activity.

Analysis of fixed overhead variance

The first step in analyzing overhead is to calculate the total variance. In this example, the total variance is $2,200, the difference between $10,200 incurred and $8,000 applied. This $2,200 may be broken down into two subvariances, the *budget variance* and the *volume variance*. A variance report may take the form of Exhibit 8-4.

EXHIBIT 8-4

M COMPANY
Machining Department
Analysis of Variance in Fixed Overhead
For the Month Ending March 31, 19x1

Item*	Actual	Budget	Variance	Explanation
Supervision	$ 1,700	$ 1,700	$ —	
Depreciation—Plant	2,000	2,000	—	
Depreciation—Equipment	5,000	5,000	—	
Property taxes	1,150	1,000	150 U	Increased assessment
Insurance—Factory	350	300	50 U	Increased coverage
	$10,200*	$10,000	$ 200 U	

Summary analysis. Normal activity is 10,000 standard hours. Standard hours allowed for output were 8,000.

(1)	(2)	(3)
	Budget:	
	Same Regardless	
Inputs × Actual Rate	of Activity Level	Outputs × Standard Rate
		(8,000 × $1.00)
$10,200	$10,000	$8,000

Budget variance, $200 U†   Activity or Volume variance, $2,000 U‡

(10,000 − 8,000 hours) × $1.00 = $2,000

Total variance, $2,200 U

*In order to simplify the example, not all possible fixed overhead items are included here.
†The *budget variance* (also called *spending variance*) for fixed overhead is the difference between the amount incurred and the budget figure. Keep in mind that the budget figure would be the same regardless of the actual level of activity.
‡The *activity variance* is also called the *volume variance,* the *utilization variance,*   and the *capacity variance.* It is the difference between fixed overhead applied and budgeted. It can also be expressed as the fixed overhead rate times the difference between normal hours and standard hours allowed.

Nature of fixed overhead variances

The major difficulty in analyzing fixed overhead variances arises from the fundamental behavior of fixed costs in relation to the dual purposes (control and product costing) of cost accounting. For control purposes, each overhead item is studied in relation to changes in activity. Budgets are devised, and results are compared with the budget. The deviations from budget are known as *budget variances*, but they are also frequently called *spending variances*. Although these fixed overhead variances are often beyond immediate managerial control, this information calls attention to changes in price factors and to possible investigation at the appropriate level of the managerial hierarchy.

Think about the flexible budget once again. How flexible is it, really? The flex in the flexible budget is confined to the variable overhead. The fixed overhead component is really static for a vast range of anticipated activity. Thus, the conventional flexible budget is really composed of two separate budgets: a really flexible budget for variable overhead plus a static budget for fixed overhead. This point is important. The analysis of fixed overhead variance differs from the analysis of variable overhead variance *because fixed costs do not behave in the same way, nor do they have the same control features*.

Let us compare the general behavior patterns of variable and fixed overhead. Exhibit 8-5 offers the appropriate comparison. Costs are plotted on the vertical axis (the y-axis) while volume is plotted on the horizontal axis (the x-axis). First, concentrate on the budget lines. Note that the budget line for variable overhead extends upward in diagonal fashion, although the budget line for fixed overhead is horizontal.

Now concentrate on the graph for variable overhead. At zero volume, no variable overhead is incurred, nor is any variable overhead applied to production—there is no production. The cost line slopes upward at the rate of $1.70 per standard direct labor hour. The equation for this budget is $y = bx$ ($y = \$1.70 \, x$); the same equation holds for overhead application, so a single line portrays *both* budgeted amounts for control and overhead application for product costing. Slope is the amount by which y increases when x increases by one unit, or the variable overhead cost per unit of product. Conceptually, there are really two lines on the graph, but the budget line and the applied line are superimposed on one another.

If incurred costs lie above the budget and overhead applied line, the budget variance is unfavorable, and vice versa.

Now let us turn to fixed overhead. For product-costing purposes, it is necessary to apply fixed overhead by using a predetermined rate which is usually based on standard hours allowed at normal activity. This predetermined rate is used to cost production regardless of the activity levels encountered. An activity variance ($2,000, in the above example) arises whenever production expressed in standard hours worked deviates from the normal activity level (or any activity level selected as the denominator for computing the product-costing rate) used for setting the predetermined rate. Because the term *volume variance* is used so widely to describe the activity variance, either term will be used here to denote this variance.

COMPARISON OF CONTROL AND PRODUCT-COSTING PURPOSES

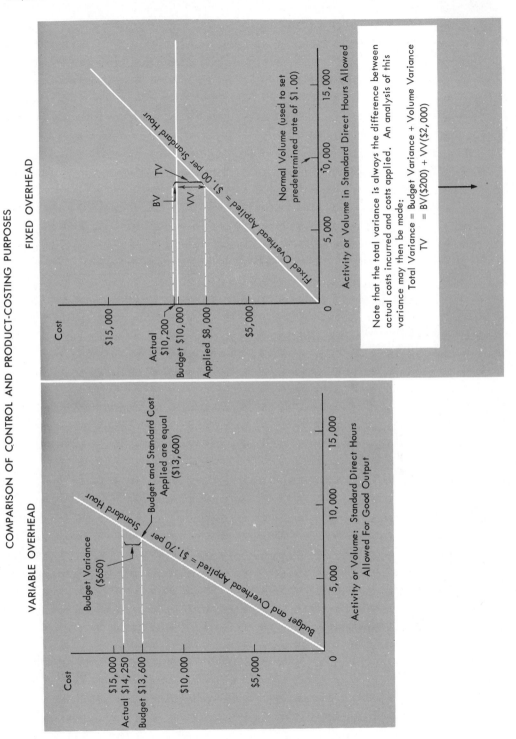

VARIABLE OVERHEAD

FIXED OVERHEAD

Cost

$15,000
Actual $14,250
Budget $13,600

$10,000

$5,000

Budget Variance
($650)

Standard Hour

Budget and Standard Cost
Applied are equal
($13,600)

Budget and Overhead Applied = $1.70 per

Activity or Volume: Standard Direct Hours
Allowed For Good Output

0   5,000   10,000   15,000

Cost

$15,000

Actual
$10,200
Budget $10,000

Applied $8,000

$5,000

BV   TV

VV

Fixed Overhead Applied = $1.00 per Standard Hour

Normal Volume (used to set
predetermined rate of $1.00)

Activity or Volume in Standard Direct Hours Allowed

0   5,000   10,000   15,000

Note that the total variance is always the difference between
actual costs incurred and costs applied. An analysis of this
variance may then be made:

Total Variance = Budget Variance + Volume Variance

TV   = BV($200) + VV($2,000)

The volume variance is a conventional measure of the cost of failure to operate at normal activity (or the benefit of operating at above-normal activity). Most companies consider volume variances to be beyond immediate control, although sometimes the top sales executive has to do some explaining or investigating because normal volume is typically geared to anticipated long-run sales. Sometimes failure to reach normal volume is caused by idleness due to poor production scheduling, unusual machine breakdowns, shortages of skilled workers, strikes, storms, and the like.

There is no volume variance for variable overhead. The concept of volume variance arises for fixed overhead because of the conflict between accounting for control (by budgets) and accounting for product costing (by application rates). Note carefully that the fixed overhead budget serves the control purpose whereas the development of a product-costing rate results in the treatment of fixed overhead *as if it were* a variable cost. In other words, the applied line in Exhibit 8-5 is artificial in the sense that, for product-costing purposes, it seemingly transforms a fixed cost into a variable cost. This bit of magic forcefully illustrates the distinction between accounting for control and accounting for product costing.

To summarize, volume variance arises because the activity level encountered (expressed as *standard hours allowed*) frequently does not coincide with the activity level used as a basis for selecting a predetermined product-costing rate for fixed factory overhead. The latter may be called *normal activity* in some companies, *master budgeted activity* in others, and *expected annual activity* in still others.

1. When normal activity and standard hours allowed are identical, there is no volume variance.
2. When standard hours allowed are less than normal activity, the volume variance is unfavorable. It is measured in Exhibit 8-5 as follows:

(Normal Activity minus Standard Hours Allowed) × Predetermined Fixed
Overhead Rate = Volume Variance

(10,000 hours − 8,000 hours) × $1.00 = $2,000

or

Budget minus Applied = Volume Variance
$10,000   − $8,000 = $2,000

3. Where standard hours allowed exceed normal activity, the volume variance is favorable because it is an index of better-than-average utilization of facilities.

Weaknesses and dangers in fixed overhead analysis

Above all, we should recognize that fixed costs are simply not divisible like variable costs; they come in big chunks and they are related to the provision of big chunks of production or sales capability rather than to the production or sale of a single unit of product.

There are conflicting views on how fixed overhead variances are best analyzed. These views are discussed in Chapter 25. Obviously, the "best" way is the one which provides management with the most insight in a particular company. Consequently, overhead analysis varies from company to company. In many companies variances are most usefully expressed in physical terms only. For instance, an activity variance could be expressed in machine-hours or kilowatt hours.

The position in this chapter has been to distinguish between fixed and variable overhead as being separate management problems. This contrasts with the tendency among many accountants to analyze variable costs and fixed costs in a parallel manner. For instance, an efficiency variance for fixed overhead is often computed, just as it is for other variable costs:

Efficiency variance[3] = (Actual hours − Standard hours allowed) ×

Hourly fixed overhead rate

However, the resulting variance is very different from the efficiency variances for material, labor, and variable overhead. Efficient usage of these three factors can affect actual cost, but short-run fixed overhead cost is not affected by efficiency. Furthermore, the managers responsible for inefficiency will be aware of its existence through reports on variable cost control, so there is little to gain from expressing ineffective utilization of facilities in historical dollar terms.

Finally, what is the economic significance of unit fixed costs? Unlike variable costs, total fixed costs do not change as production or sales fluctuate. Management would obtain a better measure of the cost of under-utilization of physical facilities by trying to approximate the related lost contribution margins instead of the related historical fixed costs. Fixed cost incurrence often involves lump-sum outlays based on a pattern of expected recoupment. But ineffective utilization of existing facilities has no bearing on the amount of fixed costs currently incurred. The economic effects of the inability to reach target volume levels are directly measured by lost contribution margins, even if these have to be approximated. The historical-cost approach fails to emphasize the distinction between *fixed cost incurrence*, on the one hand, and the objective of *maximizing the total*

---

[3] Some accountants favor computing volume variance on the basis of the difference between the fixed overhead budget ($10,000) and (actual hours worked × fixed overhead rate). In this example, the volume variance would then become $10,000 − (7,900 × $1) or $2,100 unfavorable. The remaining variance of $100 favorable [(actual hours − standard hours) × $1 overhead rate] is sometimes called the fixed overhead *efficiency* or *effectiveness* variance—the measure of the ineffective use or waste of facilities because of off-standard labor performance. This breakdown of the volume variance really attempts to separate the cost of *misused* facilities from the cost of *unused* facilities.

The author thinks this refinement is unnecessary in most cases because (a) in the short run, total fixed costs incurred are *not* changed by efficiency changes, and (b) if the budget uses standard hours as a base, the *volume* variance is more logically calculated by comparing standard hours worked with the normal standard volume which was used as a basis for setting the predetermined overhead rate. For an elaboration, see Chapter 25.

contribution margin, on the other hand. These are separable management problems, and the utilization of existing capacity is more closely related to the latter.[4]

For instance, in our example the activity variance was computed at $2,000 by multiplying a unit fixed cost of $1.00 by the 2,000-hour difference between the 10,000 hours of normal activity and 8,000 standard hours earned. This $2,000 figure may be helpful in the sense that management is alerted in some crude way to the probable costs of failure to use 10,000 hours. But the more relevant information is the lost contribution margins that pertain to the 2,000 hours. This information may not be so easy to obtain. The lost contribution margins may be zero in those cases where there are no opportunities to obtain any contribution margin from alternative uses of available capacity; in other cases, however, the lost contribution margins may be substantial. For example, if demand is high, the breakdown of key equipment may cost a company many thousands of dollars in lost contribution margins. Unfortunately, in these cases, existing accounting systems would show volume variances based on the unitized fixed costs and entirely ignore any lost contribution margins.

SUMMARY

Thorough study of the contents of this chapter should be rewarding because analysis of overhead variances must consider two major frames of reference: the flexible budget for control and the use of predetermined overhead rates for product costing. The budget variance is considered to be controllable, at least to some degree. The volume variance is considered uncontrollable in most instances. Thus, this chapter has highlighted and contrasted the many purposes that must be served in accounting for overhead. The general ledger is designed mainly to serve purposes of product costing. Yet management's major purpose, that of control, is aided by using flexible budget figures, which are not highlighted in general ledger balances. As is often the case, conventional general ledger bookkeeping for overhead often provides only a minimum of the information needed for control.

This chapter covered only some of the many methods of budgeting overhead, applying overhead, and analyzing overhead variances. How overhead is budgeted, applied, analyzed, and reported is really determined by the individual managements concerned. For further consideration of alternative versions of overhead analysis, see Chapter 25.

Note that the general ledger entries in this chapter sharply distinguish between fixed and variable overhead. This treatment is more effective for management than combining the two because it emphasizes the basic differences in cost behavior of these two kinds of overhead. Such basic differences are often important in influencing managerial decisions.

[4]For an elaboration of these ideas see Charles T. Horngren, *Accounting for Management Control: An Introduction* (Englewood Cliffs, N.J.: Prentice-Hall, Inc., 1965), pp. 247–253.

The appendix demonstrates that these distinctions can be maintained even if a combined overhead rate is used for product costing.

The worksheet analysis illustrated in Exhibit 8-6, page 246, provides a useful approach to the analysis of overhead variances. The first step is to obtain the total variance—the difference between overhead incurred and overhead applied. Then any further variance breakdowns can be added algebraically and checked against the total variance.

SUGGESTED READINGS

N.A.A. Research Series No. 11, 15, 17, 22, and *28* contain much discussion of the analysis of variances.

PROBLEM FOR SELF-STUDY

The McDermott Furniture Company has established standard costs for the cabinet department, in which one size of single four-drawer style of dresser is produced. The standard costs are used in interpreting actual performance. The standard costs of producing one of these dressers are shown below:

STANDARD COST CARD

Dresser, Style AAA

Materials: Lumber—50 board feet @ 10¢	$ 5.00
Direct labor: 3 hours at $2.00	6.00
Indirect costs:	
Variable charges—3 hours at $1.00	3.00
Fixed charges—3 hours at $.50	1.50
Total per dresser	$15.50

The costs of operations to produce 400 of these dressers during January are stated below (there were no initial inventories):

Materials purchased:	25,000 board feet @ 11¢	$2,750.00
Materials used:	19,000 board feet	
Direct labor:	1,100 hours at $1.90	2,090.00
Indirect costs:		
Variable charges		1,300.00
Fixed charges		710.00

The flexible budget for this department for normal monthly activity called for 1,400 direct labor hours of operation. At this level, the variable indirect cost was budgeted at $1,400, and the fixed indirect cost at $700.

REQUIRED: All journal entries.

Compute the following variations from standard cost. Label your answers as *favorable* or *unfavorable* (F) or (U).

1. Materials purchase price.
2. Materials usage.
3. (a) Direct labor rate;
   (b) Direct labor efficiency.
4. (a) Variable overhead budget variance;
   (b) Fixed overhead budget variance;
   (c) Fixed overhead volume variance.
5. (a) Variable overhead spending variance;
   (b) Variable overhead efficiency variance.

Solution. Journal entries are supported by pertinent variance analysis.

1. Stores control (25,000 @ $.10)	2,500	
Material purchase price variance (25,000 @ $.01)	250	
Accounts payable (25,000 @ $.11)		2,750
2. Work in process control (400 units × 50 board feet × $.10)	2,000	
Material usage variance (1,000 × $.10)		100
Stores control (19,000 × $.10)		1,900
3. Work in process control (400 units × $6.00)	2,400	
Direct labor rate variance		110
Direct labor efficiency variance		200
Accrued payroll		2,090
For analysis of variances, see Exhibit 8-6.		
4. Variable overhead control	1,300	
Accounts payable and other accounts		1,300
Work in process control	1,200	
Variable overhead applied (400 × 3 × $1.00)		1,200
5. Fixed overhead control	710	
Accounts payable and other accounts		710
Work in process control	600	
Fixed overhead applied (400 × 3 × $.50)		600

The analysis of variances in Exhibit 8-6 summarizes the characteristics of different cost behavior patterns. The approaches to direct labor and variable overhead are basically the same. Furthermore, there is no fundamental conflict between the budgetary and product-costing purposes; that is, the applied amounts in column (3) would also be the flexible budget allowances. In contrast, the behavior patterns and control features of fixed overhead require a different analytical approach. The budget is static, not flexible. There is no efficiency variance for fixed factory overhead because short-run performance cannot ordinarily affect incurrence of fixed factory overhead. Finally, there will nearly always be a conflict between the budgetary and product-costing purposes because the applied amount in column (3) for fixed overhead will differ from the static budget allowance. The latter conflict is highlighted by the volume variance, which measures the effects of working at other than the volume used to set the product-costing rate.

The following is a summary of variances:

1. Materials purchase price	$250 U
2. Materials usage	100 F
3. (a) Direct labor rate	110 F
(b) Direct labor efficiency	200 F
4. (a) Variable overhead budget variance	100 U
(b) Fixed overhead budget variance	10 U
(c) Fixed overhead volume variance	100 U
5. (a) Variable overhead spending variance	200 U
(b) Variable overhead efficiency variance	100 F

OVERHEAD VARIANCES IN THE LEDGER

There are several ways of accounting for overhead variances. The easiest way is probably to allow the departmental overhead control accounts and applied accounts to cumulate month-to-month postings until the end of the year. Monthly variances would not be isolated formally in the accounts, although monthly variance reports would be prepared. Assume that the data in the review problem are for the year rather than for the month. At the year end, isolating and closing entries could be made as follows:

Variable factory overhead applied	1,200	
Variable overhead spending variance	200	
Variable overhead efficiency variance		100
Variable factory overhead control		1,300
To isolate variances for the year.		
Fixed factory overhead applied	600	
Fixed overhead budget (or spending) variance	10	
Fixed overhead volume variance	100	
Fixed factory overhead control		710
To isolate variances for the year.		
Income summary (or Cost of goods sold)	100	
Variable overhead efficiency variance	100	
Variable overhead spending variance		200
To close.		
Income summary (or Cost of goods sold)	110	
Fixed overhead budget variance		10
Fixed overhead volume variance		100
To close.		

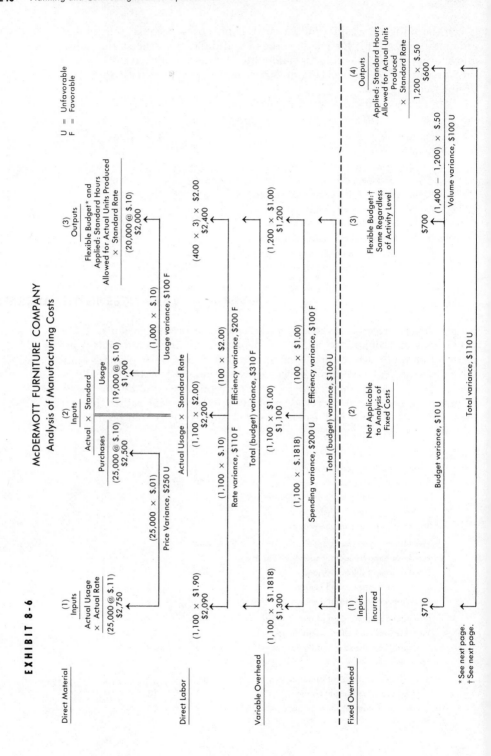

McDERMOTT FURNITURE COMPANY
Analysis of Manufacturing Costs

EXHIBIT 8-6

*Graphically, the *flexible* budget line for variable costs and the *applied* line for variable costs are identical.   For example, for variable overhead:

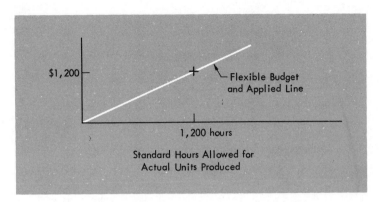

†Graphically, the flexible budget line for fixed costs is not really flexible because it is horizontal (the total budgeted fixed overhead is the same over a wide range of volume).   Hence the *budget* amount will differ from the *applied* amount when activity is not at the level (usually called *normal activity*) used to set the fixed overhead rate for product costing:

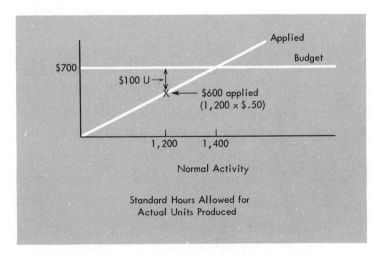

In sum, the accountant is faced with a special problem with regard to fixed overhead, which has very different cost behavior characteristics and cost control features than variable overhead.   In trying to assign fixed overhead to product, he must develop a predetermined costing rate.   In so doing, he has to select a level of activity as the denominator in his formula:

$$\text{Fixed Overhead Rate} = \frac{\text{Budget}}{\text{Normal Activity}} = \frac{\$700}{1{,}400 \text{ hours}} = \$.50 \text{ per hour}$$

Therefore, a volume variance will arise when ensuing activity differs from normal activity.

Volume variance arises only in connection with fixed overhead. There is no volume variance for variable overhead. That is why column (4) in the exhibit is extended to the right to stand alone—to highlight the fact that the *budget* and the *applied* amounts for fixed overhead will usually not be equal, in contrast to the equality of the *budget* and *applied* amounts for variable costs.

If desired, the isolation entries for monthly variances could be made monthly, although the closing entries are usually confined to the year end.

Of course, rather than being closed directly to the Income Summary or Cost of Goods Sold, in certain cases the overhead variances may be prorated at year end in a manner similar to that shown for direct material and direct labor variances in Chapter 6.

APPENDIX: COMBINED OVERHEAD RATE AND TWO-WAY AND THREE-WAY ANALYSIS

Combined rate

Many companies, while separating variable overhead and fixed overhead for control purposes, combine them for product-costing purposes and use a single predetermined overhead rate. In the example in this chapter, such a rate would be $2.70—the variable overhead rate of $1.70 plus the fixed overhead rate of $1.00. (See Exhibit 8-3.) In such cases, the overhead variance analysis would be basically the same. Therefore, this discussion appears in an appendix rather than in the body of the chapter. The study of the many varieties of overhead analysis can easily bewilder the student who is exposed to this material for the first time. The body of this chapter presents a sufficient fundamental background about overhead analysis. Do not attempt the study of this appendix until you are thoroughly familiar with the material in the body of the chapter.

The easiest way to grasp these relationships is to examine Exhibit 8-7, which is really a combination of the two graphs in Exhibit 8-5. You can readily see that what we are about to study is nothing more than a simultaneous consideration of the variable and fixed components, where the flexible budget formula is expressed as $10,000 per month plus $1.70 per hour.

Exhibit 8-8 provides a comprehensive analysis of all relationships among the combined overhead analysis and its variable and fixed parts.

Even when the actual overhead costs cannot be separated into variable and fixed components, it is still possible to generate almost all of the flexible budget analysis illustrated in the chapter. The only variances that could not be derived are the separate variable overhead spending variance and the separate fixed overhead budget variance.

Two-way and three-way analysis

Note that Exhibit 8-8 distinguishes between the so-called two-way and three-way overhead analysis. The three-way analysis is the method that was used in the body of the chapter, where three different variances were computed: spending, efficiency, and volume. The two-way analysis computes only two variances: budget and volume. The budget variance, as is clear in Exhibit 8-8, is simply the difference between actual costs and the budget allowance based on standard hours allowed. The two-way

EXHIBIT 8-7

COMBINED VARIABLE AND FIXED OVERHEAD BUDGET AND APPLICATION OF
VARIOUS MONTHLY PRODUCTION VOLUMES

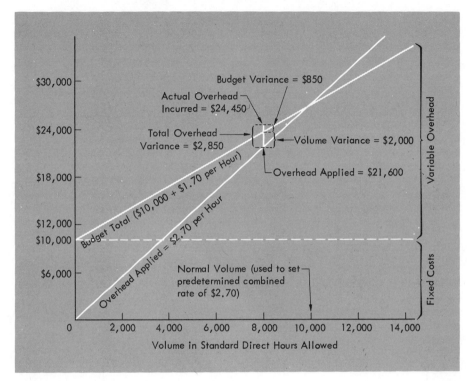

analysis stops there; it does not subdivide the budget variance into spending and efficiency variances.

Overhead analysis in nonstandard cost systems

Overhead variance analysis is possible and beneficial in both standard and normal cost systems. Analysis in the latter situations is restricted to a two-way analysis, because the budgeted and applied amounts would be expressed in actual hours only. No information on standard hours is available. Therefore, the following analysis is applicable:

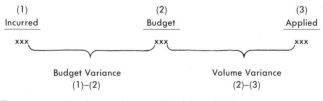

For a numerical exercise, see Problem 8-13.

EXHIBIT 8-8

WORKSHEET SUMMARY OF RELATIONSHIPS OF COMBINED OVERHEAD ANALYSIS
AND ITS VARIABLE AND FIXED PARTS

	(1) Inputs: Incurred	(2) Inputs: Budget* Based on 7,900 Actual Hours Worked	(3) Outputs: Budget* Based on 8,000 Standard Hours of Work Allowed	(4) Outputs: Applied
V	14,250	13,430	13,600	(8,000 × $1.70) = 13,600
F	10,200	10,000	10,000	(8,000 × $1.00) = 8,000
Combined	24,450	23,430	23,600	(8,000 × $2.70) = 21,600

3-way Analysis

Total Spending Variance (1)–(2)
- V 820 U
- F 200 U
- Combined 1,020 U

Total Efficiency Variance (2)–(3)
- V 170 Fav.
- F (not applicable)
- Combined 170 Fav.

Total Volume Variance (3)–(4)
- V (not applicable)
- F 2,000 U
- Combined 2,000 U

2-way Analysis

Total Budget Variance (1)–(3)
- V 650 U
- F 200 U
- Combined 850 U

Total Volume Variance (3)–(4)
- V (not applicable)
- F 2,000 U
- Combined 2,000 U

Total Variance

Total Overhead Variance (1)–(4)
- V 650 U
- F 2,200 U
- Combined 2,850 U

U = Unfavorable   V = Variable
Fav. = Favorable   F = Fixed

*Budget Formula: $10,000 per month + $1.70 per hour.

Note to Exhibit 8-8: See footnote (3) in this chapter for a discussion of an alternative way to compute the volume variance.

QUESTIONS, PROBLEMS, AND CASES

Note: There is a flock of particularly useful problems in this chapter. Especially recommended are Problems 8-4, 8-6, 8-7, 8-8, 8-15 or 8-16, and 8-20 or 8-22. Problems 8-11, 8-12, 8-14, 8-16, and 8-17 through 8-19 cover the combined overhead rate, which is discussed in the appendix.

8-1. What is the essential difficulty in applying fixed overhead to product?

8-2. Define: *normal activity, expected annual activity, practical capacity, volume variance.*

8-3. "There should be an efficiency variance for fixed overhead. A foreman can inefficiently use his fixed resources." Comment.

●**8-4. Fundamentals of Overhead Variances.** The Block Company is installing a standard cost system and a flexible overhead budget. Standard costs have been recently developed for its only product and are as follows:

Direct materials, 2 pounds @ $15	$30.00
Direct labor, 6 hours @ $3.00	18.00
Variable overhead, 6 hours @ $1.00	6.00
Fixed overhead	?
Standard cost per unit of finished product	$?

Normal activity is expressed as 12,000 standard direct labor hours per month. Fixed overhead is expected to be $18,000 per month.

REQUIRED:

1. Calculate the proper fixed overhead rate per standard direct labor hour and per unit.
2. Graph the following for activity from zero to 15,000 hours:
   (a) Budgeted variable overhead.
   (b) Variable overhead applied.
3. Graph the following for activity from zero to 15,000 hours:
   (a) Budgeted fixed overhead.
   (b) Fixed overhead applied.
4. Assume that 10,000 standard direct labor hours are allowed during a given month. $10,200 of actual variable overhead was incurred; actual fixed overhead amounted to $18,500. Calculate:
   (a) Fixed overhead budget variance.
   (b) Fixed overhead volume variance.
   (c) Variable overhead budget variance.
5. Prepare necessary journal entries to record overhead in (4).
6. Assume that 12,500 standard direct labor hours are worked during a given month. Actual overhead incurred amounted to $29,900, $18,900 of which was fixed. What is the variable overhead budget variance? Fixed overhead volume variance? Fixed overhead budget variance?

8-5. Comprehensive, Straightforward Problem on Standard Cost System. The Flagon Company uses a standard cost system. The month's data regarding its lone product follow:

Fixed overhead costs incurred, $6,150
Variable overhead applied at $.90 per hour
Standard direct labor cost, $4.00 per hour
Standard material cost, $1.00 per pound
Standard pounds of material in a finished unit, 3
Normal production per month, 2,500 units
Standard direct labor hours per finished unit, 5
Material purchased, 10,000 lbs., $9,500
Material used, 6,700 lbs.
Direct labor costs incurred, 11,000 hours, $41,800
Variable overhead costs incurred, $9,500
Fixed overhead budget variance, $100, favorable
Finished units produced, 2,000

REQUIRED:

Prepare journal entries. Prepare schedules of all variances, using the worksheet approach described in this chapter.

●8-6.   **Analysis of Fixed Overhead; Practical and Normal Capacity.**
The fixed overhead items of the lathe department of Barnes Company include for the month of January, 19x4:

Item	Actual	Budget
Supervision	$ 900	$ 800
Depreciation—Plant	750	750
Depreciation—Equipment	1,750	1,750
Property taxes	350	400
Insurance—Factory	400	300
	$4,150	$4,000

Normal activity for the lathe department is 1,000 standard hours per month. Practical capacity is 1,600 standard hours per month. Standard hours allowed for work done (good units actually produced) were 1,250.

REQUIRED:

1. Prepare a summary analysis of fixed overhead variances using normal activity as the activity base.
2. Prepare a summary analysis of fixed overhead variances using practical capacity as the activity base.
3. Explain why the budget variances in parts "1" and "2" are identical whereas the volume variances are different.

8-7.   Characteristics of Fixed Overhead Variances.   Karnes Company executives have studied their operations carefully and have been using a standard cost system for years. They are now formulating currently attainable standards for 19x1. They agree that the standards for direct material will amount to $10.00 per finished unit produced and that the standards for direct labor and variable overhead are to be $4.00 and $1.00 per direct labor hour, respectively. Total fixed overhead is expected to be $600,000. Two hours of direct labor is the standard time for finishing one unit of finished product.

REQUIRED:

1. Graph the budgeted fixed overhead for 400,000 to 800,000 standard allowed direct labor hours of activity, assuming that the total budget will not change over that activity level. What would be the appropriate product-costing rate per standard direct labor hour for fixed overhead if normal activity is 500,000 hours? Graph the applied fixed overhead line.

2. Assume that 250,000 units of product were produced. How much fixed overhead would be applied to product? Would there be a volume variance? Why? Assume that 200,000 units were produced. Would there be a volume variance? Why? Show the latter volume variance on a graph. In your own words, define volume variance. Why does it arise? Can a volume variance exist for variable overhead? Why?

3. Assume that 220,000 units are produced. Fixed overhead costs incurred were $617,000. What is the total fixed overhead variance? Budget variance? Volume variance? Use the analytical technique illustrated in the chapter.

4. Ignore parts (2) and (3). In part (1), what would be the appropriate product-costing rate per standard direct labor hour for fixed overhead if normal activity is estimated at 400,000 hours? At 600,000 hours? At 800,000 hours? Draw a graph showing budgeted fixed overhead and three "applied" lines, using the three rates just calculated. If 200,000 units are produced, and the normal activity is 600,000 standard direct labor hours, what is the volume variance? Now compare this with the volume variance in your answer to part (2); explain.

5. Specifically, what are the implications in parts (1) and (4) regarding (a) the setting of product-costing rates for fixed overhead, (b) the meaning of budget and volume variances, and (c) the major differences in planning and control techniques for variable and fixed costs?

8-8. Find the Unknowns. Consider each of the following situations independently. Data refer to operations for April. For each situation assume a standard product cost system. Also assume the use of a flexible budget for control of variable and fixed overhead based on standard direct labor hours.

			Cases			
	A	B	C	D	E	F
(1) Actual fixed overhead	—	$ 9,900	$12,550	—	$12,000	$10,600
(2) Actual variable overhead	$ 7,500	12,000	—	—	—	7 000
(3) Normal activity in hours	10,000	—	6,000	—	11,000	5,000
(4) Standard hours allowed for work done	11,000	12,000	—	6,500	—	—
Flexible budget data:						
(5) Fixed factory overhead	5,000	—	—	—	—	—
(6) Variable factory overhead (per standard hour)	70¢	—	75¢	85¢	50¢	—
(7) Budgeted fixed factory overhead	5,000	—	—	—	11,000	10,000
(8) Budgeted variable factory overhead†	—	—	—	—	—	—
(9) Total budgeted factory overhead†	—	(1)	21,000	12,525	—	—
(10) Standard variable overhead applied	—	—	9,000	—	—	7,500
(11) Standard fixed overhead applied	—	—	—	—	—	10,000
(12) Activity or volume variance	—	600F	—	500U	500F	—
(13) Variable overhead budget variance	—	—	500U	-0-	100U	—
(14) Fixed overhead budget variance	300U	—	—	300F	—	—

(1) $21,200 at 10,000 hours; $27,800 ot 16,000 hours.
†For standard hours allowed for work done.

REQUIRED:

Fill in the blanks under each case. Prepare your answer by (a) listing the numbers that are blank for each case and (b) putting the final answers next to the numbers. Prepare supporting computations on a separate sheet. For example, your answer to Case A would contain a vertical listing of the numbers 1, 8, 9, 10, 11, 12, and 13 with answers next to the appropriate numbers.

8-9. Variance Analysis. The H. G. Company uses a standard cost system in accounting for the cost of one of its products.

The standard is based on a budgeted monthly production of 100 units per day for the usual 22 work days per month. Standard cost per unit for direct labor is 16 hours at $1.50 per hour. Standard cost for overhead was set as follows:

Fixed overhead per month	$29,040
Variable overhead per month	39,600
Total budgeted overhead	$68,640
Expected direct labor cost	$52,800
Overhead rate per dollar of labor	$ 1.30
Standard overhead per unit	$ 31.20

During the month of September, the plant operated only 20 days. Cost for the 2,080 units produced were:

Direct labor, 32,860 hours @ $1.52 is	$49,947.20
Fixed overhead	29,300.00
Variable overhead	39,065.00

REQUIRED:

1. Compute the variance from standard in September for (1) direct labor cost, and (2) overhead.

2. Analyze the variances from standard into identifiable causes for (1) direct labor, and (2) for fixed and variable overhead.   [C.P.A.]

8-10. Compute Standard Cost Per Unit; Variance Analysis. X department uses a standard cost system and a flexible budget.

Normal activity is:	
Machine-hours	140
Finished pieces produced	2,800

The standard costs in connection with this production are:

Direct material	$3,360
Direct labor	315
Factory overhead (includes an allowance for variable overhead at the rate of 30¢ per piece)	1,400
	$5,075

The actual production for a month was:

Machine-hours	130
Finished pieces produced	2,860

The actual cost of this production was:

Direct material	$3,575
Direct labor	286
Factory overhead, including $573 of fixed overhead	1,573
	$5,434

Direct labor hours and machine-hours are proportional.

REQUIRED:

Answer the following questions. Be certain of the above facts and relationships before going ahead.
  1. What was the standard cost per finished piece?
For questions 2-8, use *F* or *U* to indicate whether the variance is favorable or unfavorable. Give the dollar amounts.
  2. What is total material variance?
  3. Direct labor rate variance?
  4. Direct labor efficiency variance?
  5. Variable overhead spending variance?
  6. Variable overhead efficiency variance?
  7. Fixed overhead budget variance?
  8. Fixed overhead volume variance?

8-11. Standard Costs; Journal Entries; Analysis of Variances; Combined Overhead Analysis; Income Statement. The Smith Company uses a standard cost system. The standards are based on a budget for operations at the rate of production anticipated for the current period. The company records in its general ledger: variations in material prices and usage, wage rates, and labor efficiency. Two accounts for manufacturing overhead are kept in the general ledger: Manufacturing Overhead Control and Manufacturing Overhead Applied; the month-end differences in their balances are analyzed in a supporting schedule. Three summary overhead variances are shown: spending variance, efficiency variance, and volume variance.
Current standards are as follows:

Materials:	
Material A	$1.20 per unit
Material B	2.60 per unit
Direct labor	$2.05 per hour

	Special Widgets	De Luxe Widgets
Finished products (content of each unit):		
Material A	12 units	12 units
Material B	6 units	8 units
Direct labor	14 hours	20 hours

The general ledger does not include a finished goods inventory account; costs are transferred directly from work in process to cost of sales at the time finished products are sold.

The budget and operating data for the month of August, 19x7 are summarized as follows:

Budget for 9,000 projected direct labor hours:

Fixed manufacturing overhead	$ 4,500
Variable manufacturing overhead	13,500
Selling expenses	4,000
Administrative expenses	7,500

Operating data:

Sales:

500 special widgets	$52,700
100 de luxe widgets	16,400

Purchases:

Material A	8,500 units,	$ 9,725
Material B	1,800 units,	5,635

Material requisitions:

	Material A	Material B
Issued from stores:		
Standard quantity	8,400 units	3,200 units
Over standard	400 units	150 units
Returned to stores	75 units	

Direct labor hours:

Standard (including those still in Work in Process)	9,600 hours
Actual	10,000 hours

Wages paid:

500 hours at	$2.10	
8,000 hours at	2.00	
1,500 hours at	1.90	

Other costs:

Manufacturing overhead	$20,125, including $4,625 of fixed overhead
Selling	3,250
Administrative	6,460

REQUIRED:

1. Prepare journal entries to record operations for the month of August, 19x7. Show computations of the amounts used in each journal entry. Raw material purchases are recorded at standard. (Note that there is work in process at the end of the month. Because the problem does not disclose how many units are still in process, it is impossible to reconcile standard hours worked with goods completed. This will not prevent solution of the problem, however.)

2. Prepare a statement of income for the month supported by an analysis of variations. (Treat all variations as if they were adjustments of standard cost of sales.) [C.P.A., Adapted]

8-12. Variance Analysis; Combined Overhead Rate. The Thomas Trinket Corporation makes various small novelty gifts and seasonal decorations.

The chief cost accountant has developed standards for usage of materials and for the various direct labor operations. The company uses a flexible budget as an aid in overhead control. Budgeted *total* overhead at a 40,000-standard-direct-labor-hour level is $85,500. Budgeted *variable* overhead at a 30,000-standard-direct-labor-hour level is $27,000.

The following data were available for analysis at the end of the month of June:

Volume variance	$ 3,300 (Unfavorable)
Material purchases	100,000
Direct labor costs incurred	104,400
Direct labor rate variance	4,350 (Favorable)
Total direct labor variance	600 (Favorable)
Average wage rate (10¢ less than the average standard rate)	$2.40 per hour
Total actual overhead for month	$ 88,750
Fixed overhead for the month	$ 50,000

The company uses a combined overhead rate of 80 per cent of standard direct labor cost.

REQUIRED:

Analyze all variances as far as the data permit, showing all supporting work, including amounts for costs incurred and costs applied for direct labor, variable overhead, and fixed overhead. Be sure to give a complete analysis of variable and fixed components of overhead.

8-13. Normal Costing and Overhead Analysis. The Haney Company had *budgeted* the following performance for 19x4:

Units	10,000
Sales	$120,000
Total variable production costs, including variable factory overhead of $5,000	60,000
Total fixed production costs	25,000
Gross margin	35,000
Beginning inventories	None

It is now December 31, 19x4. The factory overhead rate that was used throughout the year was $3.00 per unit. Total factory overhead incurred was $30,000. Under-applied factory overhead was $900.00. There is no work in process.

REQUIRED:

1. How many units were produced during 19x4?
2. Nine thousand units were sold at regular prices during 19x4. Assuming that the predicted cost behavior patterns implicit in the above budget have conformed to the plan (except for variable factory overhead), and that under-applied

factory overhead is written off directly as an adjustment of cost of goods sold, what is the gross margin for 19x4? How much factory overhead should be assigned to the ending inventory if it is to be carried at "normal" cost?

3. Explain *why* overhead was under-applied by $900. In other words, analyze the variable and fixed overhead variances as far as the data permit.

8-14. Variance Analysis; Journal Entries; Find Standard Time Per Unit. The Trump Electrical Company manufactures special electrical equipment. The management has established standard costs for many of its operations and uses a flexible budget. Overhead is applied on a basis of standard labor hours. The Transformer Assembly Department operates at the following standard rates:

STANDARD COSTS

One Multiplex Transformer TR-906

Materials:

4 sheets soft iron, 9 × 16 in. @ $1.12 ea.	
2 spools copper wire	@ $2.39 ea.
Direct labor rate	$2.50 per hour
Combined overhead rate	$2.10 per direct labor hour

The flexible budget indicates that total overhead would amount to $4,489 and $4,989 at production levels of 500 and 600 units, respectively. The production budget for the past month called for 2,340 direct labor hours, $2,925 variable overhead costs, and $1,989 fixed overhead costs. Only 550 transformers were produced, at the costs listed below:

Materials purchased:

3,000 sheets soft iron, $3,300.

1,500 spools copper wire, $3,600.

Materials used:

2,215 sheets soft iron.

1,106 spools copper wire.

Direct labor:

2,113 hours, $5,409.28.

Overhead:

Variable costs, $2,769.

Fixed costs, $2,110.

REQUIRED:

1. What is the standard time for assembling a transformer?
2. What is the standard unit cost?
3. What was the material price variance during the past month?
4. The material quantity variance?
5. The direct labor rate variance?
6. The direct labor efficiency variance?
7. Variable overhead spending variance?
8. Variable overhead efficiency variance?
9. Fixed overhead budget variance?
10. Fixed overhead volume variance?

8-15.   Multiple Choice; Working Backward from Given Variances.*

The Kengreen Manufacturing Company produces only one product.   Indirect costs are assigned on the basis of direct labor hours.

At normal activity, the standard cost per unit is as follows:

COST STANDARD

	Molding Department	Painting Department	Total
Direct material:			
Molding Powder, 3 lbs. @ $6 per lb.	$18.00		
Paint, 1 gallon, @ $4.00		$4.00	$22.00
Direct labor:			
4 hours, @ $2.50	10.00		
½ hour, @ $2.00		1.00	11.00
Variable indirect costs:			
4 hours, @ $1.50	6.00		
½ hour, @ $3.00		1.50	7.50
Fixed indirect costs:			
4 hours, @ 50¢	2.00		
½ hour, @ $1.00		.50	2.50
Total	$36.00	$7.00	$43.00

*Adapted from a problem prepared by Walter Kennon and David Green, Jr.

For the month of February, 19x1, the following statement presents the comparison of actual costs with standard costs.

COMPARISON OF ACTUAL AND STANDARD COSTS

Molding Department	Standard	Actual	Total Variance†
Direct material	$ 7,560.00	$ 7,869.00	$ 309.00
Direct labor	4,200.00	4,125.00	(75.00)
Variable indirect costs	2,520.00	2,640.00	120.00
Fixed indirect costs	840.00	800.00	(40.00)
Total Molding Dept. costs	$15,120.00	$15,434.00	$ 314.00
Painting Department			
Direct material	$ 1,680.00	$ 1,350.00	$(330.00)
Direct labor	420.00	500.00	80.00
Variable indirect costs	630.00	550.00	(80.00)
Fixed indirect costs	210.00	375.00	165.00
Total Painting Dept. costs	$ 2,940.00	$ 2,775.00	$(165.00)
Total	$18,060.00	$18,209.00	$ 149.00

†Favorable variances are in parentheses.

VARIANCE ANALYSIS

Direct Material:	Molding Dept.	Painting Dept.	Total
Usage	$180.00	$ 120.00	$ 300.00
Price	129.00	(450.00)	(321.00)
Total direct material variance	$309.00	$(330.00)	$ (21.00)
Direct Labor:			
Efficiency	$(75.00)	$ (20.00)	$ (95.00)
Wage rate		100.00	100.00
Total direct labor variance	$ (75.00)	$ 80.00	$ 5.00
Variable Indirect Costs:			
Efficiency	$ (45.00)	$ (30.00)	$ (75.00)
Spending	165.00	(50.00)	115.00
Total variable indirect costs	$120.00	$ (80.00)	$ 40.00
Fixed Indirect Costs:			
Budget	$	$ 75.00	$ 75.00
Volume	(40.00)	90.00	50.00
Total fixed indirect costs	$ (40.00)	$ 165.00	$ 125.00
Total variance	$314.00	$(165.00)	$ 149.00

There are no inventories of work in process at the beginning or at the end of February.

Labor wage rate standards are set according to the union contract, but new employees have to be paid a premium because of a shortage of workers.

Material price standards are set according to the company budget as to estimated material prices from regular suppliers. Prices are accepted as external to the company and not under company control.

(Support your answers with computations.)

1. The number of units produced during February were:
   - a. 423
   - b. 420
   - c. 370
   - d. None of the above, but can be determined from the data given.
   - e. Cannot be determined from the information given.

2. The pounds of molding powder used during February were:
   - a. 1,260
   - b. 1,282
   - c. 1,290
   - d. 1,305
   - e. None of the above.

3. The average wage rate for direct labor in the Painting Department was:
   - a. $2.50 per hour.
   - b. $2.00 per hour.
   - c. $1.93 per hour.
   - d. $2.27 per hour.
   - e. None of the above.

4. The unfavorable material price variance of $129.00 in the Molding Department is the responsibility of:
     a. The Molding Department foreman and workers.
     b. The engineer who designed the product.
     c. The president of the company.
     d. The controller and head accountant of the company.
     e. No one in the company organization.

5. The normal operating activity of the Painting Department is:
     a. 200 direct labor hours   d. 310 direct labor hours
     b. 210 direct labor hours   e. Cannot be determined from the
     c. 300 direct labor hours   data given.

6. The $75.00 unfavorable budget variance for fixed costs in the Painting Department represents:
     a. The actual total fixed costs in excess of the budget.
     b. The actual total fixed costs in excess of the fixed cost applied to product at the rate of $1.00 per direct labor hour.
     c. The actual direct labor hours in excess of the standard hours allowed costed at the rate of $1.00 per hour.
     d. Normal capacity less actual hours costed at the rate of $1.00 per hour.
     e. Cost over- or under-applied.

7. The $45.00 favorable efficiency variance for Variable Indirect Costs in the Molding Department represents:
     a. The amount which the Molding Department was able to save by reducing variable costs when Molding Department did not produce at full capacity.
     b. The standard time required at full capacity less the actual hours operated costed at the standard variable indirect cost rate of $1.50 per hour.
     c. Actual variable indirect cost less standard indirect cost.
     d. Actual variable indirect cost less the actual hours operated costed at the standard rate of $1.50 per hour.
     e. The amount which the Molding Department was able to save by producing in less time than the standard allowed.

8. The flexible *budget for actual hours of input* worked for Variable Indirect Costs in the Molding Department was:
     a. $2,475
     b. $2,520
     c. $2,400
     d. $2,565
     e. None of the above.

9. The budget for total fixed indirect costs in the Molding Department was:
     a. $800
     b. $825
     c. $840
     d. $855
     e. None of the above.

8-16. Variance Analysis from Fragmentary Evidence. Being a bright young man, you have just landed a wonderful job as assistant controller of Gyp-Clip, a new and promising division of Croding Metals Corporation. The Gyp-Clip Division has been formed to produce a single product, a new-model paper clip. Croding Laboratories has developed an extremely springy and lightweight new alloy, Clypton, which is expected to revolutionize the paper-clip industry.

Gyp-Clip has been in business one month; it is your first day on the job. The controller takes you on a tour of the plant and explains the operation in detail: Clypton wire is received on two-mile spools from the Croding mill at a fixed price of $40.00 a spool, which is not subject to change. Clips are bent, cut, and shipped in bulk to the Croding packaging plant. Factory rent, depreciation, and all other items of fixed factory overhead are handled by the home office at a set rate of $100,000 per month. Ten thousand tons of paper clips have been produced, but this is only 75 per cent of normal activity, since demand for the product must be built up.

The controller has just figured out the month's variances; he is looking for a method of presenting them in clear, logical form to top management at the home office. You say that you know of just the method, and promise to have the analysis ready the next morning.

Filled with zeal and enthusiasm, feeling that your future as a rising star in this growing company is secure, you decide to take your wife out to dinner to celebrate the trust and confidence that your superior has placed in you.

Upon returning home, with the flush of four martinis still upon you, you are horrified to discover your dog happily devouring the controller's figure sheet. You manage to salvage only the following fragments:

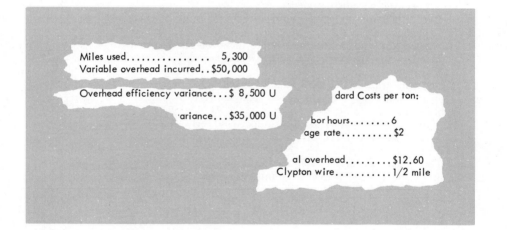

Miles used.............. 5,300
Variable overhead incurred. .$50,000

Overhead efficiency variance...$ 8,500 U

·ariance...$35,000 U

dard Costs per ton:

bor hours........6
age rate.........$2

al overhead........$12.60
Clypton wire..........1/2 mile

REQUIRED:

Don't let the controller think that you're a knucklehead; go ahead and make up your analysis of all variances.

8-17.   Combined Overhead Rate; Determine Normal Volume.   Department 385 has an overhead rate of 80 per cent of direct labor dollars for product-costing purposes. Its budgeted overhead at $25,000 of direct labor cost is $22,400; at $40,000 of direct labor cost, $27,200. What is normal volume?

8-18.   Combined Overhead Rate; Determine Overhead Behavior. A machining department has a flexible overhead budget based on direct labor cost. At direct labor cost levels of $3,500 and $4,000, budgeted overhead is $6,820 and $7,170, respectively. Factory overhead is applied to product at a rate of 165 per cent of direct labor cost.

REQUIRED:

1. Variable overhead rate per direct labor dollar.
2. Fixed overhead budget.
3. Normal activity expressed in direct labor dollars.

8-19.   Analysis of Variances; Combined Overhead Rate.   The Jones Furniture Company uses a standard cost system in accounting for its production costs.

The standard cost of a unit of furniture follows:

Lumber, 100 feet @ $150 per 1,000 feet		$15.00
Direct labor, 4 hours @ $2.50 per hour		10.00
Manufacturing overhead:		
Fixed (30% of direct labor)	$3.00	
Variable (60% of direct labor)	6.00	9.00
Total unit cost		$34.00

The following flexible monthly overhead budget is in effect:

Direct Labor Hours	Estimated Overhead
5,200	$10,800
4,800	10,200
4,400	9,600
4,000 (normal activity)	9,000
3,600	8,400

The actual unit costs for the month of December were as follows:

Lumber used (110 feet @ $120 per 1,000 feet)	$13.20
Direct labor (4¼ hours @ $2.60 per hour)	11.05
Manufacturing overhead ($10,560 ÷ 1,200 units)	8.80
Total actual unit cost	$33.05

REQUIRED:

Prepare a schedule which shows an analysis of each element of the total variance from standard cost for the month of December.   [C.P.A.]

8-20.   Working Backward from Given Variances.   The Vanguard Company manufactures one product. Its standard cost system incorporates flexible budgets and assigns indirect costs on the basis of standard direct labor hours.

At normal activity, the standard cost per unit is as follows:

Direct material, 3 lbs. @ $5.00	$15.00
Direct labor, 2 hrs. @ $4.00	8.00
Variable indirect costs, 2 hrs. @ $1.20	2.40
Fixed indirect costs, 2 hrs. @ $.80	1.60
Total	$27.00

For the month of October, 19x2, the performance report included the following information (in dollars):

	Incurred at Actual Price	Standard Costs Applied	Total Variance	Variance Analysis Price or Rate	Usage or Efficiency	Volume
Direct material used	134,400	135,000	600 F	5,600 F	5,000 U	—
Direct labor	77,900	72,000	5,900 U	1,900 U	4,000 U	—
Variable indirect costs	21,500	21,600	100 F	1,300 F	1,200 U	—
Fixed indirect costs	15,800	14,400	1,400 U	200 F*	—	1,600 U
	249,600	243,000	6,600 U	5,200 F	10,200 U	1,600 U

*Budget variance.

Direct material was quoted at $5.50 per pound throughout September and October by all suppliers. There was no purchase price variance for materials in October; the price variance shown relates solely to the materials used during October.

Wage standards were set in accordance with an annual union contract, but a shortage of workers in the local area has resulted in rates higher than standard.

There were no beginning or ending inventories of work in process.

REQUIRED:

For the month of October:
1. Number of units produced. Triple-check your computations here before proceeding.
2. Actual number of direct labor hours.
3. Actual wage rate.
4. Budget for fixed indirect costs.
5. Normal activity expressed in direct labor hours.
6. Pounds of direct material purchased.
7. Pounds of direct material used.

8-21. Standard Costing and Net Income. The Drebin Company had net income for the first ten months of 19x1 of $100,000. There were absolutely no cost variances of any kind through October 31. One hundred thousand units were produced and sold during the ten-month period. Fixed manufacturing overhead was $1,000,000 through October 31. The company uses a standard costing system. All variances are disposed of at year end as an adjustment to Standard Cost of Goods Sold. There are no ending inventories.

REQUIRED:

If a total of 25,000 units are produced and sold during the remainder of the year, what is the net income for the year likely to be?

8-22. Working Backward from Given Variances. The Jacob Company uses a flexible budget and standard costs to aid planning and control. At a 60,000-direct-labor-hour level, budgeted variable overhead is $30,000 and budgeted direct labor is $240,000.

The following are some results for August:

Variable overhead budget variance	$ 10,500 U
Variable overhead efficiency variance	9,500 U
Actual direct labor costs incurred	294,000
Material purchase price variance (based on goods purchased)	14,000 F
Material usage variance	7,500 U
Fixed overhead incurred	50,000
Fixed overhead spending variance	2,000 U

The standard cost per pound of direct material is $1.50. The standard allowance is one pound of direct material for each unit of finished product. Ninety thousand finished units were produced during August. There was no beginning or ending work in process. In July the material usage variance was $1,000, favorable, and the purchase price variance was $.20 per unit, unfavorable. In August, the purchase price variance was $.10 per unit.

In July labor troubles caused an immense slowdown in the pace of production. There had been an unfavorable direct labor efficiency variance of $60,000; there was no labor rate variance. These troubles had persisted in August. Some workers quit. Their replacements had to be hired at higher rates, which had to be extended to all workers. The actual average wage rate in August exceeded the standard average wage rate by $.20 per hour.

REQUIRED:

For August:

1. Total pounds of direct materials purchased during August.
2. Total number of pounds of excess material usage.
3. Variable overhead spending variance.
4. Total number of actual hours worked.
5. Total number of standard hours allowed for the finished units produced.

responsibility accounting, motivation, and management control systems

CHAPTER IX

In this chapter we shall see that accounting techniques for planning and control must be implemented delicately. They will be ineffective unless attention is given to two overriding features: (a) the executive's sphere of responsibility and his freedom to make decisions and (b) the executive's own motivations.

Nearly every chapter so far has emphasized that accounting figures should be compiled so that the results may be considered attributable to one person's performance. This chapter will discuss this feature in more detail. It will then consider the problem of motivation and human relations —a subject so important that it deserves explicit discussion in any text on cost accounting. We cannot overemphasize that cost accounting systems and techniques must be evaluated in relation to how they influence employee behavior.

RESPONSIBILITY ACCOUNTING

Definition

The term *responsibility accounting* (activity accounting) has become more widely used through the years. One authority on the subject has discussed responsibility accounting as follows:

> In effect, the system personalizes the accounting statements by saying, "Joe, this is what you originally budgeted and this is how you performed for the period with actual operations as compared against your budget." By definition it (responsibility accounting) is a system of accounting which is tailored to an organization so that costs

are accumulated and reported by levels of responsibility within the organization. Each supervisory area in the organization is charged only with the cost for which it is responsible and over which it has control.[1]

Illustration

The following extended illustration demonstrates the concepts and techniques of responsibility accounting.

Exhibit 9-1. The organization chart (Exhibit 9-1) will be the basis of our illustration. The boxed area represents the chain of command and responsibility in a typical manufacturing organization. It is assumed that the manufacturing vice president has a production superintendent in charge of the producing departments. The managers of the service departments are responsible directly to the manufacturing vice president.

EXHIBIT 9-1

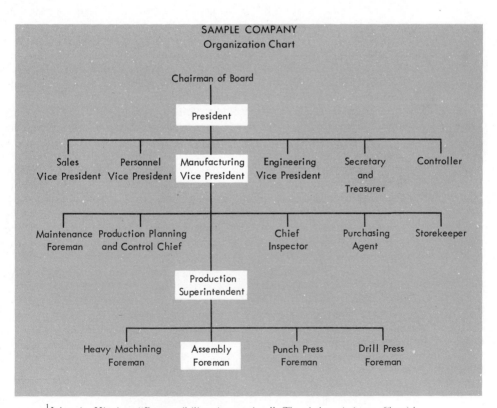

SAMPLE COMPANY
Organization Chart

[1]John A. Higgins, "Responsibility Accounting," *The Arthur Andersen Chronicle* (April, 1952). The term *activity accounting* is used by Eric Kohler and may be used interchangeably with *responsibility accounting*. See Kohler, *A Dictionary for Accountants* (3rd ed.; Englewood Cliffs, N.J.: Prentice-Hall, Inc., 1963), pp. 22–23.

Sample Company is a metal fabricator, employing 700 people and having sales of $11,000,000 per year. The company has a standard cost system and a flexible budget to aid control. Some features of control follow:

1. *Direct materials.* Prices are controlled or checked through periodic comparison of price standards with actual purchase prices. Usage standards are tight (ideal); usage variances are expected and budgeted. Issues in excess of standards are charged to departments responsible for spoiled materials and are checked against flexible budget allowances for spoiled materials.
2. *Direct labor.* Total actual costs are compared with total standard costs for each department. Variances are reported by departments and are analyzed in detail on supplementary reports.
3. *Factory overhead.* Actual costs are compared with flexible budget amounts. These reports are prepared by areas of responsibility. The responsible individual takes an active role in preparing his own budgets and standards.

Reports are tailored to the company and, within limits, each department head may determine the extent of detailed information he needs to help control his operations.

Exhibit 9-2. Exhibit 9-2 gives an over-all view of responsibility accounting and reporting. Starting with the assembly foreman and working toward the top, we shall examine how these reports may be prepared and integrated through the four managerial levels.

Exhibit 9-3. Exhibit 9-3 is a typical report for the foreman of the assembly department. The lower part of the report is a listing of the overhead items subject to the foreman's control, together with the measure of his success in meeting his budget targets. This presentation contains simple dollar amounts of variance. *Some companies prefer measuring the variances in terms of percentages of budget amounts* as well as the variance amounts themselves.

The upper part of the report contains total direct labor costs as measured against standard. The foreman is ordinarily responsible for efficient labor performance. This variance could be broken down further on this report or by supplementary analysis.

In this illustration, direct material performance is reported in a somewhat oblique way, although a third section could be added to indicate direct material usage in much the same manner as direct labor is reported. Material usage is controlled by charging *excess* issues of direct materials to producing departments and comparing these charges with flexible budget allowances. The "spoiled work" item in the controllable overhead section is the measure of excess usage of direct material. In other words, unfavorable material usage variances are anticipated and budgeted as a part of overhead.

Note that each of these four responsibility reports supplies the department head with measurements of his performance on matters subject to his control. Irrelevant items not subject to his control are removed from these performance reports. The department head concentrates on those

EXHIBIT 9-2

RESPONSIBILITY REPORTING AT VARIOUS EXECUTIVE LEVELS

PRESIDENT
(See Exhibit 9 - 6 for details.) The President receives a summary of functional performance by each of his Vice Presidents. He can trace variances to individuals.

—	x	x	x	x
—	x	x	x	x
Controllable overhead:				
—	x	x	x	x
—	x	x	x	x
—	x	x	x	x
Manufacturing	94,000	x	x	x
—	x	x	x	x
—	x	x	x	x
	235,000	x	x	x

MANUFACTURING VICE PRESIDENT
(See Exhibit 9 - 5 for details.) This man is responsible for the producing and service department costs. This report shows the performance of individuals in charge of each department. The summarized results are in turn carried upward.

$94,000

Direct labor	x	x	x	x
Materials purchased	x	x	x	x
Controllable overhead:				
—	x	x	x	x
Production superin.	39,000	x	x	x
—	x	x	x	x
—	x	x	x	x
—	x	x	x	x
—	x	x	x	x
—	x	x	x	x
	94,000	x	x	x

PRODUCTION SUPERINTENDENT
(See Exhibit 9 - 4 for details.) This report summarizes the performance of producing departments. The combined results are in turn reported to the next higher level of supervision.

$39,000

Direct labor:				
—	x	x	x	x
—	x	x	x	x
—	x	x	x	x
—	x	x	x	x
Controllable overhead:				
—	x	x	x	x
—	x	x	x	x
—	x	x	x	x
—	x	x	x	x
Assembly	8,200	x	x	x
	39,000	x	x	x

ASSEMBLY FOREMAN
(See Exhibit 9 - 3 for details.) This foreman's performance is reported to him. Totals are carried to the report of his supervisor.

$8,200

Direct labor:				
—	xx	xx	xx	xx
—	xx	xx	xx	xx
—	xx	xx	xx	xx
Controllable overhead:				
—	xx	xx	xx	xx
—	xx	xx	xx	xx
—	xx	xx	xx	xx
—	xx	xx	xx	xx
—	xx	xx	xx	xx
—	xx	xx	xx	xx
—	xx	xx	xx	xx
Total	8,200			

EXHIBIT 9-3

SAMPLE COMPANY
Assembly Department
Foreman's Monthly Responsibility Performance Report

	Standard		Variance (Over) Under Standard	
	This Month	Year to Date	This Month	Year to Date
Direct labor:				
Amount—to Exhibit 9-4	$33,000	$145,000	$(567)	$(2,735)
Hours	16,500	72,500	(200)	(1,000)
Per hour	$ 2.00	$ 2.00	$(.01)	$ (.01)

	Budget		(Over) Under Flexible Budget	
	This Month	Year to Date	This Month	Year to Date
Controllable overhead:				
Supervision—working foremen	$2,800	$12,600	$ 160	$(220)
Material handling	2,700	11,700	(30)	20
Repair and reassembly	700	2,100	(230)	(80)
Training	220	820	(40)	(10)
Idle time	60	110	(30)	(10)
Overtime premium	1,100	6,300	230	(200)
Spoiled work (excess material usage)	250	1,300	50	—
Supplies	200	650	(70)	(40)
Expendable tools	170	800	10	30
Total—to Exhibit 9-4	$8,200	$36,380	$ 50	$(510)

things subject to his influence, and he ignores data which may clutter and confuse his thinking.

Exhibit 9-4. Trace the $33,000 and the $8,200 totals from the assembly department report to the production superintendent's report. The latter report is merely a summarization of the individual reports of the four producing departments under the jurisdiction of the production superintendent. Ordinarily, the production superintendent would want copies of the detailed statements for each foreman responsible to him.

Exhibit 9-5. Trace the $84,000 and the $39,000 totals from the production superintendent's report to Exhibit 9-5, the manufacturing vice president's report. His summary report will contain figures for his own office plus all factory departments, including the service departments. The manufacturing vice president would usually desire copies (similar to Exhibit 9-4) of the detailed costs of each area. Note that material purchases are shown. The responsibility for purchases rests with the purchasing agent. The material variances shown here are price variances.

EXHIBIT 9-4

SAMPLE COMPANY
Production Department Cost Summary
Production Superintendent's Monthly Responsibility Performance Report

	Standard		Variance (Over) Under Standard	
	This Month	Year to Date	This Month	Year to Date
Direct labor:				
Drill press	$15,000	$ 60,000	$ (800)	$(4,000)
Punch press	20,000	80,000	(100)	(1,265)
Heavy machinery	16,000	65,000	67	(1,000)
Assembly	33,000	145,000	(567)	(2,735)
Total—to Exhibit 9-5	$84,000	$350,000	$(1,400)	$(9,000)

	Budget		(Over) Under Flexible Budget	
	This Month	Year to Date	This Month	Year to Date
Controllable overhead:				
Production superintendent's office	$ 4,800	$ 19,000	$ (30)	$ 230
Drill press	5,000	20,000	(50)	150
Punch press	10,000	32,000	(2,800)	(4,400)
Heavy machining	11,000	41,000	1,300	100
Assembly	8,200	36,380	50	(510)
Total—to Exhibit 9-5	$39,000	$148,380	$(1,530)	$(4,430)

EXHIBIT 9-5

SAMPLE COMPANY
Manufacturing Cost Summary
Manufacturing Vice President's Monthly Responsibility Performance Report

	Standard		Variance (Over) Under Standard	
	This Month	Year to Date	This Month	Year to Date
Direct labor—to Exhibit 9-6	$ 84,000	$ 350,000	$(1,400)	$ (9,000)
Materials purchased—to Exhibit 9-6	$420,000	$1,800,000	$ 4,000	$25,000

Exhibit 9-5 continued next page.

	Budget		(Over) Under Flexible Budget	
	This Month	Year to Date	This Month	Year to Date
Controllable overhead:				
Manufacturing vice president's office	$ 8,000	$ 32,020	$ 70	$ 600
Production superintendent's departments	39,000	148,380	(1,630)	(4,430)
Maintenance	30,000	120,000	(2,000)	(2,100)
Production planning and control	6,000	24,000	100	40
Inspection	5,000	19,000	(100)	(200)
Stores	4,000	17,000	260	—
Purchasing	2,000	7,000	—	490
Total—to Exhibit 9-6	$94,000	$367,400	$(3,300)	$(5,600)

Exhibit 9-6. Trace the $94,000 from the manufacturing vice president's report to the president's report, Exhibit 9-6. The latter statement summarizes the entire company's cost control performance. This entire system has integrated cost reports with the levels of responsibility for cost incurrence.

EXHIBIT 9-6

SAMPLE COMPANY
Departmental Cost Summary
President's Monthly Responsibility Performance Report

	Standard		Variance (Over) Under Standard	
	This Month	Year to Date	This Month	Year to Date
Direct labor	$ 84,000	$ 350,000	$(1,400)	$ (9,000)
Materials purchased	420,000	1,800,000	4,000	25,000

	Budget		(Over) Under Flexible Budget	
	This Month	Year to Date	This Month	Year to Date
Controllable overhead:				
President's office	$ 15,000	$ 60,000	$ 300	$ 1,000
Sales vice president	80,000	310,000	(7,000)	(18,000)
Personnel vice president	7,000	30,000	300	1,100
Manufacturing vice president	94,000	367,400	(3,300)	(5,600)
Engineering vice president	9,000	37,000	(900)	(3,200)
Finance vice president	30,000	110,000	100	2,000
	$235,000	$914,400	$(10,500)	$(22,700)

Controllable and uncontrollable costs

Definition of Controllable Costs.   Responsibility accounting has a natural appeal because it specifies a boundary of operations and distinguishes between controllable and uncontrollable costs. It is easy to say that a manager's performance should be judged on the basis of only those items subject to his control.   But experienced cost accountants and managers will testify that it is far from easy to decide whether an item is controllable or uncontrollable.   Moreover, there are shades of influence: an item may be controllable in whole or in part.   Therefore, do not expect to get a crystal-clear, practical concept of a controllable cost. It does not exist. Still, accountants must grapple with this problem, even though their approaches are often coarse.

Controllable costs are those which may be directly regulated at a given level of managerial authority.   Put another way, controllable costs are those that are directly influenced by a *manager* within a *given time period*. Too often, people assume that variable costs are controllable and fixed costs are uncontrollable. Such thinking may lead to erroneous conclusions. For example, rent is uncontrollable by the assembly foreman, but it may be controllable by the executive vice president, who may be assigned the responsibility of choosing plant facilities and of deciding whether to own or rent. Moreover, managers frequently have the option of trading off variable for fixed costs—for example, by purchasing labor-saving devices.

The distinction between controllability and uncontrollability also has a time dimension. Some accountants would maintain that rent is uncontrollable at any level of managerial supervision. This may be so for any given year included in a long-term lease, but over the long run, top management must determine the commitments which are reflected in such accounts as rent, depreciation, and property taxes. The level of property taxes, for example, is sometimes subject to change by management negotiation with assessors and by control over inventory levels.

In the long run, all costs are subject to at least some degree of managerial control. Long-run costs are usually incurred with special care because they are generally large and irrevocable.

In summary, controllability is a matter of degree that is affected by two major factors: the managerial area of responsibility, and the time period in question. All costs are controllable, to some degree and by somebody, over the long run. In the short run, not as many costs are controllable, and those that are controllable are subject to various degrees of influence.

In a given situation, therefore, certain costs may be regarded as controllable and others as uncontrollable.   This is a useful distinction in assigning responsibility for cost control. Modern opinion favors excluding the uncontrollable items from a performance report. The budget for which a shop foreman is responsible should show only the costs that are considered under his control. Such items as rent and taxes would not appear on his budget; from his standpoint, these are uncontrollable costs.

The countervailing view is that there may be some benefit in including the uncontrollable items to create an awareness of the whole organization and its costs. The important point is that the controllable and uncontrollable items, when appearing together, should not be commingled indiscriminately.

Difficulties in assigning costs to individual managers

The fundamental idea that individuals should be charged only with costs subject to their control is conceptually appealing. Practically, however, there are difficulties.

Few, if any, elements of cost are the sole responsibility of one person. Some guides to deciding the appropriate costs to be charged to a person (responsibility center) are as follows:

> *1. If the person has authority over both the acquisition and the use of the service, he should be charged with the cost of such services.*
>
> *2. If the person can significantly influence the amount of cost through his own action, he may be charged with such costs.*
>
> *3. Even if the person cannot significantly influence the amount of cost through his own direct action, he may be charged with those elements with which the management desires him to be concerned, so that he will help to influence those who are responsible.*[2]

The diffusion of control throughout the organization complicates the task of collecting data by responsibility centers. For example, material and supply *prices* may be influenced by the effectiveness of the purchasing officer, whereas material and supply *usage* may be most strongly influenced by the foremen. Another illustration would be the cost of operating a department which maintains and repairs machinery of producing departments. If the repair work is done under the supervision of the maintenance and repair foreman, the efficiency of the workmen is subject to his control. However, the total cost of repairs is also influenced by the day-to-day care given the machinery by the production workers.

A practical over-all guide for judging controllability is the following: Although more than one executive may regard a given cost as being within his control, *there is usually one officer in the whole organization who bears primary responsibility for control.* This is usually the executive who most closely supervises the day-to-day action which influences that cost. "Costs should be charged to the department which has the power to accept or reject the invoice or which pays for the labor required."[3] All costs which are controllable by him are also regarded as being controllable by his superior line executives.

Timing and control

Control is exercised in the form of particular actions. An action, once taken, cannot be changed by subsequent events. Performance reports,

[2]"Report of Committee on Cost Concepts and Standards," *Accounting Review*, April, 1956, p. 189.
[3]David Solomons, *Divisional Performance: Measurement and Control* (New York: Financial Executives Research Foundation, 1965), p. 55.

which provide data for appraisal, call management's attention to situations that have not been "in control." Performance reports are control mechanisms, not because they help rectify past mistakes but because they spur management to prevent future mistakes. Thus, accounting for control is oriented to the future rather than to the past. Historical data are important only insofar as they help to predict performance or help managerial investigation so that control may be better maintained in the future.

MOTIVATION

Responsibility accounting, budgets, standards, and other accounting techniques have arisen to aid management. When they are administered skillfully, they are of indispensable help. However, when they are not so administered, they may do more harm than good. We all know that organizations achieve objectives through human beings and inanimate resources like machines, buildings, accounting techniques, and materials. To do a good job, the laborer must use the materials and machines skillfully. And so it is with accounting techniques and systems; they must be administered astutely if their planning and control effectiveness is to be maximized.

Unfortunately, the human aspects of cost accounting are much more troublesome in practice than the technical phases. The purpose of this section is to examine the troubles that are encountered and to explore possible ways of preventing or minimizing these difficulties.

Need for better communication

Accountants in general need to become more cognizant of the administrative problems which evolve from the very nature of budgets and cost controls. Accounting systems put operating people on the spot—under surveillance. The natural reaction to the pinpointing of performance is self-defense. A major duty for accountants is to persuade the users of data that accounting reports really exist to aid the manager in doing a better job.

It has been said that, in today's complicated business world, accounting is the Seeing Eye dog of management. But often it's a case of the blind leading the blind. This is the accountant's greatest challenge. Accountants must communicate their techniques with care and enthusiasm, particularly to the top executives, whose attitudes often trickle down throughout the entire organization. Otherwise, the best ideas will be rejected by managers who may not comprehend their importance.

Reactions of foremen and supervisors

Budgeting and standards provide communication devices in the form of conferences and copies of budgets or other plans. Enthusiasts say that budgets are effective instruments of communication—a way to knit the views of line and staff and of upper and lower levels of management. However, this ideal picture does not always prevail. Sord and Welsch report:

> One weakness noted in some interviews concerned the inability of the budget staff to obtain line participation in developing budgets. There was a noticeable tendency in some cases on the part of line people to relinquish line budget responsibilities to the budget staff. Line personnel simply did not wish to be bothered with it. In most of these cases the budget staff have no desire to prepare budgets, and for them to do so was contrary to the intent of top management.
>
> This condition seems to be one of the major weaknesses existing in profit planning. Correction . . . involves education of management, especially at lower management levels . . . .[4]

An understanding of the foremen's and supervisors' personal views is vital in order to achieve success with a budget program. One drawback of typical control techniques has been referred to by McGregor as follows:

> It is perhaps more characteristic of (staff managers) to mistrust their managerial colleagues and to develop elaborate machinery for policing their behavior. Consider the accounting profession as an example![5]

A Controllership Foundation study has identified some of the human problems.[6] Budgetary accountants say they experience difficulty in selling budgets because factory people (a) lack education, (b) lack interest, and (c) misunderstand or mistrust budgets. Some conclusions of the study follow:

1. Budget pressure tends to unite the employees against management, and tends to place the factory supervisor under tension. This tension may lead to inefficiency, aggression, and perhaps a complete breakdown on the part of the supervisor.

2. The accounting staff can obtain feelings of success only by finding fault with factory people. These feelings of failure among factory supervisors lead to too many human relations problems.

3. The use of budgets as "needlers" by top management tends to make the factory supervisors see only the problems of their own department. The supervisors are not concerned with the other people's problems. They are not "plant-centered" in outlook.

4. Supervisors use budgets as a way of expressing their own patterns of leadership. When these patterns result in people getting hurt, the budget, in itself a neutral thing, often gets blamed.

Budgetary accountants often find it hard to see why factory executives do not speak joyously about budgets. After all, budgets are designed to help the individual improve his own abilities as well as to help the entire

---

[4]Burnard H. Sord and Glenn A. Welsch, *Business Budgeting* (New York: Controllership Foundation, Inc., 1958), p. 102.

[5]Douglas McGregor, "The Role of Staff in Modern Industry," in Shultz and Whisler (ed.), *Management Organization and the Computer* (Glencoe, Ill.: The Free Press, 1960), p. 112. This article is an excellent study of modern line-staff relationships.

[6]Chris Argyris, *The Impact of Budgets on People* (New York: Controllership Foundation, Inc., 1952), p. 25.

firm attain its objectives.   Budgets are supposed to help, not hamper, management; yet reactions such as the following exist:

> *I'm violently against the figures.   I keep away from showing them to the workers. I* know my boys *are doing a good job.   They're trying to do their best.   If I give them the heat with this stuff, they'll blow their top.   No, no, I couldn't even use a budget in front of my people.   I just wouldn't dare.   And, mind you, I don't think my top management would want us to.   We wouldn't get any production out, if we did.*

What to do about it: the importance of interpretation

Line management's attitude toward the accounting function depends on an understanding and appreciation of the reports supplied. The controller must consciously nurture effective communications between the members of his staff and line management. One effective way to improve mutual understanding is to have a member of the controller's staff personally explain and interpret reports as they are presented to line managers.

Recordkeeping is essential for cost accumulation; but interpretation is the key to enhancing management's warmth toward the accounting function. The controller's "staff" role includes being a *helper* (interpreter and analyst) *and* a *policeman* (cost accumulator and reporter). However, these two roles often clash. Therefore, wherever possible, the controller's department should divorce interpretation from recordkeeping;[7] otherwise, the day-to-day routine, the unending deadlines, and the insidious pressures of cost accumulation will shunt interpretation (with the accompanying frequent contacts between accountants and operating people) into the background and, most likely, into oblivion.

The interpretative roles (for example, explaining variances) should be manned by capable, experienced accountants who, at least to some degree, can talk the line manager's language. Indeed, the interpreters are the individuals who will establish the status of the controller's department in the company. Close, direct contacts between accountants and operating managers instill confidence in the reliability of the standards, budgets, and reports which are the measuring devices of performance.

Motivation is the key

The ability of a manger to elicit productivity from his workers has been found to depend on (a) his freedom to make decisions and (b) his own motivation.[8] The core of the problem of management is not setting a

---

[7]H. A. Simon, H. Guetzkow, G. Kozmetsky, and G. Tyndall, *Centralization vs. Decentralization in Organizing the Controller's Department* (New York: The Controllership Foundation, Inc., 1954), p. 20.

[8]George J. Benston, "The Role of the Firm's Accounting System for Motivation," *Accounting Review* (April, 1963), pp. 347–355.

Many recent articles have ably examined the psychological literature as it relates to accounting. For example, see Selwyn Becker and David Green, Jr., "Budgeting and Employee Behavior," *Journal of Business* (October, 1962), pp. 392–402. Also see the *Journal of Business* (April, 1964) for a reply by Andrew C. Stedry to the Becker and Green article, plus a rejoinder to that reply.

goal, a target, or a standard. Setting standards or budgets by themselves does not attain results. Rather it is a matter of motivation, the force that directs activity toward the standard. No action will be taken toward an objective without motivation. How can budgets and standards be used as motivating devices—as mechanisms that will influence managers and subordinates to act in accordance with the desires of top management?

Let us take a look at this word *motivation* before continuing. The word has been used loosely by many. Motivation is that within the individual, rather than that without, which directs his activity toward satisfying a need. He may survey a series of objects, some of which he selects as goals. A resulting tension is set up; this is a need: the stronger the need, the greater the motivation. Given this tension, activity is taken toward the desired goals. As commonly used, "motivation" as an idea embraces both the need and the resulting drive.

Motivation is an important, bothersome problem in practice, but there is not much literature that faces the issue as it bears on *managers*, as distinguished from laborers. The Committee on Cost Concepts of the American Accounting Association has observed:

> The basis of measurement used in providing cost data for control is often a matter of management discretion and an important consideration in motivation. Different bases may significantly affect the way in which different individuals are motivated. For this reason, the bases of measurement selected should be consistent with the type of motivation desired. For example, different types of motivation may result when maintenance costs are charged to a responsibility center on the bases of: (1) a rate per maintenance labor hour, (2) a rate per job, or (3) a single amount per month.[9]

Professor Anthony, in commenting on the committee's report, stated:

> Your committee is not made up of psychologists; in fact, its members are somewhat skeptical of some of the psychological patter. We are convinced, however, that approaching the control problem in terms of human motivation—subjective though this approach is, and different though it may seem from the customary language of debit and credit—is much more fruitful than an attempt to define "true" costs, or to say whether ideal standards are better than normal standards or any other mechanical approach.
>
> The usefulness of such an approach becomes apparent when the concepts are applied to a practical control problem. Without such an approach, one can easily become immersed in pointless arguments on such matters as whether rent should be allocated on the basis of square footage or cubic footage. There is no sound way of settling such disputes. With the notion of motivation, the problem comes into clear focus. What cost constructions are most likely to induce people to take the action that management desires? Answering this question in a specific situation is difficult . . . .[10]

Anthony has suggested that a control technique can be judged in two ways: by the *direction* and by the *strength* of its motivation. The control system should be so arranged that actions that it leads people to take, be-

[9]"Tentative Statement of Cost Concepts . . . ," *Accounting Review* (April, 1956), p. 189.

[10]Robert N. Anthony, "Cost Concepts for Control," *Accounting Review* (April, 1957), p. 234.

cause they feel that these actions are in their own best interests, are also in the best interests of the company:

> *For example, if the system signals that the emphasis should be only on reducing costs, and if the individual responds by reducing costs at the expense of adequate quality, or by reducing costs in his own department by measures that cause a more than offsetting increase in some other department, he has been motivated, but in the wrong direction. It is therefore important to ask two separate questions about a control technique: (1) What will it motivate people to do in their own selfish interests? and (2) Is this action in the best interests of the company?*[11]

MANAGEMENT CONTROL SYSTEMS

How do you judge the effectiveness and efficiency of a management control system? We need some criteria, some benchmarks, to gauge the characteristics of management control systems. Many criteria are already available in the form of highly technical checklists which explore matters like the routing of multiple copies of source documents, the assembling of data in a uniform manner, and so forth. A system may earn the highest ratings under these criteria. Nevertheless, such criteria are incomplete, and the system may be weak. Present criteria often concentrate on the minimization of errors, fraud, and waste. They focus on physical control and information handling systems—not on management control systems *in toto*.

This section raises a set of questions that both accountants and managers should ask, in addition to the traditional ones, when evaluating a particular system. Although some useful generalizations are suggested, these must be regarded as tentative hypotheses rather than as universal truths. Our state of knowledge about human behavior in organizational settings is still too fragmented to warrant much guidance beyond the "each case is different" caveat. The point is that the same questions are applicable to a wide variety of organizations, even though the answers may differ in kind or degree.

Characteristics of management control systems

Countless words have been written about the meaning of words like *organization, plan, control,* and *system.* The following terminology will be used for our purposes:

> *Planning*—the seeking and specifying of objectives together with the mapping and selecting of the best routes for their achievement.
> *Controlling*—obtaining adherence to plans.
> A comment: Planning and controlling blur into one another in the real world. The overlaps and interlocks mean that planning and con-

---

[11] Robert N. Anthony, *Management Accounting* (3rd ed.; Homewood, Ill.: Richard D. Irwin, Inc. 1964), p. 362.

trolling are basically indivisible. Nevertheless, these distinctions are useful abstractions which facilitate analysis of the management process.

System—according to *Webster's Dictionary:* "an assemblage of objects united by some form of regular interaction or interdependence; an organic or organized whole."

Process—according to *Webster's Dictionary:* "a series of actions or operations definitely conducing to an end."

A comment: Anthony neatly distinguishes between process and system.[12] The digestive system facilitates the process of digestion. In organizations, the process rather than the structure should be the determinant in systems design. That is, the structure (system) can be modified to fit whatever seems to be the best process.

Moreover, system implies a repetition of the related process. Systems are inevitably geared to the routine high-volume aspects of a process. For instance, the information-handling systems are designed to facilitate the recording of frequently encountered transactions. Hence, the isolated nonrecurring transaction is often jammed into the system in a seemingly inefficient way. In these cases, the system dominates an activity which by itself might be handled more directly. Thus, a cash purchase under a voucher system is processed through a voucher register and a check register, even though simpler techniques could be conceived.

Effectiveness—accomplishment of desired end.
Efficiency—optimum relationship between input and output.[13]

A comment: As Professor Gerald Wentworth has pointed out, killing a housefly with a sledge hammer may be effective, but it is not efficient.

The management process in its entirety varies from very complex top-level decisions regarding objectives and policies to fairly simple day-to-day supervisory chores. The complex decisions are relatively unstructured, nonrepetitive, often long-range, and often heavily dependent on "staff" expertise. The notion of systems to facilitate a process is not particularly applicable here. That is, there is little that is systematic about this activity. Anthony calls this process *strategic planning*.[14]

Management control systems are designed to facilitate the routine planning and control of operations—the process by which managers assure that resources are obtained and used effectively and efficiently in the accomplishment of the organizational objectives.[15]

Programmed and nonprogrammed activities

Elements of social psychology, economics, and engineering are especially pertinent to understanding the management control process.

[12] Robert N. Anthony, *Planning and Control Systems: A Framework for Analysis,* (Boston: Harvard Business School, 1965), p. 5.
[13] *Ibid.*, p. 28.
[14] *Ibid.*, p. 16.
[15] *Ibid.*, p. 17.

In its entirety, it is a man-machine process which entails much nonprogrammed activity and subjective decision making. *Within* this process, many activities can be engineered or made highly structured—"programmed" so that predetermined rules can closely govern day-to-day performance. As we shall see, the distinctions between programmed and nonprogrammed activities are useful because the applicable planning and control techniques are different. An important point is that the programmed activity is a subdivision of the over-all management control process even though it may be usefully separated for analysis. Exhibit 9-7 shows how the processes can be viewed as concentric circles, each being a subdivision of the larger circle. Recent business applications of mathematical models are examples of attempts to make the management process more scientific by enlarging the inner circle, which represents highly structured processes.

EXHIBIT 9-7

STRATEGIC PLANNING AND THE MANAGEMENT CONTROL SYSTEM

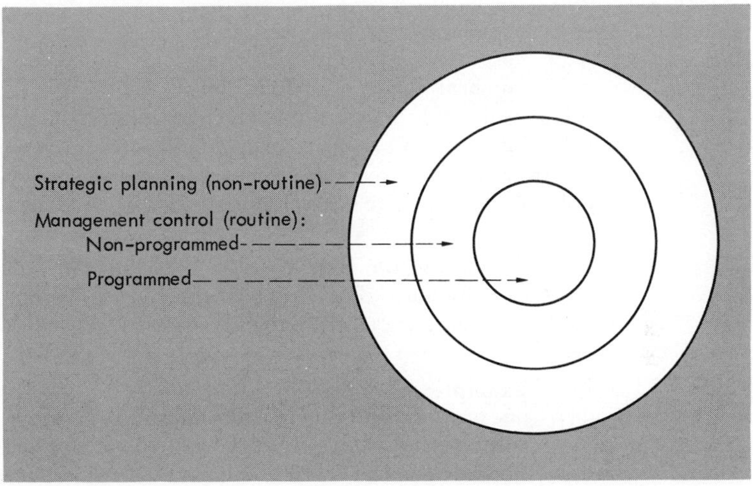

Strategic planning (non-routine)

Management control (routine):
 Non-programmed
 Programmed

Coordination and motivation are crucial in the management of a complex organization. The job of a management control system is to help management attain the harmony of goals (effectiveness) and the optimum acquisition and utilization of resources (efficiency). This is essentially coordination, which, in turn, involves problems of motivation. Motivation permeates the questions we are about to raise.

Coordination and Motivation

Over-all goal(s):

Means   I. Erecting subgoals
         II. Erecting an organization
         III. Acquiring and using resources

Goal setting

I. *Does the system provide a global emphasis, so that all major goals and their inter-relationships are considered insofar as possible when managers act? Expressed another way, does the system specify its goals and subgoals to encourage behavior that blends with top-management goals?*

Multiple Goals. The aim is to get subgoals into congruence, which requires direction and balance. It is fairly easy to assess the direction of each subgoal by itself; the trouble is that they are interdependent. Moreover, the selection of subgoals is essentially based on a series of assumptions regarding optimization which must be made at the strategic planning level. For example, General Electric Company[16] has stressed multiple goals by stating that organizational performance will be measured in the following eight areas:

1. Profitability
2. Market position
3. Productivity
4. Product leadership
5. Personnel development
6. Employee attitudes
7. Public responsibility
8. Balance between short-range and long-range goals

General Electric's efforts basically try to juggle two conflicting tendencies in goal setting. First, the overemphasis on multi-goals may lead to diffusion of effort and frustration of efficiency. Second, the overemphasis on a single goal may lead to increased efficiency but may also increase the likelihood of ineffective over-all outcomes.

Overstress on One Goal. Fixation[17] on subgoals often causes ineffective behavior. The greatest danger is overemphasis on one goal which leads to failure to attain other goals.

Example: The Soviet Union provides many cases where overstress on one or two aspects of the measurement system may lead to uneconomic behavior that focuses on a subgoal without considering over-all organizational goals. To illustrate, taxi drivers were put on a bonus system based on mileage. "Soon the Moscow suburbs were full of empty taxis barreling down the boulevards to fatten their bonuses."[18] In response to bonuses based on tonnage norms, a Moscow chandelier factory produced heavier and heavier chandeliers, until they started pulling ceilings down.

---

[16] See Wm. Travers Jerome III, *Executive Control—The Catalyst* (New York: John Wiley & Sons, Inc., 1961), Chapters 4 and 14. Also see Robert W. Lewis, "Measuring, Reporting, and Appraising Results of Operations with Reference to Goals, Plans and Budgets," *Planning, Managing and Measuring the Business, A Case Study of Management Planning and Control at General Electric Company* (New York: Controllership Foundation, Inc., 1955).

[17] Also see Yuji Ijiri, Robert K. Jaedicke, and Kenneth E. Knight, "The Effects of Accounting Alternatives on Management Decisions," in *Research in Accounting Measurement* (Evanston, Ill.: American Accounting Association, 1966).

[18] *Time*, February 12, 1965, p. 24.

The most common instance is the short-run maximization of net income or sales which hurts long-run results.

Example: There are many questionable ways to improve short-run performance. Examples include stinting on repairs, quality control, advertising, research, or training. A manager may successfully exert pressure on employees for more productivity for short spurts of time. This may have some unfavorable long-run overtones.

Tools of Coordination. The following practices are illustrations of approaches that have helped coordination:

1. If incentive rewards or punishments are directly dependent on some performance measure, such as sales, contribution to profit, or net income, the scheme should be based, at least partially, on some group (global) performance measure, such as total company net income.

2. The goal selection and constraint recognition should be interlocked explicitly. This can be achieved in many ways, from conscious informal management agreement to elaborate comprehensive budgets using linear programming. The point is that this job of goal setting and coordination is too fundamental; it should not be a product of chance or a by-product of the day-to-day extinguishing of business brush fires.

3. Rigid compartmentalization by responsibility or profit centers must be counterbalanced by explicit top-management teamwork in seeing that goals harmonize. This teamwork may take many forms. For instance, Union Carbide believes that it is necessary to have working *groups* of managers, including four at the presidential level, to achieve optimum corporate welfare.[19]

Structure of organization

II. *Is the accounting system tailored to the organizational structure to strengthen motivation? Is responsibility pinpointed? Are distinctions made between controllable and uncontrollable factors?*

Systems and Organization Changes. Ideally the organization itself and its processes must be thoroughly appraised, understood, and altered, if necessary, before a system is erected. That is, the design of a system and the design of an organizational structure are really inseparable and interdependent. The point is that the most streamlined system is not a cure-all or substitute for basic organizational ills or management ineptitude. On a practical level, there may be a powerful temptation to separate the design of systems from the design of organizational processes by assuming that the organizational structure is given. But some sad experiences with the hasty installation of computers demonstrate the weakness of such an approach.

In order to maximize efficiency and effectiveness, organizations subdivide processes and stipulate a hierarchy of managers who are ex-

---

[19]"Union Carbide's Patient Schemers," *Fortune*, December, 1965, p. 147 ff.

pected to oversee various spheres of responsibility. Some form of a responsibility accounting system usually reflects this process.

Fixing Responsibility and Cooperation versus Competition.   A fragile balance must be struck between careful delineation of responsibility, on the one hand, and too rigid separation of responsibility, on the other hand. Buck passing is a pervasive tendency that is supposedly minimized when responsibility is fixed unequivocally.

> **Example:**   A large utility used to hire college graduates and rotate them among all departments in the company during a two-year training program. Their salaries were not assigned to the departments, and individual managers took little interest in the trainees. But now it assigns the trainee to a definite department that fits his primary interest, where he is given direct responsibility as soon as possible. Both the trainees and the managers are much more satisfied with the new responsibility arrangement.

But often the motivational impact boomerangs; too much falls between the chairs. Managers often wear blinders and concentrate more than ever on their individual worlds. Family cooperation is replaced by intracompany competition.

> **Example:**   Two departments performed successive operations in a line production process making automobile frames. The frames were transferred from the first to the second department via an overhead conveyor system. Because of machine breakdowns in his department, the Department 2 manager requested the Department 1 manager to slow down production. He refused, and the frames had to be removed from the conveyor and stacked to await further processing. A bitter squabble ensued regarding which department should bear the extra labor cost of stacking the frames.

Accounting Records as Motivation Devices: Controllability and Uncontrollability.   Because the accounting system tallies performance, the records themselves become a direct mechanism of control and motivation. In many cases, particularly where activities are programmed and the measurement problems are easy, there is a favorable motivational impact from the very act of recording.

But there is also a pitfall here. There can be overdependence on an accounting system as being the prime means of motivation and the final word on the appraisal of performance. Although the system may play a necessary role in coordination and motivation, its many limitations deserve recognition, too, particularly in matters of cost allocations. A common complaint of managers, often marked by tones of discouragement, is that they are being unfairly charged with uncontrollable costs.

> **Example:**   A president of a large corporation insists that central basic research costs be fully allocated to all divisions despite objections about uncontrollability. His goal is to force division managers' interests toward such research activity. The basic question is whether the measurement system is the best vehicle for reaching such an objective. Indiscriminate cost allocations may undermine the confidence of the managers in the entire measurement system.

Acquiring and using resources

III. *Does the system properly guide managers in the acquisition and utilization of resources by providing accurate, relevant data?*

To be useful, data must be accurate, relevant, material, and timely. Here we concentrate on accuracy and relevancy, the two aspects that have the most direct bearing on the motivational influences of a system.

Does the System Encourage Accurate Recordkeeping?

Textbooks do not devote much space to the problems of obtaining accurate source documents. Yet this is easily one of the most pervasive, everlasting problems in collecting information. An accounting system will mean little to management if the scorekeeping function is haphazard.

Accurate recordkeeping is essentially a problem of motivation. The accountant and manager should be more sensitive to possible errors, more aware of the futility of trying to get usage of time and material reported accurately in small increments, and more conscious of the natural tendency of individuals to report their activities so as to minimize their personal bother and maximize their own showing.[20] The hazard of trying to get overly detailed reports extends not only to lack of confidence in individual reports themselves but to the likelihood of generating monumental contempt for the entire system.

> **Example:** "In many cases, incentive plans, while serving to increase production, are also an inducement for willful, dishonest reporting .... Therefore, for example, lost time by the fiction of 'made work' is reported as some type of productive labor."[21]

> **Example:** Interdepartmental confusion in a printing company was described by Professor George Shultz.[22] A producing department's production committee complained vigorously about the planning done by the scheduling department. Workmen objected that frequently they set up a job, only to discover that the specific paper needed was unavailable. Though paper for other jobs was available, a switch was not desirable because setup time was too great. This complaint involved other departments, so that the production committee could not correct the situation themselves. So they passed it upward to a top committee, which included the president.
>
> The head of the scheduling department was naturally upset by this complaint, so he investigated the matter thoroughly in preparation for the meeting. The worker prepares a time slip for each job, showing the total elapsed time in terms of running time, delays, and so on. The scheduling department uses this information for production planning. The scheduling department head examined the file of these slips and found that there was really extremely little delay due to "insufficient paper."

[20] Also see Sam E. Scharff, "The Industrial Engineer and the Cost Accountant," *N.A.A. Bulletin* (March, 1961), for more examples.
[21] Marion H. Simpsen, "But the Old Problems Remain," *N.A.A. Bulletin* (February, 1964), p. 13.
[22] G. P. Shultz, "Worker Participation on Production Problems," *Personnel* (1951), Vol. 28, No. 3, pp. 209–210.

At the meeting he triumphantly provided these "facts" and maintained that the complaint was insignificant. Shultz reports that this disclosure was greeted with embarrassed silence. After a long half-minute, a worker said: "Those time slips are way off. We fill them out. We were told by the foreman that he would get in trouble if we showed that delay time, so we usually added it to the running time. We've been doing it that way for years. We had no idea that you were using the slips as a basis for planning."

The foreman probably regarded the time slip procedure as a policing rather than a planning device. Likert stresses that measurements should be used primarily for self-guidance rather than policing. This will minimize the tendency to distort data to enhance personal showing. In this example, individuals now recognize the need for accuracy. Any distortion will hurt rather than help them. Moreover, new measurement techniques are more likely to be suggested, welcomed, and used, rather than feared and resisted, as is now often the case.[23] There is a self-evident need for education and communication of why the information was primarily needed.

Does the System Engender Intelligent Analysis of Relevant Data?

The accounting system should produce information that leads managers toward correct decisions regarding either evaluation of performance or selection among courses of action. Intelligent analysis of costs is often dependent on explicit distinctions between cost behavior patterns, which is more likely to be achieved via the contribution approach, described in the next chapter, than via traditional methods. The general tendency toward indiscriminate full cost allocations raises analytical dangers.

Example: An N.A.A. study cited the following instance:
"A bakery distributed its products through route salesmen each of whom loaded a truck with an assortment of products in the morning and spent the day calling on customers in an assigned territory. Believing that some items were more profitable than others, management asked for an analysis of product costs and sales. The accountants to whom the task was assigned allocated all manufacturing and marketing costs to products to obtain a net profit for each product. The resulting figures indicated that some of the products were being sold at a loss and management discontinued these products. However, when this change was put into effect, the company's over-all profit declined. It was then seen that, by dropping some products, sales revenues had been reduced without commensurate reduction in costs because the joint manufacturing costs and route sales costs had to be continued in order to make and sell the remaining products."[24]

Central corporate costs are often allocated on the basis of sales dollars because of the lack of any better basis for allocation. Too often, the product or division that is doing the best to better the organization's for-

---

[23] Rensis Likert, *New Patterns of Management* (New York: McGraw-Hill Book Company, Inc., 1961), pp. 206–210.
[24] Walter B. McFarland, "The Field of Management Accounting," *N.A.A. Bulletin*, Sec. 3 (June, 1963), p. 19.

tunes gets the heaviest dose of cost without regard to any possible cause-and-effect relationships.

> **Example:**   Beyer cites a company where in a year when all other divisions were falling greatly below their planned sales, one division's sales were booming. For some time, however, the relative profitability of the various divisions was heavily obscured by an accounting system "which in effect was charging the bulk of a volume variance against the division which was doing the most to eliminate that variance."[25]

Emphasis on Cost Behavior.   The foregoing examples demonstrate the importance of knowing the various cost behavior patterns. Intelligent cost analysis cannot be made unless the manager can distinguish between controllable and uncontrollable costs, variable and fixed costs, and separable and joint costs. Moreover, he must be able to interpret unit costs wisely.

Administration of the system

Do budgets and responsibility accounting and other modern accounting techniques foster a policed, departmental orientation rather than a positive, over-all organizational orientation? Let us ask if the *absence* of such techniques would encourage a broader orientation. The answer to such a question is indeterminate; yet it is doubtful that the lack of a budget would broaden a supervisor's horizons and would make him conscious of the organization as a whole instead of his little departmental sphere. The *administration* and *communication* of budgetary and other accounting techniques should be distinguished from the techniques themselves. The management control system embraces the techniques and their administration and communication. That is why coordination and motivation have been highlighted in this chapter.

Every system is marked in some degree by problems of conflicting goals, erroneous source documents, faulty cost analysis, and so forth. The aim is to reduce the lack of coordination and to increase the proper motivation—to improve systems with the full realization that perfection is unattainable.

In many cases of weak systems, the technical aspects of the system are not the culprits. The weaknesses are inept administration, the neglect of communication and education, and the neglect of the motivational impact of the system. The success of a management control system can be affected by both its technical perfection and by other nontechnical factors that influence management behavior.

In sum, most accountants and executives probably would agree with the following observations on costs for motivation by Simon *et al.*:

> *Interview results show that a particular figure does not operate as a norm, in either a score-card or attention-directing sense, simply because the controller's department*

[25] Robert Beyer, *Profitability Accounting* (New York: The Ronald Press Company, 1963), p. 266.

calls it a standard. It operates as a norm only to the extent that the executives and supervisors, whose activity it measures, accept it as a fair and attainable yardstick of their performance. Generally, operating executives were inclined to accept a standard to the extent that they were satisfied that the data were accurately recorded, *that the standard level was* reasonably attainable, *and that the variables it measured were* controllable *by them.*[26]

SUMMARY

Responsibility accounting accumulates and reports costs so that each supervisory area is charged only with its controllable costs.

The human aspects of budgeting and standard costs are much more troublesome in practice than the technical phases. Budgets and standards will be helpful managerial tools if managers use them skillfully. A superior tool in the hands of a clumsy oaf may do more harm than good; in the hands of a skillful artisan, it becomes an important instrument that helps toward pleasing results.

Motivation is the overriding consideration that should influence management in formulating and using performance measures and in designing management control systems. Above all, the system and techniques should impel managers toward management objectives. If this supposition is valid, any system's rules, criteria, checklists, or questionnaires should explicitly include an appraisal of the motivational influences of the system under review. Among the questions that seem especially crucial are:

    I. Does the system specify its goals and subgoals to encourage behavior that blends with top-management goals?

    II. Is the accounting system tailored to the organizational structure to strengthen motivation?

    III. Does the system properly guide managers in the acquisition and utilization of resources by providing accurate, relevant data?

Sub-questions deserving consideration would cover such commonly encountered difficulties as the overemphasis on a subgoal; the overemphasis on short-run performance; failure to pinpoint responsibility; cooperation versus competition; the lack of distinction between controllable and uncontrollable costs; limitations of records as motivation devices; inaccurate source documents; and faulty cost analysis.

SUGGESTED READINGS

Anthony, Robert N., *Planning and Control Systems: A Framework for Analysis* (Boston: Harvard Business School, 1965).

Argyris, Chris, *The Impact of Budgets on People* (New York: Controllership Foundation, Inc., 1952).

[26] Simon, *et al., op. cit.,* p. 29. But for an opposite view, see Andrew Stedry, *Budget Control and Cost Behavior* (Englewood Cliffs, N. J.,: Prentice-Hall, Inc., 1960).

Becker, Selwyn, and David Green, Jr., "Budgeting and Employee Behavior," *Journal of Business* (October, 1962), pp. 392–402. Also see the *Journal of Business* (April, 1964) for a reply by Andrew C. Stedry to the Becker and Green article, plus a rejoinder to that reply.

Benston, George J., "The Role of the Firm's Accounting System for Motivation," *Accounting Review* (April, 1963), pp. 347–355.

Beyer, Robert, *Profitability Accounting* (New York: The Ronald Press Company, 1963).

Likert, Rensis, "Measuring Organizational Performance," *Harvard Business Review* (March-April, 1958), pp. 41–50.

Simon, H. A., H. Guetzkow, G. Kosmetsky, and G. Tyndall, *Centralization vs. Decentralization in Organizing the Controller's Department* (New York: The Controllership Foundation, Inc., 1954).

Sord, Burnard H., and Glenn A. Welsch, *Business Budgeting* (New York: Controllership Foundation, Inc., 1958).

Stedry, Andrew C., *Budget Control and Cost Behavior* (Englewood Cliffs, N.J.: Prentice-Hall, Inc., 1960).

Anthony's writings are always worth reading because he has a special knack for focusing on central issues.

The Simon *et al.* book is incisive and readable. Its title is deceiving because the book covers the entire range of management accounting. Unfortunately, the book is out of print, so you may have difficulty in getting a copy.

Beyer's book offers practical coverage of responsibility accounting.

Sord and Welsch, Argyris, and Stedry discuss the role of motivation in budgeting. The studies by Argyris and by Stedry are controversial.

PROBLEM FOR SELF-STUDY

Problem.   Construct a chart with the following headings:

			Controllable Cost			
Product Cost	Variable Cost	By Sales Vice President	By Assembly Foreman	By Production Superintendent	By Manufacturing Vice President
Salesmen's commissions						
Direct material						
Punch press—Direct labor department						
Maintenance department—supplies						
Sales vice president's salary						
Straight-line depreciation—equipment in assembly department						

Assume the same organization chart as shown in Exhibit 9-1. For each account, answer "yes" or "no" as to whether the cost is a product cost, a variable cost, and a cost controllable by the four officers indicated. Thus, you will have six answers, entered horizontally, for each account.

Solution. Note particularly how the concepts of variable-fixed and controllable-uncontrollable costs differ. A variable cost is not necessarily a controllable cost. Controllability is dependent on a manager's responsibility within a given time period. Note, too, that all costs which are controllable by a manager are also regarded as being controllable by his superior line executives.

	Product Cost	Variable Cost	Controllable Cost By Sales Vice President	By Assembly Foreman	By Production Superintendent	By Manufacturing Vice President
Salesmen's commissions	No	Yes	Yes	No	No	No
Direct material	Yes	Yes	No	Yes	Yes	Yes
Punch press department —Direct labor	Yes	Yes	No	No	Yes	Yes
Maintenance department—Supplies	Yes	Yes	No	No	No	Yes
Sales vice president's salary	No	No	No	No	No	No
Straight-line depreciation—Equipment in assembly department	Yes	No	No	No	No	No*

*Note that the time element is important here. Although depreciation may not be controllable in the short run, the manufacturing vice president's policies on selection and timing of equipment purchases influence depreciation costs.

QUESTIONS, PROBLEMS, AND CASES

Note: Problems 9-21 through 9-24 and 9-28 through 9-31 are especially recommended.

9-1. Define *responsibility accounting.*

9-2. Define *controllable cost.* What two major factors help an evaluation of whether a given cost is controllable?

9-3. What guides are available in deciding the appropriate costs to be charged to a person?

9-4. "An action once taken cannot be changed by subsequent events." What implications does this have for the cost accountant?

9-5. "I think that variances should be written off as period costs except in some cases." Describe one exception that this individual probably had in mind.

9-6. List five common complaints about control budgets.

9-7. "Budgets are wonderful vehicles for communication." Comment.

9-8. Define *motivation.* How does it differ from *need?*

9-9. Give an example of how a control system can motivate a manager to behave against the best interests of the company as a whole.

9-10. In general, when will operating executives be inclined to accept a standard?

9-11. "I'm majoring in accounting. This study of human relations is fruitless. You've got to be born with a flair for getting along with others. You can't learn it!" Do you agree? Why?

9-12. "Interpretation is essential for understanding accounting reports." Suggest how the accounting function may be organized to emphasize interpretation.

9-13. Budgets as Pressure Devices. Sord and Welsch have stated: "It should be recognized that pressure on supervisors need not come from control techniques, assuming that standards of performance are not unfair or too high. Pressure on supervisors comes from the responsibilities inherent in the supervisor's job." Do you agree? Why?

9-14. Budgets as Motivators. "To accept budgets as motivators is to imply that supervisors do not have adequate interest in their job. This is seen as an insult to a man's integrity, and the factory supervisors resent it strongly." Do you agree? Why?

● **9-15. Attitudes Toward the Accountant.** A prominent financial analyst, who became very successful with his Wall Street investments, once commented:

"My experience with the accountant is that for him everything has equal importance. He is like the Lord in the Bible, where it is written that 'a thousand years are in His sight as yesterday' when it is past—except that it is just the other way around with the accountant: 10 cents in the balance sheet is just as important as a million dollars. The main thing for him is that every figure should be correct."

Elbert Hubbard, a philosopher popular early in the twentieth century, made the following remarks:

"The typical auditor is a man past middle age, spare, wrinkled, intelligent, cold, passive, non-committal, with eyes like a codfish, polite in contact, but at the same time unresponsive, cold; calm and damnably composed as a concrete post or a plaster-of-paris cast; a human petrification with a heart of feldspar and without charm of the friendly germ, minus bowels, passion, or a sense of humour. Happily, they never reproduce and all of them finally go to Hell."

In general, do you agree with the above remarks? Why?

● **9-16. Interdepartmental Conflict and Budgets.** Professor Argyris and others have pointed out that budgets help foster a *departmental* orientation rather than a *plant-wide* orientation. This causes trouble because departmental executives concentrate on the correct functioning of their individual departments but pay no attention to the functioning of individual departments in relation to one another.

For example, Argyris cites the example of the plant in which a mistake was made on a customer order. The goods were returned and a correction was made at a cost of $3,000, a large amount. Some department had to be charged with the error. But which department?

After two months of battling among the supervisors as to who was guilty, emotions became so heated that two supervisors stopped talking to each other.

The plant manager finally gave up; he decided to charge the error to no department. He explained, "I thought it might be best to put the whole thing under general factory loss. Or else someone would be hurt."

REQUIRED:

Do you agree that budgets foster too narrow an orientation? Do you agree with the action of the plant manager? Did the budget and departmental accounting system cause the trouble? Explain fully.

9-17. Inaccuracies in Source Documents.* A study was made of time reporting in the shops of a large steel and alloy plate fabricator to determine to what degree the time reporting was accurate, what kind of errors were being made, and what was the probable cause of these errors. In this company's time-reporting system, each workman reported his own time. The findings revealed that the time reported against any job could vary as much as 15 to 20 per cent from actual time without it being detected by the foreman's checking of time cards at the end of the day or by other checks, such as comparing estimated with actual hours, and so forth.

The two most glaring sources of variances were, first, inadvertently charging time to the wrong job and, second, willfully charging time to the wrong job when it was obvious that a given job was running over the estimated hours. There were numerous reasons for this being so, from improper identification of the material being worked on to workmen covering up excessive personal time. In all, some twenty-five sources of error were identified.

REQUIRED:

List four common reasons for inaccuracies in timekeeping by foremen and workmen. What should the accountant learn from the above example?

9-18. Auto Dealership Profit Centers. Many automobile dealers divide their businesses into two major divisions: (a) parts and service and (b) vehicle sales. The gross profit of the parts and service activity is looked upon as the amount which is supposed to "cover" all parts and service overhead plus all general overhead of the dealership. If this goal can be achieved, the gross profit of the vehicle division can be regarded as "gravy"—as net profit. In other words, the contribution margin of the parts and service activity is looked upon as a cost recovery, whereas the vehicle sales are regarded as the profit-making mechanism.

REQUIRED:

Evaluate the merits of this approach. If you were managing an automobile dealership, would you view your operations any differently? How?

9-19. Computation of Gross Profits on Car Sales. Many auto dealers use the "washout" concept. *Washout* is the method for computing gross profits on a series of deals starting with the sale of a new unit and ending with the straight (no trade-in) sale of the last vehicle in the series. The gross profit on the sale of the new unit and used units is totaled and stated in terms of gross profit per new unit retailed.

REQUIRED:

Evaluate the washout concept in terms of assigning responsibility to profit centers. How else could gross profit be computed?

9-20. Possible Causes of Variations. Hower, Inc., determines that the Variable Factory Overhead for the period was as follows:

*Adapted from Sam E. Scharff, "The Industrial Engineer and the Cost Accountant," *N.A.A. Bulletin* (March, 1961), p. 17.

	Dept. A.		Dept. B	
	Actual	Budget	Actual	Budget
Material handling	$5,000	$5,000	$3,000	$3,100
Idle time	510	500	1,510	500
Rework	1,300	900	130	100
Supplies	2,800	3,200	5,000	5,900
	$9,610	$9,600	$9,640	$9,600

In the period, one of the machines in Dept. A developed a twisted cutting tool which was not noted until the machine had been used for some time. This product follows an assembly-line pattern, moving from Dept. A to Dept. B.

REQUIRED:

Explain the possible causes of variations noted above in the light of information given here. Comment on the controllability of the cost elements noted.

9-21. Responsibility of Purchasing Agent.* Richards had just taken a new job as purchasing agent for The Hart Manufacturing Company. Sampson is head of the Production Planning and Control Department. Every six months Sampson gives Richards a general purchasing program. Richards gets specifications from the Engineering Department. He then selects suppliers and negotiates prices.

When he took this job, Richards was informed very clearly that he bore responsibility for meeting the general purchasing program once he accepted it from Sampson.

During Week No. 24, Richards was advised that Part No. 1234—a critical part—would be needed for assembly on Tuesday morning, Week No. 32. He found that the regular supplier could not deliver. He called everywhere, finally found a supplier in the Middle West, and accepted the commitment.

He followed up by mail. Yes, the supplier assured him, the part would be ready. The matter was so important than on Thursday of Week No. 31, he checked by phone. Yes, the shipment had left in time. Richards was reassured and did not check further. But on Tuesday of Week No. 32, the part was not in the warehouse. Inquiry revealed that the shipment had been misdirected by the railroad company and was still in Chicago.

REQUIRED:

What department should bear the costs of time lost in the plant? Why? As purchasing agent, do you think it fair that such costs be charged to your department?

9-22. A Study in Responsibility Accounting. The David Machine Tool Company is in the doldrums. Production volume has fallen to a ten-year low. The company has a nucleus of skilled tool and die men that could find employment elsewhere if they were laid off. Three of these men have been transferred temporarily to the Building and Grounds Department, where they have been doing menial

*Adapted from Raymond Villers, "Control and Freedom in a Decentralized Company," *Harvard Business Review*, Vol. XXXII, No. 2, pp. 89–96.

tasks like sweeping, washing walls, and so on, for the past month. These men have earned their regular rate of $4.40 per hour. Their wages have been charged to the Building and Grounds Department. The supervisor of Building and Grounds has just confronted the controller as follows: "Look at the cockeyed performance report you pencil-pushers have given me. The helpers' line reads:

	Budget	Actual	Deviation	
Wages of helpers	$792	$2,324	$1,532	Unfavorable

"This is just another example of how unrealistic you bookkeepers are! Those tool-and-die guys are loafing on the job because they know we won't lay them off. The regular hourly rate for my three helpers is $1.50. Now that my regular helpers are laid off, my work is piling up, so that when they return they'll either have to put in overtime or I'll have to get part-time help to catch up with things. Instead of charging me at $4.40 per hour, you should charge about $1.00 or $1.20—that's all those tool-and-die slobs are worth at their best."

REQUIRED:

As the controller, what would you do *now*? Would you handle the accounting for these wages any differently?

● **9-23. Budgets and Incentives.** You are working as a supervisor in a manufacturing department which has substantial amounts of men and equipment. You are paid a "base" salary which is actually low for this type of work. The firm has a very liberal bonus plan which pays you another $1,000 each time that you "make the budget" and two per cent of the amount you are able to save.

Your past experiences have been as follows:

Period	1	2	3	4	5	6
Budget	$40,000	$40,000	$39,000	$36,000	$36,000	$36,250
Actual	41,000	39,500	37,000	37,000	36,500	36,000
Variance	$ 1,000 U	$ 500 F	$ 2,000 F	$ 1,000 U	$ 500 U	$ 250 F

REQUIRED:

1. What would you do as a "rational man" if you were starting the job all over again from period 1 with the above information?
2. What would you recommend, if anything, be done to the system if you are now promoted to a higher job in management and required to handle the "bonus system" in this department?

9-24. Cost Savings and Compensation Plans. Amy Deere operates a reducing salon, The Gym Dandy. She used the services of three maintenance men, Sam, Jim, and Bob. Each had charge of a group of exercise and apparatus rooms similar in all regards. Miss Deere offered three methods of payment to the men:

Method A. A flat wage of $1.75 per hour.

Method B. A base rate of $1.50 per hour and 20 per cent of all reduction in expenses below a "norm" of $500 per week.

Method C. No base rate, but a bonus of $100 for meeting the "norm," plus 10 per cent of all reductions in expense below the norm.

Assume a 40-hour week. The men selected their method of compensation before commencing work.

The record for the past six weeks for the three areas follow:

	Weeks					
	1	2	3	4	5	6
Sam:						
Heat and light	150*	150	150	150	150	150
Supplies	100	100	100	100	100	100
Repairs and miscellaneous	250	200	265	220	260	305
Total	500	450	515	470	510	555
Jim:						
Heat and light	150	150	150	150	150	150
Supplies	100	100	100	100	100	100
Repairs and miscellaneous	250	250	250	250	250	250
Total	500	500	500	500	500	500
Bob:						
Heat and light	150	150	150	150	150	150
Supplies	180	20	20	260	100	20
Repairs and miscellaneous	305	250	220	265	260	200
Total	635	420	390	675	510	370

*All figures are in dollars.

REQUIRED:

1. Which payment methods were chosen by Sam, Jim, and Bob? Base your answer on an analysis of cost behavior patterns. Assume that each man chose a different plan.

2. Which method would have been most profitable for a conniving man?

3. If you bought the salon from Miss Deere, what changes would you make in the payment plan? Discuss.

9-25. Objectives of Public Accounting Firm. All personnel, including partners, of public accounting firms usually must turn in biweekly time reports, showing how many hours were devoted to their various duties. These firms traditionally have looked unfavorably on idle or unassigned staff time. They have looked favorably on heavy percentages of chargeable (billable) time because this maximizes revenue. What effect is such a policy likely to have on the behavior of the firm's personnel? Can you relate this practice to the problem of harmony of goals that was discussed in the chapter? How?

9-26. Coordination and Accountants' Attitudes. The problem of coordination is directly affected by the accountants' attitudes. Frederick G. Lesieur, an authority on the Scanlon Plan for labor compensation, has observed:

> . . . In my work, during the past eight years, I've been amazed to find how many accounting groups in companies have become so inflexible that they make very little constructive contribution. Rather than accounting servicing the company, it is often true that the company is servicing the accounting group. Why, even in some of these

situations it seems to make little difference to the accounting people whether the company was losing or making money. This may seem a little harsh, but what I am driving at is that sometimes when suggestions are made to the accounting people that a change in their system or procedure might help the company, you run into a great deal of resistance. The accountants answer: "We've got a perfect accounting system here, and under no conditions do we want to alter it." The fact that making even minor changes in procedures might help the plant was not important. The thing that seemed most important to these accounting people was "don't disturb our setup."

I share Joe Scanlon's conviction that this particular group can make a contribution that is probably unparalleled in the firm. This is the group that has the records for what is taking place in the firm. But, too often, trying to translate that record into something meaningful, which can be understood by the men and women in the plant, seems to be considered almost impossible.*

REQUIRED:

Is Lesieur justified in making these comments? Should the accountant bear all the blame? Why?

9-27.   Nature of Controllable Costs and Responsibility Accounting.
(1) Define *controllable cost*. What two major factors help decide whether a given cost is controllable?
(2) Briefly describe responsibility accounting.
(3) What guides are available to decide what costs may be appropriately charged to a person?

9-28.   Controllable or Uncontrollable Costs.   Refer to Problem 2-27. Indicate by "C" or "U" whether each item is controllable or uncontrollable by a machinery department foreman.

9-29.   Controllable Cost Concepts; Fill in Blanks.   Assume the same organization chart as shown in Exhibit 9-1. For each item listed, indicate by "Yes" or "No" whether it would be classified as a product cost, variable cost, and controllable cost. If you are in doubt about whether an item has strictly variable or strictly fixed cost behavior, decide on the basis of whether the total cost will fluctuate substantially over a wide range of volume.

			Controllable Cost			
	Product Cost	Variable Cost	By Sales Vice President	By Drill Press Foreman	By Production Superintendent	By Manufacturing Vice President
Assembly department— Polishing material	_____	_____	_____	_____	_____	_____
Secretary-Treasurer's salary	_____	_____	_____	_____	_____	_____
Chief inspector's department—Supplies	_____	_____	_____	_____	_____	_____

*Frederick G. Lesieur, "What the Plant Isn't and What It Is," *Scanlon Plan ... A Frontier in Labor-Management Cooperation* (New York: The Technology Press of Massachusetts Institute of Technology and John Wiley & Sons, Inc., 1958), p. 39.

				Controllable Cost	
	Product Cost	Variable Cost	By Sales Vice President	By Drill Press Foreman	By Production Superin-tendent	By Manu-facturing Vice President
Straight-line depreci-ation—Equipment in drill press depart-ment	_____	_____	_____	_____	_____	_____
Salesmen's travel expenses	_____	_____	_____	_____	_____	_____
Drill press department —Direct material	_____	_____	_____	_____	_____	_____

9-30. Change in Product Mix and Control of Labor Performance.*

A study was made of the control over the labor performance in a medium-sized steel manufacturing concern. The primary source of the performance (earned-hour) information in the plant under study was a supervisor's production report prepared in each cost center. Earned hours were calculated by extending and aggregating the total product of each type of output in a day's mix by the appropriate standard. Labor performance was then defined as the ratio of earned hours to actual hours worked.

Daily performance summaries of all cost centers were sent to the plant superintendent, company controller, vice president for operations, vice president for industrial relations, and president. Each of these men had a different concept of what constituted an excessively "high" or "low" performance.

Six months' data were reviewed and analyzed. Several interesting performance variations were noticed. The ill effects of inexperienced crews and summer heat on productivity were clearly revealed. Closer investigation, however, indicated the existence of certain low performance results which could not be readily explained.

Daily performance in each cost center was often found to change substantially without any explainable cause. Assume, for example, that the production during the eight hours of Day 1 was composed of five products, A, B, F, G, and J, and that the standards were relatively more difficult to meet on F and G than for products A, B, and J. A calculation of performance under these circumstances would appear as below:

Product	Mix	Standard Hours Per 1,000 lbs.	Earned Hours
A	600 lbs.	.50	0.3
B	1,000	.70	0.7
F	7,000	.30 (tight)	2.1
G	5,000	.40 (tight)	2.0
J	2,000	1.10	2.2
	15,600 lbs.		7.3
			.6

Delay allowance

$$\text{Labor performance} = \frac{7.9}{8} = 98.75\%.$$

7.9 hours

*Adapted from Trueblood and Cyert, *Sampling Techniques in Accounting* (Englewood Cliffs, N.J.: Prentice-Hall, Inc., 1957), pp. 139–143.

REQUIRED:

1. Compute the labor performance for Day 2. The only change is in the mix:

A	6,600 lbs.
B	5,000
F	1,000
G	1,000
J	2,000
	15,600 lbs.

Why should the performance change solely because of a change in mix?

2. On a particular day, the labor performance of one cost center was reported to be 161 per cent, whereas the very next day's performance dropped to 43 per cent. Assuming no change in mix, what is one very likely cause of this violent fluctuation?

9-31. Case Study: Application of Responsibility Accounting. In early 19x2 the volume of errors submitted to the Mammoth Corporation electronic data-processing center at Center, Illinois, had grown to a degree that the one employee whose task it was to correct the information and follow through on re-submittal to the computer was hard pressed to keep current with his work. Frequently overtime was necessary, and if the volume of errors persisted, an additional employee would have been needed.

It was believed that the volume of errors could be reduced but that the gravity of the matter had not been successfully communicated to the office managers at the various parts depots. A series of letters had been sent attempting to communicate this concern. Also, an attempt at education was made in a letter explaining the probable cause of each of the most frequently occurring errors.

All of these attempts were unsuccessful; errors continued to persist in approximately the same volume as before.

What could be done? (1) The errors could be sent back to the submitting parts depots for correction and re-submittal; (2) efforts could be continued to gain cooperation from the office managers to reduce the number of errors; or (3) an additional employee could be hired to cope with the increased volume of errors. Because (1) and (3) were unattractive, efforts had to be restricted to gaining help from the submitting depots.

REQUIRED:

1. Could responsibility accounting help in solving this difficulty?
2. Explain briefly how this might be done.

the contribution approach: cost allocation, inventory valuation, and pricing

CHAPTER

As organizations become more complex, various responsibility centers arise and multiple products and services are offered inside and outside the organization. One of the toughest duties of the accountant is to devise a convincing scheme for assigning costs to the various parts of an organization for appraisal of performance, product costing, and special decisions. The contribution approach—the approach that emphasizes the analysis of cost behavior patterns—provides the most insights into these matters. We shall see this again and again, especially in this chapter and in Chapters 11 through 13.

CONTRIBUTION APPROACH TO COST ALLOCATION

Objectives of allocation

Allocation means assigning one or more items of cost or revenue to one or more parts of an organization according to benefits received, services utilized, responsibilities, or some other logical method of identification. The term usually implies the subdividing of a lump sum over two or more objects.

To make intelligent decisions, a manager desires information relevant to diverse objectives. He seeks the cost of *something*: a product, a department, a product group, a territory, a division, a process, or a plant. We define this something as a segment, any line of activity or part of an organization for which a separate computation of costs or sales is sought. For example, the passenger division of a railroad is a segment; so is each train; and conceivably each car on the train could be regarded as a segment.

Because segment costs heavily influence decisions, they must be computed wisely. Particular regard must be given to the purpose of the compilation. Among the purposes are: (a) current control: evaluating the performance of a manager, a machine, a territory, a product group; (b) product costing: obtaining costs for inventory valuation and income determination; and (c) special decisions: setting prices, choosing facilities, and making various project decisions such as dropping or adding products, advertising, and selecting distribution channels. The contribution approach provides a general over-all framework suitable for all three purposes because it spotlights the cost behavior patterns and cost-volume-profit relationships that are nearly always essential to evaluating performance and to making decisions.

Exhibit 10-1 demonstrates the contribution approach to cost allocation. This is easily one of the most important exhibits in this book because it provides a sweeping glimpse of a large part of accounting for control. The stress is on cost behavior patterns. Failure to distinguish cost behavior patterns is the biggest roadblock to clarity in cost analysis.

Revenues, variable costs, and contribution margins

The allocation of revenue and of variable costs is usually straightforward, because each item is directly and specifically identifiable with a given segment of activity. The Contribution Margin, Line (1) in Exhibit 10-1, is particularly helpful for estimating the impact on net income of short-run changes in volume. Changes in net income may be quickly calculated by multiplying the change in units by the unit contribution margin or by multiplying the increment in dollar sales by the contribution margin ratio. For example, the contribution margin ratio of Product 1 is $120 \div $300 = 40 per cent. The increase in net income resulting from a $20 increase in sales can be readily computed as .40 × $20, or $8.

The contrast with traditional approach to allocation

As the Problem for Self-Study in Chapter 3 showed, the major difference between the traditional and the contribution approaches is the tendency of the traditional approach to emphasize a functional cost classification as opposed to a classification by cost behaviors. Hence, the traditional income statement would have the following pattern:

Sales	xx
Less manufacturing cost of goods sold (including fixed manufacturing overhead)	xx
Gross profit	xx
Less selling and administrative expenses	xx
Net income before income taxes	xx

EXHIBIT 10-1

THE CONTRIBUTION APPROACH: MODEL INCOME STATEMENT BY SEGMENTS*

(In thousands of dollars)

	Company as a Whole	Company Breakdown Into Two Divisions		Not Allocated	Possible Breakdown of Division B only			
		Division A	Division B		Product 1	Product 2	Product 3	Product 4
Net sales	1,500	500	1,000		300	200	100	400
Variable manufacturing cost of sales	780	200	580		120	155	45	260
Manufacturing contribution margin	720	300	420		180	45	55	140
Variable selling and administrative costs	220	100	120		60	15	25	20
(1) Contribution margin	500	200	300		120	30	30	120
Fixed expenses directly identifiable with divisions:								
Discretionary fixed costs (certain advertising, sales promotion, salesmen's salaries, engineering, research, management consulting, and supervision costs)	190	110	80	45 †	10	6	4	15
(2) Short-run performance margin	310	90	220	(45)	110	24	26	105
Other fixed costs (generally uncontrollable, such as depreciation, property taxes, insurance, and perhaps the division manager's salary)	70	20	50	20	3	15	4	8
(3) Segment margin	240	70	170	(65)	107	9	22	97
Joint fixed costs (not clearly or practically allocable to any segment except by some questionable allocation base)	135							
(4) Net income before taxes	105							

*There are two different types of segments illustrated here: *divisions* and *products*. As you read across, note that the focus becomes narrower: from the company as a whole, to Divisions A and B, to Division B only.

†Only those costs clearly identifiable to a product line should be allocated.

Note that the traditional statement does not show any contribution margin. This raises analytical difficulties in the computation of the impact on net income of changes in sales. Fixed manufacturing overhead, under traditional procedures, is unitized and assigned to products. Hence, unit costs and gross profit figures include irrelevant fixed overhead which must be removed from short-run cost-volume-profit analysis.

The contribution approach stresses the lump-sum amount of fixed costs to be recouped before net income emerges. This highlighting of total fixed costs helps to attract management attention to fixed cost behavior and control when both short-run and long-run plans are being made. Keep in mind that advocates of this contribution approach *do not maintain that fixed costs are unimportant or irrelevant*; but they do stress that the distinctions between behaviors of variable and fixed costs are crucial for certain decisions.

Advantages of contribution margins and ratios

The advantages of knowing the contribution margins and ratios of divisions and product lines may be summarized as follows:

1. *Contribution margin ratios* often help management decide on which products to push and which to de-emphasize or to tolerate only because of the sales benefits which relate to other products.

2. *Contribution margins* are essential for helping management to decide whether or not a product line should be dropped. In the short run, if a product recovers more than its variable costs, it is making a contribution to over-all profits. This information is provided promptly by the contribution approach. Under the traditional approach, the relevant information is not only difficult to gather, but there is a danger that management may be misled by reliance on unit costs, which contain an element of irrelevant fixed overhead.

3. Contribution margins may be used to appraise alternatives which arise with respect to price reductions, special discounts, special advertising campaigns, and the use of premiums to spur sales volume. Decisions such as these are really determined by a comparison of the added costs with the prospective additions in sales revenue. Ordinarily, the higher the contribution margin ratio, the better is the opportunity for sales promotion; the lower the ratio, the greater the increase in volume that is necessary to recover additional sales-promotion commitments.

4. When desired profits are agreed upon, their realism may be quickly appraised by computing the number of units which must be sold to secure the wanted profits. The computation is easily made by dividing the fixed costs plus desired profit by the contribution margin per unit.

5. Decisions must often be made as to how to utilize a given set of resources (for example, machines or materials) most profitably. The contribution approach furnishes the data for a proper decision, because the latter is determined by the product which makes the largest total contribution to profits. (However, the solution to the problem of calculating

the maximum contribution is not always intuitively obvious. This point is amplified in Chapters 13 and 28.)

      6. The contribution approach is helpful where selling prices are firmly established in the industry, because the principal problem for the individual company is how much variable cost is allowable (a matter most heavily affected in many companies by design of products) and how much volume can be obtained.

      7. Pricing will be discussed at greater length later in this chapter. Ultimately, maximum prices are set by customer demand. Minimum short-run prices are ordinarily determined by the variable costs of producing and selling. Advocates of a contribution approach maintain that the compilation of unit costs for products on a contribution basis helps managers understand the relationship between costs, volume, prices, and profits and hence leads to wiser pricing decisions.

Separable costs and joint costs

      A *separable cost* is directly identifiable with a particular segment; a *joint cost* is common to all the segments in question and is not clearly or practically allocable except on some questionable basis. Examples of typical separable costs are advertising, product research and development, sales promotion, specific management consulting, and some supervisory costs. Examples of joint costs are the salaries of the president and other top officers, basic research and development, and some central corporate costs like public relations or corporate image advertising.

      Discretionary and committed costs may be separable or joint, *depending on the segments in question.* For example, a salesman's salary may be easily identified with a particular territory. However, if he is selling a vast number of products, the allocation of his salary among such products is questionable. Consequently, there may be a limit to a given cost's separability in a given income statement. For instance, the Divisions in Exhibit 10-1 could be territorial. The salary of the salesman just described could be readily allocated to Division A or B (a territory), but it could not be allocated convincingly among the products. The point is that a given cost may be joint with respect to one segment of the organization and separable with respect to another.

Performance margin

      What version of income is most appropriate for judging performance by division managers or product managers? The short-run performance margin, keyed as item (2) in Exhibit 10-1, should be helpful, especially when it is interpreted in conjunction with the contribution margin. This is because most top managers can influence certain fixed costs, particularly *discretionary costs.* (Examples of these costs are given in Exhibit 10-1.) The incurrence of discretionary costs may have interacting effects on variable costs. For example, heavier outlays for maintenance, engineering, or management consulting may reduce repairs, increase machine speeds, heighten labor productivity, and so forth. Also, decisions on advertising, research, and sales promotion budgets necessarily are related to expected impacts on sales volumes.

Note at this stage that, although certain discretionary costs may be easily traced to divisions, they may not all be directly traceable to products. Some advertising expenses for Division B may be common to all products, whereas other advertising expenses may be confined to particular products. For example, Products 1, 2, and 3 are consumer items to which common costs apply, while Product 4 is an item sold to manufacturers by a separate sales organization with its own fixed costs.

Segment margin and net income

Segment margin, item (3) in Exhibit 10-1, is computed after deducting the directly identifiable fixed costs, which are generally considered uncontrollable in the short run. Although this figure may be helpful as a crude indicator of long-run segment profitability, it should definitely not influence appraisals of current performance.

Net income before taxes, item (4) in Exhibit 10-1, may sometimes be a helpful gauge of the long-run earning power of a whole company. However, the attempt to refine this ultimate measure by breaking it into segments (and still have the whole equal the sum of the parts) seldom can yield meaningful results.

It is difficult to see how segment performance can be judged on the basis of net income after deductions for a "fair" share of general company costs over which the segment manager exerts no influence. Examples of such costs would be central research and central headquarters costs, including salaries of the president and other high officers. Unless the general company costs are clearly separable, allocation serves no useful purpose and should not be made. Therefore, net income is not computed by segments in Exhibit 10-1.

This refusal to allocate joint costs is the most controversial aspect of the contribution approach to the income statement. Accountants and managers are used to the whole being completely broken down into neat parts that can be added up again to equal the whole. In traditional segment income statements, all costs are fully allocated, so that the segments show final net incomes that can be summed to equal the net income for the company as a whole.

Of course, if for some reason management prefers a whole-equals-the-sum-of-its-parts net income statement, the joint costs may be allocated so that the segments show net income figures that will cross-add to equal the net income for the company as a whole. The important point is that the contribution approach distinguishes between various degrees of objectivity in cost allocations. As you read downward in Exhibit 10-1, you become less and less confident about the validity and accuracy of the cost allocations. A dozen independent accountants will be most likely to agree on how the variable costs should be allocated and least likely to agree on whether and how the joint costs should be allocated.

Reports by product lines and territories

The most widely used detailed operating statements are tabulated by product lines and by sales territories. The emphasis depends on the organization of the marketing function. Some companies have distinct product lines with separate sales forces and separate advertising programs, and their operating reports emphasize contributions by products. Other companies make a multitude of products that are promoted by brand-name advertising and which are all sold by the same salesmen. Their operating reports emphasize territorial or district sales and contributions to profit.

Some guides to allocation

The following general points should guide cost allocations:

1. The fundamental distinctions between cost behavior patterns should be preserved.
2. The exactness of the breakdown in classification by segments depends on the extent of the joint costs and the clerical costs. In general, the greater the detail, the more useful the cost-allocation information. However, there is the corresponding danger—that too much detail encourages inaccurate initial recordkeeping. Costs which are really joint should not be allocated; but attempts to identify them with specific segments should be made before it is decided that the costs in question are really joint costs.

Illustrations of allocations of manufacturing costs will be found in Chapter 17; of nonmanufacturing costs, in Chapter 12.

CONTRIBUTION APPROACH TO INVENTORY VALUATION: DIRECT COSTING

Absorption costing and direct costing

The contribution approach to inventory valuation differs from the traditional approach in only one conceptual respect: fixed manufacturing overhead is excluded from the inventory cost of manufactured products. Chapter 8 demonstrated the traditional approach, whereby fixed manufacturing overhead was unitized and became absorbed as a cost of product along with the variable manufacturing overhead.

Before continuing let us consider some new terminology. There are two opposing ideas, commonly labeled as *absorption costing* and *direct costing*. Absorption costing (the traditional approach) signifies that fixed factory overhead is inventoried. In contrast, direct costing signifies that fixed factory overhead is not inventoried. These terms may be coupled with either of the two product-costing systems you have learned in this book: normal costing and standard costing, depending solely on whether a particular system inventories fixed overhead:

1. *Normal absorption costing.* Includes actual prime costs (direct material and direct labor) plus predetermined variable and fixed manufacturing overhead.
2. *Normal direct costing.* Includes actual prime costs plus predetermined variable manufacturing overhead; excludes fixed manufacturing overhead.
3. *Standard direct costing.* Includes predetermined prime costs plus predetermined variable manufacturing overhead; excludes fixed manufacturing overhead.
4. *Standard absorption costing.* Includes predetermined prime costs plus predetermined variable and fixed overhead.

Absorption costing is much more widely used than direct costing, although the growing use of the contribution approach in performance measurement and cost analysis has led to increasing use of direct costing.

Direct costing is more accurately called variable or marginal costing, because in substance it applies only the *variable* production costs to the cost of the product. Direct costing has a different impact on net income from absorption costing because fixed manufacturing is regarded as a period cost (charged against revenue immediately) rather than as a product cost (assigned to units produced).

Direct costing has been a controversial subject among accountants —not so much because there is disagreement about the need for delineating between variable and fixed cost behavior patterns for management planning and control, but because there is a question about its theoretical propriety for external reporting. Proponents of direct costing maintain that the fixed part of factory overhead is more closely related to the *capacity* to produce than to the production of specific units. Opponents of direct costing maintain that inventories should carry a fixed-cost component because both variable and fixed costs are necessary to produce goods; both these costs should be inventoriable regardless of their differences in behavior patterns. Neither the public accounting profession nor the Internal Revenue Service has approved of direct costing as a generally acceptable method of inventory valuation.

The notion of direct costing blends easily with the contribution margin approach advocated in this text. Exhibit 10-2 illustrates the principal differences between direct costing and absorption costing. Note the following points about the exhibit:

1. Under absorption costing, fixed production costs are applied to the product, to be subsequently released to expense as a part of Cost of Goods Sold. Under direct costing, fixed production costs are regarded as period costs and are immediately released to expense along with the selling and administrative expenses.
2. Under direct costing, only the variable manufacturing costs are re-

EXHIBIT 10-2

COMPARISON OF ABSORPTION AND DIRECT COSTING

(Date assumed; there is no beginning inventory; the unit *variable* manufacturing cost is $6.00.)

B COMPANY
Income Statements
For the Year Ending Dec. 31, 19x1

Absorption Costing

	Unit cost			
Sales, 1,000 units @ $10.00				$10,000
Cost of goods sold:				
Variable manufacturing costs:				
1,100 units	$6.00	$6,600		
Fixed manufacturing costs	2.00	2,200		
Cost of goods available for sale	$8.00	$8,800		
Less ending inventory:				
(100 units)	8.00	800		
			8,000	
Gross margin				$ 2,000
Less total selling and administrative expenses, including $400 of variable expenses				900
Net income				$ 1,100*

Direct Costing

Sales		$10,000
Variable manufacturing costs of goods produced	$6,600	
Less ending inventory:		
100 units @ $6.00	600	
Variable manufacturing cost of goods sold	$6,000	
Add variable selling and administrative expenses	400	
Total variable costs charged against sales		6,400
Contribution margin		$ 3,600
Less fixed costs:		
Fixed manufacturing costs	$2,200	
Fixed selling and administrative expenses	500	
		2,700
Net income		$ 900*

*The $200 difference in net income is caused by the $200 ($800 − $600) difference in ending inventories. Under absorption costing, $200 of the $2,200 fixed manufacturing costs is held back in inventory; whereas under direct costing, the $200 is released immediately as a charge against sales.

garded as product costs. Variability with manufacturing volume is the criterion used for the classification of costs into product or period categories.

3. In direct costing, the *contribution margin*—the excess of sales over variable costs—is a highlight of the income statement. Other terms for *contribution margin* include *marginal income, marginal balance, profit contribution,* and *contribution to fixed costs*.

4. The absorption costing statement in Exhibit 10-2 differentiates between the variable and fixed costs only to aid your comparison. Costs are seldom classified as fixed or variable in absorption costing statements, although such a classification is possible. Managers who are accustomed to looking at operations from a breakeven-analysis and flexible-budget viewpoint find that the absorption income statement fails to dovetail with cost-volume-profit relationships. They are then forced to take time for an attempt to reconcile and interpret two or more sets of figures which portray a single operating situation. Direct-costing proponents say that it is more efficient to present important cost-volume-profit relationships as integral parts of the major financial statements.

5. If inventories increase during a period, the direct costing method will generally report less net income than absorption costing; when inventories decrease, direct costing will report more net income than absorption costing. The differences in net income, as the note at the bottom of Exhibit 10-2 indicates, are due *solely* to the difference in accounting for *fixed* manufacturing costs.

Whether direct costing should be acceptable for external reporting need not be of paramount importance to accountants or managers. Company systems can accommodate either method; the important point is that the internal reports should use the contribution approach, which incorporates direct costing and which is the best available technique for evaluation and control.

The central issue: a question of timing

Nearly all accountants agree that distinctions between variable and fixed costs are helpful for a wide variety of managerial decisions. The conventional view recognizes this need, but takes the position that such information may be supplied without changing the conventional methods of income determination. Adherents of direct costing maintain that the importance of variable and fixed cost behavior should be spotlighted not only by changing the format of the financial statements but also by changing the basic principles or concepts whereby fixed factory overhead is written off in the period incurred rather than funneled into inventory as an integral part of inventory costs. Thus, the central question becomes, What is the proper *timing* for release of fixed factory overhead as expense: at the time of incurrence, or at the time that the finished units to which the fixed overhead relates are sold? The focus must be upon relating fixed overhead to the definition of an asset. Appendix B to this chapter discusses this conceptual issue in more detail.

Comparison of income figures

Exhibit 10-3 leads to the following generalizations about the comparative effects on net income of direct and absorption costing:[1]

1. When sales and production are in balance, direct and absorption costing methods yield the same profit. Under both methods, the amount of fixed cost incurred during the period is charged against revenue of the period. (See the first year in Exhibit 10-3.)

2. When production exceeds sales (that is, when in-process and finished inventories are increasing), absorption costing shows a higher profit than does direct costing. The reason is that, by absorption costing, a portion of the fixed manufacturing cost of the period is charged to inventory and thereby deferred to future periods. The total fixed cost charged against revenue of the period, therefore, is less than the amount of fixed cost incurred during the period. (See second year in Exhibit 10-3.)

3. When sales exceed production (that is, when in-process and finished inventories are decreasing), absorption costing shows a lower profit than does direct costing. Under absorption costing, fixed costs previously deferred in inventory are charged against revenue in the period in which the goods are sold. Total fixed costs charged against revenue, therefore, exceed the amount of fixed cost incurred during the period. (See the third and fourth years in Exhibit 10-3.)

4. When sales volume is constant but production volume fluctuates, direct costing yields a constant profit figure, because profit is not affected by inventory changes. Under the same circumstances, absorption costing yields a fluctuating profit figure, which will be directly affected by the direction and amount of the *changes* in inventories. (See the third and fourth years in Exhibit 10-3.)

5. If production volume is constant, profit moves in harmony with sales under either direct or absorption costing. The profit figures will move in the same direction but will not necessarily be the same in amount because inventory costs that are carried over from period to period will be greater under absorption costing. (See the first and fourth years in Exhibit 10-3.)

6. The divergence between periodic profit figures computed by direct and absorption costing methods tends to be smaller for long periods than for short periods, because differences between production and sales volume tend to approach equality over a long period. Thus, the difference between total profit figures computed by the two methods is usually smaller for a few years (taken together) than the difference between year-to-year profit figures. Over a period of years, the methods should give substantially the same result, because sales cannot continuously exceed production, nor can production continuously exceed sales.

---

[1]"Direct Costing." *N.A.A. Research Report No. 23, N.A.(C.)A. Bulletin* (April, 1953), p. 1116. Adapted. Also see Yuji Ijiri, Robert K. Jaedicke, and John L. Livingstone, "The Effect of Inventory Costing Methods on Full and Direct Costing," *Journal of Accounting Research* (Spring, 1965).

EXHIBIT 10-3

COMPARISON OF DIRECT COSTING AND ABSORPTION COSTING—
ANNUAL STATEMENTS

Basic production data at standard cost:

Direct material	$1.30
Direct labor	1.50
Variable overhead	.20
Fixed overhead ($150,000 ÷ 150,000 unit normal volume equals $1.00)	1.00
Total	$4.00

Sales price, $5.00 per unit.

Selling and administrative expense, assumed for simplicity as being all fixed, $100,000 per year.

	First Year	Second Year	Third Year	Fourth Year	Four Years Together
Opening inventory in units	—	—	30,000	10,000	—
Production	150,000	170,000	140,000	150,000	610,000
Sales	150,000	140,000	160,000	160,000	610,000
Closing inventory in units	—	30,000	10,000	—	—
Direct costing:					
Sales	$750,000	$700,000	$800,000	$800,000	$3,050,000
Cost of goods manufactured	$450,000	$510,000	$420,000	$450,000	$1,830,000
Add opening inventory	—	—	90,000	30,000	—
Available for sale	$450,000	$510,000	$510,000	$480,000	$1,830,000
Deduct ending inventory	—	90,000	30,000	—	—
Cost of goods sold	$450,000	$420,000	$480,000	$480,000	$1,830,000
Contribution margin	$300,000	$280,000	$320,000	$320,000	$1,220,000
Fixed factory overhead	150,000	150,000	150,000	150,000	600,000
Selling and administrative expense	100,000	100,000	100,000	100,000	400,000
Net operating income	$ 50,000	$ 30,000	$ 70,000	$ 70,000	$ 220,000
Absorption costing:					
Sales	$750,000	$700,000	$800,000	$800,000	$3,050,000
Cost of goods manufactured	$600,000	$680,000	$560,000	$600,000	$2,440,000
Add opening inventory	—	—	120,000	40,000	—
Available for sale	$600,000	$680,000	$680,000	$640,000	$2,440,000
Deduct ending inventory	—	120,000	40,000	—	—
Cost of goods sold	$600,000	$560,000	$640,000	$640,000	$2,440,000
Under- or (over-) applied overhead*	—	(20,000)	10,000	—	(10,000)
Adjusted cost of goods sold	$600,000	$540,000	$650,000	$640,000	$2,430,000
Gross margin	$150,000	$160,000	$150,000	$160,000	$ 620,000
Selling and administrative expense	100,000	100,000	100,000	100,000	400,000
Net operating income	$ 50,000	$ 60,000	$ 50,000	$ 60,000	$ 220,000

*Computation of under- or over-applied overhead based on normal volume of 150,000 units:

Second year	$20,000 over-applied: (170,000 − 150,000) × $1.00
Third year	10,000 under-applied: (150,000 − 140,000) × $1.00
Four years together	$10,000 over-applied: (610,000 − 600,000) × $1.00

Direct costing excludes fixed factory overhead from inventory. In formula form, the difference between net incomes of absorption and direct costing may be shown as follows:

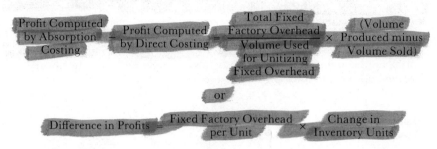

$$\begin{array}{c}\text{Profit Computed}\\\text{by Absorption}\\\text{Costing}\end{array} - \begin{array}{c}\text{Profit Computed}\\\text{by Direct Costing}\end{array} = \dfrac{\begin{array}{c}\text{Total Fixed}\\\text{Factory Overhead}\end{array}}{\begin{array}{c}\text{Volume Used}\\\text{for Unitizing}\\\text{Fixed Overhead}\end{array}} \times \begin{array}{c}\text{(Volume}\\\text{Produced minus}\\\text{Volume Sold)}\end{array}$$

or

$$\text{Difference in Profits} = \dfrac{\text{Fixed Factory Overhead}}{\text{per Unit}} \times \begin{array}{c}\text{Change in}\\\text{Inventory Units}\end{array}$$

Application of the above formula to Exhibit 10-3 is shown as follows:

	Years				Four Years
	1	2	3	4	Together
Direct cost profit	$50,000	$ 30,000	$70,000	$70,000	$220,000
Absorption cost profit	50,000	60,000	50,000	60,000	220,000
Difference	—	$(30,000)	$20,000	$10,000	—
Change in inventory in units (increase)	—	(30,000)	20,000	10,000	—
Multiply by $1.00.					
Change in amount of fixed cost in inventory*	—	$(30,000)	$20,000	$10,000	—

*Change in units × fixed overhead rate of $1.00.

Note carefully that the difference in profits does not consist merely of the volume variance computed under absorption costing. This difference is related to the change in inventory position; and this change is independent of a given volume variance.

Absorption costing is far from being uniform in its application. There are different inventory methods, such as first-in, first-out; last-in, first-out; and weighted-average. There are different assumptions as to overhead application, such as the inclusion of some administrative costs in inventory and the classification of packaging costs. These problems remain, whether direct costing or absorption costing is used. The issue thus narrows to the propriety of excluding fixed costs from inventory.

CONTRIBUTION APPROACH TO PRICING

Superiority of the contribution approach

When used intelligently, the contribution approach has distinct advantages over the absorption costing approach to guiding a pricing decision.

First, the contribution approach offers more detailed information than the absorption costing approach, because variable and fixed cost behavior patterns are delineated. Because the contribution approach is sensitive to cost-volume-profit relationships, it is a better, easier basis for developing pricing formulas.

Second, a "normal" or "target" pricing formula can be as easily developed under the contribution approach as under absorption costing. For example, assume that a company has a budget for 19x2; the absorption costing approach follows (figures assumed):

Sales	$100,000	100%
Factory cost of goods sold, including $20,000 fixed costs	60,000	60
Gross profit	$ 40,000	40%
Operating expenses, including $20,000 fixed costs	30,000	30
Net income target	$ 10,000	10%

Normal or target mark-up percentage:
$40,000 ÷ $60,000 = 66.7% of absorption cost.

The contribution approach would appear as follows:

Sales		$100,000	100%
Variable factory cost of goods sold	$40,000		
Variable selling and administrative costs	10,000	50,000	50
Contribution margin		$ 50,000	50%
Fixed costs:			
Factory costs	$20,000		
Selling and administrative costs	20,000	40,000	40
Net income		$ 10,000	10%

Normal or target mark-up percentage:
$50,000 ÷ $50,000 = 100%
of total variable costs.

Under *either* approach, the pricing decision maker will have a formula that will lead him toward the *same* target price. If he is unable to obtain such a price consistently, the company will not achieve its $10,000 net income objective.

Third, the contribution approach offers insight into short-run versus long-run effects of cutting prices on special orders. For example, assume the same cost behavior patterns as above. Assume further that a customer offers $540 for some units that have a factory cost of goods manufactured of $600 and total variable costs of $500. Should the offer be accepted? No categorical answer can be given, but more information for guidance can be generated by the contribution approach:

	Absorption Costing	Contribution Approach
Sales price	$540	$540
Factory cost of goods sold	600	
Variable costs, including selling and administrative expenses		500
Loss before deducting operating expenses	$-60	
Contribution margin		$ 40

Compare the two approaches. Under absorption costing, the decision maker has no direct knowledge of cost-volume-profit relationships. He makes his decision by hunch. On the surface, the offer is definitely unattractive because the price of $540 is $60 "below our factory costs."

Under the contribution approach, the decision maker sees a *short-run* advantage of $40 in accepting the offer. That is, net income will increase by $40 because fixed costs will be unaffected by whatever decision is made. Still, there are long-run effects to consider. Will acceptance of the offer undermine the long-run price structure in the industry? In other words, is the short-run advantage of $40 more than offset by a high probability of long-run financial disadvantages? The decision maker may think so and may reject the offer. But—and this is important—by doing so he is in effect saying that he is willing to forego $40 now in order to protect his long-run market advantages. In other words, he is *investing* $40 now because he thinks it will maximize long-run benefits. Generally, he can weigh such decisions by asking whether the expected long-run benefits are worth a present investment equal to the contribution margin ($40 in this case). Under absorption costing, he has no built-in technique that will quantify the foregone contribution.

The contribution approach or absorption costing?

A major criticism leveled at the contribution approach is that it will result in underpricing and ultimate company disaster. Such a criticism implies that full manufacturing cost is a safer guide because it does not ignore fixed factory overhead and will therefore lead to better long-run pricing decisions.

There are at least four basic weaknesses in the above argument. First, full manufacturing cost also ignores some costs: the selling and administrative costs, which are often substantial. Under absorption costing, pricing decisions are often guided by unit gross profit rather than by unit net profit.[2] Second, even when absorption costing is used, there is no single unit cost that may be used as a guide as long as volume is a variable. Third, cost accountants and businessmen give excessive emphasis to

[2] *N.A.A. Research Report No. 37, Current Application of Direct Costing* (January, 1961), p. 43.

costs as a guide to pricing. That is, they say and perhaps think that costs influence pricing decisions, but their actions show that *customer demand* and *competitor behavior* greatly overshadow costs as price-influencing factors.[3] Fourth, an N.A.A. survey (*Report No. 37*, p. 55) of 38 companies which use direct costing reported:

> *No instance of unprofitable pricing attributable to direct costing was reported but, on the contrary, opinion was frequently expressed to the effect that direct costing had contributed to better pricing decisions. However, companies restrict product cost and margin data to individuals qualified to interpret such data and responsible for pricing policy decisions.*

Our general theme of different costs for different purposes also extends into the area of pricing. To say that the contribution approach or absorption costing provides the best guide to pricing decisions is a dangerous oversimplification of one of the most perplexing problems in business. Lack of understanding and judgment can lead to unprofitable pricing regardless of the kind of cost data available or cost accounting system used.

Relating fixed costs to pricing decisions

The general relationship of prices to fixed (period) costs is complicated by the jointness of many fixed manufacturing, selling, and administrative costs. Many of these costs have only obscure relationships to various segments. In pricing, it is useful to view the ability of individual divisions, products, departments, and so forth, to contribute to the common pool of fixed costs. *N.A.A. Research Report No. 37* pointed out (pp. 42–43):

> *The ability to contribute on the part of individual segments is determined by market demand and does not necessarily correspond with the benefits received from common cost factors as measured by the bases which the accountant uses to allocate period costs . . . .*
>
> *The characteristics of period [fixed] costs . . . make it particularly important for management to have cost and income margin data which show clearly the consequences of proposed pricing decisions. Regardless of the plan of accounting used, there seems to be need for distinction between direct and period costs wherever pricing alternatives . . . involve differing volumes of production and sales.*

To summarize, the data organized in the manner shown in Exhibits 10-1 and 10-4 will be more informative and useful for pricing than the conventional data that commonly fail to distinguish between variable and fixed costs. Where feasible, there is much merit in dividing fixed costs between those clearly applicable to the segment (say, a product) and those whose application base has low reliability.

[3]For an expanded discussion, see the appendix to this chapter.

Need for clear information

Pricing decisions almost inevitably have long-run implications and thus require acute ability for proper weighting of short-run and long-run impacts. Because of the bewildering number of influencing factors, many managers are content with "satisfactory" returns rather than "maximum" returns—primarily because they are rarely sure of what the latter amounts may be. The contribution-margin approach will help clarify some factors that are not easily brought out by the conventional approach. *N.A.A. Research Report No. 37* (page 55) cited the following cases which took place before the contribution approach was adopted:

> *Instances were cited in which management had unknowingly continued selling products below out-of-pocket cost or had decided to withdraw from the market when a substantial portion of the period costs could have been recovered . . . .*
> *In one interview . . . when direct costing was introduced, analysis demonstrated that contracts which would have contributed to period costs had often been refused at times when the company had a large amount of idle capacity.*

SUMMARY

Whether direct costing ever becomes acceptable for external reporting need not influence the major point of this chapter, which is that no single version of inventory cost or income will be a valid guide to interpretation and action under all circumstances. We need different cost constructions and different income concepts for different purposes. We need a contribution approach, the approach that emphasizes the analysis of cost behavior patterns. As a minimum, the income statement should be designed to facilitate its possible use for multiple purposes. Exhibit 10-1 contains an example of the contribution approach—the direction which future income statements will probably take to facilitate performance measurement and to guide pricing and other decisions.

The contribution approach to pricing offers more helpful information than the absorption-costing approach, mainly because it quantifies the present investment needed (the foregone contribution) to protect long-run benefits.

SUGGESTED READINGS

Various issues of *Management Accounting* (formerly called the *N.A.A. Bulletin*) are permeated with articles on direct costing and the contribution approach. *N.A.A. Research Reports Nos. 23, 24,* and *37* are informative.

The Blazek Company had the following operating characteristics in 19x4 and 19x5:

Basic production data at standard cost:

Direct material	$1.30
Direct labor	1.50
Variable overhead	.20
Fixed overhead ($150,000 ÷ 150,000 units of normal volume = $1.00)	1.00
Total factory cost at standard	$4.00

Sales price, $5.00 per unit.

Selling and administrative expense is assumed for simplicity as being all fixed at $65,000 yearly except for sales commissions at 5% of dollar sales.

	19x4	19x5
In units:		
Opening inventory	—	30,000
Production	170,000	140,000
Sales	140,000	160,000
Closing inventory	30,000	10,000

There were no variances from the standard variable costs. Any under- or over-applied overhead is written off directly at year end as an adjustment to Cost of Goods Sold.

REQUIRED:

1. Income statements for 19x4 and 19x5 under direct costing and absorption costing.

2. A reconciliation of the difference in net income for 19x4, 19x5, and the two years as a whole.

3. In 19x4 a Blazek Company salesman had asked the president for permission to sell 1,000 units to a particular customer for $3.80 per unit. The president refused, stating that the price was below factory cost. Based solely on the information given, compute the effect of the president's decision on 19x4 net income. Specifically, what would be the reasoning of the contribution approach to such a decision?

1.

BLAZEK COMPANY
Comparative Income Statements (in thousands of dollars)
For the Years 19x4 and 19x5

		19x4	19x5
Direct Costing:			
Sales	(1)	700	800
Opening inventory—at variable standard cost		—	90
Add variable cost of goods manufactured		510	420
Available for sale		510	510
Deduct ending inventory		90	30
Variable cost of goods sold		420	480
Variable selling expenses—at 5% of dollar sales		35	40
Total variable expenses	(2)	455	520
Contribution margin	(3) = (1) − (2)	245	280
Fixed factory overhead		150	150
Fixed selling and administrative expenses		65	65
Total fixed expenses	(4)	215	215
Net income	(3) − (4)	30	65
Absorption Costing:			
Sales		700	800
Opening inventory—at standard absorption cost		—	120
Cost of goods manufactured		680	560
Available for sale		680	680
Deduct ending inventory		120	40
Cost of goods sold—at standard		560	640
Under- or (over-) applied overhead*		(20)	10
Adjusted cost of goods sold		540	650
Gross margin		160	150
Selling and administrative expenses		100	105
Net income		60	45

*Computation of under- or over-applied overhead based on normal volume of 150,000 units:

19x4	$20,000 over-applied (170,000 − 150,000) × $1.00
19x5	10,000 under-applied (150,000 − 140,000) × $1.00
Two years together	$10,000 over-applied (310,000 − 300,000) × $1.00

2. Reconciliation of differences in net income:

	19x4	19x5	Together
Net income under:			
Direct costing	$ 30,000	$65,000	$ 95,000
Absorption costing	60,000	45,000	105,000
Difference to be explained	$ −30,000	$20,000	$ −10,000
The difference can be reconciled by multiplying the fixed overhead rate times the *change* in the total inventory units:			
Fixed overhead rate	$1.00	$1.00	$1.00
Change in inventory units:			
Beginning inventory	—	30,000	—
Ending inventory	30,000	10,000	10,000
Change	30,000	20,000	10,000
Difference in net income explained	$ −30,000	$20,000	$ −10,000

3. The refusal of the order diminished net income by the amount of the lost contribution margin, the contribution foregone because the sales price of $3.80 exceeds the relevant unit cost of $3.19:

Sales, 1,000 units × $3.80		$3,800
Variable manufacturing costs, 1,000 units × $3.00	$3,000	
Variable selling expenses, 5% of $3.80, or $.19 per unit. 1,000 units × $.19	190	
Total variable costs		3,190
Contribution margin		$ 610

The contribution approach would reason as follows. By not accepting the order, short-run profits will be $610 lower. Therefore, the $610 foregone represents the amount Blazek Company is willing to invest now to preserve an orderly long-run price structure.

The fact that the $3.80 selling price is less than the $4.00 absorption factory cost is not relevant to this decision. Note that taking business at $.20 below factory cost will nevertheless enhance net income by $610, or $.61 per unit.

APPENDIX A: COST-PLUS FOR SETTING PRICES

Major influences on pricing

Professional economists, self-styled economists, and businessmen have been arguing for centuries about the cause-and-effect relationships between costs and prices. The problems here are intricate because of the interplay of long-run and short-run factors.

Many businessmen maintain that they use cost-plus pricing. They say that they figure their average unit costs and tack on a "fair" margin that will yield an adequate return on investment. This entails circular reasoning, because price, which influences sales, depends upon full cost, which in turn is partly determined by the *volume* of sales. Also, this "plus" in cost-plus is bothersome. It is rarely a rigid "plus." Instead, it is flexible, depending on the behavior of competitors and customers. There are at least three major influences on pricing decisions: customers, competitors, and costs.

Customers

The businessman must always examine his pricing problems through the eyes of his customers. He cannot level a shotgun at his customers and say, "Buy, or else." Customers can reject a company's product and turn to competitors' products or, perhaps, to a completely different industry for a substitute product. When coffee prices are high, many people drink one cup instead of two; others switch to tea. If a company's prices get too high, the immediate reaction of the customer is to check with competitors, who gleefully greet such inquiries. Perhaps the customer makes its own product or tries to find whether a different product will serve just as well (aluminum instead of copper). For example, buyers of welding equipment are often most heavily influenced by the way the product affects their costs. The buyer not only has alternate sources of supply within the welding equipment industry; he may not buy at all, but may keep using his existing equipment. He may substitute some other kind of equipment to accomplish his tasks; or he may manufacture the needed equipment himself.

Competitors

Rivals' reactions or lack of reactions will influence pricing decisions. In guessing a competitor's reactions, one must speculate on what the competitor's costs are, rather than be concerned with his own costs. Of course, one's own costs may be helpful in guessing, but it is the rival's costs that are relevant. Knowledge of the rival's technology, plant size, and operating policies help sharpen estimates of his costs. Companies within industries which loathe price competition have been known to swap detailed cost information for mutual benefit. Where there is no collusion, rivals' reactions and price quotations must be guessed when pricing decisions are made.

Costs

The maximum price that may be charged is the one that does not drive the customer away. The minimum price is zero. Companies occasionally will give or virtually give their products away in order to get entrenched in a market or to obtain a profitable long-run relationship with a customer. A more practical guide is gleaned from our study of cost-volume-profit relationships. In the short run, the minimum price to be quoted should be the variable costs of accepting the order or segment of available business. Any amount in excess of those variable costs directly increases net income.

Where a company has some discretion in price setting, customer demand at various price levels determines the sales volume. In these situations, study must be given to differential cost-volume-profit relationships; in turn, these relationships are dependent on market conditions, elasticity of industry demand, concentration of capacity, and rivals' reactions.

Where a company has little discretion, it accepts the price that competition has set. Then, under given economic conditions, the company ordinarily selects the level of production and sales which maximizes profits.

Example of contribution approach to pricing

Exhibit 10-4 shows an actual price-quote format used by the president and sales manager of a small job shop that bids on special machinery orders under highly competitive conditions. This approach is a tool for flexible pricing. Note that the maximum price is not a matter of cost at all; the minimum price is set by the total variable costs.

Note also, in Exhibit 10-4, that the costs are classified and tailored especially for the pricing task. Pricing duties may be in the hands of a number of different executives. Often it is a joint effort on the part of the sales manager, production manager, and general manager, with the latter

EXHIBIT 10-4

QUOTE SHEET
(Data Assumed)

Direct materials (materials only, at cost)		$25,000
Direct labor and variable overhead (direct labor hours × $3.50)		
	3,000 hrs × $3.50 =	10,500
Commission (varies with job)		3,000
Total variable costs—Minimum Price		$38,500
Add fixed costs applied (direct labor hours × $4.75)		
	3,000 hrs × $4.75 =	14,250
Total costs (including share of fixed costs)		$52,750
Add desired profit		9,250
Selling Price (What you think you can get—Maximum Price)		$62,000

The quote sheet above shows two prices, maximum and minimum. Any amount you can get over the minimum price is a contribution margin.

having the final authority. The accountant's task is to supply a format that is understandable and that involves a minimum of computations. That is why direct labor and variable overhead are lumped together in one over-all rate; all fixed costs, whether factory, engineering, selling, or administrative, are lumped together for the same reason.

Practically, when a new pricing format such as the one in Exhibit 10-4 is introduced, the ideas, forms, and procedures must be patiently sold to the pricing decision makers. Unless they wholeheartedly accept a new pricing approach, they will soon return to doing things the rough-and-ready old way. The old way too often is some version of a full-cost combination plus a "decent" margin. Such a pricing procedure is not only irrelevant, but it offers no measure of possible leeway on price quotations. It is seat-of-the-pants decision making of the worst sort.

Many managers take pride in pointing out that they only accept orders at "decent" prices, prices that promise a full cost (whatever magic figure that is) recovery plus a "fair" profit. The methodology outlined in Exhibit 10-4 is a pricing tool that helps management when they face intensive competition and crafty buyers. Inflexible pricing is a luxury that many companies cannot enjoy because customers are wise, competition is hot, and fixed costs are heavy.

As mentioned earlier, in order to survive, a company must ultimately and systematically recoup all costs. It must have some notion of a target or normal mark-up percentage. Although there are certain pricing situations where prices are set to recover only variable costs plus some margin as a contribution to the recovery of fixed costs, a consistent pricing policy which ignores fixed costs is suicide. The interplay of various types of costs and their bearing on profit-making are extremely important factors in management.

Where costs have a heavy bearing on prices, the resulting prices almost always are "target" prices which are subject to "modification." Costs can be especially helpful in competitive bidding situations in the sense that they may be the best available base for judging what the *competitors'* costs may be. Then, using knowledge of competitors' past behavior and pricing policies, the company's own pricing decisions can be formulated.[4]

In summary, the "plus" in cost-plus really should reflect what the long-run market will bear. Management would probably look to recent average returns of companies that are comparable in products, processes, and risks. The measure of competitive return that is allowable in the industry without loss of market share or invasion of markets often looms large in decision making. Finally, management cannot neglect the eyes of the union leaders and the antitrusters.

---

[4]Tools of operations research, using probability theory, may be pertinent to competitive bidding situations. For an excellent description, see Miller and Starr, *Executive Decisions and Operations Research* (Englewood Cliffs, N.J.: Prentice-Hall, Inc., 1960), pp. 223–238.

APPENDIX B: CONTROVERSY CONCERNING INCOME MEASUREMENT

Timing and definition of asset

The difference between variable (direct) and absorption costing is essentially one of timing. Proponents of absorption costing contend that fixed factory overhead costs reflect assets until the goods to which they are related are sold. Thus, the issue lies in the definition of an asset.

According to the most widely accepted definition, costs are assets if they can justifiably be carried forward to the future, if they bear revenue-producing power, if they are beneficial to future operations—if they possess service potential. Thus, the justification for treating fixed factory overhead as an asset must meet the test of service potential. The issue becomes one of service potential versus no service potential.

Absorption costers maintain that if fixed costs measure the utilization of services in the manufacture of a product, the finished good should bear a pro-rata share of these fixed costs. *The rule is that a cost which is necessary for a class of physical product must be allocated to each member of that class.* For example, the cost of a machine is obviously a part of the cost of the *total output* of that machine. Absorption costers have decided that generally what is relevant to the whole must be relevant also to each part. Therefore, they have unitized such fixed costs and assigned them to units of output.

Proponents of variable (direct) costing have adopted a totally different and conflicting rule: *a cost is relevant to (and allocable to) a unit of product if, and only if, the cost varies with the number of units produced.*

Variable-cost proponents maintain that *a cost has service potential, in the traditional accounting sense, if its incurrence now will result in future cost avoidance in the ordinary course of business.* In other words, assets (unexpired costs) ordinarily represent costs whose reincurrence is unnecessary in the future. If future cost incurrence will be unaffected by the cost in question, the cost has no relevance to future events and therefore cannot represent any benefit, any future service.

Assets and variable factory costs

In normal circumstances, direct costers and absorption costers agree that direct materials, direct labor, and variable factory overhead costs are assets. A decision to incur them in one period will reduce total future costs. Their absence would necessitate replacement expenditures to sustain normal operations as a going concern.

Assets and fixed factory overhead

Proponents of absorption costing imply that income is greater when production exceeds sales than when production is at the same level as sales, because fixed facilities are better utilized and render more benefit in the form of inventories that will bring future revenue. A portion of the fixed manufacturing cost of the period is charged to inventory and thereby deferred to future periods.

Proponents of variable costing maintain that fixed factory overhead provides capacity to produce. Whether that capacity is used to the fullest extent or not used at all is usually irrelevant insofar as the expiration of fixed costs is concerned. The salient factor is that production in advance of sale usually does not avoid any fixed factory overhead costs in future periods. The incurrence of fixed costs in a current period ordinarily has no bearing on the reincurrence of the same kind of fixed costs next period. As the clock ticks, fixed costs expire, to be replenished by new bundles of fixed costs that will enable production to continue in succeeding periods.

Relevant costing: a third approach

Relevant costing is a third approach to the accounting for fixed manufacturing overhead. The relevant-costing rule is: *any cost is carried forward as an asset if, and only if, it has a favorable economic effect on expected future cost or future revenues*.[5] Expressed another way, if the total expected future costs or revenue will be changed favorably because of the presence of a given cost, that cost is relevant to the future and is an asset; if not, that cost is irrelevant and is expired.

Any one of the following assumptions about the future would justify the inventorying of fixed factory overhead.

Assumption I: Future sales will be lost forever because of lack of inventory. That is, the absence of inventory at a certain place at a certain time will result in a permanent loss of some sales.[6]

Assumption 2: Variable production costs are expected to increase. The decision to produce now will save variable production costs amounting to the difference between incurred and expected variable costs. This difference may justifiably be capitalized. In other words, increased present utilization of fixed factors of production will result in future cost savings. But note that the savings in question are variable, not fixed, costs. This really involves capitalizing future variable cost savings, not a portion of fixed costs. Also, the capitalization of speculative future savings is far from being compatible with existing accounting practice.

Assumption 3: Future production at maximum capacity with future sales in excess of capacity by the amount of increase in ending inventory. If and when this joyful situation prevails (it ordinarily will not last long for the typical business), the utilization of the fixed factors to

---

[5]George H. Sorter and Charles T. Horngren, "Asset Recognition and Economic Attributes—The Relevant Costing Approach," *Accounting Review* (July, 1962), p. 393.
[6]For an expanded discussion, see Charles T. Horngren and George H. Sorter, "Direct Costing for External Reporting," *Accounting Review* (January, 1961), pp. 88–90.

increase inventories in a current period represents service potential. If inventory were not increased now, future sales could not be won without subcontracting or building additional plant. Both alternatives would ordinarily entail extra cost incurrence in the future period that would be avoided by an inventory build-up this period. Therefore, in these circumstances, fixed factory overhead represents service potential. Note that fixed factory overhead will be reincurred in subsequent periods. The point here is not related to reincurrence of the same type of cost; it is related to the idea that, without an inventory build-up, extra costs of some sort (apart from those fixed costs which will be reincurred anyway) would be needed in a succeeding period or else future sales would be lost (an opportunity cost).

	Period 1	Period 2	
		Case A	Case B
Full capacity is 120,000 units.			
Normal capacity is 100,000 units.			
Inventory—beginning	—	20,000	20,000
Production	100,000	80,000	120,000
Sales	80,000	100,000	140,000
Inventory—end	20,000	—	—
Fixed costs incurred	$100,000	$100,000	$100,000
Fixed costs inventoried	20,000	—	—
Fixed costs expensed as cost of sales	80,000	100,000	140,000
Fixed costs over- or under-absorbed— Capacity gain or loss		20,000 L	20,000 G
Total charges of fixed costs against revenue	80,000	120,000	120,000

Case A. If the 20,000 units of ending inventory in Period 1 could be produced in Period 2 without incurring additional fixed costs, there is no future benefit represented by Period 1's fixed costs. Future revenues clearly were not enhanced by the decision to produce 20,000 units in Period 1. The alternative of producing in Period 2 would have had the same revenue-producing effect. In fact, despite the rise in sales, the absorption-costing notion in this case results in less income (and benefit) in Period 2 because Period 2 had to bear all of the $100,000 fixed cost plus $20,000 carried over from Period 1. The $20,000 under-absorbed fixed overhead in Period 2 would be charged off as a loss from unutilized capacity. Total fixed charges to Period 2 would include a "double" charge because the $20,000 fixed costs from Period 1 were inventoried at the beginning of the period and would be expended during Period 2 together with the full $100,000 of Period 2 costs. *The scheduling decision to produce in Period 1 instead of Period 2 had no bearing on the revenue and costs of Period 2.*
Case B. Production is at full capacity. Here fixed costs in inventory imply future cost savings. The carrying of 20,000 units into Period 2 made possible sales of 140,000 units—a level that would not have been attained without the beginning inventory except by subcontracting and

incurring extra costs.   This situation is best illustrated by seasonal businesses, where interim statements may carry fixed factory overhead forward as a balance sheet item either as a part of inventory cost or as under-applied overhead or both.

Alternatively, fixed costs in inventory might be viewed as indicative of the ability to service all future sales potential. The latter is a matter of ensuring future sales revenue rather than reducing future costs.

Conclusion

By now it is evident that this writer favors relevant costing as having more *conceptual* merit than either direct or absorption costing. However, because relevant costing requires more crystal-ball gazing, it will undoubtedly not receive wide practical acceptance. The controversy between direct costing and absorption costing for external reporting will persist. The heart of the matter is in the relationship of fixed overhead to the definition of an asset. Unless the arguments come to grips with this issue, they skirt the central question.[7]

QUESTIONS, PROBLEMS, AND CASES

Note: This assignment material covers cost allocation, inventory valuation, and pricing.   There are more problems on inventory valuation because there are additional problems on cost allocation and pricing in Chapters 11, 12, and 13. However, two problems are especially recommended at this stage: 10-12 and 10-20. Other problems that deserve special mention are 10-13, 10-15, 10-19, 10-23, and 10-25.

●**10-1.**   Why is *direct costing* a misnomer?

10-2.   List four alternate terms for *contribution margin*.

10-3.   "The central issue in direct costing is *timing*." Explain.

10-4.   Distinguish between (a) contribution margin, (b) performance margin, (c) segment margin.

10-5.   "The main trouble with direct costing is that it ignores the increasing importance of fixed costs in modern business." Do you agree? Why?

10-6.   What are *programmed costs*?

10-7.   "There are at least three major influences on pricing decisions." What are they?

10-8.   What assumptions about the future are necessary to justify the inventorying of fixed factory overhead?

10-9.   "The depreciation on the paper machine is every bit as much a part of the cost of the manufactured paper as the cost of the raw pulp." Do you agree? Why?

---

[7]For expanded discussion see the articles by Sorter and Horngren, cited in the previous two footnotes. Also see Horngren and Sorter, "An Evaluation of Some Criticisms of Relevant Costing," *Accounting Review* (April, 1964), pp. 417–421, and David Green, Jr., "A Moral to the Direct Costing Controversy?" *Journal of Business* (July, 1960), pp. 218–226.

10-10. Theater prices are usually lower for matinees than for evening performances. Why? As a movie theater manager, what factors would influence your decision as to conducting matinees? To what degree are operating costs affected by the size of the audience?

10-11. Comparison of Absorption and Direct Costing. On the basis of the following information, calculate the net profit for the period and the value of finished goods on hand at the end of the period using:

1. A direct-costing system.
2. An absorption-costing system.

Sales		$128,000
Cost of goods manufactured:		
Variable costs	$48,000	
Fixed costs	32,000	$ 80,000
Selling and administrative expense (Fixed)		$ 20,000
Opening stock of finished goods		Nil
Budgeted and actual production		10,000 units
Closing stock of finished goods		2,000 units
Opening and closing stock of work in process		Nil

[S.I.C.A.]

10-12. Contribution Approach to Cost Allocation: Income Statement by Segments. Stuart Philatelic Sales, Inc. is engaged in the business of selling postage stamps and supplies to collectors on a retail basis. Stuart also makes up packets of inexpensive stamps which it sells on a wholesale basis to stamp departments of five-and-ten-cent stores.

Stuart's Retail Division has two stores, A and B, each of which has a Stamps Department and an Albums and Supplies Department. Stuart had total net sales in 19x4 of $960,000; cost of merchandise sold was $490,000; and variable operating expenses were $120,000. The company's nonvariable costs, which it fully allocated to its two divisions, were $105,000 of advertising expense and $120,000 of various committed costs. Stuart's joint discretionary and committed costs were $35,000.

The costs of merchandise sold and variable operating expenses allocated to the Retail Division were $190,000 and $50,000, respectively. Net sales of Retail were $390,000, two-thirds of which were Store A's net sales. Sixty per cent of Retail's merchandise costs and 54 per cent of its variable operating expenses were allocated to Store A. Advertising costs of $40,000 were allocated to Retail, which in turn allocated 45 per cent directly to Store A and 5 per cent to Store B; the rest of the $40,000 was unallocated. Of the $120,000 separable committed costs, 50 per cent were allocated to Retail, which in turn allocated 50 per cent of its committed costs to Store A, had $25,000 of unallocated costs, and allocated the rest to Store B.

Other information:

(1) Allocations to Store B—Stamps Department:

Net sales	$100,000
Cost of merchandise sold	$ 58,000
Variable operating expenses	$ 17,000

Allocations to Store B—Albums and Supplies Department:

Net sales	$ 30,000
Cost of merchandise sold	$ 18,000

Allocations to Store B—Albums and Supplies Department:

> Variable operating expenses $ 6,000

(2) One-half of Store B's allocated advertising expenses could not be further allocated to either Stamps or Albums and Supplies; the other half of B's allocated advertising expenses was equally divided between the two departments.
(3) Sixty per cent of Store B's committed costs were unallocated; three-fourths of the rest was allocated to the Stamps Department and one-fourth to the Albums and Supplies Department.

REQUIRED:

1. What was net income before taxes for the company as a whole?
2. Determine the contribution margin, short-run performance margin, and segment margin for each of the following:

   a. Company as a whole.
   b. Wholesale Division.
   c. Retail Division.
   d. Store A of the Retail Division.
   e. Store B of the Retail Division.
   f. Stamps Department of Store B.
   g. Albums and Supplies Department of Store B.

10-13.   The All-Fixed Company in 1996.* It is the end of 1996. The All-Fixed Company began operations in January, 1995. The company is so named because it has no variable costs. All of its costs are fixed; they do not vary with output.

The All-Fixed Company is located on the bank of a river and has its own hydroelectric plant to supply power, light, and heat. The company manufactures a synthetic fertilizer from air and river water, and sells its product at a price which is not expected to change. It has a small staff of employees, all hired on an annual-salary basis. The output of the plant can be increased or decreased by adjusting a few dials on a control panel.

The following are data regarding the operations by The All-Fixed Company:

	1995	1996†
Sales	10,000 tons	10,000 tons
Production	20,000 tons	—
Selling price	$30 per ton	$30 per ton
Costs (all fixed):		
Production	$280,000	$280,000
General and administrative	$ 40,000	$ 40,000

> †Management adopted the policy, effective January 1, 1996, of producing only as the product was needed to fill sales. During 1996, sales were the same as for 1995 and were filled entirely from inventory.

*Adapted from an article by Raymond P. Marple, "Try This on Your Class, Professor," *Accounting Review*, July, 1956.

REQUIRED:

1. Prepare three-column income statements for 1995, 1996, and the two years together,

    (a) using absorption costing;
    (b) using "direct" (variable) costing.

2. What is the breakeven point under (a) absorption costing and (b) variable costing?

3. What inventory costs would be carried on the balance sheets at December 31, 1995 and 1996, under each method?

4. Comment on the results in (1) and (2). Which costing method appears more useful?

10-14. The Semi-Fixed Company in 1996.* The Semi-Fixed Company began operations in 1995 and differs from The All-Fixed Company (described in Problem 10-13) in only one respect: it has both fixed and variable production costs. Its variable costs are $7 per ton and its fixed production costs $140,000 a year. Normal activity is 20,000 tons per year.

REQUIRED:

1. Using the same data as in Problem 10-13, except for the change in production cost behavior, prepare three-column income statements for 1995, 1996, and the two years together,

    (a) under absorption costing;
    (b) under variable costing.

2. Why did The Semi-Fixed Company earn a profit for the two-year period while The All-Fixed Company in Problem 10-13 suffered a loss?

3. What inventory costs would be carried on the balance sheets at December 31, 1995 and 1996, under each method?

4. How may the variable costing approach be reconciled with the definition of an asset as being "economic service potential"?

10-15. Direct Costing and Cost-Volume-Profit Relationships.† Fleer Company has a maximum capacity of 210,000 units per year. Normal activity is regarded as 180,000 units per year. Standard variable manufacturing costs are $11 per unit. Fixed factory overhead is $540,000 per year. Variable selling costs are $3 per unit, while fixed selling costs are $252,000 per year. Sales price is $20 per unit.

REQUIRED [Assume no variances from standard variable manufacturing costs in parts (1) through (3)]:

1. What is the breakeven point expressed in *dollar* sales?

2. How many *units* must be sold to earn a target net income of $60,000 per year.

3. How many units must be sold to earn a net income of 10 per cent of sales?

---

* *Ibid.*
†Prepared by the author and adapted for use in a CPA examination.

4. Assume the following results for a given year:

Sales, 150,000 units. Net variance for standard variable manufacturing costs, $40,000, unfavorable. Production, 160,000 units. Beginning inventory, 10,000 units.

All variances are written off as additions to (or deductions from) Standard Cost of Sales.

(a) Prepare income statements for the year under:

(1) conventional costing;
(2) "direct" costing.

(b) In fifty words or less, explain the difference in net income between the two statements.

●10-16. Comparison of Direct Costing and Absorption Costing; Volume Variance. The Davis Company uses a standard absorption costing system. Standard variable manufacturing costs are $3.00 per unit. Standard fixed factory overhead is $.50 per unit ($300,000 ÷ 600,000 units of normal activity). Sales price is $5.00 per unit. Variable selling and administrative costs are $1.00 per unit. Fixed selling and administrative costs are $120,000. Beginning inventory in 19x1 was 30,000 units; ending inventory was 40,000 units. Variances from standard variable manufacturing costs in 19x1 totaled $110,000, unfavorable. Sales in 19x1 were 540,000 units.

REQUIRED:

1. Income statement for 19x1, assuming that all variances are written off directly at year end as an adjustment to Cost of Goods Sold.
2. The president has heard about direct costing. He asks you to recast the 19x1 statement as it should appear under direct costing.
3. Explain the difference in net income as calculated in parts (1) and (2).

10-17. Pricing and Effects on Net Income. Refer to Problem 10-16. In October, 19x1, the company had been offered $20,400 for 6,000 units of production to be delivered throughout the remainder of the year. Because this was the slow season, the president was tempted to accept the offer—particularly because total selling and administrative costs would be unaffected by its acceptance. However, the president had a distate for price cutting and for accepting business that would not yield at least "full cost plus five per cent." So he rejected the order.

REQUIRED:

Using the given information, compute the effect of the president's decision on 19x1 net income. Assume that these additional 6,000 units would be produced in addition to those produced in Problem 10-16 and that they would be produced with no standard cost variances. Show the step-by-step reasoning of the contribution approach to such a decision. Do you think that the president made a wise decision? Why?

10-18. Relevance of Inventory Costs to a Business Investment Decision. Assume that a wealthy investor is contemplating buying a paper-manufacturing company. Certain inventory of the paper company is carried at $100,000, including $40,000 of variable production costs and $60,000 of fixed factory overhead.

REQUIRED:

How much should the investor pay for the inventory? Why?

10-19.   An Argument About Pricing.* Dear Miss Lovelorn: My husband and I are in constant disagreement because he drives 10 miles to work every day, and drives a mile in the opposite direction to pick up and deliver the man who rides with him. For this service the man pays $2 every other week towards gas. Bus fare would cost $5 each week, as two bus lines are involved. I say this fellow should pay at least $3 each week, which would be one-half the cost for the week's gas. But my husband says he can't just ask him for the money, so he settles for this arrangement month after month. We have three children and are in debt for several hundred dollars, and even this $3 a week would really help, as we live on a very tight budget. Am I reasonable to think the gas expense should be split 50-50?

REQUIRED:

As Miss Lovelorn, write a reply.

10-20.   Costs and Formulas for Pricing. A contractor has prepared the following budgeted figures for the current year:

Sales		$148,230
Direct material costs, including sales taxes	$40,000	
Direct labor	75,000	
Payroll taxes, insurance, and welfare contributions related to direct labor	7,500	
Other "job" overhead (variable)	2,500	
General overhead (fixed)	9,750	134,750
Target net income		$ 13,480

The contractor has followed general industry practice in his approach to pricing. He estimates the amount of material and direct labor and then adds a mark-up for overhead and another mark-up for desired net income. For example, suppose that a representative job is estimated to cost $400 for direct material and $750 for direct labor. He would prepare the following analysis for pricing:

Direct materials	$ 400.00
Direct labor	750.00
Add 10% for fringe benefits	75.00
Subtotal	$1,225.00
Add 10% for overhead	122.50
Subtotal	$1,347.50
Add 10% for net profit	134.75
Target selling price	$1,482.25

*From *Chicago Tribune*, December 29, 1959.

Note how the costs of this job parallel the cost relationships in the above budget. Assume that operations were exactly in accordance with the budget. Target selling prices were achieved on every order.

REQUIRED:

1. Prepare two budgeted income statements for the year, one with a traditional format and a second with a contribution format.

2. The contractor asks you to demonstrate at least three other ways to analyze the costs of the representative job and yet yield the same target price of $1,482.25. Include a demonstration of the so-called "contribution" approach in two of your analyses. Briefly explain why all of the different methods yield the same price; indicate which method you prefer and why.

You analyze the above data and determine that the over-all overhead rate is 26.3 per cent of direct labor; the variable overhead rate is 13.3 per cent of direct labor; the fixed overhead rate is 13.0 per cent of direct labor; the contribution margin percentage based on variable costs is 18.5 per cent; and the net income percentage based on total costs is 10.0 per cent.

As long as the over-all target net income is known, all of the possible mark-up formulas can be structured to yield the same target price. For example, a straightforward contribution approach would be to compile the total variable costs and then add a target mark-up of 18.5 per cent of variable costs.

3. Late in the year the contractor bid $1,482.25 for a subcontracting job. He was told by the general contractor: "Your price is too high. If you want the work, you'll have to do the job for $1,340." He refused to accept the $1,340 price. His refusal affected his net income for the year. By how much? Should he have accepted the $1,340 price? Why?

4. "The contribution approach to pricing is extremely dangerous because it deludes the salesmen into thinking that costs are low and it leads to suicidal price cutting." Do you agree? Why?

10-21. A Case Study in Pricing.   The Built Rite Company is a producer of aluminum storm windows and doors, paneling, and siding, which are sold extensively in the residential construction field. Built Rite had generally sold to contractors on a job order basis which required incurring substantial engineering and sales costs per order to satisfy the multiplicity of specifications required by different contractors.

In order to increase volume and reduce engineering and selling expense, Built Rite had spent considerable time and money developing standard storm windows and doors to sell to various retail outlets.

The standard windows and doors were characterized by high quality, new innovations, and ease of installation. Rapid acceptance of the standard line had been experienced. Annual sales had been approximately $1,000,000 during each of the last two years, representing about 25 per cent of the firm's net yearly sales.

The success and acceptance of the aluminum storm windows and doors had enhanced the development of severe price competition, particularly from manufacturers of relatively sleazy and low-quality goods.

At present Roe, Ward, Buck and Company, a major retail outlet, had asked for bids on approximately $200,000 worth of windows and doors. Built Rite had been their prime supplier, but the bid furnished by Built Rite was approximately 5 per cent above that of other sources. An opportunity to re-bid had been granted to Built Rite.

The engineering department was charged with the responsibility of estimating direct costs of the job. This is a rather simple procedure and yields very accurate results. Variable factory overhead is applied at a rate of 100 per cent of direct labor cost. Fixed factory overhead, which includes all engineering expense, is applied at a rate of 150 per cent of direct labor cost. Both fixed and variable overhead rates are used throughout the company for all products and are based on historical data. The rates have been in existence for the last ten years without any changes. The selling price is then computed by multiplying the total of material, labor, and overhead by 150 per cent. This factor includes allowances for profit of 20 per cent, fixed selling and administrative expense of 20 per cent, and variable selling and administrative expense of 10 per cent. This factor is the result of historical data and has been in existence without change for the past ten years.

A condensed income statement is presented in Exhibit I. It can be considered typical for the last few years. On the bid presented to Roe, Ward, Buck and Company, the president had applied the normal variable and fixed overhead rates but had shaved the mark-up factor to 140 per cent. Exhibit II gives the breakdown in the price computation.

The president is aware that he must bid less than $200,000 on the order if he is to be successful and to remain prime supplier for Roe, Ward, Buck and Company. His major concern is for the pricing on the whole standard storm window and door line. The $200,000 price is less than 4 per cent above his fully allocated cost (including allocation of fixed and variable selling and administrative expense). He is certain that the quality of the competitive windows and doors does not equal the quality of the Built Rite standard windows and doors. However, the purchasing departments of the retail outlets are unresponsive to differences in quality, and price appears to be the sole criterion for selection. The doors and windows cannot be cheapened by cuts in quality except through extensive modification in design, which in the long run would adversely affect performance and durability. He has decided he cannot afford to cut quality regardless of the outcome.

EXHIBIT I

BUILT RITE COMPANY
Income Statement
For a "Typical" Year

Net Sales		$4,021,000
Expenses:		
Direct labor	$605,000	
Materials	865,000	
Variable factory overhead	597,000	
Variable selling and administrative expense	170,000	
Fixed factory overhead	808,000	
Fixed selling and administrative expense	575,000	3,620,000
Net income (before tax)		$ 401,000

EXHIBIT II

PRICE QUOTATION
FOR
ROE, WARD, BUCK AND CO. INQUIRY

Material	$ 45,000
Direct labor	30,000
Variable overhead @ 100% of labor	30,000
Fixed overhead @ 150% of labor	45,000
Total manufacturing cost	$150,000
Selling price	$210,000

REQUIRED:

State the central problem. What should the president do?

10-22. A Study in Executive Performance; Relevant Costing (Appendix B). The following data pertain to the B. E. Company:

	Year 19x1
Selling price per unit	$ 2.00
Total fixed costs—production	$ 8,400,000.00
Total fixed costs—selling and administrative	$ 600,000.00
Variable cost per unit—selling and administrative	$ .50
Sales in units	17,000,000
Production in units	17,000,000
Normal activity in units (based on three- to five-year demand)	30,000,000
Operating loss	$ 500,000.00

No opening or closing inventories.

The board of directors has approached a competent outside executive to take over the company. He is an optimistic soul and he agrees to become president at a token salary, but his contract provides for a year-end bonus amounting to ten per cent of net operating profit (before considering the bonus or income taxes). The annual profit was to be certified by Dewey, Cheatham, and Howe, a huge public accounting firm.

The new president, filled with rosy expectations, promptly raised the advertising budget by $3,500,000, stepped up production to an annual rate of 30,000,000 units ("to fill the pipelines," the president said). As soon as all outlets had sufficient stock, the advertising campaign was launched, and sales for 19x2 increased—but only to a level of 25,000,000 units.

The certified income statement for 19x2 contained the following data:

Sales, 25,000,000 × $2.00		$50,000,000
Production costs:		
Variable, 30,000,000 × $1.00	$30,000,000	
Fixed	8,400,000	
Total	$38,400,000	
Inventory, 5,000,000 units, (1/6)	6,400,000	
Cost of goods sold		32,000,000
Gross margin		$18,000,000
Selling and administrative expenses:		
Variable	$12,500,000	
Fixed	4,100,000	
		16,600,000
Net operating profit		$ 1,400,000

The day after the statement was certified, the president resigned to take a job with another corporation having difficulties similar to those that B. E. Company had a year ago. The president remarked, "I enjoy challenges. Now that B. E. Company is in the black, I'd prefer tackling another knotty difficulty." His contract with his new employer is similar to the one he had with B. E. Company.

REQUIRED:

1. As a member of the board, what comments would you make at the next meeting regarding the most recent income statement?
2. Would you change your remarks in (1) if (consider each part independently):

   a. Sales outlook for the coming three years is 20,000,000 units per year?
   b. Sales outlook for the coming three years is 30,000,000 units per year?
   c. Sales outlook for the coming three years is 40,000,000 units per year?
   d. The company is to be liquidated immediately, so that the only sales in 19x3 will be the 5,000,000 units still in inventory?
   e. Maximum production capacity is 40,000,000 units per year, and the sales outlook for 19x3 is 45,000,000 units?

3. Assuming that the $140,000 bonus is paid, would you favor a similar arrangement for the next president? If not, and you were outvoted, what changes in a bonus contract would you try to have adopted?

10-23. Inventory Techniques and Management Planning. It is November 30, 19x4. Given the following for a company division's operations for January through November, 19x4:

DIVISION G
Income Statement
For Eleven Months Ending November 30, 19x4

	Units	Dollars	
Sales @ $1,000	1,000		1,000,000
Less cost of goods sold:			
Beginning inventory, December 31, 19x3, @ $800	50	40,000	
Manufacturing costs @ $800, including $600 per unit for fixed overhead	1,100	880,000	
Total standard cost of goods available for sale	1,150	920,000	
Ending inventory, November 30, 19x4, @ $800	150	120,000	
Standard cost of goods sold*	1,000		800,000
Gross margin			200,000
Other expenses:			
Variable, 1,000 units @ $50		50,000	
Fixed, @ $10,000 monthly		110,000	160,000
Net operating income			40,000

*There are absolutely no variances for the eleven-month period considered as a whole.

Production in the past three months has been 100 units monthly. Practical capacity is 125 units monthly. In order to retain a stable nucleus of key employees, monthly production is never scheduled at less than 40 units.

Maximum available storage space for inventory is regarded as 200 units. The sales outlook for the next four months is 70 units monthly. Inventory is never to be less than 50 units.

The company uses a standard absorption costing system. Normal production activity is 1,200 units annually. All variances are disposed of at year end as an adjustment to Standard Cost of Goods Sold.

REQUIRED:

1. The division manager is given an annual bonus which is geared to net operating income. Given the above data, assume that the manager wants to maximize the company's net income for 19x4. How many units should he schedule for production in December? Note carefully that you do not have to (*nor should you*) compute the exact net income for 19x4 in this or in subsequent parts of this question.

2. Assume that standard direct costing is in use rather than standard absorption costing. Would direct costing net income for 19x4 be higher, lower, or the same as standard absorption costing net income, assuming that production for December is 80 units and sales are 70 units? Why?

3. If standard direct costing were used, what production schedule should the division manager set? Why?

4. Assume that the manager is interested in maximizing his performance over the long run, and that his performance is being judged on an after-income-tax basis. Given the data in the beginning of the problem, assume that income tax rates will be halved in 19x5, and assume that the year-end write-offs of variances are acceptable for income tax purposes. Assume that standard absorption costing is used. How many units should be scheduled for production in December? Why?

10-24. Some Additional Requirements to Problem 10-23; Absorption Costing and Volume Variances.   Refer to Problem 10-23.

1. What net operating income will be reported for 19x4 as a whole, assuming that the implied cost behavior patterns will continue in December as they did through January-November, and assuming—without regard to your answer to requirement (1) in Problem 10-23—that production for December is 80 units and sales are 70 units?

2. Assume the same conditions as in requirement (1), except that practical capacity rather than normal activity was used in setting fixed overhead rates for product costing throughout 19x4. What volume variance would be reported for 19x4?

10-25. Computation of Net Income Under Nine Different Costing Assumptions.   The Wixkell Company began operations a year ago. There was no beginning inventory. The company has produced 100,000 units; it has sold 80,000 units for a total revenue of $680,000. Experienced executives initiated a carefully planned standard cost system at the outset. Cost data for the year follow:

Standard costs of production:

Direct material	$300,000
Direct labor	200,000
Variable indirect manufacturing costs	40,000
Fixed indirect manufacturing costs	100,000
	$640,000

Variances (all unfavorable):

Direct material	$ 30,000
Direct labor	25,000
Variable indirect manufacturing costs	10,000
Fixed indirect manufacturing costs	5,000
	$ 70,000

Selling and administrative expenses incurred:

Variable	$ 40,000
Fixed	60,000
	$100,000
Total of the three categories	$810,000

The top officers are anxious to know what the net income is for 19x1 because they know this will influence their immediate plans for seeking more capital. They have asked you to compute the company net income. You have explored various costing methods or assumptions as a part of your task. You have pinpointed the following:

A —Actual historical costs. That is, no predetermined costs are used.
B —Standard absorption costing—proration of variances

C—Standard absorption costing—without proration of variances
D—Normal* absorption costing—proration of variances
E—Normal absorption costing—without proration of variances
F—Standard variable costing—proration of variances
G—Standard variable costing—without proration of variances
H—Normal variable costing—proration of variances
I—Normal variable costing—without proration of variances

What net income (loss) would be shown under the various costing methods? Arrange your answer so that comparisons of the alternatives may be made easily.

*"Normal" costing is historical costing using predetermined overhead rates.

profit centers, performance measurement, and transfer pricing

The increased complexity of organizations has been accompanied by the development of accounting techniques for measuring the performance of individual managers. We have seen how responsibility accounting measures control performance by establishing responsibility centers for individual costs.

The basic ideas of responsibility accounting have been extended to encompass profit centers. A *profit center* is a segment of a business, usually called a division, that is responsible for both revenue and expenses. In effect, these divisions are regarded as independent businesses with a top manager who is ultimately responsible for revenue, expenses, and the resources (that is, assets) which are utilized to sustain operations.

In this chapter, we shall examine two measurement techniques that have especially facilitated the measurement of the performance of the profit centers of a business: (1) rate of return on assets, and (2) transfer pricing. Although both techniques have considerable conceptual appeal, each has practical limitations.

DIFFERENT DEFINITIONS OF INCOME AND INVESTMENT

Turnover and margins

Most managers are very much interested in the measures of dollar profits, dollar sales, and the profit margin (the ratio of profits to dollar sales). Managers are proud of sizable sales volume and hefty profit margins. However, the ultimate test of profitability is not the relationship of profit to sales. The real test is the relationship of profit to capital employed (investment). A growing number of companies are following the leads of duPont and General Motors, companies that set rate-of-return targets in relation to invested capital. These targets should be the foundations for managerial planning, policy making, and special decision making. The rate-of-return approach to an investment decision has been used for centuries by financiers and others. Yet this technique has not been very widespread in industry. Conceptually, return on investment is the best single measure of performance, because it can be compared with opportunities elsewhere, whether they be in similar projects or companies or in entirely different ventures. Practically, return on investment is an imperfect measurement and should be used in conjunction with other performance measurements.

The major advantage of the rate-of-return technique is its focus on an often neglected phase of management responsibility—the required investment in assets. For a given company at a given time, there is a best level of investment in any asset—whether it be cash, receivables, physical plant, or inventories. Cash balances, for example, may be too large or too small. The principal cost of having too much cash is the sacrifice of possible earnings; idle cash earns nothing. The principal cost of having too little cash may be lost discounts on purchases or harm to one's credit standing. For every class of asset, then, there is an optimum level of investment which, along with optimum levels of investment in other assets, helps to maximize long-run profits.

Companies take different approaches to the problem of measuring return on investment, differing mostly with respect to the appropriate measure of invested capital but also differing in the measure of income.

A useful approach to the problem may be outlined by using the following relationships:

$$\frac{\text{Sales}}{\text{Invested Capital}} \times \frac{\text{Net Income}}{\text{Sales}} = \frac{\text{Net Income}}{\text{Invested Capital}}$$

or

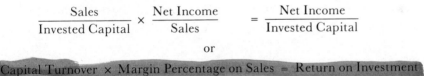

Capital Turnover × Margin Percentage on Sales = Return on Investment

Consider the components of the relationships. One may make the following obvious generalizations: any action is beneficial which (1) boosts sales, (2) reduces invested capital, or (3) reduces costs—while holding the other two factors constant. Put another way, there are two basic ingredients in profit making: turnover and margin percentages. An improvement in either without changing the other will enhance return on invested capital.

Tool for management

Assume that top management decides that a 20 per cent return on invested capital is a profit target that will yield adequate rewards and yet not invite entry into the market by new competitors. How can this return be attained? Present performance (in millions of dollars) follows:

$$\frac{\text{Sales}}{\text{Invested Capital}} \times \frac{\text{Net Profit}}{\text{Sales}} = \frac{\text{Net Profit}}{\text{Invested Capital}}$$

Present $\quad \dfrac{100}{50} \quad \times \quad \dfrac{9}{100} \quad = \quad$ 9/50 or 18%

Alternatives:

A—Increase margin by lowering expenses $\quad \dfrac{100}{50} \quad \times \quad \dfrac{10}{100} \quad = \quad$ 10/50 or 20%

B—Decrease assets $\quad \dfrac{100}{45} \quad \times \quad \dfrac{9}{100} \quad = \quad$ 9/45 or 20%

Alternative *A* demonstrates a popular way of improving performance. Margins may be increased by reducing expenses, as in this case, or by boosting selling prices, or by increasing sales volume relative to a given amount of fixed expenses.

Alternative *B* shows that controlling investments in assets may also improve performance. Management has always been very conscious of the need for increasing sales and for controlling costs so that good profit margins may be attained. But control of investment has not always received conscientious managerial attention. Too often, asset balances rise without justification. Not only do operating costs have to be controlled, but investment in cash, inventory, receivables, and fixed assets must be kept to the minimum that is consistent with effective performance. This means investing idle cash, determining proper inventory levels, managing credit judiciously, and spending carefully on fixed assets. In other words, increasing asset turnover means getting the maximum mileage in sales out of every dollar invested in business resources. For example, having too much inventory is sometimes worse than having too little. Turnover decreases and goods deteriorate or become obsolete, thus dragging the rate of return downward.

What is invested capital?

The base that is used for measuring invested capital differs between companies and within segments of the same company. Just as there may be different costs for different purposes, so there may be different rates of return for different purposes. The alternative bases that may be used include the following:

1. *Total assets available.* This base includes all business assets, regardless of their individual purpose.
2. *Total assets employed.* This base excludes excess or idle assets, such as vacant land or construction in progress.
3. *Stockholders' equity plus long-term debt.* This base is really the same as in part (1), except that current liabilities are deducted from the total assets available. In a sense, this represents an exclusion of that portion of current assets which is supplied by short-term creditors.

Some companies feel that management should not be expected to earn a return on such current assets.

4. *Stockholders' equity*. This base centers attention on the rate of return that will be earned by the business owners.

Comparison of asset and equity bases

Although an equity base is appropriate for some analytical purposes, it is not so meaningful as an asset base for appraising operating management, because (a) a company employs *total* assets to produce income, and (b) different companies have different financing policies and various capital structures.

For example, consider the following companies:

	(1)	(2)	(3)	(4)	(5)	(6)	(4) ÷ (1)	(6) ÷ (3)
							Return on	
		Equities					Investment	
		Liabil-	Stock-holders'	Income Before	6%	Net		Stock-holders'
	Assets	ities	Equity	Interest	Interest	Income	Assets	Equity
Co. A	$1,000,000	$500,000	$ 500,000	$200,000	$30,000	$170,000	20%	34%
Co. B	$1,000,000	—	$1,000,000	$200,000	—	$200,000	20%	20%

Note that when an asset base is used for measuring return, the investor sources for the assets are ignored and so is interest, which is not directly related to how efficiently the assets are used. Rate of return, as used here, means 20 per cent gross rate of return (that is, before interest expense) on total assets. The use of long-term debt can have an impact on the return based on stockholders' equity. However, the 34 per cent rate of return on stockholders' equity does not distinguish between the basic earning rate on total assets and the various costs of obtaining and using the funds. In other words, top management has two major functions: operating and financing. Measures of operating performance (how a given set of assets are employed) should not be influenced by financing decisions (how funds for obtaining the assets are acquired). Company A in effect has paid 6 per cent for the use of $500,000, which in turn has earned a gross return of 20 per cent. This method of financing benefited the stockholders handsomely. The latter is often called *trading on the equity*, which is also referred to as "using leverage." It means using borrowed money at a fixed interest rate which is less than the rate of return the company expects to earn on such funds. Trading on the equity relates only to the financing function; because it can be viewed as a separate issue, it should not influence the measurement of operating performance.

Asset bases. Exhibit 11-1 shows that some form of asset base is probably the most widely used for measuring the operating performance of a company as a whole. However, there is far from universal agreement as to the proper measurement of the assets. For example, depreciable assets may be included at original cost or at net book value or at some sort of replacement value.

EXHIBIT 11-1

INVESTMENT BASE USED IN EVALUATING PAST PERFORMANCE
FOR A COMPANY AS A WHOLE

Investment Base	Number of Companies Reporting Use of Each Base
Total assets available	28
Total assets employed (i.e., excess or idle assets eliminated)	4
Stockholders' equity plus long-term debt	6
Stockholders' equity	7
Total	45

Source: N.A.A. Research Report No. 35, *Return on Capital As a Guide to Managerial Decisions* (December, 1959), p. 8.

Price-level adjustments may be applied to a few or to all assets, although *N.A.A. Research Report No. 35* indicates that few companies use adjusted rates of return as formal recognition of the price-level problem. Yet managements are generally concerned about the impact of the dancing dollar on the significance of the rates of return.

Company accounting policies also will have a telling impact on the amount of assets included in the investment base. For example, the variety of methods of accounting for inventories, leased assets, research, depreciation, patents, secret processes, trade marks, and advertising will have an important influence on the asset base.

Fixed assets: what base?

Should assets be valued at original cost (gross value) or at net book value? The N.A.A. study showed that 18 of 28 companies use net book value as a base for valuing fixed assets. Yet there is strong disagreement as to the most useful base. Compare these two bases in Exhibit 11-2. Note the opposite effects of the gross and net methods of computation on plant performance and company performance.

Using gross assets

Some major companies, including duPont and Monsanto Chemical Company, use gross assets as an investment base. One reason often cited for using undepreciated cost is that it partially compensates for the impact of the changing price level on historical cost. However, if a company desires to use replacement cost as a base, it should not try to tailor

EXHIBIT 11-2

RATE OF RETURN ON ASSETS USING ORIGINAL COST OF FIXED ASSETS VERSUS USING NET BOOK VALUE OF FIXED ASSETS

	Fixed Assets				Plant Performance						Company Performance			
						Rate of Return					Gross Assets		Net Assets	
Year	Gross Cost	Accumulated Depreciation	Net Book Value End of Year	Average Book Value for Year	Annual Net Income	On Gross Cost	On Average Book Value	Total Cash Accumulation	Average Cash for Year*	Base	Rate of Return	Base	Rate of Return
(1)	(2)	(3)	(4) (2)−(3)	(5)	(6)	(7) (6)÷(2)	(8) (6)÷(5)	(9)	(10)	(11) (2)+(10)	(12) (6)÷(11)	(13) (4)+(9)	(14) (6)÷(13)
1	$400,000	$100,000	$300,000	$350,000	$40,000	10.0%	11.4%	$100,000	$ 50,000	$450,000	8.9%	$400,000	10.0%
2	400,000	200,000	200,000	250,000	40,000	10.0%	16.0%	200,000	150,000	550,000	7.3%	400,000	10.0%
3	400,000	300,000	100,000	150,000	40,000	10.0%	26.7%	300,000	250,000	650,000	6.1%	400,000	10.0%
4	400,000	400,000	0	50,000	40,000	10.0%	80.0%	400,000	350,000	750,000	5.4%	400,000	10.0%

(5) 1/2 (Beginning balance plus Ending balance), for example, 1/2 ($300,000 + $200,000), or $250,000, for year 2.

(9) Assume that sales and expenses except depreciation are on a cash basis, and that cash is transmitted to central headquarters in an amount equal to net income. Thus, cash in the amount of the depreciation charge will accumulate each year.

*This situation is unrealistic in the sense that idle cash is being accumulated without being reinvested to earn a return.

historical costs to the measurement problems of changing prices; the results of such a hybrid attack will be unreliable.

The reasoning in support of the gross asset base must be linked
with the purpose of its use: appraisal of company results as a whole (column 12 of Exhibit 11-2) or appraisal of a plant's or division's performance
(column 7). A company's performance as a whole is the responsibility of
top management. When profits are made, depreciation is recouped out of
sales revenue. If dividends are paid in the amount of net income, cash may
accumulate in the amount of the annual $100,000 depreciation (column 9).
(No cash is kept in the business from earnings, but there is a conversion of
fixed assets into cash as measured by depreciation.) To count original cost
plus the cash accumulation as a part of the investment base (column 11) is
duplication; it does not provide as useful a base as net assets. In contrast,
a plant manager's or division manager's performance often is best analyzed
by using gross assets as the investment base (column 7). The reinvestment
of the cash accumulation in the amount of depreciation charges may be
beyond the manager's control.

Those who favor the gross-asset base state that it facilitates comparisons among plants or divisions. If income moves downward as a plant
ages, the decrease in earning power will be evident under a gross-asset
base, while the constantly decreasing net-asset base will reflect a possibly
deceiving higher rate of return in later years (column 8).

Using net book value

The proponents of using net book value as a base maintain that it
is less confusing (a) because it is consistent with the total assets shown on
the conventional balance sheet and (b) it is consistent with net income
computations, which include deductions for depreciation.

Using net book value prevents duplication of the same asset in the
base and shows a constantly rising rate of return on plant performance.
(See column (8) of Exhibit 11-2.) Note that the inclusion of the cash accumulation and *gross fixed assets* duplicates the same item, so that the total
fixed and current gross asset base rises from year to year.

Using replacement value

Should fixed assets be measured at book value or replacement
cost? For internal purposes, there is no necessity to adhere to conventional
accounting measures. Replacement value of the services made available by
the asset is the best measure because it is the best approximation of the
current economic sacrifice. But the approximation of current replacement
values of fixed assets is not always simple. Unless there is an active market,
some price index may have to be used. However, specific appraisals by
engineers are most preferable.

This approach may be somewhat more complicated than conventional accounting measurements. However, the year-to-year updating of

such a system should not be too burdensome, particularly if the fixed assets are subdivided into broad classes. This method is not favorably regarded by industry, principally because it is too subjective. Still, it is more likely to yield an accurate approximation than either gross value or net book value.

Income and rate of return

The definition of income should be consistent with the definition of the investment base to which it is related. Thus, interest expense is ordinarily excluded in computing incomes which are related to asset bases, whereas interest expense is deducted in computing income which is related to stockholders' equity bases. Nonrecurring items are ordinarily excluded when current operating performance is to be appraised.

COMPUTING RETURN ON CAPITAL
BY PLANTS, PRODUCTS, AND DIVISIONS

Allocations are needed

Allocations of sales, costs, and assets are needed in order to develop rates of return by product lines, divisions, and plants. In other words, the corporate whole is split into individual components as if each were a separate company with its own rate-of-return target. The concept here is appealing, but implementing the concept raises many vexing problems of allocation which are solved by methods that are subject to challenge. Chapter 10 has already pointed out the problems of allocating costs to departments. The attempt to allocate assets as well as costs merely multiplies the difficulties. Just as there is a danger in holding foremen to budgets which contain uncontrollable costs, the same reasoning applies to holding managers to rate-of-return targets. Full allocations of joint costs to products or plants whereby two or more managers are responsible for a portion of the total leads to managerial resentment and disbelief. Managers are made responsible for costs and assets which are beyond their control. Although the attempt to bring rate-of-return targets down to divisional and departmental levels may be helpful as a rough guide, top management should be made aware that such refinements are subject to overwhelming limitations.

Some assets, like certain plant assets, equipment, and inventories, may be readily identified with individual segments of a company. Others, like central administrative facilities, central accounts receivable, cash, marketing facilities, and various service and research facilities, are often difficult to allocate except by an approach which is similar to reapportioning factory service department costs to productive departments. Many companies refrain from asset allocations (for example, central research facilities and central office facilities) where assets may be linked with divisions or plants only via some arbitrary base. In these cases, the arguments that ensue over the "fairness" or "equitableness" of the allocations destroy the usefulness of the rate-of-return tool. The importance of "selling" the rate-of-return notion to executives cannot be overstressed. The selling job is easier if asset allocations are made carefully.

Where the allocation of an asset (such as corporate cash or central office facilities) would be arbitrary, it is better not to allocate. Instead, a contribution approach, similar to that shown in Exhibit 10-1, should be taken. A performance margin (sales, less variable costs, less discretionary fixed costs) should be related to those assets which are clearly assignable to a given division. The resulting rate of return will reflect short-run management performance. A segment margin (sales, less variable costs, less all fixed costs directly identifiable with a division) may be used as a basis for measuring long-run performance.

Commonly used bases for allocation, when assets are not directly identifiable with a specific division, include the following:

Asset Class	*Possible Allocation Base*
Corporate cash	Budgeted cash needs; No allocation
Receivables	Sales weighted by payment terms
Inventories	Forecasted sales or usage
Fixed assets	Usage of services in terms of long-run forecasts, area occupied, hours, or service unit

Rate-of-return targets are flexible. The imprecision of the rate-of-return tool has not necessarily resulted in its rejection. Companies often limit its use to broad areas of the business where problems of allocation of assets and expenses are not overwhelming. For example, a rate of return may be easily computed for a division or a plant, but not for individual products within a product line or individual departments within a factory. Furthermore, companies tend to emphasize change in rates of return rather than absolute per cents. Thus, changes may be budgeted, actual performance may be appraised, and variances may be investigated. There are two major classes of variances: turnover and profit margins. These may be analyzed in detail to discover underlying causal factors.

Overemphasis of high rates of return may actually hurt long-run profits, because too high a return invites new competition. A company may deliberately lower its rate of return in order to preserve or enhance its long-run share of the market. Also, flexibility is desirable because the various company divisions may be in widely differing lines of business.

Harmony between goals

Motivation is the overriding consideration that should guide management in deciding (a) how assets should be allocated and (b) how the investment base should be measured. That is, the system should be designed so that the division managers will be inclined toward action which will be in harmony with over-all company goals.

For example, the use of *net* assets as an investment base may encourage incorrect decisions by divisional management. If assets are replaced or scrapped before they are fully depreciated, the division may have to show a loss. Even though, as Chapter 13 explains, such a loss is irrelevant to replacement decisions (except for its impact on timing of income tax outlays), it does affect the division's immediate profit and could influence the division manager's decision.[1]

Overemphasis on rate of return

Enthusiasts of applying the rate-of-return concept as a measurement of efficiency tend to revere the tool as a panacea for appraising managerial performance. Weaknesses of using rate of return as a sole common denominator for appraising intercompany and intracompany performance have already been indicated. *N.A.A. Research Report No. 35* shows how one company keeps the tool in perspective:

> *The company emphasizing change in return on capital employed presents a quarterly "report card" to top management. On this "report card," each division is rated for its performance in terms of seven different measures of financial performance. One of the most important of these measures is return on capital employed. Return on capital employed is not, however, presented as an absolute figure. Like the other seven measures, the percentage change in return on capital from the previous quarter is shown. The assistant controller pointed out that, in this way, no division can complain because the investment base does not reflect replacement cost, or that allocations are unrealistic. Each division is compared not with another division's performance but with its own performance in a prior period. Accordingly, the capital employed base and the allocation methods are completely comparable between periods. The division that shows the greatest improvement in return on capital employed for the quarter is ranked first for return on capital even though the absolute size of the return on capital figure may be far less than another division's. Similar rankings are prepared for the other six measures of financial performance. Then the rankings for each division for each of the seven measures are totaled to give a total rank for financial performance during the month. The division having the lowest total score "stands at the head of the class." Thus, if one division stands first in all seven measures, it will have a total score of seven. Considerable competitive spirit is generated by the division managers in their attempts to score best for the overall standing, and also to score best in certain measures, such as return on capital employed. A poll of top management and division managers revealed that none ranked return on capital less than second most important of the seven different measures.[2]*

Other measures commonly used to judge managerial performance include: plant efficiency, share of the market, employee turnover, sales volume, discovery of new products, and public relations.

[1] For an interesting discussion of various investment bases and depreciation methods plus several examples of how division managers' interests can conflict with the interests of the company as a whole, see John Dearden, "Problem in Decentralized Profit Responsibility," *Harvard Business Review* (May–June, 1960), pp. 79–86. He concludes (p. 86): "It is my belief that the only completely satisfactory method for assigning values to divisional facilities is one that uses replacement values and is not tied directly into the books of account."

[2] N.A.A. Research Report No. 35, *Return on Capital as a Guide to Managerial Decisions* (December 1, 1959), pp. 31–32.

The time period and managerial efficiency

As Chapter 9 stressed, an executive's performance should contribute to the maximization of profits, not for one quarter or for one year, but over the long run. The focus should be on long-run earning power, not on short-run profits. Yet managers switch from one executive position to another over the years; they are typically appraised in terms of those short-run factors which tend to maximize long-run earnings potential. Managers are evaluated in terms of quantifiable performance and also performance which is difficult to measure (such as public relations or employee morale).

Rate of return wraps the quantifiable factors in one convenient package. Yet short-run maximization of rate of return may not provide the best measure of managerial efficiency in many cases. For example, profitability in one year may have a direct relationship to profitability in the long run, but not necessarily. A division may increase sales by reducing quality in one period and cause a harmful effect on the corporate image. (Some observers felt that Buick made this mistake in 1955, resulting in disastrous sales in 1958–1959. Demand in 1955 resulted in record-breaking output, which was marked by poor quality control.) In these cases, the manager may deserve a low ranking, despite the division's high rate of return.

Thus, rate of return as a measure of efficiency should be studied in relation to other factors, such as budgets, standards, conformity to company policies, maintenance of quality, employee relations, customer relations, development of subordinates, and blood relationships to directors. Numerical weights are sometimes assigned to various factors and a scorecard is kept for each executive.

In summary, rate of return as a measure of efficiency cannot stand alone. Short-run profitability is only one of the factors that contributes to a company's long-run objectives. Rate of return is a short-run concept, dealing only with the past quarter or year, whereas managerial efficiency can be best expressed in terms of future results which can be expected because of present actions.[3]

TRANSFER PRICING

Intracompany transfers

Appraisal of managerial performance within a company becomes more difficult when segments of a company exchange goods and services. For example, assume that an integrated company has an iron mine which supplies ore to a steel mill, which, in turn, supplies steel to an assembly plant. Opponents of rate of return by divisions maintain that efficiency of all three divisions in this example is best measured by standard costs and budgets. Those who favor assigning profit responsibility to subdivisions of

---

[3] For an expanded discussion of the limitations of rate of return, See William J. Vatter, "Does Rate of Return Measure Business Efficiency?" *N.A.A. Bulletin* (January, 1959).

a business are often faced with the problem of pricing intracompany transfers so that each division shows sales, expenses, and profits. Transfer price has an important bearing on the profits of both the supplying and the receiving units.

Thus, the accountant is embroiled in top management policy making because the accounting techniques used often will have direct impacts on the following matters: measuring performance and profitability by divisions, measuring consequences of proposed changes in integration policy, formulating transfer pricing policies, and computing bonuses to be awarded for superior managerial performance.

There are two basic alternatives for pricing intracompany transfers: some version of cost or some version of market.

Cost bases. In the above example, the transfer of products on the basis of accumulated cost would show no returns for the mine or the steel mill, but the performance of the assembly plant would reflect the accumulated efficiencies or inefficiencies of other divisions not subject to the assembly manager's control. Transfer prices based on costs, or on cost plus some mark-up, may or may not be related to market prices. Moreover, transfer prices which insure recovery of costs often fail to provide an incentive to control costs. If pricing is not subjected to competitive comparisons at intermediate transfer points, excess costs are less likely to be discovered.

Despite the obvious limitations of the approach, transfer prices based on cost, or on cost plus some mark-up, are in common use. The main reason for their wide use is that they are understandable and convenient. Moreover, when they yield prices that, on the average, are reasonably close to market prices, they are justified because they are practical, convenient, clear, and fair.

Pricing at variable cost. Conceptually, transfers at variable cost assure the best short-run use of over-all facilities.[4] But the motivational impact of using variable costs is a thorny problem. That is, the use of variable costs hardly permits the use of profit centers as ordinarily conceived. Moreover, for long-run make-and-buy and product-line decisions, the divisional variable cost will not be the correct guide. Instead, incremental revenues and costs for the company as a whole must be analyzed. Finally, the forced transfer at variable costs may not always assure the maximization of over-all net income. For example, a product's variable cost may be $1.00 and its market value may be $2.00 at a transfer point from Division A to Division B. If Division B's variable cost of processing the product further is $1.25 and the selling price of the final product is $2.75, the Division B manager would want the product processed if the transfer price is based on variable cost. But this would contribute less to over-all net income than by selling to outsiders at the transfer point. The essential question is whether Division B should offer the final product in the market at all.

[4] The most rigorous theoretical work is that of Jack Hirshleifer, "On the Economics of Transfer Pricing," *Journal of Business* (July, 1956), pp. 172–184, and "Economics of the Divisionalized Firm," *Journal of Business* (April, 1957), pp. 96–108.

	Process Further		Sell to Outsiders at Transfer Point	
	Division B Performance	Over-all Performance	Division B Performance	Over-all Performance
Selling price	$2.75	$2.75	—	$2.00
Variable costs:				
Division A	$1.00			$1.00
Division B	$1.25			—
Total variable costs	$2.25	$2.25	—	$1.00
Contribution to net income	$ .50	$ .50	—	$1.00

Market price bases. The market price approach regards individual divisions as if they were completely separate companies. It attempts to transfer goods at a price equivalent to that prevailing in an outside market at the time of transfer, that is, at the price that the receiving division would have to pay outsiders. Put another way, the market-price approach is an attempt to approximate an arm's-length, bargained, open-market price. *A working rule is that as long as the selling division meets the price, and wants to sell internally, the buying division should have to buy internally.* The National Association of Accountants has described this method as follows:

> *Internal procurement is expected where the company's products and services are superior or equal in design, quality, performance, and price, and when acceptable delivery schedules can be met. So long as these conditions are met, the receiving unit suffers no loss and the supplier unit's profit accrues to the company. Often the receiving division gains advantages such as better control over quality, assurance of continued supply, and prompt delivery.*
>
> *If a receiving unit finds that internal sources of supply are not competitive, policy calls for one of the following actions:*
>
>   *a. It may purchase from an outside supplier after it has made a reasonable effort to bring the internal supplier unit's quotations and terms into line with those available outside.*
>
>   *b. It is free to purchase outside, but must be prepared to justify its decision. Central executives usually review such actions and have an opportunity to take action where needed.*
>
> *Normally the right to buy outside is seldom used because the advantages of integration make interunit transfers preferable for both supplying and receiving units. However, companies interviewed stated that the policy had sometimes been instrumental in bringing to light the presence of excessive costs due to obsolete or poorly located facilities, inefficient management, lack of volume, or other causes.*[5]

The usefulness of a market-price method is contingent on the availability of dependable market price quotations of other manufacturers. It is these prices which would be taken into account by parties dealing at arm's length as they establish the competitive price levels.

In sum, market prices establish the *ceiling* for transfer pricing. In

[5] *Accounting for Intra-Company Transfers*, National Association of Accountants, Research Series No. 30 (New York, June, 1956), pp. 13–14.

many instances, a lower price may easily be justified, particularly when large purchases are made, when selling costs are less, or when an advantage is obtained through an exclusive supplier contract or through a cost-plus arrangement assuring profits in all cases. These situations lead to the notion of negotiated market prices.

Negotiated market prices. Special circumstances create difficulties in ascertaining a market price that is clearly relevant to a particular transfer-pricing situation. In addition to those situations described in the previous paragraph, a division sometimes provides a product that is unavailable from outsiders or that is not sold to outsiders (for example, special parts or research). A price is then negotiated between the buying and selling divisions, or a company formula may be used for determining the price. Negotiations may be time-consuming or inflammatory, and top management may have to serve as arbitrator.

Where negotiations are necessary, some smooth-working method for arbitration of disputes is essential. The controller's department often serves as an impartial arbitrator. Appeals beyond the arbitrator to top management should be possible in exceptional circumstances.

Fictitious profit centers. The whole idea of decentralization and profit centers is based on the manager's freedom and independence. Unless he has alternatives, unless he can resort to buying and selling outside the company, his so-called profit center is fictitious; it is essentially a cost center in a centralized company. When freedom of choice is not available, the resultant transfer prices are artificial to a point which severely contaminates the rate of return or similar measures of profit performance. The measurement system will fail to distinguish controllable and uncontrollable factors.

For example, a large decentralized lumber and paper company acquired a small company which manufactured envelopes. Shortly thereafter, the envelope company was instructed to purchase all of its paper needs from a western paper division at "market" transfer prices. The quality of the paper was inferior to that previously acquired elsewhere. This adversely affected waste and machine speeds. Morale of the managers and the workmen was shaken. The envelope division manager was frustrated because he had profit responsibility without authority to purchase materials from outside sources.

The paper mill showed a handsome contribution to over-all company profit, but the envelope division's performance was poor. Bonuses were awarded to the paper mill managers but not to the envelope division managers because the central management was too far from the underlying activities to evaluate the performance in any way other than by the profit-center approach. In this case, the executive had been assigned responsibility without commensurate freedom to manage. He exerted no control over the purchasing function, and his manufacturing function suffered because of inferior raw materials.

Although over-all company net income may have benefited from these decisions, the profit centers were artificial because intracompany transfers were mandatory. Monetary rewards based on "profits" in these situations are inherently suspect. The moral is that measurement systems that do not tally with what they purport to measure are likely to have damaging influences on management attitudes and deleterious long-run effects. In this case, the manager, an effective leader by any reasonable standard, had to bellow long and threaten to resign before corrections in the measurement system were begun.

We have just seen that the notion of decentralized profit responsibility with complete freedom of action is largely make-believe. Does this mean that all the companies which use profit centers should abandon such techniques? Of course not. Very few aids for planning and control are perfect. The important point is to recognize their weaknesses and attempt to strengthen them. Those who favor the wide use of profit centers often cite the presence of internal friction and competition as a major benefit (rather than as a major defect), because, for example, exasperating transfer pricing disputes frequently focus on uneconomic activities which would not be detected by an ordinary cost center system. Profit centers tend to force managers to check outside markets, alternate suppliers, processes, and materials more often than when cost centers are used.

Coordination of objectives. Company policies concerning transfer pricing should be carefully drawn so that the division managers' decisions will meet over-all company goals. The general rule of having supplying divisions meet all bona fide outside price competition (perhaps often adjusted downward for pertinent factors such as volume or selling cost) is most likely to permit division managers to act in harmony with over-all company objectives. The point is that orders should be kept within the corporate family as long as the market price or the synthetic market price is not less than the variable manufacturing costs. This rule assumes that internal facilities would otherwise be idle.

ACCOUNTING ENTRIES FOR TRANSFERS

Transfer pricing is governed by managerial objectives, including measuring divisional performance, minimizing taxes, and controlling the rate of return. These objectives often lead to transfers at prices in excess of conventional inventory costs.

Accounting for market-based transfer prices provides another illustration of how current accounting systems are being designed primarily to aid managerial planning and control rather than to serve the needs for external financial reports. After all, from the viewpoint of the consolidated enterprise, any goods or services transferred within the enterprise and not yet sold to outsiders should be carried at cost. Thus, although intracompany transfers may be accounted for and reported in any manner that helps achieve managerial objectives, intracompany margins must be eliminated periodically when consolidated financial statements are prepared.

The basic approach may be illustrated as follows:

Data for example: Whole Company has two divisions, A and B. Goods having a manufacturing cost of $100 are transferred from A to B at a price of $135. Entries follow:

On Books of Supplier Division A

Accounts receivable—Division B	135	
Sales to Division B		135
Cost of goods sold (transferred)	100	
Inventory—Division A		100

On Books of Receiving Division B

Inventory—Division B	135	
Accounts payable—Division A		135

An examination of the above entries shows that essentially the two divisions operate as separate companies. However, if Whole Company had to prepare consolidated financial statements immediately after the above transaction, the following eliminating entries would be needed:

Accounts payable—Division A	135	
Accounts receivable—Division B		135
To eliminate intracompany receivable and payable.		
Sales to Division B	135	
Cost of goods sold (transferred)		100
Intracompany gross profit—A		35
To close and recognize Division A's intracompany gross profit.		
Intracompany gross profit—A	35	
Inventory—Division B		35
To eliminate intracompany gross profit		

SUMMARY

Conceptually, rate of return on assets employed is the best single measure of managerial operating efficiency. Practically, the measurement is fraught with limitations and should be used in conjunction with other measures such as budgets and standards, market shares, employee turnover, and the like. The *relative change* in these measures is often more significant than their *absolute* size.

Although in practice assets tend to be valued at book values for the purpose of calculating these rates of return, replacement value is a better basis.

Transfer pricing systems are needed if profit centers are to be established within companies. To insure harmony of managers' decisions with over-all company objectives, the transfer price usually is some version of market price. The trouble is that satisfactory approximations of market prices are difficult to attain. The entire area of transfer pricing is complicated by problems of human relations and the need for prices that will tend toward correct short-run and long-run decisions and appropriate evaluations of managerial performance. Transfer price policies must neither impinge unduly on executive time nor interfere with over-all company goals.

When market prices are not available as a foundation for negotiations, the resultant transfer prices are artificial to a point which severely limits the significance of rate of return or other measures of performance. In these instances, reliance on budgets and standards for all controllable phases of operations is more likely to produce sharper evaluation of performance.

Chapter 9 emphasized how motivation should be the paramount consideration that should guide management in devising appropriate performance measures. That is, the control system should be designed so that division managers will be inclined toward action that harmonizes with over-all company goals. This chapter is basically an illustration of that basic idea. The chief question to ask about which asset base is best or which transfer price is best is, "Which of the alternative measures will best induce management behavior toward over-all goals?" Unfortunately, accountants and managers must face the answer, "It depends." There are no pat answers, no canned formulas, that are universally applicable.

SUGGESTED READINGS

Anthony, R. N., J. Dearden, and R. F. Vancil, *Management Control Systems: Cases and Readings* (Homewood, Ill.: Richard D. Irwin, Inc., 1965).

Solomons, David, *Divisional Performance: Measurement and Control* (New York: Financial Executives Research Foundation, 1965). He supports the notion of residual income as being superior to the rate of return as a measure of performance. See Problem 11-23.

   N.A.A. Research Reports Nos. 30 and *35* and *Practice Report No. 14* should be enlightening.

PROBLEM FOR SELF-STUDY

Problem. An automobile division makes auto batteries; it sells them to the assembly plants and through regular market channels to outsiders. Operating details are as follows:

	To Assembly Plant		To Outsider		Total
Sales	100,000 units @ $7*	$700,000	50,000 units @ $10	$500,000	$1,200,000
Variable costs	100,000 units @ $5	$500,000	50,000 units @ $ 5	$250,000	$ 750,000
Fixed costs		150,000		75,000	225,000
Total costs		$650,000		$325,000	$ 975,000
Net operating income		$ 50,000		$175,000	$ 225,000

*The $7.00 price is ordinarily determined by the outside sale price less selling and administrative expenses wholly applicable to outside business. Note that this is an example of a "synthetic or negotiated" market price.

REQUIRED:

1. The Assembly Division manager has a chance to get a firm contract with an outside supplier at $6.50 for the ensuing period. The Battery Division manager says that he cannot sell at $6.50 because no net operating income can be earned. Should he sell at $6.50? What will be his division's net operating income? Assume that fixed costs would be unaffected by his decision. Tabulate the effects of the two alternatives on over-all corporate net operating income.

2. Suppose that the Battery Division's budgeted data are as follows:

Average available assets:	
Receivables	$300,000
Inventories	200,000
Fixed assets, net	500,000
	$1,000,000
Fixed overhead	$225,000
Variable costs	$5 per unit
Desired rate of return on average available assets	27.5%
Expected volume	200,000 units

a. What average unit sales price is needed to obtain the desired rate of return on average available assets?
b. What would be the expected turnover of assets?
c. What would be the net income percentage on dollar sales?
d. What rate of return would be earned on assets available if sales volume is 300,000 units, assuming no changes in prices or variable costs per unit?

Solution

1. Net operating income would be $175,000, a decline of $50,000, but he should sell at $6.50. If he understood cost-volume-profit relationships, he would realize that the loss of 100,000 units in volume would mean foregoing a contribution margin of $1.50 per unit ($6.50 − $5.00), a total of $150,000. Unless he can eliminate some of his fixed costs or increase his other sales, or both, to make up the $150,000 lost contribution margin, his best short-run alternative is to sell at $6.50. In the long run he would try to reduce capacity, or find more profitable ways to use available capacity, or improve production techniques to the point where the lower price becomes more profitable. To summarize:

Total Battery Division Performance
(in thousands of dollars)

	Sell to Assembly at $6.50	Refuse to Sell to Assembly	Difference
Sales	$1,150	$500	$650
Variable Costs	750	250	500
Fixed Costs ($150+$75)	225	225	—
Total Costs	$975	$475	$500
Net Operating Income	$175	$ 25	$150

The company as a whole will benefit if the sale is made internally, even though the Battery Division's net operating income declines from $225,000 to $175,000. The $50,000 decline is the 50-cent reduction in the selling price of 100,000 units.

If the facilities are idle, the Battery Division's performance will be even worse (note above that the difference in net operating income is $150,000, the contribution margin that would be foregone by failure to sell internally).

Finally, of course, the company as a whole will be hurt if the battery purchases are made outside. Variable costs would be $150,000 higher.

	Alternatives for the Company As a Whole		
	Buy from Outside	Buy Internally	Difference
100,000 units @ $6.50 variable cost	$650,000	—	
100,000 units @ $5.00 variable cost	—	$500,000	$150,000
Fixed costs, irrelevant assuming that they are unchanged	—	—	—
Total variable costs	$650,000	$500,000	$150,000

2.

(a) 27.5% of $1,000,000 = $275,000 target net income

$$\text{Let } X = \text{unit sales price}$$
$$\text{Dollar sales} = \text{Variable costs} + \text{Fixed costs} + \text{Net Income}$$
$$200,000\,X = 200,000\,(\$5) + \$225,000 + \$275,000$$
$$X = \$1,500,000 \div 200,000$$
$$X = \$7.50$$

(b) Expected asset turnover $= \dfrac{200,000 \times \$7.50}{\$1,000,000} = \dfrac{\$1,500,000}{\$1,000,000} = 1.5$

(c) Net income as a percentage of dollar sales $= \dfrac{\$275,000}{\$1,500,000} = 18.33\%$

(d) At a volume of 300,000 units:

Sales @ $7.50	$2,250,000
Variable costs @ $5.00	1,500,000
Contribution margin	$ 750,000
Fixed expense	225,000
Net income	$ 525,000
Rate of return on $1,000,000 assets	52.5%

Note that an increase of 50 per cent in unit volume almost doubles net income. This is so because fixed costs do not increase as volume increases.

QUESTIONS, PROBLEMS, AND CASES

Note: Problems 11-20, 11-22, 11-23, 11-25, 11-28, and 11-29 are especially recommended.

11-1. "Net income divided by sales is the most important single measure of business success." Do you agree? Why?

11-2. List four possible bases for computing the cost of invested capital.

11-3. "The stockholder's equity base is the best investment base for appraising operating management." Do you agree? Why?

11-4. "The use of undepreciated cost of fixed assets as part of the investment base compensates for the impact of the changing price level on historical cost." Do you agree? Why?

11-5. Under what circumstances does the gross asset base make most sense?

11-6. Proponents of net book value as an investment base usually cite two major reasons for their position. What are these reasons?

11-7. How should interest expense and nonrecurring expenses be considered in computing incomes which are related to investment bases?

11-8. "In recent years there has been a tendency toward corporate decentralization, accompanied by a setting of individual rate-of-return targets for corporate segments. This provides incentive because managers can operate their segments as if they were separate companies of their own." Do you agree? Why?

11-9. What income concept is likely to be most realistic for measuring performance of various corporate segments?

11-10. "The rate-of-return tool is so hampered by limitations that we might as well forget it." Do you agree? Why?

11-11. What measures besides rate of return are commonly used to judge managerial performance?

11-12. "Too much stress on rate of return can hurt the corporation." How?

11-13. Why are intracompany transfer prices often necessary?

11-14. What are two major bases for pricing intracompany transfers?

11-15. What is the major limitation to transfer prices based on cost?

11-16. "Company transfer pricing policies must satisfy dual objectives." What are the objectives?

11-17. Where reliable market prices cannot be ascertained for transfer pricing, what is the impact on divisional performance measurement?

11-18. What is the most common example in transfer pricing of a clash between divisional action and over-all company profitability?

11-19. Departmental Income Statement. Goodsale Limited is a retail store with three departments: basement, soft goods, and hard goods.

The basement occupies 3,000 square feet.

The soft goods occupy 2,000 square feet.

The hard goods occupy 1,000 square feet.

The store building cost $120,000. Depreciation is provided at $2\frac{1}{2}$ per cent per annum on cost.

From the company records, you are furnished with the following information for the year ended January 31, 19x2.

	Basement	Soft Goods	Hard Goods	Total
Sales	$300,000	$250,000	$150,000	$700,000
Purchases	200,000	200,000	100,000	500,000
Inventories:				
Feb. 1, 19x1	25,000	20,000	25,000	70,000
Jan. 31, 19x2	30,000	50,000	40,000	120,000
Departmental salaries	30,000	25,000	10,000	65,000
Administrative salaries				112,000
Operating expenses				12,500

Administrative salaries are to be distributed to the departments on the basis of sales; operating expenses and depreciation, on the basis of floor space.

REQUIRED:

1. A departmental statement of income for the year ended January 31, 19x2.

2. Your opinion of the aspects in which the above statement could be misleading. [S.I.C.A.]

● 11-20. **Analysis of Return on Capital; Comparison of Three Companies.***

1. Rate of return on capital is often expressed as follows:

$$\frac{\text{Income}}{\text{Capital}} = \frac{\text{Income}}{\text{Sales}} \times \frac{\text{Sales}}{\text{Capital}}$$

What advantages can you see in the breakdown of the computation into two separate components?

2. Fill in the blanks:

	Companies in Same Industry		
	A	B	C
Sales	$1,000,000	$500,000	$ —
Income	100,000	50,000	—
Capital	500,000	—	5,000,000
Income as a per cent of sales	—	—	0.5%
Turnover of capital	—	—	2
Return on investment	—	1%	—

After filling in the blanks, comment on the relative performance of these companies as thoroughly as the data permit.

11-21. Government Contracts and Profit Margins. Spokesmen for many companies which are heavily involved in government contract work often complain that defense work is not very profitable. They then cite low percentage profit margins as evidence.

*Adapted from *N.A.A. Research Report No. 35*, pp. 34–35.

REQUIRED:

Are such contentions justified? Why or why not?

11-22. Pricing, Rate of Return, and Measuring Efficiency. A large automobile company follows a pricing policy whereby "normal" or "standard" activity is used as a base for pricing. That is, prices are set on the basis of "long-run" annual-volume predictions. They are then rarely changed, except for notable changes in wage rates or material prices.

You are given the following data:

Material, wages, and other variable costs	$1,320 per unit
Fixed overhead	$300,000,000 per year
Desired rate of return on invested capital	20%
Normal volume	1,000,000 units
Invested capital	$900,000,000

REQUIRED:

1. What net income percentage based on dollar sales is needed to attain the desired rate of return?
2. What rate of return on invested capital will be earned at sales volumes of 1,500,000 and 500,000 units, respectively?
3. The company has a sizable management bonus plan based on yearly divisional performance. Assume that the volume was 1,000,000, 1,500,000, and 500,000 units, respectively, in three successive years. Each of three men has served as division manager for one year before being killed in automobile accidents. As the major heir of the third manager, comment on the bonus plan.

• **11-23. The General Electric Approach to Measuring Divisional Profitability.*** Consider the following:

	(000's omitted)	
	Division A	Division B
Total assets	$1,000	$5,000
Net annual earnings	$ 200	$ 750
Rate of return on total assets	20%	15%

REQUIRED:

1. Which is the most successful division? Why?
2. General Electric Company has chosen "residual income," the excess of net earnings over the cost of capital, as the measure of management success, as the quantity which a manager should try to maximize. The cost of capital is deducted from the net annual earnings to obtain residual income. Using this criterion, what is the residual income for each division if the cost of capital is: (a) 12 per cent,

---

*Adapted from David Solomons, *Divisional Performance: Measurement and Control* (New York: Financial Executives Research Foundation, Inc., 1965).

(b) 14 per cent, (c) $17\frac{1}{2}$ per cent? Which division is more successful under each of these rates?

11-24. Transfer Pricing. The Plastics Company has a separate division that produces a special molding powder. For the past three years, about two-thirds of the output has been sold to another division within the company. The remainder has been sold to outsiders. Last year's operating data follow:

	To Other Division		To Outsiders	
Sales	10,000 T. @ $70*	$700,000	5,000 T. @ $100	$500,000
Variable costs @ $50		$500,000		$250,000
Fixed costs		150,000		75,000
Total costs		$650,000		$325,000
Gross margin		$ 50,000		$175,000

*The $70.00 price is ordinarily determined by the outside sales price less selling and administrative expenses wholly applicable to outside business.

The Buying Division manager has a chance to get a firm contract with an outside supplier at $65.00 for the ensuing year.

REQUIRED:

Assume that the Molding Powder Division manager says that he cannot sell at $65.00, because no margin can be earned. As the Buying Division manager, write a short reply. Assume that the 10,000 tons cannot be sold by the Molding Powder Division to other customers.

11-25. Transfer Pricing Dispute. Allison-Chambers Corp., manufacturer of tractors and other heavy farm equipment, is organized along decentralized lines with each manufacturing division operating as a separate profit center. Each division head has been delegated full authority on all decisions involving the sale of his division's output to both outsiders and to other divisions of Allison-Chambers. Division C has in the past always purchased its requirement of a particular tractor engine component from Division A. However, when informed that Division A was increasing its price to $150, Division C's management decided to purchase the engine component from outside suppliers.

The component can be purchased by C for $135 on the open market. A insists that owing to the recent installation of some highly specialized equipment and the resulting high depreciation charges, A would not be able to make an adequate profit on its investment unless it raised its price. A's management appealed to top management of Allison-Chambers for support in its dispute with C and supplied the following operating data:

C's annual purchases of tractor engine component	1,000
A's variable costs per unit of tractor engine component	$120
A's fixed costs per unit of tractor engine component	$ 20

REQUIRED:

1. Assume that there are no alternative uses for internal facilities. Determine whether the company as a whole will benefit if Division C purchases the component from outside suppliers for $135 per unit.

2. Assume that internal facilities of A would not otherwise be idle. By not producing the 1,000 units for C, A's equipment and other facilities would be assigned to other production operations, which would otherwise require an additional annual expense of $18,000. Should C purchase from outsiders?

3. Assume that there are no alternative uses for A's internal facilities and that the price of outsiders drops $20. Should C purchase from outsiders?

11-26. Transfer Pricing Problem. Assume in the Allison-Chambers Corp. problem that Division A could sell the 1,000 units to other customers at $155 per unit with variable selling costs of $5 per unit. If this were the case, determine whether Allison-Chambers would benefit if C purchased the 1,000 components from outsiders at $135 per unit.

11-27. Evaluation of Transfer Pricing Policy. The Altos Chemical Company has recently been decentralized. Several profit centers have been formed. The transfer pricing system stipulates that average market prices should govern the intracompany sales; however, discounts from such prices should be made for any expenses that do not pertain to intracompany sales. Examples would be certain selling, shipping, and credit expenses.

The Fox Division, a large intracompany supplier of over 100 products, tried to develop a workable method for quoting intracompany prices. The task was complicated by the presence of many selling and manufacturing costs that were common to a number of products. The Fox Division finally proposed a flat mark-up above variable manufacturing cost as a feasible approximation of market price:

Sales to outsiders	$11,000,000
Less:	
Selling, shipping, credit, and customer service expenses not applicable to intracompany sales	1,000,000
Adjusted sales	$10,000,000
Variable manufacturing costs	6,000,000
Mark-up	$ 4,000,000

Mark-up formula: $10,000,000 \div \$6,000,000 = 167\%$ of variable manufacturing costs. This formula would be reviewed and adjusted every 120 days.

REQUIRED:

What are the strengths and weaknesses of the proposed mark-up formula? Does the formula adhere to the company policy on transfer pricing?

11-28. Conflict of Interests of Profit Centers and Company as a Whole.* Division A of a company is the only source of supply for an intermediate product which is converted by Division B into a salable final product. Most of A's costs are fixed. For any output up to 1,000 units a day, its total costs are $500 a day. Total costs increase by $100 a day for every additional thousand units made. Division A judges that its own results will be optimized if it sets its price at $0.40 a unit, and it acts accordingly.

Division B incurs additional costs in converting the intermediate product supplied by A into a finished product. These costs are $1,250 for any output up to

---

*Adapted from David Solomons, *Divisional Performance: Measurement and Control* (New York: Financial Executives Research Foundation, 1965), pp. 167–172.

1,000 units, and $250 per thousand for outputs in excess of 1,000. On the revenue side, B can increase its revenue only by spending more on sales promotion and by reducing selling prices. Its sales forecast is:

Sales in Units	Net Revenue per Thousand Units
1,000	$1,750.00
2,000	1,325.00
3,000	1,100.00
4,000	925.00
5,000	800.00
6,000	666.67

REQUIRED:

1. Prepare a schedule comparing B's costs, including its purchases from A, revenues, and net income at various levels of output.

2. What is B's maximum net income? At that level, what is A's net income? At that level, what is the corporation's aggregate net income?

3. Suppose that the company abandons its divisionalized structure. Instead of being two profit centers, A and B are combined into a single profit center with responsibility for the complete production and marketing of the product. Prepare a schedule similar to that in requirement (1). What volume level will provide the most net income?

4. Evaluate the results in (3). Why did the circumstances in requirement (1) lead to less net income than in requirement (3)? How would you adjust the transfer pricing policy to assure that over-all company net income will be maximized where separate profit centers A and B are maintained?

11-29. Evaluation of Transfer Pricing Policy. The Sunnyvale Corporation is a mammoth enterprise with over forty profit centers. A company-wide transfer pricing rule states that a selling division must always sell to a buying division at bona fide market prices.

The S Division was asked to quote prices on 10,000 standard parts (representing 10 per cent of the S Division's practical capacity) which the B Division has ordered from time to time in past years. The S Division quoted a price of $20 each, which would bring S a $60,000 total contribution margin for the 10,000 parts. However, an outside supplier quoted a price of $16, and the S Division was forced by company policy to fill the order at that price.

REQUIRED:

1. How much total contribution margin will the S Division earn at the $16 price? By how much is the net income of the Sunnyvale Corporation affected by keeping the business inside at the $16 price rather than going outside at that price?

2. The practical capacity of the S Division is 100,000 machine-hours. Suppose that it takes one machine-hour to make one of the standard parts. Suppose further that the order is indivisible; that is, the S Division must make all 10,000 parts or none—it cannot accept a third or a half of the order. Suppose, finally, that only 10,000 machine-hours of capacity were available for this production.

The S Division manager had also planned to submit a bid to an outside company for making 4,000 special parts at a selling price of $40 each, which would bring S a total contribution margin of $80,000 for the 4,000 parts. The manager felt virtually certain that he would get the order. It takes two machine-hours to make one special part. However, because he could not handle both orders, he delayed submitting his bid because of the B Division's need for the standard parts. In view of these circumstances, how were the S Division's and the Sunnyvale Corporation's net income affected by the decision to keep the standard parts order inside? How would you modify the transfer pricing rule?

11-30. Transfer Prices in an Imperfect Market.* Division A is the supplier division and Divisions B and C are the consumer divisions of a large company. After Division B deducts its own processing costs, the total net revenue and the marginal net revenue it derives from various quantities of intermediate product are:

DIVISION B

Quantity of inter-mediate processed in pounds	Total net revenue	Marginal net revenue
1000	$ 600	$600
2000	900	300
3000	1100	200
4000	1200	100

Similarly, for Division C we have:

DIVISION C

Quantity of inter-mediate processed in pounds	Total net revenue	Marginal net revenue
2000	$1200	$ —
3000	1800	600
4000	2100	300
5000	2300	200
6000	2400	100

Division A, the producing division, faces the following cost conditions:

DIVISION A

Quantity of inter-mediate produced in pounds	Total cost	Marginal cost
4000	$2000	$ —
5000	2100	100
6000	2250	150
7000	2425	175
8000	2625	200
9000	2925	300
10000	3325	400

*Adapted from David Solomons, *Divisional Performance: Management and Control* (New York: Financial Executives Research Foundation, 1965), pp. 178–179.

REQUIRED:

What transfer price should be set for A's output? Why?

11-31. The Pertinent Transfer Price. The *XYZ* Company has two divisions, A and B. For one of the company's products, Division A produces a major subassembly and Division B incorporates this subassembly into the final product. There is a market for both the subassembly and the final product, and the divisions have been delegated profit responsibility. The transfer price for the subassembly has been set at long-run average market price.

The following data are available to each division:

Estimated selling price for final product	$300
Long-run average selling price for intermediate product	200
Variable cost for completion in Division B	150
Variable cost in Division A	120

The manager of Division B has made the following calculation:

Selling price—final product		$300
Transferred-in cost (market)	$200	
Variable cost for completion	150	350
Contribution (loss) on product		$ (50)

REQUIRED:

1. Should transfers be made to Division B if there is no excess capacity in Division A? Is market price the correct transfer price?

2. Assume that Division A's maximum capacity for this product is 1,000 units per month and sales to the intermediate market are presently 800 units. Should 200 units be transferred to Division B? At what relevant transfer price?

nonmanufacturing costs

Nonmanufacturing costs include such diverse categories as selling, transportation, administrative, and research costs. These costs are more important than manufacturing costs in many industries, such as tobacco, soap, toiletries, patent medicines, and some food products. This chapter will concentrate on marketing costs, sometimes called *distribution costs*. But research costs and administrative costs will also be discussed.

COMPARISON OF MARKETING AND MANUFACTURING COSTS

The marketing function embraces all nonmanufacturing activities aimed directly at obtaining and filling sales orders. Marketing has often been described as a combination of order-getting activities and order-filling activities. *Order-getting* is the attainment of a desired sales volume and mix. It is the art of landing the order through advertising, promoting, and selling. *Order-filling* includes warehousing, packing, shipping, billing and credit extension. The latter two functions are often labeled administrative rather than marketing costs.

The basic lesson of this chapter is that fundamental concepts of planning and control are equally applicable to both manufacturing and marketing activities. Therefore, budgets, standards, performance reports, investigation of variances, and the like are used in all phases of business operations. The technicalities of such matters are covered in other chapters, so we shall not dwell on them in this chapter. For example, Chapters three and six stressed cost behavior patterns and volume-profit relationships. Chapter ten discussed the contribution approach to performance measurement and pricing. Chapter thirteen will emphasize the importance of relevance in analyzing data.

Accounting techniques for planning and control initially developed in relation to manufacturing rather than marketing. This occurred because manufacturing inputs and outputs are easier to classify and measure. The measurement of direct material and direct labor consumed and of various parts and goods produced is straightforward. The measurement of the efforts (inputs) of salesmen and of the effectiveness (outputs, usually in terms of sales or margins) of advertising and salesmen is often difficult.

Formal planning and control techniques seem more meaningful where facilities are fixed, where routine is entrenched, and where external and joint influences are minimal. They have traditionally been less meaningful where external and joint influences are overwhelming, where many short-run alternatives exist, and where courses of action (and cost incurrence) are heavily influenced by management's opinions or hunches. For example, the alternative actions in marketing are complicated by such interplaying factors as product mix, design, types of outlets, pricing, advertising, competitive behavior, customer reactions, and general economic conditions.

Marketing is generally regarded as having a more dynamic flavor than manufacturing. This common impression is reinforced by the widespread publicity that often accompanies change. For example, consider the erratic behavior of television sponsors, who seem to be adding or dropping programs incessantly. However, this aura of flexibility may be more apparent than real. Culliton and other researchers have shown that many business executives are wary of change. Managers cannot easily predict the results of a change, so they adhere to a marketing strategy that seems to be operating satisfactorily.

Marketing managers are increasingly discovering that traditional guesses, hunches, and reliance on generalized rules of thumb are no longer enough. Detailed data accumulation and analyses, including budgets and standards, point toward the products, territories, distribution channels, order sizes, divisions, departments, and employees that most sorely need attention. The use of management accounting in marketing is bound to increase because it can yield fruitful insights at little cost.

A successful marketing operation obtains the highest possible profit contribution for a given investment over the long run. Note that the objective is profit contribution, not maximization of sales alone or minimization of expenses alone. That is why marketing executives should know cost-volume-profit relationships. That is why the contribution approach to the analysis of marketing performance is superior to full-costing approaches which fail to distinguish between vital influences of various cost behavior patterns. An earlier chapter discussed the contribution approach in relation to measuring performance and to guiding price decisions. This chapter will apply these ideas to some common marketing problems.

In order to make intelligent decisions, the marketing manager must decide on his goals and on the analytical techniques that will be most helpful. Economists maintain that profit maximization is the usual goal.

This may be so, but true maximization is an ideal that is difficult to crystal-lize. Instead, the manager typically settles for improvement, a search for *better* profits without really knowing what best might be. He does this because the alternatives are often infinite, and he necessarily deals with a manageable number of alternatives which may not embrace the best possibility.

Nearly every business has multiple products. No company makes all its sales at an equal profit. The key purpose is to shift or concentrate efforts, plans, and resources toward the most profitable course of action. This cannot be done consistently without (a) formalized planning, (b) relevant revenue and cost information, and (c) experimentation. Together, these aid the manager in increasing marketing productivity, which is the "ratio of sales or net profits (effect produced) to marketing costs (energy expended) for a specific segment of the business."[1]

There is disagreement, even among managers within the same company, about the relative profitability and interrelationships among products. For example, grocers cannot agree about the profitability of frozen foods.[2] In another instance, a cost analysis indicated that 635 out of 875 products were enormously unprofitable. But the executives were reluctant to abandon the unprofitable items because of possible adverse effects on other sales. Experiments in certain territories showed that no long-run damage would result, so the unprofitable products were aban-doned.[3] Careful cost analysis and controlled experimentation in the market place are ways to replace unreliable executive hunches and con-flicting guesses about the joint factors that afflict marketing decisions. Such analysis and experimentation may be imperfect, but they are much better than no guides or the incredible folklore that managers sometimes cite as justifications for decisions.

CONTROLLING ORDER-FILLING AND ADMINISTRATIVE COSTS

Work measurement

Order-filling costs include the costs of warehousing, packing, shipping, billing, credit, and collection. Standards and budgets originated in the factory, and the application of these techniques to nonmanufacturing areas has been slow indeed. Nevertheless, many order-filling and admin-istrative duties have been measured for control purposes, especially in industries with large clerical work forces, such as banking, insurance, and utilities.

Work measurement is the careful analysis of a task, its size, the methods used in its performance, and its efficiency. Its objective is to de-

---

[1] Charles H. Sevin, *Marketing Productivity Analysis* (New York: McGraw-Hill Book Company, Inc., 1965), p. 9.
[2] *The Economics of Frozen Foods*, McKinsey-Birds Eye Study, General Foods Corpora-tion (White Plains, N.Y.: 1964), p. 1.
[3] Sevin, *op. cit.*, p. 90.

termine the work load in an operation and the number of workers needed to perform that work efficiently. The techniques used include time and motion study, observation of a random sample of the work (that is, work sampling), and the estimation, by a work-measurement analyst and a line supervisor, of the amount of time required for the work (that is, time analysis). The work load is expressed in *control factor units*, which are used in formulating the budget.

For example, the control factor units in a payroll department might include operations performed on time cards, on notices of change in the labor rate, on notices of employee promotion, on new employment and termination reports, and on routine weekly and monthly reports. All of these would be weighted. The estimated work load would then be used for determining the required labor force and budgetary allowance.

Another example of work measurement would be the physical handling of goods in warehousing, shipping, receiving, or shelving. In these instances, a "standard handling unit" may be formulated. The standard handling unit may be a case of goods; then barrels, packages, sacks, and other items "may be expressed as multiple or fractional handling units according to their time-of-handling relationship to that of the case of goods (the standard unit)."[4]

The activity measure used as a budget base may be sales dollars, product units, cases, tons, or some other unit which best reflects cost influence:

Operations	Unit of Measure (Control Factor Unit)
Billing	Lines per hour
Warehouse labor	Pounds or cases handled per day
Packing	Pieces packed per hour
Posting accounts receivable	Postings per hour
Mailing	Pieces mailed per hour

Need for measurement

The general idea of work measurement is that permanent improvement in any performance is impossible unless "scientific" measurement is used to specify the time required for the job. Measures of such items as clerical work loads and capability may be formal or informal. The latter is often achieved through a supervisor's regular observation so that he knows the productivity of his work force.

Standards for certain order-filling activities, such as packing or truck-driving, may necessarily be less refined than for such manufacturing activities as assembly work, but they still provide the best available formal tool for planning and control. For example, as Chapter 7 mentioned, short-interval scheduling has been attempted. This technique routes all work through a supervisor, who batches the work in hourly lots. This develops standards, controls backlogs, and provides close follow-up.[5] The

[4] Sevin, *op. cit.*, p. 21.
[5] Vincent Melore, "Cutting Payroll Costs in Manufacturing Staffs," *Management Services* (July–August, 1964), p. 24.

measurement of work often spurs controversy because employees do not usually welcome more stringent monitoring of their productivity.

Budgeting of order-filling and administrative costs: two approaches

There is much disagreement about how order-filling and administrative costs should be controlled. Advocates of work measurement favor a more rigorous approach, which essentially regards these costs as variable. In contrast, a discretionary cost approach, which basically regards these costs as fixed, is most often found in practice.

A comparison of the variable cost and discretionary cost approaches will be facilitated by the following example.

Assume that ten payroll clerks are employed, and that each clerk's operating efficiency *should be* the processing of the pay records of 500 employees per month. In the month of June, 4,700 individuals' pay records were processed by these ten clerks. Each clerk earns $600 per month. The variances shown by the variable cost approach and the discretionary cost approach are tabulated below and graphed in Exhibit 12-1:

EXHIBIT 12-1

	Budget as a Variable Cost (Ideal)	Budget as a Discretionary Cost (Currently Attainable)
Actual cost incurred	$6,000	$6,000
Budget allowance	5,640*	6,000
Variance	360 U	0

*Rate = $6,000 ÷ 5,000 records or $1.20 per record; total = 4,700 records @ $1.20 = $5,640.

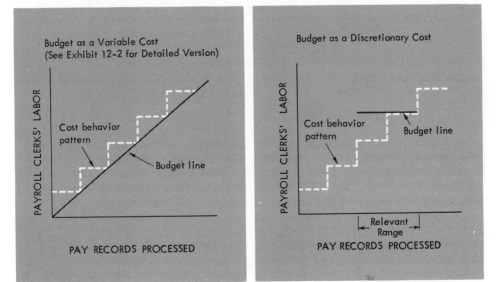

The variable cost approach: ideal standards. The step-variable cost approach to this situation is to base the budget formula on the unit cost of the individual pay record processed—$600 ÷ 500 records, or $1.20. Therefore, the budget allowance for payroll clerk labor would be $1.20 × 4,700, or $5,640. Assume that the ten employees worked throughout the month. The following performance report would be prepared:

	Actual Cost	Flexible Budget: Total Standard Quantity Allowed for Good Units Produced	Budget Variance
Payroll clerk labor	$6,000 (10 × $600)	$5,640 (4,700 × $1.20)	$360 *U*

A graphic representation of what has occurred (Exhibit 12-2 may yield insight.

EXHIBIT 12-2

STEP-VARIABLE COSTS AND VARIANCES

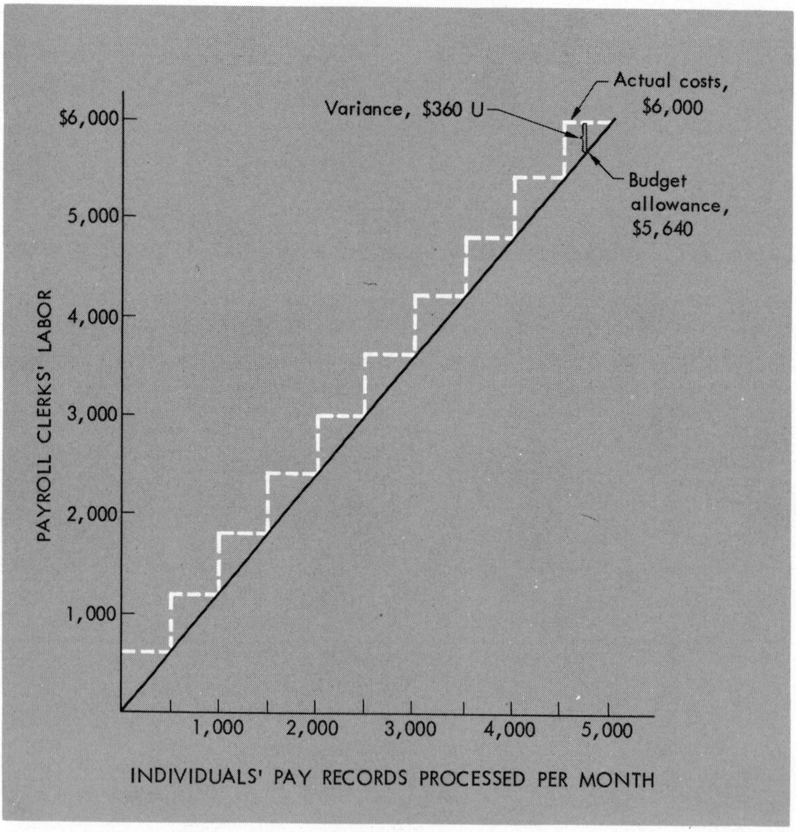

Essentially, two decisions must be made in this operation. The first is a policy decision. How many clerks do we need? How flexible should we be? How divisible is the task? Should we use part-time help? Should we hire and fire as the volume of work fluctuates? The implication of these questions is that once the hiring decision is made, the total costs incurred can be predicted easily—$6,000 in our example.

The second decision concentrates on day-to-day control, on how effectively the given resources are being utilized. The work-measurement approach is an explicit and formal attempt to measure the utilization of resources by:

1. Assuming a strictly variable budget and the complete divisibility of the work load into small units. Note that the budget line on the graph in Exhibit 12-2 is strictly variable, despite the fact that the costs are really incurred in steps.

2. Generating a budget variance that assumes a comparison of actual costs with an ideal standard—the cost that would be incurred if payroll clerk labor could be turned on and off like a faucet. In this case, the variance of $360 informs management that there was over staffing (that is, the tenth step was only partially utilized). The work load capability was 5,000 pay records, not the 4,700 actually processed. $360 is the extra cost that resulted from operating in a way which does not attain the lowest possible cost, even though this may not be the result of a conscious decision but merely the effect of producing the volume which satisfies the monthly changes in demand. Robert Beyer writes that such a variance points out "an area in which the managers should be alert for cost reduction opportunities, since alternatives may be available."[6] Such an approach provides a measure ($360) of the amount that management is currently investing to provide stability in the work force.

Admittedly, work measurement of order-filling and clerical administrative activities is not widespread. However, advocates of work measurement maintain that such an approach is the only reliable way to satisfy management's desire to plan and control such costs. The use of a tight budget based on ideal standards generates variances that upon investigation will reveal either or both of the following: (1) ineffective use or under-utilization of available personnel (for instance, perhaps 5,000 individual payroll records had to be processed, and other clerks or supervisors had to pitch in to get all the work done); (2) the cost of a management policy of deliberately retaining personnel to service long-run needs even though the volume of the current work load is insufficient (for instance, the maximum work available for payroll clerical labor may be 4,700 individual payroll records and the individual work may have been performed with complete efficiency).

The discretionary cost approach: currently attainable standards. Work-measurement techniques are not used in the vast majority of organizations. Consequently, the tendency is to rely on the experience of the de-

[6] *Profitability Accounting for Planning and Control* (New York: The Ronald Press Company, 1963), p. 162.

partment head and his superior for judging the size of the work force needed to carry out the department's functions. There is a genuine reluctance to overhire because there is a corresponding slowness in discharging or laying off people when volume slackens. As a result, temporary peak loads are often met by hiring temporary workers or by having the regular employees work overtime.

In most cases, the relevant range of activity during the budget period can be predicted with assurance, and the work force needed for the marketing and administrative functions can be readily determined. If management refuses, consciously or unconsciously, to rigidly control costs in accordance with short-run fluctuations in activity, these costs become discretionary. That is, their total amount is relatively fixed and unresponsive to short-run variations in volume.

Hence, there is a conflict between common practice and the objective of work measurement, which is to treat most costs as variable and so subject them to short-range management control. *The moral is that management's attitudes and its planning and controlling decisions often determine whether a cost is fixed or variable. A change in policy can transform a fixed cost into a variable cost, and vice versa.*

Moreover, management may regard a cost as discretionary for *cash-planning purposes* in the preparation of the master budget but may use the variable cost approach for *control purposes* in the preparation of flexible budgets for performance evaluation. These two views may be reconciled within the same over-all system. In our example, a master budget conceivably could include the following item:

Payroll clerk labor:	
Flexible budget allowance for control	$5,640
Expected flexible budget variance	
(due to deliberate over-staffing)	360
Total budget allowance for cash planning	$6,000

The common impression, which is reinforced by work measurement approaches, is that control should be constantly exerted to be effective. However, the National Association of Accountants comments:

> *In one company, where considerable study had been devoted to determining how costs ought to be affected by volume changes, it was concluded that certain costs (e.g., maintenance) which management had attempted to control with current volume could better be controlled as managed [i.e., discretionary] capacity costs. While this conclusion was contrary to management's impression that it was desirable to control costs with current volume wherever possible, trials showed savings when all relevant factors including quality and reliability of services were included in the comparison.[7]*

Follow-up of discretionary costs.   Thus, we see that control may be exercised: (1) in the commonly accepted sense of the day-to-day follow-

[7] *Accounting for Costs of Capacity*, National Association of Accountants, *Research Report No. 39* (New York, 1963), p. 13.

up that is associated with variable costs; and (2) in the special sense of periodically evaluating an expenditure, relating it to the objectives sought, and carefully planning the total amount of the cost for the ensuing period. The latter approach does not mean that day-to-day follow-up is neglected; follow-up is necessary to see that the resources made available are being used fully and effectively. It does mean that perceptive planning is stressed and that daily control is de-emphasized. Reliance is placed more on hiring capable people and less on frequent checking up.

The practical effects of the discretionary cost approach are that the budgeted costs and the actual costs tend to be very close, so that resulting budget variances are small. Follow-ups to see that the available resources are being fully and effectively utilized are regarded as the managers' responsibility, a duty that can be achieved by face-to-face control and by records of physical quantities (for example, pounds handled per day in a warehouse, pieces mailed per hour in a mailing room) that do not have to be formally integrated into the accounting records in dollar terms.

Difficulties in applying work measurement

The success of the work-measurement, variable-cost approach to order-filling and administrative costs is limited by the nature of the work being performed. Attempts have been made to measure the work of legal personnel and claims adjusters in insurance companies, of economists in a Federal Reserve Bank, and of stockboys in retail stores. Such attempts have achieved limited success because of either (1) the inability to develop a satisfactory control factor unit or (2) the diversity of tasks and objectives of such personnel or (3) the difficulty of measuring the output of lawyers or economists.

For example, consider the attempt to measure the work of clerks and stockboys in a food store. Their tasks are routine and repetitive, but they are often splintered. Attempts at measuring employee work have shown volatile results. Such results indicate that there are opportunities for better utilization of personnel. The trouble is that each employee usually performs a variety of tasks on a variety of items. He may unpack, price-mark, stock shelves, operate a cash register, bag groceries, cart groceries to automobiles, sweep floors, and watch for shoplifters.

Control-factor units may be satisfactorily established for each individual task, but the comparison of results must be made with care. For instance, a comparison showed that productivity was 14 cases of frozen food per man-hour for receiving, price-marking, and displaying in one store; in another, the productivity was 22 cases per hour.[8] These results may prompt investigation in the low-productivity store, but other factors may narrow the apparent difference in productivity. Such over-staffing may occur because, after experimentation, the store manager has decided that his local competitive situation requires a certain number of clerks and stockboys to service customers. Merchandise characteristics are

---

[8] *The Economics of Frozen Foods, op. cit.*, p. 37.

secondary, and the "case per hour" figure may reflect a more leisurely work pace simply because the alternative is idle time during a certain span of the day. The point is that an able store manager, one who can see the jointness of the problem and who is willing to experiment and to compare his practices with those of other stores, is still the key to successful operations. Work measurement is helpful, because measurement is a first step toward control. But it is only a step.

Budgets in practice: combination of variable and fixed costs

Accounting systems in practice seldom distinguish between variable and fixed cost elements for a particular selling or administrative account. Instead, these are combined into one unit rate. For instance, order-filling cost standards are often based on average conditions, so that a flat rate per piece packed or invoice typed is used as a standard instead of a two-part rate consisting of a cost, say, of $.75 per invoice plus an additional variable cost of three cents per line. When the actual activity level differs from the average level used to set standards, a volume variance appears that may be caused partially by a difference in actual mixture of conditions. Variances must be interpreted accordingly. Once again, the costs of developing highly accurate standards must be related to the value of the resulting benefits.

To illustrate standard costing where a flat rate is used, suppose that a steel warehouse labor standard is five cents per hundred pounds handled. This standard cost is based on fixed costs of $1,800 per month plus variable costs of two cents per hundred pounds. During June 7,000,000 pounds were handled at a total cost of $3,400. An analysis of the variances must be made carefully. Try to prepare your own analysis before glancing at the following:

A. Faulty Analysis	
Actual cost	$3,400
Standard cost, $.05 × 70,000	3,500
Favorable variance	$ (100)

B. Correct Analysis	
Actual cost	$3,400
Budgeted cost based on a flexible budget:	
$1,800 + ($.02 × 70,000)	3,200
Unfavorable budget variance	$ 200

The first analysis is useless from a control standpoint because it fails to recognize that *actual volume* (7,000,000 pounds) was different from the *normal volume* (6,000,000 pounds) used for developing the five-cent standard rate. By employing the flexible-budget concept for a 7,000,000-pound level, the second analysis deliberately focuses attention on the controllable aspects of performance and excludes the effect of operating at a level other than 6,000,000 pounds. The following is a reconciliation of the variances:

Actual Costs at 7,000,000 Activity		Flexible Budget at 7,000,000 Activity		Standard Costs Applied at a Flat Rate of $.05
$3,400		$3,200		$3,500
	$200, Unfavorable		$300, Favorable	
	Budget Variance		Volume Variance (Fixed cost rate of $.03 times 10,000 units)	
		Total Favorable Variance, $100		

Note that this analysis is merely an extension of the factory overhead analysis that was discussed in Chapter 8. Note also that the five-cent standard rate is useful for control purposes only if and when activity levels are close to that activity level used to set the rate. Unless this important point is kept in mind, there is a strong danger that unit costs will be used for the wrong purpose. This is especially true in nonmanufacturing situations, where many costs tend to be fixed. In other words, beware when you interpret unit costs of functions, departments, or activities.

ORDER GETTING

General characteristics of order-getting costs

The outstanding characteristic of order-getting costs is that generally they are incurred *to obtain* sales rather than *as a result of* sales. For the most part they are discretionary costs, costs that are influenced mainly by periodic management *planning* decisions. Day-to-day control has little influence on over-all order-getting cost levels (inputs). However, day-to-day control may have a considerable impact on the *effectiveness* or productivity of the costs—the quantity and quality of the sales volume obtained (outputs).

Sales performance (outputs) is influenced by many variables whose independent effects are difficult to isolate. Examples are the interlinking of advertising with other sales efforts, the actions of competitors, general business conditions, personalities of salesmen and customers, and short-run and long-run effects of order-getting activities.

Measurement difficulties become more imposing as advertising becomes more general and selling more personal. In contrast, some order-getting activities are subject to specific measurement of efforts and results. For example, some selling duties are more akin to order filling than to order getting, for instance, certain retail and wholesale selling. Also, direct-mail advertising may be evaluated by its relative effectiveness in different publications, in various timings, in various sizes of advertisements, and in various types of inquiries.

The effectiveness of advertising is usually measured by the advertising or market research department. The ideal measure is the change in net sales in relation to changes in advertising and promotion costs.

However, the unreliability of such measures is widely recognized. It is difficult to establish a singular cause-and-effect relationship between advertising and sales. Conventional accounting tools are not too helpful here. The newer statistical and mathematical approaches that show promise in this regard are described fully in the literature on operations research.[9]

Need for experimentation

Despite the obvious difficulties of measurement, experimentation in marketing is widespread. Various merchandising displays, advertisements, media, and pricing policies are attempted in different markets with the hope that the best alternative available will clearly appear. Comparisons should be made carefully, so that nothing in the experimental procedure itself will favor or bias one alternative over another.

> *Since it is not the objective in marketing experiments to arrive at absolute values, experimental techniques do* not *require recognition or even control of all the variables that are involved. . . . the actual level of the sales or profit response is, of course, affected by all the uncontrolled and unrecognized variables or factors present in the various sales territories or time periods. . . used in the experiment. But the differences in sales. . . should not be affected by these uncontrolled and unrecognized factors. With a good experimental design, all alternatives are exposed equally to the same set of uncontrolled and unrecognized variables.*[10]

The point is that good experiments are designed so that many influential factors are irrelevant because they are common to both alternatives.

Concentration on profitable opportunities: planning is crucial

Unlike many aspects of production, where control is a big phase of managerial duties, marketing is characterized by the need for highly centralized planning. Management has found that making the best commitments is paramount and more imposing than the process of fulfilling the commitments efficiently.[11] Examples include decisions on advertising, sales promotion, and product mix. Thus, the planning decisions regarding how much to spend on advertising, where to spend, and when to spend are far more important than the mechanics of implementing the advertising program.

The analysis of order-getting costs usually has a central purpose: the shifting or concentration of efforts and resources toward the most prof-

[9] Miller and Starr, *Executive Decisions and Operations Research* (Englewood Cliffs, N.J.; Prentice-Hall, Inc., 1960), p. 172. Chapter 9 of this intriguing book shows how operations research techniques can be applied to marketing problems. Also see the suggested readings for Chapter 28.

[10] Sevin, *op. cit.*, p. 121.

[11] James W. Culliton, *Management of Marketing Costs* (Boston: Harvard University, Graduate School of Business Administration, Division of Research, 1948), p. 150.

itable course of action. The problems are primarily those of planning and secondarily those of controlling.

For example, consider a typical advertising agency. The overwhelming bulk of an agency's revenue comes from a 15 per cent commission on the gross amount of advertising placed in various media. Furthermore, an agency usually can get a fairly reliable estimate of how much its various clients are budgeting for advertising in the forthcoming year. Therefore, the agency can prepare its own revenue budget with some confidence in its accuracy.

What expenses does an advertising agency incur? The principal cost is salaries, which are relatively fixed for any given year's operations. The main decisions that confront the agency top management entail the securing of creative talent that will retain and attract clients. An accompanying decision is how to react to year-to-year changes in probable revenue. Should a stable work force be maintained? Whom and when do we hire, or fire? Of course, another key analytical task is deciding on the profitability prospects for possible new clients.

The point is that the relative profitability of an agency—and, for that matter, of various company sales forces—seldom is traceable to routine day-to-day control of expenses. Instead, it is traceable to periodic policy decisions that result in discretionary costs that are not subject to day-to-day influence.

Once these discretionary costs are incurred, the job becomes one of allocating these given resources—usually, numbers of people rather than direct materials or electronic computers—to the most profitable utilization of their available time. In the case of sales forces, day-to-day control should concentrate on seeing that each man obtains the greatest possible profit contribution (usually, but not always, through highest possible sales revenue). Day-to-day control should not ordinarily concentrate on how much the salesman spent for lunch or dinner. In other words, marketing planning and control should emphasize the important sources of profit and de-emphasize the unimportant.

Budgeting order-getting costs: influential factors

The planning of order-getting costs is affected by the following factors: past experience, general economic conditions, competitor behavior, new specific objectives, market research and tests, whims of the president, and the maximum amount that may be spent in the light of desired profits.

The latter point illustrates the circularity of advertising and sales. One large soap company introduces new products which are similar to old products, so that experience with old products may be used as a guide. Basically, a forecast is prepared as follows:

Sales potential		xx
Manufacturing and other costs	xx	
Desired profit	xx	xx
Remainder available for advertising		xx

If the remainder is sufficient for the advertising necessary to attain the sales potential, the new product is introduced.

Field selling

Control of selling costs and attainment of desired sales volumes are interrelated. Selling-cost incurrence should lead to sales. Often selling costs might be deliberately increased when competition makes inroads on sales. Rigid budgetary control of selling costs is foolhardy; control must be tempered by common sense. For example, a door-to-door salesman knows that the four-cent cost per sample of shaving lotion or hand lotion is a necessary cost of getting the door open and creating a customer obligation to listen. The savings by eliminating samples would be easily offset by the lost contribution margins on sales.

A widely used technique for control of selling costs is personalizing cost incurrence. Selling costs are heavily influenced by a salesman's judgment. If he knows that his phone calls, entertainment, and traveling will be traced to him, he is more likely to be cost-conscious. Management needs reports which highlight costs by salesman and by territory. Control is hopeless after the salesman's expenses are allocated among products.

Control budgets used by territorial or product sales managers are usually for periods of from one to six months. Local conditions, population density, and the like may call for various degrees of selling effort, with costs that may vary accordingly. The problem is one of getting maximum effort —of tapping the greatest sales potential in the light of available resources. Control of selling effort involves not only directing salesmen toward increasing sales volume per hour of time but also directing salesmen toward pushing the most *profitable* product lines.

Example of control of salesmen

The ultimate measure of a salesman's effectiveness is the long-run net profit that he produces. Salesmen's performance should not be gauged by dollar sales volume alone. Salesmen should recognize that some products are more profitable than others, and the expense incurrence and time spent with customers should be tailored accordingly. For example, consider a company which sells school equipment. Simpson, its salesman who is leading in terms of dollar sales volume, ranks in the middle of the seven salesmen in terms of the ultimate net-profit criterion. He is a free spender of travel and entertainment money; he quotes the lowest possible prices; and he makes unrealistic delivery-date promises. His orders provide more trouble in follow-ups and more general confusion than any other salesman's. This raises the question of the long-run effect on repeat business. But this is hard to quantify, especially as he seems to have much genuine rapport with his customers.

In contrast, Boswick, the salesman who is the best in terms of profits, has 60 per cent of the volume of Simpson, who incidentally considers himself to be the leader despite the sales manager's attempts to correct that impression. Boswick carefully controls his expenses and allots the bulk of his time to landing orders that provide a minimum of follow-up trouble and a maximum profit.

Exhibit 12-3 compares the performance of Simpson and Boswick. Note that, *in this case*, these two men have comparable territories and sales potentials; otherwise, the quotas used would not be the same for each man. Two key quotas are used: sales volume and profit contribution. Simpson achieved an admirable volume of low-profit sales, whereas Boswick's below-quota volume contributed high-profit sales.

EXHIBIT 12-3

SALESMEN'S PERFORMANCE REPORT
FOR THE QUARTER ENDING MARCH 31, 19x1

	Simpson	Boswick
Sales	$120,000	$72,000
Per cent of $100,000 quota	120%	72%
Travel expenses (hotel, meals, etc.)	1,300	900
Entertainment	250	200
Automobile	500	450
Extra direct charges for handling, returns, etc.	2,000	200
Cost of goods sold	94,000	40,000
Total charges	$ 98,050	$41,750
Sales, less above charges	$ 21,950	30,250
Commissions (8% of prior line)	1,756	2,420
Profit contribution	$ 20,194	$27,830
Profit contribution as a per cent of sales	16.8%	38.7%
Profit contribution as a per cent of budget of $25,000 per man	80.8%	111.2%

Although travel and entertainment expenses should be carefully watched and periodically audited, the key point in controlling selling effort is directing available time toward the customers with the greatest sales and profit potential. The misdirection of effort toward sparse or unprofitable markets is much more costly to the company in terms of opportunity costs (failure to utilize time to land profitable sales) than the relatively small savings that can be wrung out of penny pinching on travel and entertainment. In this case, the sales manager's patient education of Simpson on the folly of quoting the lowest possible prices to attain high sales volume slowly bore fruit, because Simpson's profit record gradually improved as months passed. (One effective way to make salesmen profit-conscious is to tie commissions or bonuses to gross profit or contribution margin rather than to net sales. This is illustrated in Exhibit 12-3.)

Standard costs and selling effort

Standards for selling costs are more often related to effort than to results. Companies use standards to various extents, depending on the nature of the selling activity. Thus, where salesmen are primarily order takers, their daily travel schedule, number of calls, and sales techniques may be rigidly regimented. In contrast, highly trained specialist salesmen are usually subject to a minimum of overseeing.

The standards used to measure efforts and results are rarely integrated into the formal accounting system. Instead, they are used by sales managers as tools for comparisons among salesmen, territories, and techniques.

THE ROBINSON-PATMAN ACT

The Robinson-Patman Act forbids quoting different prices to competing customers unless such price discrimination is justified by differences in costs of manufacturing, sale, or delivery. Decisions of courts and the Federal Trade Commission have been based on full-costing allocations rather than on direct or differential costing.

Most of these price differentials are justified by differences in distribution costs like advertising, warehousing, and freight rather than in manufacturing costs. That is why companies with flexible pricing policies need to keep careful records of distribution costs to answer any government inquiries. However, cost justification is only one aspect of these cases. In most instances, it has been overshadowed by the issues of lessening competition and price cutting in good faith.[12]

CLASSIFICATION AND ALLOCATION

The most widely used detailed operating statements are tabulated by product lines and by sales territories. The emphasis depends on the organization of the marketing function. Some companies have distinct product lines with separate sales forces and separate advertising programs, and their operating reports emphasize contributions by products. Other companies make a multitude of products that are promoted by brand-name advertising and which are all sold by the same salesmen. Their operating reports emphasize territorial or district sales and contributions to profit.

Allocation bases: weakness of sales dollars

In any good accounting system, the need for allocation is minimized by regarding as many costs as possible as direct charges. Alloca-

---

[12] For an expanded discussion see "Price Discrimination Under Federal Law," NAM *Law Digest* (June–September 1953). Also see Herbert Taggert, "Cost Justification Under the Robinson-Patman Act," *Journal of Accountancy* (June, 1956).

tions should be based on the factor most likely to affect the cost to be allocated. Some commonly used bases for allocation are shown in Exhibit 12-4.

EXHIBIT 12-4

BASES FOR ALLOCATION OF COSTS TO TERRITORIES

Cost to be Allocated	Allocation Base
Field salesmen	Direct
Central sales management	Budgeted sales; number of men; amount of time
Central administration	Unit rate for type of service, such as billing, printing, etc.
Central warehousing	Service used as measured by quantities handled
Central advertising costs	Projected sales volume
Advertising:	
Magazine	Circulation
Radio and television	Number of set owners
Samples	Territorial sales quota

A commonly, but wrongly, used basis for allocation is dollar sales. The costs of effort are independent of the results actually obtained, in the sense that the costs are programmed by management, not determined by sales. Moreover, the allocation of costs on the basis of dollar sales entails circular reasoning. That is, the costs per segment are determined by relative sales per segment. For example, examine the effects in the following situation (figures are in millions of dollars):

YEAR 1

Product	A	B	C	Total	
Sales	$100	$100	$100	$300	(100%)
Costs allocated by dollar sales	$ 10	$ 10	$ 10	$ 30	(10%)

Assume that prices are raised on Products *A* and *B*. Their total dollar volume rises considerably. However, the direct costs and sales of Product *C* are not changed. The total costs to be allocated on the basis of dollar sales are also unchanged.

YEAR 2

Product	A	B	C	Total	
Sales	$137.5	$137.5	$100.0	$375.0	(100%)
Costs allocated by dollar sales	$ 11.0	$ 11.0	$ 8.0	$ 30.0	(8%)

The ratio between the costs allocated on the basis of dollar sales and total sales was reduced, in the second year, to 8 per cent ($30 ÷ $375), as compared with 10 per cent ($30 ÷ $300) in the first year. This resulted in less cost being allocated to Product C, despite the fact that its unit volume and directly attributable costs were approximately the same as for the first year. The point is that the product which did the worst is relieved of costs without any reference to underlying causal relationships.

Advertising is a prime example of a cost that is typically allocated on the basis of dollar sales. Basing allocation on dollar sales *achieved* may be questionable, because the unsuccessful product or territory may be unjustifiably relieved of costs. However, there is some merit in basing allocation on *potential* sales or purchasing power available in a particular territory or for a particular product. For example, there would be a consistent relationship between the advertising costs and sales volume in each territory, if all territories are equally efficient. If, however, a manager has poor outlets or a weak sales staff, one of the indicators would be a high ratio of advertising to sales.

A management consulting firm commented on the misleading information being generated by allocations based on sales dollars:

> . . . *we found that the real magnitude of this impact is often obscured by accounting practices, which frequently allocate transportation costs to stores at a fixed percentage of sales. When this happens, the profit of distant stores is often overstated, and those stores are in effect being subsidized by the understated profits of the near stores.*[13]

Functional costing: allocate with care

Although costs should be allocated as far as possible, to facilitate decision making, there are definite limitations. Some well-known consultants and writers in this field have stressed a functional costing approach, that is, the classification of costs by function (warehousing, delivery, billing, and so forth). This objective is meritorious, but the approach taken is often downright misleading. Many proponents of functional costing are grimly determined to compute a unit cost for nearly any activity, without bothering to distinguish between variable and fixed behavior patterns. All of us are familiar with glib statements such as the following (taken from an actual report): "The cost summary discloses a unit cost of $.097 for handling commercial deposits, and this is made up of the following items (functions): teller $.0658, proof $.0057, and bookkeeping $.0256." The difficulty here is not caused by interest in the costs of performing various functions; it is that cost studies are too often focused on determining the exact cost of processing an order, of posting an invoice, or of making a sales call. Too often, the attempt involves flimsy assumptions concerning what costs are pertinent and what unit should be used as the base.

The data relating to costs and the data relating to units must be examined separately before the two are expressed as costs per unit. When costs and units are studied separately, the fundamental variable, mixed, or fixed behavior of each becomes evident, the importance of joint or common costs emerges, and the variations in cost which are not due to unit

---

[13] McKinsey-General Foods Study, "The Economics of Food Distributors" (White Plains, N.Y.: General Foods Corporation, 1963), p. 7.

volume variations are revealed. The contribution approach should dominate any attempt at functional unit costing.

EXAMPLES OF CONTRIBUTION APPROACH

Need for reports

Cost reports often indicate that certain actions should be taken about unprofitable salesmen, customers, products, territories, channels, or order sizes. Yet the marketing manager may firmly believe that competition or unfavorable customer reactions prevent taking action—that over-all long-run profits may suffer. His position may be entirely irrational, or it may be valid. In any event, the accountant's duty is to be sure that management understands the relevant facts for determining its marketing policies. Then at least the manager will have an idea of the measurable costs of continuing possibly questionable procedures, and he will have a foundation for experimentation.

The following examples will demonstrate how cost classification that emphasizes cost behavior can help marketing decisions.

> **Example 1: Profitability of Distribution Channels.**[14] The marketing manager in this company had vague suspicions that one of his company's four marketing channels was unprofitable, but he had no concrete evidence to help him decide. He needed to know the contribution margin of each channel. The task was simplified because business conditions and costs were not expected to change much; thus, historical data could be a good basis for prediction. The same product at the same price was sold to the four channels.

The contribution approach requires two steps here: (1) computing variable cost behaviors, and (2) allocating them among the four channels.

There were four distribution costs: selling, office, warehousing and shipping, and delivery. Monthly data were used to make scatter charts for analyzing each cost. For example, the relationship of selling expenses to the number of sales calls had the pattern shown in Exhibit 12-5.

A line was fitted to the points: it was extended back to the vertical axis, which it intersected at $14,000. The slope of the line indicated a variable cost of $3.00 per hundred sales calls.

The same graphic analysis was applied to other distribution costs, using the following bases as indices of volume for the particular costs:

	Number of
Selling expenses	Sales calls
Office expenses	Invoices
Warehousing and shipping expenses	Cases handled
Delivery expenses	Deliveries

[14] Based on an actual case described by Charles H. Sevin, *How Manufacturers Reduce Their Distribution Costs*, Department of Commerce (Washington, D.C.: U.S. Government Printing Office, 1948), Chapter 3.

EXHIBIT 12-5

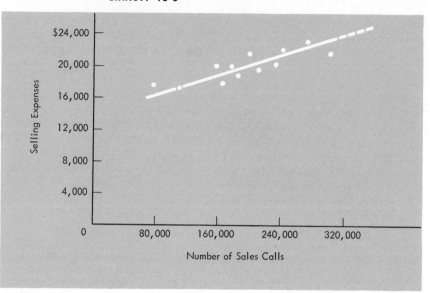

The variable portions of the above expenses were allocated to each channel by multiplying the unit variable cost in each channel by the number of units appropriate to that channel. The results (in thousands of dollars) follow:

	Total	Channels			
		A	B	C	D
Sales	1,500	750	250	300	200
Variable costs, including manufacturing costs	1,050	400	100	300	250
Contribution margin	450	350	150	0	-50
Nonvariable expenses	300				
Net income	150				

Should Channel D be dropped? The channel is not even recouping variable costs. Analysis showed that little could be done to improve profitability, so the channel was dropped. Note especially that the decision hinged on the hopeless outlook for further efforts in Channel D, not on the mere fact that the channel is currently unprofitable.

Should Channel C be dropped? The marketing manager was fully aware that the method for separating variable costs gave only crude answers. Dropping Channel C would relieve him of certain supervisory activities which could be devoted to other profit-making possibilities.

Analysis of customers in Channel C showed that eliminating low-volume customers might increase profit contribution considerably.

Examination of Channels A and B suggested that an increase in promotional effort might generate enough additional sales to make up for the lost customers in Channels C and D. The next year's results (in thousands of dollars) follow:

| | Total | Channels | | |
		A	B	C
Sales	1,260	825	315	120
Variable costs	655	415	130	110
Contribution margin	605	410	185	10
Nonvariable expenses	310			
Net income	295			

The profits almost doubled, increasing from $150,000 to $295,000 despite an over-all decline in sales. It should be remembered, however, that profit is the consequence of many forces; thus, the improved results are by no means conclusive evidence of a cause-and-effect relationship between the decision and the change in net income.

Example 2: Profit Contribution Per Unit of Retail Selling Space.
Retail managers have developed a number of practices which have often not maximized profits. McNair and May list a number of faulty practices which have arisen in department stores.
1. Overemphasis on gross margin percentages.
2. Using (1) across the board departmentally.
3. Lack of attention to costs generated by particular items.
4. No distinction between variable and fixed costs.
5. Mechanical pricing, with no regard for possible elasticities of demand.
6. General acceptance of net sales as an appropriate basis of expense allocation.
7. Overconfidence in the final departmental net profit percentages after full expense allocation.
8. Frequent tie-in of gross margin percentage with the department head's compensation.
9. Misplaced attention on ratios to sales rather than on dollars.[15]

Let us relate these points to food stores, where recent studies also show the validity of McNair's criticisms. For a given store, the objective should be to maximize the *dollar* contribution to profits, after imputing an allowance for inventory carrying costs based on average inventory value. The constraining factor or scarce resource is selling space. The ingredients of profit are the dollar contribution to profit per unit sold and the turn-over—the number of times the average inventory is sold per year.

---

[15]Malcolm P. McNair and Eleanor G. May, "Pricing for Profit: A Revolutionary Approach to Retail Accounting," *Harvard Business Review*, Vol. 35, No. 3 (May–June, 1957), p. 108.

Retail grocery chains have been making increased use of the profit-contribution-per-unit-of-space concept. Essentially the manager of a modern supermarket is concerned with maximizing the profitability of its scarce resource—selling space. Recent attempts have been made to allocate space in relation to the potential profit contribution of various products. This approach emphasizes dollar contribution, the profit per unit of space. For example, the selling price of jars of baby food minus cost of goods sold minus specifically and carefully determined handling, carrying, and other related variable expenses will yield a profit contribution. Multiplying this profit contribution by turnover and dividing by the space allotted will yield a profit contribution per unit of space. This can be assessed in the light of a target or desired average contribution for the store as a whole. To illustrate:

Target profit contribution for a store for a year	$62,400.00
Number of cubic feet of shelf space	3,000
Average annual profit contribution per cubic foot of shelf space ($62,400 ÷ 3,000)	$ 20.80
Average weekly profit contribution per cubic foot ($20.80 ÷ 52)	$ .40

The manager may use this technique to evaluate his use of space. For instance, if an item like baby food occupies three cubic feet of shelf space and contributes $.80 profit contribution per week, he will be inclined to reduce the baby food space to two cubic feet. These data may be imperfect, but the point is that at least they are relevant; they are more likely to guide the manager toward greater profits than the data he has traditionally received.

The above example was oversimplified. Complicating factors include the rating of shelf-space profitability by location and the necessity of carrying loss items as a convenience for customers. However, the supermarket's attempt to think in terms of profit contribution instead of traditional gross profits alone has sharpened insights.

For example, McKinsey & Co., Inc., a management consulting firm, conducted an intensive investigation of a typical supermarket. Profit contributions on various items were computed after allowing for such factors as inventory carrying costs, warehousing, transportation, and handling. Among the findings were the following: (1) Fast-moving baby food items do not contribute to profits because handling costs are too high; (2) a cereal carried a gross profit of $1.26 per case and profit contribution of $.25 compared to a dry soup with a gross profit of $1.21 and a profit contribution of $.71; (3) flavorings produced the highest profit contribution, $500 per cubic foot of shelf space.[16]

Incidentally, this study had a direct influence on the packaging of cereals. Until 1963, there was much empty space in an unopened package of cereal. Now smaller boxes, holding the same amount of cereal as before, are used. This saves shelf space and transportation costs.

[16] *The Economics of Food Distributors, op. cit.*

In another study,[17] the weekly dollar margin per linear shelf foot showed the following rankings:

Top Five Items	Dollar Margin Per Linear Shelf-Foot	Per- cent- age Gross Margin	Bottom Five Items	Dollar Margin Per Linear Shelf-Foot	Per- cent- age Gross Margin
Frozen orange juice	$36.91	30.1	Sanitary needs	$0.06	47.8
Frozen uncooked beef	11.83	22.6	Baby food	0.05	35.7
Frozen fruit pies	11.35	28.0	Saurkraut	0.05	40.0
Frozen turkey dinners	11.04	27.3	Cutlery	0.04	33.4
Frozen broccoli	9.99	27.1	Frozen lemon juice	0.03	14.3

Note that four of the five in the bottom group had higher gross margin percentages than any of the items in the top group.

How should costs be allocated to retail items when their relative profitability is being judged? Purchase costs, freight in, imputed inventory carrying charges, and other direct charges are easy to trace to particular items, but how and why should the costs of clerks, shelving, equipment, heat, light, and rent be allocated?

Under the contribution approach, fixed costs like rent, depreciation, heat, and light should not be allocated. But some products are clearly more difficult and time-consuming to handle within the store. Examples are flour, baby food, and frozen foods. Other products, such as bread and soup, are often cared for by vendor salesmen rather than by store personnel. Should handling costs be allocated in accordance with work-measurement techniques? That is, are labor costs variable or fixed for purposes of assessing product profitability and allocation of display space?

The McKinsey study regarded stocking labor as variable and allocated it: "Handling 1,000 cases takes twice as long and costs twice as much as 500 cases of the same product mix."[18] This exemplifies the work measurement-ideal standard attitude. This approach may indeed be the best for spurring operating improvements. However, there is evidence to show that such an approach is little more than a handy oversimplification. The real world is more complicated; it leads some managers to the view that store labor is fixed and unallocable:

> It has been found that 31 per cent of the clerks' time in a stationery store was idle time . . . that 25 per cent of the time of pharmacists in 37 drug stores was idle time. The peak demand for customer service at certain points in the day is a central factor in determining the number of clerks needed, and thus an excess of clerk time may often be available when few customers are in the store.
>
> Further, if selling activity increases sufficiently, the merchant may need to hire additional clerks to handle the peak load, even though there is idle time during

[17] Progressive Grocer, *Colonial Study* (New York: Progressive Grocer Publishing Co., 1963).
[18] *The Economics of Food Distributors, op. cit.,* p. 41.

slack periods with a lesser number of clerks ... the selling activity which affects the number of clerks needed is apparently largely determined by customer rather than by merchandise-item characteristics. That is, it appears to be difficult to trace any direct connection between a relatively small difference in the number of merchandise items carried in a retail store and the number of clerks needed to serve the customers coming into that store.[19]

RESEARCH AND DEVELOPMENT

Definition

Research and development activities have become increasingly important in modern industry. Research is no longer a frill activity; it is essential to maintain or enlarge a company's competitive position. For example, approximately half of Monsanto's $1.3 billion of sales in 1964 were of products that it did not produce ten years previously. *Research* has different meanings in different companies. It may mean fundamental or basic inquiry which has only a vague relationship to products or processes; or it may be used to describe minor efforts to improve some product part. Some of the latter effort may be called *product engineering* in one company or "research" in another company. *Development* usually takes up where research leaves off; that is, development is the transforming of research accomplishments into salable products or practical processes. The portion of the research dollar that is assigned to basic research,[20] product research, and process research varies between industries and between years. For example, in recent years petrochemical laboratories have concentrated on perfecting production processes. In attempting to outmaneuver rivals, companies have basic research and process development working closely together. That is, as basic research generates an idea, the feasibility of the result is immediately tested before allowing the basic research to continue too far.

For our purposes, research and development is a function that concentrates on bona fide research rather than on routine technical operating problems which are ordinarily tackled by an engineering department or a quality control department. Research and development embraces pure research, creation of new products, processes, and equipment, and major improvement of existing products and processes. The development phases would include costs of pilot testing.

Accounting for Research

Basic accounting for research and development is little different from other types of accounting. Costs are projected and accumulated

---

[19]Sevin, *Marketing Productivity Analysis, op. cit.*, p. 44.
[20]Industry spent only six per cent of its $15.2 billion 1966 research and development effort on basic research. Yet dollar spending on basic research rose 300 per cent in 1960–1966. Companies expect to spend $18.2 billion in 1969.

by responsibility, by nature of expenditure, and by project. But research has the following peculiar characteristics:

1. The over-all amount to be spent is appropriated by top management much as is done for advertising. The general emphasis of the research program is also settled by top management.

2. The details of execution are in the hands of the research director, who necessarily must be a *manager*, an individual who sees that his personnel work effectively. This effectiveness is difficult to measure but is essential for a successful research program. Put another way, research must be managed, and yet research workers need a stimulating, unfettered environment accompanied by a minimum of red tape. Most research workers are extremely intelligent and self-starting. They need an impelling atmosphere and enough cost-consciousness and direction to insure that company objectives will be achieved.

3. The central problem in appraising research performance is measuring effectiveness and benefit. This problem is not solved merely by comparing cost incurrence with cost budgets. A research department may consistently stay within its budget constraints and yet be ineffective. The difficulties of joint costing are overwhelming. For example, it is often hard to isolate the relative contributions of research, production, and sales effort to the success or failure of a new product. In the long run, a research program necessarily must be judged by its over-all fruitfulness. In the short run, the effective utilization of research resources is dependent on the selection of appropriate personnel and *managerial* talent on the part of its administrator.

Moreover, research spending is not a sole indicator of effectiveness. In terms of results, one good research brain at a cost of $30,000 per year may be worth considerably more than four at a cost of $10,000 each. Dr. Richard Gordon, of Monsanto, has commented: "One of the great myths of industrial research has been that if you spend enough money, something wonderful will happen. Management is beginning to realize this isn't so."[21] The attacks on the problems include (a) finding better research administrators, (b) improving motivation and organization of research scientists and engineers, and (c) encouraging coordination of research with other company activities, such as marketing and production.

Most research administrators get their start as engineers or scientists. They invariably are knowledgeable technical men as well as managers.

Research scientists, like most creative people, tend to have little patience with business routines. Consequently, the research administrator and operating management need delicate skills to maximize the researchers' motivation and productivity.

Research is only one phase of business. It cannot fluorish in isolation. For example, in 1951 Monsanto introduced a new product, Krilium, a revolutionary long-run soil conditioner developed at a cost of $3 million. It was a commercial flop. A Monsanto executive commented: "We were so excited about the product that we didn't think enough about

[21]*Fortune*, January, 1965, p. 160.

how to market it. It never occurred to us that most people just will not buy an expensive product if they can't see a benefit from it right away. If we had brought our sales people in on Krilium from the beginning they might have caught this in time for us to do something about it."[22]

Amount to be spent

Subject to the requests and opinions of interested parties, top management sets an annual research appropriation and selects the crucial areas for major research effort. Research management prepares cost estimates and implements the program through effective utilization of available talent. The cost of manpower is generally the biggest chunk of the research budget.

The lower limit of a research budget is usually the amount needed to keep a company in business. This may be zero in many instances. For example, the drug, garment, and chemical industries are marked by many companies which specialize in quickly copying other companies' new products. Consider the success of Metrecal, a new 1960 product for weight reduction. It was followed by a vast number of product imitations with lower sales prices.

It is difficult to generalize on the upper limit of a research budget, mostly because the results of research are often unpredictable. In practice, various rules of thumb are used: percentages of sales, percentages of profits, amounts spent by competitors, amounts spent by the industry as a whole, and amounts spent in previous years. Research is a continuing phenomenon; continuity is needed, so that in practice the year-to-year changes in costs are relatively slight. Most companies recognize that competitive pressures and technological change necessitate long run commitments to research that tend to creep upward. The practical rules of thumb should be mere points of departure. As a N.A.A. research study pointed out:

> . . . it is necessary to recognize that . . . research tends to be a cause rather than a result of sales volume and profits. While research expenses are often allocated to products on bases such as sales volume, cost of goods sold, or gross margin for purposes of determining product profit or loss, to apportion the research budget in the same way may not be the best way to spend research dollars. Present profits may reflect past expenditures for research, but future profits may depend on applying current research effort to products which now yield little or no income.[23]

More rigorous, analytic approaches are slowly replacing rules of thumb in setting research appropriations. Alternative acts are being weighed to understand their probable consequences and risks.

Details of current control

Most research costs consist of salaries and facilities. Current control emphasizes effective utilization of manpower and equipment rather

[22]*Ibid.*, p. 198.

[23]"Accounting for Research and Development Costs," Research Series No. 29, *N.A.(C.)A. Bulletin*, June, 1955, p. 1399.

than their fixed weekly or monthly costs. Supplies and other variable items are usually relatively minor and available on a self-service basis with a minimum of recordkeeping.

Accounting plans for current control stress expense authorization beforehand instead of typical performance reports and variance analysis. The authorization of amounts is crystallized only after consideration has been given to the pertinent research worker's judgment.

As already mentioned, keeping actual expenditures within budgeted amounts is not desirable in itself without some measure of project progress (output). About the only gauge of output is some kind of progress report, however fuzzy it may be.

Allocating research costs to divisions

Should research expenditures be allocated to divisions? Those who favor allocation maintain that it will cause division managers to take a greater interest in research activities; those who oppose allocation maintain that division managers exert no control over research costs and resent being charged with uncontrollable costs.

The decision to allocate or not to allocate depends on the individual motivational impact of the policy selected. Allocation is beneficial if it engenders active company-wide interest in research efforts; it is detrimental if it engenders negative response and misunderstanding of its purpose.

Disposition of research costs

Practically, nearly all companies charge research costs to expense as incurred, either as a part of Cost of Goods Sold, or as a part of General and Administrative Expenses, or as a separate item.

Conceptually, research costs should be classified by project. Unsuccessful projects should be written off immediately. Successful projects should be capitalized as assets. Such an accounting could also assist management in appraising the benefit of research spending.

SUMMARY

Marketing, the most important nonmanufacturing cost, has often been described as a combination of order-getting and order-filling activities. Order filling is closely akin to manufacturing and may be more easily subjected to control techniques such as work measurement. Order getting is unique in the sense that such activities generate sales rather than result from sales. Order-getting costs are mostly discretionary costs and are influenced mainly by periodic management planning decisions. The effectiveness of such costs is measured by the sales volume or contribution margins (outputs) obtained. Cause-and-effect relationships are extremely difficult to identify. That is why management accounting techniques have been more fully developed in manufacturing, where external influences are less, where routine is entrenched, and where facilities are relatively fixed.

Marketing consists of deciding on how many resources (men and money) are needed to accomplish objectives, and then allocating those resources to maximize their effectiveness.

The contribution approach is probably accounting's most helpful method for attacking these decision problems. The marketing manager should beware of any full-costing approach that fails to distinguish between such cost behavior patterns as variable, discretionary, and committed costs. The use of modern accounting techniques, plus the utilization of recently developed statistical and mathematical techniques, plus a willingness to experiment, should reduce the marketing executive's reliance on guesses or rules of thumb. The latter are no longer sufficient. Careful planning, cost analysis, and experimentation are the ingredients needed to improve performance.

SUGGESTED READINGS

Buzzell, R., W. Salmon, and R. Vancil, *Product Profitability Measurement and Merchandising Decisions* (Boston: Harvard Business School, 1965).

Gillespie, Cecil, *Cost Accounting and Control* (Englewood Cliffs, N.J.: Prentice-Hall, Inc., 1957). An annotated bibliography on distribution costs is on pp. 796–804.

McKinsey-Birds Eye Study, *The Economics of Frozen Foods* (White Plains, N.Y.: General Foods Corporation, 1964).

McKinsey-General Foods Study, *The Economics of Food Distributors* (White Plains, N.Y.: General Foods Corporation, 1963).

Schiff, Michael, and Martin Mellman, *Financial Management of the Marketing Function* (New York: Financial Executives Research Foundation, 1962).

Sevin, C. H., *Marketing Productivity Analysis* (New York: McGraw-Hill Book Company, Inc., 1965).

Taggart, Herbert, *Cost Justification* (Ann Arbor: Bureau of Business Research, University of Michigan, 1959). This is an extensive analysis of the impact of the Robinson-Patman Act on differential pricing practices and related cost allocations.

Also of interest will be *NAA Research Reports* Nos. 19, 20, 21, 25, 26, 27, 29, and 39.

PROBLEM FOR SELF-STUDY

Problem. *Clerical costs and the budgeting of variances.* The Alic Co. has many small accounts receivable. Work measurement of billing labor has shown that a billing clerk can process 2,000 customers' accounts per month. The company employs 30 billing clerks at an annual salary of $4,800 each. Next year's outlook is for a decline in the number of customers, from 59,900 to 56,300 per month.

1. Assume that management has decided to continue to employ the 30 clerks despite the drop in billings. Show two approaches, the

variable cost approach and the discretionary cost approach, to the budgeting of billing labor. Show how the *performance report* for the year would appear under each approach.

2. Some managers favor using tight budgets as motivating devices for controlling operations. In these cases, the managers really expect an unfavorable variance and must allow, in financial planning, for such a variance so that adequate cash will be available as needed. What would be the budgeted variance, also sometimes called expected variance, in this instance?

3. Assume that the workers are reasonably efficient. (a) Interpret the budget variances under the variable cost approach and the discretionary cost approach. (b) What should management do to exert better control over clerical costs?

Solution.

1. Variable cost approach:

Standard Unit Rate = $4,800 ÷ 2,000 = $2.40 per customer per year

or = $ .20 per customer per month

	Actual Cost	Flexible Budget: Total Standard Quantity Allowed for Good Units Produced × Standard Unit Rate	Budget Variance
	(30 × $4,800)	(56,300 × $.20 × 12 months)	
Billing clerk labor	$144,000	$135,120	$8,880 U

Discretionary cost approach:

	Actual Cost	Budget	Budget Variance
Billing clerk labor	$144,000	$144,000	—

2. The budgeted variance would be $8,880 unfavorable. The master budget for financial planning must provide for labor costs of $144,000; therefore, if the variable cost approach were being used for control, the master budget might specify:

Billing clerk labor:	
Control budget allowance	$135,120
Expected control budget variance	8,880
Total budget allowance for financial planning	$144,000

3. As the chapter explains, management decisions and policies are often of determining importance in categorizing a cost as being fixed or

variable. If management refuses, as in this case, to control costs rigidly in accordance with short-run fluctuations in activity, these costs are discretionary. The $8,880 variance represents the price that management, consciously or unconsciously, is willing to pay currently in order to maintain a stable work force geared to management's ideas of "normal needs."

Management should be given an approximation of such an extra cost. There is no single "right way" to keep management informed on such matters. Two approaches were demonstrated in the previous parts of this problem. The important point is that clerical work loads and capability must be measured before effective control may be exerted. Such measures may be formal or informal. The latter is often achieved through a supervisor's regular observation so that he knows how efficiently work is being performed.

QUESTIONS, PROBLEMS, AND CASES

Note: My favorites include 12-19, 12-21, and 12-27.

12-1. Why are planning and control more difficult in nonmanufacturing than in manufacturing?

12-2. "Marketing is characterized by the need for highly centralized planning." Explain.

12-3. What is the typical key purpose of the analysis of nonmanufacturing costs?

12-4. Name at least four segments of a business which are often used as a basis for reporting operating data.

12-5. Why are sales dollars usually a poor basis for cost allocation?

12-6. "The need in functional costing is for examining data relating to costs and units separately before expressing them as costs per unit." Explain.

12-7. Most order-getting costs are discretionary. Explain.

12-8. What are the two major facets in the control of order-getting costs?

12-9. "Dollar sales is the best single measure of salesmen's effectiveness." Do you agree? Why?

12-10. What are order-filling costs?

12-11. How does accounting for research differ from accounting for manufacturing?

12-12. "Research costs should not be allocated to company divisions." Do you agree? Why?

12-13. "Research costs should be charged off immediately as expenses." Do you agree? Why?

12-14. The Defense Department has used cost-plus increasingly as a basis for contracting research and development projects. What is the major weakness of this approach? What is another approach that might be used?

12-15. Product Deletion. At the beginning of the month, your company instituted a program of product deletion, as a result of which all the so-called unprofitable products were deleted from the price list on the first of the month. Profitability was determined by deducting from the sales price the estimated direct manufacturing cost of the product plus an allowance for nonmanufacturing costs based upon a percentage of the sales value. Now, at the end of the month, you find that more products have become unprofitable although there have been no changes in their prices or in the volume of their output.

REQUIRED:

1. Explain briefly why more products have become unprofitable.
2. Was the method of analysis used in this instance correct?
3. Indicate briefly the information required before proceeding with a program of product deletion.   [S.I.C.A.]

12-16. Allocation of Advertising. The *H* Company allocates national magazine advertising cost to territories on the basis of circulation weighted by an index which measures relative buying power in the territories. Does this method give cost and profit figures appropriate for the following decisions? Indicate clearly why or why not.

1. For deciding whether or not to close an unprofitable territory.
2. For deciding whether or not a territorial manager has obtained sufficient sales volume.
3. For determining how efficiently the territorial manager has operated his territory.
4. For determining whether or not advertising costs are being satisfactorily controlled.   [S.I.C.A.]

12-17. Retailing and Costs for Decision Making. You have a client who operates a large retail self-service grocery store which has a full range of departments. The management has encountered difficulty in using accounting data as a basis for decisions as to possible changes in departments operated, products, marketing methods, and so forth. List several overhead costs, or costs not applicable to a particular department, and explain how the existence of such costs (sometimes called *common costs* or *joint costs*) complicates and limits the use of accounting data in making decisions in such a store.   [C.P.A.]

12-18. Cost of Servicing a Bank Account. A bank stated that the service charge which it makes on accounts is based upon the cost of handling each account. A customer states that he does not see how it is possible to determine the cost of handling his account. Do you agree?

Discuss fully the problems involved in determining cost for such a service, including the limitations of the cost figures obtained.   [C.P.A.]

12-19. Commission Plan for New-Car Salesmen. As an automobile dealer, you are faced with the problem of formulating a new-car salesmen's commissions plan. You have listed the following alternatives:

(a) Commissions based on a flat percentage of dollar sales.

(b) Commissions based on varying percentages of dollar sales. The higher the sales price of a deal, the higher the commission rate. Also, commissions will vary depending on various accessories sold.

(c) Commissions based on net profit after allocation of a fair share of all operating expenses.

REQUIRED:

Evaluate these alternatives. Are there other methods which deserve consideration?

12-20. Selection of Product for Sales Promotion. The P. Co. plans a one-month sales promotion during which coupons worth 10 cents toward purchase of one of the company's products will be distributed to customers. Selection of the product to be promoted is being made, and the following figures have been assembled as a basis for the choice.

	Product A	Product B
Regular selling price per unit	30 cents	40 cents
Standard cost of sales	22 cents	35 cents
Contribution-margin ratio	30%	40%
Anticipated increase in sales accompanied by coupons	60,000 units	50,000 units

REQUIRED:

Tell which product should be chosen, and present appropriate figures to support your answer. [S.I.C.A.]

12-21. Analysis of Channels of Distribution and Territories. The Manning Co. has three sales territories which sell a single product. Its income statement for 19x2 contained the following data:

	Total	Territory A	Territory B	Territory C
Sales: 100,000 units, @ $11	$1,100,000	$550,000	$330,000	$220,000
Cost of goods sold, including $100,000 of fixed factory overhead	500,000	250,000	150,000	100,000
Gross margin	$ 600,000	$300,000	$180,000	$120,000
Order-filling costs:				
Freight out	$ 68,000	$ 34,000	$ 20,400	$ 13,600
Shipping supplies	50,000	25,000	15,000	10,000
Packing and shipping labor	50,000	25,000	15,000	10,000
Total	$ 168,000	$ 84,000	$ 50,400	$ 33,600
Order-getting costs:				
Salesmen's salaries	$ 50,000	$ 50,000		
Salesmen's commissions	26,400		$ 26,400	
Agents' commissions	11,000			$ 11,000
Sales manager's salary	30,000	15,000	9,000	6,000
Advertising, local	80,000	40,000	24,000	16,000
Advertising, national	100,000	50,000	30,000	20,000
Total	$ 297,400	$155,000	$ 89,400	$ 53,000
Total marketing costs	$ 465,400	$239,000	$139,800	$ 86,600
Administrative expenses:				
Variable	$ 50,000	$ 25,000	$ 15,000	$ 10,000
Nonvariable	100,000	50,000	30,000	20,000
Total administrative expense	$ 150,000	$ 75,000	$ 45,000	$ 30,000
Total expenses	$ 615,400	$314,000	$184,800	$116,600
Net operating income	$ (15,400)	$(14,000)	$ (4,800)	$ 3,400

Territory *A* contains the company's only factory and central head-quarters. This district employs five salaried salesmen.

Territory *B* is 200 to 400 miles from the factory. The district employs three salesmen on a commission basis and advertises weekly, locally.

Territory *C* is 400 to 600 miles from the factory. The district employs three manufacturers' agents. Local advertising costs are split fifty-fifty between the agents and the company. Cost per unit of advertising space is the same as in Territory *A*.

The following variable unit costs have been computed:

Freight out, per unit	$.50, $.70, and $1.10, for Territories A, B, and C, respectively
Shipping supplies, per unit	.50
Packing and shipping labor, per unit	.50
Variable administrative cost, per sales order	2.00

Territory *A* had 17,000 orders; Territory *B*, 6,000; and Territory *C*, 2,000. Local advertising costs were $60,000, $15,000, and $5,000, for Territories *A*, *B*, and *C*, respectively.

REQUIRED:

1. Mr. Manning asks you to recast the income statement in accordance with the contribution approach that he heard described at a recent sales convention. Assume that fixed manufacturing overhead, national advertising, the sales manager's salary, and nonvariable administrative expense are not allocated.

2. What is the performance margin per order in each territory? What clues for management investigation are generated by such a computation?

3. The salesmen in Territory *B* have suggested a saturation campaign in local newspaper advertising, to cost $30,000. How much must the sales volume in Territory *B* increase to justify such an additional investment?

4. Why does Territory *A* have the highest contribution margin percentage but the lowest territorial margin percentage?

5. On the basis of the given data, what courses of action seem most likely to improve profits? Should Territory *A* be dropped? Why?

● **12-22. Accounting for Research.** The Plastic Products Company maintains a research department. Research projects conducted during the accounting year 19x3 were of the following types:

    a. For development of a new product,
    b. For improvement of a product presently being manufactured, and
    c. For improvement of manufacturing methods.

Work on some of the projects was incomplete at December 31, 19x3.

What considerations are involved in selecting the accounting treatment(s) of research costs to be used by Plastic Products Company? Discuss fully, including a discussion of the various ways in which the research costs may be presented in the financial statements. [C.P.A.]

12-23. Development and Experimental Costs. A corporation was organized in 19x1 with a capital of $5,000,000 to manufacture a new type of sports automobile.

In 19x1 and 19x2 it invested $2,000,000 in a plant, machinery, and tools and expended $1,000,000 on materials, labor, advertising, and overhead costs in connection with perfecting a first or experimental model. There was no income from sales or other sources in those years. Management charged the costs of $1,000,000 to a "Development and Experimental Expense" account which appeared among "Deferred Charges" on the December 31, 19x2 balance sheet.

In January 19x3 the corporation's model was pronounced a success and its factory was ready to produce at the rate of 100 cars per year, to be sold for $5,000 per car. However, because of labor, material, and other problems, only five cars were produced and only three cars were sold. In 19x3 total sales were $15,000, purchases of materials and supplies were $100,000, factory labor was $40,000, and advertising, clerical, and overhead costs were $75,000. Management charged the net loss for the year 19x3 to the "Development and Experimental Expense" account which appeared on the balance sheet under "Deferred Charges."

During 19x4 management forecast the production and sale of 100 units. However, 80 were produced and only 20 were sold. The net operating loss for the year was $200,000, which management suggests deferring.

REQUIRED:

Assuming that you are the auditor for the company, discuss the acceptability of the accounting treatment, the disclosures, if any, you would make, and the opinion you would render as of:

1. December 31, 19x2,
2. December 31, 19x3, and
3. December 31, 19x4.   [C.P.A.]

12-24. Increase in Advertising. The following are unit costs for making and selling a single product at a normal level of 5,000 units per month:

Manufacturing costs:	
Direct materials	$40
Direct labor	24
Variable overhead	16
Fixed overhead	10
Selling and administrative expenses:	
Variable	30
Fixed	18

This product is usually sold at the rate of 60,000 units per year. Current selling price is $150.00. It is estimated that a rise in price to $160.00 will decrease volume by five per cent. How much may advertising be increased under this plan without having annual net income fall below the current level?

● **12-25. Order-Filling Costs and Minimum-Order Size.** The Independent Wholesale Drug Co. has made a time study of the cost of filling orders with the following results:

Size of Orders in Dollars	Average Time Required
$ 0.00 to $ 2.00	0.10 hours
$ 2.01 to $ 5.00	0.12 hours
$ 5.01 to $15.00	0.16 hours
$15.01 to $25.00	0.20 hours
Over $25.00	0.25 hours

Order-filling costs totaled $4,480 for the month in which the study was made, and 1,600 man-hours were worked in the Order-Filling Department. During the same period, the costs of receiving orders and of billing and posting the customers' accounts were calculated at a minimum of 16¢ per order. Gross margin (profit) on the company's merchandise averages 20 per cent.

Ignoring all considerations other than these cost data, should the company adopt a rule that it will accept orders only above some minimum size? If so, what minimum-order size would you recommend?

12-26. Order Sizes and Distribution Costs. The Inviting Cheese Company Limited has discovered that the cost of distributing its products constitutes 68 per cent of the total cost of doing business. It has therefore asked you, as its cost analyst, to make a study of various phases of distribution costs per hundred pounds of product sold.

An analysis of the number of orders, the number of items on these orders, and the total weight of the orders, indicated the following:

Size of Order	Number of Orders	Total Number of Items	Total Number of Pounds
Under 50 pounds	3,000	4,000	80,000
50 to 199 pounds	3,500	8,800	270,000
200 to 499 pounds	600	2,200	190,000
500 to 999 pounds	300	2,700	280,000
1,000 pounds and over	100	800	120,000
Total	7,500	18,500	940,000

An analysis of the various distribution expenses indicates that some of these can be allocated to the various-sized orders on the basis of the number of orders, the number of items on the orders, or the number of pounds in the orders.

The analysis provided the following breakdown of the three major groups of distribution costs and expenses:

Group of Distribution Costs	Total	Allocated on the Basis of		
		No. of Orders	No. of Items	Weight in Pounds
Direct selling expenses	$4,200	$2,200	$1,600	$ 400
Packing and shipping expenses	2,005	350	575	1,080
General and administrative expenses	2,200	1,200	600	400
Total	$8,405	$3,750	$2,775	$1,880

REQUIRED:

1. Prepare a statement to indicate the fully allocated cost of distribution per 100 pounds of cheese for each size of order.

2. If orders under fifty pounds were not accepted, would distribution costs decline by the amount of the fully allocated costs of the orders? If not, how useful

is the allocation? What information would you need to evaluate the profitability of orders under fifty pounds?   [S.I.C.A. Adapted]

12-27. Control of Discretionary Costs. The manager of a regional warehouse for a mail-order firm is concerned with the control of his fixed costs. He has recently applied work-measurement techniques and a variable cost approach to the staff of order clerks and is wondering if a similar technique could be applied to the workers who collect merchandise in the warehouse and bring it to the area where orders are assembled for shipment.

The warehouse foreman contends that this should not be done because the present work force of twenty men should be viewed as a fixed cost necessary to handle the normal volume of orders with a minimum of delay. These men work a forty-hour week at $2.50 per hour.

Preliminary studies show that it takes an average of twelve minutes for a worker to locate an article and take it to the order assembly area, and that the average order is for two different articles. At present the volume of orders to be processed is 1,800 per week.

REQUIRED:

1. For the present volume of orders, develop a discretionary cost and a variable cost approach for the weekly performance report.
2. Repeat (1) for volume levels of 1600 and 1400 orders per week.
3. What other factors should be compared with the budget variances found in (1) and (2) in order to make a decision on the size of the work force?

12-28. Standards for Order Filling; Questioning of Standard Measuring Unit. The Fremont Company has several billing clerks and has developed standard billing labor costs of $.50 per bill based on hourly labor rates of $2.00 and an average of four bills of ten lines each per hour. Each clerk has a $7\frac{1}{2}$-hour workday and a five-day work week.

The supervisor has received the following assessment of performance for a recent four-week period regarding his clerks:

	Actual	Standard	Variance
		(2,600 bills × $.50)	
Billing labor (5 clerks)	$1,500	$1,300	$200 unfavorable

The supervisor knows that his superior, the office manager, will want an explanation of the unfavorable variance together with suggestions as to how to avoid such an unfavorable variance in the future.

The supervisor has taken a random sample of 200 of the 2,600 bills that were prepared during the period in question. His count of the lines billed in the sample totaled 2,200 lines.

REQUIRED:

As the supervisor, prepare a one-page explanation of the $200 unfavorable variance, together with your remedial suggestions.

12-29. Ford Motor Company's Flexible Budget Control over Clerical Costs Through Work Measurement. This case illustrates a method by which flexible budget controls have been adapted to a nonmanufacturing operation to control costs which might normally be classed as fixed labor and operating expense. It is possible and practical to control many expenses of this nature by the use of "standard" processing rates for work performed.

The following information is presented as background material to outline the control approach followed by this company:

The parts and accessories division of Ford Motor Company controls and evaluates the performance of its branch warehouse operations by the use of "flexible labor and expense budgets." These budgetary controls are in use in both the warehousing and the accounting activities of these operations and are used for both weekly and monthly analysis.

Primarily, variable labor functions and controllable expense classifications are supervised in this manner. Fixed costs which are not controllable by local management, such as supervision, taxes, and depreciation, are administered by the use of fixed (static) budget allowances.

All variable functions of the warehousing and accounting activities have been analyzed and standardized and related to some measurable work output. By maintaining daily control of these functional productivities and related daily labor charges, the required operating reports are prepared and submitted to the general office for analysis, consolidation, and comparison to national operating budget levels.

A primary source of output statistics is obtained from a record of actual daily shipments made by the warehouse, as many accounting-function productivities are based on this measurement. The determinable output measurements are compared to the predetermined functional budget rate to calculate "budget hours generated" during the budget period under review. The operating variances are determined by comparing generated budget hours to actual functional labor charges during the same period. These variances are expressed both in hours of variance and in equivalent-persons variance. The latter variance is calculated by comparing the hourly variance amounts to the forty shift hours available in the budget period under review.

For a recent normal work week of five operating days the following output information and labor distribution detail have been accumulated for certain selected accounting department functions. The complete budget review is actually applied to approximately fifty separate and distinct activities in this operation.

Output Statistics

1. Number of orders shipped	8,640
2. Number of line items* shipped	99,280
3. Number of line items backordered in warehouse	2,720
4. Number of checks written for merchandise received	3,290
5. Number of line items on shipments received	4,960
6. Number of credit adjustments approved	975

FUNCTIONAL BUDGET RATES AND LABOR DISTRIBUTION

Function	Budget rate per hour	Actual hours worked
Invoice scheduling	135 orders shipped	68.0
Keypunch†	680 line items processed	142.0
Keyverification†	1360 line items processed	71.0
IBM machine operator†	1020 line items printed	108.0
Proofreading†	510 line items proofread	208.0
Accounts Payable:		
Invoice matching	80 line items received	
Check auditing	70 payments made	125.0
Credit adjustments	15 adjustments issued	69.0

Budgeted hourly labor rate—$2.75 per hour.
Actual payroll costs   —$2,256.00.

*Represents a single part number shipped or received regardless of quantity.
†To determine the output allowance, the 2,720 line items backordered should be added
 to the 99,280 items shipped.

REQUIRED:

1. Determine labor variance by function. Express variance in both hours and equivalent persons.
2. Calculate total labor variance in dollars.
3. Analyze the total dollar variance as determined in part 2. What portion of this variance was attributable to a labor rate variance and a labor efficiency variance?

COST ANALYSIS FOR NONROUTINE
DECISIONS AND LONG-RANGE PLANNING

relevant costs: a key concept in
special decisions

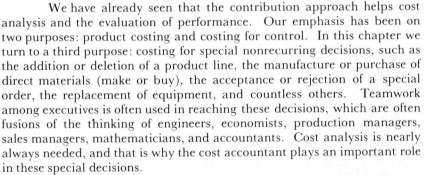

CHAPTER XIII

We have already seen that the contribution approach helps cost analysis and the evaluation of performance. Our emphasis has been on two purposes: product costing and costing for control. In this chapter we turn to a third purpose: costing for special nonrecurring decisions, such as the addition or deletion of a product line, the manufacture or purchase of direct materials (make or buy), the acceptance or rejection of a special order, the replacement of equipment, and countless others. Teamwork among executives is often used in reaching these decisions, which are often fusions of the thinking of engineers, economists, production managers, sales managers, mathematicians, and accountants. Cost analysis is nearly always needed, and that is why the cost accountant plays an important role in these special decisions.

When is an item relevant? When is it irrelevant? These distinctions are crucial to the making of intelligent decisions. The contribution approach, combined with the ability to distinguish relevance from irrelevance, will enable the accountant to reach correct conclusions in this challenging area.

THE ACCOUNTANT'S ROLE IN SPECIAL DECISIONS

Reporter of relevant data: relevance and accuracy

Accountants have an important role in the decision-making process, not as the decision makers themselves, but as collectors and reporters of relevant data. Many managers want the accountant to offer

405

recommendations about a decision even though the final choice always rests with the operating executive.

Relevance and accuracy are not identical concepts. *Relevance* means pertinence to the decision at hand. Figures are relevant if they guide the manager toward the decision that harmonizes with top-management objectives. Ideally, the data should be *relevant* (valid or pertinent) and *accurate* (precise). However, figures may be accurate but irrelevant, or inaccurate but relevant. For example, the advertising manager's salary may be exactly $45,500 per year, but this fact may have no bearing on whether to add or drop a product line.

Qualitative and quantitative factors

The consequences of each alternative may be divided into two broad categories, *qualitative* and *quantitative*. Qualitative factors are those whose measurement in dollars and cents is difficult and imprecise; yet a qualitative factor may easily be given more weight than the measurable cost savings. For example, a militant union which opposes the introduction of some labor-saving machinery may cause an executive to defer or to reject completely the contemplated installation. Or the chance to manufacture some product components at a saving below supplier quotations may be rejected because of a long-run dependency on the supplier for other important subassemblies. Quantitative factors are those which may more easily be reduced to terms of dollars and cents, such as projected alternative costs of materials, direct labor, and overhead. The accountant, statistician, and mathematician increasingly try to express as many decision factors as possible in quantitative terms. This approach reduces the number of qualitative factors to be judged.

MEANING OF RELEVANCE

Business decision making is choosing between alternative courses of action. The alternative actions take place in the future, whether the future be five seconds or a hundred years ahead; hence, the decision will be influenced by the forecast of future results to be expected under the various alternatives. The financial ingredients of the forecast must necessarily be based on expected future data. Consequently, to be relevant, a cost must be an expected future cost.

But *all* future costs are not necessarily relevant to a given decision; only those costs that will be *different* under alternatives are relevant. Thus, relevant costs may be defined as those *future* costs that will be *different* under available alternatives. The key question in determining relevance is, "What difference will it make?"

To illustrate, consider two movie theaters, each the same distance away and with equal intangible satisfactions, such as comfortable seats, courteous employees, and clean washrooms. You are considering going to one of the two theaters tonight. They are showing identical programs.

You have attended both theaters recently and found their admission prices to be ninety cents at one and fifty cents at the other. You assume, therefore, that these admission prices have not changed. The relevant costs are ninety cents and fifty cents, the future costs that will be different under the two alternatives. You use your past experience as the best guide to predict the relevant costs. Note that the pertinent costs are not what you paid in the past but what you *expect to pay* tonight.

You also may have the habit of purchasing popcorn at the theater. The cost *is expected to be* a quarter for the same quality popcorn at either theater. This, too, is an expected future cost, but it is irrelevant because it will be the same under either alternative—it does not involve an element of difference.

As another illustration, assume that a company is thinking of re-arranging its plant facilities. Accounting records show that past direct labor costs were $2.00 per unit. No wage-rate changes are expected, but the rearrangement is expected to reduce direct labor usage by 25 per cent. Direct material costs of $5.00 per unit will not change under either alternative. An analysis follows:

	Relevant Costs Per Unit	
	Do Not Rearrange	Rearrange
Direct labor	$2.00	$1.50

The cost comparison above is one of *expected future costs* that will *differ* under alternatives. The $2.00 direct labor charge may be the same as in the past, and the past records may have been extremely helpful in pre-paring the $2.00 forecast. The trouble is that most accountants and managers view the $2.00 past cost as the future cost. But the crucial point is that the $2.00 is an expected future cost, not a past cost. *Historical costs in themselves are irrelevant, though they may be the best available basis for estimating future costs.*

The direct material costs of $5.00 per unit are expected future costs, not historical costs. Yet these future costs are irrelevant because they will not differ under alternatives. There may be no harm in preparing a comparative analysis that includes both the relevant direct labor cost forecast and the irrelevant direct material cost forecast:

	Cost Comparison Per Unit	
	Do Not Rearrange	Rearrange
Direct material	$5.00	$5.00
Direct labor	2.00	1.50

However, note that we can safely ignore the direct material cost, because it is not an element of difference between the alternatives. The point is that irrelevant cost may be included in cost comparisons for deci-sions, provided that they are included properly and do not mislead the decision maker. A corollary point is that concentrating solely on relevant costs may eliminate bothersome irrelevancies and may sharpen both the accountant's and the manager's thinking regarding costs for decision making.

In summary, the chart below shows that relevant costs for decisions are expected future costs that will differ under alternatives. Historical costs, although helpful in predicting relevant costs, are always irrelevant costs per se:

Past Costs		Expected Future Costs	
(often used as a guide for prediction)			
		Do Not Rearrange	Rearrange
Direct material	$5.00	$5.00*	$5.00*
			Second Line of Demarcation
Direct labor	2.00	2.00	1.50

First Line
of
Demarcation in a Conceptual
Approach to Distinction Between
"Relevant" and "Irrelevant"

*Although these are expected future costs, they are irrelevant because they are the same for both alternatives. Thus, the second line of demarcation is drawn between those costs that are the same for the alternatives under consideration and those that differ; only the latter are relevant costs as we define them.

This idea of relevance, coupled with the contribution approach, arms the manager and the accountant with a powerful general weapon for making special decisions. The rest of this chapter will show how to apply these notions to some commonly encountered decisions.

ILLUSTRATIONS OF RELEVANCE: CHOOSING ACTIVITY LEVELS

Decisions that affect activity levels are made under a given set of conditions which include certain plant capacity, equipment, and basic operating conditions. Such decisions are essentially short-run in nature; but they have long-run overtones that should never be overlooked.

The special order

Management is sometimes faced with the problem of price quotations on special orders when there is idle capacity.

Example: X Company manufactures overshoes. The current operating level, which is below full capacity of 110,000 pairs per year, promises the following results for the year:

		Per Unit
Sales, 80,000 pairs @ $1.00	$80,000	$1.00
Manufacturing costs:		
Variable, 80,000 pairs @ $.50	$40,000	.50
Fixed	25,000	.3125
Total manufacturing cost of goods sold	65,000	$ .8125
Gross margin		$ .1875
Variable selling expenses*	$ 4,000	.05
Fixed selling expenses	8,000	.10
Total selling expenses	12,000	$ .15
Total expenses	$77,000	.9625
Net operating income	$ 3,000	$ .0375

*Consists only of shipping expenses of 5¢ per pair.

A mail-order chain offers to buy 20,000 pairs @ 75¢. The buyer will pay for the shipping expenses. The president is reluctant to accept that order because the 75¢ price is below the $.8125 factory unit cost. Should the offer be accepted?

Exhibit 13-1 shows a report that might be presented to management as a guide for decision making. The relevant items of cost are those that will be affected by taking the special order: the variable *manufacturing* costs. The fixed manufacturing costs and the variable selling expenses are irrelevant. The only relevant figures are revenue and variable manufacturing costs.

EXHIBIT 13-1

COMPARATIVE ANNUAL INCOME STATEMENTS

	Without Special Order	Difference		With Special Order
Sales	$80,000	20,000 @ $.75	$15,000	$95,000
Variable costs:				
Manufacturing, 80,000 pairs @ $.50	$40,000	20,000 @ $.50	$10,000	$50,000
Selling	4,000		—	4,000
Total variable costs	$44,000		$10,000	$54,000
Contribution margin	$36,000		$ 5,000	$41,000
Fixed costs:				
Manufacturing	$25,000		—	$25,000
Selling	8,000		—	8,000
Total fixed costs	$33,000		—	$33,000
Net income	$ 3,000		$ 5,000	$ 8,000

Differential cost

Differential cost (sometimes called *incremental cost*) in any given situation is commonly defined as the *change* in total cost under each alternative. The Difference column of Exhibit 13-1 shows that the differential revenue is $15,000, the differential cost is $10,000, and the differential margin is $5,000. Notice that *differential cost* is the algebraic difference between the relevant costs for the alternatives under consideration.

Fixed expenses and unit costs

Exhibit 13-1 also illustrates the irrelevance of fixed costs in a decision of this kind. The fixed costs remain the same under both alternatives (acceptance or rejection); therefore, the $33,000 is irrelevant. The fixed costs here perhaps may involve future outlays, but they will not change regardless of what decision is made. You may substitute $1,000,000 for the $33,000 fixed cost without changing the result.

Note also that the full factory unit cost at the 80,000-unit activity level was $.8125. If such a cost were used as a guide in deciding, the offer would have been unwisely rejected on the grounds that the $.75 prospective selling price is well below the $.8125 unit cost. In most cases it is safer to compare *total* costs rather than *unit* costs. Thus, fixed costs must be analyzed carefully, because their behavior is unique. The spreading of the $25,000 fixed manufacturing cost over 100,000 units instead of 80,000 units resulted in the lowering of the unit cost from $.8125 to $.75 for all units produced. But how fixed costs are attached to units of product has no bearing on special decisions.

Short run and long run

Many of the decisions that affect activity levels reduce themselves so that all variable costs are relevant and all fixed costs are irrelevant. This preconceived attack may be handy, but it is far from being foolproof. For instance, this special-order example is not merely a case of saying that the variable costs are relevant and the fixed costs are irrelevant. The selling costs are variable but irrelevant because they are not affected by this special order.

Economists and accountants agree that, if the length of time under consideration becomes long enough, no type of cost is fixed. Yet management is faced with the task of making decisions when the length of time under consideration is short enough so that many conditions and costs are fixed. What role should fixed costs play in decision making? No categorical answer may be given to this question. About the most useful generalization is that fixed costs should be considered when they are altered under the problem at hand. If activity levels change so that additional supervision, plant, equipment, insurance, and property taxes are needed, these new fixed costs are relevant. For example, sales or production may expand to the point where a new delivery truck may be bought.

Qualitative factors

Of course, in these cases there are many other considerations which are important but difficult to measure. For example, possible ill effects on regular customer goodwill, price breaks on regular business, and illegal price cutting would tend toward rejection of the order. On the other hand, the possibility of a profitable long-run relationship as supplier to a national retail chain would favor acceptance of the offer. Also, there may be a need to maximize use of facilities in order to keep a stable work force. These various qualitative factors are often the determining ones, rather than the immediate effects on net income. However, as Chapter 10 pointed out, the contribution approach to the special order would be as follows: "Mr. Manager, acceptance of this order will increase immediate net income by $5,000. If you do not accept, in effect you are saying that the immediate benefits fail to outweigh long-term disadvantages. Your rejection amounts to investing $5,000 now to preserve the long-run pricing structure."

Reports for decision making

The assumption in this book is that management seeks to max-imize long-run return on investment. The illustrations in this chapter assume a stable investment base, so we shall concentrate on the effects on net income only. Thus, ideally the alternatives under every decision would be compared as in Exhibit 13-1 by preparing a separate income statement for each alternative, as well as showing the differences. This provides the ultimate test, but short cuts may emphasize *differences* in order to spotlight only the relevant factors that *influence* the final results shown on these separate income statements. A short-cut analysis would be con-fined to the middle column in Exhibit 13-1. The point here is that concen-tration on differential revenues and differential costs in analyzing data does not necessarily mean that the final reports submitted to the decision-making executives should contain only these differential items. The final reports should be tailored to managerial quirks and wants. There is no single way to present data. The right way is that which is most under-standable and meaningful to the executives concerned. However, as Chap-ter 10 emphasized, the contribution approach tends to facilitate under-standing.

Dropping a product line

Assume that a company has three product lines, all produced in one factory. Management is considering dropping Product C, which has consistently shown a net loss. The present income picture follows:

		Product		
	A	B	C	Total
Sales	$500,000	$400,000	$100,000	$1,000,000
Variable expenses	295,000	280,000	75,000	650,000
Contribution margin	$205,000(41%)	$120,000(30%)	$ 25,000(25%)	$ 350,000(35%)
Fixed expenses (salaries, depreciation, property taxes, insurance)	165,000	90,000	45,000*	300,000
	$ 40,000	$ 30,000	$(20,000)	$ 50,000

*Includes product line supervisory salaries of $10,000.

Assume that the only available alternatives are to drop Product C or to continue with Product C. Assume further that the total assets invested will not be affected by the decision. Thus, the issue becomes one of selecting the production combination that will provide maximum profits. Comparisons follow:

Income Statements	Keep Product C	Difference	Drop Product C
Sales	$1,000,000	−$100,000	$900,000
Variable expenses	$ 650,000	−$ 75,000	$575,000
Fixed expenses	300,000	− 10,000	290,000
Total expenses	$ 950,000	−$ 85,000	$865,000
Net income	$ 50,000	−$ 15,000	$ 35,000

The above data reveal that dropping unprofitable Product C would make matters worse instead of better. Why? Because all of the fixed expenses would continue except for the $10,000 that would be jarred loose through discharging supervisory help. Product C now contributes $25,000 toward the coverage of fixed overhead; thus, the net effect of dropping Product C would be to forego the $25,000 contribution in order to save the $10,000 salaries. The result would be a $15,000 drop in over-all profit, from $50,000 to $35,000.

Another important factor that was not included in the two alternatives discussed above is the possibility of dropping Product C, keeping the supervisor, and using the vacant facilities to produce, say, Product A to satisfy its expanding demand. If this happened, and if sales of Product A are expanded by $100,000, income would increase by $16,000, as follows:

	Total, Keep Product C	Difference		Total, Drop C, Produce More A
		Drop C	More A	
Sales	$1,000,000	−$100,000	+$100,000	$1,000,000
Variable expenses	$ 650,000	−$ 75,000	+$ 59,000	$ 634,000
Fixed expenses	300,000			300,000
Total expenses	$ 950,000	−$ 75,000	+$ 59,000	$ 934,000
Net income	$ 50,000	−$ 25,000	+$ 41,000	$ 66,000

Note that a short-cut solution to this problem could be found by concentrating on the differences shown in the two middle columns of the tabulation. These make up the final $16,000 difference in net income.

Note further that, with given facilities and given fixed expenses, the emphasis on products with higher contribution margins apparently maximizes net income. Although this may be true in many instances, the matter is not quite that simple, as our next section demonstrates.

Contribution per unit of constraining factor

When a multi-product plant is being operated at capacity, decisions must often be made as to which orders to accept. The contribution approach supplies the data for a proper decision, because the latter is determined by the product which makes the largest *total* contribution to profits. This does *not* necessarily mean that the products to be pushed are those with the biggest contribution margin ratios per unit of product or per sales dollar. The objective is to maximize total profits, which depend on getting the highest contribution margin per unit of the *constraining (scarce, limiting,* or *critical) factor.* The following example may clarify the point. Assume that a company has two products:

	Product	
Per Unit	A	B
Selling price	$10	$15
Variable expenses	7	9
Contribution margin	$ 3	$ 6
Contribution margin ratio	30%	40%

At first glance, B looks more profitable than A. However, if you were the division manager, had 1,000 hours of capacity available, and knew that you could turn out 3 units of A per hour and only 1 unit of B per hour, your choice would be A, because it contributes the most margin per *hour*, the constraining factor in this example:

	A	B
Contribution margin per hour	$ 9	$ 6
Total contribution for 1,000 hours	$9,000	$6,000

The constraining factor is that item which restricts or limits the production or sale of a given product. *Thus the criterion for maximum profits, for a given capacity, is the greatest possible contribution to profit per unit of the constraining factor.* The constraining factor in the above example may be machine-hours or labor hours. It may be cubic feet of display space; in such cases, a ratio such as the contribution margin ratio is an insufficient clue to profitability. The ratio must be multiplied by the stock turnover (number of times the average inventory is sold per year) in order to obtain comparable measures of product profitability.

The success of the suburban discount department stores illustrates the concept of the contribution to profit per unit of constraining factor. These stores have been satisfied with subnormal mark-ups because they have been able to increase turnover and thus increase the contribution to profit per unit of space. Exhibit 13-2 demonstrates this point and assumes that the same total selling space is used in each store.

EXHIBIT 13-2

	Regular Department Store	Discount Department Store
Retail price	$4.00	$3.50
Cost of merchandise	3.00	3.00
Contribution to profit per unit	$1.00(25%)	$ .50(14 + %)
Units sold per year	20,000	44,000
Total contribution to profit	$20,000	$22,000

As you may imagine, there may be many constraining factors which may have to be utilized by each of a variety of products. The problem of formulating the most profitable production schedules and the mixes of raw materials are essentially those of maximizing the contribution in the face of many constraints. These complications are solved by linear programming techniques, which are discussed in Chapter 28.

Make or buy and idle facilities

Manufacturers are often confronted with the question of whether to make or buy a product—whether, for example, to manufacture their own parts and subassemblies or buy them from vendors. The qualitative factors may be of paramount importance. Sometimes the manufacture of parts requires special knowhow, unusually skilled labor, rare materials, and the like. The desire to control the quality of parts is often the determining factor in the decision to make them. On the other hand, companies hesitate to destroy mutually advantageous long-run relationships by the erratic order giving which results from making parts during slack times and buying them during prosperous times. They may have difficulty in obtaining any parts during boom times, when there are shortages of materials and workers and no shortage of sales orders.

What are the quantitative factors relevant to the decision of whether to make or buy? The answer, again, depends on the context. A key factor is whether there are idle facilities. Many companies make parts only when their facilities cannot be used to better advantage.

Assume that the following costs are reported:

COST OF MAKING PART NO. 300

	Per Unit	10,000 Units
Direct materials	$ 1	$ 10,000
Direct labor	8	80,000
Variable overhead	4	40,000
Fixed overhead, separable	2	20,000
Fixed overhead, joint but allocated	3	30,000
Total costs	$18	$180,000

Another manufacturer offers to sell *B* Co. the same part for $16. Should *B* Co. make or buy the part?

Although the above figures seemingly indicate that the company should buy, the answer is rarely obvious. The key question is the difference in future costs as between the alternatives. If the $3 fixed overhead assigned to each unit represents those costs (for example, depreciation, property taxes, insurance, and reapportioned executive salaries) that will continue regardless of the decision, the entire $3 becomes irrelevant.

Again, it is risky to say categorically that only the variable costs are relevant. Perhaps all of the $2 of directly identifiable fixed costs will be saved if the parts are bought instead of made. In other words, fixed costs that may be avoided in the future are relevant.

For the moment, let us assume that the capacity now used to make parts will become idle if the parts are purchased. The relevant computations follow:

	Per Unit		Totals	
	Make	Buy	Make	Buy
Direct material	$ 1		$ 10,000	
Direct labor	8		80,000	
Variable overhead	4		40,000	
Fixed overhead that can be avoided by not making	2		20,000	
Total relevant costs	$15	$16	$150,000	$160,000
Difference in favor of making		$1	$10,000	

Essence of make or buy: opportunity cost

The choice in our example is really not whether to make or buy; it is how best to utilize available facilities. Although the above data indicate that making the part is the better choice, the figures are not conclusive —primarily because we have no idea of what can be done with the manufacturing facilities if the component is bought. Only if the released facilities are to remain idle are the above figures valid.

On the other hand, if the released facilities can be used advantageously in some other manufacturing activity or can be rented out, there is an opportunity cost of continuing to make the part. An *opportunity cost* is the measurable sacrifice in rejecting an alternative; it is the maximum amount foregone by forsaking an alternative; it is the maximum earning that might have been obtained if the productive good, service, or capacity had been applied to some alternative use.

The decision to manufacture might entail the rejection of an opportunity to rent the given capacity to another manufacturer for $5,000 annually. The opportunity cost of making the parts is the sacrifice of the chance to get $5,000 rental.

Although no dollar outlay is involved, the opportunity cost is relevant to the decision. It can be considered in two ways, depending on the preference of the analyst.

a. The two courses of action have become three, and can be analyzed in the following summary form:

	Make	Buy and not Rent	Buy and Rent
Obtaining of parts	$150,000	$160,000	$160,000
Rent revenue	—	—	(5,000)
Total relevant costs	$150,000	$160,000	$155,000

b. The opportunity cost approach yields the same results, but the format of the analysis differs:

	Make	Buy
Obtaining of parts	$150,000	$160,000
Opportunity cost: rent foregone	5,000	
Total relevant costs	$155,000	$160,000

Note that opportunity costs are not ordinarily incorporated in formal accounting systems. Such costs represent incomes foregone by rejecting alternatives; therefore, opportunity costs do not involve cash receipts or outlays. Accountants usually confine their recording to those events that ultimately involve exchanges of assets. Accountants confine their history to alternatives selected rather than those rejected, primarily because of the impracticality or impossibility of accumulating meaningful data on what might have been.

Policy making for make or buy

Costs must be related to time. A cost which is fixed over a short period may be variable over a longer period. Profits may increase momentarily by applying the contribution margin approach to decisions but, over the long run, profits may suffer by inordinate use of such an approach. Thus, companies develop long-run policies for the use of capacity:

> One company stated that it solicits subcontract work for other manu-
> facturers during periods when sales of its own products do not fully
> utilize the plant, but that such work cannot be carried on regularly
> without expansion of its plant. The profit margin on subcontracts is not
> sufficiently large to cover these additional costs and hence work is ac-
> cepted only when other business is lacking. The same company some-
> times meets a period of high volume by purchasing parts or having
> them made by sub-contractors. While the cost of such parts is usually
> higher than the cost to make them in the company's own plant, the addi-
> tional cost is less than it would be if they were made on equipment
> which could be used only part of the time.[1]

Beware of unit costs

Unit costs should be analyzed with care in decision making. There are two major ways to go wrong: (*a*) the inclusion of irrelevant costs, such as the $3 allocation of fixed costs in the make-or-buy comparison, which would result in a unit cost of $18 instead of the relevant unit cost of $15; and (*b*) comparisons of unit costs not computed on the same basis. Generally, it is advisable to use total costs rather than unit costs. Then, if desired, the total may be unitized. Machinery salesmen, for example, often brag about the low unit costs of using their new machines. Sometimes they neglect to point out that the unit costs are based on outputs far in excess of the volume of activity of their prospective customer. The unitiza-tion of fixed costs in this manner can be particularly misleading. The lesson here is to use total costs, not unit costs, in relevant cost analysis when possible.

IRRELEVANCE OF PAST COSTS

Book value of old equipment

A relevant cost is (1) an expected future cost which will (2) differ between alternatives. The contribution aspect of relevant cost analysis has shown that those expected future costs which will not differ among alternatives are irrelevant. Now we return to the idea that all past costs are also irrelevant. For the first time, our data extend beyond one year.

Assume that there is a machine, with a cost of $120,000, two-thirds depreciated on a straight-line basis, with a book value of $40,000, and with a remaining useful life of four years. The old machine has a $4,000 disposal value now; in four years, its disposal value will be zero. A new machine is available that will dramatically reduce operating costs. Annual

---

[1] *The Analysis of Cost-Volume-Profit Relationships,* National Association of Accountants, Research Series No. 17 (New York, 1949), p. 552.

revenue of $100,000 will not change regardless of the decision. The new machine will cost $60,000 and have zero disposal value at the end of its four-year life. The new machine promises to slash variable operating costs from $80,000 per year to $56,000 per year. Many managers and accountants would not replace the old machine because it would entail recognizing a $36,000 "loss on disposal," whereas retention would allow spreading the $40,000 over four years in the form of "depreciation expense" (a more appealing term than "loss on disposal").

Under our definition of relevant costs, book value of old fixed assets is always irrelevant in making decisions. This proposition is by far the most difficult for managers and accountants alike to accept. The real concept of importance here is that *all* historical costs are irrelevant. At one time or another we all like to think that we can soothe our wounded pride arising from making a bad purchase decision by *using* the item instead of replacing it. The fallacy here is in erroneously thinking that a current or future action can influence the long-run impact of a past outlay. All past costs are down the drain. *Nothing* can change what has already happened.[2]

We can apply our definition of relevance to four commonly encountered items:

1. Book value of old equipment. Irrelevant, because it is a past (historical) cost.
2. Disposal value of old equipment. Relevant (ordinarily), because it is an expected future inflow which usually differs between alternatives.
3. Gain or loss on disposal. This is the algebraic difference between (1) and (2). It is therefore a meaningless combination of book value, which is always irrelevant, and disposal value, which is usually relevant. The combination form, *loss* (or gain) *on disposal*, blurs the distinction between the irrelevant book value and the relevant disposal value. Consequently, it is best to think of each separately.[3]
4. Cost of new equipment. Relevant, because it is an expected future outflow that will differ between alternatives.

Exhibit 13-3 should clarify the above assertions.

Book value of old equipment is irrelevant regardless of the decision-making technique used. The Difference columns in Exhibit 13-3 show that book value of old equipment is not an element of difference between alternatives and could be completely ignored without changing the $10,000 difference in average annual net income. No matter what the *timing* of the charge against revenue, the *amount* charged is still $40,000 regardless of any available alternative. In either event, the undepreciated cost will

---

[2]For simplicity, we ignore income tax considerations and the effects of the interest value of money in this chapter. But book value is irrelevant even if income taxes are considered, because the relevant item is then the tax cash flow, not the book value. For elaboration, see Chapter 15.

[3]The loss or gain will affect the *income tax cash flow*, which is relevant, but the loss or gain on disposal is irrelevant per se. For elaboration, see Chapter 15.

EXHIBIT 13-3

COST COMPARISON—REPLACEMENT OF MACHINE,
INCLUDING RELEVANT AND IRRELEVANT ITEMS
(In Thousand of Dollars)

	Four Years Together			Annualized (Divided by 4)		
	Keep	Replace	Difference	Keep	Replace	Difference
Sales	$400	$400	$ —	$100	$100	$ —
Expenses:						
Variable	$320	$224	$ 96	$ 80	$ 56	$ 24
Old machine (book value):						
Periodic write-off	40		—	10		—
or						
Lump-sum write-off		40*			10	
Disposal value		− 4*	4	—	− 1	1
New machine, written off periodically as depreciation	—	60	− 60	—	15	− 15
Total expenses	$360	$320	$ 40	$ 90	$ 80	$ 10
Net income	$ 40	$ 80	$ 40	$ 10	$ 20	$ 10

The advantage of replacement is $40,000 for the four years together; the *average* annual advantage is $10,000.

*In a formal income statement, these two items would be combined as "loss on disposal" of $36,000.

be written off with the same ultimate effect on profit.[4]   The $40,000 creeps into the income statement either as a $40,000 offset against the $4,000 proceeds to obtain the $36,000 *loss on disposal* in one year or as $10,000 depreciation in each of four years. But how it appears is irrelevant to the replacement decision. In contrast, the $15,000 annual depreciation on the new equipment *is* relevant because the total $60,000 depreciation may be avoided by not replacing.

Examining alternatives over the long run

The foregoing is the first example that has looked beyond one year. A useful technique is to view the alternatives over their entire lives and then to compute annual average results. In this way, peculiar nonrecurring

[4]We are deliberately ignoring income tax factors for the time being. If income taxes are considered, the *timing* of the writing off of fixed asset costs may influence *income tax* payments. In this example, there will be a small real difference: the present value of $40,000 as a tax deduction now versus the present value of a $10,000 tax deduction each year for four years. But this difference in *future* income tax flows is the *relevant* item—not the book value of the old fixed asset per se. See Chapter 15.

items (such as loss on disposal) will not obstruct the long-run view that necessarily must be taken in almost all special managerial decisions.

Exhibit 13-4 concentrates on relevant items only. Note that the same answer (the $40,000 net difference) will be produced even though the book value is completely omitted from the calculations. The only relevant items are the variable operating costs, the disposal value of the old equipment, and the depreciation on the new equipment.

EXHIBIT 13-4

COST COMPARISON—REPLACEMENT OF MACHINE: RELEVANT ITEMS ONLY
(In Thousands of Dollars)

	Four Years Together			Annualized (Divided by 4)		
	Keep	Replace	Difference	Keep	Replace	Difference
Variable expenses	$320	$224	$ 96	$ 80	$ 56	$ 24
Disposal value of old equipment	—	− 4	4		− 1	1
Depreciation—new equipment	—	60	− 60		15	− 15
Total relevant expenses	$320	$280	$ 40	$ 80	$ 70	$ 10

THE PROBLEM OF UNCERTAINTY

It is vitally important to recognize that, throughout this chapter and the next, dollar amounts of future sales and operating costs are assumed in order to highlight and to simplify various important points. In practice, the forecasting of these key figures is generally the most difficult aspect of decision analysis. For elaboration, see Chapter 26.

SUMMARY

The accountant's role in special decisions is basically that of a technical expert on cost analysis. His responsibility is to see that the manager uses relevant data in guiding his decisions.

To be relevant to a particular decision, a cost must meet two criteria: (1) it must be an expected *future* cost; and (2) it must be an element of *difference* between alternatives. The key question is, "What difference does it make?" All *past (historical)* costs are irrelevant to any decision about the future.

The role that past costs play in decision making is an auxiliary one; the distinction here should be definitive, not fuzzy. Past (irrelevant) costs are useful because they provide empirical evidence that often helps sharpen predictions of future relevant costs. But the expected future costs are the *only* cost ingredients in any analysis of alternatives.

The ability to distinguish relevant from irrelevant items and the use of the contribution approach to cost analysis are twin foundations for tackling many various decisions.

In decisions about activity levels (the special order, make or buy, and adding or dropping a product line) there may be a temptation to say that variable costs are always relevant and that fixed costs are always irrelevant. This is a dangerous generalization, because fixed costs are often affected by a decision. For example, plans to buy a second car for family use should be most heavily influenced by the new set of fixed costs that would be encountered. Conceivably, if the total family mileage were unaffected, the variable costs could be wholly irrelevant.

For a given set of facilities or resources, the key to maximizing net income is to obtain the largest possible contribution per unit of constraining factor.

Generally, in cost analysis it is advisable to use total costs, not unit costs, because unitized fixed costs are often erroneously interpreted as if they behaved like variable costs. A common activity or volume level must underlie the comparison of equipment.

The book value of old equipment is always irrelevant in replacement decisions. Disposal value, however, is usually relevant.

Incremental or differential costs are the differences in total costs under each alternative.

An opportunity cost is the sacrifice in rejecting an alternative; it is the earning that might have been obtained if the productive good, service, or capacity had been put to some alternative use.

Cost reports for special decisions may concentrate on relevant items only (Exhibit 13-4), or they encompass both relevant and irrelevant items (Exhibit 13-3). The best format depends on individual preferences. The short-cut approach concentrates only on the Difference column, because it summarizes the relevant items. The problem of uncertainty, which is discussed in Chapter 26, complicates prediction and is easily the gravest practical difficulty.

PROBLEM FOR SELF-STUDY

Problem. A toy manufacturer specializes in making fad items. He has just acquired a special-purpose molding machine for $50,000 cash. It automatically produces a special toy. The machine will be useless after the 100,000-unit total market potential, spread evenly over four years, is exhausted.

Expected annual operating data are as follows (in thousands):

Sales		$90.0
Direct materials	$10.0	
Direct labor	20.0	
Variable manufacturing overhead (75% of direct labor)	15.0	
Fixed manufacturing overhead*	7.5	
Depreciation, straight-line	11.9	
Selling and administrative expenses:		
Variable	4.0	
Fixed	8.0	76.4
Net income		$13.6

*Exclusive of depreciation on machine.

The disposal value of the machine is $6,000 now and will be $2,400 four years from now. The machine has been used to produce one unit. Suddenly a machine salesman appears. He says, "I have a new machine that is ideally suited for this production problem. My machine will be useless after your 100,000-unit total market potential is exhausted. But it has distinct operating superiority over your 'old' machine. It will reduce material usage by ten per cent, produce twice as many units per hour, will cost $44,000, and will have zero disposal value at the end of four years."

The toy manufacturer responds, "I don't want your new machine. I must retain the $50,000 machine because we've got to keep using it to recover our investment."

REQUIRED:

1. How will net income be affected if the "old" machine is scrapped and the new machine is purchased? Show computations for the four years taken together and on an average annual basis.

2. Evaluate the toy manufacturer's reaction to the proposal.

Solution.

1. Exhibits 13-5 and 13-6 show that net income would be enlarged by $8,400 annually and $33,600 for the four years together. Study these exhibits carefully, particularly to prove to yourself that the $50,000 book value is indeed irrelevant. Note also that the selling and administrative expenses are common to both alternatives and are therefore irrelevant, even though they contain both variable and fixed elements.

Take particular notice of how the difference in disposal values is handled. In effect, the decline in deposal value of $3600 is the net relevant amount.[5]

2. A common reaction in this example would be to retain the $50,000 machine because "we have got to keep using it to recover our investment" or "we have got to get our money out of it" or "it is not fully depreciated yet." In the light of subsequent events, nobody will deny that the original $50,000 investment was unwise. A little luck or foresight would have resulted in buying the new machine without previously acquiring the old machine. But what's done is done. The next question is whether or not the company will still be better off by buying the new machine. Management would have been much happier had the $50,000 never been spent in the first place, but the decision to buy the new machine will improve the long-run profitability of the firm. The original mistake should not be compounded by keeping the old machine.

Substitute $300,000 or $1,000,000 or $3,000 for the $50,000 original investment in the above example. No matter what the past cost was,

[5]Some experts would look at this $3,600 decline and say that "depreciation on old equipment based on disposal value" totals $3,600, at a rate of $900 per year. This author dislikes such terminology because "depreciation" connotes write-off of original cost. This decline is not depreciation but a recognition that keeping the old equipment entails a foregoing of the opportunity to sell it for $6,000 now. The measure of this *opportunity cost* is $6,000 less $2,400, a total of $3,600 or $900 per year.

EXHIBIT 13-5

COST COMPARISON—REPLACEMENT OF MACHINE: RELEVANT AND IRRELEVANT ITEMS

(In thousand of Dollars)

	Four Years Together			Annualized (Divided by 4)		
	Keep	Replace	Difference	Keep	Replace	Difference
Sales	$360.0	$360.0	$ —	$ 90.0	$ 90.0	$ —
Expenses:						
Direct materials	$ 40.0	$ 36.0	$ 4.0	$ 10.0	$ 9.0	$ 1.0
Direct labor	80.0	40.0	40.0	20.0	10.0	10.0
Variable manufacturing overhead	60.0	30.0	30.0	15.0	7.5	7.5
Fixed manufacturing overhead	30.0	30.0	—	7.5	7.5	—
Old machine (book value):						
Periodic write-off	50.0*			12.5*		
or						
Lump-sum write-off		50.0†	—		12.5†	—
Disposal values of old machine	− 2.4*	− 6.0†	3.6	− .6*	− 1.5†	.9
New machine, periodic write-off	—	44.0	−44.0	—	11.0	−11.0
Selling and administrative expenses:						
Variable	16.0	16.0	—	4.0	4.0	—
Fixed	32.0	32.0	—	8.0	8.0	—
Total expenses	$305.6	$272.0	$ 33.6	$ 76.4	$ 68.0	$ 8.4
Net income	$ 54.4	$ 88.0	$ 33.6	$ 13.6	$ 22.0	$ 8.4

The advantage of replacement is $33,600 for the four years together; the *average* annual advantage is $8,400.

*In a formal income statement, these two items would be combined as "depreciation" of $11,900 annually. They are separated here because book value is irrelevant and disposal value is relevant.

†In a formal income statement, these two items would be combined as "loss on disposal" of $44,000. But this combination form blurs the distinction between irrelevant book value and relevant disposal value. Therefore, it is safest to think of each separately.

EXHIBIT 13-6

COST COMPARISON—REPLACEMENT OF MACHINE: RELEVANT ITEMS ONLY
(In Thousands of Dollars)

	Four Years Together			Annualized (Divided by 4)		
Relevant Costs	Keep	Replace	Difference	Keep	Replace	Difference
Direct material	$ 40.0	$ 36.0	$ 4.0	$10.0	$ 9.0	$ 1.0
Direct labor	80.0	40.0	40.0	20.0	10.0	10.0
Variable manufacturing overhead	60.0	30.0	30.0	15.0	7.5	7.5
Disposal value of old equipment	−2.4	−6.0	3.6	−.6	−1.5	.9
Depreciation—new equipment	—	44.0	−44.0	—	11.0	−11.0
Total relevant costs	$177.6	$144.0	$33.6	$44.4	$36.0	$ 8.4

it will not change the advantage of buying the new machine. The future-cost approach taken here will always minimize long-run losses or maximize long-run gains.

Finally, note that the question in the requirement was phrased carefully. It did not ask whether the new machine should be purchased; it asked simply for the effect on future net income. Whether the new machine should be purchased depends on whether the increase in future net income is sufficiently large to warrant the increase in investment. We consider this problem in Chapter 14.

APPENDIX: COST TERMS USED FOR DIFFERENT PURPOSES

Because costs must be tailored to the decision at hand, many terms (too many!) have arisen to describe different types of cost. The author believes that the variety of terms is more confusing than illuminating; yet the varying usage of such terms necessitates a familiarity with them. Whenever you are confronted by these terms in practice, you will save much confusion and wasted time if you find out their exact meaning in the given case. For that matter, this word of caution applies to all the weird accounting terms used from company to company. Individual companies frequently develop their own extensive and distinctive accounting language. This language is not readily understood by accountants outside the company. The following terms will be related to other terms used previously in this book.

Imputed cost is a cost that does not appear in conventional accounting records and does not entail dollar outlays. A common example is the inclusion of "interest" on ownership equity as a part of operating expenses.

The terms *opportunity costs* (described in the chapter) and *imputed costs*[6] are used interchangeably in many other situations (for example, charging operations with rent or interest that could be gained from alternate uses of resources). However, there is a distinction in some cases. The opportunity-cost notion is demand-oriented; it is the measure of profits foregone. Sometimes the imputed-cost notion is the same as the opportunity-cost idea. At other times, however, it is cost-oriented, closer to the internal situation rather than the external situation. For example, transfer prices between departments or divisions of the same company could be imputed in a number of ways. Assume that an iron-ore mining division produces ore for a steel-producing division of Ford Motor Company. There are at least three ways of charging the steel-producing division for iron ore: (a) at cost in the conventional sense, (b) at imputed cost based on the lowest alternative supplier price (opportunity-cost idea), and (c) at imputed cost based on some arbitrary mark-up over mining cost (arbitrary imputed-cost idea).

Out-of-pocket costs, a short-run concept, are those costs which entail current or near-future outlays for the decision at hand. For example, the

---

[6]Some accountants may say that *imputed cost* is a narrow term because it refers only to "interest" charges that do not involve out-of-pocket expenditures.

acceptance of an order so that otherwise idle facilities may be used would entail a compilation of the out-of-pocket costs which otherwise could be avoided by not accepting the order; the depreciation on the machinery and equipment used for production would be irrelevant because it does not entail out-of-pocket outlays as a result of the decision.

Joint cost is the term most often applied to the costs of manufactured goods which are produced by a single process and which are not identifiable as individual types of products until a certain stage of production known as the *split-off point* (point of separation) is reached. Examples of such products are soap and glycerin, kerosene and gasoline, chemicals, and lumber. Joint costs are total costs incurred up to the point of separation. Inasmuch as joint costs by their very nature cannot be directly traced to units worked on, any method of apportioning such costs to various units produced is essentially arbitrary. The usefulness of joint-cost apportionment is limited to purposes of inventory costing. Such apportionment is useless for cost-planning and control purposes.

Viewed broadly, joint costs plague the accountant throughout his work. Few costs are not joint in relation to some other factor such as time or facilities. The entire problem of allocating the costs of fixed assets to months, years, departments, and products is essentially that of joint costing. Sometimes the term *common cost* is used instead of *joint cost* to describe another aspect of joint costing, such as the problem of determining unit cost of such services as bank accounts. Any allocation method is arbitrary, because many facilities and services are shared by many revenue-producing activities. The entire problem of reapportioning service department costs among producing departments is really one of joint cost.

Postponable costs are those which may be shifted to the future with little or no effect on the efficiency of current operations. The best example of these is maintenance and repairs. Railroads sometimes go on an economy binge and cut their sizable maintenance budgets. But it is really a matter of deferral and not avoidance. Eventually some overhauls must be made and tracks must be repaired.

Discretionary costs are those which are generally regarded as not being absolutely essential. They are usually incurred because of top-management decisions, and they may be easily escapable or avoidable. This category of cost is difficult to isolate and is subjective to a large degree. For example, supporting a company country club for employees may be regarded as absolutely essential for morale, but most executives would regard such a cost as discretionary. Dire times would probably cause such an endeavor to be dropped.

Avoidable costs are those that may be saved by not adopting a given alternative. For example, by not adopting a new product line, the appropriate direct material, direct labor, and variable overhead costs could be avoided. The criterion here is the question: which costs can be saved by not adopting a given alternative?

Sunk cost is another term for a past cost which is unavoidable because it cannot be changed no matter what action is taken. The author dislikes this term because it often beclouds the distinction between historical and future costs. However, *sunk cost* is discussed here because it is one of the most widely used terms in special decision making.

To illustrate, if old equipment has book value of $600,000 and scrap value of $70,000, what is the sunk cost? There are two ways of looking at the $600,000 book value of old equipment. This author agrees with a minority view which would maintain that the entire $600,000 is sunk because it represents an outlay made in the past which cannot be changed; the $70,000 scrap value is a future factor to be considered apart from the $600,000 sunk cost. The majority view maintains that $530,000 of the $600,000 is sunk, whereas $70,000 is not sunk because it is immediately recoverable through scrapping. Thus, the sunk part of an historical cost is that which is irrecoverable in a given situation. The latter view is that the two factors (book value and present scrap value) are complementary in replacement decisions; that is, book value minus scrap value equals sunk cost.

In the author's opinion, the term *sunk cost* should not be used at all. It muddles the task of collecting proper costs for decision making. Because all past costs are irrelevant, it is fruitless to introduce unnecessary terms to describe past costs. The issue of what part of a past cost is sunk need not arise. The essence of the distinction between past and future, irrelevant and relevant, costs was described earlier in this chapter. These distinctions are all that are needed for approaching special decisions. The term *sunk cost* is often more befuddling than enlightening. If it is going to be used, *sunk cost* should have the same meaning as *past cost*.

QUESTIONS, PROBLEMS, AND CASES

Note: Problems 13-7, 13-10, 13-15, and 13-18 are particularly recommended.

13-1. Distinguish briefly between *quantitative* and *qualitative* factors in decision making.

13-2. Define *relevant cost* as the term is used in this chapter. Why are historical costs irrelevant?

13-3. What is a *differential cost*? Distinguish it from a relevant cost.

13-4. "All future costs are relevant." Do you agree? Why?

13-5. Questions on Disposal of Assets.
1. A company has an inventory of 1,000 assorted missile parts for a line of missiles that has been junked. The inventory cost $100,000. The parts can be either (a) re-machined at total additional costs of $30,000 and then sold for a total of $35,000 or (b) scrapped for $2,000. What should be done?
2. A truck, costing $10,000 and uninsured, is wrecked the first day in use. It can be either (a) disposed of for $1,000 cash and replaced with a similar truck costing $10,200, or (b) rebuilt for $8,500 and be brand-new as far as operating characteristics and looks are concerned. What should be done?

13-6. Operation of Concession. The *M* Co., manager of an office building, is considering putting in certain concessions in the main lobby. An accounting study produces the following estimates, on an average annual basis:

Salaries		$ 7,000
Licenses and payroll taxes		200
Cost of merchandise sold:		
Beginning inventory	$ 2,000	
Purchases	40,000	
Available	$42,000	
Ending inventory	2,000	40,000
Share of heat, light, etc.		500
Pro rata building depreciation		1,000
Concession advertising		100
Share of company administrative expense		400
Sales of merchandise		49,000

The investment in equipment, which would last 10 years, would be $2,000.

As an alternative, a catering company has offered to lease the space for $750 per year for ten years, and to put in and operate the same concessions at no cost to the *M* Co. Heat and light are to be furnished by the office building at no additional charge.

What is your advice to the *M* Co.? Explain fully.   [C.P.A.]

13-7. The Careening Bookkeeping Machine.* "A young lady in the accounting department of a certain business was moving a bookkeeping machine from one room to another. As she came alongside an open stairway, she carelessly slipped and let the machine get away from her. It went careening down the stairs with a great racket and wound up at the bottom in some thousands of pieces, completely wrecked. Hearing the crash, the office manager came rushing out, and turned rather white when he saw what had happened. 'Someone tell me quickly,' he yelled, 'if that is one of our fully amortized units.' A check of the equipment cards showed that the smashed machine was, indeed, one of those which had been written off. 'Thank God!' said the manager."

REQUIRED:

Explain and comment on the point of Professor Paton's anecdote.

13-8. Disposal of Unsalable Merchandise. A clothing manufacturer's inventory includes 2,000 highly styled ladies' dresses carried at a cost of $10·each. The dresses are unsalable at normal mark-ups in their present form. Management is considering the following alternatives:

1. Re-style the dresses in one manner at an additional cost of $7.00 apiece. Management feels confident that a national chain will buy all the re-styled dresses at $13.00 apiece, F.O.B. factory.

2. Re-style the dresses in another manner at an additional cost of $2.00 apiece. Management feels equally confident that the dresses can be moved by their salesmen at a selling price of $10 apiece, F.O.B. factory, subject to a 10 per cent sales commission.

3. Sell the dresses to an exporter "as is" at $5.00 each, F.O.B. factory.

4. Donate the dresses to local charities.

*From W. A. Paton, "Restoration of Fixed Asset Values to the Balance Sheet," *Accounting Review* (April, 1947), pp. 194–210.

REQUIRED:

Considering only the facts as outlined, which alternative is most desirable? Why?

13-9. Determination of Relevant Costs. The Frel Company makes a standard line of gauges. A large aircraft company has asked for competitive bids on an order of 10,000 special gauges for use in the manufacture of aircraft parts. Frel Company wants to know the minimum price to bid that will insure at least a $5,000 increase in net income.

The operating picture, as it will appear for the year if the extra order is not landed, is as follows:

FREL COMPANY
Income Statement
For the Year Ending December 31, 19x1

1.	Sales (40,000 gauges)		$600,000
	Cost of sales:		
2.	Direct material	$100,000	
3.	Direct labor	200,000	
4.	Variable overhead (varies with direct labor hours)	50,000	
5.	Fixed overhead	100,000	450,000
	Gross margin		$150,000
	Selling and administrative expenses:		
6.	Variable (including shipping costs of 40¢ per unit)	$ 30,000	
7.	Fixed	80,000	110,000
	Net income		$ 40,000

Assume that the cost behavior patterns will not be changed by the additional order, except as follows:

(a) Shipping costs, which are ordinarily borne by the Frel Company, will be paid for and borne by the aircraft company.

(b) Special setup costs and the cost of special tools (that will not be reusable) will total $5,000.

(c) Direct labor charges on these gauges will be 20 per cent higher because of more time needed per unit.

REQUIRED:

1. Prepare a new income statement, assuming that the order is landed after quoting the minimum price. Set up your solution in the following manner:

	Column		
	(a) Old Income Statement	(b) Change	(c) New Income Statement
1. Sales			
Cost of sales:			
2. Direct material			
3. Direct labor			
(and so forth)			

2. Examine the format of your answer to requirement (1). How else could the information be presented?

13-10. Relevance of Equipment Costs. The Auto Wash Company has just installed a special machine for washing cars. The machine cost $20,000. Its operating costs, based on a yearly volume of 100,000 cars, total $15,000, exclusive of depreciation. The machine will have a four-year useful life and no residual value.

After the machine has been used one day, a machine salesman offers a different machine that promises to do the same job at a yearly operating cost of $9,000, exclusive of depreciation. The new machine will cost $24,000 cash installed. The "old" machine is unique and can be sold outright for only $10,000, less $2,000 removal cost. The new machine, like the old one, will have a four-year useful life and no residual value.

Sales, all in cash, will be $150,000 per year and other cash expenses will be $110,000 annually, regardless of this decision.

REQUIRED:

1. Prepare income statements as they would appear for each of the next four years under both alternatives. What is the net difference in income for the four years taken together?

2. Prepare cash-flow (cash receipts and disbursements) statements as they would appear for each of the next four years under both alternatives. What is the net difference in cash flow for the four years taken together?

3. What are the irrelevant items in each of your presentations in (1) and (2)? Why are they irrelevant?

4. Describe your thoughts on the role of book value in replacement of equipment.

5. Should the new equipment be bought if the difference in its favor is $2,400 for the four years taken together? Why?

● **13-11. Make or Buy Decision.** When you had completed your audit of The Scoopa Company, management asked for your assistance in arriving at a decision whether to continue manufacturing a part or to buy it from an outside supplier. The part, which is named Faktron, is a component used in some of the finished products of the Company.

From your audit working papers and from further investigation you develop the following data as being typical of the Company's operations:

1. The annual requirement for Faktrons is 5,000 units. The lowest quotation from a supplier was $8.00 per unit.

2. Faktrons have been manufactured in the Precision Machinery Department. If Faktrons are purchased from an outside supplier, certain machinery will be sold and would realize its book value.

3. Following are the total costs of the Precision Machinery Department during the year under audit when 5,000 Faktrons were made:

Materials	$67,500
Direct labor	50,000
Indirect labor	20,000
Light and heat	5,500
Power	3,000
Depreciation	10,000
Property taxes and insurance	8,000
Payroll taxes and other benefits	9,800
Other	5,000

4. The following Precision Machinery Department costs apply to the manufacture of Faktrons: material, $17,500; direct labor, $28,000; indirect labor, $6,000; power, $300; other, $500. The sale of the equipment used for Faktrons would reduce the following costs by the amounts indicated: depreciation, $2,000; property taxes and insurance, $1,000.

5. The following additional Precision Machinery Department costs would be incurred if Faktrons were purchased from an outside supplier: freight, $.50 per unit; indirect labor for receiving, materials handling, inspection, etc., $5,000. The cost of the purchased Faktrons would be considered a Precision Machinery Department cost.

REQUIRED:

1. Prepare a schedule showing a comparison of the total costs of the Precision Machinery Department (1) when Faktrons are made, and (2) when Faktrons are bought from an outside supplier.

2. Discuss the considerations in addition to the cost factors that you would bring to the attention of management in assisting them to arrive at a decision whether to make or buy Faktrons. Include in your discussion the considerations that might be applied to the evaluation of the outside supplier. [C.P.A.]

13-12. Operating a Salesman's Car. Following are representative total costs for operating a salesman's car for 20,000 miles in a year:

Gasoline: 1,333 gallons @ 30¢	$ 400.00
Oil (changed every 2,000 miles)	25.00
Tire wear (based on life of 25,000 miles; a new set of 4 will cost $100)	80.00
Grease jobs (every 1,000 miles)	30.00
Regular maintenance and repair	150.00
Washing and waxing	30.00
Licenses	50.00
Garage rent and parking fees	255.00
Auto insurance	130.00
Depreciation ($2,800 − $600) ÷ 4-year life	550.00
	$1,700.00

Unit cost is $1,700 ÷ 20,000 miles, or 8.5 cents.

REQUIRED:

1. If the salesman drives 30,000 miles per year, what would be the average unit cost per mile? If he drives 10,000 miles?

2. He takes his car on a 100-mile journey with a friend who agrees to share the cost of the trip. How much should the friend pay?

3. The salesman's wife wants a similar car for shopping and other errands that the husband now performs. If he buys the second car, it will be driven 3,000 miles per year, but the total mileage of the two cars taken together will still be 20,000 miles. What will be the annual cost of operating the second car? The average unit cost?

4. List other possible costs of car ownership that are not included in the above tabulation.

5. What costs are relevant to the question of selling the car at the end of one year (market value, $2,000) and using other means of transportation?

6. Assume that the salesman has no car. What costs are relevant to the question of buying the car described versus using other means of transportation?

7. The salesman has no car. He is thinking of either buying the $2,800 car described at the beginning of this problem or renting the same car for two years at $79.50 per month. The lessor bears costs of oil, grease, maintenance, repairs, tires, licenses, and insurance. All other costs are borne by the salesman. Should the salesman buy or rent?

8. Assume the same facts as in (7), except that the salesman now owns the car. It is one year old and he can get $1,800 for it. Should he continue to own or rent?

13-13. Discontinuing a Department; Make or Buy. Ace Publishing Company is in the business of publishing and printing guidebooks and directories. The board of directors has engaged you to make a cost study to determine whether the company is economically justified in continuing to print, as well as publish, its books and directories. You obtain the following information from the company's cost accounting records for the preceding fiscal year:

	Departments			
	Publishing	Printing	Shipping	Total
Salaries and wages	$275,000	$150,000	$25,000	$ 450,000
Telephone and telegraph	12,000	3,700	300	16,000
Materials and supplies	50,000	250,000	10,000	310,000
Occupancy costs	75,000	80,000	10,000	165,000
General and administrative	40,000	30,000	4,000	74,000
Depreciation	5,000	40,000	5,000	50,000
	$457,000	$553,700	$54,300	$1,065,000

Additional Data

1. A review of personnel requirements indicates that, if printing is discontinued, the publishing department will need one additional clerk at $4,000 per year to handle correspondence with the printer. Two layout men and a proofreader will be required, at an aggregate annual cost of $17,000; other personnel in the printing department can be released. One mailing clerk, at $3,000, will be retained; others in the shipping department can be released. Employees whose employment was being terminated would immediately receive, on the average, three months' termination pay. The termination pay would be amortized over a five-year period.

2. Long-distance telephone and telegraph charges are identified and distributed to the responsible department. The remainder of the telephone bill, representing basic service at a cost of $4,000, was allocated in the ratio of 10 to publishing, 5 to printing, and 1 to shipping. The discontinuance of printing is not expected to have a material effect on the basic service cost.

3. Shipping supplies consist of cartons, envelopes, and stamps. It is estimated that the cost of envelopes and stamps for mailing material to an outside printer would be $5,000 per year.

4. If printing were discontinued, the company would retain its present building but would sublet a portion of the space at an annual rental of $50,000.

Taxes, insurance, heat, light, and other occupancy costs would not be significantly affected.

   5. One cost clerk would not be required ($5,000 per year) if printing is discontinued. Other general and administrative personnel would be retained.

   6. Included in administrative expenses is interest expense on a five per cent mortgage loan of $500,000.

   7. Printing and shipping room machinery and equipment having a net book value of $300,000 can be sold without gain or loss. These funds in excess of termination pay would be invested in marketable securities earning five per cent.

   8. The company has received a proposal for a five-year contract from an outside printer, under which the volume of work done last year would be printed at a cost of $550,000 per year.

   9. Assume continued volume and prices at last year's level.

REQUIRED:

   Prepare a statement setting forth in comparative form the costs of operation of the printing and shipping departments under the present arrangement and under an arrangement in which inside printing is discontinued. Summarize the net saving or extra cost in case printing is discontinued.   [C.P.A.]

   13-14. Different Cost Terms.   *Instructions:* You are to match each of the nine numbered "items" which follow with the *one* term listed below (A through R) which *most specifically* identifies the cost concept indicated parenthetically. (Caution: An item of cost may be classified in several ways, depending on the purpose of the classification. For example, the commissions on sales of a proposed new product line might be classified as *direct, variable,* and *marginal,* among others. However, if such costs are being considered specifically as to the amount of *cash outlay* required in making a decision concerning adoption of the new line, the commissions are *out-of-pocket costs.* That would be the *most* appropriate answer in the context.) The same term may be used more than once.

   Indicate your choice of answer for each item by printing beside the item numbers the *capital letter* which identifies the term you select.

Terms

A. By-product costs	J. Indirect costs
B. Common or joint costs	K. Opportunity costs
C. Controllable costs	L. Original cost
D. Direct costs	M. Out-of-pocket costs
E. Estimated costs	N. Prime costs
F. Fixed costs	O. Replacement costs
G. Historical cost	P. Standard costs
H. Imputed costs	Q. Sunk costs
I. Differential cost	R. Variable costs

Items

   1. The management of a corporation is considering replacing a machine which is operating satisfactorily with a more efficient new model. Depreciation on the cost of the existing machine is omitted from the data used in judging the proposal, because it has little or no significance with respect to such a decision. (*The omitted cost.*)

   2. One of the problems encountered by a bank in attempting to establish the cost of a commercial-deposit account is the fact that many facilities and

services are shared by many revenue-producing activities. (*Costs of the shared facilities and services.*)

3. A company declined an offer received to rent one of its warehouses and elected to use the warehouse for storage of extra raw materials to insure uninterrupted production. Storage cost has been charged with *the monthly amount of the rental offered.* (*This cost is known as ?*)

4. A manufacturing company excludes all "fixed" costs from its valuation of inventories, assigning to inventory only *applicable portions of costs which vary with changes in volume of product.* (*The term employed for the variable costs in this context by advocates of this costing procedure.*)

5. The sales department urges an increase in production of a product and, as part of the data presented in support of its proposal, indicates the total additional cost involved for the volume level it proposes. (*The increase in total cost.*)

6. A C.P.A. takes exception to his client's inclusion in the cost of a fixed asset of an "interest" charge based on the client's own funds invested in the asset. The client states that the charge was intended to obtain a cost comparable to that which would have been the case if funds had been borrowed to finance the acquisition. (*The term which describes such interest charges.*)

7. The "direct" production cost of a unit includes those portions of factory overhead, *labor, and materials* which are obviously traceable directly to the unit. (*The term used to specify the last two of the named components.*)

8. Calling upon the special facilities of the production, planning, personnel, and other departments, a firm estimated its future unit cost of production and used this cost (analyzed by cost elements) in its accounts. (*The term used to specify this scientifically predetermined estimate.*)

9. A chemical manufacturing company produces three products originating in a common initial material mix. Each product gains a separate identity part way through processing and requires additional processing after the "split." Each contributes a significant share of revenue. The company plans to spread the costs up to the "split" among the three products by the use of relative market values. (*The term used to specify the costs accumulated up to the point of the split.*)　　　　　　　　　　　　　　　　　　　　　　　[C.P.A.]

13-15. Multiple Choice; Comprehensive Problem on Relevant Costs. The following are Class Company's *unit* costs of making and selling a given item at a level of 20,000 units per month:

Manufacturing:	
Direct materials	$1.00
Direct labor	1.20
Variable indirect cost	.80
Fixed indirect cost	.50
Selling and other:	
Variable	1.50
Fixed	.90

The following situations refer only to the data given above—there is *no connection* between the situations. Unless stated otherwise, assume a regular selling price of $6.00 per unit.

Choose the answer corresponding to the most nearly acceptable or correct answer in each of the nine items. Support each answer with summarized computations.

1. In presenting an inventory of 10,000 items on the balance sheet, the unit cost conventionally to be used is:

a) $2.20   b) $3.00   c) $3.50   d) $5.00   e) $5.90

2. The unit cost relevant to setting a *normal* price for this product, assuming that the implied level of operations is to be maintained, is:

a) $5.90   b) $5.00   c) $4.50   d) $3.50   e) $3.00

3. This product is usually sold at the rate of 240,000 units per year (an average of 20,000 per month). At a sales price of $6.00 per unit, this yields total sales of $1,440,000, total costs of $1,416,000, and a net margin of $24,000, or 10¢ per unit. It is estimated by market research that volume could be increased by 10 per cent if prices were cut to $5.80. Assuming the implied cost behavior patterns to be correct, this action, if taken, would:

(a) Decrease profits by 20¢ per unit, $48,000, but increase profits by 10 per cent of sales, $144,000; net, $86,000 increase.
(b) Decrease unit fixed costs by 10 per cent or 14¢ per unit and thus decrease profits by 20¢ − 14¢, or 6¢ unit.
(c) Increase sales volume to 264,000 units, which at the $5.80 price would give total sales of $1,531,200; costs of $5.90 per unit for 264,000 units would be $1,557,600, and a loss of $26,400 would result.
(d) Decrease profits by a net of $7,200.
(e) None of the above.

4. A cost contract with the government (for 5,000 units of product) calls for the reimbursement of all costs of production plus a fixed fee of $1,000. This production is part of the regular 20,000 units of production per month. The delivery of these 5,000 units of product increases profits from what they would have been, were these units not sold, by

a) $300   b) $1,000   c) $2,500   d) $3,500   e) None of these.

5. Assume the same data as in (4) above, except that the 5,000 units will displace 5,000 other units from production. The latter 5,000 units would have been sold through regular channels for $30,000 had they been made. The delivery to the government increases (or decreases) net profits from what they would have been, were the other 5,000 units sold, by

a) $500 increase   b) $4,000 decrease   c) $3,000 increase   d) $6,500 decrease   e) None of these.

6. The company desires to enter a foreign market, in which price competition is keen. An order for 10,000 units of this product is being sought on a minimum unit-price basis. It is expected that shipping costs for this order will amount to only 75¢ per unit but that fixed costs of obtaining the contract will be $4,000. Domestic business will be unaffected. The minimum basis for break-even price is:

a) $3.00   b) $3.50   c) $4.15   d) $4.25   e) $5.00

7. The company has an inventory of 1,000 units of this item left over from last year's model. These must be sold through regular channels at reduced prices. The inventory will be valueless unless sold this way. The unit cost that is relevant for establishing the minimum selling price would be:

a) $5.90   b) $4.50   c) $4.00   d) $3.00   e) $1.50

8. A proposal is received from an outside supplier who will make and ship this item directly to Class Company's customers as sales orders are forwarded

from Class's sales staff. Class's fixed selling costs will be unaffected, but its variable selling costs will be slashed 20 per cent. Class's plant will be idle, but its fixed factory overhead would continue at 50 per cent of present levels. To compare with the quotation received from the supplier, the company should use a unit cost of:

     a) $5.35   b) $4.75   c) $3.95   d) $2.95   e) None of these.

     9. Assume the same facts as in (8) above, except that, if the supplier's offer is accepted, the present plant facilities will be used to make a product whose unit costs will be:

Variable manufacturing costs	$5.00
Fixed manufacturing costs	1.00
Variable selling costs	2.00
Fixed selling costs	.50

Total fixed factory overhead will be unchanged, while fixed selling costs will increase as indicated. The new product will sell for $9.00. This minimum desired net profit on the two products taken together is $50,000 per year. What is the maximum purchase cost per unit that Class Company should be willing to pay for subcontracting the old production?

     13-16. Best Production and Sales Mix. The Marcia Company has asked your assistance in determining an economical sales and production mix of their products for 19x4. The Company manufactures a line of dolls and a doll dress sewing kit.

     The Company's sales department provides the following data:

Doll's Name	Estimated Demand for 19x4 (Units)	Established Net Price (Units)
Laurie	50,000	$5.20
Debbie	42,000	2.40
Sarah	35,000	8.50
Kathy	40,000	4.00
Sewing kit	325,000	3.00

     To promote sales of the sewing kit there is a 15 per cent reduction in the established net price for a kit purchased at the same time that a Marcia Company doll is purchased.

     From accounting records you develop the following data:

     1. The production standards per unit:

Item	Material	Labor
Laurie	$1.40	$ .80
Debbie	.70	.50
Sarah	2.69	1.40
Kathy	1.00	1.00
Sewing kit	.60	.40

     2. The labor rate of $2.00 per hour is expected to continue without change in 19x4. The plant has an effective capacity of 130,000 labor hours per year on a single-shift basis. Present equipment can produce all of the products.

3. The total fixed costs for 19x4 will be $100,000. Variable costs will be equivalent to 50 per cent of direct labor cost.

4. The Company has a small inventory of its products that can be ignored.

REQUIRED:

a. Prepare a schedule computing the contribution to profit of a unit of each product.

b. Prepare a schedule computing the contribution to profit of a unit of each product per labor dollar expended on the product.

c. Prepare a schedule computing the total labor hours required to produce the estimated sales units for 19x4. Indicate the item and number of units that you would recommend be increased (or decreased) in production to attain the Company's effective productive capacity.

d. Without regard to your answer in "c," assume that the estimated sales units for 19x4 would require 12,000 labor hours in excess of the Company's effective productive capacity. Discuss the possible methods of providing the missing capacity. Include in your discussion all factors that must be taken into consideration in evaluating the methods of providing the missing capacity.

[C.P.A. Adapted]

● **13-17. Relevant Cost Analysis and Pricing.** You have been engaged to assist the management of the Stenger Corporation in arriving at certain decisions. The Stenger Corporation has its home office in Philadelphia and leases factory buildings in Rhode Island, Georgia, and Illinois. The same single product is manufactured in all three factories. The following information is available regarding 19x4 operations:

	Total	Rhode Island	Illinois	Georgia
Sales	$900,000	$200,000	$400,000	$300,000
Fixed costs:				
Factory	180,000	50,000	55,000	75,000
Administration	59,000	16,000	21,000	22,000
Variable costs	500,000	100,000	220,000	180,000
Allocated home office expense	63,000	14,000	28,000	21,000
Total	802,000	180,000	324,000	298,000
Net profit from operations	$ 98,000	$ 20,000	$ 76,000	$ 2,000

Home office expense is allocated on the basis of units sold. The sales price per unit is $10.

Management is undecided whether to renew the lease of the Georgia factory, which expires on December 31, 19x5 and will require an increase in rent of $15,000 per year if renewed. If the Georgia factory is shut down, the amount expected to be realized from the sale of the equipment is greater than its book value and would cover all termination expenses.

If the Georgia factory is shut down, the Company can continue to serve customers of the Georgia factory by one of the following methods:

1. Expanding the Rhode Island factory, which would increase fixed costs by 15 per cent. Additional shipping expense of $2.00 per unit will be incurred on the increased production.

2. Entering into a long-term contract with a competitor who will serve the Georgia factory customers and who will pay the Stenger Corporation a commission of $1.60 per unit.

The Stenger Corporation is also planning to establish a subsidiary corporation in Canada to produce the same product. Based on estimated annual Canadian sales of 40,000 units, cost studies produced the following estimates for the Canadian subsidiary:

	Total Annual Costs	Per Cent of Total Annual Cost That Variable
Material	$193,600	100%
Labor	90,000	70
Overhead	80,000	64
Administration	30,000	30

The Canadian production will be sold by manufacturer's representatives who will receive a commission of 8 per cent of the sales price. No portion of the United States home office expense will be allocated to the Canadian subsidiary.

REQUIRED:

1. Prepare a schedule computing the Stenger Corporation's estimated net profit from United States operations under each of the following procedures:
   a. Expansion of the Rhode Island factory.
   b. Negotiation of long-term contract on a commission basis.
2. Management wants to price its Canadian product to realize a 10 per cent profit on the sales price. Compute the sales price per unit that would result in an estimated 10 per cent profit on sales.
3. Assume that your answer to part "2" is a sales price of $11 per unit. Compute the breakeven point in sales dollars for the Canadian subsidiary. [C.P.A.]

13-18. Selection of Most Profitable Product. The Flabbo Co. produces two basic types of reducing equipment, G and H. Pertinent data follow:

	Per Unit	
	G	H
Sales price	$100.00	$70.00
Expenses:		
Direct material	$ 28.00	$13.00
Direct labor	15.00	25.00
Variable factory overhead*	25.00	12.50
Fixed factory overhead*	10.00	5.00
Selling expenses (all variable)	14.00	10.00
	$ 92.00	$65.50
Net margin	$ 8.00	$ 4.50

*Applied on the basis of machine-hours.

The diet craze is such that enough of either G or H can be sold to keep the plant operating at full capacity. Both products are processed through the same production centers.

Which product should be produced? If more than one should be produced, indicate the proportions of each. Briefly explain your answer.

13-19.   Relationship of Disposal Value, Book Value, and Net Loss on Old Equipment.   Scott Harshaw is the president of a small plastics company. He wants to replace an old special-purpose molding machine (original cost, $18,700; eight years old; book value, $9,100; straight-line depreciation, $1,200 per year; residual value at end of useful life, $700) with a new, more efficient machine. The new machine has an expected useful life of only seven years, but it promises savings in cash operating costs of $2,257 per year.   Operating costs with the new machine are $30,000; with the old machine, $32,257.   The cost of the new machine is $8,800. The old machine can be sold outright for $2,300 less $200 removal cost. It is estimated that the old machine would have a net disposal value of $700 seven years from now; the new machine, a value of $750 seven years from now.

Vladimar Galoot, controller, opposes replacement because no advantage is apparent. His analysis shows:

Cost of new investment:	
Outlay	$ 8,800
Loss on old machine ($9,100 minus $2,100)	7,000
Total cost	$15,800
Savings: $2,257 per year × 7 years	$15,800 (rounded)
Net advantage of replacement	$ –0–

He also added, "I can't ever see disposing of fixed assets at a loss before their useful life expires. Plant and equipment are bought and depreciated with some useful life in mind. We are in business to maximize income (or minimize loss). It seems to me that the alternatives are clear: (a) disposal of a fixed asset before it diminishes to zero or residual book value often results in a loss; (b) keeping and *using* the same fixed asset avoids such a loss. Now, any sensible person will have brains enough to avoid a loss when his other alternative is recognizing a loss. It makes sense to use a fixed asset till you get your money out of it."

Yearly sales are $90,000 and cash expenses, excluding the data given above, are $50,000.

REQUIRED: (Ignore income tax effects):

1. How will net income be affected if the old machine is scrapped and the new machine is purchased? Show computations for the seven years taken together and on an average annual basis.

2. Prepare columnar income statements for years 1 through 7 under both alternatives, as follows:

Year 1	Each Year, 2–7	7 Years Together

3. Generalize as to the role of disposal value on old equipment in these decisions.

4. Generalize as to the role of (a) book value in these decisions and (b) net loss on disposal of old fixed assets.

5. Critize Galoot's schedule and his comments.

6. What important cost factor has been ignored in your answers (1) and (2)?

introduction to capital budgeting
(project selection)

CHAPTER XIV

The problem of measuring the profit potential of long-range in-vestment proposals has been receiving increased attention. This tendency is likely to enlarge because of growing mechanization and automation in industry. This chapter's objective is to introduce the latest thinking in this area, as reflected by the definite surge in industry toward using discounted cash-flow techniques for these decisions instead of some version of conventional accounting approaches.

One word of assurance before you begin: do not be afraid of the discounted cash-flow techniques discussed here. We shall confine our study to present value tables, which may seem imposing but which are simple enough to be taught in many grade-school arithmetic courses.

CONTRASTS IN PURPOSES OF COST ANALYSIS

At this stage, we again focus on purpose. Income determination and the planning and controlling of operations primarily have a *current time-period* orientation. Special decisions and long-range planning primarily have a *project* orientation with a far-reaching time span.

William D. McEachron, of Standard Oil Co. (Ind.), has illustrated these distinctions with a chart (Exhibit 14-1).

The project and time-period orientations of Exhibit 14-1 represent two distinct cross sections of the total corporate assets. The vertical dimension signifies the total investment (assets) of the company, which may be subdivided into divisions, product lines, departments, buildings, a fleet of trucks, or a machine. These parts of an organization's resources are in-

439

dividual *projects*, or investment decisions. The horizontal dimension repre-sents successive years in a company's life.

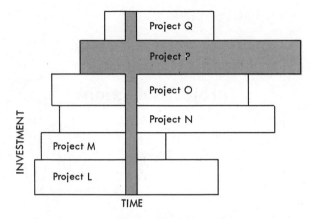

EXHIBIT 14-1

THE PROJECT ORIENTATION OF CAPITAL BUDGETING

Source: William D. McEachron, "Profitability Index in Investment Evaluation," *The Controller*, Vol. XXIX, No. 10 (October, 1961), p. 478.

The black horizontal rectangle shows that many projects entail commitments over a prolonged span of time, not just one year. The focus is on a single cross section, a lone investment venture, throughout its life. The interest which can be earned over a period of time (that is, the time value of money) often looms large in special decisions and in long-range planning.

The black vertical rectangle illustrates the focus of income deter-mination and current planning and control. The cross-sectional emphasis is upon the company's over-all performance and status for a year or less. The time period is relatively short, and the interest value of money is usually not directly involved.

The point of all this is that our ordinary accounting systems and techniques have been designed to determine the cost and income of prod-ucts for current planning and control. There is a great danger of using the existing general-purpose accounting system incorrectly—that is, of using data indiscriminately for solving special problems.

So in this chapter we shall shift gears. We shall take a fresh look at the purpose of the special decision, and then we shall decide what tools seem best for achieving that purpose.

DEFINITION OF CAPITAL BUDGETING

Capital budgeting is long term planning for making and financing proposed capital outlays. Most expenditures for plant, equipment, and other long-lived assets affect operations over a series of years. They are large, permanent commitments that influence long-run flexibility and earning power. Decisions in this area are among the most difficult, primarily because the future to be foreseen is distant and hard to perceive. Because the unknowable factors are many, it is imperative that all the knowable factors be collected and properly measured before a decision is reached.

The profitability of a business decision depends on two vital factors: (1) future net increases in cash inflows or net savings in cash outflows; and (2) required investment. Thus, a chance to receive an annual return of $5,000 on a bond or stock can be judged only in relationship to how much money need be committed to obtain the $5,000. If the required capital is $10,000, the $5,000 (50 per cent) return may be extremely appealing. If the required investment is $1 million, the $5,000 ($\frac{1}{2}$ per cent) return probably will be unappealing. Depending on risk and available alternatives, individuals and corporate investors usually have some notion of a minimum rate of return that would make various projects desirable investments.

The quantitative approach to the selection of projects is, generally, to estimate the effect of the alternatives on cash flows in relation to the required investments. Thus, all projects whose rate of return exceeds the minimum rate of return would be desirable, and vice versa. A project which promises a return of 25 per cent would ordinarily be more desirable than one which promises a return of 12 per cent. The problem of choosing the minimum acceptable rate of return (more a problem of finance than of accounting) is extremely complex. In this book we shall assume that the minimum acceptable rate of return is given to the accountant by management, and that it represents the rate that can be earned by alternative uses of investment capital.

There are several different ways of approaching the capital-budgeting decision. Although we shall discuss: (a) urgency and persuasion; (b) discounted cash flow; (c) payback; and (d) the accounting method (see Appendix A), we shall concentrate on discounted cash flow because it is conceptually superior to the others.

URGENCY AND PERSUASION

Many phases of business operations are managed in the same manner that many individuals care for their cars. How many of us keep cars going until that bald tire becomes suddenly useless, the old battery refuses to perform, or the sticky valves keep the car from starting in cold weather? Then, what happens? Stop-gap action may be taken so that the car can be back in service quickly. When a machine part fails, a belt breaks, or a generator wears out, routine replacements are made to avoid disruption in production. If the old machine on the assembly line suddenly disintegrates, there may be a fast but uneconomic replacement so that down time is minimized. All repairs, maintenance, and replacements should be implementations of an over-all equipment policy which considers future cost comparisons and timing. The repair of the moment is only one of a series that are upcoming. All of these outlays should be considered together and matched against future benefits and alternatives. Because of widespread ignorance and faulty criteria for replacement decisions, many businesses keep equipment far longer than they should.

Often the urgent action taken is correct on logical grounds. But it is correct by coincidence rather than by methodical analysis. The pressures of the moment lead to quick remedial action. Then too, common-sense action such as replacing worn gaskets to prevent oil leakage is too obvious to warrant formal pro-and-con analysis. However, when a contemplated outlay is large and far-reaching in its effects, urgency should not be a convincing influence.

The individual manager's power of persuasion is a key factor where urgency or postponability is paramount in influencing the spending decisions of top management. The managers who are best at selling their own projects to the decision maker get the lion's portion of the available money, whereas the rest of the managers either get nothing or wait, and then wait some more. Economic considerations become secondary as individual managers war with words and with impressive operating performance that may or may not be relevant to the capital-budgeting problem at hand.

DISCOUNTED CASH FLOW

Time value of money

The discounted cash-flow method for capital budgeting recognizes that the use of money has a cost (interest), just as the use of a building or an automobile may have a cost (rent). A dollar in the hand today is worth more than a dollar to be received (or spent) five years from today. For instance, in the interim a dollar can be invested in a savings institution; the dollar would grow markedly during a five-year span because of the interest it would earn. *Because the discounted cash-flow method explicitly and routinely weighs the time value of money, it is the best method to use for long-range decisions.*

Another major aspect of the cash-flow method is its focus on *cash* inflows and outflows rather than on *net income* as computed in the conventional accounting sense. As we shall see, the student without a strong accounting background has an advantage here. He does not have to unlearn the accrual concepts of accounting, which the accounting student often wrongly tries to inject into discounted cash-flow analysis.

There are two main variations of the discounted cash-flow method: (a) time-adjusted rate of return; and (b) net present value. A brief summary of the tables and formulas used is included in Appendix B at the end of this chapter. *Before reading on, be sure you understand Appendix B.*

Time-adjusted rate of return

Example A. A manager is considering buying a new special-purpose machine, which will have a five-year useful life, have zero disposal value, and result in cash operating savings of $1,000 annually. If the machine will cost $3,791 now, what is the time-adjusted rate of return on this project?

EXHIBIT 14-2

TWO PROOFS OF TIME-ADJUSTED RATE OF RETURN

Original investment	$3,791	
Useful life	5 years	
Annual cash inflow from operations	1,000	
Rate of return	10% [a]	

PROOF 1:   Discounting Each Year's Cash Inflow Separately*

	Present Value of $1, Discounted at 10%	Total Present Value	Sketch of Cash Flows					
End of Year			0	1	2	3	4	5
Cash flows:								
Annual cash savings	.909	$ 909		$1,000				
	.826	826			$1,000			
	.751	751				$1,000		
	.683	683					$1,000	
	.621	621						$1,000
Present value of future inflows		$3,791‡						
Initial outlay	1.000	(3,791)	$(3,791)					
Net present value (the zero difference proves that the rate of return is 10 per cent)		$ 0						

PROOF 2:   Using Annuity Table†

Annual cash savings	3.791	$3,791	$1,000 $1,000 $1,000 $1,000 $1,000
Initial outlay	1.000	(3,791)	$(3,791)
Net present value		$ 0	

*Present values from Table 14-2, Appendix B to Chapter 14.
†Present values of annuity from Table 14-4, Appendix B to Chapter 14.
‡Sum is really $3,790, but is rounded.
[a] The rate of return would be computed by trial-and-error methods; this is explained later in the chapter.

The time-adjusted rate of return may be defined as "the maximum rate of interest that could be paid for the capital employed over the life of an investment without loss on the project.[1] This rate corresponds to the effective rate of interest so widely computed for bonds purchased or sold at discounts or premiums.

Note in Exhibit 14-2 that $3,791 is the present value, at a rate of return of ten per cent, of a five-year stream of inflows of $1,000 in cash per year. Ten per cent is the rate that equates the amount invested ($3,791) with the present value of the cash inflows ($1,000 per year for five years). In other words, *if* money were borrowed at an effective interest rate of 10 per cent, the cash inflow produced by the project would exactly repay the hypothetical loan plus interest over the five years. If the minimum desired rate of return[2] is less than 10 per cent, the project will be profitable. If the cost of capital exceeds 10 per cent, the cash inflow will be insufficient to pay interest and repay the principal of the hypothetical loan. Therefore, 10 per cent is the time-adjusted rate of return for this project.

Explanation of compound interest

The time-adjusted rate of return is computed on the basis of the funds in use from period to period instead of on the original investment. (See Exhibit 14-3). The return in that exhibit is 10 per cent of the capital invested during each year. The cash flows in excess of the 10 per cent "rent" on the invested capital are regarded as recoveries of the original investment. In this example, the five-year cash inflow recovers the original investment plus annual interest at a rate of 10 per cent on the yet unrecovered capital.

Depreciation and discounted cash flow

Students are often perplexed by the seeming exclusion of depreciation from discounted cash-flow computations. A common homework error is to discount cash flows less depreciation. This tendency betrays a lack of understanding of a basic idea of the time-adjusted rate of return. Discounted cash-flow techniques and tables *automatically* provide for recoupment of principal in computing time-adjusted rates of return. Conse-

---

[1] *Research Report 35, Return on Capital as a Guide to Managerial Decisions*, National Association of Accountants (December, 1959), p. 57. *Rate of return* may alternatively be defined as the discounting rate that makes the present value of a project equal to the cost of the project.

[2] Minimum desired rate of return (cost of capital) is discussed in Chapter 15. For now, we assume the cost of capital as given; it is the minimum desired rate of return. Any project whose rate of return exceeds the cost of capital is desirable. Cost of capital usually is a long-run weighted average based on both debt and equity. Cost of capital is *not* typically a piecemeal computation based on the market rate of interest; that is, cost of capital is not "interest expense" on borrowed money as the accountant usually conceives it to be. For example, a mortgage-free house still has a cost of capital—the amount that could be earned with the proceeds if the house were sold.

EXHIBIT 14-3

RATIONALE UNDERLYING TIME-ADJUSTED RATE OF RETURN
(Same data as in Exhibit 14-2)

	Original investment			$3,791	
	Annual cash inflow from operations			1,000	
	Useful life			5 years	
	Rate of return			10%	

	(1)	(2)	(3)	(4)	(5)
				Amount of Investment	Unrecovered
	Unrecovered		Return at	Recovered	Investment
	Investment	Annual	10% per	at End	at End
	at Beginning	Cash	Year	of Year	of Year
Year	of Year	Inflow	(1) × 10%	(2) – (3)	(1) – (4)
1	$3,791	$1,000	$ 379	$ 621	$3,170
2	3,170	1,000	317	683	2,487
3	2,487	1,000	249	751	1,736
4	1,736	1,000	173	827	909
5	909	1,000	91	909	0
		$5,000	$1,209	$3,791	

Assumptions: Unrecovered investment at beginning of each year earns interest for whole year. Annual cash inflows are received at the end of each year. For simplicity in the use of tables, all operating cash inflows or outflows are assumed to take place at the end of the years in question. This is unrealistic because such cash flows ordinarily occur uniformly throughout the given year, rather than in lump sums at the end of the year. Compound interest tables especially tailored for these more stringent conditions are available,[3] but we shall not consider them here.

quently, *it is unnecessary to deduct depreciation charges from cash inflows before consulting present value tables.* For example, re-examine Exhibit 14-3. Note that at the end of year one, the $1,000 cash inflow represents a 10 per cent ($379) return on the $3,791 unrecovered investment at the beginning of year one *plus* a $621 recovery of principal. (The latter is akin to the depreciation provision in conventional accounting.)

    This difficult point warrants another illustration. Assume that a company is considering investing in a project with a two-year life and no residual value. Cash flow is to be received in equal payments of $3,000 at the end of each of the two years. How much would the company be willing to invest in order to earn a time-adjusted rate of return of 6 per cent? A quick look at the table for either the present value of $1 (Appendix B, Table 14-2) or the present value of an ordinary annuity of $1 (Table 14-4) will show:

P.V. of annuity of $3,000 for 2 years at 6% is: $3,000 × 1.833 = $5,499

or

P.V. of $3,000 at end of year 1: $3,000 × .943 = $2,829
P.V. of $3,000 at end of year 2: $3,000 × .890 =   2,670 $5,499

[3] For example, see J. C. Gregory, *Interest Tables for Determining Rate of Return* (The Atlantic Refining Company).

The following is an analysis of computations that are automatically considered when present value tables are used:

Year	Investment at Beginning of Year	Operating Cash Inflow	Return at 6% per Year	Amount of Investment Received at End of Year	Unrecovered Investment at End of Year
1	$5,499	$3,000	.06 × $5,499 = $330	$3,000 − $330 = $2,670	$5,499 − $2,670 = $2,829
2	$2,829	$3,000	.06 × $2,829 = $170	$3,000 − $170 = $2,830	$2,829 − $2,830 = −$1*

*Discrepancy due to rounding.

A study of these computations will show that discounted cash-flow techniques do consider recovery of investment in rate-of-return computations and that the discount tables have built-in provisions for recovery of investment.

Net present value method

Another type of discounted cash-flow approach may be called the net present value method. Computing the exact time-adjusted rate of return entails trial and error and, sometimes, cumbersome hand calculations and interpolations within a compound interest table. In contrast, the net present value method assumes some minimum desired rate of return. All expected cash flows are discounted to the present, using this minimum desired rate. If the result is positive, the project is desirable because its return exceeds the desired minimum. If the result is negative, the project is undesirable.

Example A will also be used to demonstrate the net present value approach. The new machine will cost $3,791. Exhibit 14-4 indicates a net present value of $202; therefore, the investment is desirable. The manager would be able to invest $202 more, or a total of $3,993 (that is, $3,791 + $202), and still earn 8 per cent on the project.

The higher the minimum desired rate of return, the less the manager would be willing to invest in this project. At a rate of 12 per cent, the net present value would be $−185 (that is, $1,000 × 3.605, the present value factor from Table 14-4, = $3,605, which is $185 less than the required investment of $3,791). When the desired rate of return is 12 per cent, rather than 8 per cent, the machine is undesirable at its selling price of $3,791.

COMPARISON OF NET
PRESENT VALUE AND TIME-ADJUSTED METHODS

Example B. As we have seen, there are two discounted cash-flow methods: time-adjusted rate of return and net present value. Now we shall compare them and also review what this chapter has covered so far. The Block Company is thinking of buying at a cost of $22,000 some new material-handling equipment that promises to save $5,000 in cash

EXHIBIT 14-4

NET PRESENT VALUE TECHNIQUE

Original investment	$3,791
Useful life	5 years
Annual cash inflow from operations	1,000
Minimum desired rate of return	8%

Approach 1: Discounting Each Year's Cash Inflow Separately*

	Present Value of $1, Discounted @ 8%	Total Present Value	Sketch of Cash Flows					
End of Year			0	1	2	3	4	5
Cash flows:								
Annual cash savings	.926	926		$1,000				
	.857	857			$1,000			
	.794	794				$1,000		
	.735	735					$1,000	
	.681	681						$1,000
Present value of future inflows		$3,993						
Initial outlay	1.000	(3,791)	$(3,791)					
Net present value		$ 202						

Approach 2: Using Annuity Table†

Annual cash savings	3.993	$3,993		$1,000	$1,000	$1,000	$1,000	$1,000
Initial outlay	1.000	(3,791)	$(3,791)					
Net present value		$ 202‡						

*Present values from Table 14-2, Appendix B to Chapter 14.
†Present annuity values from Table 14-4.
‡Rounded.

operating costs per year. Its estimated useful life is ten years, and it will have zero disposal value.

REQUIRED:

1. Time-adjusted rate of return.
2. Net present value if the minimum desired rate of return is 16 per cent.

Solution

1. Time-adjusted rate of return:
   $22,000 = P.V. of annuity of $5,000 at X per cent for 10 years, or what

factor (F) in the table of present values of an annuity (Table 14-4) will satisfy the following equation:

$$\$22,000 = \$5,000 \ (F)$$
$$F = \$22,000/\$5,000 = 4.400$$

Now on the ten-year line in the table for the present value of an annuity (Table 14-4), find the column that is closest to 4.400. You will find that 4.400 lies somewhere between a rate of return of 18 per cent and one of 20 per cent. Interpolate as follows:

18%	4.494	4.494
True rate ⟶		4.400
20%	4.192	
Difference	.302	.094

True rate:	18% plus .094/.302 (2%)	
	18% plus .31 (2%)	
	18% plus .62%, or	18.62%

The time-adjusted rate (18.62 per cent) is the rate that equates the amount invested ($22,000) with the present value of the cash inflows ($5,000 per year for ten years). In other words, if money were borrowed at an effective interest rate of 18.62 per cent, the cash inflow (or savings) produced by the project would exactly repay the loan and interest over the ten years. If the cost of capital is less than 18.62 per cent, the project will be profitable at a rate measured by the difference between the cost of capital and the rate earned by the investment (18.62 per cent). If the cost of capital exceeds 18.62 per cent, the cash inflow (or savings) will not be enough to pay interest and repay the principal of the hypothetical loan. Therefore, 18.62 per cent is the rate of return in this instance.

2. Net present value:

This method takes the same basic equation used in (1):

$$\$22,000 = \text{P.V. of annuity of } \$5,000 \text{ at } X \text{ per cent for 10 years.}$$

However, this time we shall replace the $22,000 with an unknown and replace X per cent with the minimum desired rate of return (assumed to be 16 per cent):

$$X = \text{P.V. of annuity of } \$5,000 \text{ at 16 per cent for 10 years.}$$

The computed present value is compared to the required investment. If the present value exceeds the required investment, the project is desirable, and vice versa:

Consult the table for the present worth of an annuity. Find the 16% column and the 10-year row. The factor is 4.833. Substitute in the equation:

$$X = \$5,000 \ (4.833)$$
$$X = \$24,165$$

Net present value = $24,165 minus $22,000 = $2,165

We can summarize the practical guidance offered by these two methods as follows:

<table>
<tr><td>Time-Adjusted Rate of Return</td><td>Net Present Value</td></tr>
<tr><td>

1. Using present value tables, compute the time-adjusted rate of return by trial and error interpolation.

2. If this rate equals or exceeds the minimum desired rate of return, accept the project; if not, reject the project.

</td><td>

1. Calculate the net present value, using the minimum desired rate of return as the discount rate.

2. If the net present value is zero or positive, accept the project; if negative, reject the project.

</td></tr>
</table>

We emphasize the net present value method in this text because it has distinct advantages over the time-adjusted rate of return. The net present value approach does not entail scouring tables and solving for the "true" rate of return by trial and error. Also, its rationale is a bit easier for most individuals to understand. It can be applied to any situation, regardless of whether there is uniform cash flow (present value of annuity) or some uneven cash flows. The latter is more tedious, as Example C demonstrates, because it calls for taking the future cash flows for *each* year in the contemplated project and discounting them to the present. (See the next chapter for a more detailed comparison.)

THE NET PRESENT VALUE COMPARISON OF TWO PROJECTS

Incremental versus Total Project Approach

The mechanics of compound interest may appear formidable to those readers who are encountering them for the first time. However, a little practice with the interest tables should easily clarify the mechanical aspect. More important, we shall now blend some relevant cost analysis with the discounted cash-flow approach.

> **Example C.** A company owns a packaging machine, which was purchased three years ago for $56,000. The machine has a remaining useful life of five years, but will require a major overhaul at the end of two more years of life, at a cost of $10,000. Its disposal value now is $20,000; in five years its disposal value is expected to be $8,000. The cash operating costs of this machine are expected to be $40,000 annually.
>
> A salesman has offered a substitute machine for $51,000, or for $31,000 plus the old machine. The new machine will slash annual cash operating costs by $10,000, will not require any overhauls, will have a useful life of five years, and will have a disposal value of $3,000.

REQUIRED:

Assume that the minimum desired rate of return is 14 per cent. Using the net present value technique, show whether the new machine should be purchased, using: (1) a total project approach; (2) an incremental approach. Try to solve before examining the solution.

Solution. A difficult part of long-range decision making is the structuring of the data. We want to see the effects of each alternative on future cash flows. The focus here is on bona fide *cash* transactions, not on opportunity costs. Using an opportunity cost approach may yield the same answers, but repeated classroom experimentation with various analytical methods has convinced the author that the following steps are likely to be the clearest:

> *Step 1. Arrange the relevant cash flows by project, so that a sharp distinction is made between total project flows and incremental flows.* The incremental flows are merely algebraic differences between two alternatives. (There are *always* at least two alternatives. One is the *status quo*, the alternative of doing nothing.) Exhibit 14-5 shows how the cash flows for *each* alternative are sketched.

> *Step 2. Discount the expected cash flows and choose the project with the least cost or the greatest benefit.* Both the total project approach and the incremental approach are illustrated in Exhibit 14-5. Which approach you use is a matter of preference. However, to develop confidence in this area, you should work with both at the start. In this example, the $8,425 net difference in favor of replacement is the ultimate result under either approach.

Analysis of typical items under discounted cash flow

1. Future disposal values. The disposal value at the date of termination of a project is an increase in the cash inflow in the year of disposal. Errors in forecasting disposal value are usually not crucial because the present value is usually small.

2. Current disposal values and required investment. In a replacement decision, how should the current disposal value affect the computations? For example, suppose that the current disposal value of old equipment is $5,000 and that new equipment is available at $40,000. There are a number of correct ways to analyze these items, all of which will have the same ultimate effect on the decision. Generally, the required investment is most easily measured by offsetting the disposal value of the old assets against the gross cost of the new assets ($40,000) and by showing the net cash outgo at $35,000.

3. Book value and depreciation. Depreciation is a phenomenon of accrual accounting that entails an allocation of cost, not a specific cash outlay. Depreciation and book value are ignored in discounted cash-flow approaches for the reasons mentioned earlier in this chapter.

4. Income taxes. In practice, comparison between alternatives is best made after considering tax effects, because the tax impact may alter the picture. (The effects of income taxes are considered in Chapter 15 and may be studied now if desired.)

5. Overhead analysis. In relevant cost analysis, only the overhead that will differ between alternatives is pertinent. There is need for careful study of the fixed overhead under the available alternatives. In practice, this is an extremely difficult phase of cost analysis, because it is difficult to relate the individual costs to any single project.

EXHIBIT 14-5

Total Project versus Incremental Approach to Net Present Value
(Data from Example C)

End of Year	Present Value Discount Factor, @ 14%	Total Present Value	0	1	2	3	4	5
						Sketch of Cash Flows		
TOTAL PROJECT APPROACH								
A. *Replace*								
Recurring cash operating costs, using an annuity table*	3.433	$(102,990)		($30,000)	($30,000)	($30,000)	($30,000)	($30,000)
Disposal value, end of Year 5	.519	1,557						3,000
Initial required investment	1.000	(31,000)	($31,000)					
Present value of net cash outflows		$(132,433)						
B. *Keep*								
Recurring cash operating costs, using an annuity table*	3.433	$(137,320)		($40,000)	($40,000)	($40,000)	($40,000)	($40,000)
Overhaul, end of Year 2	.769	(7,690)			(10,000)			
Disposal value, end of Year 5	.519	4,152						8,000
Present value of net cash outflows		$(140,858)						
Difference in favor of replacement		$ 8,425						
INCREMENTAL APPROACH								
A—B *Analysis Confined to Differences*								
Recurring cash operating savings, using an annuity table*	3.433	$ 34,330		$10,000	$10,000	$10,000	$10,000	$10,000
Overhaul avoided, end of Year 2	.769	7,690			10,000			
Difference in disposal values, end of Year 5	.519	(2,595)						(5,000)
Incremental initial investment	1.000	(31,000)	($31,000)					
Net present value of replacement		$ 8,425						

*Table 14-4, p. 474.

6. Unequal lives. Where projects have unequal lives, comparisons may be made either over the useful life of the longer-lived project or over the useful life of the shorter-lived project. For our purposes, let us estimate what the residual values will be at the end of the longer-lived project. We must also assume a reinvestment at the end of the shorter-lived project. This makes sense primarily because the decision maker should extend his time horizon as far as possible. If he is considering a longer-lived project, he should give serious consideration to what actually could be done in the time interval between the termination dates of the shorter-lived and longer-lived projects.

7. Mutually exclusive projects. When the projects are mutually exclusive, so that the acceptance of one automatically entails the rejection of the other (for example, buying Dodge or Ford trucks), the project which maximizes wealth measured in net present value in dollars should be undertaken.

8. A word of caution. The foregoing material has been an *introduction* to the area of capital budgeting, which is, in practice, complicated by a variety of factors: unequal lives; mutually exclusive investments; major differences in the size of alternative investments; peculiarities in time-adjusted rate-of-return computations; various ways of allowing for uncertainty (see Chapter 26); changes, over time, in desired rates of return; the indivisibility of projects in relation to a fixed over-all capital budget appropriation; and more. These niceties are beyond the scope of this introductory chapter, but the next chapter will help you pursue the subject in more depth.

PAYBACK

Uniform cash inflows

Payback, sometimes called *payout* or *payoff*, is a rough-and-ready method that is looked upon with disdain by many academic theorists. Yet payback is the most widely used method, and it certainly is an improvement over the criterion of urgency or postponability. Furthermore, it is a handy device (1) where precision in estimates of profitability is not crucial and preliminary screening of a rash of proposals is necessary; (2) where a weak cash and credit position has a heavy bearing on the selection of investment possibilities; and (3) where the contemplated project is extremely risky.

Assume that $4,500 is spent for a machine which has an estimated useful life of ten years. It promises cost savings of $1,000 a year in *cash flow from operations* (depreciation is ignored). The payback calculations follow:

$$P = I/O_c$$
$$P = \$4,500/\$1,000 = 4.5 \text{ years}$$

P is the payback time; I is the initial incremental amount invested; and O_c is the uniform annual incremental cash inflow from operations.

Essentially, payback is a measure of the time it will take to recoup in the form of cash from operations only the original dollars invested. Given the useful life of an asset and uniform cash flows, the less the payout period, the greater the profitability; or, given the payback period, the greater the useful life of the asset, the greater the profitability.

Although the payback method may often yield clues to profitability, it should not be used blindly. Note that payback does not measure profitability; it does measure how quickly investment dollars may be recouped. An investment's main objective is profitability, not recapturing the original outlay. If a company wants to recover its investment outlay rapidly, it need not bother spending in the first place. Then the payback time is zero; no waiting time is needed.

The major weakness of the payback approach is its neglect of profitability. The mere fact that a project has a satisfactory payback does not mean that it should be selected in preference to an alternative project with a longer payback time. To illustrate, consider an alternative to the $4,500 machine mentioned earlier. Assume that this other machine requires only a $3,000 investment and will also result in gross earnings of $1,000 per year before depreciation. Compare the two payback periods:

$$P_1 = \$4,500/\$1,000 = 4.5 \text{ years}$$
$$P_2 = \$3,000/\$1,000 = 3.0 \text{ years}$$

The payback criterion would favor buying the $3,000 machine. However, one fact about this machine has been purposely withheld. Its useful life is only three years. Ignoring the complexities of compound interest for the moment, one finds that the $3,000 machine results in zero profits, whereas the $4,500 machine yields profits for five and one-half years beyond its payback period. Despite these criticisms, a form of the payback method, called the *payback reciprocal*, discussed later in this chapter, is useful in many situations.[4]

Nonuniform cash inflows

The payback formula is designed for uniform cash inflows. When cash inflows are not uniform, the payback computation takes a cumulative form. That is, each year's net cash inflows are accumulated until the initial investment is recovered. For example, assume that the $4,500 machine produces a total cash savings of $10,000 over ten years, but not at a rate of $1,000 annually. Instead, the inflows are as follows:

Year	Cash Savings	Accumulated	Year	Cash Savings	Accumulated
1	$2,000	$2,000	6	$ 800	$ 8,300
2	1,800	3,800	7	600	8,900
3	1,500	5,300	8	400	9,300
4	1,200	6,500	9	400	9,700
5	1,000	7,500	10	300	10,000

[4] Also see Alfred Rappaport, "The Discounted Payback Period," *Management Services* (July–August, 1965), pp. 30–35.

The payback time is slightly beyond the second year. Straight-line interpolation within the third year reveals that the final $700 (that is, $4,500 − $3,800) needed to recover the investment would be forthcoming in 2.47 years (that is,

$$\frac{\$700}{\$1,500} \times 1 \text{ year} = .47 \text{ years}).$$

The bail-out factor: a better approach to payback

The typical payback computation tries to answer the question: "How soon will it be before I can recoup my investment *if operations proceed as planned*?" However, a more fundamental question is: "Which of the competing projects has the best bail-out protection if things go wrong? In other words, which has the least risk?" To answer such a question, we must consider the salvage value of the equipment throughout its life, an item that is ignored in the usual payback computations.

For instance, salvage values of general-purpose equipment far exceed those of special-purpose equipment. These salvage values can be incorporated in a bail-out approach to payback as follows:

Assume that Equipment A (General-Purpose) costs $100,000 and that Equipment B (Special-Purpose) costs $150,000. Each has a ten-year life. A is expected to produce uniform annual cash savings of $20,000; B, of $40,000. A's salvage value is expected to be $70,000 at the end of year 1; it is expected to decline at a rate of $10,000 annually thereafter. B's salvage value is expected to be $80,000 at the end of year 1; it is expected to decline at a rate of $20,000 annually. Note the difference in results under the traditional payback and the bail-out payback methods. The "bail-out payback time" is reached when the cumulative cash operating savings plus the salvage value at the end of a particular year equals the original investment:

Traditional Payback	Bail-out Payback

Traditional Payback

If operations go as expected:

$$A: P = \frac{I}{O_c} = \frac{\$100,000}{20,000} = 5 \text{ years}$$

$$B: P = \frac{I}{O_c} = \frac{\$150,000}{40,000} = 3.75 \text{ years}$$

Bail-out Payback

If the project fails to meet expectations:

	At end of	Cumulative Cash Operating Savings	Salvage Value	Cumulative Total
A:	Year 1	$ 20,000 +	$70,000 =	$ 90,000
	Year 2	40,000 +	60,000 =	100,000

Therefore, payback is 2 years.

	At end of	Cumulative Cash Operating Savings	Salvage Value	Cumulative Total
B:	Year 1	$ 40,000 +	$80,000 =	$120,000
	Year 2	80,000 +	60,000 =	140,000
	Year 3	120,000 +	40,000 =	160,000

Therefore, payback is 2.75 years, assuming that the salvage value would also be $40,000 at the end of that time.

The above analysis demonstrates how different interpretations of the payback method can produce different results. If the objective is to measure risk (in the sense of how to avoid loss), the bail-out method is better than the traditional method.

Annuity formula and payback reciprocal

The much maligned traditional payback method has received increasing attention[5] and approval as being useful for a wide number of situations.

The major argument in favor of payback is based on the equation for the present value of an annuity.

General formula for present value of annuity:

$$P_N = O_c \left(\frac{1 - \dfrac{1}{(1 + R)^N}}{R} \right) \quad (1)$$

Restated:

$$P_N = \frac{O_c}{R} - \frac{O_c}{R}\left(\frac{1}{(1 + R)^N}\right) \quad (2)$$

Multiply by R:

$$RP_N = O_c - O_c\left(\frac{1}{(1 + R)^N}\right) \quad (3)$$

Solve for R:

$$R = \frac{O_c}{P_N} - \frac{O_c}{P_N}\left(\frac{1}{(1 + R)^N}\right) \quad (4)$$

P_N = investment; O_c = annual *cash* savings or cash inflow from operations; R = rate of return; N = life of investment in years.

Note in equation (4) that the first right-hand term is the reciprocal of the payback period. The second right-hand term is the same reciprocal multiplied by $\dfrac{1}{(1 + R)^N}$. Now, if either R or N is large, this second term becomes small; therefore, *in these cases*, the rate of return will be closely approximated by the payback reciprocal. (Will the payout reciprocal be larger or smaller than the true rate of return?)

Limitations of payback reciprocal

A project with an infinite life would have a rate of return exactly equal to its payback reciprocal because the second right-hand term, in equation (4), becomes zero. Thus, in practice, the payback reciprocal is a

---

[5]Myron Gordon, "Payoff Period and Rate of Profit," *Journal of Business* (Oct., 1955), pp. 253–260. Professor Gordon's article is cited often in the following two references:
Spencer and Siegelman, *Managerial Economics* (Homewood, Ill.: Richard D. Irwin, Inc., 1964), pp. 390–395. *N.A.A. Research Report 35, op. cit.*, pp. 75–82.

helpful tool in quickly estimating the true rate of return where the project life is *at least twice the payback period*.

The payback reciprocal has wide applicability as a meaningful though rough tool. But its major limitations should be kept in mind:

1. It is valid only when the useful life of the project is at least twice the payback period. In any event, the payback reciprocal will always exceed the true rate of return.
2. It assumes that earnings or savings are constant over the investment's life.

Relationships of payback reciprocal to rate of return

Exhibit 14-6 shows the relationships of the payback reciprocal to the rate of return for a project with a five-year payback period (payback reciprocal is 20 per cent) and various useful lives. Note that the payback reciprocal gives a reasonable approximation of the time-adjusted rate of return only if the useful life of the project is at least ten years—twice the payback period. Otherwise, the regular time-adjusted computations must be made.

EXHIBIT 14-6

RECIPROCAL OF PAYBACK PERIOD COMPARED WITH RATE OF RETURN

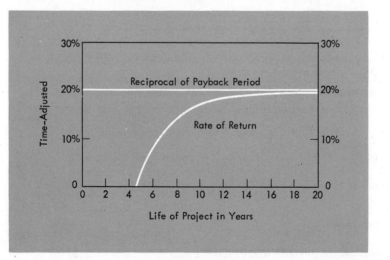

Source: *N.A.A. Research Report 35, Return on Capital as a Guide to Managerial Decisions*, p. 78.

The table in Exhibit 14-7 shows various combinations of payback periods and time-adjusted rates of return. The table is based on one used by a company that uses the payback period in approximating the rate of return.

EXHIBIT 14-7

TABLE FOR APPROXIMATING RATE OF RETURN

Useful Life in Years	Time-Adjusted Rate of Return (Per Cent)										
3	0										
4	15	11	7	3	0						
5	23	19	15	12	9	6	4	2	0		
6	27	23	20	17	15	12	10	8	6	3	0
7	29	26	23	20	18	15	13	11	10	7	4
8	30	27	25	22	20	18	16	14	13	10	8
9	31	28	26	23	21	19	18	16	15	12	10
10	32	29	27	24	22	21	19	18	16	14	11
15	33	30	28	25	25	23	22	20	19	16	15
20	33	30	28	26	25	23	22	20	19	18	16
Over 20	34	31	29	27	26	24	23	21	20	19	17
Payback Period in Years	3	$3\frac{1}{4}$	$3\frac{1}{2}$	$3\frac{3}{4}$	4	$4\frac{1}{4}$	$4\frac{1}{2}$	$4\frac{3}{4}$	5	$5\frac{1}{2}$	6

Source: Adapted from *N.A.A. Research Report 35, Return on Capital as a Guide to Managerial Decisions,* p. 76.

Example 1. (Same facts as plotted in graph in Exhibit 14-6.) Project savings expected to last ten years; computed payback period is five years (a payback reciprocal of 20%). Enter table at ten-year row and five-year column. Table shows 16% time-adjusted rate of return. (The relationships on the graph in Exhibit 14-6 can also be found in the five-year column of this table.)

Example 2. Project savings expected to last 12 years. Computed payback period is 4.7 years. Enter table using nearest values; that is, use 10 years for savings and 4¾ years for payback period. Table shows 18% time-adjusted rate of return. For more accurate computations, interpolation may be used.

Returning to the Block Company example discussed earlier in this chapter:

$$\text{Payback Reciprocal} = O_c/I = \frac{\$5,000}{\$22,000} = \underline{\underline{22.73\%}}$$

Note that this rate is closer to the time-adjusted rate (18.62 per cent) of return than either answer provided by the accounting method, discussed in Appendix A.

Note also that the table in Exhibit 14-7 would be used as follows:

$$\text{Payback period} = \frac{\$22,000}{\$5,000} = 4.400 \text{ or } 4\tfrac{1}{2} \text{ years}$$

The useful life is ten years. The table's ten-year row and $4\tfrac{1}{2}$-year column indicate a time-adjusted rate of return of 19 per cent, a very accurate approximation.

Payback is widely used in industry. Prudent use of the device shows that it may be very helpful:

> This company uses the rate of return on "book investment," (i.e., the accounting method) exclusively for projects costing over $25,000. For smaller projects, it uses the payback period. The controller stated that, as a general guide, the company "should get its money back in no more than half the expected life of the project" and that furthermore this payback period should be a relatively short period of years. Apparently he realized that, where the life of the project is substantially in excess of the payback period, the payback period varies inversely with rate of return and, by keeping the payback period short, the company insures a fairly high rate of return.[6]

ADMINISTRATION OF CAPITAL BUDGETS

Although ordinary budget procedures are well entrenched in many companies, formal capital budgeting is still quite undeveloped, largely because it has flowered fairly recently.

The first feature of dynamic capital budgeting administration is the awareness on the part of all management members that long-run expenditures are generators of long-run profits. This engenders a constant search for new methods, processes, and products.

Approval of over-all capital budgets usually is the responsibility of the board of directors. Depending on the amounts involved, individual projects receive approval at various managerial levels. Requests are usually made semiannually or annually. They are reviewed as they pass upward through managerial levels until they reach a committee that examines capital budget requests and submits recommendations to the president. In turn, the president submits final recommendations to the board of directors.

Of course, most companies will have a set of forms and a timetabled, uniform routine for processing capital budgets.

When projects are authorized, there is a need for follow-up on two counts. First, control is needed to see that spending and specifications conform to the plan as approved. Second, the very existence of such follow-up will cause capital spending requests to be sharply conceived and honestly estimated.

Systematic procedures are needed not only to implement capital budgets but to appraise (audit) the profitability performance of projects.

[6] For other examples of company uses of payback methods, see *N.A.A. Research Report 35, op. cit.*, pp. 80–81.

This is *vital* to a successful capital budgeting program. The follow-up comparison of performance with original estimates not only better insures careful forecasts but also helps sharpen the tools for improving future forecasts.

SUMMARY

Product costing, income determination, and the planning and controlling of operations have a current time-period orientation. Special decisions and long-range planning have primarily a project orientation. There is a danger in using ordinary accounting data for special purposes. Discounted cash-flow techniques have been developed for the making of special decisions and for long-range planning because the time value of money becomes extremely important when projects extend beyond one year.

The field of capital budgeting is important because lump-sum expenditures on long-life projects have far-reaching effects on profitability and flexibility. It is imperative that management develop carefully laid plans based on reliable forecasting procedures.

Urgency, favoritism, and subjectivity should be minor criteria in the selection of capital projects.

Capital budgeting is long-term planning for proposed capital outlays and their financing. Projects are accepted if their rate of return exceeds a minimum desired rate of return.

Because the discounted cash-flow method explicitly and automatically weighs the time value of money, it is the best method to use for long-range decisions. The overriding goal is maximum long-run net cash inflows.

The discounted cash-flow approach has two variations; time-adjusted rate of return and net present value. Both approaches take into account the timing of cash flows and are thus superior to other methods.

The payback method is the most widely used approach to capital spending decisions. It is simple and easily understood, but it neglects profitability.

The payback reciprocal has wide applicability as a rough measure of the time-adjusted rate of return.

The accounting rate of return (discussed in Appendix A) is widely used, although it is more cumbersome and much cruder than discounted cash-flow methods. It fails to recognize explicitly the time value of money. Instead, the accounting method depends on averaging techniques that may yield inaccurate answers, particularly when cash flows are not uniform through the life of a project. The accounting method is adequate where the return plainly far exceeds the minimum desired rate or where projects are not subject to close competition from other projects.

The estimate of cost savings (differential cash flows) is the key measurement for capital budgeting. Factors that must be considered in these calculations include income taxes and different capacities of plant and equipment, as well as the usual recurring operating costs. The use of probability theory can help approach and measure the uncertainty that plagues this work.

The difficult forecasting problem makes capital budgeting one of the most imposing tasks of management. Although judgment and attitudes are important ingredients of capital budgeting, the correct application of the techniques described here should crystallize the relevant factors and help management toward intelligent decision making.

Special problems in relevant costs and capital budgeting, including income tax factors, are discussed in Chapter 15. A suggested reading list is given at the end of Chapter 15.

PROBLEM FOR SELF-STUDY

Use the data in the Problem for Self-Study from Chapter 13 (p. 421).

REQUIRED:

1. Assume that the minimum rate of return desired is 18 per cent. Using discounted cash-flow techniques, show whether the new equipment should be purchased. Use a total project approach and an incremental approach.
2. What is the traditional payback period for the new equipment?

Solution

1. The first step is to analyze all relevant operating *cash* flows and align them with the appropriate alternative:

SCHEDULE OF ANNUAL OPERATING CASH OUTFLOWS

	(1) Present Situation	(2) New Situation	(3) Increment
Sales (irrelevant)			
Expenses:			
Direct materials	$10,000	$ 9,000	$ 1,000
Direct labor	20,000	10,000	10,000
Variable overhead	15,000	7,500	7,500
Fixed overhead (irrelevant)			
Selling and administrative expenses (irrelevant)			
Total relevant operating cash outflows	$45,000	$26,500	$18,500

The next step is to sketch the *other* relevant cash flows, as shown in Exhibit 14-8. Either the total project approach or the incremental approach results in the same $10,527 net present value in favor of replacement.

EXHIBIT 14-8

SOLUTION TO REQUIREMENT 1 OF PROBLEM FOR SELF-STUDY

End of Year	Present Value Discount Factor, @ 18%	Total Present Value	Sketch of Cash Flows 0	1	2	3	4
TOTAL PROJECT APPROACH							
A. *New Situation*							
Recurring cash operating costs, using an annuity table*	2.690	$ (71,285)		($26,500)	($26,500)	($26,500)	($26,500)
Disposal value of old equipment now	1.000	6,000	$ 6,000				
Cost of new equipment	1.000	(44,000)	($44,000)				
Present value of net cash outflows		$(109,285)					
B. *Present Situation*							
Recurring cash operating costs, using an annuity table	2.690	$(121,050)		($45,000)	($45,000)	($45,000)	($45,000)
Disposal value of old equipment four years hence	.516	1,238					$ 2,400
Present value of net cash outflows		$(119,812)					
Difference in favor of replacement		$ 10,527					
INCREMENTAL APPROACH							
A—B Analysis Confined to Differences							
Recurring cash operating savings, using an annuity table*	2.690	$ 49,765		$18,500	$18,500	$18,500	$18,500
Disposal value of old equipment now	1.000	6,000	$ 6,000				
Cost of new equipment	1.000	(44,000)	($44,000)				
Disposal value of old equipment foregone four years hence	.516	(1,238)					($ 2,400)
Net present value of replacement		$ 10,527					

*From Table 14-4.

Note that the book value of the old machine is irrelevant, and so it is completely ignored. In the light of subsequent events, nobody will deny that the original $50,000 investment could have been avoided, with a little luck or foresight. But nothing can be done to alter the past. The next question is whether the company will nevertheless be better off by buying the new machine. Management would have been much happier had the $50,000 never been spent in the first place, but the original mistake should not be compounded by keeping the old machine.

2. The payback formula can be used because the operating savings are uniform:

$$P = \frac{I}{O_c} = \frac{\$44,000 - \$6,000}{\$18,500} = 2.1 \text{ years}$$

Note that the payback formula is an *incremental* formula.

APPENDIX A. ACCOUNTING METHOD OF RATE OF RETURN

Equations

Although discounted cash-flow approaches to business decisions are being increasingly used, they are still relatively new, having been developed and applied for the first time, on any wide scale, in the 1950's. There are other techniques with which the accountant and manager should be at least somewhat familiar, because they are entrenched in many businesses.

The technique we are about to discuss is conceptually inferior to discounted cash-flow approaches. Then why do we bother studying it? First, changes in business practice occur slowly. Where older methods, such as payback or the accounting method, are in use, they should be used properly, even if there are better tools available. Many managers use the accounting method because they regard it as satisfactory for their particular needs. In other words, they feel that the use of this tool is adequate for guiding their decisions even though the more refined discounted cash-flow tools are available. In such cases, care should be taken so that the cruder tool is used properly. The situation is similar to using a pocket knife instead of a scalpel for removing a person's appendix. If the pocket knife is used by a knowledgeable and skilled surgeon, the chances for success are much better than if it is used by a bungling layman.

The label for the *accounting method* is not uniform. It is also known as the *financial statement method*, the *book value method*, the *rate-of-return on assets method*, the *approximate rate-of-return method*, and the *unadjusted rate-of-return method*. Its computations supposedly dovetail most closely with conventional accounting methods of calculating income and required investment. However, the dovetailing objective is not easily attained because the purposes of the computations differ. The most troublesome aspects are depreciation and decisions concerning capitalization versus expense. For example, advertising and research are usually expensed, even though they often may be viewed as long-range investments.

The equations for the accounting rate of return are:

Accounting rate of return $=$

$$\frac{\text{Increase in future average annual net income}}{\text{Initial increase in required investment}} \qquad (1)$$

$$R = \frac{O_c - W - S}{I} \qquad (2)$$

where $R =$ Average annual rate of return on initial incremental investment
$O_c =$ Average annual incremental cash inflow from operations
$W =$ Average annual write-off of incremental investment (akin to depreciation except that salvage value is handled separately)
$S =$ Average annual incremental effects of salvage values

Assume the same facts as in our payback illustration: cost of machine, \$4,500; useful life, ten years; estimated disposal value, zero; and expected annual cash inflow from operations, \$1,000. Substitute these amounts into Eq. (2):

$$R = \frac{\$1,000 - \$450 - 0}{\$4,500} = 12.2\%$$

The denominator: investment base

Many advocates of the accounting method would not use \$4,500 in the denominator. Instead, they would halve the original investment, because only about half the \$4,500, or \$2,250, is the average amount invested in the machine over its ten-year life. Their reasoning is that depreciable assets do not require a permanent investment of the original amount. The funds are gradually recovered as the earnings are realized.[7] Under this approach, the rate of return would obviously be doubled, as follows:

$$R = \frac{\$1,000 - \$450 - 0}{\$2,250} = 24.4\%$$

Initial investment as a base

Although our examples in this appendix will use the initial investment base, practice is not uniform as to whether initial investment or average investment in fixed assets should be used in the denominator. Com-

[7] The measure of funds recovered in the above example is \$450 a year, the amount of the annual depreciation. Consequently, the average funds committed to the project would decline at a rate of \$450 per year from \$4,500 to zero; hence, the average investment would be the beginning balance plus the ending balance (\$4,500 + 0) divided by 2, or \$2,250.

panies defend the use of the initial investment base because it does not change over the life of the investment; therefore, follow-up and comparison of actual rate of return against predicted rate of return is facilitated. This follow-up is crucial for control and for improving future capital planning and comparison on a year-to-year, plant-to-plant, and division-to-division basis. The initial base is not affected by depreciation methods.

In most cases, the rankings of competing projects will not differ regardless of whether the gross or average investment base is used. Of course, using the average base will show substantially higher rates of return; however, the desirable rate of return used as a cut-off for accepting projects is also higher.

Current assets as a part of investment base

Current assets, such as cash, receivables, and inventories, often are expanded in order to sustain higher activity levels. In our example, if a $1,000 increase in current assets is required, the denominator will be $4,500 plus $1,000, or $5,500. This $1,000 increase in current assets will be fully committed for the life of the project; so, under the average investment method, the average base would be $3,250 ($2,250 average investment in equipment plus $1,000 average investment in current assets).

Danger of understating investment

The gross or initial investment in the project should include the following: all additional required current assets, fixed assets, research costs, engineering costs, market-testing costs, start-up costs, initial costs of sales promotion, and so forth. The omission of any of these items from the base can give misleading results.

Although the *accounting method's* approach to investment decisions tries to approximate the figures as they will eventually appear in financial statements, there is not always an exact agreement between figures on conventional statements and figures used for decision making. The tendency in accounting practice is to write costs off to expense quickly. Thus, the assembly of figures for special decisions requires care to see that investment is not understated. Often the investment base for decision making should include items, like research and sales promotion costs, that the accountant ordinarily writes off immediately as expenses.

Accounting method is an averaging technique

The unadjusted method ignores the time value of money. Expected future dollars are unrealistically and erroneously regarded as equal to present dollars. The discounted cash-flow method explicitly allows for the force of interest and the exact timing of cash flows. In contrast, the unadjusted method is based on *annual averages*.

Compare the time-adjusted rate of return in Example B, 18.62 per cent, with the accounting rate of return:

Based on initial investment

$$R = \frac{O_c - W - S}{\text{Initial } I} = \frac{\$5,000 - \$2,200 - 0}{\$22,000} = 12.727\%$$

Based on average investment

$$R = \frac{O_c - W - S}{\text{Average } I} = \frac{\$5,000 - \$2,200 - 0}{.5\,(\$22,000)} = 25.455\%$$

Note how the accounting rate of return, however calculated, can produce results that differ markedly from the time-adjusted rate of return.

To demonstrate how the accounting method is basically an averaging technique that ignores the time value of money, re-examine Example C:

Incremental Effects	Five Years Together	Annual Average	
Recurring cash operating savings	$50,000	$10,000	
Overhaul avoided, end of year 2	10,000	2,000	
Average annual incremental cash inflow from operations		$12,000	= O_c
Incremental initial investment ($51,000 − $20,000)	31,000		= I
Average annual write-off of incremental investment		6,200	= W
Difference in disposal values: new equipment, $3,000; old equipment, $8,000	5,000		
Average annual incremental effects of disposal values		1,000	= S

$$R = \frac{O_c - W - S}{I} = \frac{\$12,000 - \$6,200 - \$1,000}{\$31,000} = \frac{\$4,800}{\$31,000} = 15.48\% \text{ or } 15\%*$$

*Because we deal with uncertainty about expected future data, computations to the nearest whole per cent should be satisfactory.

Note in the illustration that net disposal value of old assets should be offset against the gross cost of new assets in computing the *incremental* (additional) initial investment base. *One of the most frequent mistakes in the accounting method is to fail to relate the proper investment base to the proper operating figures.* The $4,800 net annual advantage should be related to the $31,000 *additional* investment, not the $51,000 total investment.

Conflict of concepts and purposes

The discounted cash-flow method is more objective because its answer is not directly influenced by decisions as to depreciation methods, capitalization-versus-expense decisions, and conservatism. (These decisions do influence income tax cash flows, however.) Erratic flows of revenue and expense over the project's life are directly considered under discounted cash flow but are "averaged" under the accounting method. "The [accounting method] utilizes concepts of capital and income which were originally designed for the quite different purpose of accounting for periodic income and financial position."[8] Thus, in the accounting method the initial capital may be computed differently, the force of interest may be ignored, and the approximation of the average rate of return may be far from the real mark. The degree of error often becomes larger where the cash inflows do not have a uniform pattern. Equipment becomes much more desirable where cash savings are bigger in early years than where they are spread evenly throughout the useful life. Yet the accounting method would not make this distinction in computing average annual effects.

EXHIBIT 14-9

COMPARISON OF RATES OF RETURN BY
ACCOUNTING METHOD AND DISCOUNTED CASH-FLOW METHOD*

	Project A	Project B	Project C
Amount invested	$ 75,000	$ 75,000	$ 75,000
Cumulative† cash inflow from operations:			
Years 1–5	$160,000	$ 80,000	$ 40,000
6–10	100,000	80,000	80,000
11–15	80,000	80,000	120,000
16–20	40,000	80,000	100,000
21–25	20,000	80,000	60,000
Totals	$400,000	$400,000	$400,000
Average annual cash flow	$ 16,000	$ 16,000	$ 16,000
Less depreciation ($75,000 ÷ 25)	3,000	3,000	3,000
Average annual net income	$ 13,000	$ 13,000	$ 13,000
Rate of return on original investment ($13,000 ÷ $75,000)	17.3%	17.3%	17.3%
Rate of return on average investment ($13,000 ÷ $37,500)	34.7%	34.7%	34.7%
Rate of return by discounted cash-flow method‡	40.5%	21.4%	16.6%

*Source: **N.A.A. Research Report 35, Return on Capital as a Guide to Managerial Decisions**, p. 67.
†For example, Project A's cash inflow is $32,000 annually for the first five years, $20,000 annually for the next five years, and so forth.
‡These time-adjusted rates could be computed by trial-and-error methods. As you can imagine, this is a tedious process if you use hand calculations. In this case, the N.A.A. used tables that assumed cash inflows to be forthcoming *throughout* the year rather than at the *end* of the year. Table 14-4 assumes the latter; this would produce slightly lower rates. (Why?)

[8] *N.A.A. Research Report 35, op. cit.*, p. 64.

Uneven cash flows

Discounted cash-flow techniques can more readily compare projects having different lives and having different timings of cash inflows because discounting allows comparisons to be made at the same point in time. See Exhibit 14-9 for an illustration of the effect of different timings of cash flows. Some projects, such as mines and oil wells, have heavy earnings in early years. Other projects, like new product lines and new stores, take more time to produce maximum earnings.

Postaudit

The accounting method usually facilitates follow-up, because the same approach is used in the forecast as is used in the accounts. Yet exceptions to this ideal situation often occur. The most common exceptions arise from the inclusion, in the forecast, of some initial investment items that are not handled in the same manner in the subsequent accounting records. For example, the accounting for trade-ins and disposal values varies considerably. In practice, test checks are frequently used on key items. An interesting suggestion on the problem of postaudit follows:

> When a major project is undertaken, it seems desirable to prepare project cost and income budgets employing the usual accounting classifications so that subsequent actual figures drawn from the accounts can be compared directly with estimates. Rates of return can also be computed by the [accounting method], using the budgeted and actual data. Thus . . . the discounted cash flow method would be used as a basis for project selection and rate of return based upon a financial budget for the project would be used as a goal against which to compare subsequent performance.[9]

Understandability

There is general agreement that the accounting method is easier to understand and apply than the discounted cash-flow method. Yet proponents of discounted cash flow maintain that its difficulty is overestimated, that reluctance to use it is based more on unfamiliarity than on inherent complexity. (Experience in the author's classes indicates that the student has far more difficulty understanding the accounting method than the discounted cash-flow methods.) Tables and short cuts are available to reduce the pencil pushing. Also, the estimation of cash flows does not require a knowledge of the intricacies of accounting concepts and conventions.

The choice of method is ultimately dependent on personal preference and on the danger of making wrong decisions by using the less precise accounting method. *In any event, the isolation and measurement of relevant revenue and cost factors are usually more important than which evaluation technique is used.* Because we are dealing only with future costs, all the compiled figures are

[9] *N.A.A. Research Report 35, op. cit.*, pp. 72–73.

necessarily estimated (forecasted) and clouded by varying degrees of uncertainty;[10] any intricate compound interest techniques applied to these estimates are useful only insofar as the basic data are reliable.

PROBLEM FOR SELF-STUDY FOR APPENDIX A

Problem. Using the data in the Problem for Self-Study in Chapter 13 (see Exhibits 13-5 and 13-6), compute the accounting rate of return based on initial investment.

Solution. All data in the numerator are from the final column in Exhibit 13-6:

$$R = \frac{(\$1,000 + \$10,000 + \$7,500) - (\$11,000) - (\$900)}{\$44,000 - \$6,000}$$

$$R = \frac{\$18,500 - \$11,000 - \$900}{\$38,000}$$

$$R = \frac{\$6,600}{\$38,000} = 17.4\%$$

Note that the denominator is always the incremental investment and that the entire concept, like payback, is an incremental or differential approach. The numerator is similar to the numerator in the payback approach, except that depreciation (new) and disposal values are also introduced.

APPENDIX B: NOTES ON COMPOUND INTEREST

Interest

Interest is the cost of using money. It is the rental charge for funds, just as rental charges are made for the use of buildings and equipment. Whenever a time span is involved, it is necessary to recognize interest as a cost of using invested funds. This applies even if the funds in use represent ownership capital and if the interest does not entail an outlay of cash. The reason why interest must be considered is that the selection of one alternative automatically commits a given amount of invested funds which otherwise could be invested in some other opportunity. The measure of the interest in such cases is the return foregone by rejecting the alternative use.

Interest often is unimportant when short-term projects are under consideration, but it looms large when long-run plans are being con-

[10] See Chapter 26 for an extended discussion of how to deal with uncertainty. Also see Bierman and Smidt, *The Capital Budgeting Decision* (2nd ed., New York: The Macmillan Company, 1966), and David B. Hertz, "Risk Analysis in Capital Investment," *Harvard Business Review* (January-February, 1964), pp. 95–106. Hertz uses a simulation approach which yields an expected value together with a range of minimum and maximum probable values.

sidered. Because of this, the rate of interest in question is of telling import. The rate used often will influence the ultimate decision. For example, $100,000 invested now and compounded annually for ten years at 3 per cent will accumulate to $134,392; at 7 per cent, to $196,715.

Interest tables

Four basic tables are used for computations involving interest. Tables 14-2 and 14-4 are the most pertinent for our purposes.

Table 14-1—Amount of $1. Table 14-1 shows how much $1 invested now will accumulate to in a given number of periods at a given compounded interest rate per period. The future proceeds of an investment of $1,000 for three years at 8 per cent compound interest could be sketched as follows:

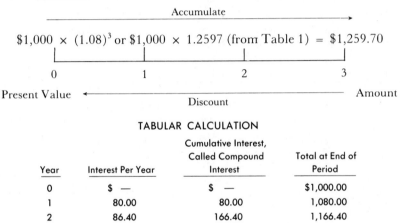

$$\$1,000 \times (1.08)^3 \text{ or } \$1,000 \times 1.2597 \text{ (from Table 1)} = \$1,259.70$$

TABULAR CALCULATION

Year	Interest Per Year	Cumulative Interest, Called Compound Interest	Total at End of Period
0	$ —	$ —	$1,000.00
1	80.00	80.00	1,080.00
2	86.40	166.40	1,166.40
3	93.30	259.70	1,259.70

Note that what is really being done in the tabular presentation is a series of computations that could appear as follows:

$$S_1 = 1,000\,(1.08)$$
$$S_2 = 1,000\,(1.08)^2$$
$$S_3 = 1,000\,(1.08)^3$$

The formula for the "amount of 1," often called the "future value of 1," can be written:

$$S = P(1 + r)^n$$
$$S = 1,000\,(1 + .08)^3 = \$1,259.70$$

S is the *amount*, the future worth; P is the present value, $1,000 in this case; r is the rate of return; n is the number of periods.

Fortunately, tables make key computations readily available, so that a facility in selecting the *proper* table will minimize computations. Check the accuracy of the above answer against Table 14-1.

TABLE 14-1

AMOUNT OF $1.00. $S = P(1 + r)^n$

Periods	2%	4%	5%	6%	8%	10%
1	1.0200	1.0400	1.0500	1.0600	1.0800	1.1000
2	1.0404	1.0816	1.1025	1.1236	1.1664	1.2100
3	1.0612	1.1249	1.1576	1.1910	1.2597	1.3310
4	1.0824	1.1699	1.2155	1.2625	1.3605	1.4641
5	1.1041	1.2167	1.2763	1.3382	1.4693	1.6105
6	1.1262	1.2653	1.3401	1.4185	1.5869	1.7716
7	1.1487	1.3159	1.4071	1.5036	1.7138	1.9488
8	1.1717	1.3686	1.4775	1.5938	1.8509	2.1436
9	1.1951	1.4233	1.5513	1.6895	1.9990	2.3589
10	1.2190	1.4802	1.6289	1.7908	2.1589	2.5938
11	1.2434	1.5395	1.7103	1.8983	2.3316	2.8532
12	1.2682	1.6010	1.7959	2.0122	2.5182	3.1385
13	1.2936	1.6651	1.8856	2.1329	2.7196	3.4524
14	1.3195	1.7317	1.9799	2.2609	2.9372	3.7976
15	1.3459	1.8009	2.0709	2.3966	3.1722	4.1774
16	1.3728	1.8730	2.1829	2.5404	3.4259	4.5951
17	1.4002	1.9479	2.2920	2.6928	3.7000	5.0545
18	1.4282	2.0258	2.4066	2.8543	3.9960	5.5600
19	1.4568	2.1068	2.5270	3.0256	4.3157	6.1160
20	1.4859	2.1911	2.6533	3.2071	4.6610	6.7276
30	1.8114	3.2434	4.3219	5.7435	10.0627	17.4495
40	2.2080	4.8010	7.0400	10.2857	21.7245	45.2597

Table 14-2—Present Value of $1. In the previous example, if $1,000 compounded at 8 per cent per annum will accumulate to $1,259.70 in three years, then $1,000 must be the present value of $1,259.70 due at the end of three years. The formula for the present value can be derived by reversing the process of *accumulation* (getting the amount) that we just finished. Look at the earlier sketch to see the relationship between accumulating and discounting.

If

$$S = P(1 + r)^n,$$

then

$$P = \frac{S}{(1 + r)^n};$$

$$P = \frac{\$1,259.70}{(1.08)^3} = \$1,000.$$

Use Table 14-2 to check this calculation.

When accumulating, we advance or roll forward in time. The difference between our original amount and our accumulated amount is called *compound interest*. When discounting, we retreat or roll back in time. The

TABLE 14-2

PRESENT VALUE OF $1.00. $P = \dfrac{S}{(1 + r)^n}$

Periods	4%	6%	8%	10%	12%	14%	16%	18%	20%	22%	24%	26%	28%	30%	40%
1	0.962	0.943	0.926	0.909	0.893	0.877	0.862	0.847	0.833	0.820	0.806	0.794	0.781	0.769	0.714
2	0.925	0.890	0.857	0.826	0.797	0.769	0.743	0.718	0.694	0.672	0.650	0.630	0.610	0.592	0.510
3	0.889	0.840	0.794	0.751	0.712	0.675	0.641	0.609	0.579	0.551	0.524	0.500	0.477	0.455	0.364
4	0.855	0.792	0.735	0.683	0.636	0.592	0.552	0.516	0.482	0.451	0.423	0.397	0.373	0.350	0.260
5	0.822	0.747	0.681	0.621	0.567	0.519	0.476	0.437	0.402	0.370	0.341	0.315	0.291	0.269	0.186
6	0.790	0.705	0.630	0.564	0.507	0.456	0.410	0.370	0.335	0.303	0.275	0.250	0.227	0.207	0.133
7	0.760	0.665	0.583	0.513	0.452	0.400	0.354	0.314	0.279	0.249	0.222	0.198	0.178	0.159	0.095
8	0.731	0.627	0.540	0.467	0.404	0.351	0.305	0.266	0.233	0.204	0.179	0.157	0.139	0.123	0.068
9	0.703	0.592	0.500	0.424	0.361	0.308	0.263	0.225	0.194	0.167	0.144	0.125	0.108	0.094	0.048
10	0.676	0.558	0.463	0.386	0.322	0.270	0.227	0.191	0.162	0.137	0.116	0.099	0.085	0.073	0.035
11	0.650	0.527	0.429	0.350	0.287	0.237	0.195	0.162	0.135	0.112	0.094	0.079	0.066	0.056	0.025
12	0.625	0.497	0.397	0.319	0.257	0.208	0.168	0.137	0.112	0.092	0.076	0.062	0.052	0.043	0.018
13	0.601	0.469	0.368	0.290	0.229	0.182	0.145	0.116	0.093	0.075	0.061	0.050	0.040	0.033	0.013
14	0.577	0.442	0.340	0.263	0.205	0.160	0.125	0.099	0.078	0.062	0.049	0.039	0.032	0.025	0.009
15	0.555	0.417	0.315	0.239	0.183	0.140	0.108	0.084	0.065	0.051	0.040	0.031	0.025	0.020	0.006
16	0.534	0.394	0.292	0.218	0.163	0.123	0.093	0.071	0.054	0.042	0.032	0.025	0.019	0.015	0.005
17	0.513	0.371	0.270	0.198	0.146	0.108	0.080	0.060	0.045	0.034	0.026	0.020	0.015	0.012	0.003
18	0.494	0.350	0.250	0.180	0.130	0.095	0.069	0.051	0.038	0.028	0.021	0.016	0.012	0.009	0.002
19	0.475	0.331	0.232	0.164	0.116	0.083	0.060	0.043	0.031	0.023	0.017	0.012	0.009	0.007	0.002
20	0.456	0.312	0.215	0.149	0.104	0.073	0.051	0.037	0.026	0.019	0.014	0.010	0.007	0.005	0.001
21	0.439	0.294	0.199	0.135	0.093	0.064	0.044	0.031	0.022	0.015	0.011	0.008	0.006	0.004	0.001
22	0.422	0.278	0.184	0.123	0.083	0.056	0.038	0.026	0.018	0.013	0.009	0.006	0.004	0.003	0.001
23	0.406	0.262	0.170	0.112	0.074	0.049	0.033	0.022	0.015	0.010	0.007	0.005	0.003	0.002	
24	0.390	0.247	0.158	0.102	0.066	0.043	0.028	0.019	0.013	0.008	0.006	0.004	0.003	0.002	
25	0.375	0.233	0.146	0.092	0.059	0.038	0.024	0.016	0.010	0.007	0.005	0.003	0.002	0.001	
26	0.361	0.220	0.135	0.084	0.053	0.033	0.021	0.014	0.009	0.006	0.004	0.002	0.002	0.001	
27	0.347	0.207	0.125	0.076	0.047	0.029	0.018	0.011	0.007	0.005	0.003	0.002	0.001	0.001	
28	0.333	0.196	0.116	0.069	0.042	0.026	0.016	0.010	0.006	0.004	0.002	0.002	0.001	0.001	
29	0.321	0.185	0.107	0.063	0.037	0.022	0.014	0.008	0.005	0.003	0.002	0.001	0.001	0.001	
30	0.308	0.174	0.099	0.057	0.033	0.020	0.012	0.007	0.004	0.003	0.002	0.001	0.001	0.001	
40	0.208	0.097	0.046	0.022	0.011	0.005	0.003	0.001	0.001						

difference between the future amount and the present value is called *compound discount*. Note the following formulas:

$$\text{Compound interest} = (1 + r)^n - 1 = \$259.70$$

$$\text{Compound discount} = 1 - \frac{1}{(1 + r)^n} = \$259.70.$$

Table 14-3—Amount of Annuity of $1. An (ordinary) *annuity* is a series of equal payments (receipts) to be paid (or received) at the *end* of successive periods of equal length.

TABLE 14-3

AMOUNT OF ANNUITY OF \$1.00 IN ARREARS. $S_n = \dfrac{(1 + r)^n - 1}{r}$

Periods	2%	4%	5%	6%	8%	10%
1	1.0000	1.0000	1.0000	1.0000	1.0000	1.0000
2	2.0200	2.0400	2.0500	2.0600	2.0800	2.1000
3	3.0604	3.1216	3.1525	3.1836	3.2464	3.3100
4	4.1216	4.2465	4.3101	4.3746	4.5061	4.6410
5	5.2040	5.4163	5.5256	5.6371	5.8666	6.1051
6	6.3081	6.6330	6.8019	6.9753	7.3359	7.7156
7	7.4343	7.8983	8.1420	8.3938	8.9228	9.4872
8	8.5830	9.2142	9.5491	9.8975	10.6366	11.4360
9	9.7546	10.5828	11.0266	11.4913	12.4876	13.5796
10	10.9497	12.0061	12.5779	13.1808	14.4866	15.9376
11	12.1687	13.4864	14.2068	14.9716	16.6455	18.5314
12	13.4121	15.0258	15.9171	16.8699	18.9771	21.3846
13	14.6803	16.6268	17.7130	18.8821	21.4953	24.5231
14	15.9739	18.2919	19.5986	21.0151	24.2149	27.9755
15	17.2934	20.0236	21.5786	23.2760	27.1521	31.7731
16	18.6393	21.8245	23.6575	25.6725	30.3243	35.9503
17	20.0121	23.6975	25.8404	28.2129	33.7502	40.5456
18	21.4123	25.6454	28.1324	30.9057	37.4502	45.6001
19	22.8406	27.6712	30.5390	33.7600	41.4463	51.1601
20	24.2974	29.7781	33.0660	36.7856	45.7620	57.2761
30	40.5681	56.0849	66.4388	79.0582	113.2832	164.4962
40	60.4020	95.0255	120.7998	154.7620	259.0565	442.5974

Assume that $1,000 is invested at the end of each of three years at 8 per cent:

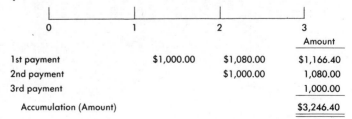

	0	1	2	3
				Amount
1st payment		$1,000.00	$1,080.00	$1,166.40
2nd payment			$1,000.00	1,080.00
3rd payment				1,000.00
Accumulation (Amount)				$3,246.40

The arithmetic shown above may be expressed algebraically as the amount of an ordinary annuity of $1,000 for three years = $1,000 $(1 + r)^2 + \$1,000(1 + r)^1 + \$1,000$.

We can develop the general formula for S_n, the amount of an ordinary annuity of $1, by using the above example as a basis:

(1) $S_n = 1 + (1 + r)^1 + (1 + r)^2$

(2) Substitute: $S_n = 1 + (1.08) + (1.08)^2$

(3) Multiply (2) by $(1 + r)$: $(1.08)S_n = 1.08 + (1.08)^2 + (1.08)^3$

(4) Subtract (2) from (3): $1.08S_n - S_n = (1.08)^3 - 1$
Note that all terms on
right-hand side are re-
moved except $(1.08)^3$
in equation (3) and 1
in equation (2).

(5) Factor (4): $S_n(1.08 - 1) = (1.08)^3 - 1$

(6) Divide (5) by $(1.08 - 1)$: $S_n = \dfrac{(1.08)^3 - 1}{1.08 - 1} = \dfrac{(1.08)^3 - 1}{.08}$

(7) The general formula for
the amount of an ordi-
nary annuity of $1
becomes: $S_n = \dfrac{(1 + r)^n - 1}{r}$ or $\dfrac{\text{Compound Interest}}{\text{Rate}}$

This formula is the basis for Table 14-3. Look at Table 14-3 or use the formula itself to check the above calculations.

Table 14-4—Present Value of an Ordinary Annuity of $1. Using the same example as for Table 14-3, we can show how the formula of P_n, *the present value of an ordinary annuity,* is developed.

$$\vert\underset{0}{\quad}\quad\underset{1}{\vert}\quad\underset{2}{\vert}\quad\underset{3}{\vert}$$

	Present Value				
1st payment:	$\dfrac{1,000}{1.08} = \$\ 926.14$	$1,000		
2nd payment:	$\dfrac{1,000}{(1.08)^2} = \$\ 857.52$		$1,000	
3rd payment:	$\dfrac{1,000}{(1.08)^3} = \$\ 794.00$			$1,000
	$\$2,577.66$				

P_N = sum of present values of each item.

For the general case, the present value of an ordinary annuity of $1 may be expressed:

(1) $P_n = \dfrac{1}{1 + r} + \dfrac{1}{(1 + r)^2} + \dfrac{1}{(1 + r)^3}$

TABLE 14-4

Present Value of Annuity of $1.00 in Arrears. $P_n = \dfrac{1}{r}\left[1 - \dfrac{1}{(1+r)^n}\right]$

Periods	4%	6%	8%	10%	12%	14%	16%	18%	20%	22%	24%	25%	26%	28%	30%	40%
1	0.962	0.943	0.926	0.909	0.893	0.877	0.862	0.847	0.833	0.820	0.806	0.800	0.794	0.781	0.769	0.714
2	1.886	1.833	1.783	1.736	1.690	1.647	1.605	1.566	1.528	1.492	1.457	1.440	1.424	1.392	1.361	1.224
3	2.775	2.673	2.577	2.487	2.402	2.322	2.246	2.174	2.106	2.042	1.981	1.952	1.923	1.868	1.816	1.589
4	3.630	3.465	3.312	3.170	3.037	2.914	2.798	2.690	2.589	2.494	2.404	2.362	2.320	2.241	2.166	1.849
5	4.452	4.212	3.993	3.791	3.605	3.433	3.274	3.127	2.991	2.864	2.745	2.689	2.635	2.532	2.436	2.035
6	5.242	4.917	4.623	4.355	4.111	3.889	3.685	3.498	3.326	3.167	3.020	2.951	2.885	2.759	2.643	2.168
7	6.002	5.582	5.206	4.868	4.564	4.288	4.039	3.812	3.605	3.416	3.242	3.161	3.083	2.937	2.802	2.263
8	6.733	6.210	5.747	5.335	4.968	4.639	4.344	4.078	3.837	3.619	3.421	3.329	3.241	3.076	2.925	2.331
9	7.435	6.802	6.247	5.759	5.328	4.946	4.607	4.303	4.031	3.786	3.566	3.463	3.366	3.184	3.019	2.379
10	8.111	7.360	6.710	6.145	5.650	5.216	4.833	4.494	4.192	3.923	3.682	3.571	3.465	3.269	3.092	2.414
11	8.760	7.887	7.139	6.495	5.988	5.453	5.029	4.656	4.327	4.035	3.776	3.656	3.544	3.335	3.147	2.438
12	9.385	8.384	7.536	6.814	6.194	5.660	5.197	4.793	4.439	4.127	3.851	3.725	3.606	3.387	3.190	2.456
13	9.986	8.853	7.904	7.103	6.424	5.842	5.342	4.910	4.533	4.203	3.912	3.780	3.656	3.427	3.223	2.468
14	10.563	9.295	8.244	7.367	6.628	6.002	5.468	5.008	4.611	4.265	3.962	3.824	3.695	3.459	3.249	2.477
15	11.118	9.712	8.559	7.606	6.811	6.142	5.575	5.092	4.675	4.315	4.001	3.859	3.726	3.483	3.268	2.484
16	11.652	10.106	8.851	7.824	6.974	6.265	5.669	5.162	4.730	4.357	4.033	3.887	3.751	3.503	3.283	2.489
17	12.166	10.477	9.122	8.022	7.120	6.373	5.749	5.222	4.775	4.391	4.059	3.910	3.771	3.518	3.295	2.492
18	12.659	10.828	9.372	8.201	7.250	6.467	5.818	5.273	4.812	4.419	4.080	3.928	3.786	3.529	3.304	2.494
19	13.134	11.158	9.604	8.365	7.366	6.550	5.877	5.316	4.844	4.442	4.097	3.942	3.799	3.539	3.311	2.496
20	13.590	11.470	9.818	8.514	7.469	6.623	5.929	5.353	4.870	4.460	4.110	3.954	3.808	3.546	3.316	2.497
21	14.029	11.764	10.017	8.649	7.562	6.687	5.973	5.384	4.891	4.476	4.121	3.963	3.816	3.551	3.320	2.498
22	14.451	12.042	10.201	8.772	7.645	6.743	6.011	5.410	4.909	4.488	4.130	3.970	3.822	3.556	3.323	2.498
23	14.857	12.303	10.371	8.883	7.718	6.792	6.044	5.432	4.925	4.499	4.137	3.976	3.827	3.559	3.325	2.499
24	15.247	12.550	10.529	8.985	7.784	6.835	6.073	5.451	4.937	4.507	4.143	3.981	3.831	3.562	3.327	2.499
25	15.622	12.783	10.675	9.077	7.843	6.873	6.097	5.467	4.948	4.514	4.147	3.985	3.834	3.564	3.329	2.499
26	15.983	13.003	10.810	9.161	7.896	6.906	6.118	5.480	4.956	4.520	4.151	3.988	3.837	3.566	3.330	2.500
27	16.330	13.211	10.935	9.237	7.943	6.935	6.136	5.492	4.964	4.524	4.154	3.990	3.839	3.567	3.331	2.500
28	16.663	13.406	11.051	9.307	7.984	6.961	6.152	5.502	4.970	4.528	4.157	3.992	3.840	3.568	3.331	2.500
29	16.984	13.591	11.158	9.370	8.022	6.983	6.166	5.510	4.975	4.531	4.159	3.994	3.841	3.569	3.332	2.500
30	17.292	13.765	11.258	9.427	8.055	7.003	6.177	5.517	4.979	4.534	4.160	3.995	3.842	3.569	3.332	2.500
40	19.793	15.046	11.925	9.779	8.244	7.105	6.234	5.548	4.997	4.544	4.166	3.999	3.846	3.571	3.333	2.500

(2) Substituting, $P_n = \dfrac{1}{1.08} + \dfrac{1}{(1.08)^2} + \dfrac{1}{(1.08)^3}$

(3) Multiply by $\dfrac{1}{1.08}$: $P_n \dfrac{1}{1.08} = \dfrac{1}{(1.08)^2} + \dfrac{1}{(1.08)^3} + \dfrac{1}{(1.08)^4}$

(4) Subtract (3) from (2): $P_n - P_n \dfrac{1}{1.08} = \dfrac{1}{1.08} - \dfrac{1}{(1.08)^4}$

(5) Factor: $P_n\left(1 - \dfrac{1}{1.08}\right) = \dfrac{1}{1.08}\left[1 - \dfrac{1}{(1.08)^3}\right]$

(6) or $P_n\left(\dfrac{.08}{1.08}\right) = \dfrac{1}{1.08}\left[1 - \dfrac{1}{(1.08)^3}\right]$

(7) Divide by $\dfrac{.08}{1.08}$: $P_n = \dfrac{1}{.08}\left[1 - \dfrac{1}{(1.08)^3}\right]$

The general formula for the present worth of an annuity is:

$$P_n = \frac{1}{r}\left(1 - \frac{1}{(1+r)^n}\right) = \frac{\text{Compound Discount}}{\text{Rate}}$$

Solving $P_n = \dfrac{.2062}{.08} = 2.577$

This formula is the basis for Table 14-4. Check the answer in the table. The present value tables, Tables 14-2 and 14-4, are used most frequently in capital budgeting.

Note that the tables for annuities are not really essential. That is, with Tables 14-1 and 14-2, compound interest and compound discount can be readily computed. Then it is simply a matter of dividing either of these by the rate to get values equivalent to those shown in Tables 14-3 and 14-4.

QUESTIONS, PROBLEMS, AND CASES

Note: Problems 14-8, 14-10, 14-11, 14-12, 14-18, 14-24, and 14-25 cover the basic points. The problem of determining what is relevant is far more imposing than any difficulties of using present value tables. Additional basic problems on capital budgeting and joint products are in Chapter 18. Problems 14-26 through 14-30 cover the accounting method, which is not covered in the other problems.

14-1. Define *capital budgeting.*

14-2. What is the payback method? What is its main weakness?

14-3. Define *time-adjusted rate of return.*

14-4. "The payback reciprocal has wide applicability as a meaningful approximation of the time-adjusted rate of return. But it has two major limitations," What are the two limitations?

14-5. "The trouble with discounted cash-flow techniques is that their use ignores depreciation costs." Do you agree? Why?

14-6. "Accelerated depreciation provides higher cash flows in early years." Do you agree? Why?

14-7. "A project with a useful life of sixty years would have a time-adjusted rate of return practically exactly equal to its payback reciprocal." Why?

14-8. Exercises in Compound Interest. To be sure that you understand how to use the tables in the appendix to this chapter, solve the following exercises. Do the exercises on your own before checking your answers. The correct answers rounded to the nearest dollar are printed after Problem 14-30.

1. You have just won $5,000. How much money will you have at the end of ten years if you invest it at six per cent compounded annually? Ignore income taxes in this and other parts of this problem.

2. Ten years from now, the unpaid principal of the mortgage on your house will be $8,955. How much do you have to invest today at six per cent interest compounded annually just to accumulate the $8,955 in ten years?

3. You plan to save $500 of your earnings each year for the next ten years. How much money will you have at the end of the tenth year if you invest your savings compounded at six per cent per year?

4. If the unpaid mortgage on your house in ten years will be $8,955, how much money do you have to invest annually at six per cent to have just this amount on hand at the end of the tenth year?

5. You hold an endowment insurance policy which will pay you a lump sum of $20,000 at age 65. If you invest the sum at six per cent, how much money can you withdraw from your account in equal amounts each year so that at the end of ten years there will be nothing left?

6. You have estimated that for the first ten years after you retire you will need an annual income of $2,720. How much money must you invest at six per cent at age 65 to just realize this annual income?

7. The table below shows two schedules of prospective operating cash inflows, each of which requires the same initial investment:

Year	Annual Cash Inflows	
	Plan A	Plan B
0	$ 1,000	$ 5,000
1	2,000	4,000
2	3,000	3,000
3	4,000	2,000
4	5,000	1,000
Total	$15,000	$15,000

The minimum desired rate of return is six per cent compounded annually. In terms of present values, which plan is more desirable? Show computations.

14-9. Payback Period. A manager is considering three mutually exclusive investment projects, A, B, and C, each promising a cash flow of $20,000 per year for an initial investment of $100,000. Useful lives are as follows:

Project	Years
A	5
B	6
C	7

REQUIRED:

1. Compute the payback period for each project. If payback time is the sole criterion for the decision, which project is most desirable?

2. Which project offers the highest rate of return?

14-10. Comparison of Approaches to Capital Budgeting. Refer to Problem 13-10. Using all data given there, compute:

1. Payback period.

2. Time-adjusted rate of return by trial and error.

3. Net present value of future savings discounted at a 10 per cent minimum desired rate of return.

• **14-11. Comparison of Approaches to Capital Budgeting.** The Gehrig Company estimates that it can save $2,800 a year in cash operating costs for the next ten years if it buys a special-purpose machine at a cost of $11,000. No residual value is expected. The company's minimum desired rate of return is 14 per cent.

REQUIRED:

(Round all computations to the nearest dollar. Ignore income taxes):

1. Payback period.

2. Using discounted cash flow:
   a. Time-adjusted rate of return.
   b. Net present value.

3. Payback reciprocal.

14-12. Different Approaches to Capital Budgeting; Proper Investment Base. Ruth Company has been operating a small lunch counter for the convenience of employees. The counter occupies space which is not needed for any other business purpose. The lunch counter has been managed by a part-time employee whose annual salary is $3,000. Yearly operations have consistently shown a loss as follows:

Receipts		$20,000
Expenses for food, supplies (in cash)	$19,000	
Salary	3,000	22,000
Net loss		$(2,000)

A company has offered to sell Ruth automatic vending machines for a total cost of $13,000, less $1,000 trade-in allowance on old equipment (which was carried at zero book value and which could be sold outright for $1,000 cash) now used in the lunch counter operation. Sales terms are cash on delivery. The old equipment will have zero disposal value ten years from now.

The useful life of the equipment is estimated at 10 years, with zero scrap value. The equipment will easily serve the same volume that the lunch counter handled. A catering company will completely service and supply the machines. Prices and variety of food and drink will be the same as those that prevailed for the lunch counter. The catering company will pay five per cent of gross receipts to the Ruth Company and will bear all costs of foods, repairs, and so forth. The part-time employee will be discharged. Thus, Ruth's only cost will be the initial outlay for the machines.

REQUIRED:

Consider only the two alternatives mentioned.
1. Prospective annual income statement under new plan. What is the annual income difference between alternatives?
2. Compute the payback period.
3. Compute:
   a. Present value under discounted cash-flow method if relevant cost of company capital is 20 per cent.
   b. Rate of return under discounted cash-flow method.
4. Compute the payback reciprocal. Compare your answer with the result in 3(b).
5. What other considerations may influence the decision?

14-13. Choosing an Automobile. Having given the matter some thought, you decide that you would be equally happy buying:
   (a) A Cadillac and trading every sixth year.
   (b) A Pontiac and trading every third year.
   (c) A Rambler and trading every second year.

You have decided to base your decision on the present value of the expected future costs. You have estimated your costs as follows:

	Cadillac	Pontiac	Rambler
Original cost	$6,500	$4,500	$3,000
Market value at trade-in time	1,000	2,000	1,500
Annual operating costs, excluding depreciation	600	700	500
Overhaul, fourth year	500		
Overhaul, second year		150	

Minimum desired rate of return is 6%.

REQUIRED:

Select the alternative that promises the greatest financial advantage. Show computations.

14-14. Replacement of Machine. The Maris Company is considering the purchase of a vertical milling machine to replace an obsolete milling machine. The machine currently being used for the operation is in good working order and will last, physically, for at least ten years. However, the proposed machine will perform the operations so much more efficiently that Maris Company engineers estimate that labor, material, and other direct costs of the operation will be reduced $2,000 a year if the proposed machine is installed. The proposed milling machine costs $10,000 delivered and installed. The Company expects to earn 20 per cent on all investments. Taxes are to be disregarded. The new machine's useful life is ten years.

Note: The present value of $1 received annually for ten years at various interest rates is:

15%	16%	18%	20%	22%	25%
5.019	4.833	4.494	4.192	3.923	3.571

1. Assuming that the present machine is being depreciated at a rate of $800 per year, that it has a book value of $8,000 (cost, $18,000; accumulated

depreciation, $10,000), and that it has zero net salvage value today, what action should be taken? What time-adjusted rate of return would be earned on the investment in the new machine?

2. Data of (1), except that the net salvage value of the old machine today is $2,000, and if retained for ten years its salvage value will be zero. How is your answer to (1) altered?

14-15. Two Sizes of Machines; Uneven Revenue Stream; Price-Level Change. The Kubek Company has developed a new product for which a growing demand is anticipated. During the first year, sales are expected to be 20,000 units; the second year, 30,000 units; the third year, 50,000 units; the fourth year and each year thereafter, 80,000 units.

The Kubek Company must choose between two alternative production arrangements:

1. Buy a big, heavy-duty machine with a capacity of 90,000 units and an estimated useful life of six years. This machine costs $250,000.

2. Buy a smaller machine with a capacity of 50,000 units and an estimated useful life of three years. Three years from today buy two such machines to replace the one that will be worn out. The smaller machines now cost $100,000 each.

Property taxes and insurance per year are expected to be $8,000 per year on the big machine and four per cent of original cost of equipment in use on the small machines. Maintenance cost is expected to be $2,000 per year on the big machine and $1,200 per year on each of the smaller machines. Variable production costs per unit will be $3.00 with the big machine and $3.10 with the smaller machines. Both machines will have zero disposal values at the end of their respective useful lives.

Prices on this type of machinery have been increasing at the rate of four per cent compounded annually. Which alternative is more attractive? Show all computations clearly, using the total present values of all outlays for each alternative. The minimum desired rate of return is 10 per cent. Assume that all outlays take place at the end of the accounting periods. Round off present value factors to two decimal places.

14-16. Elimination of Department. The Howard Pharmacy is considering eliminating its soda fountain. The proprietor feels that the space can be devoted to more profitable use if he expands his displays of over-the-counter pharmaceuticals. The income statement is presented below:

	Prescriptions	Over-the-Counter Pharmaceuticals	Fountain	Total
Sales	$50,000	$70,000	$40,000	$160,000
Less: Cost of sales	28,000	56,000	20,000	104,000
Gross profit	$22,000	$14,000	$20,000	$ 56,000
Variable expenses	$11,000	$ 8,000	$16,000	$ 35,000
Fixed expenses*	3,000	2,000	5,000	10,000
Depreciation	500	1,000	1,800	3,300
Total expenses	$14,500	$11,000	$22,800	$ 48,300
Net profit	$ 7,500	$ 3,000	$(2,800)	$ 7,700

*Exclusive of depreciation.

From past experience, the proprietor feels that he can increase his sales of over-the-counter pharmaceuticals by the following amounts:

Year 1	$30,000
Year 2	40,000
Year 3 and thereafter	50,000

Variable expenses are expected to rise by the following amounts:

Year 1	$1,000
Year 2	1,200
Year 3 and thereafter	1,500

It is expected that the cost of sales in this department will remain at the same proportion that it now is. Fixed expenses are expected to remain at the same level.

The fountain's present book value is $10,000. Its present disposal value is $2,000. Its expected useful life is five years, and its expected salvage value is $1,000.

The cost of renovating the store is $18,000. The market value of the new fixtures in five years is estimated at $5,000.

The minimum desired rate of return is 10 per cent.

REQUIRED:

Should the proprietor of the Howard Pharmacy go through with his plan? Support your answer by calculations showing the effect of discounted cash flows for the next five years. Use incremental analysis.

14-17.   A Study of the Potential Economic Usefulness of an Invention. A store manager of a large grocery chain has invented a labor-saving machine. It is designed to cut automatically the tops and bottoms from cases of grocery merchandise. These tops and bottoms, with their one and one-half-inch edges, are used as trays to hold 12 and 24 cans each. These filled trays are then stacked directly onto the shelves. Production time is improved as a result of handling 12 or perhaps 24 in one motion as opposed to hand-stacking the same number of cans in from three to six separate motions.

This "tray-pack" method of shelf-stocking and display-building is not new to the grocery business. Up until now, however, the trays had to be cut by hand, which is difficult, tedious work that often has unsightly results. The electric tray-cutter is fastened to the roller conveyor in the back room and adjusts itself automatically to any case-size. It cuts trays just about as quickly as stock can be pulled by two men in a grocery back room, simply slicing off the trays as the merchandise rolls by on the conveyor.

Some elementary time-study work was necessary to verify that the machine was indeed a time-saver and to give comparative production figures for the job. The following estimates were made of the annual depreciation and maintenance expenses:

Machine cost	$950.00
Depreciation (annual, straight-line)	200.00
Installation cost	50.00
Annual repair and electricity expense	50.00
Scrap value	00.00

The weekly savings experienced in an average store, cutting about 600 cases of tray-pack merchandise each week, are as follows:

Manual-cutting rate	2 cases per minute
Machine-cutting rate	12 cases per minute

The current labor cost is $2.00 per hour plus $.20 in fringe benefits.

Assume a 20 per cent minimum desired rate of return. Also assume that the labor savings are real, that is, that the labor costs under investigation are variable costs.

REQUIRED:

1. Compute: payback time, payback reciprocal, and the net present value for the average store.

2. What is the lowest volume of cases per week which could be handled and still make the installation desirable? Show computations.

14-18. Capital Investment in a Baseball Player. William Voock, president of the Chicago Chartreuse Sox, is currently considering a player deal in which he will acquire Bill Bantle, a great gate attraction, from the New York Confederates in exchange for $500,000 cash plus George Bumble, a regular Sox outfielder who is currently receiving a salary of $15,000 a year. Bantle is to be Bumble's replacement in the regular outfield. Voock and his fellow executives have assembled the following data.

Estimated useful life of Bantle	5 years
Estimated residual value of Bantle	$20,000
Estimated useful life of Bumble	5 years
Estimated residual value of Bumble	None
Current cash offer for Bumble received from the Atlanta Carpetbaggers Baseball Club	$50,000
Applicable minimum desired rate of return	10%

Other data:

Year	Bantle's Salary	Additional Club Gate Receipts Because of Bantle	Additional Expenses of Handling Higher Volume
1	$60,000	$330,000	$33,000
2	70,000	300,000	30,000
3	80,000	200,000	20,000
4	80,000	100,000	10,000
5	72,000	40,000	4,000

REQUIRED (Ignore income taxes):

1. Based on the data as given, should the Sox buy Bantle? Use the following present value factors:

Year	Present Value of 1 at 10%
1	.91
2	.83
3	.75
4	.68
5	.62

2. What other factors should be considered before making the decision? How much confidence do you have in the available data?

14-19. Purchase of New Furnace; Different Capacities. Different Useful Lives. The Glen Manufacturing Company is using a single gas-fired furnace at present, but, owing to expected increases in output, it is considering the following alternatives:

(a) Purchase a new electric furnace with double the capacity of the present furnace, and sell the present furnace.

(b) Purchase a new gas furnace similar to the present one, and operate the two gas furnaces.

The following information is available to aid in making the decision:

1. All furnaces are assumed to have a ten-year life with zero salvage value at the end of that time.

2. The old furnace had a cost of $4,000 four years ago. It can be sold outright for $2,400 cash.

3. The price of a new gas furnace is $4,680. This price is expected to increase at a rate of four per cent compounded annually.

4. Repair and maintenance costs for a gas furnace used regularly during the year are $1,400 per year.

5. The price of the new electric furnace is $22,400; annual repair and maintenance costs are expected to be $1,200.

6. Comparative variable costs per charge (the unit of heating) are:

	Gas	Electric
Purchase power source	$ 6.80	$12.40
Supplies	2.60	1.20
Labor	10.60	4.40
	$20.00	$18.00

7. Property taxes are estimated to be $150 per gas furnace and $700 per electric furnace per year.

8. Minimum desired rate of return is six per cent.

9. It is estimated that machine usage over the next ten years will be at the rate of 700 units (charges) per year.

REQUIRED (To ease computations, round off all factors from the compound interest tables to two decimal places):

1. The "payout" or "payback" time. The payback reciprocal. What can you conclude from the reciprocal?

2. The net present value of the electric furnace.

3. Indicate for *each* of the following whether the use of the *gas* furnace system would become more or less desirable. You may justify your answer by a *one*-sentence explanation.

(1) Property tax rates advance.
(2) New labor contract raises wage rates.
(3) Interest rates advance.
(4) Demand for product increases, so that machine usage is increased to 800 units.
(5) FPC authorizes an increases in natural gas rates.

● **14-20. Compute Minimum Desired Rate of Return.** The Hilliard Company has used the net present value method in making capital investment decisions. The company rejected an offer of a machinery salesman who had convincing evidence that his $12,500 lifting equipment would save the company $3,000 in cash operating costs per year for ten years. The disposal value of the machine was $2,000 at the end of ten years. In applying the net present value method, the company computed a negative net present value of $457. What was the minimum desired rate of return? Show computations.

14-21. When to Cut a Tree. Del Doller, a wealthy capitalist, bought land and put it in the conservation reserve. He was told that if he planted trees on the land, he would get a yearly check, and the government would not come to inspect for 20 years.

A large industrial firm that needs lumber has approached Del. The firm's employees will plant and care for trees on Del's land. In return for the use of the land they will pay 10¢ a board foot for the lumber they cut. They will cut at Del's discretion.

The number of board feet of lumber in a tree depends upon the age of the tree in years. Assuming an average growth, the growth function for trees is $f(n) = 300\sqrt{n} - 900$, n being years. $f(n)$ is the number of board feet.

REQUIRED:

Del wants to know the most profitable time for cutting the trees. Del uses a 20 per cent minimum desired rate of return.

n	$\sqrt{n}$	n	$\sqrt{n}$
10	3.162	16	4.000
11	3.317	17	4.123
12	3.464	18	4.243
13	3.606	19	4.359
14	3.742	20	4.472
15	3.873		

14-22. Replacement Decision for Railway Equipment. The Milwaukee Railroad is considering replacement of a Kalamazoo Power Jack Tamper, used in connection with maintenance of track, with a new automatic raising device which can be attached to a production tamper.

The present power jack tamper cost $18,000 five years ago and has an estimated life of twelve years. After the sixth year the machine will require a major overhaul estimated to cost $5,000. Its disposal value now is $2,500. There will be no value at the end of twelve years.

The automatic raising attachment has a delivered selling price of $24,000 and an estimated life of twelve years. Because of anticipated future developments in combined maintenance machines, it is felt that the machine should be disposed of at the end of the seventh year to take advantage of newly developed machines. Estimated sale value at the end of seven years is $5,000.

Tests have shown that the automatic raising machine will produce a more uniform surface on the track than the power jack tamper now in use. The new equipment will eliminate one machine operator and one laborer, whose combined annual salary is $9,500.

Track-maintenance work is seasonal and the equipment normally works from May 1 to October 31 each year. Machine operators and laborers are transferred to other work after October 31, at the same rate of pay.

The salesman claims that the annual normal maintenance of the new machine will run about $1,000 per year. Because the automatic machine is more complicated than the manually operated machine, it is felt that it will require a thorough overhaul at the end of the fourth year at estimated cost of $7,000.

Records show the annual normal maintenance of the Kalamazoo machines to be $1,200. Fuel consumption of the two machines is equal.

Should the Milwaukee keep or replace the Kalamazoo Power Jack Tamper? A 10 per cent rate of return is desired.

The Milwaukee is not currently paying any income tax.

14-23. Decision to Sell a Business. Mr. H. Closet is the sole proprietor of a medium-sized plumbing and heating business. Owing to the increasing amount of government contract work in his business territory and the fact that the Federal Government requires union-scale wages be paid on all government work, Closet is being pressured to unionize his shop.

Sensing Closet's distate for unions and knowing that his age is near that of retirement, a syndicate promoter, the Ulm Company, has extended a $100,000 cash offer for his business.

Closet, however, sees a large amount of business coming his way if he unionizes and receives the government contracts. He decides that if he does stay in business, he will definitely sell out in eight years. His investment in current assets (cash, inventory, accounts receivable) will be expanded by $24,000 because of the increased volume of business. His equipment will not be in very good condition eight years hence. He therefore expects to sell the business at the end of the eighth year for $40,000.

KEYSTONE PLUMBING & HEATING WORKS
Income Statement
(Last Year)

Sales		$400,000
Cost of goods sold:		
Direct material	$125,000	
Direct labor	175,000	
Variable overhead	30,000	
Fixed overhead	54,000	384,000
Gross margin		$ 16,000
Selling & administrative expense, fixed		17,000*
Net income (loss)		$ (1,000)

*Includes a $10,000 salary paid to Closet.

Closet estimates that the government contract work will result in a $200,000 increase in yearly sales. Nongovernmental sales will remain constant at $400,000 a year. Direct material costs are proportional to sales. His direct labor costs are proportional to sales but will increase by 10 per cent for all labor because of higher unionized wages. Variable overhead is assumed to vary with sales, and annual fixed overhead will total $60,000. Straight-line depreciation will increase from $8,000 per year to $10,000 per year, because new equipment must be purchased for $16,000. All fixed assets will be fully depreciated at the end of eight years. Selling and administrative expenses will remain at $17,000. Neglect any tax effects.

REQUIRED:

1. Prepare an income statement, assuming that there will be $200,000 of government contract work and that all costs will vary as stated above. This statement will be applicable to any of the next eight years.

2. Assume that his minimum desired rate of return is 8 per cent and that Closet considers his annual net cash flow as his $10,000 salary plus any cash flow from operations. Should Closet sell his business now, or continue in business for another eight years as a union shop? If he sold out, Closet would retire and not work elsewhere. Assume that all additional investments in the business by Closet will be made immediately.

3. Discuss the limitations of the analysis that influenced your recommendation.

14-24. Three Alternatives, Effects on Inventory Investments. The Dull Company has a very stable operation that is not marked by detectable variations in production or sales.

Dull Company has an old machine with a net disposal value of $5,000 now and $1,000 five years from now. A new Rapido machine is offered for $25,000 cash or $20,000 with a trade-in. The new machine promises annual operating cash outflows of $2,000 as compared with the old machine's annual outflow of $10,000. A third machine, the Quicko, is offered for $45,000 cash or $40,000 with a trade-in; it promises annual operating cash outflows of $1,000. The disposal values of the new machines five years hence will be $1,000 each.

Because the new machines will produce output more swiftly, the average investment in inventories will be as follows:

Old machine	$100,000
Rapido	80,000
Quicko	50,000

The minimum desired rate of return is 20 per cent. The company uses discounted cash-flow techniques to evaluate decisions.

REQUIRED:

Which of the three alternatives is most desirable? Show calculations. This company uses discounted cash-flow techniques for evaluating decisions. When more than two machines are being considered, the company favors computing the present value of the future costs of each alternative. The most desirable alternative is the one with the least cost.

PV of $1 at 20% for 5 years,	.40	Amount of $1 at 20% for 5 years,	2.20
PV of annuity of $1 at 20% for 5 years,	3.00	Amount of annuity of $1 at 20% for 5 years,	8.00

14-25. Cost-Volume-Profit Analysis and Discounted Cash Flow. The Susan Company wants to make doughnuts for its chain of restaurants in Los Angeles. Two machines are proposed for the production of the doughnuts: semi-automatic and automatic. The company now buys doughnuts from an outside supplier at $.04 each. Manufacturing costs would be:

	Semi-Automatic	Automatic
Variable costs per doughnut	$.02	$.0125
Fixed costs:		
Annual cash operating outlays	$2,500	$ 3,500
Initial cost of machines	$6,000	$15,000
Useful life of machines in years	4	4
Salvage value at the end of 4 years	—	$ 3,000

REQUIRED:

1. The president wants to know how many doughnuts must be sold in order to have total average annual costs equal to outside purchase costs for the (a) semi-automatic machine and (b) automatic machine.

2. At what annual volume of doughnuts would the total annual costs be the same for both machines?

3. Assume that the sales forecast over the next four years is 400,000 doughnuts per year. The minimum desired rate of return is 10 per cent. Should the automatic machine be purchased? Why? Show calculations. Ignore income taxes.

P.V. of $1.00 at 10% for 4 periods is	.7
P.V. of annuity of $1.00 at 10% for 4 periods is	3.2

Note: Problems 14-26 through 14-30 cover the accounting method, which is discussed in Appendix A.

14-26. Accounting Rate of Return. Refer to Problem 14-11. Using the data there, compute the accounting rate of return based on (a) average investment, (b) initial investment.

14-27. Accounting Rate of Return. Refer to Problem 13-10. Using the data there, compute the accounting rate of return based on (a) initial investment, (b) average investment.

14-28. Accounting Rate of Return. Refer to Problem 14-12. Using the data there, compute the accounting rate of return based on (a) average investment, (b) initial investment.

14-29. Accounting Rate of Return. Refer to Problem 13-19. Using the data there, compute the accounting rate of return based on (a) average investment, (b) initial investment.

14-30. Choice of Machines. Comparison of Discounted Cash-Flow and Accounting Method. India Manufacturing Co. is considering the purchase of a machine for their factory. Two courses are available.

(a) Machine A is being offered at a special price of $50,000 with an estimated life of seven years and a disposal value estimated at $1,000. The cash operating expenses would amount to $30,000 annually. The machine would require major repairs every two years at a cost of $5,000.

(b) Machine B is available for a price of $75,000 with an estimated life of seven years and a disposal value of $5,000. The cash operating expenses with this machine would amount to $26,000 annually. Major repairs cost $3,500 every third year.

Assume the same revenue flow in all years for both alternatives. Assume that the minimum desired rate of return is 10 per cent.

REQUIRED:

1. Compute the average annual return on the extra \$25,000 needed to buy Machine B, using the accounting method and an "initial" investment base.
2. Using discounted cash flow, compute the present value of all future costs under both alternatives. Also compare the alternatives on an incremental basis.

Answers to exercises in compound interest (Problem 14-8)

The general approach to these problems centers about a key question: which of the four basic tables am I dealing with? No computations should be made until after this basic question is answered with confidence.

1. \$8,954. From Table 1. The \$5,000 is a present value. The value ten years hence is an *amount* or *future worth*.

$S = P(1 + r)^n$; the conversion factor, $(1 + r)^n$, is on line 10 of Table 1.

Substituting: $S = 5,000\,(1.7908) = \$8,954.$

2. \$4,997. From Table 2. The \$8,955 is an *amount* or *future worth*. You want the present value of that amount.

$P = \dfrac{S}{(1 + r)^n}$. The conversion factor, $\dfrac{1}{(1 + r)^n}$, is on line 10 of Table 2.

Substituting: $P = \$8,955\,(.558) = \$4,997.$

3. \$6,590. From Table 3. You are seeking the *amount* or *future worth* of an annuity of \$500 per year.

$$S_n = \$500\ F,\ \text{where}\ F\ \text{is the conversion factor.}$$
$$S_n = \$500\,(13.1808) = \$6,590.$$

4. \$679. From Table 3. The \$8,955 is a future worth. You are seeking the uniform amount (annuity) to set aside annually.

$$S_n = \text{Annual deposit}\ (F).$$
$$\$8,955 = \text{Annual deposit}\ (13.1808).$$

$$\text{Annual Deposit} = \frac{\$8,955}{13.1808} = \$679.$$

5. \$2,717. From Table 4. When you reach age 65, you will get \$20,000. This is a present value at that time. You must find the annuity that will just exhaust the invested principal in ten years.

$$P_n = \text{Annual withdrawal}\ (F).$$
$$\$20,000 = \text{Annual withdrawal}\ (7.360).$$

$$\text{Annual withdrawal} = \frac{\$20,000}{7.360} = \$2,717.$$

6. $20,019. From Table 4. You need to find the present value of an annuity for ten years.

$$P_n = \text{Annual withdrawal } (F).$$
$$P_n = \$2,720 \ (7.360).$$
$$P_n = \$20,019.$$

7. Plan B is preferable. Its present value exceeds that of Plan A by $1,038:

Year	P.V. Factors at 6% From Table 2	P.V. of Plan A	P.V. of Plan B
0	1.000	$ 1,000	$ 5,000
1	.943	1,886	3,772
2	.890	2,670	2,670
3	.840	3,360	1,680
4	.792	3,960	792
		$12,876	$13,914

a closer look at capital budgeting

CHAPTER **XV**

This chapter will consider a variety of interrelated problems of capital budgeting, including income tax factors, rationing capital, multiple alternatives, unequal lives, and cost of capital.

INCOME TAX FACTORS

Importance of income taxes

As any businessman will be quick to remark, income taxes are major disbursements that often have a tremendous influence on decisions. Even where tax rates and timing are the same for all alternatives, the before-tax differences between alternatives are usually heavily slashed by application of current income tax rates, so that after-tax differences become narrower. This reduction of differences often results in rejection of alternatives that are seemingly attractive on a pre-tax basis. Thus, a 50 per cent tax rate reduces the net attractiveness of $100,000 in cash operating savings to $50,000.

There are two major aspects to the role of income taxes in decision making: the impact of income taxes (a) on the *amount* of cash inflow or outflow, and (b) on the *timing* of cash flows. In short, the role of taxes in capital budgeting is no different from that of any other cash disbursement.

The intricacies of the income tax laws are often bewildering. This chapter will concentrate on a few pertinent provisions of the law in order to highlight a general approach to the problem. Our discussion will be confined to corporations rather than partnerships or individuals.

489

The applicable tax rate to be used in estimating cash flows is dependent on the income tax bracket of the taxpayer and on the type of income in question. For example, the federal rates on ordinary corporate net income in the late 1960's were 22 per cent on the first $25,000 and 48 per cent on the excess. But most states also levy income taxes, with rates that vary considerably. Thus, the combined tax effect on ordinary income in excess of $25,000 may easily exceed 50 per cent.

Timing and different depreciation methods

Exhibit 15-1 shows the relationship between net income before taxes, income taxes, and depreciation. Assume that a company has a single fixed asset, purchased for $90,000 cash, which has a five-year life and

EXHIBIT 15-1

BASIC ANALYSIS OF INCOME STATEMENT, INCOME TAXES, AND CASH FLOWS
(Data assumed)

Traditional Income Statement

(S)	Sales	$100,000
(E)	Less: Expenses, excluding depreciation	$ 62,000
(D)	Depreciation (straight-line)	18,000
	Total expenses	$ 80,000
	Net income before income taxes	$ 20,000
(T)	Income taxes at 40 per cent	8,000
(I)	Net income after income taxes	$ 12,000

Net after-tax cash inflow from operations is either

$$S - E - T = \$100,000 - \$62,000 - \$8,000 = \$30,000$$

or

$$I + D = \$12,000 + \$18,000 \qquad = \$30,000$$

Analysis of the Above for Capital Budgeting

Cash Effects of Operations

(S − E)	Cash inflow from operations: $100,000 − $62,000 =	$38,000
	Income tax effects, at 40 per cent	15,200*
	After-tax effects of cash inflow from operations	$22,800

Tax Shield

(D)	Straight-line depreciation: $90,000 ÷ 5 = $18,000	
	Income tax savings, at 40 per cent	$ 7,200*
	Total cash effects	$30,000

*Net cash outflow for income taxes, $15,200 − $7,200 = $8,000.

zero disposal value. The purchase cost, less any estimated disposal value, is tax-deductible in the form of yearly depreciation. This deduction has been aptly called a *tax shield*, because it protects that amount of income from taxation.

As Exhibit 15-2 shows, the cost of the asset represents a valuable future tax deduction of $90,000. The present value of this deduction depends directly on its specific yearly effects on future income tax payments. Therefore, the present value is influenced by the depreciation method selected, the tax rates, and the discount rate.

The best depreciation method

The three most widely used depreciation methods are straight-line, sum-of-the-years'-digits, and double-declining-balance. The effects of the first two are shown in Exhibit 15-2. Note that the present value of the tax shield is greater if straight-line depreciation is *not* used. The accelerated depreciation methods generally will maximize present values as compared with the straight-line method. The cumulative dollar tax bills may not change, but the early write-offs defer tax outlays to future periods. The measure of the latter advantage depends on the rate of return that can be gained from funds that otherwise would have been paid as income taxes. The general rule in shrewd income tax planning is: When there is a legal choice, take the deduction sooner rather than later.

Effects of income taxes on cash flow

The effects of income taxes on cash flow may best be visualized by a step-by-step analysis of a simple example. The following example is similar to those in Chapter 14. However, all income tax effects will now be considered and an after-tax cost of capital is used.

> **Example 1.** The Lindo Company is considering replacing an old packaging machine with a new, more efficient machine. The old machine originally cost $22,000. Accumulated straight-line depreciation is $12,000 and the remaining useful life is five years. The old machine can be sold outright now for $4,000. The estimated residual value at the end of five years is $600; however, the company has not used a residual value in allocating depreciation for tax purposes. Annual cash operating costs are $50,000 per year.
>
> Company engineers are convinced that the new machine, which costs $15,000, will have annual cash operating costs of $46,000 per year. The new machine will have a useful life of five years with an estimated residual value of $700. Sum-of-the-years' digits depreciation would be used for tax purposes, with no provision for residual value.

REQUIRED:

Assume that the minimum desired rate of return, after taxes, is 10 per cent. Using the net present value technique, demonstrate which

EXHIBIT 15-2

TAX-SHIELD EFFECTS OF TWO DEPRECIATION METHODS

Straight-Line Depreciation

Annual depreciation $90,000 ÷ 5 = $18,000
Tax Shield: savings in income taxes @ 40% = $7,200

	10% Discount Factor	Present Value at 10%
	3.791	$27,295

Sketch of Cash Flows

Year 1	Year 2	Year 3	Year 4	Year 5
$ 7,200	$7,200	$7,200	$7,200	$7,200

Sum-of-the-Years'-Digits Depreciation

Year	Multiplier*	Deduction	Income Tax Savings @ 40%	10% Discount Factor	Present Value at 10%
1	5/15	$30,000	$12,000	.909	$10,908
2	4/15	24,000	9,600	.826	7,930
3	3/15	18,000	7,200	.751	5,407
4	2/15	12,000	4,800	.683	3,278
5	1/15	6,000	2,400	.621	1,490
					$29,013

Sketch of Cash Flows

Year 1	Year 2	Year 3	Year 4	Year 5
$12,000	$9,600	$7,200	$4,800	$2,400

*The general formula for obtaining the denominator of the multiplier under the sum-of-the-digits method is:

$$S = n\left(\frac{n+1}{2}\right) \text{ when}$$

$$S = \text{sum of the digits,}$$
$$n = \text{number of years of estimated useful life.}$$

$$S = 5\left(\frac{5+1}{2}\right) = 5 \times 3 = 15$$

action is more profitable with a total project approach and with an incremental approach. Assume that the zero residual values are acceptable for tax purposes. Assume a 40 per cent tax rate on ordinary income and a 25 per cent tax rate on capital gains.

Solution. See Exhibits 15-3 and 15-4 for the complete solution. The following steps are recommended. The pertinent income tax aspects are considered for each step.

Step 1. General Approach. The inclusion of tax consideration does not change the general approach to these decisions. Review Chapter 14.

Step 2. Cash Operating Costs and Depreciation. Cash operating costs and their income tax effects are separated from the depreciation tax shield. These could be combined if preferred. However, the treatment illustrated facilitates comparisons of alternative depreciation effects and allows the use of annuity tables for the cash operating costs if they are equal per year.

In this illustration we assume that any cash flow and the related tax flow occur in the same period. For simplicity, we are neglecting the possibility that some tax payments related to the pre-tax operating cash inflows of Year 1 may not actually occur until sometime in Year 2. The analysis could be refined to account for any possible lags.

Step 3. Disposals of Equipment. In general, gains and losses on disposal of equipment are taxed in the same way as ordinary gains and losses.[1]

Exhibit 15-7 shows an analysis of the alternative dispositions of the old equipment. Disposal at the end of Year 5 results in a taxable gain, the excess of the selling price over book value (zero in this case). The cash effect is the selling price less the 40 per cent tax on the gain.

Immediate disposal of the old equipment results in a loss which is fully deductible from current income. The net loss must be computed to isolate its effect on current income tax, but the total cash inflow is the selling price plus the current income tax benefit.

Step 4. Total Project or Incremental Approach? Exhibits 15-3 and 15-4 demonstrate these approaches. Both result in the same net present value in favor of replacement. Where there are only two alternatives, the incremental approach is faster. However, the incremental approach rapidly becomes unwieldy when there are multiple alternatives or when computations become intricate.

---

[1]In this case, the old equipment was sold outright. Where the old equipment is traded-in on new equipment of like kind, no gain or loss can be recognized for tax purposes in the year of the transaction. Rather, the new equipment is capitalized at the book value of the old equipment plus the cash payment. Any gain or loss is then spread over the life of the new equipment through the new depreciation charges.

Before 1962, gains from disposal of equipment were taxed at the capital gains rate, 25 per cent. Since then, the gain on sale of equipment is not considered a capital gain except in special circumstances. This complication frequently results in part of the gain being taxed at ordinary income tax rates and part at capital gains rates. For simplicity, this chapter does not introduce the latter complication. We assume that gains on disposal are taxed at ordinary rates.

EXHIBIT 15-3

LINDO COMPANY, AFTER-TAX ANALYSIS OF EQUIPMENT REPLACEMENT: TOTAL PROJECT APPROACH

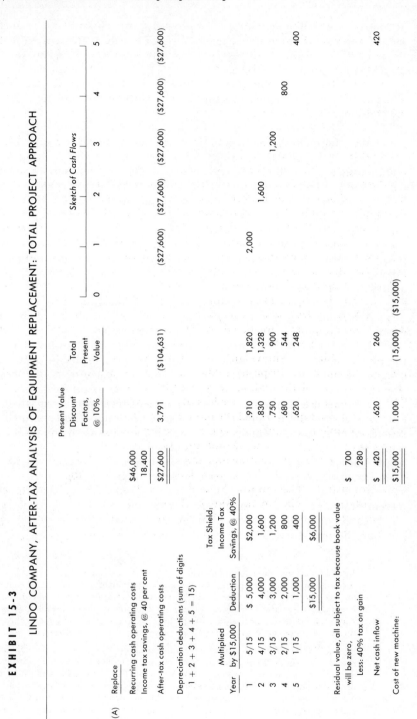

(A) Replace

		Present Value Discount Factors, @ 10%	Total Present Value	Sketch of Cash Flows — 0	1	2	3	4	5
Recurring cash operating costs	$46,000								
Income tax savings, @ 40 per cent	18,400								
After-tax cash operating costs	$27,600	3.791	($104,631)		($27,600)	($27,600)	($27,600)	($27,600)	($27,600)

Depreciation deductions (sum of digits 1 + 2 + 3 + 4 + 5 = 15)

Year	Multiplied by $15,000	Deduction	Tax Shield: Income Tax Savings, @ 40%								
1	5/15	$ 5,000	$2,000	.910	1,820		2,000				
2	4/15	4,000	1,600	.830	1,328			1,600			
3	3/15	3,000	1,200	.750	900				1,200		
4	2/15	2,000	800	.680	544					800	
5	1/15	1,000	400	.620	248						400
		$15,000	$6,000								

		Present Value Discount Factors, @ 10%	Total Present Value	0	1	2	3	4	5
Residual value, all subject to tax because book value will be zero,	$ 700								
Less: 40% tax on gain	280								
Net cash inflow	$ 420	.620	260						420
Cost of new machine:	$15,000	1.000	(15,000)	($15,000)					

Disposal of old equipment:

			Factor	Present value	Year 1	Year 2	Year 3	Year 4	Year 5
Book value now		$10,000							
Selling price		4,000							
Net loss		$ 6,000							
Tax savings		× .40							
		2,400							
Net immediate cash effects, including tax saving		$ 6,400	1.000	6,400					
Total present value of all cash flows				($108,131)	6,400				

(B) Keep

			Factor	Present value	Year 1	Year 2	Year 3	Year 4	Year 5
Recurring cash operating costs		$50,000							
Income tax savings, @ 40%		20,000							
After-tax cash operating costs		$30,000	3.791	($113,730)	($30,000)	($30,000)	($30,000)	($30,000)	($30,000)
Depreciation deductions	$2,000								
Income tax savings, @ 40%	× .40	$ 800	3.791	3,033	800	800	800	800	800
Residual value, all subject to tax		$ 600							
Less: 40% tax on gain		240							
Net cash inflow		$ 360	.620	223					360
Total present value of all cash flows				($110,474)					
Difference in favor of replacement				$ 2,343					

EXHIBIT 15-4

LINDO COMPANY, AFTER-TAX ANALYSIS OF EQUIPMENT REPLACEMENT: INCREMENTAL ANALYSIS

		Present Value Discount Factors, @ 10%	Total Present Values	Sketch of Cash Flows					
				0	1	2	3	4	5
Analysis Confined to Differences between (A) and (B) in Exhibit 15-3:									
Recurring operating savings,									
$50,000 – $46,000	$4,000								
Income tax, @ 40%	1,600								
After-tax operating savings	$2,400	3.791	$9,098		$2,400	$2,400	$2,400	$2,400	$2,400

Differences in depreciation:

Year	Replace	Keep	Difference	Income Tax Effect, @ 40%	Discount Factors @ 10%	Total Present Values	0	1	2	3	4	5
1	$5,000	$2,000	$3,000	$1,200	.910	1,092		1,200				
2	4,000	2,000	2,000	800	.830	664			800			
3	3,000	2,000	1,000	400	.750	300				400		
4	2,000	2,000	—	—	.680	—					—	
5	1,000	2,000	(1,000)	(400)	.620	(248)						(400)

	Present Value Discount Factors, @ 10%	Total Present Values	0	5
Difference in disposal value, end of Year 5				
(see Exhibit 15-3 for details): $420 – $360 = $60	.620	37		60
Incremental initial investment				
(see Exhibit 15-3 for details): $15,000 – $6,400 = ($8,600)	1.000	(8,600)	($8,600)	
Net present value of replacement		$2,343		

[Income tax complications]

The foregoing illustration deliberately excluded many possible complications. Income taxes are affected by many factors, including progressive tax rates, loss carrybacks and carryforwards, many depreciation options, state income taxes, short- and long-term gains, distinctions between capital assets and other assets, offsets of losses against related gains, exchanges of property of like kind, and exempt income. Moreover, most fixed asset purchases in the 1960's have qualified for an "investment credit," which is an immediate income tax credit of 7 per cent of the initial cost; furthermore, the full original cost, less the estimated disposal value, is deductible as yearly depreciation.

Managers have a responsibility to avoid income taxes. Avoidance is not *evasion*. Avoidance is the use of legal means to minimize tax payments; evasion is the use of illegal means. Because income tax planning is exceedingly complex, professional tax counsel should be sought whenever the slightest doubt exists.

RATIONING CAPITAL AMONG PROJECTS

Chapter 14 indicated that the attractiveness of capital projects is best measured by discounting at the minimum desired rate of return; *any* project with a positive net present value should be undertaken. This is a general rule. Like all general rules, this is subject to qualifications. We shall now see how this rule is applied in various situations.

Budget constraint

Many companies specify an over-all limit on the total budget for capital spending. There is no conceptual justification for such a budget ceiling. All projects that enhance long-run profitability should be accepted. This is the only decision rule that makes economic sense. To the extent that capital rationing exists, it should be a "short-run phenomenon, limiting expenditures only to the current year or two."[2]

There are no hard-and-fast rules to be found in practice regarding the selection of an over-all constraint. The net present values (or some similar measure such as time-adjusted rate of return) may strongly influence the over-all budget amount. For example, a flock of projects with huge net present values would probably result in a much higher over-all budget than would a group of projects that all slightly exceeded zero.

[Other interrelated factors that influence the amount of total funds to be committed in a single year include:]

1. Top management's philosophy toward capital spending. (Some managements are highly growth-minded, whereas others are very conservative.)

[2]H. Martin Weingartner, "The Excess Present Value Index—A Theoretical Basis and Critique," *Journal of Accounting Research* (Autumn, 1963), p. 214.

2. The outlook for future investment opportunities that may not be feasible if extensive current commitments are undertaken.
3. The funds provided by current operations less dividends.
4. The feasibility of acquiring additional capital through borrowing or sale of additional stock. Lead times and costs of financial market transactions can influence spending.
5. Period of impending change in management personnel, when the status quo is maintained.

Different sizes of projects and budget constraints

Various writers have suggested using the following ranking devices: (a) time-adjusted rate of return, which was introduced in Chapter 14, and (b) the excess present value index, also sometimes called the profitability index:

$$\text{Excess present value index} = \frac{\text{Total present value}}{\text{Investment required}}$$

We shall now compare the results under the excess present value index and the net present value methods.

EXHIBIT 15-5

ALLOCATION OF CAPITAL BUDGET: COMPARISON OF TWO ALTERNATIVES

		Allocation of $5,000,000 Budget					
	Alternative One				Alternative Two		
Projects[3]	Investment Required	Excess Present Value Index	Total Present Value at 10%	Project	Investment Required	Excess Present Value Index	Total Present Value at 10%
C	600,000	167%	$1,000,000	C	$ 600,000	167%	$1,000,000
A(GP)	1,000,000	140%	1,400,000				
D	400,000	132%	528,000	D	400,000	132%	528,000
				A(SP)	3,000,000	130%	3,900,000
F	1,000,000	115%	1,150,000	F	1,000,000	115%	1,150,000
					$5,000,000*		$6,578,000‡
E	800,000	114%	912,000	E	800,000	114%	Reject
B	1,200,000	112%	1,344,000	B	1,200,000	112%	Reject
	$5,000,000*		$6,334,000†				
H	550,000	105%	Reject	H	550,000	105%	Reject
G	450,000	101%	Reject	G	450,000	101%	Reject
I	1,000,000	90%	Reject	I	1,000,000	90%	Reject

*Total budget constraint.   †Net present value, $1,334,000.   ‡Net present value, $1,578,000.

[3]Each of the specific plans for the projects listed may have been selected from alternative mutually exclusive proposals. For example, Project D may be for new Dodge trucks, selected after considering competing brands. Thus, the capital budget is the crystallization of many "sub-capital-budgeting" decisions.

Mutually exclusive alternatives and budget constraints

Assume that a company is considering two projects that are mutually exclusive, that is, where the acceptance of one alternative automatically results in the rejection of the other(s). The company can invest in either special-purpose equipment or general-purpose equipment, as follows:

	(1) Cost	(2) Present Value at 10% Cost of Capital	(2) ÷ (1) Excess Present Value Index	(2) − (1) Net Present Value
GP Equipment	$1,000,000	$1,400,000	140%	$400,000
SP Equipment	3,000,000	3,900,000	130%	900,000

The GP equipment promises a higher return per dollar invested; if all other things, like risk, alternative uses of funds, and the like, were equal, the GP equipment seems an obvious choice. But "all other things" are rarely equal.

Assume that $5,000,000 is the total capital budget for the coming year, and that the allocation of resources, using GP equipment for Project A, is as shown under Alternative One in Exhibit 15-5.

Note that the rationing used in Alternative Two is superior to Alternative One, despite the greater profitability per dollar invested of general-purpose equipment compared with special-purpose equipment. Why? Because the $2,000,000 incremental investment in special-purpose equipment has an incremental present value of $500,000, whereas the $2,000,000 would otherwise be invested in Projects E and B, which have a lower combined incremental present value of $256,000:

	Cost	Present Value	Increase in Net Present Value
SP Equipment	$3,000,000	$3,900,000	
GP Equipment	1,000,000	1,400,000	
Increment	$2,000,000	$2,500,000	$500,000
Project E	$ 800,000	$ 912,000	
Project B	1,200,000	1,344,000	
Total	$2,000,000	$2,256,000	$256,000

The above example illustrates that decisions involving mutually exclusive investments of different sizes cannot be based on the excess present value index (or the time-adjusted rate of return, for that matter). The net present value method is the best general guide.

Investment indivisibilities

In general, any ranking procedure by excess present value indices or rates of return or net present value is approximal because of investment indivisibilities. For example, assume that five projects are available, as follows:

Project	Cost	Present Value	Excess Present Value Index	Net Present Value
V	$6,000	$8,400	140%	$2,400
W	3,000	4,050	135%	1,050
X	2,000	2,600	130%	600
Y	2,000	2,560	128%	560
Z	1,000	1,000	100%	—

Now, if $10,000 is available for capital spending, there are two likely combinations. The natural tendency would be to select V, W, and Z and reject X and Y. But this would not yield the optimum answer:

		Allocation of $10,000 Budget					
		Alternative One			Alternative Two		
	Cost	Cost	Present Value	Index	Cost	Present Value	Index
V	$6,000	$ 6,000	$ 8,400		$ 6,000	$ 8,400	
W	3,000	3,000	4,050				
X	2,000				2,000	2,600	
Y	2,000				2,000	2,560	
Z	1,000	1,000	1,000				
Total available funds		$10,000	$13,450	134.5%	$10,000	$13,560	135.6%
Net present value			$ 3,450			$ 3,560	

Given a budget constraint, it may be wisest to accept smaller, though less attractive, projects to use the limited funds completely in order to maximize total returns. In our example, the optimum solution rejected Projects W and Z, whose combined excess present value index and whose combined net present values were less than those of both X and Y.[4]

MULTIPLE ALTERNATIVES

The basic approach to choosing among alternatives is the same, regardless of the number of alternatives available. However, comparisons become more intricate when three or more alternatives are under consideration.

[4] Integer programming would be the best attack on these difficulties. See Weingartner, *op. cit.*, p. 215. Linear programming techniques are also helpful in reaching an optimum solution when there are many variables and many constraints. See Charnes, Cooper, and Miller, "Application of Linear Programming to Financial Budgeting and the Costing of Funds," *Journal of Business* (January, 1959), pp. 20–46.

Illustration of over-all versus incremental approach

A retail outlet is considering extending credit to its customers for the first time in its history. A careful study of competitors' experience with a variety of credit plans shows the expected increases in net profits under various plans, as illustrated in Exhibit 15-6. Which choice would you make? Why? Decide before reading on.

EXHIBIT 15-6

MULTIPLE ALTERNATIVE INVESTMENTS

Line	Plan	A	B	C	D	E
			Minimum Desired Rate of Return—14%			
1	Total investment in receivables	$10,000	$30,000	$50,000	$80,000	$100,000
2	Annual net income	$ 500	$ 4,200	$ 7,800	$12,120	$ 14,320
3	Rate of return	5.0%	14.0%	15.6%	15.2%	14.3%
4	Incremental investment over preceding plan		$20,000	$20,000	$30,000	$ 20,000
5	Incremental net income		$ 3,700	$ 3,600	$ 4,320	$ 2,200
6	Rate of return on incremental investment		18.5%	18.0%	14.4%	11.0%

Incremental approach is best

Where multiple alternatives of similar risk are available, the key to the correct decision is the incremental approach. Total investment should be increased, increment by increment (as long as each increment meets the minimum desired rate of return) until the incremental rate of return falls below the cut-off rate (14 per cent in this case).

In our example, the incremental approach assumes *that the total $100,000 funds available can be invested in some phase of the business at 14 per cent with comparable risk.* Our approach would result in choosing Project D, because the incremental rate of return thereafter falls below 14 per cent. The desirability of this choice can be proven as follows:

Line	Plan	A	B	C	D	E
1	Total funds to invest	$100,000	$100,000	$100,000	$100,000	$100,000
2	Amount invested	10,000	30,000	50,000	80,000	100,000
3	Difference	$ 90,000	$ 70,000	$ 50,000	$ 20,000	$ —
	Return on amount in line (2)	$ 500	$ 4,200	$ 7,800	$ 12,120	$ 14,320
	Plus 14% return on investment shown in line (3)	12,600	9,800	7,000	2,800	—
		$ 13,100	$ 14,000	$ 14,800	$ 14,920	$ 14,320
	Rate on $100,000	13.1%	14.0%	14.8%	14.92%	14.32%

Danger of using over-all approach

Using over-all rates of return as a guide will not yield an optimum choice, no matter what interpretation of over-all rate of return is used. Some analysts, interested in maximum over-all rate of profitability, would choose Project C (15.6 per cent). Such a choice rejects the investment of an additional $30,000 (Project D) at an incremental rate of return of 14.4. The latter is a better rate than the 14 per cent available in other phases of the business at comparable risk.

Other analysts, recognizing that the maximum of $100,000 is available for investment, and that the appropriate cut-off rate is 14 per cent, would select Project E (14.3 per cent). Failure to concentrate on *differences* results in the inclusion of a final $20,000 incremental investment[5] that earns only an 11 per cent return.

Any approach based solely on the over-all rate of profitability will not necessarily yield an optimum choice. In our example, all alternatives except Project A promise a rate of return in excess of the assumed minimum desired rate of 14 per cent.

RANKING DIFFICULTIES AND UNEQUAL LIVES

Conflict of ranking techniques

Conceptually, it is sensible to rank proposals by profitability and then accept or reject them by using a minimum desired rate of return as a cut-off rate. However, many people have a tendency to think that the two variations of the discounted cash-flow approach will give equivalent results. Exhibit 15-7 shows a case where the net present value approach and the rate-of-return approach show completely different rankings. (Use tables to check the validity of the computations in Exhibit 15-7.)

---

[5]The incremental approach also assumes that the *previous* increment earned at least the cut-off rate. Otherwise, optimum choices will not be made. To illustrate, using the facts in our example, assume an intervening plan (Plan DD) between D and E.

Plan	D	DD	E
1. Total investment	$80,000	$90,000	$100,000
2. Annual net income	$12,120	$12,600	$ 14,320
3. Rate of return	15.2%	14.0%	14.3%
4. Incremental investment		$10,000	$ 10,000
5. Incremental net income		$ 480	$ 1,720
6. Rate of return on incremental investment		4.8%	17.2%

Choosing Plan E is unwise because it really means making an investment in DD also, a combined incremental investment of $20,000 showing a combined return of only 11.0 per cent (as shown in Exhibit 15-6). For an expanded discussion, see Grant and Ireson, *Principles of Engineering Economy* (4th ed., New York: Ronald Press Company, 1960), Chapter 12.

EXHIBIT 15-7

Project	Life	Annual Net Cash Earnings	Investment	Ranking by Rate of Return		Ranking by Net Present Value		
				Rate of Return	Ranking	Present Value of Earnings at 10% Minimum Desired Rate	Net Present Value	
							Amount	Rank
A	5	$1,000	$2,864	22%	1	$3,791	$ 927	3
B	10	1,000	4,192	20%	2	6,145	1,953	2
C	15	1,000	5,092	18%	3	7,606	2,514	1

What is the essential difference between these two variations of the discounted cash-flow method? Essentially, differing assumptions are made with respect to the *rate of return on the reinvestment* of the cash proceeds at the end of the shorter investment's life. Both methods make different implicit assumptions as to the reinvestment rate of return.

The rate-of-return approach assumes that the reinvestment rate is equal to the indicated rate of return for the shorter-lived project. The net-present-value approach assumes that the funds obtainable from competing projects can be reinvested only at the rate of the company's minimum desired rate of return. Comparison follows:

Comparison of Projects A and C

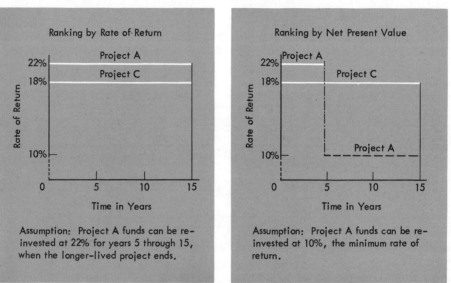

Assumption: Project A funds can be re-invested at 22% for years 5 through 15, when the longer-lived project ends.

Assumption: Project A funds can be re-invested at 10%, the minimum rate of return.

Unequal lives and reinvestment

As shown in Exhibit 15-7 and in the above graphs, where alternate projects have unequal lives, the two methods show different rankings.[6] Let us see how these contradictory results occur. At the end of fifteen years, the original investment in Project A will accumulate to more than Project C under the rate-of-return method, because it is assumed that the *Project A amount at the end of the fifth year can be reinvested to earn a 22 per cent rate of return.* On the other hand, the net-present-value method assumes that the Project A amount at the end of the fifth year can be reinvested to earn only the *10 per cent minimum desired rate of return.* Thus, as long as projects under consideration promise rates of return in excess of the cut-off rate, the rate-of-return method has a built-in assumption in favor of short-lived projects

---

[6] Also recall that similar conflicting results can occur when the terminal dates are the same but the sizes of the investment outlays differ (see Exhibit 15-5).

like Project A, whereas the net-present-value method has a built-in minimum rate of return that would favor longer-lived projects.

How may we reconcile these two approaches? Ideally, the answer
is to reject both assumptions as to the reinvestment rate of return and predict a tailor-made rate of return for the time between the termination of
the shorter-lived project and the termination of the longer-lived project.
In other words, there is a need for a common terminal date and for explicit
assumptions as to the appropriate reinvestment rates of funds. Solomon
comments:

1. *The valid comparison is not simply between two projects but between two alternative courses of action. The ultimate criterion is the total wealth that the investor
   can expect from each alternative by the terminal date of the longer-lived project* ⋯.
2. If the rate of return *is to be used as an index of profitability, then the relevant
   rate is the per annum yield promised by each alternative course of action from its
   inception to a common terminal date in the future (usually the terminal date of the
   longer-lived project).*
3. If the present value *is to be used as an index of relative profitability, the expected reinvestment rate or set of rates should be used as the discounting factor.
   These rates will be equal to the company's present cost of capital only by coincidence.*[7]

The practical difficulties of estimating future profitability on *reinvestment* are greater than those of estimating profitability of immediate
projects. But reinvestment opportunities should be considered where they
may be foreseen and measured.

Equipment replacement

Equipment-replacement decisions are often complicated by unequal lives of competing equipment.[8] One way of approaching the problem
of unequal lives is to estimate the residual value of the new equipment at
the end of the remaining useful life of the old equipment. Then a comparison is made only over the remaining life of the old equipment.

Still another approach is to compare over the longer time span,
including an estimate of replacement cost for the old machine at a later
date. In essence, this is the approach described by Solomon above.

Of course, the crux of the problem in replacement decisions is the
lack of a realistic common terminal date for both proposals. Thus, some
estimate of residual value is necessary, whether the comparison is made
over the remaining life of old equipment or the useful life of the new equipment. If new equipment is to last eight years and old equipment five years,
a decision to retain old equipment implies that replacement will be made
in five years. Therefore, if a comparison is to be made over eight years,
the future replacement cost (five years hence) of the old equipment has to

---

[7]Ezra Solomon, "Arithmetic of Capital Budgeting Decisions," *Journal of Business*
(April 1956), p. 127.

[8]George Terborgh has called the old equipment already owned the *defender*, and the
new equipment being considered the *challenger*.

be estimated and also the terminal value of that replacement at the end of the eight-year span under review. This vicious difficulty goes on and on;[9] the practical answer is to make realistic assumptions regarding residual values at a common terminal date. The common date should be as distant as can be considered with confidence.

Reinvestment outlook

Capital budgeting decisions in one year have chain reactions that may affect investment opportunities and availability of capital in future years. Such diverse factors as price-level changes, technological changes, and future investment choices may strongly influence current capital-spending decisions.

For example, in Exhibit 15-7, if investment opportunities five years hence are expected to return less than 15 per cent, Project C, which promises a return of 18 per cent for fifteen years, may be preferable to Project A, which promises a return of 22 per cent for five years. In contrast, if opportunities to invest at 22 per cent or more are anticipated in five years, the shorter-lived Project A might be more desirable than Project C, even if Project A promised only, say, a 16 per cent rate of return. In the latter case, Project C would require a much bigger investment than would be committed for a prolonged period.

RECAPITULATION

The above examples have demonstrated the weaknesses of the excess present value index (see Exhibit 15-5 for instance) and the time-adjusted rate of return[10] (see Exhibit 15-7). The net present value criterion is the best general rule for choosing projects, whether the complexity involves an over-all budget limit, different sizes of outlays, different terminal dates, or mutually exclusive investments. This general rule should be used on an increment-by-increment basis and should be modified where there are investment indivisibilities in relation to a fixed over-all capital budget appropriation.[11]

The above guides still do not provide answers to some fundamental questions. How do you consider uncertainty? How do you grapple with

[9]Some writers favor handling this problem by assuming an infinitely continuous replacement cycle. Thus, alternatives are compared by using perpetuity formulae. Although this is conceptually most appealing, it probably is too unrealistic to serve as a practical technique.

[10]James H. Lorie and Leonard J. Savage, "Three Problems in Rationing Capital," *Journal of Business* (October, 1955), have demonstrated a number of weaknesses of the time-adjusted rate of return. Of special interest is the phenomenon where *two* rates of return can be calculated for *one* project; this can occur when a project, such as an oil well, may entail heavy outlays at termination date.

[11]For a full discussion see H. Martin Weingartner, *Mathematical Programming and the Analysis of Capital Budgeting Problems* (Englewood Cliffs, N.J.: Prentice-Hall, Inc., 1963).

changes, over time, in desired rates of return? How do you decide on the appropriate minimum desired rate of return? These difficulties will be considered in the next section, but do not expect any fully satisfying answers. There are none. These are subjects of controversy.

MINIMUM DESIRED RATE OF RETURN: COST OF CAPITAL

Importance of concept

Thus far in our study of capital budgeting a "minimum desired rate of return" has been somehow given or assumed for use in the analysis of investment proposals. It has been used either as a discount rate under the net present value method or as a cut-off under the time-adjusted rate of return method. In any event, the minimum desired rate (k) plays a crucial role in determining the acceptability of an investment proposal.

What is k and how should it be measured? Solomon claims that this is "clearly the central question facing financial management."[12] Descriptive terms for k include minimum desired rate of return, cut-off rate, target rate, hurdle rate, financial standard, and cost of capital. The latter term is probably used most frequently.

Complexity of measuring

The use of a cut-off rate implies that the objective of management is to maximize the wealth of company stockholders. This objective will be obtained by acceptance of projects that promise a rate of return in excess of the cost of capital. In this way, the value of the firm, as measured by the market values of stock and debt, will be maximized.

The measure of the cost of capital is far more complex than the accountant's usual notion; he ordinarily thinks of the cost of capital as being the interest expense that appears on the conventional income statement.

Opinions differ immensely as to what cost of capital should be used for capital-budgeting purposes. A few managers cling to the notion that the cost of capital is the mere out-of-pocket interest and financing charges on any debt arising from an undertaking. This position implies that any ownership funds are cost-free—a dangerous position because it ignores the alternative earnings that could be had from the funds. Thus, a home buyer with a $20,000, six per cent term mortgage may regard the $1,200 annual interest outlay as his financing charge. But the homeowner with a mortgage-free $20,000 home also bears a real cost of capital, even though no interest outlay is involved. He could sell his home and invest the $20,000 in four per cent bonds or perhaps reap a bonanza on a mining stock. The sacrifice of these alternative earnings becomes his cost of capital as far as home ownership is concerned.

[12] Ezra Solomon, *The Theory of Financial Management* (New York: Columbia University Press, 1963), p. 27.

Computation of cost of capital

There are really two basic approaches to computing the cost of capital. The short-run, marginal approach considers each financing as a separate problem; the key criterion is the effect of the project and financing on earnings per share. The long-run approach develops an average cost of capital.

The principal objection to the short-run approach is the insidious effect of low-cost debt financing on projects over a series of years. To illustrate, the cost of 100 per cent financing by four per cent bonds is only two per cent after applying a tax rate of 50 per cent. If unlimited debt could be arranged in a given year, any project with an after-tax of return over two per cent would be accepted. Next year, the debt limit for an optimum capital structure may already be reached, and equity financing may show a high cost of 20 per cent after taxes. This would mean that any project that could not produce such a high rate would be automatically rejected.

The reasoning underlying the calculation of a long-run average cost of capital is complex and subject to disagreement. A thorough treatment is beyond the scope of this text. The following paragraphs summarize Solomon's fundamental approach.[13] A prime feature of this approach is the attempt to measure cost in terms of its net effect on common shareholders. The rationale is that newly employed funds must generate incremental earnings at a rate equal to that now applicable to existing equity capital, as computed in Example 2 below.

Example 2. The following is a general approach to measuring the cost of capital. Suppose that Company W has:

Market Values

B =	total market value of bonds outstanding	$5,000
S =	total market value of stockholders' equity	5,000
V =	total market value of the firm	$10,000

Annual Income Data

O =	expected annual net operating income	$1,000
F =	expected annual interest charges on debt	200
E =	expected annual net income for stockholders	$ 800

[13] Solomon's approach is a widely used technique. However, disputes as to the best technique were rampant among specialists in economics and finance in the 1950's and continue to rage in the 1960's. The approach used here is that cost of capital is ultimately determined by the investors in the capital markets, not by the firm itself. Most scholars in the area agree with this concept. However, there is disagreement as to the market effects of leverage (use of debt) on the cost of capital. See F. Modigliani and M. Miller, "The Cost of Capital, Corporation Finance, and the Theory of Investment," *American Economic Review*, XLVIII, pp. 261–297, and their "Dividend Policy, Growth, and the Valuation of Shares," *Journal of Business (October, 1961), pp. 411–433,* for a thorough discussion of the issues.

For the moment we ignore the effects of corporate income taxes and the presence of any growth elements in the income data. Three costs of capital (k) can be computed:

$$k_f = \frac{\$200}{\$5,000} = 4\%, \text{ the bond yield.}$$

$$k_e = \frac{\$800}{\$5,000} = 16\%, \text{ the rate of return on equity.}$$

$$k_o = \frac{\$1,000}{\$10,000} = 10\%, \text{ the over-all company rate, also called the weighted-average rate.}$$

The first rate, k_f, is the effective yield on the company's bonds.

The third rate, k_o, reflects the basic business uncertainty of the company. This rate is higher than k_f because the risk of earning k_o is higher than the risk of earning the service charges on the debt. The higher the risk or uncertainty, the higher the cost of capital.

The second rate, k_e, is the rate at which the anticipated residual income to owners is capitalized. If there is no debt, k_e equals k_o. If debt exists, the residual income "is subject not only to business uncertainty but to the additional financial uncertainty caused by borrowing."[14]

The rate k_o can also be stated as a weighted average of k_e and k_f, with the stock and bond components of total market value used as weights:

	(1) Market Value	(2) Proportion of Market Value	(3) Cost of Capital	(2) × (3) Weighted Average
Bonds	$5,000	$w_1 = 50\%$	$k_f = 4\%$	$w_1 k_f = 2\%$
Stock	5,000	$w_2 = 50\%$	$k_e = 16\%$	$w_2 k_e = 8\%$
				$k_o = 10\%$

This can be expressed:

$$k_o = k_f w_1 + k_e w_2$$

Another way to express the equity rate k_e is in terms of the over-all rate k_o plus an adjustment for uncertainty:

$$k_e = k_o + (k_o - k_f)\frac{B}{S}$$

$$k_e = .10 + (.10 - .04) \cdot 1 = .16$$

Here the adjustment for financial uncertainty is equal to the debt-equity ratio multiplied by the spread between k_o and k_f.

In this example, k_o, is the appropriate measure for the minimum rate of return that should be required on the new projects which offer returns of the same uncertainty as those anticipated from existing assets.

[14]Solomon, *op. cit.*, p. 73.

The problem of growth

The key figure in the computation of k_e is estimated *future* earnings divided by present market price. Current earnings may be used *only* if they are the best estimate of future earnings. This precludes such computations as taking Polaroid's, IBM's, Xerox's, or some other growth company's current earnings, dividing them by market prices of the common stock, and calling the result the cost of equity capital. Such computations can produce ridiculously low costs of equity capital; they are patently invalid where the market is obviously valuing the stock in terms of some future expected income stream.[15]

When we move from the foregoing example to the real world, we must contend with a number of complications. Among these are (a) the variations in uncertainty among individual projects, (b) the variations in debt financing available for individual projects, and (c) the effects of income taxes.

Borrowing rate and lending rate

Literature on cost of capital is somewhat confusing because the same term is used to describe two distinct concepts.

The first concept, described in the previous paragraphs, is the "borrowing" rate—the weighted-average rate that a company must pay for long-run capital. This is an indicator of the over-all minimum return that the company must earn if the stockholder's rate of return is going to be maintained. It is stockholder-oriented inasmuch as it is determined by market prices, which in turn are influenced by the investor's opportunities.

The *lending rate* is basically an opportunity-cost concept; it is the rate that can be earned on alternative investments *having a like degree of risk*. It is the *investment rate*, which varies with risk, that should be used for purposes of discounting future cash flows to the present under the net-present-value method.

Degree of risk or uncertainty

Capital budgeting would be simplified if all projects bore the same degree of risk or uncertainty.[16] Then a single cut-off rate k_o could be used for a company-wide rationing process. But k_o reflects average uncertainty,

---

[15] See Modigliani and Miller, *op. cit.*, and Solomon, *op. cit.*, for demonstrations of how the elements of growth can be considered in the computation of the cost of capital.

[16] Various definitions of *risk* have been offered in the literature. Some writers like to distinguish between risk (objective) and uncertainty (subjective). As used here, risk is thought of as the probability of obtaining a future income stream. An investment in United States bonds is risk-free because the probability of getting the interest income is nearly 100 per cent, whereas an investment in a single oil well is risky because the variability of prospective income is immense.

and all competing projects do *not* bear the same uncertainty. In practice, there are many ways[17] of adjusting for this fact of business life. The effective way by which managers grapple with uncertainty is probably more intuitive than scientific. In any event, in practice there is no single rate that is used as a guide for sifting among all projects. Instead, projects are classified by degree of risk or uncertainty, with different minimum rates being used for different classes of projects. Conceivably, investments could be made in certain low-risk ventures (for example, installment accounts receivable financing) whose discount rate (lending rate) would be below the weighted-average borrowing rate. In other cases, high-risk ventures would have higher discount rates than the weighted-average borrowing rate.

John McLean, vice president of Continental Oil Company, provides a summary of a big company's approach to acceptable rates of return:[18]

> As a starting point, we recommended that approximately 10% after taxes be regarded as the minimum amount we should seek to earn on investments involving a minimum of risk, such as those in new service stations and other marketing facilities. We further recommended that the minimum acceptable level of returns should be increased as the risks involved in the investment projects increased. Accordingly, we set substantially higher standards for investments in manufacturing, petrochemical, and exploration and production ventures.
>
> We arrived at these bench-mark figures:
>
> Our long-term borrowing costs.
>
> The returns which Continental and other oil companies have customarily earned on their borrowed and invested capital (substantially more than 10%).
>
> The returns which must be earned to make our business attractive to equity investors.
>
> The returns which must be earned to satisfy our present shareholders that the earnings retained in the business each year are put to good use.
>
> In this latter connection it may be noted that, whenever we retain earnings instead of paying them out as dividends, we in effect force our stockholders to make a new investment in the Continental Oil Company. And clearly, we have little justification for doing that unless we can arrange to earn as much on the funds as the stockholders could earn by investing in comparable securities elsewhere.

Note that McLean's first paragraph is lending-rate oriented, whereas the remainder of the quotation is borrowing-rate oriented. Continental Oil Company's "lending" rates are 10 per cent for marketing and

---

[17] Ways of adjusting for risk include requiring higher rates of return for longer-lived projects, artificially short payback periods or useful lives, deliberate ignoring of salvage values, and so forth. Solomon, *op. cit.*, p. 76, comments, "Unfortunately, we know little about how to apply these adjustments or about how k_o itself varies with uncertainty. Nor are we likely to find out much more." See also David B. Hertz, "Risk Analysis in Capital Investment," *Harvard Business Review* (January-February, 1964), pp. 95–106. Chapter 26 shows how subjective probabilities could be applied systematically to specific estimates of future cash flows. In this way, the use of haphazard techniques, such as using higher arbitrary discount rates, could be minimized.

[18] John G. McLean, "How to Evaluate New Capital Investments," *Harvard Business Review* (November-December, 1958), pp. 67 and 69.

pipeline facilities, 14 per cent for refining facilities, and 18 per cent for development wells and petrochemical facilities. Its "borrowing" rate, approximately 10 per cent, was arrived at through consideration of optimum capital structure and shareholder alternatives, as described in the quotation above.

The disparity among cut-off rates is evident from a study of pricing objectives in large companies:

Company	Target Rate of Return on Investment
U. S. Steel	8 per cent after taxes
General Electric	20 per cent after taxes
Alcoa	20 per cent after taxes; higher on new products
General Motors	20 per cent after taxes
International Harvester	10 per cent after taxes
Sears Roebuck	10–15 per cent after taxes
Kroger	20 per cent before taxes
Johns-Manville	15 per cent after taxes; higher on new products

Source: Lanzilotti, "Pricing Objectives in Large Companies," *American Economic Review*, XLVIII (December, 1958), pp. 921–940.

Using equity rate as cost of capital

Solomon maintains that using k_e, the equity rate, is the most promising way to calculate cost of capital:

> *The tax factor can be taken into account quite directly . . . on an after-tax basis. It can also handle the fact that different proposals should be charged different rates of interest, depending on the actual rates at which borrowed funds are available.*
>
> *The rate* k_e *reflects the combined effect of business uncertainty and financial uncertainty contained in the expected equity yield on existing assets. Each new asset under consideration offers operating earnings whose quality may differ from that reflected in* k_o. *By "allowing" each new proposal a different proportion of debt financing varying from zero to high proportions of debt, it is possible to adjust the over-all level of business plus financial uncertainty contained in any given proposal so that the net yield it offers can be compared directly against the over-all uncertainty reflected in* k_e.[19]

The following formula can be used on an after-tax basis:

$$\frac{(1 - t)(\Delta O - Iw_1 k_f)}{Iw_2} > k_e(1 - t)$$

New terms: t = income tax rate;
  I = required investment in project.

[19] Solomon, *op. cit.*, p. 77. See also Alexander A. Robichek and John G. McDonald, "The Cost of Capital Concept: Potential Use and Misuse." *Financial Executive* (June, 1965), for an expanded discussion with several examples.

Example 3. Consider the following example, where the same basic data apply as were used in Example 2. New data:

$$\text{Income tax rate} = 40\% = t$$
$$\text{Investment} = \$2000 = I$$
$$\text{Increase in } O = \$\ 300 = \Delta O$$

Substituting into the formula:

$$\frac{(1 - .4)\,[\$300 - \$2000\,(.5)(.04)]}{\$2000\,(.5)} > .16\,(1 - .4)$$

$$\frac{.6\,(300 - 40)}{1000} > .096$$

$$.156 > .096$$

This says that the new project's rate of return on equity is 15.6 per cent after taxes, which exceeds the 9.6 rate that might be considered as an appropriate cut-off.

The w_1 is the debt ratio which "equates the over-all uncertainty (business plus financial) of the net earnings promised by the proposal to the over-all uncertainty of expected net earnings on existing assets, and k_f is the actual rate of interest payable on funds borrowed for the proposal. A specific rate may or may not exist. If it does, it should be used. If it does not, the appropriate measure for k_f is the average rate of interest payable on all existing debt."[20]

Clearly, the calculation and use of cost of capital are unsettled, frustrating issues. Still, by the acts of decision making, management inplicitly or explicitly uses some cost of capital. The increasing tendency to explicitly measure the cost of capital is another example of how folklore and hunches are minimized in well-managed organizations.[21]

---

[20] *Ibid.*, p. 77. If preferred stock is in the capital structure, it is regarded as debt for purposes of this analysis. There is an income tax benefit from the use of debt because interest is deductible in the computation of income taxes. In contrast, dividends are not deductible. Consider the effects of using $100 of debt versus $100 of preferred stock:

	Principal	4% Return	Income Needed Before 50% Tax
Bonds	$100	$4	$4
Preferred Stock	$100	$4	$8

In other words, a company would need pre-tax income of $8 to pay dividends on the preferred stock. In contrast, a company would need only $4 of pre-tax income to pay interest on the bonds.

Another way of viewing the picture is to say that the after-tax cost of a 4 per cent Bond is only 2 per cent; for a 4 per cent Preferred Stock, it is 4 per cent.

[21] But see S. J. Pullara and L. R. Walkep, "The Evaluation of Capital Expenditure Proposals: A Survey of Firms in the Chemical Industry," *Journal of Business* (October, 1965), p. 406: "For the chemical industry, a surprisingly large proportion of firms rely on subjective judgment and are willing to admit it."

SUMMARY

The uncertainty about long-run events makes capital budgeting a difficult but challenging area. The imprecision of prediction should over-hang any analyst's tendency to split hairs concerning controversial aspects. However, there are a few guideposts that should help toward intelligent decisions. Some are summarized at the end of Chapters 13 and 14. Others were discussed in this chapter.

Income tax factors almost always play an important role in deci-sion making. It is dangerous to assume that income taxes are irrelevant or insignificant.

Decisions on types of production equipment often are only re-motely related to cash receipts, if at all. Thus, the decision becomes one of cost minimization. A logical approach, especially if there are income tax complications and several alternative investments available, is to compare all projects, discounting each to the present and choosing the project with the least cost.

Two interrelated constraints for rationing capital are over-all funds available and a minimum desired cut-off rate(s) of return. Capital ration-ing has no conceptual justification; that is, all desirable projects should be undertaken and the needed funds acquired if possible. Investment indi-visibilities often necessitate juggling project selections to obtain optimum over-all results.

Incremental approaches are very useful in checking among multiple alternatives, to be certain that each separable investment is earn-ing the minimum desired rate of return and that over-all funds available are earning a maximum amount.

Comparisons of projects with unequal lives necessitate predictions of reinvestment of proceeds of shorter-lived projects and a comparison to the terminal date of the longer-lived project.

Cost of capital is used for purposes of determining the cut-off rate in the selection of projects. There is no agreement as to how to compute a magic, single-figured cost of capital. But it is agreed that recognition should be given to a "cost" of equity capital as well as debt. In practice, projects are classified by degree of risk, with different minimum cut-off rates being used for different classes of projects. Probabilistic approaches, which formally and explicitly recognize the dispersion in estimated data, have just begun to be used.[22]

SUGGESTED READINGS

Bierman, H., *Topics in Cost Accounting and Decisions* (New York: McGraw-Hill Book Company, 1963).

Bierman, H., and C. Bonini, and L. Fouraker, and R. Jaedicke, *Quantitative Analysis for Business Decisions* Rev. ed. (Homewood, Illinois: Richard D. Irwin, Inc., 1965).

[22]Hertz, *op. cit.*

Bierman, H., and S. Smidt, *The Capital Budgeting Decision*. (New York: 2nd ed., The Macmillan Co., 1966).

Clark, J. M., *Studies in the Economics of Overhead Costs* (Chicago: University of Chicago Press, 1923).

Dean, Joel, *Capital Budgeting* (New York: Columbia University Press, 1951).

Grant, E. L., and W. G. Ireson, *Principles of Engineering Economy* (4th ed., New York: Ronald Press Company, 1960).

Lutz, F. and V., *The Theory of Investment of the Firm* (Princeton, N.J.: Princeton University Press, 1951).

National Association of Accountants, *Research Report 35, Return on Capital as a Guide to Managerial Decisions* (New York: the Association, 1959).

Solomon, Ezra, (ed.), *The Management of Corporate Capital* (Glencoe, Ill.: Free Press, 1959).

Solomon, Ezra, *The Theory of Financial Management* (New York: Columbia University Press, 1963).

Terborgh, George, *Business Investment Analysis* (Washington, D.C.: Machinery and Allied Products Institute, 1958). This book describes the widely used MAPI formula for equipment-replacement decisions.

Weingartner, H. Martin, *Mathematical Programming and the Analysis of Capital Budgeting Problems* (Englewood Cliffs, N.J.: Prentice-Hall, Inc., 1963).

PROBLEMS FOR SELF-STUDY

Review Examples 1, 2, and 3, and the other illustrations.

APPENDIX: THE FINANCIAL LEASE

Leases are frequently classified as operating or financial.[23]　An operating lease is one that is cancelable or that terminates before the rental payments have repaid the purchase price. Examples are telephone equipment and monthly rentals of automobiles. For capital-budgeting purposes, the cash flows of operating leases can be analyzed just like ordinary operating cash flows.

The financial lease, according to Vancil, is noncancelable; it obligates the lessee to rentals which in total equal or exceed the purchase price of the asset leased. Examples of assets which are often subject to financial lease arrangements are jet aircraft, sports arenas, office buildings, and grocery stores. We are concerned here with the financial lease only.

Example: Suppose that it is a tax-free world.　A company with a weighted-average cost of capital of 10 per cent is contemplating the acquisition of a machine which will save $2,400 in cash operating costs annually over its useful life of four years. The machine will have no residual value. The machine may be bought outright for $6,500 cash; it is also available

---

[23]See Richard F. Vancil, "Lease or Borrow—New Method of Analysis," *Harvard Business Review* (September–October, 1961), pp. 122–133, and Richard S. Bower, Frank C. Herringer, and J. Peter Williamson, "Lease Evaluation," *The Accounting Review* (April, 1966), pp. 257–265, for thorough examinations of these distinctions and for consideration of income tax factors.

on a four-year, noncancelable lease at $2,000 annually. Should the company buy or lease?

Solution 1. The time-adjusted rate of return of leasing may be calculated as follows:

Net cash operating savings	$2,400
Lease payments	(2,000)
Net increase in cash flow per year	$ 400
Outlay at time zero	0
Time-adjusted rate of return	infinite

Something is wrong here. Intuitively, we know that this proposition does not bear an infinite rate of return.[24]

Solution 2. The lease arrangement is clearly more attractive. The present value of the lease payments at 10 per cent is $2,000 × 3.170 (from Table 14-4), or $6,240, which is less than the $6,500 purchase price. Note that the discounting of lease payments at the lessee's weighted-average cost of capital will lead to leasing rather than buying in all instances where the lessee's cost of capital exceeds the lessor's implicit contractual interest rate.

Solution 3. Perplexing implications arose in the two preceding solutions because of the failure of the prospective lessee to separate the *investment* decision from the *financing* decision. The biggest pitfall is to fail to distinguish these two aspects.

The financial-lease decision is complicated because each rental payment has two components: the implicit interest charged by the lessor and the amortization of the principal sum. In effect, the lessor is a seller of an asset and a lender of money. The rent must provide him with a recovery of the selling price of the asset plus interest on the money advanced.

The recommended general approach by the lessee to the buy-lease decision is as follows:

1. *The investment decision.* Decide whether to acquire the asset *without regard for how the purchase will be financed*:

   a. Determine an outright cash purchase price.

   b. Discount the future cash flows at the minimum desired rate of return (weighted-average cost of capital, in this example).

   c. If the net present value of (a) plus (b) is positive, acquire the asset. If negative, stop at this point; do not even consider leasing.

2. *The financing decision.* The lease itself is just another means of obtaining financing.

   Note that the decision is not whether to buy or lease, despite the fact that advertisements for leasing usually describe the decision in this way. The decision is a twofold one: (1) whether

[24] See Robert N. Anthony, John Dearden, and Richard F. Vancil, *Management Control Systems* (Homewood, Ill.: Richard D. Irwin, Inc., 1966), pp. 467–474 and 507–516.

to acquire the asset or not to acquire the asset and (2) whether to lease or borrow.

Bierman and Smidt comment on this lease-or-borrow phase as follows:

Since the lease is presumed to require a contractually predetermined set of payments, it is reasonable to compare the lease with an alternative type of financing available. . . that also requires a contractually predetermined set of payments, i.e., a loan. It follows that the interest rate at which the firm would actually borrow, if it chose to acquire the asset by buying and borrowing, is an appropriate discount rate to use in this analysis. The recommendation holds even if the firm chooses to use some other discount rate for ordinary capital budgeting decisions.[25]

The present value of the rentals should be discounted at a relatively low loan rate rather than at the weighted-average cost-of-capital rate. Therefore, the steps necessary for making the financing decision are:

a. Approximate the lowest rate at which cash could be borrowed in an amount equal to the purchase price of the equipment.

b. Discount the rentals to determine the "equivalent purchase price" of the equipment. (Any excess over the actual purchase price is the "lessor's premium.") If this "equivalent purchase price" is less than the purchase cost in step 1 (a), leasing is desirable.[26]

The preferred solution, therefore, is:

1. Investment decision:
   a. Purchase price, $6,500.
   b. Discount future cash flows, $2,400 at 10 per cent for four years, $2,400 × 3.170 = $7,608.
   c. Net present value, $7,608 − $6,500 = $1,108. Therefore, continue the analysis.

2. Financing decision:
   a. Approximate the company loan rate. Suppose that the rate is 6 per cent.
   b. "Equivalent purchase price" is $2,000 at 6 per cent for four years, $2,000 × 3.465 = $6,930, which exceeds the purchase price by $430. Therefore, do not lease.

The analysis of leases can become vastly more complicated by the introduction of income taxes and residual values. However, because leasing is basically a problem of finance rather than of cost accounting, we terminate our study at this point.

QUESTIONS, PROBLEMS, AND CASES

Note: Problems 15-11, 15-13, 15-15, 15-17, and 15-18 cover the essential points. Problems 15-14 and 15-20 through 15-23 deal with cost of capital; these

[25] Harold Bierman, Jr., and Seymour Smidt, *The Capital Budgeting Decision* (2nd ed., New York: The Macmillan Company, 1966), p. 220.
[26] Vancil, *op. cit.*, p. 136.

may be skipped if the instructor wishes to concentrate on the *investment* aspects of capital budgeting rather than the *financing* aspects. Problem 15-24 deals with the financial lease; it should be attempted only after reading the appendix to this chapter. Compound interest tables are on pages 470–474.

15-1. What are the two major aspects of the role of income taxes in decision making?

15-2. "It doesn't matter what depreciation method is used. The total dollar tax bills are the same." Do you agree? Why?

15-3. In general, what is the impact of the income tax on disposals of fixed assets?

15-4. "In the case of mutually exclusive investments, smaller profitability indexes may enhance over-all economic returns." How?

15-5. "The crux of the problem in replacement decisions is the lack of a realistic common terminal date for both proposals." Briefly describe two practical approaches to the problem.

15-6. "Cost of capital is the out-of-pocket interest charge on any debt arising from an undertaking." Do you agree? Why?

15-7. The short-run, marginal approach considers each financing as a separate problem. What is the principal objection to the short-run approach?

15-8. Should retained earnings bear a cost of capital? Why?

15-9. Distinguish between the borrowing rate and the lending rate with respect to cost of capital.

15-10. "In practice there is no single rate that is used as a guide for sifting among all projects." Why? Explain.

● **15-11. Tax Impact of Depreciation Policies.** The Mays Company estimates that it can save $2,800 a year in cash operating costs for the next ten years if it buys a special-purpose machine at a cost of $11,000. No residual value is expected. Assume that income tax rates average two-sevenths of taxable income, and that the minimum desired after-tax rate of return is 10 per cent.

REQUIRED (Round all computation to the nearest dollar.):

A. Answer all questions below, assuming straight-line depreciation.
1. Payback period.
2. Using discounted cash flow,
   (a) Time-adjusted rate of return;
   (b) Net present value.
3. Payback reciprocal.
B. Answer all questions in Part A, assuming sum-of-the-years'-digits depreciation.

15-12. Bargaining Range for Sale of Business. George Weber controls 100 per cent of the stock of a company whose sole business is the operation of a huge apartment building on leased land. The lease will expire, and the building will become fully depreciated, in four years. The building is in excellent condition and fully occupied at favorable rental rates. There has been considerable appreciation in the value of the property. Because depreciation is based on costs of thirty-six years ago, the date of construction of the building, the corporation's taxable income is unusually large. Weber believes that the building and the balance of the leasehold could be sold at a price that would effect a substantial tax advantage to the corporation while still leaving a profitable operation to the buyer for the balance of the four years, when title to the building will revert to the University of Chicago, the owner of the land. There has been only slight variation in profits for each of the past six years. (Because of a special tax provision, gains on the sale of buildings and leaseholds held more than ten years are subject to income taxes at the capital gains rate rather than at ordinary income tax rates.)

Average of Income Statements
For the Past Six Years

Rental revenue		$1,200,000
Expenses:		
Operations	$500,000	
Administration	50,000	
Property taxes	133,333	
Depreciation (straight-line)	100,000	783,333
Net income before taxes		$ 416,667
Income taxes at 52%		216,667
Net income after taxes		$ 200,000

REQUIRED:

You are to indicate a proper range of bargaining as to price, based on the averages of the income statements, assuming no change in income, expenses, or tax rates. The sale, if made, would be a cash sale. Ignore any possible relationship between buyer and seller and any residual value of furnishings at the expiration of the lease.

1. In this part, ignore interest or discount, alternative uses of the funds by either the buyer or the seller, and any other variables.
   a. What is the most the buyer should pay?
   b. What is the least the seller should take?

2. In this part, assume that the minimum desired rate of return (the cost of capital) for both buyer and seller is 10 per cent per annum.
   a. What is the most the buyer should pay?
   b. What is the least the seller should take?

	At 10%	
Periods	P.V. of $1	P.V. of Annuity of $1
1	.91	.91
2	.83	1.74
3	.75	2.49
4	.68	3.17

15-13. Comparison of Projects with Unequal Lives. The manager of the Robin Hood Company is considering two investment projects, which happen to be mutually exclusive.

The cost of capital to this company is 10 per cent, and the anticipated cash flows are as follows:

Project No.	Investment Required Now	Cash Flows (Income)			
		Year 1	Year 2	Year 3	Year 4
1	$10,000	$12,000	0	0	0
2	$10,000	0	0	0	$17,500

REQUIRED:

1. Calculate the time-adjusted rate of return of both projects.
2. Calculate the net present value of both projects.
3. Comment briefly on the results in (1) and (2). Be specific in your comparisons.

15-14. Computing Cost of Capital. The Capital Budget Committee of the Walton Corporation was established to appraise and screen departmental requests for plant expansions and improvements at a time when these requests totaled $10 million. The Committee thereupon sought your professional advice and help in establishing minimum performance standards which it should demand of these projects in the way of anticipated rates of return before interest and taxes.

The Walton Corporation is a closely held family corporation in which the stockholders exert an active and unified influence on the management. At this date, the company has no long-term debt and has 1,000,000 shares of common capital stock outstanding. It is currently earning $5 million (net income before interest and taxes) per year. The applicable tax rate is 50 per cent.

Should the projects under consideration be approved, management is confident that the $10 million of required funds can be obtained either:

(1) *By borrowing*—via the medium of an issue of $10 million, four per cent, twenty-year bonds.

(2) *By equity financing*—via the medium of an issue of 500,000 shares of common stock to the general public. It is expected and anticipated that the ownership of these 500,000 shares would be widely dispersed and scattered.

The company has been earning $12\frac{1}{2}$ per cent return after taxes. The management and the dominant stockholders consider this rate of earnings to be a fair capitalization rate (eight times earnings) as long as the company remains free of long-term debt. An increase to 15 per cent, or six and two-thirds times earnings, would constitute an adequate adjustment to compensate for the risk of carrying $10 million of long-term debt. They believe that this reflects, and is consistent with, current market appraisals.

REQUIRED:

1. Prepare columnar schedules comparing minimum returns, considering interest, taxes, and earnings ratio, which should be produced by each alternative to maintain the present capitalized value per share.
2. What minimum rate of return on new investment is necessary for each alternative to maintain the present capitalized value per share?   [C.P.A.]

15-15. Approach to Income Taxes and Discounted Cash Flow. Charles Company is trying to decide whether to launch a new household product. Through the years, the company has found that its products have a useful life of six years, after which the product is dropped and replaced by other new products. Available data follow:

1. The new product will require new special-purpose factory equipment

costing $900,000. The useful life of the equipment is six years, with a $140,000 estimated disposal value at that time. However, the Internal Revenue Service will not allow a write-off based on a life shorter than nine years. Therefore, the new equipment would be written off over nine years for tax purposes, using the sum-of-the-years'-digits depreciation and no salvage value.

2. The new product will be produced in an old plant already owned. The old plant has a book value of $30,000 and is being depreciated on a straight-line basis at $3,000 annually. The plant is currently being leased to another company. This lease has six years remaining at an annual rental of $9,000. The lease contains a cancellation clause whereby the landlord can obtain immediate possession of the premises upon payment of $6,000 cash (fully deductible for tax purposes). The estimated sales value of the building is $80,000; this price should remain stable over the next six years. The plant is likely to be kept for at least ten more years.

3. Certain nonrecurring market research studies and sales promotion activities will amount to a cost of $500,000 during year 1. The entire amount is deductible in full for income tax purposes in the year of expenditure.

4. Additions to working capital will require $200,000 at the outset and an additional $200,000 at the end of two years. This total is fully recoverable at the end of six years.

5. Net cash inflow from operations before depreciation and income taxes will be $400,000 in years 1 and 2, $600,000 in years 3 through 5, and $100,000 in year 6.

The company uses discounted cash-flow techniques for evaluating decisions. For example, in this case tabulations of differential cash flows would be made from year 0 through year 6. Yearly cash flows are estimated for all items, including capital outlays or recoveries. An applicable discount rate is used to bring all outlays from year 1 through year 6 back to year 0. If the summation in year 0 is positive, the project is desirable, and vice versa.

The minimum desired after-tax rate of return is 12 per cent. Income tax rates are 60 per cent for ordinary income.

REQUIRED:

Using an answer sheet, show how you would handle the data listed above for purposes of the decision. Note that you are *not* being asked to apply discount rates. You are being asked for the detailed impact of each of items (1) through (5) on years 0 through 6.

Note, too, that each item is to be considered separately, including its tax ramifications. *Do not combine your answers to cover more than one item.*

Assume that all cash flows take place at the end of each period. Assume that income taxes are due or refundable at the end of the period to which they relate.

SAMPLE ANSWER SHEET FOR PROBLEM 15-15

Item	Explanation	Net Present Value	Cash Flows in Year						
			0	1	2	3	4	5	6
1.	* (Allow ample								
2.	space between								
3.	items.)								
4.									
5.									

15-16. Case Study of Business Flying. The president of a medium-sized Chicago aircraft supply company is seriously considering the purchase of a five-passenger Beechcraft twin-engine airplane. He and his three top executives travel extensively in representing their products to the base operators at airports all over the country. Since he and two of the other executives have twin-engine and instrument-pilot ratings, he has been tempted to purchase a plane for some time, but has been afraid that his business was not large enough to afford plane ownership.

Feeling a burning desire to grasp those twin throttles again, he calls for his secretary to bring in their detailed travel records for the past year. These reveal that the four executives have been flying a total of 400,000 man-miles a year on commercial airlines. They have gone alone 50 per cent of the mileage; 25 per cent of the mileage has been traveled by two men together; 15 per cent of the mileage has been traveled by three men together; and all four men traveling to and from conferences accounted for 10 per cent of the total mileage.

They have used:

> Air-coach for 50 per cent of the mileage at 5.5 cents/mile,
> First class for 40 per cent of the mileage at 7.5 cents/mile,
> Jet service for 10 per cent of the mileage at 7.7 cents/mile.

The controller (who is secretly afraid to fly in a small plane) states that it is ridiculous to take anything but a 600-miles-per-hour jet, "as we did most of the time last year." Whereupon the president requested the controller to submit an analysis of the percentage usage of the main types of airliners and the block-to-block (air terminal building-to-air terminal building) speed that each type of aircraft averages. He found the following:

Percentage of Total Mileage Traveled	Type of Aircraft	Block-to-Block Speed
50%	DC-6 (Coach)	200 m.p.h.
25%	Convair (First class)	110 m.p.h.
15%	Electra (First class)	280 m.p.h.
10%	707 or DC-8 jets (First class)	400 m.p.h.

The executive vice president looked at the above data and exclaimed, "Let's be sure to count our time saved by the faster speed on the airlines. Oh, sure, I know it takes longer to go by cab to Midway or O'Hare Fields than it does to go to Meigs, where we would moor the new plane if we buy it, but we can count the cost of the extra time against commercial air travel."

All four executives agree that their time savings are worth an average of $10.00 per hour to the company before company income taxes. That is, each hour saved would add $10.00 to the company's taxable income.

They also agree that the time wasted on a commercial flight, compared with a flight in their own plane, totals about two hours. The increased distance to the airport accounts for about 45 minutes; they have to be at the airport half an hour before plane time for a commercial flight; they waste another half-hour arranging for tickets and picking them up; and they have to wait a quarter of an hour for baggage when they arrive at their destination. In the preceding year, the men made a total of 300 round trips (600 flights).

Average additional cab fares to Midway or O'Hare Fields are $2.50. The men have been riding one, two, three, or four in a cab in the same proportions that they travel on airliners. Therefore, the relevant extra cab fare is:

Round Trips		
150	solo	$ 750
38	duo	190
15	trio	75
7	for four	35
	Total	$1,050

The vice president in charge of sales stated, "I've flown the type of aircraft we are considering buying. It's a 200-m.p.h. honey. Beech figures its block-to-block speed at 185 m.p.h. I believe it would pay, as we take half of our mileage traveling in two's to four's. We pay a lot of money each year to travel at the convenience of the airlines."

Purchase cost of the five-seat plane they are considering buying, equipped for night and instrument flight, is $59,165. The company plans to use it for five years, depreciating it in straight-line fashion to a salvage value of $9,165.

Direct operating costs are:

> Gasoline: 18 gallons/hour at 35 cents/gallon.
>
> Oil (allowing for changes): 37 cents/hour.

Indirect operating costs are:

> Mooring rental, at home and away: $1,740 per year.
>
> Inspections, repairs, parts, and engine overhauls: $4.48
>   per air-hour.
>
> Insurance: $1.00 per air-hour.

The controller was overhead remarking as he calculated the depreciation on the private plane, "Now, here is one place where taxation helps us. It will cut the net ownership cost by plenty." The company is subject to a flat 40 per cent tax rate.

REQUIRED:

1. Prepare a schedule showing the yearly cost to the company of using commercial airlines and of flying their own plane. Do not consider any costs except those specifically mentioned in the problem. Assume that the mileage and cost figures of the problem will not change in the next five years.

2. Assume a desired after-tax rate of return of 10 per cent. Using discounted cash-flow procedures, show whether the plane should be purchased. Assume that yearly expenses are paid at the *start* of the year.

3. What factors other than the ones considered in (1) and (2) should be considered in reaching a decision? This is an important question, so give it more than cursory thought.

15-17. Choosing New Equipment; Complex Considerations.* The Playboy Autocar Company has developed a unique engine which it intends to use

*Prepared by Professor David Green, Jr.

in a new model. Two proposals for the necessary manufacturing equipment have been prepared. One, Plan A, considers the use of general-purpose equipment. These machines could be used in the manufacture of other Playboy models or sold on the active "used equipment" market if the new model is not a success. Plan B envisions highly specialized, automated equipment of use only on this prototype. If the new model is not a success, the Plan B equipment will have to be junked.

Costs for each plan (assuming an output of 50,000 units a year) are as follows:

	Plan A	Plan B
Machinery costs	$1,850,000	$4,600,000
Annual variable costs:		
Labor	$2,000,000	$ 500,000
Material	1,500,000	1,350,000
Other	1,000,000	750,000
	$4,500,000	$2,600,000
Annual nonvariable costs:		
Supervision	$ 500,000	$ 600,000
Insurance, taxes, etc.	250,000	500,000
Depreciation on machinery	?	?

Additional Data

1. A conference with representatives of the Internal Revenue Service indicates that the general-purpose machinery (Plan A) is to be depreciated over ten years and the Plan B machinery over five years; for depreciation computations, salvage value is estimated to be $200,000 for Plan A equipment and $100,000 for Plan B. The sum-of-the-years'-digits method of calculating depreciation is to be used.

2. Estimated salvage if the machinery is sold is as follows:

At End of Year	Plan A	Plan B
1	$1,200,000	$300,000
2	1,200,000	300,000
3	1,000,000	250,000
4	1,000,000	200,000
5	800,000	200,000
6	800,000	175,000
7	600,000	150,000
8	400,000	100,000
9	400,000	100,000
10	200,000	100,000

3. A new corporation is to be formed and operated as a wholly owned subsidiary. The new equipment will be purchased by the subsidiary. The engines will be sold, as finished, to the parent company for $125 cash.

4. Income tax rates are assumed to be 50 per cent on ordinary income.

5. For purposes of this situation, the factors in the present value tables may be rounded to two decimal places.

REQUIRED:

1. (a) Prepare an analysis that will show which plan is most advantageous, after taxes, assuming that 50,000 units a year will be sold, that the engine will be manufactured for five years, and that the minimum desired rate of return is 10 per cent.

(b) What additional information should be supplied the board of directors to assist them in their decision?

2. One of the directors says, "These new-fangled approaches don't answer the real questions." He asks that you calculate the payout in years for each plan, assuming that 50,000 units a year will be produced and sold.

15-18. Ranking Projects.* Assume that the following six projects have been submitted for inclusion in the coming year's budget for capital expenditures.

	Year	A	B	C	D	E	F
Investment	0	$(100,000)	$(100,000)	$(200,000)	$(200,000)	$(200,000)	$(50,000)
	1	0	20,000	70,000	0	5,000	23,000
	2	10,000	20,000	70,000	0	15,000	20,000
	3	20,000	20,000	70,000	0	30,000	10,000
	4	20,000	20,000	70,000	0	50,000	10,000
	5	20,000	20,000	70,000	0	50,000	
Per year	6–9	20,000	20,000		200,000	50,000	
	10	20,000	20,000			50,000	
Per year	11–15	20,000					
Time-adjusted rate of return		14%	?	?	?	12.6%	12.0%

REQUIRED:

1. Rates of return (to the nearest half per cent) for Projects B, C, and D and a ranking of all projects in descending order. Show computations. What approximations of rates of return for Projects B and C do you get by using payback reciprocals?

2. Based on your answer in (1), which projects would you select, assuming a 10 per cent cut-off rate:

(a) If $500,000 is the limit to be spent? (b) If $550,000? (c) If $650,000?

3. Assuming a 16 per cent minimum desired rate of return, and using the net-present-value method, compute the net present values and rank all the projects. Which project is more desirable, C or D? Compare your answer with your ranking in (2). If Projects C and D are mutually exclusive proposals, which would you choose? Why?

4. What factors other than those considered in (1) through (3) would influence your project rankings? Be specific.

15-19. Buy or Rent a Computer. The Gercken Corporation sells computer services to its clients. The Company completed a feasibility study and

*Adapted from *N.A.A. Research Report No. 35*, pp. 83–85.

decided to obtain an additional computer on January 1, 1965. Information regarding the new computer follows:

1. The purchase price of the computer is $230,000. Maintenance, property taxes, and insurance will be $20,000 per year. If the computer is rented, the annual rent will be $85,000 plus 5 per cent of annual billings. The rental price includes maintenance.

2. Owing to competitive conditions, the Company feels it will be necessary to replace the computer at the end of three years with one which is larger and more advanced. It is estimated that the computer will have a resale value of $110,000 at the end of the three years. The computer will be depreciated on a straight-line basis for both financial reporting and income tax purposes.

3. The income tax rate is 50 per cent.

4. The estimated annual billing for the services of the new computer will be $220,000 during the first year and $260,000 during each of the second and third years. The estimated annual expense of operating the computer is $80,000 in addition to the expense mentioned above. An additional $10,000 of start-up expenses will be incurred during the first year.

5. If it decides to purchase the computer, the Company will pay cash. If the computer is rented, the $230,000 can be otherwise invested at a 15 per cent rate of return.

6. If the computer is purchased, the amount of the investment recovered during each of the three years can be reinvested immediately at a 15 per cent rate of return. Each year's recovery of investment in the computer will have been reinvested for an average of six months by the end of the year.

7. The present value of $1.00 due at a constant rate during each year and discounted at 15 per cent is:

Year	Present Value
0–1	$.93
1–2	.80
2–3	.69

The present value of $1.00 due at the end of each year and discounted at 15 per cent is:

End of Year	Present Value
1	$.87
2	.76
3	.66

REQUIRED:

1. Prepare a schedule comparing the estimated annual income from the new computer under the purchase plan and under the rental plan. The comparison should include a provision for the opportunity cost of the average investment in the computer during each year.

2. Prepare a schedule showing the annual cash flows under the purchase plan and under the rental plan.

3. Prepare a schedule comparing the net present values of the cash flows under the purchase plan and under the rental plan.

4. Comment on the results obtained in parts "1" and "3." How should the computer be financed? Why?   [C.P.A.]

15-20. Computation of Cost of Capital. Company Y expects net operating income to be approximately $2 million over the next few years. Annual interest on bonds will be $400,000. The market value of the bonds outstanding is $8 million; of common stock, $12 million. The book value of the bonds is $10,000,000; of the stock, $10,000,000.

REQUIRED:

1. Effective yield on bonds, rate of return on common equity, and over-all weighted-average cost of capital.

2. Express the equity capitalization rate in terms of the over-all capitalization rate plus an adjustment for financial uncertainty.

15-21. After-tax Cost of Equity Capital. Assume the same facts as in Problem 15-20. The income tax rate is 40 per cent.

REQUIRED:

1. After-tax rate of return on common equity.

2. The company is considering investing $100,000 in a proposed project, which will increase net operating income by $12,000. Should the project be undertaken?

15-22. Cost of Capital.

1. If a firm's marginal cost of capital were plotted on the following graph, describe the line or curve that would likely result.

Note: A sketch will be acceptable as a description of the line or curve.

2. Give a reason to explain the behavior of the line or curve you described in part (a).

3. If a firm were contemplating raising additional capital by issuing bonds, how would the cost of this debt capital likely be affected if the firm issued a significant amount of common stock prior to offering the contemplated bond issue? *State your reason.*   [C.G.A.A. Adapted]

15-23. Cost of Capital After Taxes. A company is considering a project costing $100,000. The market value of outstanding bonds is $5,000,000; of stock, $5,000,000. The interest on debt is 4 per cent. The required after-tax rate on equity is 10 per cent. The income tax rate is 50 per cent. The project is expected to produce $12,000 in earnings, before interest and taxes in perpetuity. Ignore depreciation.

REQUIRED:

1. The over-all after-tax cost of capital for the company.
2. The over-all after-tax rate of return on the project.
3. The after-tax rate on equity for the project.

15-24. The Financial Lease. The Vanthony Company has a weighted-average cost of capital of 12 per cent. Its basic loan rate is six per cent. The financial vice president is trying to decide whether to buy or lease some machinery. The purchase price is $14,000. A noncancelable lease is also available for six years at $3,000 annually. The useful life of the machine is six years; it will have no residual value. Annual cash operating savings are expected to be $4,000.

The salesman is encouraging the lease. He says: "No matter how you look at it, you can't lose by leasing. You take in $4,000 annually, pay out $3,000 annually, and make no down payment. Your rate of return is infinite."

Should the Vanthony Company buy or lease? Show computations.

SPECIAL TOPICS
FOR FURTHER STUDY

SECTION

inventory planning, control, and valuation

CHAPTER **XVI**

There is an optimum level of investment for any asset, whether it be cash, physical plant, or inventories. For example, even cash balances may be too large or too small. The principal cost of having too much cash is the sacrifice of earnings; idle cash earns nothing. The principal cost of having too little cash may be lost discounts on purchases or harm to one's credit standing. For every asset class, then, there is a conceptual optimum investment which, when considered with optimum levels in other asset classes, helps to maximize long-run profits.

The major goal of "inventory control" is to discover and maintain the optimum level of inventory investment.[1] Two limits must be imposed in controlling inventory levels, because there are two danger points that management usually wants to avoid. The first danger is that of inadequate inventories, which disrupt production and perhaps lose sales. The second danger is that of excessive inventories, which introduce unnecessary carrying costs and obsolescence risks. The optimum inventory level lies somewhere between the two danger points. Our major purpose in this chapter will be to see how this optimum inventory level is computed and maintained. We shall also consider the various methods of inventory valuation.

CHARACTERISTICS OF INVENTORIES

Need for inventories

If production and delivery of goods were instantaneous, there would be no need for inventories except as a hedge against price changes.

[1]Throughout this chapter, the term "inventory control" will refer to both planning inventory investment and executing the plans.

Despite the marvels of computers, automation, and scientific management, the manufacturing and merchandising processes still do not function quickly enough to avoid the need for having inventories. Inventories must be maintained so that the customer may be serviced immediately, or at least quickly enough so that he does not turn to another source of supply. In turn, production operations cannot flow smoothly without having inventories of work in process, direct materials, finished parts, and supplies.

Inventories are cushions (1) to absorb planning errors and unforeseen fluctuations in supply and demand, and (2) to facilitate smooth production and marketing operations. Further, inventories help isolate or minimize the interdependence of each part of the organization (for example, departments or functions) so that each may work effectively. For example, many parts and subassemblies may be purchased or manufactured, stored, and used as needed.

Inventory records and control

Inventory records are only a means to the end of inventory control. A company may have thousands of impressive stores cards whose balances are always in precise agreement with physical counts taken in its immaculate storeroom. The requisition, purchasing, receiving, and material-handling duties may be at peak efficiency. Despite errorless paper shuffling and diligent employees, inventory control may still be inadequate. Management's major duty with respect to inventory control is not clerical accuracy. (In many cases, it is possible to attain excellent inventory control through visual inspection rather than through elaborate perpetual inventory records.) The major inventory control problem is to maximize profitability by balancing inventory investment against what is needed to sustain smooth operations.

Functional viewpoints

Four main functions of business—sales, production, purchasing, and finance—generate four views of inventories that often are in conflict. The sales manager has a natural desire to have plenty of everything on hand so that no customer is ever turned away or forced to wait because of lack of stock. The production manager likes to concentrate on continuous, single-product runs so as to spread such costs as setups, changeover, spoilage, and learning over longer runs of product. The purchasing officer often prefers to buy in large quantities to take advantage of quantity discounts and lower freight costs. Sometimes he would like to outguess changing market prices and to postpone or accelerate purchases accordingly. The financial manager wants to pry loose as much inventory capital from inventory investment as is feasible so that it may be channeled into other profitable opportunities. Because of these conflicting functional objectives, any inventory control policy must be carefully drawn if it is to benefit the business as a whole.

CONTROL CLASSIFICATIONS: THE ABC METHOD

Sometimes it is difficult to comprehend the enormous number of items that companies must keep in stock—up to 50,000 and more. Any effective inventory control system will not have all items in the inventory treated in the same manner under the same control techniques. For example, some items are often controlled by the "two-bin" system. Some companies do not bother maintaining perpetual inventory cards; instead, two bins are kept where withdrawal from the second bin necessitates a reorder. Or, physical control is exercised through having a red line painted in a bin at a reorder level. Another example would be keeping reorder quantities in a special package; when these quantities are finally invaded, an attached purchase requisition for replenishment is immediately forwarded to the purchasing department.

Many companies find it useful to divide materials, parts, supplies, and finished goods into subclassifications for purposes of stock control. For example, Exhibit 16-1 shows direct materials, which are subclassified

EXHIBIT 16-1

ABC ANALYSIS OF MATERIAL INVENTORY

Step 1.   Multiply average usage times unit price to obtain total cost:

Item	Average Usage	Unit Price	Total Consumption Cost (See note.)
H20	10,000	$10.00	$100,000
H21	1,000	.05	50
H22	10,000	.02	200
H23	11,000	1.00	11,000
H24	110,000	.10	11,000

(and so forth)

Step 2.   Group above items in descending order of total consumption cost and then divide into three classes:

Class	Items Number of Items	Per Cent of Total	Dollars Total Cost	Per Cent of Total
A	5,000	10%	$14,400,000	72%
B	10,000	20%	3,800,000	19%
C	35,000	70%	1,800,000	9%
	50,000	100%	$20,000,000	100%

Special note: The total annual cost of raw materials consumed is dependent on two main factors: physical quantity needed and cost per unit. It is the *total* cost rather than the *unit* cost that matters. Thus, 11,000 units @ $1.00 requires the same investment as 110,000 units @ $.10.

in step-by-step fashion by (1) itemizing total annual purchase cost of each item needed and (2) grouping in decreasing order of annual consumption cost. This technique is often called the *ABC method*, although it also has other labels.

The final A, B, C classification in Exhibit 16-1 demonstrates that only 10 per cent of the items represents 72 per cent of the total cost. In general, the greatest degree of continuous control would be exerted over these "A" items which account for high annual consumption costs and correspondingly high investment in inventories. This type of control would mean frequent ordering, low safety stocks, and a willingness to incur expediting costs on "A" items because the costs of placing and following up orders are relatively low in comparison with costs of carrying excess inventories. At the other extreme, where the total yearly purchase cost is relatively low, there would be less frequent ordering, higher safety stocks, and less paper work ("C" items).

Type "A" and "B" items are ordered according to budget schedules prepared by the production planning department.[2] Essentially, sales forecasts are the cornerstone for production scheduling.[3] In turn, these production schedules are "exploded" (a commonly used term for detailed breakdowns of data) into the various direct material, parts, and supply components. These explosions result in purchase schedules for major items. These purchase schedules are adjusted for lead times, planned changes in inventories, and normal waste and spoilage. Purchases are made accordingly, and follow-ups are instituted by the purchasing department as needed. In other words, Type "A" and "B" items are budgeted almost on a hand-to-mouth basis, because carrying costs are too high to warrant inventories which are sizable in terms of many days' usage.

Stores cards are usually kept for Type "A" and "B" items. It is noteworthy that such cards increasingly carry physical unit balance only. More managements are doubtful that the added clerical costs of carrying actual unit prices on stores cards are worth while.

ORDER QUANTITY

Associated costs

The most straightforward approach to computing optimum investment in inventory is to select the inventory level that minimizes total long-run costs. Comparisons of total annual costs often serve as a practical guide. Inventories entail two types of associated costs: those of carrying

[2]Ford Motor Company uses four inventory classes and keeps two days' supply of "A" items; five days supply of "B"; 10 days' supply of "C"; and 20 or more days' supply of "D" items.

[3]An effective production planning and control system is an intricate mechanism. It depends on accurate demand forecasts expressed in units of production capacity, a production budget which establishes inventory levels and production activity, and a control procedure for adjusting inventory levels when errors in the demand forecast cause inventories to exceed or fall below budget.

and those of not carrying enough. The optimum solution minimizes the
total of these two classes of costs:

Cost of Carrying plus	*Cost of Not Carrying Enough*
1. Risk of obsolescence	1. Foregone quantity discounts*
2. Desired rate of return on investment*	2. Disruptions of production with extra costs of expediting, over-time, setups, hiring, and train-ing
3. Handling and transfer	
4. Space for storage	3. Contribution margins on lost sales*
5. Personal property taxes	
6. Insurance	4. Extra costs of uneconomic pro-duction runs
7. Clerical costs	5. Loss of customer goodwill*
	6. Extra purchasing and transporta-tion costs
	7. Foregone fortuitious purchases*

*Costs which often do not explicitly appear on formal accounting records.

Note the conflicting behavior of these two classes of costs. For
example, if management decides to carry huge inventories, many costs of
carrying will soar while many costs of not carrying will fall.

The measurement problem

Many of the relevant costs influenced by inventory levels usually
are not apparent in the accounting records. For example, ordinary accounting records will not contain opportunity costs such as the desired
rate of return on·investment (which is usually the highest cost of carrying
additional inventory), foregone quantity discounts, contribution margins
on lost sales, and the like. Then, too, even if the accountant recognizes
that such costs are relevant to inventory policy, some of these costs are
extremely difficult to identify and to measure.

Relevant costs for inventory decisions

The size of many relevant costs will differ depending on the length
of time under consideration and the specific alternative uses of resources.
For example, if storage space is owned and cannot be used for other
profitable purposes, differential space costs are zero. But if the space
may be used for other productive activities, or if there is rental cost
geared to the space occupied, a pertinent cost of space usage for inventory purposes must be recognized.

To the extent that money is invested in inventories, there is an
interest cost of carrying stock. But how is this to be measured? In
practice, this rate may be based on current borrowing rates, the long-run
average cost of capital, or some "appropriate" rate selected by management. The proper rate should depend on investment opportunities avail-

able to management; it may be small or large, depending on specific circumstances.

Other costs that may or may not be relevant in policy decisions include overtime premiums on rush orders that would be unnecessary if bigger inventories were carried, idle time caused by material shortages, emergency expediting, extra transportation costs (for example, air freight), extra physical count-taking, obsolescence risks, and extra moving and handling costs.

As in any policy-making situation, inventory costs that are common to all alternatives are irrelevant and may be ignored. Costs that are often irrelevant because they will not be affected by the inventory decision include salaries of store record clerks, storekeepers, and material handlers, depreciation on building and equipment, and fixed rent.

In practice, however, for purposes of inventory planning most of the wage costs are unitized on a per-order or a per-unit-handled basis. Thus they are regarded as fully variable costs. Whether this is justified depends on specific circumstances. Surely the cost of processing 4,000 orders per period will be strikingly greater than the cost of processing 1,000 orders. The basic question often is whether in the same situation the cost of processing 3,400 orders will be notably different from the cost of processing 3,000 orders. This is simply another example of the importance of determining what is relevant in any given decision-making situation.

A salient feature of inventory control is that production and inventory decisions are rarely affected by minor variations in cost factors.[4] At the same time, the lack of precise cost data does not justify its haphazard use.[5]

There are two central questions which must be faced in designing an inventory control system: (1) How much should we buy (or manufacture) at a time? (2) When should we buy (or manufacture)? Now we turn to the first of these questions.

How much to order?

A key factor in inventory policy is computing the optimum size of either a normal purchase order for raw materials or a shop order for a production run. This optimum size is called the *economic order quantity*, the size which will result in minimum total annual costs of the item in question.

---

[4]Note that a total of minor variations may reveal two things: (1) a large total variation and (2) a trend of costs that may be important.

[5]It is easy to critize various mathematical approaches to problems of inventory control on the grounds that the relevant costs are impossible to measure. But such criticisms are invalid in nearly all situations. Optimum inventory policies can be achieved without knowledge of "true costs." For an interesting discussion see Miller and Starr, *Executive Decisions and Operations Research* (Englewood Cliffs, N.J.; Prentice-Hall, Inc., 1960), pp. 262–270.

Example 1: Economic Order Quantity. A refrigerator manufacturer buys certain steel shelving in sets from outside suppliers at $4.00 per set. Total annual needs are 5,000 sets at a rate of 20 sets per working day.

The following cost data are available:

Desired annual return on inventory investment,		
10% × $4.00	$.40	
Rent, insurance, taxes, per unit per year	.10	
Carrying costs per unit per year		$ .50
Costs per purchase order:		
Clerical costs, stationery, postage, telephone, etc.		$10.00
What is the economic order quantity?		

Tabulation of Lowest Annual Cost. Exhibit 16-2 shows a tabulation of total costs under various alternatives. The column with the least cost will indicate the economic order quantity.

EXHIBIT 16-2

ANNUALIZED COSTS OF VARIOUS STANDARD ORDERS
(250 working days)

					Least Cost					
Symbols					↓	↓				
E	Order size	50	100	200	400	500	600	800	1,000	5,000
E/2	Average inventory in units*	25	50	100	200	250	300	400	500	2,500
A/E	Number of purchase orders	100	50	25	12.5	10	8.3	6.7	5	1
S(E/2)	Annual carrying cost @ $.50	$ 13	$ 25	$ 50	$100	$125	$150	$200	$ 250	$1,250
P(A/E)	Annual purchase order cost @ 10.00	1,000	500	250	125	100	83	67	50	10
C	Total annual expenses	$1,013	$525	$300	$225	$225	$233	$267	$ 300	$1,260

E = Order size.
A = Annual quantity used in units.
S = Annual cost of carrying one unit in stock one year.
P = Cost of placing an order.
C = Total annual expenses.

*Assume that stock is zero when each order arrives. (Even if a certain minimum inventory were assumed, it has no bearing on the choice here as long as the minimum is the same for each alternative.) Therefore, the average inventory relevant to the problem will be one-half the order quantity. For example, if 600 units are purchased, the inventory on arrival will contain 600. It will gradually diminish until no units are on hand. The average inventory would be 300; the storage cost, $.50 × 300 or $150.

Exhibit 16-2 shows minimum costs at two levels, 400 and 500 units. The next step would be to see if costs are lower somewhere between 400 and 500 units—say, at 450 units:

Average inventory, 225 × $.50   = $113 Carrying costs
Number of orders (5,000/450), 11.1 × $10 =   111 Purchase order costs

$224 Total annual expenses

The dollar differences here are extremely small, but the approach is important. The same approach may be shown in graphic form. See Exhibit 16-3. Note that in this case total cost is at a minimum where total purchase order cost and total carrying cost are equal.

Order-size formula

The graphic approach has been expressed in formula form. The total annual cost (for any case, not just this example) is differentiated with respect to order size. Where this derivative is zero, the minimum annual cost is attained.[6] The widely used formula approach to the order-size problem may be expressed in a variety of ways, one of which follows:

$$E = \sqrt{\frac{2AP}{S}}$$

E = order size; A = annual quantity used in units; P = cost of placing an order; and S = annual cost of carrying one unit in stock one year.
Substituting:

$$E = \sqrt{\frac{2(5,000)\,(\$10)}{\$.50}} = \sqrt{\frac{\$100,000}{\$.50}} = \sqrt{200,000}$$

E = 448, the economic order quantity.

As we may expect, the order size gets larger as A or P gets bigger or as S gets smaller.

Recapitulation of economic order quantity

Note in Exhibit 16-3 that the approach to economic lot size centers on locating a minimum cost *range* rather than a minimum cost *point*.

[6]The formula may be derived as follows:
The tabular and graphic approaches may be expressed:

(1) $C = \dfrac{AP}{E} + \dfrac{ES}{2}$ (4) $SE^2 = 2AP$

(2) $\dfrac{dC}{dE} = \dfrac{-AP}{E^2} + \dfrac{S}{2}$ (5) $E^2 = \dfrac{2AP}{S}$

(3) Set $\dfrac{dC}{dE} = 0$; $\dfrac{S}{2} - \dfrac{AP}{E^2} = 0$ (6) $E = \sqrt{\dfrac{2AP}{S}}$

The total cost curve tends to flatten between 400 and 800 units. In practice, there is a definite tendency to (a) find the range and (b) select a lot size at the lower end of the range. In our example, there would be a tendency to select a lot size of 400 or slightly more.

An analytical approach such as has been outlined here is useful even if cost factors used are approximations. Total annual expenses of inventory control are fairly insensitive to moderate changes in order size. In other words, these tools let us hit the target at least, even if we never score a bull's eye. To illustrate, going back to our data in Exhibit 16-3, assume that the carrying cost is erroneously estimated at $1 per unit instead of 50¢. Substituting in our formula, we would get $\sqrt{\dfrac{\$100,000}{\$1.00}}$, or $E = 333$ units. Now the correct annual cost at 333 units would be:

Carrying cost, 167 × $.50   = $ 83
Purchase order cost, 5,000/333 or 15 orders × $10 =   150
                                                                           ‾‾‾‾‾
                                                                           $233

Compared with optimum cost of $224, the $9 difference is an error of 4 per cent, which is certainly not catastrophic.

EXHIBIT 16-3

GRAPHIC SOLUTION OF ECONOMIC LOT SIZE

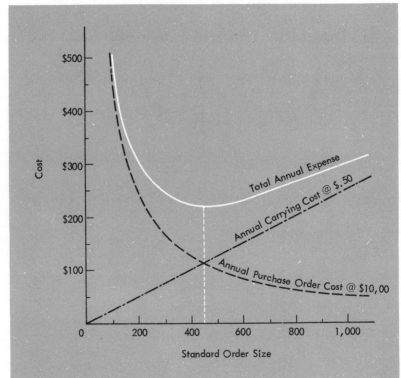

Production runs

The economic-order-quantity approach may also be applied to production runs. For example, assume the same facts as in our steel-shelving example (Exhibit 16-2), except that the shelving is manufactured rather than purchased. The setup costs (for example, labor costs for adjusting machines) are $50. The same formula may be used; the only difference is substituting a $50 setup cost for the $10 cost of placing an order.

$$E = \sqrt{\frac{2(5,000)\,\$50}{\$.50}} = \sqrt{\frac{\$500,000}{\$.50}}$$

$$E = \sqrt{1,000,000} = \underline{\underline{1,000}} \text{ units per production run.}$$

Incidentally, historically in various machine shops the high cost of setup time has been a critical factor that tends to boost the size of production runs and the optimal size of inventory. The increasing use of automated machine tools, which are set up and controlled by computer programs, has reduced setup time enormously. It is now much easier to switch from the production of one item to another. This phenomenon has led toward lower production runs and lower optimal inventory sizes.

Quantity discounts

Quantity discounts affect unit prices; in general, the bigger the size of the order, the lower the unit price. The price usually falls between brackets; within each bracket, a uniform unit price prevails.

The basic formula used previously can be adapted to such situations, but its complexities will not be described further here. For our purposes, the following approach will be easiest to understand.

First, compute annual basic expenses in the manner illustrated in Exhibit 16-2. Then merely add the additional expenses of *foregoing* quantity discounts. The economic order quantity will be that which offers the lowest expenses. See Exhibit 16-4, alternative 1. Or, the total yearly delivered cost may be computed, which is then added to the annual basic expenses. This method is shown in Exhibit 16-4, alternative 2. Both alternatives are fundamentally the same and, of the alternatives tabulated, yield the same economic order quantity, 800 units. (The optimum size is really 601 units, which would entail total expenses of $233 plus $500, or $733.)

SAFETY STOCKS

When to order?

Although we have seen how to compute economic order quantity, we have not yet answered another key question: When to order? This

EXHIBIT 16-4

ANNUAL COSTS OF VARIOUS STANDARD ORDERS

Facts: Carrying costs per unit per year $ .50
       Costs per purchase order $10.00

Cost of shelving per set:	Total Cost	Foregone Discount
In orders of 400 or less	$4.00	.20
401– 600	3.95	.15
601–1,000	3.90	.10
1,001–5,000	3.80	—

Alternative 1:

Order size	50	100	200	400	500	600	800	1,000	5,000
Annual basic expenses (from Exhibit 16-2)	$ 1,013	$ 525	$ 300	$ 225	$ 225	$ 233	$ 267	$ 300	$ 1,260
Foregone discount per unit × 5,000 annual need	1,000	1,000	1,000	1,000	750	750	500	500	—
Total expenses	$ 2,013	$ 1,525	$ 1,300	$ 1,225	$ 975	$ 983	$ 767	$ 800	$ 1,260

Alternative 2:

	50	100	200	400	500	600	800	1,000	5,000
Yearly delivered cost of inventory (5,000 units)	$20,000	$20,000	$20,000	$20,000	$19,750	$19,750	$19,500	$19,500	$19,000
Annual basic expenses (from Exhibit 16-2)	1,013	525	300	225	225	233	267	300	1,260
Total expenses	$21,013	$20,525	$20,300	$20,225	$19,975	$19,983	$19,767	$19,800	$20,260

Note that the difference in total expenses between alternatives 1 and 2 is a constant $19,000; that is, 5,000 units multiplied by the $3.80 unit cost when there is no foregone discount.

question is easy to answer only if we know the *lead time*—the time interval between placing an order and receiving delivery—know the economic order quantity, and are *certain* of demand during lead time. The graph in Exhibit 16-5 will clarify the relationships between the following facts:

Economic order quantity	448 sets of steel shelving
Lead time	2 weeks
Average usage	100 sets per week

Exhibit 16-5, Part A, shows that the *reorder point*—the quantity level that automatically triggers a new order—is dependent on expected usage during lead time; that is, if shelving is being used at a rate of 100

EXHIBIT 16-5

DEMAND IN RELATION TO INVENTORY LEVELS

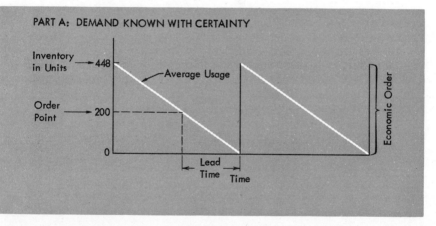

PART A: DEMAND KNOWN WITH CERTAINTY

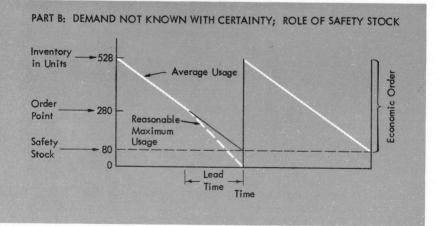

PART B: DEMAND NOT KNOWN WITH CERTAINTY; ROLE OF SAFETY STOCK

sets per week and the lead time is two weeks, a new order would be placed when the inventory level reaches 200 sets.

Minimum inventory: safety allowance for fluctuations in demand

Our previous example assumed that 100 sets would be used per week—a demand pattern that was known with certainty. Businesses are seldom blessed with such accurate forecasting. Instead, demand may fluctuate from day to day, from week to week, or from month to month. Thus, the company will run out of stock if there are sudden spurts in usage beyond 100 per week, delays in processing orders, or delivery delays. Obviously, then, nearly all companies must provide for some safety stock—some minimum or buffer inventory as a cushion against reasonable expected maximum usage. Part B of Exhibit 16-5 is based on the same facts as Part A, except that reasonable expected maximum usage is 140 sets per week. The safety stock would be 80 sets (excess usage of 40 sets per week × 2 weeks). The reorder point is commonly computed as safety stock plus the average usage during the lead time.[7]

Computation of safety stock

In our example, we used 80 sets as a safety stock. The computation of safety stocks hinges on demand forecasts. The executive will have some notion—usually based on past experience—of the range of daily demand: what percentage chance (probability) exists for usages of various quantities.

A frequency distribution based on prior daily or weekly changes in demand will offer data for constructing the associated costs of maintaining safety (minimum) stocks. Once again, there are two major costs: the costs of carrying, sometimes called the *cost of overstock*, which are primarily interest on investment, obsolescence write-offs, and space costs; and the costs of not carrying (*stockout costs*), which include expensive expediting, loss of contribution margins, and loss of customer goodwill. The latter costs are difficult to measure, but statisticians and mathematicians have used statistical probability techniques on this problem with some success.[8]

[7] This handy but special formula does not apply where the receipt of the standard order fails to increase stocks to the order-point quantity; for example, where the lead time is three months and the standard order is a one-month supply. In these cases, there will be overlapping of orders. The order point will be: average usage during lead time plus safety stock minus orders placed but not received. The latter is really the general formula for computing the reorder point. In most cases, a simplified version is used because the last term in the general formula is zero. For elaboration, see Magee, *Production Planning and Inventory Control* (New York: McGraw-Hill Book Company, Inc., 1958), p. 71.

[8] Thomson M. Whitin, *Theory of Inventory Management* (2nd ed.; Princeton, N.J.: Princeton University Press, 1957), p. 95, advances the idea that the rational entrepreneur should attempt to vary his inventory levels with the square root of sales rather than with sales. This is based on the relationships expressed in the economic-lot-size formula, discussed earlier, where the optimum lot size increased in proportion to the square root of the annual quantity used.

The optimum safety stock level exists where the costs of carrying an extra unit is exactly counterbalanced by the expected costs of not carrying.

The most difficult cost to determine is *stockout cost,* consisting mainly of the foregone present and future contribution to profit from losing an order because of lack of inventory:

> But if there is no demand during the period an item is out of stock, there is no lost profit, and reliable information on unfilled demand is seldom maintained. Where there is unfilled demand, but the customer is willing to wait or accept a substitute, there may be no immediate loss of profit. But there may be loss of future business as a result of dissatisfied customers. Because of these difficulties, most of the practical inventory management systems specify a customer service level (percentage of items in stock) that they wish to meet rather than trying to minimize a total cost that includes stockout cost.[9]

A practical approach to setting levels of safety stock is shown in the following example.

Example 2: Safety Stock. Suppose that a company has the following distribution of weekly retail sales for one item in a department store for 100 weeks:

Number of Weeks	Weekly Sales in Units
2	0
7	1
15	2
20	3
18	4 = weighted-average sales
16	5
11	6
6	7 11% of the time sales > 6 units
3	8 5% of the time sales > 7 units
1	9
0	10 2% of the time sales > 8 units
1	11

The lead time for reorder was a constant one week. Average sales were four items per week, and actual sales equaled this average in 18 of the 100 weeks, or 18 per cent of the time. Weekly sales exceeded six units in 11 per cent of the weeks and exceeded eight units in only 2 per cent of the weeks.

The reorder point would be based on a safety stock, plus average sales of four units during the one-week lead time. Because sales of more than eight units occur only 2 per cent of the time, a safety stock of four units (eight units minus average sales of four units) should result in weekly potential sales in excess of inventory on hand only 2 per cent of the time. A stockout occurs when the safety stock is fully depleted before the inventory is replaced. Stockouts would occur whenever weekly sales exceeded seven units, or about 5 per cent of the time. Note that a stockout at a sales level of exactly eight units would do no harm in the sense that the safety stock

[9] N.A.A. Research Report 40, *Techniques in Inventory Management,* p. 14.

might be exhausted just as the replenishment arrives. In any event, for an item with a constant lead time, a knowledge of the sales distribution permits a setting of a safety stock which provides a specific level of protection against stockouts.[10]

Under the ABC inventory classification, different levels of protection may be specified for different classes, depending on objectives. Thus some firms may specify a 99 per cent in-stock condition for the fast-moving A items, 90 per cent for B items, and 80 per cent for C items. "Other companies that are more concerned with controlling the investment in inventory might set the lowest safety stock levels, along with the highest frequency of reorders, for the high cost Class A items and spend less reordering effort, at the cost of proportionately higher safety stocks, for the lowest cost Class C Items."[11]

Constant order-cycle system

The foregoing discussion of inventory control revolved around the so-called two-bin or constant order-quantity system: when inventory levels recede to X, then order Y. There is another widely used model in practice, the constant order-cycle system: for example, in Exhibit 16-6 every month

EXHIBIT 16-6

CONSTANT ORDER-CYCLE SYSTEM
Item AB-34

Reorder date—10th of each month.
Reorder quantity—enough to bring the quantity on hand and on order, up to 12 units.

Date	Received	Shipped	On Hand	On Order	On Hand and on Order
6/1	11	3	8		8
6/8		4	4		4
6/10*			4	8	12
6/13	8		12		12
6/20		6	6		6
7/10*			6	6	12
7/11		2	4		10
7/13	6		10		10
7/26		8	2		2
8/10*			2	10	12

*Constant Order Date.

[10] This example was adapted from Joseph Buchan and Ernest Koenigsberg, *Scientific Inventory Management*, (Englewood Cliffs, N.J.: Prentice-Hall, Inc., 1963), pp. 7–8. The authors point out: "The tedious process of compiling the distribution of historical sales data for every item in an inventory in order to set buffer levels can often be avoided." They refer to short cuts that may be taken because many sales distributions are either Poisson, exponential, or normal. The book contains numerous case illustrations of applications of inventory control systems.

[11] *NAA Research Report No. 40, op. cit.*, p. 11.

review the inventory level on hand and order enough to bring the quantity on hand and on order up to twelve units. The reorder date is fixed and the quantity ordered depends on the usage since the previous order and the outlook during the lead time. Demand forecasts and seasonal patterns also should be considered in specifying the size of orders during the year.

The minimization of the total associated costs of inventories is still the prime objective, regardless of the system used. A constant order-cycle system may be adopted instead of a constant order-quantity system where (a) the cost of continuous surveillance is too high or (b) transportation and ordering economies may be gained through regular ordering of several different items from the same supplier. The major disadvantage of the constant order-cycle system is that it may require carrying more safety stock to protect against stockouts not only during the replenishment lead time (for example, between the tenth and thirteenth of the month in Exhibit 16-6) but also during the period between the placing of the orders. In contrast, in an order-quantity system, safety stock is needed only to protect against stockouts during the replenishment period.[12]

Inventory turnover

Note that the emphasis in this chapter is on the word *optimum*, not *minimum*. Contrast this with the commonly used index of inventory management—inventory turnover, the number of times the average inventory is sold or used in a year. The traditional rule has been: "The higher the turnover, the better the inventory management." Consider the following comments:

> An infinite turnover can be achieved by carrying no inventory whatsoever. But such an inventory policy would not be a good policy because a company with no inventory would be continuously buying, expediting. . . . Turnover is worth improving, yes, but only if there is no substantial increase in ordering cost and only if there is no substantial loss of sales resulting from excessive stockouts.[13]

SUMMARY OF OPTIMUM INVESTMENT IN INVENTORIES

The practical objective of inventory control is to minimize the total associated costs of inventories: the costs of carrying plus the costs of not carrying.

The basic approach described here is applicable to all types of inventories: materials, supplies, parts, work in process, and finished goods.. For example, the economic-order-quantity approach may be applied to problems of buying materials or of manufacturing finished units. There are two major sub-areas for cost analysis: computing economic order quantity (how much to order), and computing optimum safety stocks (when to order). For the "fixed economic order-quantity system," average

[12] *Ibid.*, p. 90.
[13] *Ibid.*, p. 96.

inventory quantities will be half the economic order quantity plus the safety stock.

THE MECHANICS OF THE SYSTEM

Fixing responsibility

As a business becomes more complex, the interdependent problems of production planning and inventory control become imposing enough to warrant appointing an executive to assume sole responsibility for implementing a coordinated inventory control policy. The scope of this position varies from company to company. In some firms, he may be a vice president in charge of production planning and control. In other firms, the planning and control functions may be separated. Duties of purchasing, receiving, and storing may be the responsibility of a single executive, although day-to-day duties may be delegated to various officers, such as a purchasing agent, a receiving-room foreman, and a storeroom foreman.

An important aspect of inventory and production control systems is that they may be largely dehumanized. For example, when reorder points, economic order quantities, safety stocks, and other technicalities are calculated, the entire system may be automated with the help of a digital computer. The system can then operate with a minimum dependence on human judgment. That is why inventory control systems are being increasingly computerized. However, human judgment cannot be eradicated altogether. The ingredients (costs, demand) of the model do frequently change and a constant surveillance for the sensitivity of the model to such changes is an important, and not too automatic, part of an effective control system.

Internal check

Just as in production operations, inventory control procedures should be systematized in order to promote efficiency and reduce errors, fraud, and waste. Commonly followed internal control rules[14] should be applied in setting up an inventory system. For example, the stores record clerk should not have access to the physical storeroom, nor should the storeroom employees have access to the formal stores records.

There is a temptation at this point to discuss a typical company system in detail, including descriptions of the routing of multi-copies of requisitions, purchase orders, vouchers, invoices, and receiving reports. However, we shall refrain from such a detailed study because (a) such descriptions belong in a book on accounting systems, (b) each system must be tailored to the specific needs of a company, and (c) dwelling on details

[14] For a discussion of internal control, see Chapter 22.

EXHIBIT 16-7

SAMPLE ROUTINE FOR PURCHASING MATERIALS

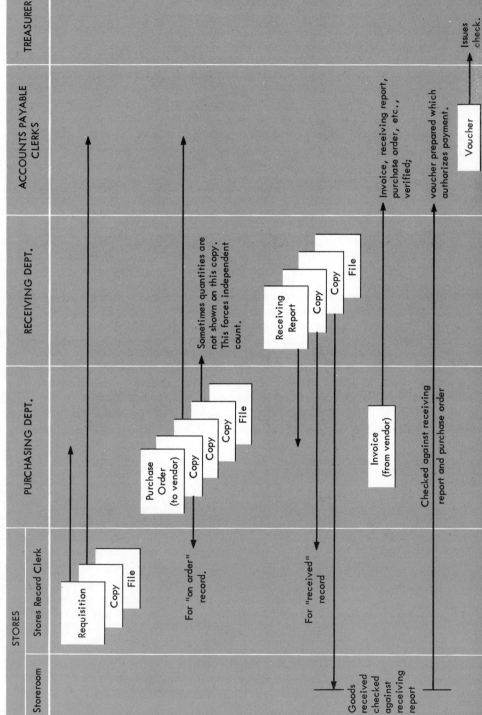

of paper work often beclouds the important general concepts that need the spotlight.

Purchase records

The purchasing department is responsible for getting favorable prices, following up irregularities, using approved suppliers, and taking advantage of discounts. Separate, sequential records for each item may be kept by purchase lots, showing dates, source, quantity, unit price, total costs, discounts, and special remarks. Thus, all pertinent data for control are kept on a current basis at the point where control is supposed to be exercised.

The paper-work routine for purchasing and receiving is shown in Exhibit 16-7. Purchasing agents should be free to devote their energies to obtaining optimum prices, investigating sources, and studying market conditions. Their buying should be triggered strictly by purchase requisitions. In general, inventory levels and purchase requisitions are ultimately the responsibility of production planning and control, not of the purchasing department.

Factory usage

An effective method of controlling material usage was described in Chapter 5, but we shall summarize it here. Production planning departments or foremen present standard bills (requisitions) of materials, including allowances for normal spoilage, to the storeroom. If standards are not met, different-colored excess material requisitions are used to obtain additional material. These should be routed to the foreman's superior so that immediate follow-up may be made. Any material left over is returned to the storeroom by inspectors or foremen.

INVENTORY VALUATION METHODS

Purpose of discussion of inventory methods

Management makes policy decisions, at one time or another, regarding methods of inventory valuation. These decisions are important because they directly affect the way income will be computed.

We have already seen how price fluctuations in inventories are accounted for under standard costing. The following discussion surveys alternate approaches to valuation of materials acquired at various prices.[15] The intention here is to demonstrate methodology rather than to dwell on important theoretical issues of inventory valuation which are discussed

---

[15] Fifo and weighted-average techniques under process costing are discussed in Chapters 19 and 20.

at length in typical introductory, intermediate, and advanced accounting texts. Also, the influence of income taxes, which is immense, is not discussed at length here.

Question of timing

With few exceptions, the differences between inventory methods are merely ones of timing cost releases in relation to income determination.[16] In short, when do inventory costs become expenses? Where it is impractical to identify inventories with specific usage or sales, some assumption is made for transferring certain costs out of inventory. The most commonly used assumption is one of the following three:

1. *First-in, first-out (FIFO)*. The earliest-acquired stock is assumed to be used first; the latest-acquired stock is assumed to be still on hand.

2. *Last-in, first-out (LIFO)*. The earliest-acquired stock is assumed to be still on hand; the latest-acquired stock is assumed to have been used immediately. The Lifo method releases the most recent (or last) inventory costs as cost of goods used or sold. It attempts to match the most current cost of obtaining inventory against sales for a period. As compared to Fifo, Lifo will result in less income during periods of rising prices and more income in periods of falling prices.

3. Some version of an *average-inventory method*. An example would be the *moving-average method*, whereby each purchase is lumped with the former inventory balance so that a new average unit price is used to price subsequent issues of inventory. This method may be used with a perpetual inventory system. A *weighted-average method* is often used with a periodic inventory system; this average is computed by dividing the total cost of the beginning inventory plus purchases by the total number of units in those two classes.

These methods are best understood through illustration.

Try to solve the problem yourself before consulting the answers that follow.

Example 3: Inventory Valuation (adapted from an A.I.C.P.A. examination). The Saunders Corporation uses raw material A in a manufacturing process. Information as to balances on hand, purchases, and requisitions of material A are given in the following table. You are to answer each question on the basis of this information.

(1) If a perpetual inventory record of material A is operated on a Fifo basis, it will show a *closing inventory* of:

(a) $150   (b) $152   (c) $159   (d) $162   (e) $170
(f) Answer not given.

(2) Assume that no perpetual inventory is maintained for material A, and that quantities are obtained by an annual physical count. The

---

[16] Certain last-in, first-out inventory situations where base stocks are temporarily depleted call for departures from strict historical costing.

Raw Material A

Date	Quantities			Dollars			
	Received	Issued	Balance	Unit Price	Received	Issued	Balance
Jan. 1			100	$1.50			$150
Jan. 24	300		400	1.56	$468		
Feb. 8		80	320				
Mar. 16		140	180				
June 11	150		330	$1.60	240		
Aug. 18		130	200				
Sept. 6		110	90				
Oct. 15	150		240	1.70	255		
Dec. 29		140	100				

accounting records show information as to purchases but not as to issues. On this assumption, the *closing inventory* on a Fifo basis will be:

(a) $150 (b) $156 (c) $159 (d) $160 (e) $170
(f) Answer not given.

(3) If a perpetual inventory record of material A is operated on a Lifo basis, it will show a *closing inventory* of:

(a) $150 (b) $152 (c) $156 (d) $160 (e) $170
(f) Answer not given.

(4) Assume that no perpetual inventory is maintained for material A, and that quantities are obtained by an annual physical count. The accounting records show information as to purchases but not as to issues. On this assumption, the *closing inventory* on a Lifo basis will be:

(a) $150 (b) $152 (c) $156 (d) $160 (e) $170
(f) Answer not given.

(5) If a perpetual inventory record of material A is operated on a moving-average basis, it will show a *closing inventory* which is:

(a) Lower than on the Lifo basis. (b) Lower than on the Fifo basis.
(c) Higher than on the Fifo basis. (d) Answer not given.

(6) The exact closing inventory in question (5) is $ _____ .

(7) Assume that no perpetual inventory is maintained, and that quantities are obtained by an annual physical count. The accounting records show information as to purchases but not as to issues. On this assumption, the closing inventory on a weighted-average basis will be $ _____ .

Answers and comments.

1. (e) $170. Under Fifo, the ending inventory valuation may be most easily obtained by first working back from the closing date until the number of units purchased equals the number of units in ending inventory. Then, by applying the appropriate unit purchase costs, the total dollar amount is obtained. In this example, 100 units @ $1.70 is $170.

2. (e) $170. The answer is identical under perpetual and periodic systems. Under a periodic inventory method, files must be combed for recent invoices until 100 units are tallied. In this case, the most recent invoice would suffice. In other cases, more than one invoice may be needed to cover the 100 units in the ending inventory.

3. (b) 90 units @ $1.50 plus 10 units @ $1.70 equals $152. Under Lifo, the ending inventory valuation generally may be obtained by working forward from the beginning inventory until the total number of units equals the number of units in ending inventory. Then, by applying the appropriate beginning inventory unit costs and the early current-purchase unit costs, the total dollar amount is obtained.

However, under a perpetual Lifo method, a temporary reduction (September 6) below the number of units in the beginning inventory calls for the assignment of the base-inventory price to the number of units released from the base inventory.

4. (a) 100 units @ $1.50, or $150. Under a periodic Lifo method, *a temporary* reduction below the number of units in the beginning inventory will have no effect upon the valuation of the ending inventory as long as the number of units in the count of ending inventory for the year as a whole is at least equal to the beginning inventory.

5. (b) Fifo assigns earliest costs to cost of sales and latest costs to inventory. Unit prices have been rising during the period. Therefore, more of the earlier and lower-cost units will be contained in the ending inventory under the moving-average method than under Fifo.

6. $165.125. This technique requires the computation of a new average unit cost after each acquisition; this unit cost is used for all issues until the next purchase is made.

MOVING-AVERAGE

Perpetual Method

Date	Received Units	Received Price	Received Amount	Issued Units	Issued Price	Issued Amount	Balance Units	Balance Price	Balance Amount
Jan. 1							100	$1.50	$150.00
Jan. 24	300	$1.56	$468				400	1.545	618.00
Feb. 8				80	$1.545	$123.60	320	1.545	494.40
Mar. 16				140	1.545	216.30	180	1.545	278.10
June 11	150	1.60	240				330	1.57	518.10
Aug. 18				130	1.57	204.10	200	1.57	314.00
Sept. 6				110	1.57	172.70	90	1.57	141.30
Oct. 15	150	1.70	255				240	1.65125	396.30
Dec. 29				140	1.65125	231.175	100	1.65125	165.125

Recapitulation

Costs to account for: $150 + $468 + $240 + $255 = $1,113.000

Deduct: Issues   947.875

Ending balance $ 165.125

7. $159. (100 units × $1.59.)

WEIGHTED-AVERAGE

Periodic Method

Date	Units	Unit Price	Dollars
Jan. 1	100	$1.50	$ 150
Jan. 24	300	1.56	468
June 11	150	1.60	240
Oct. 15	150	1.70	255
To account for	700		$1,113

Weighted Unit Cost, $1,113 ÷ 700   = $159

Costs released	600 @ $1.59	$ 954
Costs in ending inventory	100 @ $1.59	159
Costs accounted for		$1,113

Note that the assumption of a weighted-average approach is subject to criticism because the October 15 purchase influences the costing of issues throughout the year, even though, strictly speaking, the cost of earlier issues would not have been affected by purchases made later in the year.

Lifo versus Fifo

If unit prices would not fluctuate, all inventory methods would show identical results. Price changes appear in the financial records in different ways, depending on the specific inventory method used. Lifo ordinarily reflects current purchase prices in current operating results, whereas Fifo delays recognition of price effects. If price changes are volatile, year-to-year incomes may differ dramatically between Lifo and Fifo approaches.

Balance sheet presentations are also affected by the choice of Lifo or Fifo. Lifo usage results in older and older, and hence meaningless, prices being shown in inventory if stocks grow through the years, whereas Fifo tends to reflect more nearly current prices on the balance sheet.

If prices are rising, Lifo shows less income than Fifo, and thus it minimizes income taxes. Also, the periodic Lifo method permits immediate influencing of net income by timing of purchases, a feature that has not received the attention it deserves. For example, if prices are rising and a company desires to show less income in a given year because of income tax or other reasons, all that need be done is to buy a large amount of inventory near the end of the year—thus releasing higher costs to expense than ordinarily.

It should also be recognized that neither Fifo or Lifo isolates and measures the effects of price fluctuations as special managerial problems. For example, when prices rise, Fifo buries price gains in the regular income figure, whereas Lifo excludes the effects of price changes from the income statement:

		Lifo		Fifo	
Sales, 5,000 @ 20¢		$1,000		$1,000	
Inventory, beginning	1,000 @ $.10 = $100		$100		
Purchases	5,000 @ $.15 = 750		750		
	$850		$850		
Inventory, ending	1,000 @ $.10 = 100	750	1,000 @ $.15 = 150	700	
Gross margin		$ 250		$ 300	

The $50 price gain (which is attributable to the 1,000 units in ending inventory @ $.05) is submerged in the $300 Fifo gross margin figure and is ignored in the $250 Lifo gross margin figure.

Here again we see the benefit of a standard cost approach. When currently attainable standards are in use, standard costing automatically provides a measure of price "gains" or "losses" that can be reported separately on an income statement. This has two advantages: (a) it prevents price changes from influencing appraisals of efficiency in operations; (b) it spotlights and measures the impact of some price changes on over-all company results.

SUMMARY

Inventory control is primarily concerned with optimizing inventory balances so that net income is maximized. Recordkeeping in itself is only one of the important phases of inventory control. Top management's task is to formulate inventory policies that will result in optimum inventory investment, will promote efficiency, and will avoid errors, fraud, and waste.

Associated costs which are affected by various inventory policies are headed by the opportunity cost of interest on investment. Other costs include quantity discounts, contribution margins on lost sales, space costs, overtime premiums, idle time, expediting, transportation, obsolescence, handling, training, learning, setup, order processing, order filling, personal property taxes, insurance, and handling. These costs are often difficult to isolate and measure, especially with regard to their differential behavior between alternatives. However, attempts at sensible measurement at least cast light on a *range* of optimum alternatives.

Different control policies may be applied to different segments of the inventory. Thus, a variety of purchase timing, storing, receiving, and recording techniques may be employed at the same time within the same company.

Modern mathematical methods, especially linear programming, have been applied on a wide front to the problems of production planning and inventory control. The complexity of inventory control is such that many consulting firms specialize in the area to the extent of studying a business's inventory problems and tailor-making a special slide rule for computing economic order quantities.

The subject matter of this chapter again shows how the field of managerial accounting spills over and invades allied fields such as engineering, modern mathematics, and business policies. The complexities of modern business make it increasingly difficult to construct fences around technical specialties.

First-in, first-out, last-in, first-out, and various average methods of inventory valuation are used to contend with fluctuations in unit prices. However, none of these methods pinpoint a measure of price "gains" or "losses" that can be reported separately. Standard costing, on the other hand, does automatically provide helpful information about price changes.

PROBLEMS FOR SELF-STUDY

Problem 1. Review Example 1 in the chapter. Suppose that the annual purchase order cost was $20.00 per order instead of $10.00. What is the economic order quantity?

Problem 2. Review Example 2 in the chapter. Suppose that management specified that stockouts should occur about 11 per cent of the time. What safety stock should be provided?

Problem 3. Review Example 3.

Solution 1.

$$E = \sqrt{\frac{2\,(5,000)\,\$20}{\$.50}} = \sqrt{\frac{\$200,000}{\$.50}} = \sqrt{400,000} = 633$$

Note that the higher the order cost, the higher the economic order quantity.

Solution 2. Weekly sales exceeded six units 11 per cent of the time and seven units 5 per cent of the time. If the safety stock is three units (seven units minus average sales of four units), stockouts will occur whenever weekly sales exceed six units, or about 11 per cent of the time.

Solution 3. See the solution which follows Example 3.

QUESTIONS, PROBLEMS, AND CASES

Note: Problems 16-13 through 16-18 cover inventory valuation. Problems 16-19 through 16-26 cover planning and control. Problem 16-26 is especially recommended.

16-1. "There are two danger points that management usually wants to avoid in controlling inventories." Explain.

16-2. "Inventory records are only a means to the end of inventory control." Explain.

16-3. Certain costs associated with inventory policies do not appear on formal accounting records. Enumerate at least three.

16-4. "Identical space costs for inventory can be zero during some months and sizable during other months." Explain.

16-5. Define *economic order quantity*.

16-6. "The practical approach to determining economic order quantity is concerned with locating a minimum cost *range* rather than a minimum cost *point*." Explain.

16-7. Define: *lead time, reorder point*.

16-8. What is a *safety stock?* What techniques are used to compute safety stocks?

16-9. Describe a "two-bin" inventory system.

16-10. What are the major responsibilities of the purchasing department?

16-11. Distinguish between the *moving-average* and the *weighted-average* inventory methods.

16-12. "Standard costing is superior to both Lifo and Fifo for isolating and measuring the effects of price fluctuations as special managerial problems." Why?

16-13. Cost Elements of Materials Stores. You have a client who wishes to include, as part of the cost of raw material in stores, all of the cost of acquiring and handling incoming material. You are asked to:

1. Name the principal items which may enter into the cost of material acquisition and handling.

2. Give the arguments favoring the inclusion of these items as a part of the cost of raw material in stores.

3. Give the arguments against the inclusion of these items as a part of the cost of raw material in stores.   [C.P.A.]

16-14. Comparison of Lifo and Fifo. The Kiner Coal Co. does not maintain a perpetual inventory system. The inventory of coal on June 30 shows 1,000 tons at $6 per ton. The following purchases were made during July:

July 5	2,000 Tons @ $7 per ton
July 15	500 Tons @ $8 per ton
July 25	600 Tons @ $9 per ton

A physical inventory on July 31 shows a total of 1,200 tons on hand. Revenue from sales of coal for July totals $30,000.

REQUIRED: Compute the inventory value as of July 31, using:

1. Lifo—Last in, First Out.
2. Fifo—First in, First Out.

16-15. Inventory Card, Moving-Average. Steel Stores Limited is a dealer in steel products.

The company purchases its steel from various mills. Prices are f.o.b. point of shipment. On January 1, freight costs were $5.00 per ton; but on January 14, they advanced 10 per cent. The steel industry uses the standard 2,000-pound ton.

During the month of January, the following transactions in Hot Rolled Sheets, 60" long and 36" wide, took place:

Jan. 1	Inventory	10 tons at $6.00 per 100 lbs.
Jan. 2	Purchased	3 tons at $5.50 per 100 lbs.
Jan. 3	Sold	2 tons
Jan. 5	Purchased	2 tons at $5.60 per 100 lbs.

Jan.	6	Sold	3 tons
Jan.	10	Purchased	8 tons at $5.55 per 100 lbs.
Jan.	12	Sold	8 tons
Jan.	15	Purchased	2 tons at $5.55 per 100 lbs.
Jan.	16	Sold	2 tons
Jan.	30	Purchased	5 tons at $5.60 per 100 lbs.
Jan.	31	Sold	7 tons

Sales prices are determined by applying a mark-up of 30 per cent to laid-down costs at the beginning of each month.

REQUIRED:

1. Show these transactions as they would appear on a perpetual inventory card, using the moving-average cost method. Calculations should be made to the nearest cent.

2. Calculate the gross profit for the month.

3. Name two methods other than the moving-average cost method which could have been used in pricing the issue transactions above.   [S.I.C.A.]

16-16. Multiple-Choice; Comparison of Inventory Methods. The Berg Corporation *began business on January 1, 19x4.* Information about its inventories under different valuation methods is shown below. Using this information, you are to choose the phrase which best answers each of the following questions. For each question, insert on an answer sheet *the letter which identifies the answer you select.*

INVENTORY

	Lifo Cost	Fifo Cost	Market	Lower of Cost or Market
Dec. 31, 19x4	$10,200	$10,000	$ 9,600	$ 8,900
Dec. 31, 19x5	9,100	9,000	8,800	8,500
Dec. 31, 19x6	10,300	11,000	12,000	10,900

1. The inventory basis which would show the *highest net income for 19x4* is:

    (a) Lifo cost   (b) Fifo cost
    (c) Market   (d) Lower of cost or market

2. The inventory basis which would show the *highest net income for 19x5* is:

    (a) Lifo cost   (b) Fifo cost
    (c) Market   (d) Lower of cost or market

3. The inventory basis which would show the *lowest net income for the three years combined* is:

    (a) Lifo cost   (b) Fifo cost
    (c) Market   (d) Lower of cost or market

4. For the year 19x5, how much higher or lower would profits be on the *Fifo cost basis* than on the *lower-of-cost-or-market basis?*

    (a) $400 higher   (b) $400 lower   (c) $600 higher
    (d) $600 lower   (e) $1,000 higher   (f) $1,000 lower
      (g) $1,400 higher   (h) $1,400 lower

5. On the basis of the information given, it appears that *the movement of prices* for the items in the inventory was:

(a) Up in 19x4 and down in 19x6   (b) Up in both 19x4 and 19x6

(c) Down in 19x4 and up in 19x6   (d) Down in both 19x4 and

19x6   [C.P.A.]

16-17.   Reconciliation of Inventory Records.   As part of a test of inventory control, you examined the perpetual inventory records of stockroom M. A full set of records (subsidiary and control) is maintained in the factory while a controlling account is also kept in the accounting department.

You are required to set up a summarizing schedule in money amounts which simultaneously reflects the flow of materials (starting with initial inventory and ending with final inventory) and reconciles the accounting department records with those of the factory in regard to opening inventory, receipts, withdrawals of materials, and ending inventory.

The items to be considered in preparing this schedule are as follows:

(1) Receipts of materials in stockroom M, entered properly on factory records but treated by the accounting department as stockroom N, $240.

(2) Correction made by the accounting department of an error in a prior period. The error was the recording of an $800 withdrawal of materials as $500. The original item had been correctly entered by the factory record clerk.

(3) A shortage of item M-143, amounting to $45, which was noted and entered during the period on the factory records but information on which had not been transmitted to the accounting department.

(4) An initial inventory, according to factory records, of $11,000 in stockroom M. Receipts were $14,000 and withdrawals were $13,000, according to the records of the accounting department.   [C.P.A.]

16-18.   Prepare Correcting Journal Entries.   Consider each of the following situations separately. Prepare any correcting general journal entries called for by the following information:

1. During December, there were raw materials costing $1,000 which had been returned to vendors for which no entry appeared on the books.

2. Freight out of $300 paid on shipments sold f.o.b. destination to customers was charged to Stores.

3. The debit side of the Stores Control account had been overfooted (*overfooted* means "over-added") by $100.

4. A $10,000 shipment of raw materials received from vendors was charged to Selling Expense Control and credited to Accounts Payable.

5. Some goods returned by customers for credit had been recorded as follows:

dr. Returned sales	$1,000	
cr. Accounts receivable		$1,000
(To credit their accounts at selling price.)		
dr. Stores	$ 700	
cr. Cost of goods sold		$ 700
(To increase our inventory by the factory cost of goods returned.)		

6. On December 28, 19x1, a company clerk discovered that Job #109 (100 units), which was completed and half of which was sold in October, had accumulated $200 of direct material cost and $300 of direct labor cost but had

not been assigned any overhead. The overhead rate is 50 per cent of direct labor cost. Half the units of Job #109 are still in finished stock.

16-19. Reorder Point and Economic Lot Size. An automobile manufacturer has a planned usage of 500,000 automobile tires of a certain size during the next year. The incremental cost of placing an order is $8.00. The cost of storing one tire for one year is $2.00. Lead time on an order is five days, and the company is going to keep a reserve supply of two days' usage.

Usage is assumed to be constant over a 250-workday year.

REQUIRED:

1. Calculate the reorder point.
2. Calculate the economic order quantity.
3. Graph the inventory level (Y-axis) against time (X-axis) through two complete inventory cycles. Show the reorder points.

16-20. Miscellaneous Inventory Control Computations. Lt. Brighteyes, supply officer at a remote radar site, has been informed that the lead time for his supplies will be reduced from the present 180 days to 90 days.

The maximum daily usage of 12AU6 Pentodes has been 10 per day; average, 8 per day; minimum, 6 per day. Average inventory during the past two years has been 1360 tubes. Determine the minimum inventory, reorder point, normal maximum stock level, absolute maximum stock level, and the economic order quantity which Lt. Brighteyes has been submitting.

Do the same for the new 90-day level, *assuming that the economic size is unchanged.*

16-21. Stabilizing Production. The cost of manufacturing a durable seasonal product for which there is a predictable seasonal demand is 20 per cent for material, 60 per cent for highly skilled direct labor, and 20 per cent for overhead. The banker on whom the manufacturer relies for additional working capital when necessary is urging him to stabilize inventories; the plant manager is urging him to stabilize production.

List and describe briefly:
1. The advantages of *stabilizing* inventories.
2. The advantages of *stabilizing* production.   [C.P.A.]

16-22. Economic Order Quantity; Price Discounts. A medium-sized manufacturing company uses 50 barrels of soap a year in one of their plants. It costs them $1.00 a year to store a barrel and a purchase order costs $10.00 to process.

The following discount schedule applies to the purchase price of the soap:

Quantity	Discount
1– 9	None
10–49	$0.50 per barrel
50–99	$1.00 per barrel
100–up	$2.00 per barrel

REQUIRED:

Determine the economic order quantity, and briefly show why it is where it is.

16-23.   Inventory Planning and Monthly Cost Savings.   Grossman Drug Stores, Inc., buys a large, economy-sized tooth-paste package to market under its own brand name. Monthly sales of this product in all of their stores is about 60,000 units and quite steady.

The company now purchases this item in lots of 60,000 at a unit price of $1.00 and delivery of 15 days. An 18,000-unit base inventory is kept at all times, so that the reorder point is 48,000 units.

The supplier has offered to sell Grossman Drug Stores, Inc., this item for 90¢ a unit if they will increase the order size to 300,000 units and accept 30-day delivery. If they accept this plan, they will still have to maintain an 18,000-unit minimum inventory.

If the company goes through with the proposed change, it will have to rent extra storage space at a cost of $6,000 per year. Other expenses associated with the increased space will total $4,000 per year.

Also, if the new plan is adopted, handling costs will be increased $0.83 $\frac{1}{3}$ per hundred on units sold.

REQUIRED:

1. Calculate the monthly savings (loss) if the new plan is adopted.
2. Grossman Stores, Inc., expects, and can obtain, a return of 12 per cent per annum on invested capital elsewhere. The company policy is to impute a 1 per cent per month interest charge on average inventory investment in computing the net monthly saving. What is the monthly saving (or loss)? Would you recommend that the new plan be adopted?

16-24.   Make or Buy.   The Gamma Company is considering the feasibility of purchasing from a nearby jobber a component which it now makes. The jobber will furnish the component in the necessary quantities at a unit price of $4.50. Transportation and storage costs would be negligible.

Gamma produces the component from a single raw material. The firm at present orders material in economic lots of 1,000 units at a unit cost of $1.00; average annual usage is 10,000 units. The yearly storage cost (including rent, taxes, and return on inventory investment) is computed at $.50 per unit. The minimum inventory is set at 200 units. Direct labor costs for the component are $3.00 per unit; fixed manufacturing overhead is applied at a rate of $2.00 per unit based on a normal annual activity of 10,000 units. In addition to the above costs, the machine on which the components are produced is leased at a rate of $100 per month.

Should Gamma make or buy the component?

16-25.   Inventory Control and Television Tubes.   The Nemmers Co. assembles private-brand television sets for a retail chain, under a contract requiring delivery of 100 sets per day for each of 250 business days per year. Each set requires a picture tube which Nemmers buys outside, for $20 each. The tubes are loaded on trucks at the supplier's factory door and are then delivered by a trucking service at a charge of $100 per trip, regardless of the size of the shipment. The cost of storing the tubes (including the desired rate of return on investment) is $2 per tube per year. Because production is stable throughout the year, the average inventory is one-half the size of the truck lot. Tabulate the relevant annual cost of various truck-lot sizes at 5, 10, 15, 25, 50, and 250 trips per year. Show your results graphically. (Note that the $20 unit cost of tubes is common to all alternatives and hence may be ignored.)

16-26.   Comprehensive Study of Inventory Planning and Control.
The Ward Company is trying to obtain better means of controlling inventory
levels and attendant costs for an expensive part which they have been using for
some time. Studies of cost behavior patterns reveal the following information:

Variable costs of placing and following up purchase orders (stationery,
postage, telephone, etc.) total $3.00 per order.   Other clerical costs, such as
salaries and related office equipment expenses, have a step cost behavior as
follows:

For every additional 200 orders processed per week, there is a $70.00
increase in purchasing costs, a $60.00 increase in accounting costs, and
an $80.00 increase in receiving costs.

Insurance and taxes on inventory are 4 per cent of average inventory
value per year.

The factory is rented at a cost of $60,000 per year.   It contains 100,000
square feet of floor space, of which 3,000 square feet is reserved for storing this
item.   Excess storage space is available in the neighborhood at 75¢ per square
foot per year.   Extra handling costs for using excess storage space will be 2½¢
per inventory unit in excess storage space per year.   The article requires storage
space, allowing for aisles, of three square feet each and can be stacked six
units high.

Breakage, obsolescence, and deterioration amount to about 2 per cent of
average inventory per year.

The company's average cost of capital is 10 per cent per annum.   The
company uses this rate for inventory investment decisions.

Ward Company works 52 weeks a year, 5 days per week.   It uses an
average of 100 subassemblies per workday, but usage fluctuates from as low as
50 to as high as 150 per day.   Many suppliers are available; but, regardless
of the source of supply and the size of the order, it will take two weeks from
the time a purchase order is placed until delivery.   Top management wants to
keep an ordinary minimum stock of 1,500 units.

The purchasing agent is anxious to take advantage of savings in unit
invoice and freight costs by purchasing in large quantities.   Pertinent purchasing
data are as follows:

	Invoice Cost		Freight Cost	
Lot Size	Unit Cost	Total Cost	Unit Cost	Total Cost
1,000	$55.00	$ 55,000.00	$5.00	$ 5,000.00
2,000	55.00	110,000.00	5.00	10,000.00
4,000	55.00	220,000.00	5.00	20,000.00
5,000	54.00	270,000.00	5.00	25,000.00
6,000	54.00	324,000.00	4.40	26,400.00
8,000	54.00	432,000.00	4.00	32,000.00
10,000	54.00	540,000.00	3.80	38,000.00
13,000	53.50	695,500.00	3.80	49,400.00
26,000	52.00	1,352,000.00	3.50	91,000.00

REQUIRED:

Special Note: Assume that the base stock is already on hand and is therefore irrelevant.   The average inventory that is relevant is exclusive of the base.

Assume, too, that the maximum inventory to be computed for commitments to excess storage space will be the *absolute* maximum, computed as follows: order point less minimum usage + standard order.

1. What order size should Ward Company use? Support your answer by tabular analysis of the relevant costs for each lot size given above from 1,000 to 26,000.

2. What considerations other than the quantitative data may influence the decision here?

3. Comment on the cost behavior patterns in the situation. Which costs appear to be the most crucial?

alternative methods of overhead application and reapportionment

This chapter explores the following facets of overhead accounting: (a) different production bases for overhead application, (b) departmental overhead rates, (c) service department costs, and (d) proper volume level for developing overhead rates. Although the major issues discussed are primarily related to the product-costing purpose of cost accounting, the problem of control of service department costs is also covered.

Manufacturing overhead items, by definition, are those factory costs which are necessary for production but which are not conveniently traceable to specific physical units. Basically, the accountant lumps all individual overhead items together and applies them to products through the use of averages. In its simplest form, this means that a $100,000 overhead total would be spread over 100,000 units at a rate of $1.00 per unit. But the application of overhead is usually far from simple. The very nature of the relationship of indirect costs and physical products necessitates some assumptions when overhead rates are being developed. Nevertheless, the choice of assumptions is crucial because individual product cost computations, rightly or wrongly, do influence pricing policies in many businesses —particularly job shops—and do influence reported income and inventory valuations.

DIFFERENT PRODUCTION BASES FOR OVERHEAD APPLICATION

Because individual overhead costs cannot be traced directly to physical units, some factor common to both physical units and to fluctuations in overhead cost as a whole should be used as the basis for overhead application. This common denominator differs between companies, but the most widely used bases are selected after considering (a) the factors already associated with the individual products or jobs (for example, direct material and direct labor), (b) necessary clerical costs and effort in application, and (c) differences in final results. Where results do not differ significantly, the easier method is used. *The most important criterion for selecting a base is: relate overhead to its most causal factor.*[1]

The following bases are widely used. Two or more bases may be used by a company for applying different classes of overhead.

Physical units produced

The formula used is as follows: Total Overhead ÷ Total Units Produced = Overhead Rate. This base is valid only when the units produced are homogeneous and receive nearly identical attention and effort.

Direct labor hours

Most overhead costs are more closely related to time expiration than to any other factor. Fixed costs such as depreciation, rent, taxes, and insurance relate to a given time period. Indirect labor and supply usage are most closely related to the input of hours of effort. That is why time devoted to specific products is often the most reasonable factor for correlating overhead with products. Time is traced to specific products by using work tickets for direct labor. Overhead rates are developed by dividing total estimated overhead by total estimated direct labor hours. Thus, the amount of overhead applied to any given product is dependent on the amount of time devoted to an operation or product.

Machine hours

In these days of mechanized production, machine time is often a better indicator of overhead cost incurrence than direct labor time. Depreciation, property taxes, supply usage, and indirect labor frequently are more closely related to machinery utilization than to direct labor usage. In theory, then, machine time may be the most valid base for overhead application.

In practice, however, machine time is not used as often as labor time because of the added clerical cost and the difficulty of computing ma-

[1] It is an oversimplification to say that there is a single cause-and-effect relationship between overhead incurrence and the application base used. William J. Vatter, "Limitations of Overhead Allocation," *Accounting Review* (April, 1945), pp. 164–165, observed: "Every cause has a number of effects; every event arises from many causes; all incidents and observations are bound together by many ties. All costs are more or less interwoven in a complex fabric; in large measure, costs are joint as to their incurrence, as well as to their associations with various costing units."

chine time on individual jobs. Machine time may be ignored where the relationship of labor time or labor costs to machine time is unchanging between jobs; that is, the final overhead application to a given type of job would not differ (for example, one direct laborer runs two similar machines). This neglect of machine time as a base is acceptable only as long as the final job costs are not greatly distorted.

Direct labor cost

If labor rates are nearly uniform for every operation, the use of a labor *dollar* base for overhead application yields the same results as using direct labor *hours*. Otherwise, direct labor *hours* is the better base in most instances. For example, a senior worker may earn $3.00 per hour while a junior worker may earn $2.50 per hour. If a 200-per-cent-of-direct-labor-cost rate is in effect, the overhead cost of a given job which requires one hour of direct labor would be $6.00 if the senior worker were used and $5.00 if the junior worker were used. Standard or average labor rates generally prevent such ridiculous results.

Direct labor *dollars* as an overhead base may be conceptually better than labor *hours* where many overhead items represent fringe labor costs, which are primarily tied to direct labor *cost* or where high-cost direct laborers make the greatest use of high-cost facilities and complex machinery.

Direct material

Unless the labor and equipment needed for material handling are a major part of overhead, the use of direct material dollars or weights is not a valid theoretical basis for overhead application. Again, material may be used as a base where the final results are the same regardless of the overhead base adopted. Sometimes storeroom and material-handling overhead is separated from other factory overhead and is applied to jobs on the basis of direct material weight or bulk. The remaining overhead items would be applied by using some other base.

Comparison of bases

If all data are accurate and planned capacity is achieved, the annual overhead will be fully applied to jobs regardless of the base selected. The major problem in choosing a proper base is to relate overhead to its most closely related causal factor. (Avoid the misconception that it is correct to use the number of tranquilizer tablets consumed by the president as a base if it best correlates with overhead behavior. Such coincidences may lead to misleading overhead rates, because the apparent relationship is mere happenstance and not a continuing one. Apparent correlation is only part of the check.)

As long as all of the possible causal factors are used proportionately on individual jobs, each job will get a proper amount of overhead. Exhibit 17-1 shows that the job cost would be the same regardless of the base used because all of the possible bases are used proportionately.

Exhibit 17-1 illustrates the following important points:

1. Either direct labor dollars or direct labor time may be used as a basis for overhead application as long as the direct labor dollars and hours vary in direct proportion, that is, as long as labor rates are uniform on similar jobs.

2. Where costs related to machines are the predominant overhead factor, machine-hours should be used instead of labor hours if both do not fluctuate in proportion. In other words, if one operator runs one machine for a certain job and three similar machines for another job, other things being equal, the machine-hour base is more rational than a labor base.

3. If labor time has a proportionate relationship to machine time, it is unnecessary to use machine-hours because the final costs of a job will not differ.

4. The base factor which is easiest and cheapest to apply should be selected as long as individual job costs are not significantly affected. Note in Exhibit 17-1 that the final results are the same on a specific job because all base factors are used proportionately. But if the possible bases are not used proportionately on individual jobs, certain jobs may receive distorted amounts of overhead. This latter point is not illustrated specifically in the exhibit. However, the point can be readily seen by changing the number of machine-hours on Job No. 2 from five to six. This would change the overhead application, using a machine-hour rate, from $25 to $30.

DEPARTMENTAL OVERHEAD RATES

Plant-wide rate versus departmental rates

Most factories produce more than one product. The variety of products command varying attention and effort, different material usages, and different production routings. These situations call for refinement of overhead application by departments or cost centers so that different products may bear their related share of factory overhead.

Assume that one job is routed through two departments: Machining and Finishing. The Machining Department is heavily mechanized with costly semi-automatic and automatic equipment. The Finishing Department contains a few simple tools and is dependent on painstaking skilled workmanship. Overhead costs would be relatively large in machining and small in finishing.

Now consider two jobs: the first requires one hour of machining time and ten hours of finishing time. The second requires nine hours of machining time and two hours of finishing time. If a single, plant-wide, blanket overhead rate based on labor hours is used, each job would receive the same total overhead application. But this would not be sensible, because Job No. 1 made light use of overhead-incurring factors while Job

EXHIBIT 17-1

COMPARISON OF OVERHEAD APPLICATION WHEN BASES ARE USED PROPORTIONATELY

Annual overhead budget data:	Total	Possible Rates
Total overhead	$100,000	
Direct labor cost	$200,000	50% of direct labor cost
Direct labor hours	100,000	$1.00 per DLH
Direct material usage	$400,000	25% of direct material
Machine hours	20,000	$5.00 per machine-hour

Job data:

Job No. 1		
Direct labor hours		5
Machine-hours		1
Direct material	$ 20	
Direct labor cost	10	
Prime cost	$ 30	

Possible Overhead Application Using Following Bases:

	Direct Material	Direct Labor Hours	Direct Labor	Machine-Hours
Overhead	.25($20) = $5	$1.00(5 hr.) = $5	.50($10) = $5	1 hr.($5) = $5
Total job cost	$ 35			

Job No. 2		
Direct labor hours		25
Machine-hours		5
Direct material	$100	
Direct labor cost	50	
Prime cost	$150	
Overhead	.25($100) = $25	$1.00(25 hr.) = $25	.50($50) = $25	5 hr.($5) = $25
Total job cost	$175			

No. 2 made heavy use of such services. Departmental rates, as shown in Exhibit 17-2 result in a more acceptable linking of overhead with specific jobs when products do not move uniformly through the plant.

EXHIBIT 17-2

PLANT-WIDE OVERHEAD RATE VERSUS DEPARTMENTAL OVERHEAD RATES

	Plant-Wide Rate		Departmental Rates		
	Machining	Finishing	Machining	Finishing	
Budgeted annual overhead	$100,000	$ 8,000	$100,000	$ 8,000	
Direct labor hours	10,000	10,000	10,000	10,000	
Blanket rate per DLH: $108,000 ÷ 20,000	$ 5.40				
Departmental rates per DLH			$ 10.00	$ .80	
Overhead application:					
Job No. 1					
Labor time, 11 hours @ $5.40	$59.40				
or Labor time:					
Machining, 1 hour @ $10.00			$ 10.00		Total
Finishing, 10 hours @ $.80				$ 8.00	$18.00
Job No. 2					
Labor time, 11 hours @ $5.40	$59.40				
or Labor time:					
Machining 9 hours @ $10.00			$ 90.00		
Finishing, 2 hours @ $.80				$ 1.60	$91.60

To summarize, when products are heterogeneous, receiving uneven attention and effort as they move through various departments or cost centers, departmental or cost-center overhead rates are necessary to achieve representative product costs.

Different bases for different departments

Some companies use different overhead bases for different departments. Exhibit 17-2 used direct labor hours as the base for the Machining Department because it was assumed that direct labor time was proportionate to machine time. In Exhibit 17-2, if labor time was not proportionate to machine time, machine-hours would be the overhead base in the Machining Department whereas labor hours would continue to be the base in the Finishing Department. Some machines may be almost entirely automatic; or an operator may be able to run two or three machines simultaneously on some jobs while he may be able to run only one machine at a time on other jobs.

SERVICE DEPARTMENT COSTS

Service departments exist to facilitate production. Examples of service departments are Cafeteria, Maintenance, Personnel, Medical, Production Control, Production Planning, Storerooms, Building and Grounds, and Tool Rooms. These departments render services which benefit operations as a whole, even though products do not physically flow through any service departments. Service department costs are, therefore, (a) accumulated by departmental responsibility for control purposes and (b) reapportioned to producing departments for product-costing purposes. Thus, predetermined overhead rates are based, not only on producing department overhead, but also on the producing department's "fair" share of service department costs. The premise for this inclusion of service department costs in overhead rates is that the service department cost is every bit as much a product cost as are the lubricants used by the Machining Department. First, let us consider the relationships of service departments to product costing; then we shall consider problems of control.

SERVICE DEPARTMENTS AND PRODUCT COSTING

The relationships of various overhead items to physical products are not all alike. It is fairly easy to see a relationship between a product

EXHIBIT 17-3

TYPICAL BASES FOR REAPPORTIONMENT OF SERVICE DEPARTMENT
COSTS TO PRODUCTION DEPARTMENTS

Service Department	Base for Reapportionment of Costs
Building and Grounds	Square footage or cubic footage.
Cafeteria	Number of workers.
Cost Accounting	Labor hours.
Engineering	*Analysis of services rendered each department; labor hours.
Maintenance	Direct charges on basis of materials used plus hours worked for each department.
Material Handling	Units carried; tonnage; hours of service rendered.
Medical	Number of employees; labor hours; number of cases.
Personnel or Employment	Number of workers; rate of labor turnover; number of workers hired; *analysis of time spent for each department.
Production Planning and Control	Machine-hours; labor hours; analysis of services rendered.
Power	Metered usage; capacity of equipment; machine-hours; formula weighting capacity and machine-hours.
Receiving, Shipping, and Stores	Pounds handled; requisitions; receiving slips; issues.
Tool Room	Requisitions.

*Sometimes detailed analyses or surveys are made of services rendered over two, six, or twelve months; the results of the "sample" are used as a basis for reapportionment until conditions warrant another sample survey.

and the salaries of material handlers, the power costs of running equipment, and the consumption of small cutting tools. Relationships between product and overhead costs become more hazy and tenuous when one tries to link the factory nurse's salary, the costs of personnel testing, the loss from the factory cafeteria, and the cost of the factory picnic to specific products. Still, the general opinion prevails that service departments facilitate production and that no product cost should be relieved of an "equitable" share of these auxiliary costs.

The general idea is to somehow funnel all factory costs, whether they originate in service departments or production departments, to the *production departments*. In turn, these costs are applied to *products*, using overhead rates that encompass both production and service department costs:

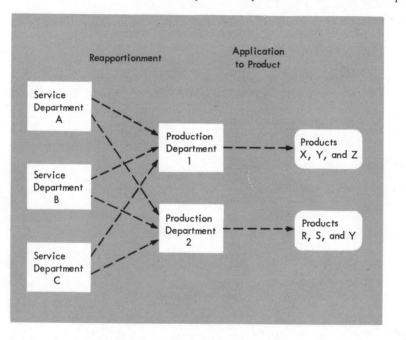

Criteria for selection of reapportionment bases

As can be seen in Exhibit 17-3, there is a wide variety of commonly used bases. Criteria for selection of a base include (a) physical identification or use, as evidenced by repair orders, requisitions, and power meters; (b) facilities provided, as evidenced by square feet occupied and rated capacity of electrical equipment; and (c) ease of reapportionment, as evidenced by using number of employees as bases for reapportioning personnel, medical, and cafeteria costs when more refined bases could be theoretically developed. The latter criterion, ease of reapportionment, is often overriding. This should temper the accountant's natural inclination to revere the "accuracy" of resultant product costs.

Assume that a company has four departments. The two service departments are General Factory Administration and Engineering. The two production departments are Machining and Assembly. Overhead costs are budgeted on a flexible basis and are accumulated by department responsibility for control purposes. For product-costing purposes, the service department costs at levels that support normal production activity are reapportioned to other departments. The base for reapportionment is the common denominator that best measures the relative benefits received by the other service and producing departments. The data for our example follow:

	Service Departments		Producing Departments		
	General Factory Administration	Engineering	Machining	Assembly	
	1	2	A	B	Totals
Overhead costs before reapportionment of service department costs	$600,000	$116,000	$400,000	$200,000	$1,316,000
Proportions of service furnished: By Department 1(based on total man-hours):					
Total man-hours		24,000	12,000	36,000	72,000
Proportion		$\frac{2}{6}$	$\frac{1}{6}$	$\frac{3}{6}$	$\frac{6}{6}$
By Department 2 (based on engineering hours worked for each department):					
Engineering hours	2,000		16,000	2,000	20,000
Proportion	10%		80%	10%	100%

Direct reapportionment — method 1

Direct reapportionment, or some similar method, is the most widely used method for reapportionment of service department costs. This method ignores any service rendered by one service department to another; it reapportions each service department's total costs directly to the producing departments. Note in Exhibit 17-4 that this method ignores the service rendered by the General Factory Administration Department to the Engineering Department and also the service rendered by Engineering to General Factory Administration. The base used for reapportionment of General Factory Administration costs is the 48,000 man-hours worked in the producing departments. Distinguish between *total* labor hours (which includes indirect hours) and *direct* labor hours. Total labor hours are often used as bases for reapportionments, whereas direct labor hours are often used as bases for developing predetermined overhead rates in producing departments for product-costing purposes.

EXHIBIT 17-4

DIRECT METHOD OF REAPPORTIONMENT

			Department		
	1	2	A	B	Total
Overhead costs before reapportionment	$600,000	$116,000	$400,000	$200,000	$1,316,000
Reapportionment:					
Department 1 $(\frac{1}{4}, \frac{3}{4})$*	($600,000)		1'50,000	450,000	
Department 2 $(\frac{8}{9}, \frac{1}{9})$†		($116,000)	103,111	12,889	
Total overhead of producing departments			$653,111	$662,889	$1,316,000
Computation of predetermined overhead rates for product-costing purposes:					
Divide by machine-hours			40,000		
Divide by direct labor hours				30,000	
Rate			$ 16.328	$ 22.096	

* Base is (12,000 + 36,000) or 48,000 hours.
† Base is (16,000 + 2,000) or 18,000 hours.

Step method—method 2

Many companies use the *step method* of reapportionment, which recognizes services rendered by service departments to other service departments. This method is more complicated, because a sequence of reapportionments must be chosen. The sequence typically begins with the department that renders service to the greatest number of other service departments; the sequence continues in step-by-step fashion and ends with the reapportionment of costs of that service department which renders service to the least number of other departments. Thus, departments like Building and Grounds and Personnel would be reapportioned earlier than Production Control or Product Engineering.

Exhibit 17-5 shows the step method. Note that Department 1 costs are reapportioned to another service department as well as to the producing departments. Note also that, once Department 1 costs are reapportioned, Department 2 costs include a share of Department 1 costs. The new total for Department 2 is then reapportioned to *subsequent* departments only. *Once a service department's costs have been reapportioned, no subsequent service department costs are recirculated back to it.*

EXHIBIT 17-5

STEP METHOD OF REAPPORTIONMENT

	1	2	A	B	Total
Overhead costs before reapportionment	$600,000	$116,000	$400,000	$200,000	$1,316,000
Reapportionment:					
Department 1 ($\frac{2}{6}, \frac{1}{6}, \frac{3}{6}$)	(600,000)	200,000	100,000	300,000	
Department 2 ($\frac{8}{9}, \frac{1}{9}$)		($316,000)	280,889	35,111	
Total overhead of producing departments			$780,889	$535,111	$1,316,000
Computation of predetermined overhead rates for product-costing purposes:					
Divide by machine-hours			40,000		
Divide by direct labor hours				30,000	
Rate			$ 19.522	$ 17.837	

Note, further, that *in this case* the overhead rates for product-costing purposes are significantly different under the two methods. For example, the machine-hour rate is $16.33 under the direct method and $19.522 under the step method. Note further that Department A's rate is higher under the step method while Department B's rate is lower. The step method would be preferable because it recognizes the service rendered to Engineering by General Factory Administration whereas the direct method ignores this relationship.

Arbitrary rules

The entire methodology of reapportionment of service department costs is plagued by the necessity of reliance on some arbitrary rules which are designed to charge producing departments in some "equitable" manner. Some common denominator is sought which will provide for acceptable parceling of service department costs. Thus, Personnel Department costs are usually reapportioned on the basis of the number of employees in each of the other departments. The underlying assumption here would be that each employee receives his pro-rata share of the Personnel Department's attention. Of course, this is rarely realistic, because labor turnover and types of skilled and unskilled employees may heavily influence the Personnel Department's efforts and time. Yet it is an expedient oversimplification to use number of employees as a base. The additional refinement of the measuring stick seldom garners enough change in the final reapportionment to be worthwhile or meaningful.

The whole matter of reapportionment is complicated by many computations. The reader should remember that reapportionment is necessary solely for product-costing purposes; control of individual overhead costs is rarely influenced by how scrupulously service costs are reapportioned. Therefore, the aura of precision, which is heightened by elaborate working papers and several decimal places, should not overimpress anybody. Reapportionments are laced with many assumptions which severely limit the usefulness of the resulting product costs.

FURTHER ILLUSTRATION OF REAPPORTIONMENT

Now we turn to a more complicated illustration, shown in Exhibit 17-6. Observe that costs are first accumulated by departmental responsibility; then the service department costs are reapportioned to other departments.

Difficulties arise when there are two or more service departments that serve the same number of other departments. Which department's costs are to be reapportioned first? Generally, when two or more departments serve the same number of other departments, the one with the biggest total cost is reapportioned first, because the costliest department supposedly provides the largest amount of service.[2] However, in Exhibit 17-6, Repair and Maintenance is reapportioned first because it renders more service to Building and Grounds than the latter renders to Repair and Maintenance.

Exhibit 17-6 also shows that the basis for reapportionment differs, depending on the service department in question. The selection of the base is a matter of determining what factor (for example, number of employees, direct man-hours, number of orders, or requisitions) offers the most rational and practical measure of relative benefits received.

Meaning of "direct"

The word *direct*, as it is used in overhead accounting, refers to the convenient, obvious tracing of an individual overhead cost to a *department*.

[2]This criterion has been criticized as follows: "It is not the absolute size of the balance in any service department which is of consequence; it is the relative importance of the service balance due *from* other service departments in excess of the amount due *to* others which minimizes the error." See Carl Thomas Devine, *Cost Accounting and Analysis* (New York: The Macmillan Company, 1950), Chapter III, for a thorough discussion.

For example, supplies (as shown in Exhibit 17-6) would be *direct* with respect to the department which requisitions them; the factory superintendent's salary would be a *direct* charge to Factory Administration but *indirect* to the Assembly Department. The superintendent's salary is aggregated with other Factory Administration charges; the latter departmental total is then reapportioned to production departments.

Some classes of overhead items may be partly direct and partly indirect. For example, depreciation on certain equipment may be charged directly to the Machining Department, whereas depreciation on the plant building may first be charged to a service department called "Building and Grounds" and then reapportioned as a part of the total costs of the Building and Grounds Department.

Computation techniques

Lines 20–22 of Exhibit 17-6 show the two computation techniques for reapportionment. Building and Grounds is reapportioned on the basis of the departmental percentage of total square footage. An alternate method would be to develop a rate per square foot, $5,592 divided by 100,000 square feet, or $.05592 per square foot. Then the square footage in each department would be multiplied by the rate. The two calculations are logically identical, and they give the same results. Personal preference determines the arithmetical method used in a specific case.

Setting departmental overhead rates for product costing

Besides demonstrating how service department costs are reapportioned, Exhibit 17-6 also illustrates how overhead rates for the producing departments are developed. The bases used in this illustration are standard direct labor hours in each department. Note that product-costing rates are used only for producing departments, because products flow only through producing departments.

Reciprocal services

The step method is not theoretically accurate, because many service departments render reciprocal services. For example, the Factory Administration Department serves the employees of the Building and Grounds Department, while the Factory Administration Department occupies some floor space and has janitorial attention. If reciprocal services between service departments are significant, elaborate schemes of reapportionment involving simultaneous equations may be adopted. Ordinarily, however, the step method will not distort the final charges to the producing departments; consequently, intricate methods of reapportionment are rarely used in practice. The step method is considered more than adequate in most instances, but electronic computers now permit the

EXHIBIT 17-6

SAMPLE COMPANY
Factory Overhead Budget—Step Method of Reapportionment
(Normal Month)

Line	(Distribution Basis)	Service Departments			Production Departments			Total
		Repair & Maintenance	Buildings & Grounds	Factory Administration	Machining	Assembly	Finishing	
1	Indirect labor [Direct to Departments (payroll analysis or work tickets)]	$ 400	$ 960	$2,200	$ 4,900	$ 1,000	$ 360	$ 9,820
2	Supplies [Direct to Departments (requisitions)]	640	700	240	3,500	400	1,400	6,880
3	Power (Meters or horsepower ratings)	130	1,600	25	1,800	200	500	4,255
4	Payroll taxes (Department payrolls)	200	50	200	1,300	300	100	2,150
5	Overtime premium (Department payrolls)	100	–	60	600	140	50	950
6	Rework (Direct to responsible department)	–	–	–	300	150	40	490
7	Fuel	–	100	–	–	–	–	100
8	Total variable overhead	$1,470	$3,410	$2,725	$12,400	$ 2,190	$ 2,450	$24,645
9	Property taxes and Insurance	140	770	760	600	100	100	2,470
10	Depreciation	150	700	300	2,300	400	300	4,150
11	Supervisor	700	220	4,015	1,800	1,010	550	8,295
12	Total direct department overhead	$2,460	$5,100	$7,800	$17,100	$ 3,700	$ 3,400	$39,560

							Total
Reapportionment of service department costs (See Note A):							
13	Repair and Maintenance (Maintenance service, current month)	$2,460	492	25	1,476	246	221
14	Building and Grounds (Square footage occupied)		$5,592	559	3,355	1,119	559
15	Factory administration (Direct labor hours)*			$8,384	6,708	838	838
16	Total Production Department overhead				$28,639	$5,903	$5,018	$39,560
17	Application bases—estimated standard direct labor hours				24,000	3,000	3,000
18	Overhead rate per standard direct labor hour.				$1.1933	$1.9677	$1.6727
	Note A: Percentage used for reapportionment:							
19	Repair and Maintenance, based on specific maintenance service	100%	20%	1%	60%	10%	9%
20	Building and Grounds, based on square footage in each department			10,000	60,000	20,000	10,000	100,000
21	Using rate method, $5,592 ÷ 100,000 sq. feet = $.05592 per sq. ft. or (.05592 × 10,000),(.05592 × 60,000), (.05592 × 20,000),(.05592 × 10,000)		100% —				
22	Percentages based on square footage			10%	60%	20%	10%
23	Factory Administration, based on direct labor hours			100%	80%	10%	10%

*Other possible bases might be number of employees or total labor hours.

practical use of the reciprocal method; however, the resulting high degree of accuracy can be misleading if it is not evaluated carefully in relation to the calculations' purpose.[3]

Direct method

Exhibit 17-7 illustrates the direct method of reapportionment. As mentioned previously, this method reapportions each service department's total costs to the producing departments without having such costs pass through a series of other service departments in step-by-step fashion. As long as the final overhead rates will not be significantly influenced by this short-cut method, the step method or some elaborate time-consuming variation thereof may be justly avoided. For example, a comparison of the overhead rates in Exhibits 17-6 and 17-7 reveals only a hairsplitting difference between the final overhead rates for product costing. The overhead rate for the Machining Department is $1.1933 per direct labor hour under the step method and $1.1920 under the direct method. Of course, before adopting the easier method, a company should prove to itself that the direct method and the step method yield substantially the same results. The simple way is naturally the most appealing, but simplicity is beneficial only when it does not impinge on the usefulness of the results.

DUAL RATES FOR REAPPORTIONMENT

So far, our examples have pooled all overhead items together regardless of individual behavior. This method is straightforward, simple, and useful for the determination of product costs for inventory and ordinary pricing purposes. However, many companies find it useful to have two overhead rates: one for applying variable portions of overhead and another for applying fixed portions of overhead. These rates are not difficult to develop for companies which use flexible overhead budgets. They supply more useful data because product costs may be broken down more minutely for a variety of decision-making purposes—especially for decisions on regulating volume. In addition, dual rates permit closer dovetailing of cost accounting for product-costing purposes and for budgetary control purposes.

Further, dual rates permit using different bases for reapportionment of service department costs. Although this refinement may be unimportant in many cases, it may be warranted in some instances. To illustrate the difference in results, consider the adaptation of a CPA examination question on page 580.

[3] See Neil C. Churchill, "Linear Algebra and Cost Allocations: Some Examples," *Accounting Review* (October, 1964), pp. 894–904, and Rene P. Manes, "Comment on Matrix Theory and Cost Allocation," *Accounting Review* (July, 1965), pp. 640–643.

EXHIBIT 17-7

SAMPLE COMPANY
Factory Overhead Budget—Direct Method of Reapportionment
(Normal Month)

	Service Departments			Production Departments			Total
	Repair & Maintenance	Buildings & Grounds	Factory Administration	Machining	Assembly	Finishing	
Total direct department overhead from line 12 of Exhibit 17-6	$2,460	$5,100	$7,800	$17,100	$3,700	$3,400	$39,560
Reapportionment of service department costs (See Note A below):							
Repair and Maintenance	$2,460			1,869	311	280	
Building and Grounds		$5,100		3,400	1,133	567	
Factory Administration			$7,800	6,240	780	780	
Total Production Department overhead				$28,609	$5,924	$5,027	$39,560
Application basis—standard direct labor hours				24,000	3,000	3,000	
Overhead rate per standard labor hour				$1.1920	$1.9745	$1.6754	
Note A: Percentages used for reapportionment:							
Repair and Maintenance, based on production departments' relative use of maintenance services, $6/79$, $10/79$, and $9/79$, respectively	100%			75.94%	12.66%	11.40%	
Building and Grounds, based solely on production departments' relative floor space		100%		66.67%	22.22%	11.11%	
Factory Administration, based on direct labor hours			100%	80%	10%	10%	

Given below are the details pertaining to the Power Service Department.

SCHEDULE OF HORSEPOWER HOURS

	Total	Producing Departments		Service Departments	
		A	B	X	Y
Needed at capacity production	50,000	10,000	20,000	12,000	8,000
Used during the month of April	30,000	8,000	9,000	7,000	6,000

During the month of April, the costs of operating the Power Service Department amounted to $15,000; of this amount, $9,000 were considered to be fixed costs.

What dollar amounts of the Power Service Department costs should be apportioned to each producing department and service department? Try to answer this question before looking at the discussion that follows.

The dual-rate approach to reapportionment considers the $9,000 fixed cost as that of providing ability to serve all other departments at capacity production. The fixed cost is not related to the amount of service rendered in a given month. The proper reapportionment base for fixed costs is the horsepower hours needed at capacity production. The $6,000 variable cost is directly related to service rendered. Therefore, its proper reapportionment base is the horsepower hours actually used. The dual-rate reapportionment appears in Exhibit 17-8, followed by two possible conventional single-rate reapportionments. Exhibit 17-8 shows striking differences in results, depending on the alternative base selected.

CONTROL OF SERVICE DEPARTMENT COSTS

Performance evaluation and cost analysis must be conducted carefully where service department costs are reapportioned. As you may imagine, practices vary widely. The methods of reshuffling costs among departments for product-costing purposes do not necessarily give meaningful data or charges for cost control purposes. Distinctions between variable, fixed, controllable, and uncontrollable costs are always difficult, but the difficulties of jointness are compounded when service departments are involved. For example, a maintenance department may render service upon demand throughout a company. Who controls such costs—the user or the supplier? Probably both. The user largely affects the quantity of such services, and the supplier largely affects the quality and unit cost. Most companies assign responsibility by billing the user departments for actual usage at some standard or estimated unit rate. In this way, the user is primarily responsible for the quantity, and the supplier is primarily responsible for quality and cost control. The flexible budget concept can be easily integrated in such a system.

EXHIBIT 17-8

COMPARISON OF THREE ALTERNATE BASES FOR REAPPORTIONMENT, OF POWER
SERVICE DEPARTMENT COSTS, FOR THE MONTH ENDING APRIL 30, 19x1

	Total	Producing Departments		Service Departments	
		A	B	X	Y
Bases available in horsepower hours:					
Needed at capacity production	50,000	10,000	20,000	12,000	8,000
Used during April	30,000	8,000	9,000	7,000	6,000
Reapportionment of costs:					
Alternative No. 1, Dual Rates:					
Variable costs:					
20¢ per hour used ($6,000 ÷ 30,000 hours)	$ 6,000	$1,600	$1,800	$1,400	$1,200
Fixed costs:					
18¢ per hour of capacity provided ($9,000 ÷ 50,000 hours)	9,000	1,800	3,600	2,160	1,440
	$15,000	$3,400	$5,400	$3,560	$2,640
Alternative No. 2, Single Rate:					
Based on Usage: 50¢ per hour ($15,000 ÷ 30,000 hours)	$15,000	$4,000	$4,500	$3,500	$3,000
Alternative No. 3, Single Rate:					
Based on Capacity Provided: 30¢ per hour ($15,000 ÷ 50,000 hours)	$15,000	$3,000	$6,000	$3,600	$2,400

The following points highlight some fruitful approaches to the control of service department costs:

1. Production department managers exert little or no influence over some service department costs. Examples are services which are predominately discretionary, such as cost accounting, personnel, production planning and control, engineering, heating, and similar services. Top management, rather than first-line supervisors, usually decides the extent of such services. The individual service department head usually works with his superiors in formulating his budget, which is largely static (programmed for a particular planning period). These costs may be reapportioned for product-costing and long-run pricing purposes, but they usually should not be regarded as being controllable by production department managers.

2. The costs of steadily available services, such as power, steam, compressed air, repairs, and similar items whose utilization varies with production activity, are, as already described, charged to the consuming

department at a standard unit rate. The costs of rendering such services are usually stipulated in the service department flexible budgets. The accuracy of the budget estimates depends on the type of services. For example, power can ordinarily be budgeted precisely, but the services of mechanics and electricians are more difficult to predetermine because their operations are often not easily standardized.[4]

3. Where market prices are readily obtainable, they may be utilized as the standard transfer prices in the above system. This in effect makes the service department a profit center, permits an evaluation of its efficiency in relation to its flexible budget and in relation to its outside competitors, and allows regular assessment of whether services should be acquired inside or outside the company.

4. Where service department fixed overhead is relatively large, special care must be taken in reapportionment. Generally, these costs represent a stable of available services whose cost is little affected by short-run changes in production volume. Therefore, if the activity or volume of the services is used as a basis for reapportionment, disputes are likely to arise because the amount of the reapportioned charge is too directly dependent on changes in activity levels of the individual producing departments vis-à-vis each other. For example, assume that the personnel department costs are prorated among three producing departments on the basis of total labor hours as follows in 19x1:

		Producing Department		
	Personnel	1	2	3
Personnel department costs	$(300,000)	$100,000	$100,000	$100,000
Total labor hours		500,000	500,000	500,000

Suppose that the activity of Department 1 is severely restricted in the middle of 19x2, requiring many layoffs and much employee counseling. However, by the end of 19x2, operations have returned to normal. If the same base for reapportionment is used, Departments 2 and 3 would receive a bigger chunk of the personnel department costs, despite the fact that more personnel time was devoted to Department 1 in 19x2 than in 19x1:

		Producing Department		
	Personnel	1	2	3
Personnel department costs	$(300,000)	$ 60,000	$120,000	$120,000
Total labor hours		250,000	500,000	500,000

Departments 2 and 3 would have a strong foundation for disputing the charges.

---

[4] For an expanded discussion see "The Analysis of Manufacturing Cost Variances," *NAA Research Series Report No. 22* (August, 1952), pp. 1550–51.

The fixed portion of service department costs are often reapportioned in lump sums to the various production departments in relation to the individual long-run expected usage envisioned when the fixed costs were incurred. This provides a stable apportioned amount, minimizes the likelihood of disputes over departmental charges, and helps perspective for the evaluation of product-line profitability. Beyer points out that such an allocation recognizes the long-term readiness to serve which must be maintained in all departments. He adds:

"Furthermore, the amount allocated to a product line will not vary widely from year to year because of temporary shifts in volume between departments or between product lines. A product manager, faced with the problem of setting selling prices and earning a proper return on investment, should not be confronted each year with substantial changes in the amount of standby [fixed] cost allocated to his product line as a result of temporary volume changes."[5]

Attempts to use a single reapportionment plan to fulfill both product-costing and control purposes generally will not succeed because foremen of producing departments will resist being held responsible for those service department costs which are not controllable by the producing departments. Arguments about the fairness of a given reapportionment of service department charges are fruitless and frustrating. They are not only unnecessary, but they may have a lasting, damaging effect on the managerial usefulness of the over-all accounting system. If the foreman is suspicious of a few reapportionment charges, he begins to question the validity of all the figures and eventually looks upon the accountants with disdain and distrust.

Therefore, great care is needed in defining responsibility for incurrence of service department costs. It is probably safer to confine reports for supervisors to controllable costs only. Responsibility reporting for control should in most instances be clearly separated from the problem of reapportionment of service costs for product-costing purposes.

PROPER ACTIVITY LEVEL FOR OVERHEAD APPLICATION

Characteristics of capacity

The choice of a capacity size is usually the result of capital-budgeting decisions, which are reached after studying the expected impact of these capital outlays on operations over a number of years. The choice may be influenced by a combination of two major factors, each involving trade-off decisions and each heavily depending on long-range forecasts of demand, material costs, and labor costs.

1. Provision for seasonal and cyclical *fluctuations* in demand. The trade-off is between (a) additional costs of physical capacity versus (b) the costs of inventory stockouts and/or the carrying costs of inventory

[5] Robert Beyer, *Profitability Accounting for Planning and Control* (New York: The Ronald Press Co., 1963), p. 202.

safety stocks of such magnitude to compensate for seasonal and cyclical variations, the costs of overtime premium, subcontracting, and so on.
2. Provision for upward *trends* in demand. The trade-off is between (a) the costs of constructing too much capacity for initial needs versus (b) the later extra costs of satisfying demand by alternative means. For example, should a factory designed to make color television tubes have an area of 100,000, 150,000, or 200,000 square feet?

Although it can be defined and measured in a particular situation, capacity is an illusive concept. Consider, for example, the following:

> Capacity planning requires definition and measurement of capacity in a manner relevant to questions which arise in the planning process. This problem has two aspects. First, it is necessary to specify capacity in terms of how much the company should be prepared to make and to sell. Second, the capacity of specific facilities available or to be acquired must be determined . . . . A variety of alternative combinations of capacity and operating patterns is usually possible.[6]

There is much fluidity in the above quotation. To most people, the term *capacity* implies a constraint, an upper limit. We sometimes hear: "I'm working to capacity now. I simply can't do more." This same notion of capacity as a constraint is commonly held in industry.

Although the term *capacity* is usually applied to plant and equipment, it is equally applicable to other resources, such as men and materials. A shortage of direct labor, executive time, or raw material may be determining in limiting company production or sales.

The upper limit of capacity is seldom absolutely rigid, at least from an engineering viewpoint. That is, ways and means—such as overtime, subcontracting, or premium prices for raw materials—can usually be found to expand production. But the latter may be totally unattractive from an economic viewpoint. Hence, the upper limit of capacity is *specified* by management for current planning and control purposes after considering engineering and economic factors. The upper limit is usually *imposed* by management, not by external forces.

In our subsequent discussion, let us consider the word *capacity* as representing *practical capacity* (sometimes called *practical attainable capacity*), the maximum level at which the plant or department can realistically operate most efficiently. Practical capacity allows for unavoidable operating interruptions such as repair time or waiting time (down time).

Two commonly used[7] levels of capacity utilization, discussed originally in Chapter 8, are:

1. *Normal activity*, which is the level of capacity utilization that will satisfy average consumer demand over a span of time (often five years) that includes seasonal, cyclical, and trend factors; and

---

[6] *Accounting for Costs of Capacity, NAA Research Series Report No. 39* (New York: National Association of Accountants, 1963), p. 10.
[7] For an analysis of practice see Charles R. Purdy, "Industry Patterns of Capacity or Volume Choice: Their Existence and Rationale," *Journal of Accounting Research* (Autumn, 1965), pp. 228–241.

2. *Expected annual activity*, which is the anticipated level of capacity utilization for the coming year.

There are likely to be differences in terminology between companies, so be sure to obtain an understanding of terms in a given situation.

Normal activity versus expected annual activity for overhead application

Expected annual activity is the basis for applying all fixed overhead to products in any given *year*, while the overhead rate based on *normal activity* attempts to apply fixed overhead by using a *longer-run* average expected activity. Conceptually, the *normal rate* results in over-applications in some years which are offset by underapplications in other years.

Consider the following data. We shall deal with fixed overhead only, because variable overhead fluctuates with changes in activity while fixed overhead does not. *Thus, the entire problem of using expected annual activity or normal activity is raised by the presence of fixed overhead.* (If you will recall, the idle capacity or volume variance in Chapter 8 was confined to fixed overhead.)

Fixed factory overhead	$500,000
Practical capacity per year	100,000 standard direct labor hours
Normal activity	90,000 standard direct labor hours
Expected annual activity for specific year	(Fluctuates from year to year)
Normal overhead rate is $500,000 ÷ 90,000 hours	$5.55
Expected annual overhead rate	(Varies from year to year)

Exhibit 17-9 shows that, if normal activity is the base, the overhead rate of $5.55 would be used for costing inventory. In the second year there would be an under-applied fixed overhead balance of $5.55 times 20,000 hours, or $111,000. This would be considered the measure of the cost of *not* producing—the loss from idle capacity. Inventories would be costed with a $5.55 rate instead of a $7.15 rate. Under the expected annual activity method, if volume fluctuates from year to year, product and inventory costs will gyrate solely because of differences in utilization of facilities. Using a normal rate will avoid capricious changes in unit costs and will also provide a yearly and monthly measure of the cost of idle capacity.

Note carefully that Exhibit 17-9 is designed to stress only the computation of overhead rates under different activity bases. It deliberately avoids introducing changes in budgeted fixed overhead costs; instead, it assumes that total fixed costs are constant from year to year. Actually, year-to-year changes in the prices paid for fixed overhead items and services can affect the overhead rate, regardless of whether expected annual activity, normal activity, or some other activity base is used to set the rate.

EXHIBIT 17-9

COMPARISON OF EXPECTED ANNUAL AND NORMAL ACTIVITY
FOR OVERHEAD APPLICATION

Year	Standard Labor Hours Worked*	Expected Annual Activity Basis				Normal Activity Basis		
		Over-head Rate	Total Applied	Under-(Over-) Applied	Over-head Rate	Total Applied	Under-(Over-) Applied†
1	90,000	$5.55	$500,000	$ —	$5.55	$500,000	$ —
2	70,000	7.15	500,000	—	5.55	389,000	111,000
3	100,000	5.00	500,000	—	5.55	555,000	(55,000)
4	80,000	6.33	500,000	—	5.55	445,000	55,000
5	100,000	5.00	500,000	—	5.55	555,000	(55,000)
6	100,000	5.00	500,000	—	5.55	555,000	(55,000)
				$ —			$ —0—

*For illustrative purposes, we assume that expected annual activity and standard labor hours worked are equal.

†Debit under-applied or credit over-applied overhead directly to Income Summary as a measure of gain or loss from under- or over-utilization of capacity.

Selection of activity base

The activity base to be used depends largely on the nature of the business. Fixed costs measure the capacity to make and sell. They usually include at least depreciation and a core of salaried payroll costs. The total fixed cost commitment is influenced by the long-run sales outlook. The conventional view is that all products should receive some "equitable" portion of fixed overhead.

If the total sales volume does not change greatly from year to year, *expected annual activity* for each year is a rational base because expected annual activity and normal activity coincide. In these cases, even if the companies have seasonal sales patterns, all fixed factory overhead is exactly applied to product by the end of the year. See Exhibit 17-9.

Many accountants reject the normal activity notion and maintain that each year must stand by itself; that is, each year's overhead must be applied to each year's production, written off as a loss, or both. This attitude arises from (a) the widespread conviction that the year is the key time period and (b) adherence to the idea that overhead costs for a given year generally must cling or attach to the units produced during that year regardless of the relationship of that year's activity to average long-run activity.

A more convincing reason for using expected annual activity as a base is the overwhelming measurement problem that accompanies the determination of normal activity. Sales not only fluctuate cyclically, but they have trends over the long run. In effect, the use of normal activity implies an acute talent for accurate long-run forecasting. Many account-ants and executives who reject the normal activity idea as a base claim that the nature of their company's business precludes accurate forecasts beyond one year.

Where companies use normal activity, the objective is to choose a period long enough to average out sizable fluctuations in volume and to allow for trends in sales. The uniform rate for applying fixed overhead supposedly provides for "recovery" of fixed costs over the long run. General Motors' pricing policy uses this approach. Companies expect that over-applications in some years will be offset by under-applications in other years.

Conceptually, when *normal activity* is the base, the yearly over- or under-applied overhead should be carried forward on the balance sheet. Practically, however, year-end balances are closed directly to Income Summary because the accounting profession (and the internal revenue de-partment) generally views the year as being the terminal time span for allocation of under- or over-applied overhead. In year 2 in Exhibit 17-9, the year-end journal entry for closing the Fixed Factory Overhead accounts may appear as follows:

Fixed factory overhead applied	389,000	
Idle capacity loss (to income summary)	111,000	
Fixed factory overhead control		500,000

The journal entry for the end of year 3 would appear as follows:

Fixed factory overhead applied	555,000	
Gain from over-utilization of capacity		55,000
Fixed factory overhead control		500,000

The logical question that should arise at this point is: why use normal activity at all if the yearly over- or under-applications are written off at year-end anyway? Are the yearly results not the same, whether expected annual activity or normal activity are used? The Problem for Self-Study shows the fundamental answer: "There is still a difference be-cause inventory costs are different."

Practical capacity

Many managements want to keep running at full capacity, which really means practical capacity. Their "normal activity" for applying fixed costs is "practical capacity"; anything less reduces profits and is undesirable. Therefore, the overhead costing rates are relatively lower than if lesser activity levels were used as a base. Where product costs are used as guides for pricing, some managers say that this policy results in more competitive pricing, which maximizes both volume and profits in good times and bad. The accounting effects of such a policy are lower unit costs for inventory purposes and the almost perpetual appearance of "Loss from idle capacity" on the income statements.

Significance of activity base for product costing and control

We can conclude from the above discussion that the proper activity base for product costing is largely a matter of opinion. Given a set of facts, a dozen accountants could easily reach twelve different activity bases as being appropriate for product-costing purposes. At least, the accountants are likely to come within a range of agreement if they have discussed their opinions among themselves.

The selection of a base probably becomes crucial where product costs heavily influence managerial decisions—particularly, pricing decisions. For example, in a cyclical industry, the use of expected annual activity rather than normal activity as a base would tend to cause a company to quote low prices in boom years and high prices in depression years—in obvious conflict with good business judgment. That is why normal capacity makes more sense as an overhead base when there are wide swings in business volume through the years, even though the yearly over- and under-applied overhead is not carried forward in the balance sheet from year to year.

In the realm of current planning and control, however, normal activity is an empty concept. Normal activity is used as a basis for long-range plans. It depends on the time span selected, the forecasts made for each year, and the weighting of these forecasts. In Exhibit 17-9, a comparison in year 2 of the 70,000-hour expected actual activity with the 90,000-hour normal activity might be suggested as the best basis for auditing long-range planning. However, normal activity is an average that has no particular significance with respect to a follow-up for a particular year. The pertinent comparison is a particular year's expected annual activity with that year's activity level used in the authorization for the acquisition of facilities. This comparison may be done project by project. It need not be integrated in the accounting system on a routine basis. Furthermore, attempting to use normal capacity as a reference point for judging current performance is an example of misusing a long-range measure for a short-range purpose.

The expected annual activity, rather than normal activity or practical capacity, is more germane to the evaluation of current results. Expected annual activity is the basis for the year's master budget—the principal short-run planning and control tool. Managers feel much more obligated to reach the levels stipulated in the master budget, which should have been carefully set in relation to the maximum opportunities for sales in the current period. In contrast, normal activity and practical capacity are not so pertinent to current operating problems because they are not usually incorporated in the comprehensive or master budget—the focus of attention.

SUMMARY

Common denominators most frequently used as bases for overhead application include direct labor hours, machine-hours, and direct labor cost. The major problem in choosing a proper base is to relate overhead to its most closely related causal factor.

Where products receive uneven attention and effort as they move through departments, departmental overhead rates rather than plant-wide rates should be used.

The entire methodology of reapportionment of service department costs is plagued by the necessity of reliance on some working rules which are designed to charge producing departments in some equitable manner. Some common denominator is sought which will provide for the rational parceling of service department costs.

The whole matter of reapportionment is complicated by many computations. Reapportionment is necessary solely for product-costing purposes; control of individual overhead costs is rarely influenced by how scrupulously service costs are reapportioned.

The control of service department costs raises some vexing problems. For example, the foreman of the maintenance department may have control over the efficiency of repair work but little control over the total demand by other departments for his department's repair services. The control mechanism used in these instances usually takes some form of billing the consuming departments at standard rates for service rendered and using a flexible budget for appraising the efficiency of the repair and maintenance department.

Three commonly used activity bases for developing product-costing overhead rates are (1) expected annual activity, (2) normal activity over three to five years, and (3) practical capacity. The selection is essentially a matter of opinion. The choice will influence inventory valuations and resultant timing of income recognition.

PROBLEMS FOR SELF-STUDY

Problem 1. Consider the following case, adapted from a CPA examination:

You have been engaged to install a cost system for Martin Company. Your investigation of the manufacturing operations of the business discloses these facts:

(1) The company makes a line of lighting fixtures and lamps. The material cost of any particular item ranges from 15 per cent to 60 per cent of total factory cost, depending on the kind of metal and fabric used in making it.

(2) The business is subject to wide cyclical fluctuations, for the sales volume follows new housing construction.

(3) About 60 per cent of the manufacturing is normally done in the first quarter of the year.

(4) For the whole plant, the wage rates range from $1.25 to $3.75 an hour. However, within each of the eight individual departments, the spread between the high and low wage rates is less than 5 per cent.

(5) Each of the products made uses all eight of the manufacturing departments but not proportionately.

(6) Within the individual manufacturing departments, factory overhead ranges from 30 per cent to 80 per cent of conversion cost.

Based on the above information, you are to prepare a statement or letter for the president of the company explaining whether in its cost system Martin Company should use:

a. A normal overhead rate or an expected-actual-capacity annual overhead rate;

b. An over-all overhead rate or a departmental overhead rate;

c. A method of factory overhead application based on: direct labor hours; direct labor cost; or prime cost.

Include the reasons supporting *each* of your three recommendations.

Problem 2.   The Shane Co. incurs fixed manufacturing overhead of $500,000 annually. Practical capacity is 100,000 standard direct labor hours; normal activity, 90,000 hours; and expected annual activity, 70,000 hours. In 19x1, 70,000 units were produced (in 70,000 standard hours) and 60,000 units were sold. Standard hours worked were 70,000. There was no beginning inventory.

REQUIRED:

a. Prepare a three-column comparison of the various methods of applying fixed overhead to product. Designate which methods would result in the highest and lowest net income. For each method, show the amounts that would be charged to:

> Cost of sales (expense)
> Loss from idle capacity, volume variance (loss)
> Ending inventory

b. Why is expected annual activity better than either practical capacity or normal activity for judging current operating performance?

Solution 1.

Dear Sir:

From a study of the manufacturing operations of Martin Company, it is my recommendation that, in applying its manufacturing overhead, the company use normal departmental overhead rates applied as percentages of the *direct labor cost*.

The company should use normal rather than expected actual overhead rates because of the wide seasonal and cyclical fluctuations in its business. Expected actual rates would, owing to the large fixed overhead expenses, make the per-unit overhead costs high in the low-production periods and low in the high-production periods. The use of normal rates would apply the same per-unit overhead costs regardless of month-to-month and year-to-year fluctuations. Both for quoting prices and for pricing inventories, it is best to use per-unit costs neither inflated by the costs of available but unused factory facilities nor deflated by the gains of better-than-normal use of the factory facilities.

The company should use departmental overhead rates because the rates obviously vary so markedly between the departments. If a blanket rate were used as an average rate, it would not be correct for any department. Because the company's overhead is a large part of factory cost, the inaccuracy in the per-unit costs caused by the use of a blanket rate would be substantial. If all the products made used all the departments proportionately, a blanket rate would result in substantially accurate total (but not departmental) unit overhead costs. However, in Martin Company, the products do not use all the departments proportionately.

As the wage rates are substantially uniform within the separate departments, the labor costs in each department are closely proportionate to the labor time. Therefore, the per-cent-of-direct-labor-cost method of applying the factory overhead would in this case effect about as accurate an application as would the rate-per-direct-labor-hour method. The clerical expense of the per-cent-of-direct-labor-cost method would be low, because the method does not require accumulation of the number of direct labor hours applicable to each job.

The per-cent-of-prime-cost method of overhead application is not recommended because of the wide differences in the costs of the materials that may be used to make a given lamp or fixture. Factory overhead is primarily the cost of using factory facilities. The factory facilities applied to make a lamp of silver are not more than those used to make the same lamp of copper. For this reason, the use of prime cost (because it includes materials cost) would result in an excessive charge to lamps using expensive materials.

Very truly yours,

Solution 2.

a. Exhibit 17-10 shows that the use of different activity bases for developing product-costing overhead rates results in different *inventory valuations* and resultant different net incomes. Further, the measure of utilization of facilities, "Loss (or Gain) from idle capacity," will differ markedly. In Exhibit 17-10, income is lowest where practical capacity is the overhead base and highest when expected annual activity is the overhead base because a smaller portion of overhead is held back as an asset in inventory when a lower overhead rate is used.

The exhibit also indicates that the accounting effects of using practical capacity are lower unit costs for inventory purposes and the steady appearance of "Loss from idle capacity" on the income statement.

b. As is explained more fully in the chapter, expected annual activity is more pertinent to current operating problems because it is usually the notion of activity that is incorporated in the master budget. Therefore, it has more current meaning to the department managers who must live with the budget.

EXHIBIT 17-10

SOLUTION TO SELF-STUDY PROBLEM 2(a)

Income Statement Effects of Using Various Activity Bases for Overhead Application

	Expected Annual Activity[1] Using a $7.15 Overhead Rate	Normal Activity[2] Using a $5.55 Overhead Rate	Practical Capacity[3] Using a $5.00 Overhead Rate
Sales	$ xxx	$ xxx	$ xxx
Production costs:			
Direct material, direct labor, variable overhead	$ xxx	$ xxx	$ xxx
Fixed overhead applied to product	500,000	389,000	350,000
Total production costs — 70,000 units	$ xxx	$ xxx	$ xxx
Ending inventory — fixed overhead component — 10,000 units	71,500	55,555	50,000
Total fixed overhead component of cost of sales	428,500	333,445	300,000
Loss from idle capacity (shown separately on income statements)	None	111,000	150,000
Total fixed overhead charged to the period's sales	$428,500	$444,445	$450,000
Net income	Highest	Middle	Lowest
Recapitulation:			
Total overhead to account for	$500,000	$500,000	$500,000
Accounted for as follows:			
Charged to Cost of Sales (expense)	$428,500	$333,445	$300,000
Charged to Loss from Idle Capacity, volume variance (loss)	None	111,000	150,000
Charged to Ending Inventory (asset)	71,500	55,555	50,000
Overhead accounted for	$500,000	$500,000	$500,000

[1] $500,000 ÷ 70,000 hours worked = $7.15 (rounded)
[2] $500,000 ÷ 90,000 hours normal activity = $5.55
[3] $500,000 ÷ 100,000 hours practical capacity = $5.00

QUESTIONS, PROBLEMS, AND CASES

Note: Problems 17-11, 17-13, and 17-17 cover the essential points. Problems 17-15, 17-18, and 17-19 also deserve consideration.

17-1. What is the most important criterion for selecting an overhead base?

17-2. Why are departmental overhead rates generally preferable to plant-wide rates?

17-3. "Service department costs shouldn't be reapportioned." Do you agree? Why?

17-4. What are the criteria for selecting reapportionment bases for service department costs?

17-5. "In order to save time and effort, we use a single reapportionment plan to fulfill both product-costing and control purposes." Discuss.

17-6. "I don't understand what the fuss concerning ideal, practical, normal, or expected annual activity is all about." What causes the problem in the first place?

17-7. "Why use normal activity at all if the yearly over- or underapplications are written off at year end anyway?" Discuss.

17-8. A prominent economist once said, "Not even Almighty God can tell a railroad the cost of moving a hundred tons of freight from Boston to New York." Do you agree? Why?

17-9. Comparison of Overhead Bases. Some manufacturing businesses identify or allocate all manufacturing overhead to productive departments. An overhead rate then may be established for each productive department based on direct labor cost. Using this rate, overhead is then applied to jobs or products.

Discuss the possible advantages and disadvantages of the direct-labor-cost basis for applying overhead to jobs or products as opposed to other commonly used bases for overhead distribution, such as machine-hours or cost of material used.

[C.P.A.]

17-10. Selection of Most Suitable Application Base.* The manufacturing operations of this company are highly seasonal; production reaches a peak in April, May, and June of each year. The following are typical data concerning production activities over a year.

	Indirect Costs Incurred	Direct Labor Cost	Direct Man-Hours	Machine-Hours
January	$ 8,800	$ 8,000	6,500	3,600
February	8,400	7,600	6,200	3,200
March	9,600	8,600	7,400	3,800
April	11,200	10,000	7,800	4,600
May	12,000	11,600	8,100	6,000
June	11,600	12,000	8,500	7,800
July	10,000	9,000	7,500	5,600
August	9,200	8,200	6,800	4,200
September	9,400	8,600	7,200	5,000
October	8,600	7,200	6,300	3,400
November	8,000	6,000	6,000	3,300
December	7,200	4,000	5,000	2,500
	$114,000	$100,800	83,300	53,000

*From William J. Vatter, *Managerial Accounting* (Englewood Cliffs, N.J.: Prentice-Hall, Inc., 1950), p. 386.

REQUIRED:

1. Prepare predetermined overhead application rates, using three different bases or methods.

2. For a given batch of product involving direct materials costing $84, direct labor cost of $72, 40 direct labor man-hours, and 20 machine-hours, what would be the total cost as assigned by the use of each of the rates computed in (1)?

3. Which of these three rates is in your opinion most suitable for establishing the cost of product for purposes of determining income, assuming a constant price level for all cost factors? Why?

17-11. Reapportion Service Department Costs.   The X Company has prepared departmental overhead budgets for normal activity levels before reapportionments as follows:

Building and grounds	$ 10,000
Personnel	1,000
General factory administration[1]	26,090
Cafeteria—operating loss	1,640
Storeroom	2,670
Machining	34,700
Assembly	48,900
	$125,000

[1] To be reapportioned before cafeteria.

Management has decided that the most sensible product costs are achieved by using departmental overhead rates. These rates are developed after appropriate service department costs are reapportioned to production departments.

Bases for reapportionment are to be selected from the following:

Department	Direct Labor Hours	Number of Employees	Square Feet of Floor Space Occupied	Total Labor Hours	Number of Requisitions
Building & grounds	—	—	—	—	
Personnel[1]		—	2,000	—	
General factory administration		35	7,000	—	
Cafeteria— operating loss		10	4,000	1,000	
Storeroom		5	7,000	1,000	
Machining	5,000	50	30,000	8,000	2,000
Assembly	15,000	100	50,000	17,000	1,000
	20,000	200	100,000	27,000	3,000

[1] Basis used is number of employees.

REQUIRED:

1. Using a worksheet, reapportion service department costs by the step method. Develop overhead rates per direct labor hour for machining and assembly.

2. Same as in (1), using the direct method.

3. What would be the blanket plant-wide factory overhead application rate, assuming that direct labor hours are used as a base?

4. Using the following information about two jobs, prepare three different total overhead costs for each job, using rates developed in (1), (2), and (3) above.

	Direct Labor Hours	
	Machining	Assembly
Job 88	18	2
Job 89	3	17

17-12. Comparison of Departmental and Plant-wide Overhead Rates. The Sayther Company manufactured two products, A and B, during the first year of its operations. For purposes of product costing, an overhead rate of application of $1.70 per direct labor hour was used, based on budgeted factory overhead of $340,000 and 200,000 budgeted direct labor hours, as shown below:

	Budgeted Overhead	Budgeted Hours
Department 1	$240,000	100,000
Department 2	100,000	100,000
Total	$340,000	200,000

The number of labor hours required to manufacture each of these products was:

	Product A	Product B
In Department 1	4	1
In Department 2	1	4
	5	5

At the end of the year there was no work in process and 2,000 and 6,000 finished units, respectively, of products A and B on hand. Assume that budgeted activity was attained.

REQUIRED:

1. What was the effect on the Company's income of using a plant overhead rate instead of departmental overhead rates?

2. Assume that materials and labor cost per unit of Product A are $10 per unit and that the selling price is established by adding 40 per cent to factory overhead costs to cover profit and selling and administrative expenses. What difference in selling price would result from the use of departmental overhead rates?

3. Explain briefly but clearly why departmental overhead rates are generally preferable to plant-wide rates.   [C.G.A.A.]

17-13. Reapportionment; Departmental versus Plant-Wide Applications. The following are pertinent data for the Alou Company:

Budget Data for 19x7	(S1) Factory Personnel	(S2) Production Planning & Control	(P1) Machining	(P2) Assembly
Estimated overhead	$51,000	$198,500	$2,235,500	$755,000
Machine-hours			300,000	—
Direct labor hours			40,000	500,000
Orders to be processed			8,000	2,000
Number of employees		10	30	300

Factory Personnel Department costs are to be reapportioned on the basis of number of employees; Production Planning and Control, on the basis of orders processed. The step basis is used for reapportionment.

This company produces a wide variety of products on a job-order basis. Management has always used a single, plant-wide overhead application rate based on direct labor hours.

Recently, however, customer complaints on price quotations, plus the outside auditor's criticism of the plant-wide rate, has prompted management to ask you, the controller, to re-study the situation before setting rates for 19x7.

You decide that departmental overhead ·rates should be developed, at least as a method of attack. You think that a machine-hour rate should be used for the Machining Department, which contains costly automatic and semi-automatic equipment manned by a few workers who tend and control many machines simultaneously.

The workers may operate a couple of machines at a time on certain jobs, and as many as six machines or more on other jobs. Because the Assembly Department requires painstaking workmanship but little equipment, you think that direct labor hours is the most proper overhead base there.

The budget data for 19x7 are little different from those for 19x6, so you pick five representative jobs worked on during December, 19x6 as a basis for comparing the blanket rate with departmental rates. You keep careful records of machine-hours as well as of the direct labor hours. The results follow:

Job Number	Machining Machine-Hours	DLH	Assembly DLH
300	5	2	10
301	40	4	40
302	10	2	30
303	7	1	5
304	15	11	30

REQUIRED (Show and label computations):

1. Departmental overhead rates.
2. Blanket plant-wide rate.
3. A detailed summary by jobs of (a) total overhead applied, using departmental rates; (b) total overhead applied, using a plant-wide rate; (c) difference between (a) and (b).
4. What is the total difference for the jobs taken together?
5. What overhead application base would you recommend? Why?

17-14. Overhead Reapportionments Already Given; Determine Bases Used. Listed below are the Kurt Company's departmental overhead budg-

ets for a normal activity level, overhead costs reapportioned by department utilizing predetermined rates, and a few operating and plant statistics for the period
concerned. Assume that 15,000 direct labor hours were worked in each producing
department.

				Reapportioned Costs (Step Method)				
	Budgeted Normal Activity	Employ- ment Service	General Plant Adminis- tration	Lunch- room	Store- room	Vulcan- izing Depart- ment	Assembly Depart- ment
Janitorial Service	$ 8,000	$300	$600	$ 900	$1,600	$2,300	$ 2,300
Employment Service	3,700		300	200	200	1,300	2,000
General Plant Adm.	19,100			1,000	750	8,250	10,000
Lunchroom	1,400				200	1,300	2,000
Storeroom	250					2,100	900
Vulcanizing Dept.	14,750						
Assembling Dept.	22,800						
	$70,000						

Total number of square feet	80,000
Total number of employees	200
Total number of labor hours	40,000
Total direct labor hours	30,000
Total number of requisitions	1,000

REQUIRED:

1. In tabular fashion:
    (a) Determine the most logical bases for reapportionment.
    (b) List the total costs reapportioned to each plant operation.
    (c) Compute rates for reapportionment (that is, janitorial service
        is 10¢ per square foot, and so on).
    (d) List the following data for *each* plant operation:

        Number of the square feet utilized.
        Number of employees assigned.
        Number of total labor hours assigned.
        Number of direct labor hours utilized.
        Number of requisitions initiated.

2. Compute the overhead rate per direct labor hour for the two departments.

3. Compute a plant-wide overhead application rate with direct labor
hours as the base.

17-15.   Dual Reapportionment.   Given below are the details pertaining to the Power Service Dept.

SCHEDULE OF HORSEPOWER HOURS

	Producing Depts.		Service Depts.	
	A	B	X	Y
Needed at capacity production	10,000	20,000	12,000	8,000
Used during month of April	8,000	13,000	7,000	6,000

During the month of April, the expenses of operating the Power Service Department amounted to $9,300; of this amount, $2,500 were considered to be fixed costs.

What dollar amounts of the Power Service Department expense should be reapportioned to each producing and service department?   [C.P.A.]

17-16. Different Activity Bases. The production manager of a small company realizes that although various bases (such as direct labor hours or machine-hours) can be used to apply factory overhead to product costs, another problem of fundamental importance exists in the way in which each of these bases will be expressed. That is, should the base decided upon be expressed in terms of "expected annual activity," "average or normal activity," or "practical capacity?" The manager is uncertain, however, how the use of overhead rates based on each of these capacity-utilization concepts may give different results.

The following information related to the planned operations of the company during 19x4:

	Hours
Maximum capacity utilization, based on absolute physical potential	100,000
Practical capacity utilization, after allowance for normal breakdowns, maintenance, loss time, etc.	95,000
Average or normal activity, based on the average production requirements for 5 years	75,000
Expected activity, based on the 19x4 production requirements	85,000

REQUIRED:

Explain fully why the use of each of the three (3) capacity-utilization concepts referred to in the first paragraph above will cause different total variances between actual and applied overhead for the year 19x4.   [S.I.C.A. Adapted]

17-17. Overhead Rates and Cyclical Business. It is a time of severe business depression throughout the capital goods industries. A division manager for a large corporation in a heavy-machinery industry is confused and unhappy. He is distressed with the controller, whose cost department keeps feeding the manager costs that are of little use because they are higher than ever before. At the same time, the manager has to quote lower prices than before in order to get any business.

REQUIRED:

1. What activity base is probably being used for application of overhead?

2. How might the overhead by applied in order to make the cost data more useful in making price quotations?

3. Would the product costs furnished by the cost department be satisfactory for the costing of the annual inventory?

17-18. Argument About Proper Activity Base. The president, controller, and assistant controller have studied possible alternative activity bases for overhead application to products. Until now the company has applied all actual overhead to products on a month-to-month basis. The three executives have different views as to the most appropriate base. They briefly summarized their thinking as follows:

President: "The only time I'm satisfied is when we are operating at peak capacity. If we're not, our profits are less than what they should be. As I understand it, the use of practical capacity as a base will result in lower product costs. This will allow us to price more competitively, and at the same time we'll have some idea of the loss from our inability to utilize full capacity."

Controller: "The only proper base for overhead application is expected activity for the year. Each year's costs are borne to benefit each year's production. The only sensible way to track yearly overhead costs is to pool them and then use an annual average rate to funnel them to products as they are manufactured. Any major year-end over- or under-absorbed overhead should be prorated over the year's production by an adjusting entry."

Assistant Controller (who plans to resign next week): "You're both wrong! Anybody who thinks this matter through realizes that the core of the question is the sticky, almost unalterable behavior of fixed overhead. Commitments like fixed assets, research costs, and executive salaries not only do not change from month to month; they do not even change materially from year to year. These commitments are made to sustain a level of operations for three or four years ahead. We should use normal activity as a base. Furthermore, major year-end under- or over-absorbed overhead should be carried forward on the balance sheet from year to year. Over a three- or four-year period, such overhead will be largely counterbalanced."

Pertinent data on factory overhead for this company follow:

	Year	Variable Overhead	Fixed Overhead	Total Overhead	Standard Direct Labor Hours
Past data:					
	1	$ 500,000	$1,000,000	$1,500,000	500,000
	2	1,000,000	1,100,000	2,100,000	1,000,000
	3	800,000	1,200,000	2,000,000	800,000
Future Estimates:					
	4	880,000	1,300,000	2,180,000	800,000
	5	1,100,000	1,300,000	2,400,000	1,000,000
	6	1,320,000	1,400,000	2,720,000	1,200,000

REQUIRED:

As a management consultant who specializes in cost accounting difficulties, write a concise report supporting the most proper overhead activity base to be used in this case. As an appendix, write a brief answer to each of the contentions of the president, controller, and assistant controller. Assume that practical capacity is 1,300,000 hours.

17-19. Control of Service Department Costs. Hotpoint Company, a division of General Electric, is operated on a "departmental" basis. The principal departments involved in this accounting situation are:

> Plant 1, Production of washers and dryers.
> Plant 2, Production of ranges, ovens, etc.
> Plant 3, Production of component parts.
> Plant 6, Relations and Utilities Department.
> Plant 8, Production of refrigerators.

The production departments are self-explanatory. The purpose of the R. and U. Department centers around ownership of office buildings, maintenance of buildings and machines, and production of steam. When employees of R. and U. perform work for a productive department, R. and U. bills the productive department. Against these billings, R. and U. incurs costs for plumbers, electricians, carpenters, and so forth.

Being a service department, as opposed to a productive department, R. and U. does not generate income as ordinarily conceived. The book profit or loss remaining at the end of the year is reapportioned to the productive departments.

The Relations and Utilities Department usually presented a problem to the productive departments. In some instances similar work could be contracted for with outside vendors for less costs. The executives of the R. and U. Department maintained that they were required to have a standby maintenance crew for emergencies. They also maintained that, if their charges were slightly high, any book profits were redistributed to the productive departments.

Against this background the accounting problems that arose concerned the production of steam. R. and U. accumulated all the costs relative to steam in one account. The credits to this account arose when the productive departments were billed for the steam.

The production of steam presented a slightly unique problem. A group of men were assigned to the steam facilities. A few men were "floaters." These men worked at various boiler rooms during the course of the week. In summer, when less steam was required, these men supposedly maintained the equipment, although the maintenance work was never recorded.

The productive departments had the following accounting procedure for all utility expenses. The utility expenses *including steam* were accumulated in a clearing account. This account was credited and manufacturing operations were charged during the year based on units produced or budgeted.

The R. and U. Department had a similar accounting procedure for accumulating steam costs. All steam costs incurred were also accumulated in a clearing account. The R. and U. clearing account was credited when the productive departments were billed for their steam usage. At year-end, the R. and U. clearing account balance was apportioned to the productive departments.

The problem encountered with the present accounting procedure was control. Steam costs, which included labor (firemen), gas, oil, water, depreciation, maintenance, and so forth, amounted to one million dollars a year.

The R. and U. Department constructed a very general budget or schedule of steam costs to be incurred during the coming year. The amount of steam to be produced was estimated based on prior years. The productive departments followed the same pattern. Utility costs in their budget were based on prior years.

At year-end the manufacturing operations absorbed the over- or under-absorbed utility and steam expenses. If the clearing account was over-absorbed, everyone was happy and no questions were asked. If the clearing account was under-absorbed, it was chalked up to experience.

REQUIRED:

How do you control such costs? Is a nonprofit service department desirable? Would you make any organizational or accounting changes in the current setup?

17-20. Indirect Costs and Government Contracts.   The president of
a large university commented on the previous year's operations as follows:

"I should point out that, if the Congress had not recently reduced
the ceiling on indirect cost recovery in connection with research grants
by the Department of Defense and the Independent Agencies from 25 per
cent, as it now is for the National Science Foundation and the National
Aeronautics and Space Administration, to 20 per cent, income for the
next academic year would have come close to cancelling the anticipated
deficit. This is another way of saying that government research grants
require some sharing of the cost from general University funds, for our
calculated indirect costs are about 32 per cent.   In other words, we
recover only 63 per cent of the true indirect costs.

"How do we obtain these funds?   The answer is, through careful
planning and hard work on the part of many people, including trustees,
officers, deans, chairmen, faculty, the Development Office, the Alumni
Fund, and friends of the University."

For example a research contract that formerly called for $100,000 direct
costs plus $25,000, or $125,000, now would be $100,000 plus $20,000,
or $120,000.

REQUIRED:

Evaluate the president's comments. Do you agree with his analysis? Why
or why not?

joint-product costs and
by-product costs

CHAPTER XVIII

Nearly every manufacturing operation produces two or more products. But ordinarily all the manufacturing costs of these multiple products are applied to a single product. For example, as cloth or metal is cut or formed, the excess is regarded as waste or scrap. The minor cost that might be applied to the waste or scrap is usually ignored, and all the production cost is applied to, say, the coat or the lamp that is eventually manufactured.

Whether the accountant applies costs individually among multiple products is dependent on their relative revenue-producing power. When a group of individual products is simultaneously produced, with each product having significant relative sales values, the outputs are usually called *joint products*. The products are not identifiable as different individual products until a certain stage of production known as the *split-off point*. Their joint manufacturing cost is allocated carefully among the members of the product group. A distinguishing characteristic is that no one of the products may be produced without an accompanying appearance of the other products in the joint group, though perhaps in variable proportions. Examples include chemicals, lumber, petroleum products, flour milling, copper mining, meat packing, leather tanning, soap making, gas manufacturing, canneries, and tobacco manufacturing. A meat-packing company cannot kill a pork chop; it has to slaughter a hog, which supplies various cuts of dressed meat, hides, and trimmings.

We shall see that any method of assigning truly joint costs to various units produced is useful only for purposes of inventory costing. *Such assignment is useless for cost-planning and control purposes.*

The term *by-products* is usually confined to those multiple products that have very minor sales values as compared with that of the major or chief product(s).

In this chapter we shall examine (a) the methods of assigning joint costs to products, (b) the impact of joint costs on decision making, and (c) accounting for by-products.

METHODS OF ASSIGNING JOINT COSTS TO PRODUCTS

Definition of joint-product cost

Viewed broadly, joint costs plague the accountant throughout his work. The entire problem of allocating the costs of fixed assets to months, years, departments, and products is essentially that of joint costing. Sometimes the term *common cost* is used instead of *joint cost* to describe aspects of joint costing where facilities are shared, such as in computing unit cost of services like bank accounts. Any allocation method is limited in usefulness, because many facilities and services are shared by many revenue-producing activities. Another example of joint-cost problems is the difficulty of re-apportioning service department costs to producing departments. Still another illustration is the application of overhead to job orders. Essentially factory overhead items are costs that are jointly shared by all products flowing through the factory. However, we shall confine the term *joint-product cost* to the costs of a single process or series of processes that simultaneously produces two or more products of significant relative sales values. Joint-product costs are total costs incurred up to the point of separation of the different products.

Example 1.

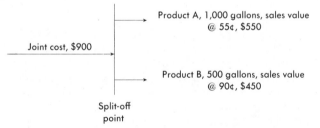

Example 1 shows the joint costs of a chemical process that produces Products A and B; both become finished goods at the split-off point. How much of the $900 joint cost is assignable to A? How much to B? The $900 cannot be physically identified or traced to either individual product, because the products themselves were not separated before the split-off point. Yet the accountant chooses to select some systematic means of splitting the $900 between the two products so that ending inventories may be costed and income determined. Two basic approaches are commonly used, although there are many variations of both: (1) physical measures and (2) relative sales values.

Physical measures

In Example 1, the $900 cost produced 1,500 gallons of product on a physical-quantity basis; therefore, the unit cost is 60¢ per gallon. Costs are assigned as follows: $600 to A, $300 to B. These computations may be shown in a different manner as follows:

	Production	Weighting	Costs Assigned
A	1,000 gal.	1,000/1,500 × $900	$600
B	500 gal.	500/1,500 × $900	300
	1,500 gal.		$900

Assume that one-tenth of the output is unsold at the end of the month. A product-line income statement would appear as follows:

INCOME STATEMENT FOR JOINT PRODUCTS
For the Month Ending _____

	A		B		Total
Sales	900 gals.,	$495	450 gals.,	$405	$900
Joint costs:					
Production costs	1,000 gals.,	$600	500 gals.,	$300	$900
Less inventory	100 gals.,	60	50 gals.,	30	90
Cost of sales	900 gals.,	$540	450 gals.,	$270	$810
Gross margin		($ 45)		$135	$ 90
Gross margin percentages				33.3%	10%

Note that the use of physical weighting for assignment of joint costs may have no relationship to the revenue-producing power of the individual products. Thus, if the joint cost of a hog were assigned to its various products on the basis of weight,[1] center-cut pork chops would have the same unit cost as pigs' feet, lard, bacon, ham, and so forth. Fabulous profits would be shown for some cuts, although losses would consistently be shown for other cuts.

Relative sales value approach

In the sense that inventory figures should be indicators of sales-generating power, the relative sales value approach gives the best practical approximation to the objective of getting a meaningful allocation of joint costs. Traditionally, accountants and managers have felt that costs are incurred with the expectation of recovery at a mark-up. Therefore, *the*

[1] Sometimes one joint product may be a liquid while another may be a solid. This situation necessitates converting all physical measures into common terms, such as pounds, gallons, square feet, and the like.

relative sales value method of joint-cost assignment is most widely used, because it assumes that all end products should show some profit margin under typical marketing conditions.   In effect, the relative sales value method assigns costs in proportion to a product's ability to absorb the costs. The popularity of the relative sales value method may be attributed to the search for a way to assign a cost to each of the final products that is an index of the product's ability to generate revenue:

	Production in Terms of Sales Value	Weighting	Costs Assigned
A	$ 550	550/1,000 × $900	$495
B	450	450/1,000 × $900	405
	$1,000		$900

	A	B	Total
Sales	$495.0	$405.0	$900.0
Production costs	$495.0	$405.0	$900.0
Less inventory	49.5	40.5	90.0
Cost of sales	$445.5	$364.5	$810.0
Gross margin	$ 49.5	$ 40.5	$ 90.0
Gross margin percentage	10%	10%	10%

Compare this income statement with the previous one; note that the gross margin percentage is the same for both products under the relative sales value method.   Exhibit 18-1 compares the two methods for assigning joint costs.

EXHIBIT 18-1

COMPARISON OF TWO METHODS FOR ASSIGNING JOINT COSTS

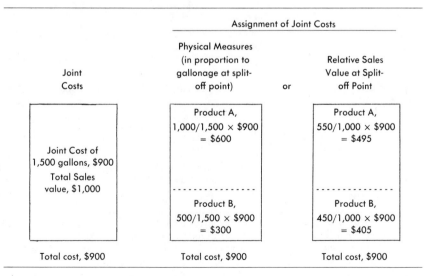

Costs beyond split-off

The relative sales value method becomes more intricate when joint products are processed individually beyond the split-off point. A conventional approach to this problem follows (all costs are processing costs):

Example 2.

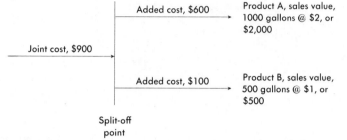

Although Example 2 is basically the same as Example 1, it assumes that the products are unsalable in their stage of completion at the split-off point. Further processing costs are needed to put them into salable form. *This assumption is important because, when sales price quotations (or replacement prices) at the split-off point are known or can be determined, they should be used as a basis for splitting joint costs.* That is, the best approach to assigning joint costs is the relative sales values *at the split-off point.* If these values are not explicitly available because there is no market for Products A and B at the split-off point or because the products cannot be purchased from outsiders, the *next best* alternative—for product-costing purposes only—is to take the ultimate relative sales values at the point of sale and work backward to *approximate* (computed) relative sales values at the split-off point. The conventional way of doing this is as follows:

	Production in Terms of Sales Values	Less Costs Beyond Split-off Point	Approximate Relative Sales Value at Split-off Point	Weighting	Joint Costs Assigned
A (1,000 gallons @ $2.00)	$2,000	$600	$1,400	1,400/1,800 × $900	$700
B (500 gallons @ $1.00)	500	100	400	400/1,800 × $900	200
	$2,500	$700	$1,800		$900

Exhibit 18-2 shows a product-line income statement as prepared under this "conventional approximated relative sales value" method, [2] assuming no ending inventories.

[2] There is another approximated relative sales value technique that may be applied in these situations. It entails (a) deducting an *over-all profit margin* from the sales values, obtaining the total costs that each product line should bear, and (b)

EXHIBIT 18-2

INCOME STATEMENT

For the Month Ending_____

		Product	
	Total	A	B
Sales	$2,500	$2,000	$500
Cost of goods sold:			
Joint costs	$ 900	$ 700	$200
Separable costs	700	600	100
Cost of goods sold	$1,600	$1,300	$300
Gross margin	$ 900	$ 700	$200
Gross margin percentage	36%	35%	40%

If bona fide selling prices are unavailable at the split-off point, as Exhibit 18-2 and footnote (2) assume, the computed (approximated) relative sales values should not be used for sell-or-process further decisions or for judging the performance of either the joint or the separable processes. The relative profitability of joint and separable processes cannot be determined by using artificial market prices, which incorporate shaky assumptions. The latter may be needed for product-costing purposes, but they are useless for planning and control. The relative profitability of joint processing and further separable processing must incorporate an incremental analysis of the level of bona fide selling prices (if there are none, analysis is impossible) at the split-off point and after separable processing.

---

deducting the separable costs from the total costs to obtain the joint-cost assignment. The data from Example 2 and Exhibit 18-2 would yield the following results under this *over-all margin* method:

	Total		A		A
Sales value	$2,500	1,000 @ $2.00,	$2,000	500 @ $1.00,	$500
Over-all gross margin percentage (from Exhibit 18-2)					
(36%)	900	(36%)	720	(36%)	180
Total cost	$1,600		$1,280		$320
Special processing cost	700		600		100
Joint cost	$ 900		$ 680		$220

A favorable aspect of the *over-all profit margin* technique is cited by Carl Thomas Devine, in *Cost Accounting and Analysis* (New York: The Macmillan Company, 1950), p. 116, as follows: "Uniform markup on all products is desirable for inventory purposes. Regardless of the composition of finished goods, equal inventory values (costs) will indicate equal sales possibilities."

Once this approach is understood, it is slightly easier to use than the conventional relative sales value method. Both techniques rest on arbitrary basic assumptions.

Costing joint products at realizable values

Because the various schemes for joint-cost allocations are subject to so many valid criticisms, many companies refrain from the attempt entirely. Instead, they carry all inventories resulting from joint processing at sales values or at net realizable values (ultimate sales values less estimated separable costs to complete and sell). The meat-packing industry is the primary example, but the canning and mining industries provide other examples. This realizable-value approach ignores joint production costs altogether. It is difficult to criticize this approach when one compares it with the pitfalls of trying to assign joint costs to products.

However, it should be pointed out that accountants ordinarily frown on carrying inventories at sales values, because in this way profit is recognized before sales are made. When compared with generally accepted inventory-costing methods, the realizable-value approach results in higher profits as inventory is increased and lower profits as inventory is decreased. Using selling prices or variations thereof as bases for inventory valuation is more justifiable where differences between costs and selling prices are small and where turnover is high (for example, in the meat-packing and other food-product industries).

Probably the most sensible method is followed by the many companies which carry their inventories at *net realizable values less a normal profit margin* to counteract the criticism that the net realizable value method recognizes profits before goods are sold.

IRRELEVANCE OF JOINT COSTS IN DECISION MAKING

No technique that is applicable to the problem of joint-product costing should be used for managerial decisions regarding whether a product should be sold or processed further. When a product is an inherent result of a joint process, the decision to process further is not influenced by either the size of the total joint costs or the portion of the joint costs assigned to particular products.

The decision to incur added costs beyond split-off is a matter of comparing the revenue available (if any) at the split-off point with the differential income attainable beyond the split-off point. In Example 2, zero revenue was available at the split-off point, whereas differential revenue for Product B ($500) less differential costs ($100) yields a differential income of $400. In other words, the company is better off by $400, the income that would be foregone if Product B were dumped in the river upon split-off. The amount of joint costs and how they are allocated are completely irrelevant with respect to these decisions.

Many manufacturing companies constantly face the decision of whether to process a joint product further. Meat products may be sold as cut or may be smoked, cured, frozen, canned, and so forth. Petroleum refiners are perpetually trying to adjust to the most profitable product mix. The refining process necessitates separating all products from crude oil even though only one or two may be desired. The refiner must decide what combination of processes to use to get the most profitable quantities of gasoline, lubricants, kerosene, naphtha, fuel oil, and the like. In addition, at times he may find it profitable to purchase distillates from some other refiner and process them further. Profitability depends on producing the proper product in the proper quantities at the proper time.

[In serving management for these decisions, the accountant must concentrate on opportunity costs rather than on how historical joint costs are to be split among various products. The only relevant costs are the additional costs (including the "cost" of capital) as compared with additional revenue. In turn, these must be compared with the revenue foregone by rejecting other alternatives.]

To illustrate the importance of the relevant-cost viewpoint, consider another example:

Example 3.

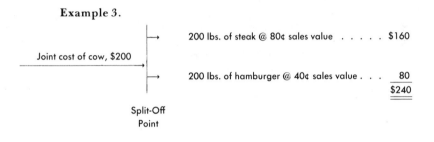

Conventional joint-cost allocations[3] would be:

	By Weight			By Sales Value		
	Pounds	Weighting	Joint Cost	Sales Value	Weighting	Joint Cost
Steak	200	2/4 × $200	$100	$160	16/24 × $200	$133
Hamburger	200	2/4 × $200	100	80	8/24 × $200	67
	400		$200	$240		$200

The packer is faced with the choice of selling the 200 pounds of hamburger at 40 cents ($80) or slicing, freezing, and packaging the hamburger as 200 packages of sandwich steaks. The total additional costs of converting bulk hamburger into sandwich steaks would be $30, while the sales price per package would be 60¢ (total revenue, $120).

Conventional methods of joint-cost allocation are not only irrelevant here, but allowing joint-cost allocations to influence the decision will yield inconsistent results. For example, the weight method would show a

[3] As already mentioned, meat packers typically carry inventory at selling prices less costs of disposal rather than use the two approaches here. However, the cow or hog example of a joint cost is useful for illustrative purposes.

loss for sandwich steaks, whereas the relative sales value method would show a profit:

	By Weight		By Relative Sales Value	
Sales, 200 lbs, @ 60¢		$120		$120
Joint cost	$100		$67	
Added cost	30	$130	30	$ 97
Profit		$(10)		$ 23

The only approach that will give valid results is to compare the incremental revenue with incremental costs. In this case:

Incremental revenue, 20¢ × 200 pounds	$40
Incremental costs, added processing	30
Additional margin	$10

Another way of looking at the same problem:

Sandwich steak revenue, 200 lbs. @ 60¢		$120
Costs:		
Added processing	$30	
Opportunity cost, foregoing of hamburger sales (200 × 40¢)	80	110
Difference in favor of added processing		$ 10

The validity of this approach may be proven as follows:

	Total Income Computations		
	Sell Hamburger	Sell Sandwich Steaks	
Sales	$240	($160 + $120)	$280
Total costs	200	($200 + $ 30)	230
Margin	$ 40		$ 50
Difference in margin,	$ 10		

[In summary, it is profitable to extend processing or to incur additional distribution costs on a joint product as long as the incremental revenue exceeds the total of incremental explicit costs and the incremental opportunity costs of required additional capital.]

ACCOUNTING FOR BY-PRODUCTS

Problems of definition

The distinction between joint products, by-products, and scrap is largely influenced by the relative sales values of the products in question. However, these distinctions are not firm; the variety of terminology and accounting practice is bewildering. For example, valuable brass turnings may be called *scrap* in one company and *by-products* in another. Glycerin, which is ordinarily a *by-product* of soap manufacture, may become at least a *joint product* during wartime production. Many sewage plants that regarded their products as waste have developed the waste into joint-product stature as valuable fertilizer. Kerosene once was a major petroleum product; now it is a by-product.

Kroehler Company, manufacturers of furniture, provides an example of the impact of technological change on importance of products. Traditionally, there has been 40 per cent wastage of wood in a furniture factory. Kroehler now compresses almost all of these wood scraps into cultured wood, which is used for bottoms and backs of drawers and other purposes. Previously, two-thirds of the scraps were incinerated at a cost of $2 per ton while the other third was used to fire steam boilers.

By-products are multiple products that have minor sales value as compared with that of the major or chief product(s). Examples are mill-ends of cloth and carpets; cotton meal and cotton hulls in processing of cotton oil; tar, naphtha, and kerosene in gasoline production; minor chemicals, gas, and tar from coke manufacture. The distinction between scrap and by-products is often difficult to establish. A view that is sometimes helpful is that by-products (a) have relatively more sales value than scrap and (b) are often subject to additional costs beyond the split-off point whereas scrap is usually sold outright. The basic accounting for scrap and for by-products is the same. *The net realizable values of both are best treated as deductions from the cost of the main product.* The rest of this discussion will be confined to accounting for by-products.

Accounting methods for by-products

There are many methods of accounting for by-products. A comparison of the methods is given in Exhibit 18-3. If the by-product is really a minor product, the differences in results between by-product methods are not significant enough to get excited about.

The following representative methods are illustrated in Exhibit 18-3.

Method
Illustrated

1	By-product income shown as additional revenue.
2	By-product income shown as other income.
3	By-product income shown as a deduction from cost of sales.
4	By-product income shown as a deduction from cost of production.
5	Net realizable value of by-products produced shown as a deduction from cost of production.
6	Same as (5), except that ending inventory of main product is based on Net Cost of production rather than on Gross Cost of production.

Conceptually, the best method is probably number 6, where the sales value less costs of disposal is deducted from the total costs of production of the main product. This method eliminates the lag between production and sales and directly matches the cost-reduction power of by-products against the production costs of the main product. The real effect of this approach is to recognize by-product inventory as an asset valued at selling price (or a variation thereof). Furthermore, if the realizable-value method is carried to its logical end, the main-product inventory should be based on the net cost of production and not on the gross cost. Nevertheless, the extra clerical effort involved in the more refined approaches such as (5) and (6) often results in the practical choice being made among the other methods.

Comparison of methods

As in so many phases of accounting, the conceptual issue here is one of timing the recognition of revenue and expenses. Methods (1) through (4) have identical impacts on net margin. It may be helpful to compare these methods with (5) and (6). Assume that the company ceases operations and merely sells its ending inventory in the ensuing period. See Exhibit 18-3, page 613, before examining the following analysis:

INCOME STATEMENT—SECOND PERIOD

		Methods		
		(1) through (4)	(5)	(6)
	Main product:			
	Sales, 10,000 units	$15,000	$15,000	$15,000
	Cost of sales (from ending inventory of prior period—Exh. 18-3)	10,000	10,000	9,880
(a)	Gross margin	$ 5,000	$ 5,000	$ 5,120
	By-product:			
	Sales, 300 units	$ 450	$ 450	$ 450
	Less:			
	Costs of disposal	90	90	90
	Inventory cost	–	360	360
(b)	Income from by-product sales	$ 360	$ 0	$ 0
	Net margin (a) + (b)	$ 5,360	$ 5,000	$ 5,120
	Net margin for first period	$30,840	$31,200	$31,080
	Net margin for two periods	$36,200	$36,200	$36,200

The two periods taken together show the same income by all methods. The variations in methods raise some provocative theoretical problems concerning matching of revenues and expenses, but expediency usually dictates the method actually used in practice.

The reader who prefers expediency but likes to recognize conceptual niceties will probably prefer either method (3) or method (4).

Both of these recognize that by-product margins are somehow reductions of cost of the main product, even though these methods are not very fussy about problems of timing such cost offsets.

EXHIBIT 18-3

COMPARISON OF ACCOUNTING METHODS FOR BY-PRODUCTS

Data for Illustration

No beginning inventories.

Main product:

Production	10,000 units	Production cost (gross)	$100,000
Sales	9,000 units	Cost of sales (gross)	90,000
Ending inventory	1,000 units	Sales	120,000

By-product:

Production	1,000 units		
Sales	700 units		
Ending inventory	300 units	By-product sales, 700 @ $1.50	$ 1,050
Sales value	$1.50 per unit	Costs of disposal, 700 @ $.30	210
Costs of disposal	$ .30 per unit	Net income from by-product sales	$ 840

Income Statements (in dollars)

Method (See text for description.)

	(1)	(2)	(3)	(4)	(5)	(6)
Sales	120,000	120,000	120,000	120,000	120,000	120,000
Income from by-product sales*	840					
Sales and other income	120,840	120,000	120,000	120,000	120,000	120,000
Cost of sales:						
Production costs, gross	100,000	100,000	100,000	100,000	100,000	100,000
Income from by-product sales*				(840)		
Net realizable value of by-product produced†					(1,200)	(1,200)
Production costs (net) of major product				99,160	98,800	98,800
Ending inventory—main product	(10,000)	(10,000)	(10,000)	(10,000)	(10,000)	(9,880)
Cost of sales (gross)	90,000	90,000	90,000			
Income from by-product sales*			(840)			
Cost of sales (net)			89,160	89,160	88,800	88,920
Gross margin	30,840	30,000	30,840	30,840	31,200	31,080
Other income:						
Income from by-product sales*		840				
Net margin	30,840	30,840	30,840	30,840	31,200	31,080

*By-product sales	$1,050	†Income from by-product sales		$ 840
Costs of disposal	210	Realizable value of ending inventory,		
		300 units × ($1.50 − $.30)		360
Income	$ 840	Net realizable value of by-products produced		$1,200

Methods (1) and (2) are supported by expediency alone. By-product accounting is an excellent example of how expediency may be the most important criterion in selecting an accounting method. Not much real harm is done if theory is warped in practice, as long as we are confident that the results do not differ significantly between the theoretical method and the practical method. This is the case in by-product accounting because by definition by-products are minor and thus should be immaterial—their sales values are small in relation to the major product(s).[4]

SUMMARY

Joint costs permeate accounting. Costs are joint with respect to time, facilities, and products. Accountants attempt to split joint costs among products having relatively important sales values. Where the joint product is valueless (for example, waste), all costs are applied to the major product. Where the joint product has minor value, it is often called a *by-product*; its net realizable value or income from sales is frequently deducted from the cost of the major product.

No matter what the joint-production situation, any assignment of a joint cost is useless for purposes of managerial decision making. The only use for allocating joint-product costs is for purposes of "reasonable" inventory valuations and income determinations. The *relative sales value method* is the technique most frequently used for assigning joint costs to products.

Only opportunity and incremental costs are relevant to the decisions on whether to incur additional separable costs beyond the split-off point. As long as the differential revenue exceeds the differential costs (including the appropriate cost of capital), additional cost incurrence will be warranted.

PROBLEM FOR SELF-STUDY

The Alden Oil Company buys crude vegetable oil. The refining of this oil results in four products, A, B, and C, which are liquids, and D, which is a heavy grease. The cost of the oil refined in 19x9 was $27,600

[4]However, "Determining the Cost of Gasoline," Statement of Tidewater Oil Company before the Federal Trade Commission, May, 1965 (available from Tidewater Oil Company, Los Angeles), describes and favors a linear programming computer method as the standard method for deriving the cost of gasoline in FTC pricing investigations. This method is applied to appropriate marginal or incremental raw materials, product values, and product yields. The linear programming method, in effect, computes total incremental variable costs and subtracts total by-product (such as fuel oil) value; the cost that remains is allocated to gasoline. Note that these results are the same as those obtained by using the by-product method described in this chapter, when applied to the same data. The results are the same because, for a given gasoline volume, the linear programming computer models increase by-product output until profit no longer increases. The models are designed to stop at a level of output at which the by-products literally break even.

For additional economic analysis of the over-all problem of costing joint products, see Rene P. Manes and Vernon L. Smith, "Economic Joint Cost Theory and Accounting Practice," *Accounting Review* (January, 1965), pp. 31–35.

and the refining department had total processing costs of $70,000. The output and sales for the four products in 19x9 were as follows:

Product	Output	Sales	Additional Processing Cost
A	500,000 gal.	$115,000	$30,000
B	10,000 gal.	10,000	6,000
C	5,000 gal.	4,000	—
D	9,000 gal.	30,000	1,000

REQUIRED:

1. Assume that the conventional approximated relative sales value of allocating joint costs is used. What is the net income for Products A, B, C, and D? Joint costs total $97,600.

2. The company had been tempted to sell at split-off directly to other processors. If that alternative had been selected, sales per gallon would have been: A, 15¢, B, 50¢, C, 80¢, and D, $3. What would the net income have been for each product under this alternative?

3. The company expects to operate at the same level of production and sales in the forthcoming year. Could the company increase net income by altering its processing decisions? If so, what would be the expected over-all net income? Which products should be processed further and which should be sold at split-off? Assume that all costs incurred after split-off are variable.

Solution.

1.

Sell Beyond Split-off

	(a)	(b)	Relative Sales Value at Split-off	(c)		a – (b + c)
	Sales Value	Separable Costs	(c)	Allocation of Joint Costs		Net Profit
A	$115,000	$30,000	$ 85,000	85/122 × $97,600 = $68,000		$17,000
B	10,000	6,000	4,000	4/122 × 97,600 =	3,200	800
C	4,000	—	4,000	4/122 × 97,600 =	3,200	800
D	30,000	1,000	29,000	29/122 × 97,600 =	23,200	5,800
	$159,000	$37,000	$122,000		$97,600	$24,400

2.

Sell at Split-off

	(a) Relative Approximated Sales Value at Split-off	(b) Allocation of Joint Costs	(a) – (b) Net Profit
A	500,000 ($ .15) = $ 75,000	75/111 × $97,600 = $65,947	$ 9,053
B	10,000 ($ .50) = 5,000	5/111 × 97,600 = 4,396	604
C	5,000 ($ .80) = 4,000	4/111 × 97,600 = 3,517	483
D	9,000 ($3.00) = 27,000	27/111 × 97,600 = 23,740	3,260
	$111,000	$97,600	$13,400

3. Note that comparing (1) and (2) in the manner computed above is irrelevant. For example, Product C's profit above is $483 or $800, despite the fact that the same amount is sold at the same price in either case. The only proper way to compare is to use an incremental approach:

	Sales Beyond Split-off	Sales at Split-off	Incremental Sales	Separable Costs Beyond Split-off	Incremental Gain or (Loss)
A	$115,000	$75,000	$40,000	$30,000	$10,000
B	10,000	5,000	5,000	6,000	(−1,000)
D	30,000	27,000	3,000	1,000	2,000
Increase in profit from further processing					$11,000

Based on the given data, the company income, before considering cost of capital for further processing, could be further improved by $1,000 by selling Product B at the split-off point instead of processing it further.

QUESTIONS, PROBLEMS, AND CASES

Note: Problems 18-9, 18-10 or 18-11, and 18-15 cover the major points. Problems 18-14 and 18-18 through 18-20 deal with joint products and capital-budgeting decisions. When the term "approximated relative sales value" is used, it refers to the conventional method illustrated in Exhibit 18-2.

18-1. "The problem of accounting for depreciation is one of joint costs." Do you agree? Why?

18-2. "Nearly every manufacturing operation produces two or more products." Do you agree? Why?

18-3. List four methods of accounting for by-products.

18-4. What is the main weakness of the relative sales method of joint-cost allocation?

18-5. Define *net realizable value*.

18-6. "The relative sales value method of joint-cost allocation is the best method for managerial decisions regarding whether a product should be sold or processed further." Do you agree? Why?

18-7. Difference Between Joint Products and By-Products.

1. Explain the basic difference between the method of accounting for joint products and that for by-products.

2. State the conditions under which an item should be treated as a by-product rather than as a joint product.

3. Explain the two principal methods of assigning joint costs to the joint products, and state the circumstances under which each would be appropriate.
[C.P.A.]

• **18-8. Relative Sales Value Method.** A company produces two joint products, A and B. The joint cost is $24,000. Added processing costs: A, $30,000; B, $7,500. A sells for $50 per unit; B sells for $25 per unit.

If the company produces 1,000 units of A and 500 units of B, what is the proper amount of joint cost that should be allocated to B, assuming that the approximated relative sales value method of allocation of joint costs is used?

• **18-9. Joint-Product Costs: Ending Inventories.** The Darl Company operates a simple chemical process to reduce a single basic material into three separate items, here referred to as X, Y, and Z (all three end products being separated simultaneously at a single split-off point).

Y and Z are ready for sale immediately upon split-off without further processing or any other additional cost. Product X, however, is processed further before being sold.

The selling prices quoted below have not changed for three years, and no future changes are foreseen.

During 19x3 the selling prices of the items and the total number sold were as follows:

X	120 T. sold for $1,600 per T.
Y	340 T. sold for $1,000 per T.
Z	175 T. sold for $800 per T.

There were no beginning inventories whatsoever of X, Y, Z.

The total joint manufacturing costs for the year were $505,000. An additional $30,000 was spent in order to finish product X.

At the end of the year, the following inventories of completed units were on hand: X, 180 tons; Y, 60 tons; Z, 25 tons. There was no ending work in process.

REQUIRED:

Prepare a computation of the "cost" of inventories X, Y, and Z for balance sheet purposes as of December 31, 19x3. Include in your presentation a summary of the cost of goods sold by product line. (The Darl Company uses the "approximated relative sales value" method of allocating joint costs to end products.)

18-10. Mark-ups and Allocation of Joint Costs.

1. Refer to the data and comments about Exhibit 18-2. Suppose that market prices were available at split-off of 70¢ for Product A and 40¢ for Product B. What is the joint cost applicable to A? to B? To what would you attribute the gross margin, the joint process or the separable process?

2. Refer to footnote 2 in the chapter. Suppose that market prices were available at split-off of 68¢ for Product A and 44¢ for Product B. What is the joint cost applicable to A? to B? To what would you attribute the gross margin, the joint process or the separable process? What is the role of bona fide market prices at split-off in management planning and control? Of computed approximate market prices?

18-11. Introduction to Joint Costing Techniques. The Wood Spirits Company produces two products, turpentine and methanol (wood alcohol), by a joint process. Joint costs amount to $12,000 per batch of output. Each batch totals 10,000 gallons, being 25 per cent methanol and 75 per cent turpentine. Both products are processed further without gain or loss in volume. Added processing costs: methanol, 30¢ per gallon; turpentine, 20 ¢ per gallon. Methanol sells for $2.10 per gallon; turpentine sells for $1.40 per gallon.

REQUIRED:

1. What joint costs per batch should be assigned to the turpentine and methanol, assuming that joint costs are assigned on a physical-volume basis?

2. If joint costs are to be assigned on an approximated relative sales value basis, what amounts of joint cost should be assigned to the turpentine and the methanol?

3. Prepare product-line income statements per batch for requirements (1) and (2).

4. The company has discovered an additional process by which the methanol (wood alcohol) can be made consumable and into a pleasant-tasting alcoholic beverage. The new selling price would be $6 a gallon. Additional processing would increase separable costs 90¢ a gallon, and the company would have to pay taxes of 20 per cent on the new selling price. Assuming no other changes in cost, what is the joint cost applicable to the wood alcohol? Should the company use the new process?

18-12. Joint Products and By-Products; Selection of Costing Method. A and B are joint products. Their cost for the period up to the point of separation was $30,000. There were no costs beyond this point. The production of A was 20,000 units. The production of B was 40,000 units. A's selling price is $5. B's selling price is 20¢ (twenty cents!).

Use this information in answering the four questions which follow. Each question is independent of all others except as noted. Only the above information is common to all the questions.

1. If there is no ending inventory of A and B (that is, all of the units were sold during the period), what allocation of cost would be made to A and B?

2. If the inventory at the end of the period was 10,000 units of A and 20,000 units of B, what valuation figure should be used for the total inventory (that is, A and B together)? Why?

3. If the ending inventory was 10,000 units of A and 10,000 units of B, what would the valuation of A be for balance sheet purposes? The valuation of B? Use the approximated relative sales value method.

4. If B is considered a *by-product* of A, would your answer to "3" have been different? If so, what would the valuation of A now be for balance sheet presentation? The valuation of B?

18-13. Christmas Trees; Allocating Joint Costs. S. Claus is a retired gentleman who has rented a lot in the center of a busy city for the month of December, 19x0, at a cost of $5,000. On this lot he sells Christmas trees and wreaths. He buys his trees by the bundle for $5 each. A bundle is made up of two big trees (average height, seven feet), four regular-sized trees (average height, five feet), and broken branches. The shipper puts in the broken branches merely to make all of the bundles of uniform size for shipping advantages. The amount of branches varies from bundle to bundle.

Mr. Claus gets 50¢ a foot for the trees. He takes home the broken branches. He and Mrs. Claus, Donner, Blitzen, and the rest sit about the fire in the evenings and make wreaths, which Mr. Claus sells for $3.50 each. Except for Christmas Eve, these evenings are a time when there is nothing else to do; therefore, their labor is not a cost.

During the course of the season Mr. Claus buys 1,000 bundles of trees and makes 2,000 wreaths. In addition to the broken branches, the wreaths contained pine cones (100 pounds, total cost $200), twine (4,000 yards @ 5¢ a yard), and miscellaneous items which amounted to $600.

In 19x0, Claus sold 1,800 of the seven-foot trees, all of the regular-sized ones, and half of the wreaths (the local Boy Scouts were also selling wreaths). The department store next door says that they will buy the rest of the wreaths, if Claus will preserve them, for $3 each. The preservative spray costs $2,000 for enough to do the job.

REQUIRED:

1. What unit cost should Claus assign to each of his items?
2. What is the inventory cost on January 1, 19x1, if he doesn't sell to the department store?
3. Should he sell to the department store?

18-14. Joint Costs; Change in Product Mix. The Laissez Faire Perfume Company processes a secret blend of flower petals into three products. The process works in such a way that the petals are broken down into a high-grade perfume, "Charm" and a low-grade flower oil. The flower oil is then processed into a low-grade perfume "Wild Scent" and "Personally" cologne.

The company used 10,000 pounds of petals last month. The costs involved in reducing the petals into "Charm" and flower oil were:

Direct material	$150,000
Direct labor	90,000
Indirect costs	60,000
	$300,000

The costs of producing "Wild Scent" and "Personally" from the flower oil were:

Direct material	$15,000
Direct labor	35,000
Indirect costs	20,000
	$70,000

Total production for the month, with no ending work in process inventory, was:

Charm	10,000 ounces
Wild Scent	20,000 ounces
Personally	50,000 ounces

The sales price of "Charm" is $40 an ounce; of "Wild Scent," $10 an ounce; and of "Personally," $1 an ounce.

Additional costs, entirely separate for each product, of processing and selling are:

Charm	$ 20,000
Wild Scent	160,000
Personally	40,000
	$220,000

REQUIRED:

1. Joint cost of "Charm," "Wild Scent," and "Personally," using the approximated relative sales value method.
2. Product-line income statement, assuming no beginning or ending inventories.

3. The management, completely ignorant of cost accounting, is considering the possibility of increasing the quality of "Wild Scent" at an increase in final processing cost of $2 per ounce. The selling price would increase to $12 an ounce. This would result in a different product mix of "Wild Scent" and "Personally." Every 10,000 pounds of petals would then result in 10,000 ounces of "Charm," 18,000 ounces of "Wild Scent," and 60,000 ounces of "Personally." The separable costs of "Personally" and "Wild Scent" are completely variable. All prices and costs not specifically mentioned will remain unchanged. Should this alternative be selected?

18-15. Sell or Process Further. Mow Company produced three joint products at a joint cost of $100,000. Two of these products were processed further. Production and sales were:

	Weight	Sales	Additional Processing Costs
A	300,000 lbs.	$245,000	$200,000
B	100,000 lbs.	30,000	None
C	100,000 lbs.	175,000	100,000

1. Assume that the approximated relative value of allocating joint costs is used. What is the net income for Products A, B, and C?

2. The company had been tempted to sell at split-off directly to other processors. If that alternative had been selected, sales would have been: A, $50,000 B, $30,000, and C, $60,000. What would the net income have been for each product under this alternative?

3. The company expects to operate at the same level of production and sales in the forthcoming year. Could the company increase net income by altering its processing decisions? If so, what would be the expected over-all net income? Which products should be processed further and which should be sold at split-off? Assume that all costs incurred after split-off are variable.

18-16. Sell or Process Further; Allocation of Fixed Costs. The Space Parts Co. receives cold worked steel in sheet form from a nearby steel mill. They have a special patented machine which takes the sheet steel and produces three missile parts simultaneously. Part A is taken from the machine and further processed to make it available for sale at $3.50; the additional processing cost for Part A is $495. Parts B and C are run through a vat containing a secret "dip" developed by one of the company engineers to make them heat-resistant. This dip costs 20¢ per cubic foot of product. Part B sells for $5 and part C for $8.25.

Additional Information

Material	$ 8,000
Direct labor	1,600
Maintenance and depreciation	1,200
	$10,800 cost of running special machine for month.

Month's production and sales (which is the typical product mix):

Part A	600 units
Part B	800 units
Part C	1,000 units

Part B has a volume of 0.50 cu. ft.

Part C has a volume of 0.75 cu. ft.

The vat is being depreciated at the rate of $60 per month, requires three men for its operation, at a total salary of $1,500 per month, and necessitates other operating expenses of $165 per month. All these costs are fixed.

REQUIRED:

1. Joint costs assignable to each part for the month's operations. Use the approximated relative sales value method.
2. The company has a chance to sell part B undipped at split-off at $4.70 each on a long-run basis. Should the company adopt this alternative?

18-17. Computation of Breakeven Point for Joint Processes. (Adapted from a problem prepared by Professor James March.) The March-I Company processes soybeans to obtain oil, meal, and chaff. There are three processes. In the cleaning process the chaff and foreign materials are separated from the beans. In the pressing process soybean oil and soybean cake are produced. The oil is stored in tanks and later pumped into tank cars for shipment. In the grinding process the soybean cake is dried and then ground into meal.

The standard yield from a ton (2,000 lbs.) of beans is 100 pounds of chaff, 800 pounds of meal, and 100 gallons of oil. The following selling prices have been chosen for the purpose of calculations: Beans delivered to plant, $120 a ton; chaff, $10 a ton; oil, $1.20 a gallon; and meal, $200 a ton. Budgeted costs of processing are:

	Variable costs per unit	Fixed costs per month
Cleaning	10¢ per ton of beans	$ 500
Pressing	$2 per ton of cleaned beans	2,000
Grinding	$2 per ton of meal	1,500

Assume that there are no work in process inventories and that selling and administrative expenses are: fixed costs of $1,800 monthly and variable costs of 10 per cent of dollar sales in the case of oil sales and meal sales and zero in the case of chaff sales.

REQUIRED:

1. Chart of physical flow.
2. How many tons of beans must be processed monthly in order to break even? Show computations clearly.

18-18. Comparing Alternatives; Discounted Cash Flow. Pottsville Process, Inc., processes an ore which yields 60 per cent product A, 20 per cent product B, and 20 per cent complete waste. Willo, Inc., the sole customer and a mere intermediate link in the distribution chain, purchases the entire output of products A and B.

A Pottsville company engineer has developed a process that will produce a 70 per cent yield of product A from the ore—a new product A that is in a form that can be sold directly to the prime user. This will eliminate Willo, Inc., as a customer for both products; there is no other available market for product B. The required investment to provide the capital equipment and the necessary expansion is $4,000,000. These new facilities have an estimated life of 20 years, exactly the remaining life of the present equipment. This money can be obtained at a rate of 4 per cent. However, the company's average cost of capital is 10 per cent.

COMPARATIVE COST DATA

Present

Processed: 1,000,000 tons per year.

Cost Data:	Per Ton
Variable manufacturing cost	$ 5.00
Fixed manufacturing cost other than depreciation	6.00
Depreciation on equipment (straight-line)	.30
	$11.30

"New Process"

Processed: 1,000,000 tons per year.

Cost Data:	
Variable manufacturing cost	$10.00
Fixed manufacturing cost other than depreciation	9.00
Depreciation—including new equipment (straight-line)	.50
	$19.50

PRICE DATA

Present:

Product A—$20.00 per ton.

Product B —$ 3.00 per ton.

"New Process":

"New Product" A—$30.00 per ton.

REQUIRED:

1. Prepare comparative annual income statements for the two alternatives.

2. Analyze the alternatives on a discounted cash-flow basis, using the present value technique.

3. Would your decision in (2) be changed if product B in the amount produced under the present process could also be sold under the new process?

18-19. Joint Costs and Discounted Cash Flow. The Faia Company manufactures products A, B, and C. These products all derive from the same basic raw material and are then processed into final products. Current operating data are displayed below:

Joint costs of production: $200,000 for 100,000 gallons.

	Per Unit	
	Selling Price	Cost Past Split-Off
A	$15	$10
B	10	4
C	6	2

Every 10 gallons of raw material produces 2 gallons of A, 5 gallons of B, and 3 gallons of C.

The Shrewd Co. has offered to lease a patented device to the Faia Company which will increase the yield from the common raw material by 50 per cent for an initial fee of $100,000 plus a royalty of 20¢ per gallon of yield. In addition, Shrewd Co. wants an exclusive contract as a term of the license to purchase all of the firm's final output of A at a price of $8 for the next six years. At the end of this time, Shrewd Co. would grant the Faia Company a rebate of $10,000. If the offer were accepted, the Faia Company could scrap existing equipment with a disposal value of $10,000, a remaining useful life of six years, and an expected disposal value of zero then.

The Faia Company expects that it will be able to market all of the additional output at existing prices. The sales manager of the Faia Company has indicated that he will turn down the offer, as it involves selling product A to Shrewd Co. at a price below out-of-pocket costs.

The Faia Company's minimum desired rate of return is 10 per cent.

REQUIRED:

Ignoring income taxes and using discounted cash flow, prepare data that will aid the president in making a correct decision. Include your recommendations as to the proper course of action.

18-20. Relative Sales Value Method; Discounted Cash-Flow Approach to Joint Process Replacement.

1. The *A* Company produces two items, X and Y. The items first go through joint processing. Then each receives separable processing. All of production is sold, and no inventories are carried. Annual joint costs are $100,000.

	X	Y
Yearly sales	$100,000	$300,000
Annual separable costs	$ 50,000	$150,000

What is the gross margin of each product, using the approximated relative sales value method?

2. A new joint process has been developed to replace the currently used joint process. It will reduce annual joint costs by 50 per cent, but it requires an initial investment of $200,000. Its useful life is five years. Annual additional processing costs of X will be reduced by $15,000 but those of Y will increase by $20,000. Sales will not be affected. Minimum desired rate of return is 10 per cent.

Should the new method be adopted? (Use discounted cash-flow calculations.) How has the reallocation of joint costs affected the decision?

18-21. Complex Physical Process; By-Product Accounting. The McLean Processing Company produces a chemical compound, Supergro, that is sold for $4.60 per gallon. The manufacturing process is divided into the following departments:

1. Mixing Department. The raw materials are measured and mixed in this department.

2. Cooking Department. The mixed materials are cooked for a specified period in this department. In the cooking process there is a 10 per cent evaporation loss in materials.

3. Cooling Department. After the cooked materials are cooled in this department under controlled conditions, the top 80 per cent in the cooling tank is

syphoned off and pumped to the Packing Department. The 20 per cent residue, which contains impurities, is sold in bulk as a by-product, Groex, for $2 per gallon.

4. Packing Department. In this department, special one-gallon tin cans costing 60¢ each are filled with Supergro and shipped to customers.

The Company's Research and Development Department recently discovered a new use for the by-product if it is further processed in a new Boiling Department. The new by-product, Fasgro, would sell in bulk for $5 per gallon.

In processing Fasgro, the top 70 per cent in the cooling tank would be syphoned off as Supergro. The residue would be pumped to the Boiling Department, where one-half gallon of raw material, SK, would be added for each gallon of residue. In the Boiling Department process there would be a 40 per cent evaporation loss. In processing Fasgro, the following additional costs would be incurred:

Material SK . . . . $1.10 per gallon
Boiling Department variable processing costs. . . . . . . $1.00 per gallon of input
Boiling Department fixed processing costs . . . . $2,000 per month

In recent months, because of heavy demand, the Company has shipped Supergro and Groex on the same day that their processing was completed. Fasgro would probably be subject to the same heavy demand.

During the month of July, 19x3, which was considered a typical month, the following raw materials were put into process in the Mixing Department:

Material FE — 10,000 gallons @ $ .90 per gallon
Material QT— 4,000 gallons @ $1.50 per gallon

July processing costs per gallon of departmental input were:

Mixing Department . . . . $.40
Cooking Department. 50
Cooling Department 30
Packing Department 10

For accounting purposes the Company assigns costs to its by-products equal to their net realizable value.

REQUIRED:

Prepare a statement computing total manufacturing costs and gross profit for the month of July that compares (1) actual results for July, and (2) estimated results if Fasgro had been the by-product. [C.P.A.]

18-22. Compute Maximum Price to Be Paid for Raw Material. The Nerg Fertilizer Company buys special silt and dehydrates, sorts, and bales it for sale as powerful fertilizer. The silt is separated into three grades, the separation being dependent upon the relative content of foreign matter. The three grades of fertilizer have the following list prices per ton: (1) $200, (2) $150, and (3) $125. Standards provide for 110 tons to be purchased for every 100 tons yield of baled fertilizer. Processing costs are $40 per ton of baled fertilizer and handling costs are $5 per ton of silt.

Selling and administrative expenses are 15 per cent of sales; target income is 10 per cent of sales.

The purchasing agent for the Nerg Company has been offered 2 carloads of silt at a cost of $80 per ton. Tests indicate that this silt will yield 60 per cent of grade 1 and 20 per cent each of grades 2 and 3; however, waste will be 10 per cent higher than present levels. Should the agent accept this offer in light of the target income?

18-23. Maximum Purchase Price for Ton of Material. The management of the Southern Cottonseed Company has engaged you to assist in the development of information to be used for managerial decisions.

The Company has the capacity to process 20,000 tons of cottonseed per year. The yield of a ton of cottonseed is as follows:

Product	Average Yield Per Ton of Cottonseed	Average Selling Price Per Trade Unit
Oil	300 lbs.	$ .15 per lb.
Meal	600 lbs.	50.00 per ton
Hulls	800 lbs.	20.00 per ton
Lint	100 lbs.	3.00 per cwt.
Waste	200 lbs.	

A special marketing study revealed that the Company can expect to sell its entire output for the coming year at the listed average selling prices.

You have determined the Company's costs to be as follows:

Processing costs
    Variable: $9 per ton of cottonseed put into process.
    Fixed: $108,000 per year.
Marketing costs
    All variable: $20 per ton sold.
Administrative costs
    All fixed: $90,000 per year.

From the above information you prepared and submitted to management a detailed report on the Company's breakeven point. In view of conditions in the cottonseed market, management told you that they would also like to know the average maximum amount that the Company can afford to pay for a ton of cottonseed.

Management has defined the average maximum amount that the Company can afford to pay for a ton of cottonseed as the amount that would result in the Company's having losses no greater when operating than when closed down under the existing cost and revenue structure. Management states that you are to assume that the fixed costs shown in your breakeven-point report will continue unchanged even when the operations are shut down.

REQUIRED:

1. Compute the average maximum amount that the Company can afford to pay for a ton of cottonseed.

2. You also plan to mention to management the factors, other than the costs that entered into your computation, that they should consider in deciding whether to shut down the plant. Discuss these additional factors.

[C.P.A. adapted.]

18-24. Joint Costs and Relevant Costs. The Curling Chemical Company begins all production in Department A. At the end of processing in Department A, Products X and Y appear. Both can be sold immediately, but X can also be processed further in Department B, where products X-1 and X-2 appear at the end of processing. X-1 is then immediately sold; X-2 can also be (a) sold in bulk to another processor, (b) packaged and sold as a consumer good, or (c) be aged for one year and reintroduced as raw material (Mysto) in Department A. One unit of aged X-2 is equal to one unit of Mysto.

Production and sales have been stable for the past few years, and the basic demand for all products does not look as though it will change for quite a few more years.

Data for the past year include the following:

Processing costs—Department A:

Variable	$ 75,000
Fixed	45,000

Processing costs—Department B (not including transferred-in costs):

Variable	$ 58,000
Fixed	150,000

Unit data:

	In Units	
	Production	Ending Inventories
X	220,000	20,000
Y	200,000	5,000
X-1	70,000	1,000
X-2	30,000	2,000

Selling prices per unit (unchanged throughout this year):

X (net of separable selling expenses)	$ .20
Y (net of separable selling expenses)	$ .44
X-1 (after deducting $.10 variable packaging costs)	$2.00
X-2 in bulk	$4.30
X-2 as consumer good	$5.00

Purchase costs:

Mysto: $4.00 per unit

5,500 units of Mysto were needed last year for production operations in Department A.

Selling costs of X-2, all variable, 10% of selling price.

Packaging costs of X-2 for consumer sales, 50¢ per unit.

The company's average cost of capital is 10%.

Packaging costs are considered as manufacturing costs by this company.

REQUIRED:

Unless otherwise stated, consider each situation below independently. State any special assumptions that you make.

1. The company uses "market value at split-off point" as a basis for allocating joint production costs to products. What are the appropriate total ending inventory values for Products X, Y, X-1, and X-2? Show computations *clearly*. For products X-1 and X-2, show a breakdown in total inventory costs between the Department A portion and the Department B portion.

2. Assume that the outside purchase cost of Mysto is going to rise. Based on the given information, how high will the price of Mysto have to go before the Curling Chemical Company should seriously consider aging X-2 and using it in Department A? Explain.

3. The company is considering adding another material at a cost of $1.00 per unit to Product X-1, packaging the resulting product at a variable cost of 42¢ per unit, and selling it through manufacturer's agents at a straight commission of 10 per cent of selling price. The prospective selling price will be $3.80 per finished unit. Should the company adopt this plan? Why? Show computations.

4. The company has been offered some new processing equipment for Department A. The salesman says that the new equipment will slash unit costs by 3.5¢. The new equipment will replace old equipment which has a remaining useful life of seven years, has zero disposal value now, and is being depreciated on a straight-line basis at $10,000 per year. The new equipment's straight-line depreciation would be $25,000 per year. It would last seven years and have no disposal value. The salesman pointed out that over-all unit costs now are slightly over 28.5¢ per unit of product in Department A, whereas the new equipment is being used by one of Curling's competitors at a unit cost of production of only 25¢ per unit of product, computed as follows:

Variable costs	$ 60,060
Fixed costs	76,440*
Total costs	$136,500
Divide by total units of X and Y produced	546,000
Cost per unit	25¢

*The $76,440 includes $25,000 depreciation on the new equipment in question. Curling's supervisory payroll is $6,000 less than this competitor's.

The salesman went on to point out that a saving of $3\frac{1}{2}$¢ per unit would add $14,700 to Curling's annual profits.

a. Show *specifically* how the salesman made his computations of Department A unit costs.

b. As adviser to Curling's management, evaluate the salesman's contentions and prepare a quantitative summary to support your recommendations for Curling's best course of action.

process costing:
a type of product costing

CHAPTER XIX

Process-costing techniques are used for inventory costing when there is continuous mass production of like units, in contrast to the production of tailor-made or unique goods. This chapter will cover the major *product-costing* approaches that may be used in process cost systems. It will be concerned only incidentally with *planning and control*, because the latter techniques have already been discussed and are applicable to all product-costing systems regardless of whether process costing or job order costing is used.

GENERAL CHARACTERISTICS OF PROCESS COSTING

All product costing is averaging

The most important point is that product costing is an averaging process. The unit cost used for inventory purposes is the result of taking some accumulated cost and dividing it by some measure of production. The basic distinction between job order costing and process costing is the breadth of the denominator: in job order costing, it is small; but in process costing, it is large.

The two polar extremes of product costing are usually labeled *job order costing* and *process costing*. As we saw in Chapter 4, job order costing is concerned with individual units or batches, each receiving various degrees of attention and skill. In contrast, process costing deals with the mass production of like units which usually pass in continuous fashion through a series of production steps called *operations* or *processes*. Process costing is most often found in such industries as chemicals, oil, textiles, paints, flour, canneries, rubber, steel, glass, food processing, mining, and cement.

If a company mass-produces only one uniform product, the product-costing task at first glance is simple. Obtain a unit cost by dividing the total manufacturing costs by the total units produced. Then use the resultant unit cost to compute the costs of inventories and the cost of goods sold. Indeed, it is simple, provided that there are (a) no work in process inventories or no significant changes between the levels of the beginning and ending work in process inventories and (b) no abnormal spoilage, shrinkage, or waste. However, if the foregoing two conditions do not hold, the product-costing task becomes more difficult.

Equivalent units: the key

Consider the following example:

Example 1.

Beginning inventory, in process	0
Units placed in process	40,000
Units finished	38,000
Units in process, end, ½ finished	2,000

Total costs to account for, $39,000. Assume that the flow of all costs is a continuous and constant stream.

In deriving average unit cost, it is evident that the units in process should not be weighted the same as the finished units. The partially completed units have received only half the attention and effort that the finished units have received. Thus, the notion of "equivalent performance" or "equivalent units" is used as a technique for establishing the cost per unit. In substance, the notion of equivalent units is the expression of physical units in terms of *doses* or *charges* of work applied thereto. So a physical unit is viewed by an accountant as a bundle of work charges, as a collection of the factors of production (material and conversion costs). Equivalent units are calculated as follows:

Units finished, charged with full dose of cost	38,000
Units in process, end, each unit is ½ completed:	
2,000 × ½	1,000
Total equivalent unit performance	39,000
Unit cost, per equivalent unit ($39,000/39,000)	$ 1.00
Costs to be attached to finished units:	
38,000 × $1.00	$38,000
To work in process:	
1,000 × $1.00	1,000
Total costs accounted for	$39,000

Note that unit cost is *not* calculated on the basis of physical units. It *is* calculated on the basis of equivalent unit performance—that is, on the basis of "charges" or "doses" of cost needed to finish a given unit. Therefore, a finished unit gets a full charge while a half-finished unit is assigned one-half a charge.

Five basic steps to solution

Many process cost situations contain complex production flows. It is essential to understand the production cycle itself before making any calculations; a sketch of the physical flow of units is often helpful. In making computations, the reader should concentrate on physical flow and equivalent units at the outset. *Disregard dollar amounts until equivalent units are computed.*

Building in self-checks in a step-by-step solution is an extremely helpful technique. Such self-checks are woven into the five-step uniform approach outlined below. Use caution as you study these steps. There is a real danger in clinging to the five steps as a mechanical technique without understanding *why* nearly all process cost problems can be solved with the five-step method. The reasoning will be explained as the discussion progresses. If the basic nature of accounting for process costs is understood, the five steps may be developed at any time. Memorization will not be necessary.

As can readily be seen in our examples, most process cost problems can be solved by a uniform approach as follows:

Step 1. Physical Flow. Trace the physical flow of production (Where did units come from? Where did they go?). In other words, (a) What are the units to account for? and (b) How are they accounted for? Draw flow charts as a preliminary step, if necessary.

Step 2. Equivalent Units. Convert the physical flow, as accounted for in Step 1(b) above, into equivalent units of production. Thus, if 6,000 physical units are two-thirds complete as to materials and one-half complete as to conversion costs, it means that 4,000 *doses* of material and 3,000 *doses* of conversion costs have been applied. (See Example 2 below.)

Step 3. Total Costs to Account For. Summarize, using material, labor, overhead, and so forth, the *total* costs to be accounted for.

Step 4. Cost Per Equivalent Whole Unit. Divide the data in Step 3 by the equivalent units calculated in Step 2. The result will be the cost per equivalent whole unit.

Step 5. Build the TOTAL Cost of Production and Inventories. Apply the unit costs obtained in Step 4 to inventories and to goods transferred out. Be sure to *total* these figures to see that they agree with the *grand total* obtained in Step 3.

Using the five steps

The above steps are noted parenthetically by number in the examples that follow.

In the actual presentation of a complete solution, Steps 1 and 2 and Steps 3 and 4 may be combined to make two schedules for the four steps.

It is not claimed that this five-step approach is the only or the fastest way to solve process cost problems. Nevertheless, it is logical and has self-checks. By applying the five-step approach, you will develop confidence and comprehension. Armed with this approach, you should be able to handle adequately any process cost situation. Short cuts should be applied wherever feasible. But it is difficult to generalize on short-cut methods, because they differ depending upon the specific problem and the student's ability to use them.

Beginning inventories

Calculations become more complicated when beginning inventories exist. There are two commonly used methods of tracing beginning inventory costs: *weighted average* and *modified first in, first out* (Fifo). The former will now be presented. The latter is discussed in the appendix to this chapter. The data in Example 2 will be used. *For the time being, concentrate on the data for Department A only.*

> **Example 2.** A company has two processes. Material is introduced at the *beginning* of the process in Department A, and additional material is added at the *end* of the process in Department B. Conversion costs are applied uniformly throughout both processes. As the process in Department A is completed, goods are immediately transferred to the next department; as goods are completed in Department B, they are transferred to Finished Goods.
>
> Data for the month of March, 19x1, include the following:

	Department A	Department B
Work in process, beginning	10,000 units	12,000 units
	2/5 completed, $7,500	2/3 completed, $21,000
	(Materials, $6,000;	(Transferred-in costs,
	conversion costs, $1,500)	$9,800; conversion
		costs, $11,200)
Units completed during March	48,000	44,000
Units started during March	40,000	?
Work in process, end	2,000, 1/2 complete	16,000, 3/8 completed
Materials cost added	$22,000	$13,200
Conversion costs added	$18,000	$63,000

REQUIRED:

Compute the cost of goods transferred out of each department. Also show journal entries for the transfers. Compute ending inventory costs for goods remaining in each department. Assume weighted-average costing.

WEIGHTED-AVERAGE METHOD

Description

As Exhibit 19-1 shows, the weighted-average method treats the beginning Work in Process as if it were begun and finished during the current period. The beginning work in process inventory is looked upon as being part and parcel of current production, regardless of the fact that it was begun prior to the current period. Therefore, beginning inventory costs are mingled with current costs. When equivalent units are calculated, work done in the past is regarded as if it were done currently.[1]

Interdepartmental transfers

Now we turn to Department B in Example 2. Most process cost situations have two or more departments in the production cycle. Ordinarily, as goods move from department to .department, related costs are also transferred. Exhibit 19-1 shows how such a transfer is handled under the weighted-average inventory method.

Transferred-in costs tend to give students much trouble, so special study is needed here. As far as Department B is concerned, units coming in from Department A may be viewed as if they were the raw material of Department B. Costs transferred from Department A to Department B are similar to the material costs brought into Department A, although they are called *transferred-in* or *previous department* costs, not material costs. That is, one might visualize the situation as if Department B bought the goods from an outside supplier. Thus, Department B's computations must provide for transferred-in costs for any new material costs added in Department B and for conversion costs added in Department B.

Journal entries and transfers

The journal entries under the weighted-average method are:

Department B—Work in process control	45,982	
Department A—Work in process control		45,982
To transfer costs from Department A.		
For detailed computations, see Exhibit 19-1.		
Finished goods control	119,403	
Department B—Work in process control		119,403
To transfer costs of goods finished.		

[1] William J. Vatter, *Managerial Accounting* (Englewood Cliffs, N.J.: Prentice-Hall, Inc., 1950), p. 434, calls the weighted-average method the "roll-back" method because "the averaging of cost doses is 'rolled back' to include the work carried over from last month."

EXHIBIT 19-1

PRODUCTION COST REPORT
For the Month Ending March 31, 19x1   Weighted-Average Method

Department A

Quantities	(Step 1) Physical Flow	(Step 2) Equivalent Units — Materials	Conversion Costs
Work in process, beginning	10,000(2/5)*		
Units started (or transferred in)	40,000		
To account for	50,000		
Units completed	48,000	48,000	48,000
Work in process, end	2,000(1/2)*	2,000	1,000
	50,000	50,000	49,000

Details

Costs	Totals	Materials	Conversion Costs	Equivalent Whole Unit
Work in process, beginning	$ 7,500	$ 6,000	$ 1,500	
Current costs	40,000	22,000	18,000	
(Step 3) Total costs to account for	$47,500	$28,000	$19,500	
(Step 4) Divide by equivalent units		÷50,000	÷49,000	
Cost per equivalent unit		$ .56	$ .398	$ .958

(Step 5) Summary of costs

Units completed (48,000)	$45,982†	48,000($.958)
Work in process, end (2,000):		
Transferred-in costs	$ —	
Materials	1,120	2,000($.56)
Conversion costs	398	1,000($.398)
Total cost of work in process	$ 1,518	
Total costs accounted for	$47,500	

Department B

Quantities	(Step 1) Physical Flow	(Step 2) Equivalent Units — Transferred-in Costs	Materials	Conversion Costs
Work in process, beginning	12,000(2/3)*			
Units started (or transferred in)	48,000			
To account for	60,000			
Units completed	44,000	44,000	44,000	44,000
Work in process, end	16,000(3/8)*	16,000	—	6,000
	60,000	60,000	44,000	50,000

Details

Costs	Totals	Transferred-in Costs	Materials	Conversion Costs	Equivalent Whole Unit
Work in process, beginning	$ 21,000	$ 9,800	$ —	$11,200	
Current costs	122,182	45,982	13,200	63,000	
(Step 3) Total costs to account for	$143,182	$55,782	$13,200	$74,200	
(Step 4) Divide by equivalent units		÷60,000	÷44,000	÷50,000	
Cost per equivalent unit		$ .9297	$ .30	$ 1.484	$2.7137

(Step 5) Summary of costs

Units completed (44,000)	$119,403	44,000($2.7137)
Work in process, end (16,000):		
Transferred-in costs	$ 14,875	16,000($.9297)
Materials	—	
Conversion costs	8,904	6,000($1.484)
Total cost of work in process	$ 23,779	
Total costs accounted for	$143,182	

*Degree of completion on conversion costs.
†Rounded from 45,984 for decimal discrepancy.

Sometimes a problem requires that the Work in Process account be split into Work in Process—Materials, Work in Process—Labor, and Work in Process—Overhead. In these cases, the journal entries would contain this greater detail, even though the underlying reasoning and techniques would be unaffected.

Production cost reports

The format in Exhibit 19-1 attempts to make a step-by-step worksheet also serve the purpose of a formal production cost report. However, as process cost situations become more complex, the details become more intricate and unwieldy for jamming into a worksheet that can also serve as a cost report. The point is that a step-by-step, no-short-cut approach to process costing computations is needed. Therefore, the exhibit is concerned primarily with stressing the logic and the need for built-in checks; the format is of much less importance, principally because production cost reports vary considerably from company to company anyway.

STANDARD COSTS AND PROCESS COSTS

Standards are useful

Previous chapters demonstrated that the use of standard costing is completely general; that is, it can be used in job order situations or in process-costing situations, and with absorption costing or direct costing. Standard cost procedures tend to be most effective when they are adapted to process-costing situations. Mass, continuous, and repetitive production conditions lend themselves rather easily to setting meaningful physical standards. Price tags may then be applied to the physical standards to develop standard costs. Such standard costs would allow for normal shrinkage, waste, evaporation, or spoilage.

The intricacies and conflicts between weighted-average and fifo costing methods (discussed in the appendix to this chapter) are eliminated by using standard costs. Further, weighted-average and fifo techniques become very complicated when used in industries that produce a variety of products. Standard costing is especially useful where there are various combinations of materials, operations, and product sizes. March points out:

> *A steel rolling mill uses various steel alloys and produces sheets of various sizes and of various finishes. The items of raw material are not numerous; neither are the operations performed. But used in various combinations they result in too great a variety of products to permit the use of the averaging procedure of historical process cost accounting. Elsewhere in modern industry similar conditions are frequently found as, for example, in plants manufacturing rubber goods, textiles, ceramics, paints, and packaged-food products.*[2]

[2] James H. March, *Cost Accounting* (New York: McGraw-Hill Book Company, Inc., 1949), p. 171.

Process costing in practice

The weighted-average method and the fifo method (particularly) have been extensively covered by cost accounting texts, including the first edition of this book. However, the time has come for their de-emphasis; more attention should be given to standard costing because it is more useful for both product costing and control. There is some evidence to support this assertion. In 1965 some of my students personally interviewed accounting executives at fourteen process-costing companies in the Chicago area:

Chemicals	2
Steel	1
Food processing	6
Meat packing	1
Glass	1
Rubber	1
Petroleum	1
Paint	1
	14

The over-all product-costing systems were distributed as follows:

Weighted-average (actual):		
Absorption costing	3	
Direct costing	1	4
Standard:		
Absorption costing	5	
Direct costing	4	9
Hybrid: Actual for material, standard for labor, and predetermined overhead rate		1
Total		14

Note that no companies used fifo. Note, too, the tendency toward direct costing. Furthermore, a student's survey of company process-costing practices as described in individual articles in the N.A.A. Bulletins from 1955 to 1965 revealed that not a single company out of forty used a fifo process-costing system.

Clearly, there is a wide diversity in practice, and standard costing is likely to be growing in importance in process-costing industries. Therefore, because of its conceptual and practical appeal, standard costing deserves our study. Because we have already seen how standard costing aids planning and control, we shall concentrate on its product-costing aspects.

Computations under standard costing

Example 3.   The facts are basically the same as those for Department A in Example 2, except that standard costs have been developed for the process as follows:

	Per Unit
Direct materials, introduced at start of process	$ .53
Conversion costs, incurred uniformly throughout process	.37
Standard cost per unit	$ .90
Work in process, beginning, 10,000 units, 2/5 completed, (materials, $5,300; conversion costs, $1,480)	$ 6,780
Units completed during March	48,000
Units started during March	40,000
Work in process, end	2,000, 1/2 complete

REQUIRED:

(a) Compute the standard cost of goods completed and of goods in process at end.

(b) If "actual" material costs added during the month were $22,000 and conversion costs were $18,000, show a summary schedule of total material variance and total conversion cost variance.

The formal solution is shown in Exhibit 19-2. Requirement (b) appears at the bottom of the exhibit. Careful study of Exhibit 19-2 will readily reveal that a standard cost system greatly simplifies process cost computations. A standard cost system not only eliminates the intricacies of weighted-average versus fifo inventory methods; it also erases the need for burdensome computations of costs per equivalent unit. The standard cost *is* the cost per equivalent unit. In addition, a standard-costing approach facilitates control.

ADDITIONAL ASPECTS OF PROCESS COSTING

Estimating degree of completion

This chapter's illustrations plus almost all process cost problems blithely mention various degrees of completion for inventories in process. The accuracy of these estimates depends on the care and skill of the estimator and the nature of the process. Estimating the degree of completion is usually easier for materials than for conversion costs. The conversion sequence usually consists of a number of standard operations or a standard number of hours, days, weeks, or months for mixing, heating, cooling, aging, curing, and so forth. Thus, the degree of completion for conversion costs depends on what proportion of the total effort needed to complete one unit or one batch has been devoted to units still in process. In industries where no exact estimate is possible, or, as in textiles, where vast quantities in process prohibit costly physical estimates, all work in process in every department is assumed to be either $1/3$, or $1/2$, or $2/3$

EXHIBIT 19-2

STANDARD COSTS IN A PROCESS COST SYSTEM
Department A, Production Cost Report (at standard),
For the Month Ending March 31, 19x1

Quantities	Physical Flow	Equivalent Units Material	Equivalent Units Conversion Costs
Work in process, beginning	10,000(2/5)		
Units started	40,000		
To account for	50,000		
Units completed:			
From beginning inventory	10,000*	— *	6,000*
From current production	38,000	38,000	38,000
Work in process, end	2,000(½)	2,000	1,000
Units accounted for	50,000	40,000	45,000

Costs	Totals	Materials	Details Conversion Costs	Equivalent Whole Unit
Standard cost per equiv-alent unit (given)		$.53	$.37	$.90
Equivalent units		× 40,000	× 45,000	
Current standard costs	$37,850	$21,200	$16,650	
Beginning inventory	6,780	$ 5,300	$ 1,480	
	$44,630			

Summary of Costs

Units completed (48,000)	$43,200			48,000($.90)
Work in process, end (2,000):				
Materials	$ 1,060	2,000($.53)		
Conversion costs	370		1,000($.37)	
Total cost of work in process	$ 1,430			
Total costs accounted for	$44,630			

Summary of Variances for Current Performance:

Current output in equivalent units		40,000	45,000
Current output at standard costs		$21,200	$16,650
Costs charged to department for the month		$22,000	$18,000
Total variance†		$ 800U	$ 1,350U

*Note that, to obtain a measure of current output, a first-in, first-out physical flow is usually as-sumed in standard costing situations. Therefore, because all material is added at the beginning of the process, no equivalent units of material are added during the current period for the be-ginning Work in Process; similarly, only 6,000 units of conversion costs are added.
†These could be broken down further into price, rate, quantity, and efficiency variances, depending upon details that may be available.

complete. In other cases, continuous processing entails little change of work in process levels from month to month. Consequently, work in process is safely ignored and monthly production costs are assigned solely to goods completed.

The company survey mentioned earlier disclosed the following practices concerning the valuation of work in process:

Method of Valuation	Number of Companies
Raw material input	3
Standard cost to the extent completed	3
Deduct estimated costs to complete from ultimate cost when finished	2
Not applicable or of negligible value	5
No information available	1
	14

Overhead and predetermined rates

Labor and overhead tend to be lumped together as conversion costs for process-costing purposes. In many process cost industries continuous, uniform production results in little fluctuation of total factory overhead from month to month. In such cases, there is no need to use predetermined overhead rates. Of course, where overhead costs and production vary from period to period, predetermined overhead rates are used in order to get representative unit costs.

Overhead and cost flow

The assumption that all conversion costs are incurred uniformly in proportion to the degree of product completion is difficult to justify on theoretical grounds. For example, this implies that a wide variety of overhead cost incurrence is directly related to labor cost incurrence. Although such a direct cause-and-effect relationship may not exist, refinements of overhead application beyond this assumption are usually impractical and inexpedient. When more precision is attempted, it is usually confined to developing a predetermined overhead rate to be loaded on material cost to cover such indirect costs as purchasing, receiving, storing, issuing, and transferring materials. In such cases, one overhead rate would be applied along with material costs while a separate overhead rate would be applied along with labor costs.

SUMMARY

Process-costing techniques are used for inventory costing when there is continuous, mass production of like units. The key concept in process costing is that of equivalent units, the expression of physical units in terms of doses or charges of work applied thereto.

Five basic steps may be used in solving process cost problems. Process costing is complicated by uneven flow of cost factors, by the presence of beginning inventories, and by the presence of costs transferred-in from prior departments.

Two widely advocated costing techniques are known as the *weighted-average* and *first-in, first-out* methods. As the appendix shows, for product-costing purposes, the weighted-average method is vastly superior to fifo in most instances.

The use of standard costs in process cost systems is simpler and more useful than other techniques for both product-costing and control purposes.

PROBLEMS FOR SELF-STUDY

Review each example in this chapter and obtain the solutions on your own. Then check your work against the solutions, which appear in the various exhibits.

APPENDIX: MODIFIED FIRST-IN, FIRST-OUT

Illustration of fifo

The fifo method regards the beginning inventory as if it were a batch of goods separate and distinct from goods started and finished within the same period. Fifo is really a step in the direction of job order costing, because it distinguishes batches whereas the weighted average method does not.

Example 3: Study the data in Example 2, page 631. Assume first-in, first-out costing and compute the solution for both departments.

The solution for Department A in Exhibit 19-3 carries costs separately for (a) goods carried over in beginning work in process and for (b) goods started and finished in the current month. The unit costs differ for each portion (batch) of the total goods completed during the month. As may be seen by comparing computations for Department A in Exhibits 19-1 and 19-3, the weighted-average method is far easier to use than fifo for process costing.

Transfers' effect: modification of fifo

In a series of interdepartmental transfers, each department is regarded as a distinct accounting entity. All transferred-in costs during a given period are carried at one unit cost, regardless of whether weighted-average or fifo techniques were used by previous departments.

Thus, although the fifo method as used by Department A may show batches of goods accumulated and transferred at different unit costs, these goods are typically costed by Department B at *one* average unit cost,

PRODUCTION COST REPORT
For the Month Ending March 31, 19x1 — Modified First-in, First-out Method

EXHIBIT 19-3

Quantities

	Department A				Department B				
	(Step 1) Physical Flow	(Step 2) Equivalent Units Materials	Conversion Costs	Equivalent Whole Unit	(Step 1) Physical Flow	(Step 2) Equivalent Units Transferred-in Costs	Materials	Conversion Costs	Equivalent Whole Unit
Work in process, beginning	10,000(2/5)*				12,000(2/3)				
Units started (or transferred in)	40,000				48,000				
To account for	50,000				60,000				
Units completed:									
From beginning inventory	10,000	—	6,000		12,000	—	12,000	4,000	
From current production	38,000	38,000	38,000		32,000	32,000	32,000	32,000	
Work in process, end	2,000(1/2)	2,000	1,000		16,000(3/8)	16,000	—	6,000	
Units accounted for	50,000	40,000	45,000		60,000	48,000	44,000	42,000	

Costs

Department A:

	Totals	Materials	Conversion Costs	Equivalent Whole Unit
Work in process, beginning	$ 7,500			
Current costs:	40,000	$22,000	$18,000	
(Step 3) Total costs to account for	$47,500			
(Step 4) Divide by equivalent units		÷40,000	÷45,000	
Cost per equivalent unit		$ .55	$ .40	$ .95
(Step 5) Summary of costs:				
Units completed (48,000):				
From beginning inventory (10,000)	$ 7,500			
Current costs added:				
Materials	—			
Conversion costs	2,400		6,000($.40)	
Total from beginning inventory	$ 9,900			
Started and completed (38,000)	36,100			38,000 ($.95)
Total costs transferred out	$46,000			
Work in process, end (2,000):				
Transferred-in costs				
Materials	$ 1,100	2,000($.55)		
Conversion costs	400		1,000($.40)	
Total cost of work in process	$ 1,500			
Total costs accounted for	$47,500			

Department B:

	Totals	Transferred-in Costs	Materials	Conversion Costs	Equivalent Whole Unit
Work in process, beginning	$ 21,000				
Current costs:	122,200	$ 46,000	$13,200	$63,000	
(Step 3) Total costs to account for	$143,200				
(Step 4) Divide by equivalent units		÷48,000	÷44,000	÷42,000	
Cost per equivalent unit		$.958333	$ .30	$ 1.50	$2.75833
(Step 5) Summary of costs:					
Units completed (48,000):					
From beginning inventory (12,000)	$ 21,000				
Current costs added:					
Materials	3,600		12,000($.30)		
Conversion costs	6,000			4,000($1.50)	
Total from beginning inventory	$ 30,600				
Started and completed	88,267				32,000 ($2.75833)
Total costs transferred out	$118,867				
Work in process, end (16,000):					
Transferred-in costs	$ 15,333	16,000($.95833)			
Materials	—				
Conversion costs	9,000			6,000($1.50)	
Total cost of work in process	$ 24,333				
Total costs accounted for	$143,200				

*Degree of completion on conversion costs.

as Exhibit 19-3 demonstrates. In other words, a departmental fifo method may be used, but in practice the strict fifo method is modified to the extent that subsequent departments use weighted-average methods for cost transferred in during a given period. If this were not done, the attempt to trace costs on a strict fifo basis throughout a series of processes would become too burdensome and complicated. For example, a four-department process-cost system could have at least eight or more batches, which would need separate costing by the time costs are transferred to and out of the final department. However, as goods are transferred from the last process to Finished Goods, the records of finished stock could be kept on a strict first-in, first-out method if desired. The clerical burden alone is enough to cause most process cost industries to reject strict fifo as a costing method. More will be said about the weakness of fifo in the appendix to the next chapter concerning spoilage.

In summary, although the so-called fifo method is sometimes used in process-costing situations, only rarely is an application of strict fifo ever encountered. It should be called a *modified* or *departmental fifo* method. Fifo techniques are applied within a department to cost goods transferred *out*, but goods transferred *in* during a given period usually bear a single average unit cost as a matter of convenience.

Comparison of weighted-average and fifo

The most apparent cause of any significant difference in results between fifo and weighted-average methods is the erratic price behavior of raw materials. However, in such cases, the company is likely to rely on some special technique (usually some version of standard or estimated prices) for costing production so as to isolate the influence of price variances on production costs.

Except for raw material prices, the differences in results between fifo and weighted-average methods are usually insignificant because of the inherent characteristics of industries using process costing. Process cost situations usually entail mass production of a continuous nature. Beginning and ending inventory levels are not likely to change radically from month to month. Furthermore, conversion costs per unit are not likely to fluctuate wildly from month to month.

For *cost-control* purposes, fifo is generally superior to the weighted-average method because current performance should be judged solely on the basis of current cost incurrence. However, neither the fifo nor the weighted-average method is as effective as standard process costing for purposes of cost control.

Finally, those readers who plan to take the CPA examination should recognize that the modified fifo method is frequently required on the examination, even though it is seldom encountered in practice.

Pitfalls to avoid in working problems

1. Remember to include transferred-in costs from previous departments in your calculations. Such costs should be treated as if they were

another kind of material costs, because each department is treated as a separate entity. In other words, when successive departments are involved, transferred goods from one department become all or a part of the raw material of the next department, although they are called *transferred-in costs*, not raw material.

2. Material and conversion costs (labor and overhead) are often not applied at the same rates. Special care should be used, therefore, in expressing work in process in terms of equivalent units. For material doses, the degree of completion may be 100 per cent (if all material is added at beginning of the production cycle) for some material and 0 per cent for material which will not be added until the end of the process. At the same time, conversion doses may be 50 per cent or 75 per cent.

3. In calculating costs to be transferred on a first-in, first-out basis, do not overlook the costs attached at the beginning of the period to goods that were in process but are now included in the goods transferred.

4. Unit costs may fluctuate between periods. Therefore, transferred goods may contain batches accumulated at different unit costs (see point 3). These goods, when transferred to the next department, are typically valued by that next department at *one* average unit cost.

5. Units may be expressed in terms of pounds in one department and gallons in the next. Consider each department separately. Unit costs would be based on pound measures in the first department and gallons in the second. As goods are received by the second department, they may be converted to the gallon unit of measure.

6. If the problem calls for first-in, first-out calculations, do not use the weighted-average approach, and vice versa.

QUESTIONS, PROBLEMS, AND CASES

Note: Problems 19-6, 19-8, 19-9, 19-14, and 19-15 cover basic notions of process costing. Problems 19-10 and 19-13 deal with standard costing. Notice that, when standard costing is applied to process cost situations, there is very little new to learn. Problems on fifo process costing appear in a separate category at the end of this group.

19-1. "Standard cost procedures are particularly applicable to process-costing situations." Do you agree? Why?

19-2. What are some virtues of standard costs as used in process costing?

19-3. "There is no need for using predetermined overhead rates for product costing in process-cost industries." Do you agree? Why?

19-4. Why should the accountant distinguish between *transferred-in costs* and *new raw material* costs for a particular department?

19-5. What is the feature of the first two steps of the five-step uniform approach that distinguishes them from the final three steps?

●**19-6. Introductory Process Costing: Material Introduced at Start of Process.** A certain process incurred $40,000 of production costs during a month. Materials costing $22,000 were introduced at the start of processing, while conversion costs of $18,000 were incurred at a uniform rate throughout the production cycle. Of the 40,000 units of product started, 38,000 were completed and 2,000 were still in process at the end of the month averaging one-half complete.

REQUIRED:

In step-by-step fashion, prepare a production cost report showing cost of goods completed and cost of ending work in process.

19-7. Introductory Process Costs; Single Department. The following data pertain to the Mixing Department for July:

Units:	
Work in process, July 1	0
Units started	50,000
Completed and transferred to Finishing Department	35,000

Costs:	
Material P	$200,000
Material Q	$ 70,000
Direct labor and overhead	$135,000

Material P is introduced at the start of the process, while Material Q is added when the product reaches a three-fourths stage of completion. Conversion costs are incurred uniformly throughout the process.

REQUIRED:

Cost of goods transferred during July. Cost of work in process as of July 31. Assume that ending work in process is one batch, two-thirds completed.

19-8. Process Costing, Budgeting and Control.* The Dopern Company uses departmental budgets and performance reports to help plan and control its process-costing operations. Department A has the following budget for January's contemplated production of 1,000 whole units of equivalent performance, which represents a normal month's volume.

Variable and controllable costs	
Direct material	$20,000
Direct labor	10,000
Indirect labor	2,000
Power	200
Supplies	800
	$33,000

Fixed and uncontrollable costs	
Rent	$ 400
Supervision	1,000
Depreciation	500
Other	100
	$ 2,000
Total budgeted costs	$35,000

*Prepared by the author and adapted for use in the May, 1965, CPA examination.

Direct material is introduced at the start of the process. All conversion costs are assumed to be incurred uniformly throughout the process. Production fluctuates from month to month, so that the fixed overhead is applied at a rate of $2 per equivalent unit.

There were no beginning inventories. Eleven hundred units were started during the month; 900 were completed, and the 200 still in process at the end of the month were estimated to be three-fourths completed. There is no material shrinkage or spoilage, and no waste of materials.

The following performance report was prepared:

	Budget	Actual	Variance
Direct material	$20,000	$22,550	$2,550 U
Direct labor	10,000	10,500	500 U
Indirect labor	2,000	2,100	100 U
Power	200	210	10 U
Supplies	800	840	40 U
	$33,000	$36,200	$3,200 U

U = unfavorable.

A total of $2,000 of fixed conversion costs were incurred during January.

REQUIRED:

1. Cost of goods completed during January.
2. Cost of ending work in process.
3. Amount of under- or over-applied overhead at January 31.
4. Comment on the performance report in 150 words or less. What *specific* conclusions can you draw from the performance report?

19-9. Comparison of Two Process-Costing Techniques. The following information relates to one department operating under a process-cost system: Work in process, December 1, 19x1, 1,000 units, 40 per cent complete, consisting of $8,703 of materials and $5,036 of conversion costs. Production completed for December, 8,200 units; work in process, December 31, 19x1, 800 units, 20 per cent complete.

All materials are introduced at the start of the process, while conversion costs are incurred uniformly throughout the process. Materials added during December were $72,000; conversion costs were $83,580.

REQUIRED:

1. Using weighted averages, show a schedule of equivalent performance, unit costs, and summary of costs. Also prepare a summary entry for the transfer of completed goods to finished stock.
2. Assume standard costs per finished unit as follows: Direct material, $8.50; Conversion costs, $10.00.
   (a) Compute standard costs of goods transferred and still in process.
   (b) Give the total variances for current performance on direct material and conversion costs.

19-10. Weighted Averages; Standard Costs. The Dyer Processing Company had work in process at the beginning and end of 19x1 as follows:

	Percentage of Completion	
	Material	Conversion Costs
January 1, 19x1 — 3,000 units	40%	10%
December 31, 19x1 — 2,000 units	80%	40%

The company completed 40,000 units of finished goods during 19x1. Manufacturing costs incurred during 19x1 were: materials, $242,600; conversion costs, $445,200. Inventory at January 1, 19x1 was carried at a cost of $10,600 (materials, $7,000; conversion costs, $3,600).

Part One. Assuming weighted average:

1. Compute equivalent production for 19x1 for (a) materials and (b) conversion costs.

2. What is the proper cost of ending goods in process?

Part Two. (Consider independently of requirements in Part One.)

If the standard cost for materials is $5 per finished unit and the standard cost for conversion costs is $10 per finished unit, what would be the total standard cost of work *performed during* 19x1?

19-11. Weighted-Average Process-Costing Method. Bright Paint Co. uses a process-cost system. Materials are added at the beginning of a particular process and conversion costs are incurred uniformly. Work in process at the beginning and end is assumed 50 per cent complete. One gallon of material makes one gallon of product.

Data:

Beginning inventory	900 gallons
Materials added	9,900 gallons
Ending inventory	450 gallons
Conversion costs incurred	$18,000
Cost of materials added	$20,000
Conversion costs, beginning inventory	$ 800
Cost of materials, beginning inventory	$ 1,600

REQUIRED:

Prepare a cost of production report for the weighted-average method.

19-12. Weighted-Average Process Costing. The B Lunder Co. Ltd. manufactures a product which requires processing in three departments. In Department C, materials are added at the very beginning of the Department C processing. Conversion costs are added continuously throughout the process. Manufacturing overhead is applied to units in process in Department C at the rate of 125 per cent of direct labor costs.

The following data pertain to the operations of Department C for the month of July:

In process, July 1: 4,000 units, 60% converted costs:

Dept. B costs	$15,340
Dept. C materials	2,273
Dept. C direct labor	2,764
Dept. C applied overhead	?

During the month, 12,000 units were received from Department B at a cost of $45,460.

Costs incurred by Department C during July included:

Direct materials requisitioned	$ 8,975
Direct labor	11,124

On July 31 there were 6,000 units left in process, 40 per cent converted. No units were spoiled or lost in processing.

REQUIRED:

Using the weighted-average method of costing, prepare a production cost report for July.   [C.G.A.A. Adapted]

19-13.   Process Costs; Standard Costs; Analysis of Variances. The Jammer Company uses standard costs and produces a chemical from a secret formula. Material A is introduced at the start of the single process, while Material B is added when the conversion process is 80 per cent completed. Conversion costs are applied uniformly throughout the process.

Standard costs per finished unit:	
Materials:	
A, five gallons @ 40¢	$ 2.00
B, one pound	10.00
Conversion costs:	
Labor, 2 hours	5.00
Variable overhead*	1.00
Fixed overhead*	4.00
	$22.00

*Applied as a percentage of standard direct labor cost.

Beginning inventory in process, July 1, 19x1, consisted of 1,000 units, all 30 per cent completed. Fifty-two thousand gallons of A were added during July. Twelve thousand pounds of B were added during July. Nine thousand units were completed. Two thousand units were still in process, 90 per cent completed, at the end of July.

Actual costs incurred by the production department were as follows:

Material A, $26,000
Material B, $108,000
Direct labor, 22,000 hours @ $2.50 = $55,000
Variable overhead, $10,850
Fixed overhead, $47,800

Normal activity is 12,000 finished units per month.

REQUIRED:

Expression of production in terms of equivalent units for:
1. Material A.
2. Material B.
3. Conversion costs.

Give dollar amounts and use F or U to denote whether the following variances are favorable or unfavorable:

4. Material A price variance (Assume that this company recognizes price variances for materials as they are used rather than as they are purchased.)
5. Material A usage variance.
6. Material B price variance.
7. Material B usage variance.
8. Labor rate variance.
9. Labor efficiency variance.
10. Variable overhead spending variance.
11. Variable overhead efficiency variance.
12. Fixed overhead spending variance.
13. Fixed overhead volume variance.

19-14. Two Departments; Two Months.* One of the products of this company is manufactured by passing it through two processes. The materials are started into production at the beginning of Process 1 and are passed directly from Process 1 to Process 2 without inventory between the processes. Operating data for two months are given below:

January

Process 1. No initial work in process. During the month, 800 units were put into process and $8,000 was charged to this account. Operations during the month cost $2,800. Six hundred units were finished and passed on to Process 2. The work in process at January 31 was one-half finished.

Process 2. No work in process on January 1. The work transferred from Process 1 was received and costs of $2,000 were incurred in operations to complete 300 units. At the end of the month, 300 units one-third finished remained in process.

February

Process 1. Six hundred units of material were put into process at a total price of $6,000. Other costs incurred were $2,550. At the end of the month, there were 300 units still within the process, two-thirds finished.

Process 2. Costs charged to operations in this process for February were $2,640. On February 28 there were 300 units still within the process, two-thirds finished.

There is no spoilage or shrinkage in either of the processes; all units unfinished at the beginning of the month are completed within that month.

*William J. Vatter, *Managerial Accounting*, © 1950. Prentice-Hall, Inc., Englewood Cliffs, N.J. Reprinted by permission.

REQUIRED:

Calculations of production costs for each process for each month on a weighted-average basis.

19-15. Joint Costs and Process Costs; First-in, First-out; Sell or Process Further. The Chemo Company manufactures two principal products, known as Gummo and Yummo. The company has three producing departments, A, B, and C. Raw material is started in process in Department A. Upon completion of joint processing in that department, two distinct chemicals are produced. One-fourth of the output goes to Department B, where it is made into Gummo; the other three-fourths goes to Department C, where it becomes Yummo. As Gummo and Yummo are completed, they are immediately transferred to finished stock.

The company assigns Department A costs to Gummo and Yummo in proportion to their net sales values at point of separation, computed by deducting costs to be incurred in subsequent processes from the sales value of the products.

The following information concerns the operations during May, 19x1:

INVENTORIES

	April 30		May 31
	Units	Cost	Units
Department A	None		None
Department B	500*	$10,000	700†
Department C	1,000*	11,300	700†
Finished goods—Gummo	800	19,200	500
Finished goods—Yummo	600	13,200	800

*Each unit is 1/5 completed.
†Each unit is 3/5 completed.

COSTS INCURRED IN MAY

	Materials Used	Conversion Costs
Department A	$72,000	$72,000
Department B	—	$15,600
Department C	—	$12.00 per equivalent unit

Twelve thousand units of material were produced in Department A.

	Sales Prices
Gummo	$25.00 per unit
Yummo	$22.00 per unit

Prices as of May 31 are unchanged from those in effect during the month.

The company uses first-in, first-out to cost out production.

REQUIRED:

1. For May production, conversion cost per equivalent unit in Department B.

2. Conversion cost per equivalent unit in Department A.

3. Total costs transferred to Department B.

4. Costs transferred from Department B to finished stock.

5. The company is considering a chance to sell the product that now goes into Department C at the split-off point instead of processing it into Yummo. (Gummo would continue to be processed as usual.) If the long-run selling price at split-off point will be $10, should the company close down Department C and sell at split-off? Why? Answer in seventy words or less.

19-16. Process Costs, Joint Products, and Applicable Costs for Bidding on a Government Contract. The "Dart Company" problem requirements: (1) Calculate the quantities of raw material ingredients to be placed in process in each of the departments. (2) Complete the problem as required in problem instructions.

From the following information concerning Dart Company, prepare a statement showing the estimated cost of producing 13,500 tons of X product for the purpose of bidding on a government contract.

Dart Company manufactures X, a main product, and Y, a by-product. X is produced and sold by the ton (2,000 lbs.). The raw material used in production consists of three ingredients, "H", "I", and "J", contained in both the finished main product and the finished by-product in proportions and at estimated costs per ton set forth below:

> "H"—40% at $8 per ton
> "I"—36% at $5 per ton
> "J"—24% at $7 per ton

The contract for 13,500 tons of X represents 60 per cent of the budgeted 19x2 production of X by Dart Company.

Main product X is manufactured through four processes, as follows:

Process No. 1: Ingredients "H" and "I" are issued at the outset of Process No. 1; completed work in process is transferred to Process No. 2.

Process No. 2: Ingredient "H" at the end of process No. 2 suffers a 5 per cent weight loss due to evaporation, and 10 per cent of the remaining work in process is sold as waste at a nominal amount of $6 per ton; completed work in process is transferred to process No. 3.

Process No. 3: Ingredient "J" at the outset of process No. 3 is mixed with work in process. Ingredient "J" loses 4 per cent of its original weight owing to evaporation at the end of process No. 3.

Process No. 4: In this final process, the material is separated into main product X and by-product Y in the proportions of 80 per cent and 20 per cent, respectively, and such products are placed in salable form.

Estimated direct labor per ton by processes is as follows:

Process No.	Direct Labor Cost per Ton
1	$5.00
2	2.50
3	3.00
4	4.00

Manufacturing overhead expense at normal capacity, that is, 75 per cent of a total plant capacity of 25,000 tons annually of X, is as follows:

Process No.	Variable	Fixed	Total
1	$ 60,000	$30,000	$ 90,000
2	62,000	18,000	80,000
3	50,000	20,000	70,000
4	40,000	16,000	56,000
Total	$212,000	$84,000	$296,000

At the normal activity level, general manufacturing overhead applicable to the factory as a whole amounts to $60,000, of which 40 per cent is fixed.

It is expected that the units called for by the government contract, coupled with the company's curtailed civilian production during 19x2, will reach 90 per cent of total-plant capacity measured in finished units of product X.

Product Y is expected to sell for an estimated $20.00 per ton, before deduction for handling, selling, and administrative expenses of $2.50 per ton.

Carry all computations to two decimal places.

Assume that direct labor cost is applied to the total weight at the beginning of each process. [C.P.A.]

19-17. Fifo Computations. Refer to Problem 19-9. Repeat requirement (1), using the modified first-in, first-out method.

19-18. Fifo Computations. Repeat Problem 19-11, using the modified first-in, first-out method.

19-19. Fifo Computations. Repeat Problem 19-14, using the modified first-in, first-out method.

19-20. Fifo Process Costing. Bisto Corporation manufactures valves and pumps for liquids. On December 1, 19x4, Bisto paid $25,000 to the Poplen Company for the patent for its Watertite Valve. Bisto planned to carry on Poplen's procedure of having the Valve casing and parts cast by an independent foundry and doing the grinding and assembling in its own plant.

Bisto also purchased Poplen's inventory of the Valves at 80 per cent of its cost to Poplen. The purchased inventory was comprised of the following:

	Units
Raw material (unfinished casings and parts)	1,100
Work in process:	
Grinding (25% complete)	800
Assembling (40% complete)	600
Finished Valves	900

Poplen's cost accounting system provided the following unit costs:

	Cost per Unit
Raw material (unfinished casings and parts)	$2.00
Grinding costs	1.00
Assembling costs	2.50

Bisto's cost accounting system accumulated the following costs for the month of December, which do not include cost of the inventory purchased from Poplen:

Raw material purchases (casings and parts for 5,000 units)	$10,500
Grinding costs	2,430
Assembling costs	5,664

Bisto's inventory of Watertite Valves at December 31, 19x4 follows:

Raw material (unfinished casings and parts)	2,700
Work in process:	
Grinding (35% complete)	2,000
Assembling (33-⅓ % complete)	300
Finished Valves	2,250

No Valves were spoiled or lost during the manufacturing process.

REQUIRED:

(Bisto uses the modified fifo process-costing method in its accounting system.)

Prepare a schedule to compute the equivalent units produced, the costs incurred per unit, and a summary of costs for the month of December, 19x4.

[C.P.A. Adapted]

spoilage, waste, defective units, and scrap

CHAPTER XX

Problems of waste, scrap, or spoilage are found in nearly all manufacturing businesses, regardless of the specific production techniques used. Because there is a general approach to this entire area, this chapter views the problem as a whole before considering the peculiar difficulties in process-costing and job-costing situations.

The conceptual ideas of accounting for spoilage, scrap, and waste primarily center about distinguishing between abnormal and normal spoilage. Abnormal spoilage is controllable by first-line supervision, whereas normal spoilage is not. Accounting for spoilage, defective units, and the like varies considerably in practice. This chapter will consider these matters from both product-costing and control viewpoints.

TERMINOLOGY

Terminology and accounting in this area are not at all precise or uniform. This chapter distinguishes between the various terms as follows:

Spoilage. Production that does not meet dimensional or quality standards and that is junked and sold for disposal value. Net spoilage cost is the difference between costs accumulated to point of rejection less disposal value (sometimes called *salvage value*).

Defective Units. Production that does not meet dimensional or quality standards and that is subsequently reworked and sold through regular channels as firsts or seconds, depending on the characteristics of the product and on available alternatives.

Waste. Material that either is lost, evaporates, or shrinks in a manu- facturing process or is a residue that has no measurable recovery value;

for example, gases, dust, smoke, and unsalable residues. Sometimes waste disposal entails additional costs; for example, atomic waste.

Scrap. Material residue from certain manufacturing operations that has measurable but relatively minor recovery value. For example, outlined metal from a stamping operation, shavings, filings, turnings, borings, sawdust and short lengths from woodworking operations, and sprues and "flash" from foundry and molding processes. Scrap may be either sold or reused.

SPOILAGE IN GENERAL[1]

Management implications and factor combination

Most production processes generate some bad as well as good units as an unavoidable result of the most economical combination of the factors of production. Although it may be technically possible to eliminate spoilage altogether in many instances, it may be uneconomical to do so because the costs of lowering spoilage rates are greater than the costs of eliminated spoilage. Thus, beer bottles sometimes explode, defective castings inevitably appear, and impure as well as pure chemicals and food arise. The problem of spoilage is important from many aspects, the most important being that of managerial planning and control. Managers must first select the most economical production method or process. They then must see that spoilage is controlled within chosen predetermined limits so that excessive spoilage does not occur.

Normal spoilage

Working within the selected set of production conditions, management must establish that rate of spoilage which is to be regarded as *normal*. *Normal spoilage* is that which arises under efficient operating conditions; it is an inherent result of the process and is thus uncontrollable in the short run. Costs of normal spoilage are typically viewed as a part of the costs of *good* production because the attaining of good units necessitates the simultaneous appearance of spoiled units. In other words, normal spoilage is planned spoilage in the sense that the choosing of a given combination of factors of production entails a spoilage rate that management is willing to accept.

Abnormal spoilage

Abnormal spoilage is that which should not arise under efficient operating conditions; it is regarded as unnecessary and thus controllable even in the short run. Costs of abnormal spoilage are "lost costs," meas-

[1] The writer acknowledges the helpful suggestions of Professor Samuel Laimon, of the University of Saskatchewan.

ures of inefficiency that should be written off directly as losses for the period. The Loss From Abnormal Spoilage account should appear on a detailed income statement as a separate loss item, preferably below Net Operating Income.

General accounting procedures for spoilage

Before discussing debits and credits for spoiled goods, let us try to relate spoiled goods to the two major purposes of cost accounting: control and product costing. Accounting for control is primarily concerned with charging responsibility centers for costs as *incurred*. Product costing is concerned with *applying* to inventory or other appropriate accounts the costs already incurred. Where does costing for spoiled goods fit into this framework? First, it must be made clear that the costs of both normal and abnormal spoiled goods are *product costs* just like costs of acceptable finished goods. Thus, product costs can represent either good product or bad product. The existence of spoiled goods does not involve any additional cost beyond the amount already incurred.[2] Therefore, in accounting for spoiled goods:

(1) We are dealing with cost application and reallocation rather than new cost incurrence.

(2) We want to distinguish between costs of normal spoilage (which should be added to the cost of good units) and abnormal spoilage (which should be written off as a loss).

(3) We want to accumulate data to spotlight the cost of spoilage so that management is made aware of its magnitude.

Depending on the product(s) or departments involved, there is a bewildering mass of treatments in practice which vary from being inexcusable to being highly informative. This chapter cannot possibly cover all the theoretical and practical ramifications. It will try to contrast conceptual treatments with some methods used in practice.

A study of the conceptual entries in Exhibit 20-1 will show that, when a product is spoiled, some debit must be made to balance the necessary credit to work in process. Further, some means must be found to charge normal spoilage to good inventory and abnormal spoilage to a loss account. The entries in the conceptual treatment use a Cost of Spoiled Goods account to highlight the nature of the problem and to stress the notion that the costs applied to work in process are initially product costs which are then reallocated either to Finished Goods or to a loss account. In practice, this account is not used, and the second set of entries in Exhibit 20-1 are more likely to be found.

[2]Where spoilage is not detected until completion of goods, spoiled units require the same effort as good units. In other words, a laborer can be performing with equal efficiency on all goods and yet turn out some spoiled units because of inferior materials, worn cutting tools, and the like. Thus, a workman can efficiently turn out spoiled goods. That is, labor efficiency may be very satisfactory, but spoilage may nevertheless be a major problem.

EXHIBIT 20-1

GENERAL ACCOUNTING FOR SPOILAGE

Assume:	Units worked on		1,100
	Good units completed	1,000	
	Normal spoilage	30	
	Abnormal spoilage	70	1,100

Assume a unit cost of $10, not including any spoilage allowance.

CONCEPTUAL TREATMENT			PRACTICAL TREATMENT			
1. Work in process	11,000		1.	(Same.)		
Stores, Accrued payroll,						
Applied overhead		11,000				
1,100 units worked on.						
2. Cost of spoiled goods	1,000		2.3.4.	Finished goods	10,300	
Work in process		1,000		Work in process		10,300
100 units spoiled.				1,000 good units		
3. Finished goods	10,000			completed @ $10		
Work in process		10,000		plus normal spoil-		
1,000 good units completed.				age of 30 units		
4. Finished goods	300			@ $10. Total		
Cost of spoiled goods		300		costs of 1,000		
Normal spoilage allowance,				good units is thus		
30 units.				$10,300.		
5. Loss from abnormal spoilage	700		5.	Loss from ab-		
Cost of spoiled goods		700		normal spoilage*	700	
Abnormal spoilage,				Work in process		700
70 units.				Abnormal spoilage,		
				70 units.		

*In practice, abnormal spoilage is often not isolated at all. Instead, the $700 cost is lumped with the other costs to show a total cost of $11,000 and a unit cost of $11 for the 1,000 good units produced.

JOB COSTING AND SPOILAGE

Spoiled units sold for salvage: treatment in practice

Job cost accounting for spoilage in practice varies considerably. Where spoiled goods have a disposal value,[3] the net cost of spoilage is computed by deducting disposal value from the costs of the spoiled goods accumulated to the point of rejection.

Where spoilage is considered to be a normal characteristic of a

[3] In practice, the words *scrap* and *spoilage* are sometimes used indiscriminately. Thus, *spoilage costs* may be thought of as total accumulated cost of spoiled work. Yet the spoiled goods may be "scrapped" (that is, sold for whatever can be recovered—"scrap" value). Thus, *net spoilage cost* is total spoilage cost less scrap recovery.

given production cycle, and where causes of spoilage are attributable to work done on all jobs, net spoilage cost is budgeted as a part of overhead, so that the predetermined overhead rate includes a provision for spoilage costs. Therefore, spoilage costs are spread, through overhead application, over all jobs rather than being loaded on particular jobs only. The rationale is thus provided for the debit, to the overhead control account, of the net spoilage cost in the following journal entry made when spoilage is considered to be normal in character:

Stores control (spoiled goods at disposal value)	150	
Department factory overhead control (normal spoilage)	350	
Work in process		500

Assume that 5 pieces out of a lot of 50 were spoiled. Costs accumulated to point where spoilage was detected were $100 per unit. Salvage value is estimated at $30 per unit. Items in parentheses indicate subsidiary postings.

Another alternative used where management finds it helpful for control or for pricing is to credit specific jobs with only the resale value of spoiled units, thus forcing the remaining good units in the job to bear net normal spoilage costs. The journal entry, with the same data as were just used, follows:

Stores control (spoiled goods at disposal value)	150	
Work in process		150

Criticism of practical treatment under job costing

Conceptually, the prevailing treatments just described can be criticized primarily because *product costs* are being charged back to Department Factory Overhead Control, which logically should accumulate only *costs incurred*, rather than both cost incurrence and product costs. If this distinction is not maintained, Department Factory Overhead Control will include duplicate charges for overhead. For example, as both good units and those units which will be spoiled are worked on, the various production costs (including applied overhead) are charged to the departmental work in process account. Then, when the normal spoilage is detected, the conventional treatment results in charging back these same product costs (including applied overhead), in an amount equal to the actual net spoilage cost, to the departmental overhead control account.[4]

To illustrate, assume that the actual net spoilage cost of $350 is exactly equal to a predetermined normal spoilage cost allowance for the

[4] For an extended criticism of the duplication of charges to Department Factory Overhead Control, see Alfred P. Koch, "A Fallacy in Accounting for Spoiled Goods," *Accounting Review* (July, 1960), pp. 501–502.

completed production of forty-five good units of product. The more logical conceptual treatment would be as follows:

1. Work in process   5,000
         Stores, Accrued payroll, Applied overhead   5,000
    50 units worked on at costs of $100 each.

2. Stores (5 spoiled units at disposal value of $30 per unit)   150
    Cost of spoiled goods   350
         Work in process   500
    5 units spoiled @ $100 accumulated costs.
    Net spoilage cost is $100 less $30, or $70 each.

3. Finished goods [45 × $100 plus (5 × $70) normal
       spoilage allowance]   4,850
         Work in process   4,500
         Cost of spoiled goods   350
    45 good units completed with normal spoilage allowance. If spoilage were abnormal, it would be written off as a loss. If spoilage consisted of $300 normal and $50 abnormal, the debits would be split between Finished Goods and a loss account accordingly.

This conceptual treatment does not bury a normal spoilage allowance in the factory overhead application rate and does not charge actual net normal spoilage costs to the overhead control account. Instead, it deals with spoilage as a problem separate and distinct from cost incurrence. It isolates net spoilage costs as a special bundle of product costs already incurred and applies (allocates) normal spoilage to good units produced through a special predetermined normal spoilage rate (the credit entry being to Cost of Spoiled Goods or, if desired, to a Cost of Spoiled Goods Applied account which is subsequently closed against Cost of Spoiled Goods in a manner similar to the closing of applied overhead accounts).[5]

DEFECTIVE UNITS

Defective units are subsequently reworked and transformed into units to be sold as "firsts" or "seconds." Management needs effective control over such actions because foremen are tempted to rework rather than to junk spoiled units. If control is not exercised, foremen may rework many

[5] In an unpublished paper, Professor Samuel Laimon evaluates the views expressed by Koch and expands the conceptual treatment described above. Laimon recognizes the existence of two kinds of normal and abnormal spoilage in job order accounting: spoilage peculiar to the job and spoilage common to all jobs. He suggests the provision of separate normal spoilage allowances for each of these and, therefore, the use of two special predetermined normal spoilage application rates. The accounting for spoilage costs is fraught with joint-cost problems and control problems that are among the most difficult in the entire field of cost accounting.

bad units instead of having them sold for salvage at a greater economic advantage. Rework should either be authorized by the foreman's superior or be undertaken only in accordance with prescribed operating procedures.

Unless there are special reasons for charging rework to the jobs or batches that contained the bad units, extra materials, labor, and other costs in practice are usually charged to overhead.[6] Thus, once again we see that rework is usually spread over all jobs or batches as a part of a predetermined overhead rate. Assume that the five spoiled pieces used in our prior illustration are reworked and sold as firsts through regular channels. Entries follow:

Original cost accumulations:	Work in process control	500	
	Stores control		200
	Accrued payroll		200
	Factory overhead applied		100
Rework: (Figures assumed)	Departmental factory overhead control (rework)	190	
	Stores control		40
	Accrued payroll		100
	Factory overhead applied		50
Transfer to finished stock:	Finished goods control	500	
	Work in process control		500

ACCOUNTING FOR SCRAP

Scrap is residue from manufacturing operations that has measurable but relatively minor recovery value. There are two major aspects of accounting for scrap: control and costing. Items like metal chips, turnings, filings, and borings should be quantified by weighing, counting, or some other expedient means. Norms or standards should be determined, because excessive scrap indicates inefficiency. *Scrap tickets* are prepared as source documents for periodic scrap reports that summarize the amount of scrap and compare it with predetermined norms or standards. Scrap should be returned to the storeroom to be held for sale or for re-use. Scrap should be accounted for in some manner, not only from the point of view of efficiency, but because scrap is often a tempting source for embezzlement by workers.

[6] The criticisms of the practical treatment for spoiled goods are also applicable to the above treatment—but only in the sense that the overhead incurred and applied accounts may be padded for amounts that in themselves did not necessitate overhead incurrence. In other words, the extra materials, labor, and variable overhead may represent extra cost incurrence, but fixed overhead will not be affected. Also, any accounting entry that simultaneously involves a debit to department overhead and a credit to overhead applied tends to blur the primary purpose of the overhead control account—that of only accumulating overhead costs *as incurred*.

There are many methods of accounting for scrap. Typically, scrap is not assigned any cost; instead, its sales value is regarded as an offset to factory overhead, as follows:

Scrap returned to storeroom:	No journal entry.		
	(Memo of quantity received is entered on the perpetual record.)		
Sale of scrap:	Cash	xx	
	Department factory overhead control		xx
	Posting made to subsidiary record - "Sale of Scrap" column on departmental cost sheet.		

This method is both simple and accurate enough in theory to justify its wide use. A normal amount of scrap is an inevitable result of production operations. Basically, this method does not link scrap with any particular physical product; instead, because of practical difficulties, all products bear regular production costs without any particular credit for scrap sales except in an indirect manner. What really happens in such situations is that sales of scrap are considered when setting predetermined overhead rates. Thus, the predetermined overhead rate is lower than it would be if no credit for scrap sales were allowed in the overhead budget.

An alternate method in a job cost situation would be to trace sales of scrap to the jobs that yielded the scrap. This method is used only when it is feasible and economically desirable. For example, there may be agreements between the company and particular customers that provide for charging specific, difficult jobs with all scrap or spoilage costs and crediting such jobs with all scrap sales arising therefrom. Entries follow:

Scrap returned to storeroom:	No journal entry.		
	(Memo of quantity received and related job made on perpetual record.)		
Sale of scrap:	Cash	xx	
	Work in process		xx
	Posting made to specific job order.		

The above illustrations assume that no inventory value is assigned to scrap as it is returned to the storeroom. Where there is a significant time lag between storing scrap and selling it, there is justification for inventorying scrap at some conservative estimate of net realizable value so that production costs and related scrap recovery may be recognized in the same period.

Some companies tend to delay sales of scrap until the price is most attractive. Violent price fluctuations are typical for scrap metal. In these cases, if scrap inventory becomes significant, it should be inventoried at some "reasonable" value—a difficult task in the face of volatile market prices.

SOME APPLICATIONS TO STANDARD COSTS

Shrinkage and waste

When standard cost systems are used, allowance is made in the standard product costs for a standard shrinkage. Actual shrinkage is usually computed by working back from product output. Shrinkage in excess of standard is a material usage or quantity variance. Unlike spoilage and scrap, shrinkage cannot be tagged and traced by physical identification.

Examples of waste that are not traced and specifically costed include paint or varnish adhering to the sides of their containers, mill-ends, shavings, evaporation, and so forth. Excess material consumption is usually revealed through excess-material requisitions or through standard-yield percentages for such materials as lumber, chemicals, and ores. Thus, where 15,000 gallons of raw chemicals ordinarily produce 12,000 gallons of good finished product, the standard-yield percentage could be expressed as 80 per cent of normal input. On the other hand, the waste percentage could be expressed as 20 per cent of normal input or as 25 per cent of good output.

Note that these percentages provide a physical standard that may be used without worrying about price changes. Further, such a standard is easily understood and can be readily used as a timely index of efficiency—on an hourly or batch basis if desired.

Scrap

Material usage standards usually include allowances for scrap. Although the allowance may be computed in various ways, standards are based on a careful study of the operation(s), not on historical data alone or on wild guesses. The standard cost of direct material thus becomes (a) standard unit price times the standard input per finished unit less (b) standard scrap price per unit times standard scrap weight loss per finished unit.

To illustrate, assume that the metal rod is fed into an automatic screw machine. About five inches (ten ounces) at the end of each 105-inch rod (210 ounces) are clutched by the chuck and cannot be used. The standard-lot size is 1,000 units. The first ten units are scrapped in setting up the run. It takes five ounces of metal to produce a finished unit that weighs four ounces. Standard cost computations follow:

	Ounces	Assumed Price Per Ounce	Total Cost
Standard cost per unit:			
Finished piece	4.00		
Turnings	1.00		
Crop loss (10 oz. ÷ 40 units per rod)	0.25		
Scrap piece loss (10 units ÷ 1,000) × 5	.05		
	5.30	$.0300*	$.1590
Less credit for scrap	1.30	.0020†	.0026
Standard cost per finished unit	4.00		$.1564

*Or 48¢ per lb.
†3.2¢ per lb.

Although standards for direct materials are built in this way for each operation, it is usually inexpedient to trace scrap to specific lots or operations. Comparisons are usually limited to monthly, or sometimes weekly, comparisons of standard costs of good work produced with the total "actual" charges to the department.[7]

Spoilage

In practice, allowances for net spoilage costs and for rework are often incorporated into the flexible budget for overhead. Spoiled units are removed from Work in Process at standard costs and charged to Factory Overhead. Periodic comparisons of budget allowances with actual spoilage provide summary information for managerial control. If no spoilage is allowed, the budget provided may be zero. Rework is controlled in a similar manner. Day-to-day control is aided by spoilage tags prepared at point of inspection. These tags, or a summary thereof, are promptly shown to the foreman and other interested parties.

This procedure really spotlights spoilage and rework as special managerial problems as opposed to, say, material quantity variances that are related to good units. For example, the standard cost for a product is as follows:

Direct materials, 1 pound	$ 5.00
Direct labor, 1 hour	3.00
Factory overhead – variable	1.50
Factory overhead – fixed	1.50
Standard cost per unit	$11.00

[7] For an extended discussion of spoilage and standard costs, see Stanley B. Henrici, *Standard Costs for Manufacturing* (New York: McGraw-Hill Book Company, Inc., 1960), pp. 275–280, 303–308.

Assume that no spoilage occurs, but that it takes 1,150 pounds of material to produce 1,000 good units:

Direct materials:

Actual, 1,150 pounds @ $5.00	$5,750	
Standard, 1,000 pounds @ $5.00	5,000	
Usage variance	$ 750	

Assume, instead, that 1,100 units were produced, but that 100 were spoiled because of careless machine operation. There would be two alternatives for analyzing such a variance. First consider the figures:

	Incurred Costs	Standard Costs— Good Output	Total Variance
*Direct material, 1,150 lbs.	$ 5,750	$ 5,000	$ 750 U
Direct labor, 1,100 hours	3,300	3,000	300 U
Factory overhead – variable	1,650	1,500	150 U
Factory overhead – fixed	1,650	1,500	150 U
	$12,350	$11,000	$1,350 U

*Standard material allowed for good units	1,000 lbs.
Standard material allowed for spoiled units, which were spoiled by careless labor	100 lbs.
Excess material used in producing 1,100 units	50 lbs.
Total	1,150 lbs.

Analysis One. Analyze variances on the basis of good output only. This is the familiar way:

Direct material quantity variance	$5,750 – $5,000	$ 750
Direct labor efficiency variance	$3,300 – $3,000	300
Variable overhead total variance	$1,650 – $1,500	150
Fixed overhead total variance	$1,650 – $1,500	150
Total variance explained		$1,350

Analysis Two. Isolate a separate variance for spoilage, $1,100, consisting of the four elements shown above. This would entail setting up a special Spoilage Variance account in the ledger. This account would represent the standard cost of spoiled work. Thus the other variance accounts would not reflect any spoilage effects:

	Spoilage Variance	Other Variances		Total Variance Explained
Direct material	$ 500	Usage	$250 U	$ 750
Direct labor	300		—	300
Variable overhead	150		—	150
Fixed overhead	150		—	150
	$1,100		$250	$1,350

PROCESS COST ACCOUNTING PROCEDURES AND SPOILAGE

Distinguish between normal and abnormal spoilage

Although this discussion of process costing will emphasize accounting for spoilage, the ideas here are equally applicable to waste (shrinkage, evaporation, or lost units).

Again we must distinguish between control and product costing. For control, most companies use some version of estimated or standard costs which incorporates an allowance for normal spoilage, shrinkage, or waste in the estimate or standard. This section emphasizes product costing in so-called actual process-costing systems. A conceptual framework is stressed because it is needed to judge the many compromises necessary in practice.

As a general rule, it is sensible to trace and build the costs of spoilage separately. Then allocate normal spoilage costs to Finished Goods or Work in Process, depending on where in the production cycle the spoilage is assumed to take place. Spoilage is typically assumed to occur at the stage of completion where inspection occurs because spoilage is recognized at this point. Normal spoilage need not be allocated to units that have not yet reached this point in the production process, because the spoiled units are related solely to the units that have passed inspection.

Many writers on process costing advocate ignoring the computation of equivalent units for spoilage, shrinkage, or waste. The reason cited in favor of this short-cut technique is that it automatically spreads normal spoilage costs over good units through the use of higher equivalent unit costs. However, the results of this short cut are inaccurate unless (a) no work in process inventories exist or (b) material, conversion costs, *and* spoilage are all incurred uniformly throughout the production cycle. To illustrate, assume that a department has no beginning inventory. It starts 1,000 units: 500 are completed, 400 are in process, half completed, and 100 are spoiled. The 100 units represent normal spoilage. Spoilage is detected upon completion. Material costs are $1,800 and conversion costs are $1,400. All material is introduced at the start of the process.

The solution in Exhibit 20-2 shows that ignoring spoilage lowers total equivalent performance; when the latter is divided into the production costs, a higher *unit cost* results. The effective result is to load higher unit costs on work in process that has not reached the inspection stage of completion. At the same time, total charges to completed units are too low. Therefore, ending work in process contains costs of spoilage ($130 in this example) that do not pertain to such units and that properly should be charged to completed goods. Further, ending work in process that has not reached inspection undoubtedly contains some units that will subsequently be recognized as spoiled. Thus, work in process is being loaded with spoilage ($130) that should be charged to completed goods. In effect, work in process is being doubly charged, because it already contains spoilage that will be recognized and allocated when inspection occurs.

In summary, when spoilage occurs, trace the units spoiled as well as the units finished and in process. Compute both normal and abnormal

EXHIBIT 20-2

COMPARISON OF ACCOUNTING FOR SPOILAGE

	Accurate Method: Count Spoilage			Less Accurate Method: Ignore Spoilage		
	Equivalent Performance			Equivalent Performance		
Units	Physical Flow	Material	Conversion Costs	Physical Flow	Material	Conversion Costs
Completed	500	500	500	500	500	500
Normal spoilage	100	100	100	100	–	–
In process, end (½)	400	400	200	400	400	200
Accounted for	1,000	1,000	800	1,000	900	700

		Details			Details	
Costs:	Totals	Material	Conversion Costs	Totals	Material	Conversion Costs
Current costs	$3,200	$1,800	$1,400	$3,200	$1,800	$1,400
Divide by equivalent units		1,000	800		900	700
Cost per equivalent unit		$1.80	$1.75		$2.00	$2.00
Summary of Costs:						
Units completed (500):				$2,000	500 ($2.00)	500 ($2.00)
Costs before spoilage	$1,775	500 ($1.80)	500 ($1.75)			
Add normal spoilage	355	100 ($1.80)	100 ($1.75)			
Total costs transferred out	$2,130					
Work in process, end (400):						
Materials	$ 720	400 ($1.80)		$ 800	400 ($2.00)	
Conversion costs	350		200 ($1.75)	400		200 ($2.00)
Total cost of work in process	$1,070			$1,200		
Total costs accounted for	$3,200			$3,200		

spoiled units. Build separate costs of spoiled units. Then reallocate
normal spoilage costs to good units produced; charge off abnormal spoilage costs as a loss. Even if no abnormal spoilage exists, it is helpful to
compute normal spoilage costs separately before reallocation. In this way,
management will be constantly reminded of the normal spoilage costs of a
given process.

Base for computing normal spoilage

Normal spoilage should be computed from the good output, or
from the *normal* input—not from the total input. Total input includes the

abnormal as well as the normal spoilage and is therefore irrational as a basis for computing normal spoilage. For example, if the normal rate of spoilage of polio vaccine is sloppily stated as 5 per cent, an input of 100,000 cubic centimeters would be expected to produce 5,000 cubic centimeters of spoilage. Now, if 85,500 cubic centimeters of good units are produced, normal spoilage is not 5,000 cubic centimeters (five per cent of 100,000), because it should have taken only 90,000 cubic centimeters of input to get 85,500 cubic centimeters of good vaccine. If normal spoilage is expressed as 5 per cent of input, then good output should be 95 per cent of normal input. In this case, abnormal spoilage would be 10,000 cubic centimeters and normal spoilage would be 4,500 cubic centimeters. These relationships may be clarified by the following:

			Relationships
Input	100,000 c.c.		
Output:			
Good units	85,500 c.c.		95%
Normal spoilage	4,500 c.c.	90,000 c.c.*	5% 100%
Abnormal spoilage		10,000 c.c.	
		100,000 c.c.	

*Normal input.

Thus, we could express the normal spoilage rate more accurately either as five per cent of *normal input* or as $^5/_{95}$ of good output.[8]

Illustration of process accounting for spoilage

Example 1. B Company. The costs of producing one of the *B* Company's products are accumulated on a process cost basis. Materials for this product are put in at the beginning of the cycle of operations; labor and indirect costs are assumed to flow evenly over the cycle. Some units of this product are spoiled as a result of defects not ascertainable before inspection of finished units. Normally the spoiled units are one-tenth of the good output.

At January 1, the inventory of work in process on this product was $29,600, representing 2,000 pounds of material ($15,000) and conversion cost of $14,600 representing four-fifths completion. During January, 8,000 pounds of material ($61,000) were put into production. Direct labor of $40,200 was charged to the process. Indirect costs are assigned at the rate of 100 per cent of direct labor cost. The inventory at January 31 consisted of 1,500 pounds, two-thirds finished. Seventy-two hundred pounds of good product were transferred to finished goods stock after inspection.

REQUIRED:

Using the weighted-average technique, show calculations of:
(1) The dollar and unit amount of the abnormal spoilage during January.

[8]This is merely an extension of the flexible budget concept, whereby the standard or norm may be adapted to any level of output.

(2) Total product costs transferred to finished stock.
(3) The work in process inventory at January 31.
(4) Journal entries for transfers out of work in process inventory.
Example 1 illustrates a spoilage situation in process cost account-

EXHIBIT 20-3

B COMPANY

Production Cost Report
For the Month Ending January 31, 19x1
Weighted-Average Method

Quantities:	(Step 1) Physical Flow	(Step 2) Equivalent Units Materials	Conversion Costs
Work in process, beginning	2,000($^4/_5$)		
Units started	8,000		
To account for	10,000		
Abnormal spoilage	580	580	580
Normal spoilage	720	720	720
Good units completed	7,200	7,200	7,200
Work in process, end	1,500($^2/_3$)	1,500	1,000
Accounted for	10,000	10,000	9,500

Costs:	Totals	Materials	Details Conversion Costs	Equivalent Whole Unit
Work in process, beginning	$ 29,600	$15,000	$14,600	
Current costs	141,400	61,000	80,400	
(Step 3) Total costs to account for	$171,000	$76,000	$95,000	
Divide by equivalent units		÷10,000	÷ 9,500	
(Step 4) Cost per equivalent unit		$7.60	$10.00	$17.60

(Step 5) Summary of Costs:

	Totals	Materials	Conversion Costs	Equivalent Whole Unit
Abnormal spoilage (580)	$ 10,208			580 ($17.60)
Units completed (7,200):				
Costs before adding spoilage	$126,720			7,200 ($17.60)
Normal spoilage	12,672			720 ($17.60)
Total cost transferred out	$139,392			
Work in process, end (1,500):				
Materials	$ 11,400	1,500 ($7.60)		
Conversion costs	10,000		1,000 ($10.00)	
Total cost of work in process	$ 21,400			
Total costs accounted for	$171,000			

.[9]   Exhibit 20-3 employs the weighted-average techniques.   The
uested journal entries follow:

Finished goods	139,392	
Processing department—Work in process		139,392
To transfer good units completed in January.		
Loss from abnormal spoilage	10,208	
Processing department—Work in process		10,208
To recognize abnormal spoilage in January.		

erim fluctuations in spoilage rates

There is a tendency among accountants to seize a single figure or a
gle rate as the standard or index of normal efficiency, when in reality the
standard or norm is in the middle of a range. Thus, normal spoilage may
average 10 per cent, but random influences may cause deviations from the
10 per cent norm in a range of, say, 6 per cent to 14 per cent. Over an
extended period, say, a year, the rate should center around 10 per cent.

This situation, as shown in Exhibit 20-4, calls for using a predetermined 10 per cent normal spoilage cost rate for charging spoilage costs to

EXHIBIT 20-4

ILLUSTRATION OF ACCOUNTING FOR SPOILAGE FLUCTUATIONS
(Equivalent Unit Cost: $10)

Let us assume that a single department process produces 1,000 good
units per month, but that spoilage fluctuates. Normal spoilage averages
10 per cent, with the normal range considered to be from 6 per cent to
14 per cent. The company's cost behavior is such that all units are produced at an equivalent unit cost of $10. All spoilage is detected upon
completion. The company uses a Spoilage Random Fluctuations account
and costs completed units as if they were all accompanied by a 10 per
cent normal spoilage factor.   Possible situations and general ledger
entries are shown below:

Case	(1)	(2)	(3)	(4)
Total units completed	1,100	1,130	1,170	1,060
Good units completed	1,000	1,000	1,000	1,000
Actual spoilage	100	130	170	60
Normal spoilage	100	100	100	100
General ledger entries:				
Finished goods	$11,000 dr.	$11,000 dr.	$11,000 dr.	$11,000 dr.
Spoilage random fluctuations	—	300 dr.	400 dr.	400 cr.
Loss from abnormal spoilage	—	—	300 dr.	—
Department—Work in Process	11,000 cr.	11,300 cr.	11,700 cr.	10,600 cr.

[9]This illustration assumes inspection upon completion. In contrast, inspection
may take place at some other stage, say, at the halfway point in the production
cycle. In such a case, normal spoilage costs would be reallocated to completed
goods and to the units in process that are more than half completed.

good units produced throughout the year regardless of actual month-to-month fluctuations within the normal range. The differences between normal spoilage costs charged to production and those actually incurred within the normal range would rest in a temporary general ledger account called Spoilage Random Fluctuations. It should have a zero balance by the end of a year. If a balance tends to build up, it would indicate that an erroneous normal rate of spoilage was being used.

If a Spoilage Random Fluctuations account were used, abnormal spoilage would usually be recognized only when actual spoilage exceeded the top of the normal range (14 per cent in this example; see Case (3) in Exhibit 20-4).

The handling of subnormal spoilage is shown in Case (4) of Exhibit 20-4.

SPOILAGE RANDOM FLUCTUATIONS

(2)	300		(4)	400
(3)	400			

This account should balance out to zero over a period of, say, 12 months.

SUMMARY

Nearly every manufacturing company has some problems of waste, scrap, or spoilage as a consequence of management's choice of those factors of production that will render the most economic benefit. Hence, some waste, scrap, or spoilage is a normal result of efficient production. Yet there is a need to distinguish between, for example, normal and abnormal spoilage. Standards or norms must be computed so that performance may be judged and costs properly accounted for. Normal spoilage, then, is that which is unavoidable under a given set of efficient production conditions; abnormal spoilage is that which is avoidable through efficient use of available resources. Laxity in setting careful standards often results in too liberal allowances for normal spoilage.

Abnormal spoilage is controllable by first-line supervision, whereas normal spoilage is controllable only by those managers who determine the nature of products and processes.

Managerial cost accounting must distinguish between normal and abnormal spoilage, primarily for keeping management informed but also for proper product costing.

Accounting for spoilage, defective units, and the like varies considerably. Practically, most of these net costs are allowed for in predetermined overhead rates; or, where standard costs are employed, scrap and spoilage allowances are often incorporated in the standard costs for direct material, direct labor, and overhead.

Conceptually, some practical treatments are faulty because they muddle the distinction between product costs and costs for control by charging product costs back to Department Factory Overhead Control.

PROBLEMS FOR SELF-STUDY

Review each example in this chapter and obtain the solutions on your own. Then check your work against the solutions, which appear in the text.

APPENDIX: FIFO PROCESS COSTING AND SPOILAGE

Re-examine Example 1 and Exhibit 20-3. Try to solve the problem using the first-in, first-out technique.

A comparison of methodology used in Exhibits 20-3 and 20-5 will show that the fifo method necessitates an arbitrary assumption in order to split normal spoilage costs between those goods completed from current production during a given period and those completed from beginning work in process. The most widely used assumption is to load spoilage on all good units at current unit costs. But to do this is inconsistent with the fifo assumption; examine the footnote to Exhibit 20-5 for an illustration of the inconsistencies that arise.

In contrast, the weighted-average method does not necessitate splitting normal spoilage costs between two batches of good units completed because the initial inventory is merged with the current costs to determine unit costs. The more one examines process costing, the more one becomes convinced that weighted-average costing is generally superior to first-in, first-out costing for *product-costing* purposes. Moreover, standard costing is superior to either weighted-average costing or first-in, first-out costing for *control* purposes.

QUESTIONS, PROBLEMS, AND CASES

Note: Problems 20-11 and 20-13 cover the basic points. Problems 20-20 through 20-23 cover fifo.

20-1. "Management has two major planning and control problems regardingspoilage." What are the two problems?

20-2. "Normal spoilage is planned spoilage." Discuss.

20-3. "Costs of abnormal spoilage are lost costs." Explain.

20-4. "In accounting for spoiled goods, we are dealing with cost application and reallocation rather than cost incurrence." Explain.

20-5. "Total input includes the abnormal as well as the normal spoilage and is therefore irrational as a basis for computing normal spoilage." Do you agree? Why?

20-6. Explain the operation of a Spoilage Random Fluctuations account.

20-7. "The practical treatments of spoilage in job order costing can be criticized on conceptual grounds." What is the major criticism?

[10] Werner Frank shows how the approach in this chapter can be applied on a computer in his "A Computer Application in Process Cost Accounting," *Accounting Review* (October, 1965), pp. 854–862.

EXHIBIT 20-5

B COMPANY
Production Cost Report for the Month Ending January 31, 19x1 — Modified Fifo Method

	(Step 1) Physical Flow	(Step 2) Equivalent Units Materials	(Step 2) Equivalent Units Conversion Costs
Quantities			
Work in process, beginning	2,000($^4/_5$)		
Units started	8,000		
To account for	10,000		
Abnormal spoilage	580	580	580
Normal spoilage	720	720	720
Good units completed:			
From beginning inventory	2,000	–	400
Started and completed	5,200	5,200	5,200
Work in process, end	1,500($^2/_3$)	1,500	1,000
Accounted for	10,000	8,000	7,900

	Totals	Details Materials	Details Conversion Costs	Equivalent Whole Unit
Costs:				
Work in process, beginning	$ 29,600			
Current costs	141,400	$61,000	$80,400	
Total costs to account for (Step 3)	$171,000			
Divide by equivalent units		÷8,000	÷7,900	
Cost per equivalent unit (Step 4)		$7.625	$10.1772	$17.8022

(Step 5)   Summary of Costs:

(A) Abnormal spoilage (580)	$ 10,325.28		580 ($17.8022)
Units completed (7,200):			
From beginning inventory (2,000):			
Current costs added	$ 29,600.00	400 ($10.1772)	
	$ 4,070.88		
Total cost from beginning inventory before spoilage	$ 33,670.88		
Started and completed before spoilage (5,200)	92,571.56		5,200 ($17.8022)
*Normal spoilage	12,817.58		720 ($17.8022)
(B) Total costs transferred out	$139,060.02		
Work in process, end (1,500):			
Materials	$ 11,437.50	1,500 ($7.625)	
Conversion costs	10,177.20	1,000 ($10.1772)	
(C) Total cost of work in process	$ 21,614.70		
(A) + (B) + (C) Total costs accounted for	$171,000.00		

*Note that normal spoilage really should be split between the two batches of good units completed if fifo is to be followed thoroughly. But to split spoilage costs on a pro-rata basis implies that all spoilage traceable to beginning inventory is costed on the basis of full current costs, not past costs. This is inconsistent with the fifo assumption which states that past costs should be kept separate from current costs. In effect, using current costs for attaching normal spoilage costs to beginning inventory assumes that all spoilage traceable thereto was begun and completed during the current period — an obvious contradiction of the fifo concept.

Special Note: For a computer application to solving this process cost problem, see Werner Frank, "A Computer Application in Process Cost Accounting," *Accounting Review* (October 1965), pp 854–862.

20-8. Describe the general accounting for scrap where no inventory value is assigned to scrap.

20-9. How is scrap usually accounted for under standard costing?

20-10. Two Ways of Accounting for Spoilage. In manufacturing activities, a portion of the units placed in process is sometimes spoiled and becomes practically worthless. Discuss two ways in which the cost of such spoiled units could be treated in the accounts, and describe the circumstances under which each method might be used. [C.P.A.]

20-11. Process Costing and Spoilage. The Alston Company operates under a process cost system. It has two departments, Cleaning and Milling. For both departments, conversion costs are applied in proportion to the stage of completion. But materials are applied at the *beginning* of the process in the Cleaning Department, and additional materials are added at the *end* of the Milling process. Following are the costs and unit production statistics for May. All unfinished work at the *end* of May is one-fourth completed. All beginning inventories (May 1) were four-fifths completed as of May 1. All completed work is transferred to the next department.

Beginning Inventories:	Cleaning	Milling
Cleaning: $1,000 materials, $800 conv. costs	$1,800	
Milling: $6,450 previous dept. cost (transferred-in cost) and $2,450 conv. costs		$8,900
Current Costs:		
Material	$9,000	$ 640
Conversion costs	$8,000	$4,950
Units in beginning inventory	1,000	3,000
Units started this month	9,000	7,400
Total units finished and transferred	7,400	6,000
Normal spoilage	500	400
Abnormal spoilage	500	0

Additional Factors

1. Spoilage is assumed to occur at the *end* of *each* of the two processes, when the units are inspected.

2. Assume that there is no other waste, shrinkage, evaporation, or abnormal spoilage than that indicated in the tabulation above.

3. Carry unit cost calculations to three decimal places where necessary. Calculate final totals to the nearest dollar.

REQUIRED:

Using the weighted-average method, show for *each* department:

(1) Analysis of physical flows and an analysis of equivalent performance.

(2) Calculations of *unit* costs.

(3) *Detailed* presentation of the *total* values assigned to goods transferred out and the total values assigned to ending work in process.

Be certain that your solution is presented in step-by-step fashion so that your reasoning can be followed easily.

20-12. Allocating Spoilage. The *ABC* Company operates under a process cost system for one of its products. During the period in question for this product, 3,850 units were put into production. During the period, 3,000 finished units were turned out. Inspection of this product occurs at the halfway point in the process. Normally, rejects amount to 10 per cent of the good units passed. The inspection department informs us that the process did in fact function normally during this period. The department foreman estimates that units still in process are on the average two-thirds complete. All, however, are at least one-half done.

Costs for the period were:

Material:	$38,500	—Applied at the beginning of the process
Conversion cost:	35,080	—Applied uniformly during the process
	$73,580	

REQUIRED :

Determine the cost of goods completed and the cost of the ending inventory of work in process. Assume that there were no beginning inventories.

20-13. Multiple Choice; Weighted-Average Method; Spoilage. The data that follow are to be used in answering questions 1–9, inclusive. Support your answers with a statement of production costs.

The manufacture of product XT-123 is begun in Department No. 1. From there it goes to Department No. 2, where the product is completed. Upon completion it is then sent to finished goods storage in the warehouse. At the end of processing in each department, the units of products are inspected; only those which pass inspection are sent to Department No. 2 and finished goods storage, respectively. The spoiled units (both normal and abnormal spoilage) cannot be salvaged, have no scrap value, and are thrown away.

Below are listed the pertinent data regarding the production of XT-123 for the month of December, 19x3:

	Department No. 1	Department No. 2
Costs applied to product:		
Material	At the beginning of processing in the department.	At 50% completion of processing in the department.
Other costs	Evenly throughout entire period of processing.	Evenly throughout entire period of processing.
Work in process, December 1, 19x3:		
Number of units	600 units	2,000 units
Per cent complete	$66\frac{2}{3}\%$	25%
Accumulated cost:		
Department No. 1 material	$2,844	$30,280
Department No. 1 other cost	$3,120	
Department No. 2 material		None
Department No. 2 other cost		$ 6,200
Work in process, December 31, 19x3:		
No. of units	1,400 units	800 units
Per cent complete	50%	75%

	Department No. 1	Department No. 2
Normal spoilage (detected by inspection of product upon completion of processing in each department)	140 units	40 units
Abnormal spoilage:		
Number of units	60 units	None
Per cent complete	100%	
Units of finished product transferred to finished goods warehouse	—	3,960 units
December cost applied to product (exclusive of accumulated cost of work in process at December 1, 19x3):		
Material	$19,800	$15,140
Other costs	34,260	52,860

Indicate your answer by letter.

1. The actual number of units transferred to Department No. 2 from Department No. 1 during the month was:

    a. 2,760   c. 2,800   e. 3,000
    b. 3,960   d. 2,860

2. The actual number of units begun in Department No. 1 during the month was:

    a. 3,620   c. 3,760   e. 4,400
    b. 3,520   d. 3,800

Note: Questions 3–9, inclusive, refer to answers you would secure using the weighted-average method. (Round off unit costs to the nearest cent.)

3. In Department No. 1 the total equivalent performance for "other costs" was:

    a. 3,700   c. 2,800   e. 3,000
    b. 4,400   d. 4,200

4. In Department No. 1 the equivalent unit cost for materials was:

    a. $8.09   c. $5.39   e. $7.71
    b. $5.15   d. $5.22

5. In Department No. 1 the cost of work in process at December 31, 19x3, was:

    a. $18,396   c. $14,616   e. $14,280
    b. $17,864   d. $14,378

6. The cost of goods transferred from Department No. 1 to Department No. 2 during the month of December was:

    a. $43,615   c. $42,010   e. $42,700
    b. $44,100   d. $44,835

7. In Department No. 2 the total equivalent performance for materials (only those materials *added* by Department No. 2) was:

    a. 4,000   c. 4,400   e. 4,800
    b. 5,000   d. 4,600

8. In Department No. 2 the equivalent unit cost for "other costs" (only those "other costs" *added* by Department No. 2) was:

    a. $12.84   c. $13.42   e. $14.91
    b. $12.30   d. $12.95

9. In Department No. 2 the total cost of units transferred to the finished goods warehouse was:

    a. $63,960   c. $145,544   e. $125,294
    b. $63,310   d. $126,560

20-14. Process Costs; Weighted Average. The *H* Co. Ltd. manufactures a single product that is processed in three departments. The process cost procedure in use bases inventory values on the weighted-average cost method. The following cost and production data are available for Department 2 for the month of April.

Opening work in process inventory— 1,500 units:	
Cost from preceding department	$12,000
Dept. 2 material (added at the beginning	
of the process)	2,041
Dept. 2 labor and applied overhead	4,168
(These units were 40% complete as to	
conversion costs.)	
Transferred-in during April from Dept. 1:	
6,000 units	46,800
Department 2 costs for April:	
Material	8,459
Labor and applied overhead	41,727

Production Data:

  5,900 units were completed and transferred to Dept. 3; 1,000 units were still in process (20 per cent complete) at the end of April; the balance were spoiled units, detected at the end of the Dept. 2 processing. One-half of the spoilage is abnormal in nature and is to be charged to an Abnormal Spoilage Loss Account.

REQUIRED:

Prepare a Cost of Production Report for April.   [C.G.A.A.]

20-15. Different Ways of Accounting for Spoilage. The D. Hayes Cramer Company manufactures product C, whose cost per unit is $1 of material, $2 of labor, and $3 of overhead costs. During the month of May, 1,000 units of product C were spoiled. These units could be sold for 60¢ each.

  The accountant said that the entry to be made for these 1,000 lost or spoiled units could be one of the following four:

Entry No. 1		
Spoiled goods	$ 600	
Work in process—Materials		$ 100
Work in process—Labor		200
Work in process—Overhead		300

Entry No. 2

Spoiled goods	$ 600	
Manufacturing expenses	5,400	
Work in process—Materials		$1,000
Work in process—Labor		2,000
Work in process—Overhead		3,000

Entry No. 3

Spoiled goods	$ 600	
Loss on spoiled goods	5,400	
Work in process—Materials		$1,000
Work in process—Labor		2,000
Work in process—Overhead		3,000

Entry No. 4

Spoiled goods	$ 600	
Receivable	5,400	
Work in process—Materials		$1,000
Work in process—Labor		2,000
Work in process—Overhead		3,000

REQUIRED:

Indicate the circumstance under which each of the four above solutions would be appropriate.   [C.P.A.]

20-16.   Spoilage; Two Departments. The Mantis Manufacturing Company manufactures a single product that passes through two departments: extruding and finishing-packing. The product is shipped at the end of the day in which it is packed. The production in the extruding and finishing-packing departments does not increase the number of units started.

The cost and production data for the month of January are as follows:

Cost Data	Extruding Department	Finishing-Packing Department
Work in process, January 1:		
Cost from preceding department	—	$60,200
Material	$ 5,900	—
Labor	1,900	1,500
Overhead	1,400	2,000
Costs added during January:		
Material	20,100	4,400
Labor	10,700	7,720
Overhead	8,680	11,830
Percentage of completion of work in process:		
January 1:		
Material	70%	0%
Labor	50	30
Overhead	50	30

Cost Data	Extruding Department	Finishing-Packing Department
January 31:		
Material	50	0
Labor	40	35
Overhead	40	35
January Production Statistics		
Units in process, January 1	10,000	29,000
Units in process, January 31	8,000	6,000
Units started or received from preceding department	20,000	22,000
Units completed and transferred or shipped	22,000	44,000

In the extruding department, materials are added at various phases of the process. All lost units occur at the end of the process when the inspection operation takes place.

In the finishing-packing department, the materials added consist only of packing supplies. These materials are added at the midpoint of the process when the packing operation begins. Cost studies have disclosed that one-half of the labor and overhead costs apply to the finishing operation and one-half to the packing operation. All lost units occur at the end of the finishing operation when the product is inspected. All of the work in process in this department at January 1 and 31 was in the finishing-operation phase of the manufacturing process.

REQUIRED:

(The Company uses the average costing method in its accounting system.)
1. Compute the units lost, if any, for each department during January.
2. Compute the equivalent units for the calculation of unit costs for each department by January.
3. Prepare a cost of production report for both departments for January. The report should disclose the departmental total cost and cost per unit (for material, labor, and overhead) of the units (1) transferred to the finishing-packing department and (2) shipped. Assume that January production and costs were normal. (Submit all supporting computations in good form.)   [C.P.A. Adapted]

● **20-17. Normal and Abnormal Spoilage.** The Van Brocklin Company manufactures one style of long, tapered wax candle which is used on festive occasions. Each candle requires a two-foot-long wick and one pound of a specially prepared wax. Wick and melted wax are placed in molds and allowed to harden for twenty-four hours. Upon removal from the molds, the candles are immediately dipped in a special coloring mixture which gives them a glossy lacquer finish. Dried candles are inspected, and all defective ones are pulled out. Because the coloring mixture penetrates into the wax itself, the defective candles cannot be salvaged for re-use. They are destroyed in an incinerator. Normal spoilage is reckoned as 3 per cent of the number of candles which pass inspection.

Cost and production statistics for a certain week were as follows:

Raw materials requisitioned (including wicks and wax)	$3,340.00
Direct labor and indirect costs (applied at a constant rate during the hardening process)	1,219.50
Total cost incurred	$4,559.50

During the week 7,800 candles were completed; 7,500 passed inspection, and the remainder were defective. At the end of the week 550 candles were still in the molds; they were considered 60 per cent complete. There was no beginning inventory. Show computations.

1. Which of the following is the normal cost of the 7,500 candles which passed inspection?

  a. $4,125.00
  b. $4,217.85
  c. $4,248.75
  d. $4,290.00
  e. $4,333.73

2. Which of the following is the normal cost of the candles still in the molds at the end of the week?

  a. $185.13
  b. $269.50
  c. $274.72
  d. $300.30
  e. $393.25

20-18. Process Costs; Abnormal Spoilage. The Quebec Manufacturing Company produces a single product. There are two producing departments, Departments 1 and 2, and the product passes through the plant in that order.

There were no work in process inventories at the beginning of the year.

In January, materials for 1,000 units were issued to production in Department 1 at a cost of $5,000. Direct labor and factory overhead costs for the month were $2,700. During the month, 800 units were completed and transferred to Department 2. The work in process inventory at the end of the month contained 200 units complete in material and one-half complete in labor and overhead.

Direct labor and factory overhead in Department 2 amounted to $6,250 in January. During the month, 500 units were completed and transferred to finished stock. At the end of the month, 200 units remained in process, one-quarter complete. Ordinarily, in Department 2, spoilage is recognized upon inspection at the end of the process, but in January there was an abnormal loss of 50 units when one-half complete. The effect of abnormal loss is not to be included in inventory.

REQUIRED:

Prepare a detailed cost of production report for the month of January.

                [S.I.C.A.]

20-19. Standard Process Costing; Spoilage.* The Sharbill Company uses standard process costing in accounting for its costs of production. One product only is manufactured, with standard costs, *per thousand units*, as follows:

Material A,	15 lbs. @ 80¢		$12.00
Material B,	4 lbs. @ $2.25		9.00
Direct labor,	5 hours @ $3.60		18.00
Variable overhead,	5 hours @ $2.00		10.00
Fixed overhead,	5 hours @ $1.60		8.00
Normal spoilage,	10% of Material A	$1.20	
	5% of Conversion costs	1.80	3.00
Total standard cost per 1,000 units			$60.00

*Prepared by Professor Samuel Laimon.

The standards for materials and conversion costs are exclusive of spoilage costs. The latter costs are allowed for separately in the standard. Material A is added at the beginning of the process. Labor and overhead are added evenly throughout the process. Inspection at the 50 per cent stage of completion removes all spoiled units. Normal spoilage amounts to 10 per cent of all *good* units passing the inspection point. Immediately after the removal of spoiled units, Material B is added to the remaining good units, and the processing of these units is then completed.

Production data for April, 19x1, were as follows:

Beginning work in process inventory	400,000 units—40% complete	
Put into process during April	500,000	
Transferred to finished goods	600,000	
Spoiled units	100,000	
Ending work in process inventory	200,000	—60% complete.

Cost Data

1. Materials: All price variances on materials are recognized at the time of purchase.

> (a) Material A: Beginning inventory, 2,000 pounds.
> Purchased, 10,000 lbs. @ 84¢ = $8,400.
> Issued to production, 8,000 pounds.
>
> (b) Material B: Beginning inventory, 1,000 pounds.
> Purchased, 4,000 lbs. @ $2.00 = $8,000.
> Issued to production, 3,100 pounds.

2. Direct labor payroll: 3,100 hours @ $3.50 = $10,850.
3. Overhead costs incurred:

> (a) Variable, $6,500
> (b) Fixed, $5,610

4. Budget data: Planned production for the month was 675,000 units.
5. Variance disposition: All variances are charged to the period of their incurrence.

REQUIRED:

1. Presentation at standard cost of:
   (a) Abnormal spoilage.
   (b) Units transferred.
   (c) Ending work in process.
2. Summary analysis of all variances, including detailed breakdown of direct labor and overhead variances.

20-20. Re-do Problem 20-11, using fifo.

♥**20-21. First-in, First-out Process Costing; Multiple Choice.** The Meara Company uses a process cost system (first-in, first-out) in costing its sole product. Materials for the product are added at the beginning of the operating cycle; conversion costs are assumed to accrue evenly over the cycle. Spoilage is detected by inspection upon completion of the product. Normally the spoiled units are equal to one-tenth of the good output.

At January 1, the inventory of work in process was 2,000 units of product, representing an average of three-fourths complete. The cost of these units was $32,200, being $17,000 for raw material and $15,200 for conversion cost (direct labor and indirect cost). During January, 8,000 additional units of product were begun. During January, material cost of $64,000 was requisitioned from stores and charged to operations. Direct labor costs for the month were $38,000. Indirect costs are assigned at the rate of 100 per cent of direct labor cost.

At January 31, the work in process consisted of 1,500 units of product, two-thirds complete. During the month, 7,200 units of good product were transferred to finished goods stock after inspection.

Select the answer that correctly completes each of the following statements (identify your answer by letter). Support your over-all answer with a production cost report.

1. Units of normal spoilage amounted to:

    a. 1,000   d. 720
    b.   950   e. 580
    c.   800

2. Units of abnormal spoilage amounted to:

    a.   580   d. 800
    b. 1,000   e. 950
    c.   720

3. The total equivalent performance for materials cost was:

    a. 8,500   d.   8,000
    b. 9,500   e. 10,000
    c. 9,000

4. The total equivalent performance for conversion costs was:

    a. 9,000   d. 7,500
    b. 8,500   e. 8,000
    c. 7,000

5. The equivalent unit cost for materials was:
    a. $8.50   d. $8.25
    b. $6.40   e. $8.00
    c. $8.10

6. The cost of products transferred to finished goods was:
    a. $138,550   d. $140,550
    b. $127,950   e. $140,184
    c. $108,350

20-22. Fifo Process Costs; Lost Units. The Biltimar Company manufactures gewgaws in three steps or departments. The Finishing Department is the third and last step before the product is transferred to finished goods inventory.

All material needed to complete the gewgaws is added at the beginning of the process in the Finishing Department, and lost units, if any, occur only at this point. The company uses the fifo cost method in its accounting system and has accumulated the following data for July for the Finishing Department:

	Units
1. Production of gewgaws:	
In process, July 1 (labor and manufacturing expense three-fourths complete)	10,000
Transferred from preceding departments during July	40,000
Finished and transferred to finished goods inventory during July	35,000
In process, July 31 (labor and manufacturing expense one-half complete)	10,000

2. Cost of work in process inventory, July 1:	
Cost from preceding departments	$ 38,000
Costs added in Finishing Department prior to July 1:	
Materials	21,500
Labor	39,000
Manufacturing expense	42,000
Cost of work in process inventory, July 1	$140,500

3. Gewgaws transferred to the Finishing Department during July had costs of $140,000 assigned from preceding departments.

4. During July, the Finishing Department incurred the following production costs:	
Material	$ 70,000
Labor	162,500
Manufacturing expense	130,000
Total	$362,500

REQUIRED:

    1. The cost of the gewgaws lost in production during July.

    2. The cost of the gewgaws transferred to finished goods inventory in July.

    3. The cost of the work in process inventory at July 31.   [C.P.A.]

20-23.   Process Costs; Spoilage; Fifo and Weighted Average.   The King Process Company manufactures one product, processing it through two processes—No. 1 and No. 2.

For each unit of Process No. 1 output, 2 units of raw material X are put in *at the start* of processing. For each unit of Process No. 2 output, 3 cans of raw material Y are put in *at the end* of processing. Two pounds of Process No. 1 output are placed in at the start of Process No. 2 for each unit of finished goods started.

Spoilage generally occurs in Process No. 2 when processing is approximately 50 per cent complete.

In-process accounts are maintained for raw material, conversion costs, and prior department costs.

The company uses fifo basis for inventory valuation for Process No. 1 and finished goods, and average cost for inventory valuation for Process No. 2.

Data for March:

  (1) Units transferred: From Process No. 1 to Process No. 2   2,200 lbs.

                  From Process No. 2 to Finished Goods   900 gallons

                  From Finished Goods to Cost of Goods Sold   600 gallons

  (2) Units spoiled in Process No. 2—100 gallons.

  (3) Raw material unit costs: X—$1.51 per unit; Y—$2.00 per can.

(4) Conversion costs: Process No. 1—$3,344; Process No. 2—$4,010.

(5) Spoilage recovery: $100 (treated as cost reduction).

(6) Inventory data:

	Process No. 1		Process No. 2		Finished Goods	
	Initial	Final	Initial	Final	Initial	Final
Units	200	300	200	300	700	1,000
Fraction complete conversion costs	½	⅓	½	⅔		
Valuation:					$13,300	
Materials	$560		0			
Conversion costs	$108		$ 390			
Prior-department costs			$2,200			

REQUIRED:

Journalize March entries to record the transfer of costs from Process No. 1 to Process No. 2, from Process No. 2 to Finished Goods, and from Finished Goods to Cost of Goods Sold. Prepare schedules of computations to support your entries. Regard spoilage as normal spoilage. [C.P.A.]

sales mix and production mix
and yield variances

CHAPTER XXI

Most companies have more than one finished product, and many companies blend two or more raw materials when manufacturing a particular product. Therefore, over-all sales plans and production standards usually assume some given or normal combination of products or ingredients. Consequently, the analysis of subsequent results should detect any variances from the original expectations. The purpose of isolating these variances is to explain how mix, quantity, and price factors cause deviations from revenue or cost targets. We are already familiar with quantity and price variances. Now we concentrate on the complications that arise when mix factors differ from original plans. The basic approach is to hold two of the three major factors (mix, quantity, and price) constant when calculating the third factor.

CHANGES IN SALES MIX

Sales mix is the relative combination of the quantities of a variety of company products that compose total sales. The best way to study the influence of sales mix on income is by example.

Example 1. Suppose that a company has the following budget:

	Product X			Product Y			Total		
	Units	Price	Total	Units	Price	Total	Units	Price*	Total
Sales	1,000	$3.00	$3,000	3,000	$2.00	$6,000	4,000	$2.25	$9,000
Variable costs	1,000	1.20	1,200	3,000	1.00	3,000	4,000	1.05	4,200
Contribution margin	1,000	$1.80	$1,800	3,000	$1.00	$3,000	4,000	$1.20	$4,800
Contribution margin percentage		60%			50%			53.3%	

*Weighted average obtained by dividing total sales or costs by total units.

683

Now consider three different sets of actual results:
a. Change in mix only;
b. Changes in mix and in quantity sold;
c. Changes in mix, in quantity sold, and in selling and cost prices.

a. Change in Mix Only. Suppose that 4,000 units were actually sold, 2,000 of X and 2,000 of Y:

	Product X			Product Y			Total		
	Units	Price	Total	Units	Price	Total	Units	Price	Total
Sales	2,000	$3.00	$6,000	2,000	$2.00	$4,000	4,000	$2.50	$10,000
Variable costs	2,000	1.20	2,400	2,000	1.00	2,000	4,000	1.10	4,400
Contribution margin	2,000	$1.80	$3,600	2,000	$1.00	$2,000	4,000	$1.40	$ 5,600
Contribution margin percentage		60%			50%			56%	

The total contribution margin is $5,600 instead of the $4,800 originally budgeted for the 4,000 units. This $800 difference is attributable solely to the change in sales mix. One way to obtain this $800 figure is to multiply 4,000 units by the 20¢ difference in average contribution margin ($1.40 actual − $1.20 budgeted). How can we obtain a general approach or formula that pinpoints the effects on profit of a change in mix?

Compare the budgeted with actual mix percentages:

	Budgeted	Actual
X	25%	50%
Y	75%	50%

The mix variance for each product may be defined and generalized as:

[(Budgeted mix percentage × Actual *total* quantity) −

Actual *product* quantity] × Budgeted price*

X's mix variance = [(.25 × 4,000) − 2,000] × $1.80 = $1,800 F
Y's mix variance = [(.75 × 4,000) − 2,000] × $1.00 = 1,000 U

Total mix variance $ 800 F

F = Favorable; U = Unfavorable.

This may appear to be an unnecessarily elaborate way to compute a mix variance—and it is, in this case. However, the next two steps will show that this type of analysis can become complicated very rapidly. That is why this formula is introduced with this simple example.

b. Changes in Mix and in Quantity Sold. Suppose that 6,000 units were actually sold, 3,000 of X and 3,000 of Y:

*In this and in the following example, "price" refers to the contribution margin per unit.

	Product X			Product Y			Total		
	Units	Price	Total	Units	Price	Total	Units	Price	Total
Sales	3,000	$3.00	$9,000	3,000	$2.00	$6,000	6,000	$2.50	$15,000
Variable costs	3,000	1.20	3,600	3,000	1.00	3,000	6,000	1.10	6,600
Contribution margin	3,000	$1.80	$5,400	3,000	$1.00	$3,000	6,000	$1.40	$ 8,400
Contribution margin percentage		60%			50%			56%	

The total contribution margin is $8,400 instead of the $4,800 originally budgeted for the 4,000 units. This $3,600 difference is attributable to two factors: a $1,200 change in sales mix and a $2,400 change in the quantities sold:

Mix variance = [(Budgeted mix percentage ×

  Actual total quantity) − Actual product quantity] × Budgeted price

$$X = [(.25 \times 6,000) - 3,000] \times \$1.80 = \$2,700 \text{ F}$$
$$Y = [(.75 \times 6,000) - 3,000] \times \$1.00 = \underline{\quad 1,500} \text{ U}$$

  Total mix variance $1,200 F

Quantity variance = [(Budgeted mix percentage ×

  Actual total quantity) − Budgeted product quantity] × Budgeted price

$$X = [(.25 \times 6,000) - 1,000] \times \$1.80 = \$ \ 900 \text{ F}$$
$$Y = [(.75 \times 6,000) - 3,000] \times \$1.00 = \underline{\quad 1,500} \text{ F}$$

  Total quantity variance $2,400 F

Note that the mix variance computation holds the other variables, prices and quantities, constant; it concentrates solely on the effects of changes in mix on the actual quantity attained—without worrying about whether the actual quantities attained agreed with the budget. In contrast, the quantity variance computation holds the other variables, prices and mix, constant; it concentrates solely on the effects of volume—as if the mix percentage had not changed at all.

The analysis of Product Y is especially revealing. Even though the 3,000 units originally budgeted for Y have been sold, there is nevertheless both a mix and a quantity variance. The mix variance occurred because the actual mix percentage was 50 per cent rather than the 75 per cent originally budgeted. The quantity variance occurred because, of 6,000 over-all units sold, the company should have sold the original mix of 75 per cent—4,500 units of Y instead of the 3,000 attained.

c. Changes in Mix, in Quantity Sold, and in Selling and Cost Prices. Suppose that 6,000 units were actually sold, 3,000 of X and 3,000 of Y. However, all unit prices differed from the budget:

	Product X			Product Y			Total		
	Units	Price	Total	Units	Price	Total	Units	Price	Total
Sales	3,000	$2.80	$8,400	3,000	$2.10	$6,300	6,000	$2.45	$14,700
Variable Costs	3,000	1.10	3,300	3,000	1.20	3,600	6,000	1.15	6,900
Contribution margin	3,000	$1.70	$5,100	3,000	$ .90	$2,700	6,000	$1.30	$ 7,800
Contribution margin percentage		60.7%			52.9%			53.1%	

The total margin is $7,800 instead of the $4,800 originally budgeted for the 4,000 units. This $3,000 difference is attributable to the mix and quantity variances computed in (b) plus the price-cost variances that appear here and that are computed in the usual way:

Price-cost variance = Difference in unit contribution margin ×

Actual product quantity

X = ($1.80 − $1.70) × 3000 =	$ 300 U
Y = ($1.00 − $ .90) × 3000 =	300 U
Total price-cost variance	$ 600 U [1]
Total mix variance (from part (b))	1,200 F
Total quantity variance (from part (b))	2,400 F
Total variance explained [2]	$3,000 F

CHANGES IN MATERIAL MIX AND YIELD

Manufacturing processes often entail the combination of a number of different materials to obtain a unit of finished product. Chemicals, plastics, lumber, fruit, vegetables, rubber, and fabrics, for example, can sometimes be combined in various ways without affecting the specified quality characteristics of a finished product. Yield is the quantity of finished product manufactured from a given combination and amount of materials. Sometimes trade-offs between the mix of materials and the quantity (yield) of finished product are made. That is, a favorable mix variance may more than offset an unfavorable yield variance, and vice versa. For instance, a shoe manufacturer may try some variations in the grades of leather if the potential savings exceed the potential excessive waste or rejects.

[1] This example has focused on the contribution margin. A more detailed breakdown can be easily formulated:

Sales price:	X = ($3.00 − $2.80) × 3,000 =	$600 U
	Y = ($2.10 − $2.00) × 3,000 =	300 F
Cost:	X = ($1.20 − $1.10) × 3,000 =	300 F
	Y = ($1.20 − $1.00) × 3,000 =	600 U
		$600 U

The advantage of this breakdown is that these variances can be dovetailed precisely with the further breakdowns that occur in detailed variance analysis concerning price and efficiency factors. See James B. Hobbs, "Volume-Mix-Price/Cost Budget Variance Analysis: A Proper Approach," *Accounting Review* (October, 1964), pp. 905–913.

[2] Note that the method of computing these three variances considers them as independent variables; but surely these mix, quantity, and price variances are mutually dependent. For example, sales mix is a function of the quantity sold and the sales prices charged, so that if prices change, mix will also change, causing additional changes in volume, and so on. The variances as computed do not directly consider this interdependence.

Mix variances will arise when deliberate changes in input are attempted or where humidity, temperature, molecular structure, or other physical characteristics result in various combinations of raw materials to produce a given output.

As the following example shows, there is basically no difference between the analysis of a change in sales mix and the analysis of a change in material mix:

Example 2.   Suppose that a company has the following standards:

5 gallons of Material F at $ .70 = $3.50
3 gallons of Material G at   1.00 =   3.00
2 gallons of Material H at   .80 =   1.60

$8.10 for 10 gallons of standard mix, which should produce 9 gallons of finished product at a standard cost of $.90 ($8.10 ÷ 9) a gallon.

Suppose, for simplicity, that no inventories of raw materials are kept. Purchases are made as needed, so that all price variances relate to materials used.   Actual results showed that 100,000 gallons were used during a period:

45,000 gallons of F at actual cost of $ .80 = $36,000
33,000 gallons of G at actual cost of $1.05 =   34,650
22,000 gallons of H at actual cost of $ .85 =   18,700

100,000 $89,350

Good output was 92,070 gallons at standard
cost of $.90   82,863

Total material variance to be explained $ 6,487 U

Explained as follows:

Mix variance	$1,100 U
Quantity (yield) variance	1,863 F
Price variance	7,250 U
Total explained	$6,487 U

Mix variance = [(Budgeted mix percentage × Actual *total* quantity) −
                          Actual *product* quantity] × Standard price

F = [(.50 × 100,000) − 45,000] × $ .70 = $3,500 F
G = [(.30 × 100,000) − 33,000] × $1.00 =   3,000 U
H = [(.20 × 100,000] − 22,000] × $ .80 =   1,600 U

Total $1,100 U

Note that the budgeted input must be that normally needed to produce 92,070 gallons, or 92,070 ÷ .9, or 102,300 gallons. Material F's budgeted share would be .50 × 102,300, or 51,150 gallons; G's, .30 × 102,300, or 30,090; and so forth:

Quantity (yield) variance = [(Budgeted mix percentage ×
Actual *total* quantity) − Budgeted product quantity] × Standard price

$$
\begin{array}{ll}
\text{F} = (50,000 - 51,150) \times \$ .70 = \$ & 805 \text{ F} \\
\text{G} = (30,000 - 30,690) \times \$1.00 = & 690 \text{ F} \\
\text{H} = (20,000 - 20,460) \times \$ .80 = & 368 \text{ F} \\
\hline
\text{Total} & \$1,863 \text{ F}^1
\end{array}
$$

Price variance = Difference in unit price × Actual product quantity

$$
\begin{array}{ll}
\text{F} = (\$ .80 - \$ .70) \times 45,000 = \$4,500 \text{ U} \\
\text{G} = (\$1.05 - \$1.00) \times 33,000 = \ 1,650 \text{ U} \\
\text{H} = (\$ .85 - \$ .80) \times 22,000 = \ \underline{1,100} \text{ U} \\
 & \ \$7,250 \text{ U}
\end{array}
$$

In this example, the unfavorable mix variance of $1,100 was more than offset by the favorable yield variance of $1,863.

DIRECT LABOR AND VARIABLE OVERHEAD VARIANCES

Refinements in the usual direct labor and variable overhead usage variances may be computed when actual product yields vary from standard expectations:

Example 3. Suppose that in Example 2 the following direct labor and variable overhead factors prevailed:

	Direct Labor	Variable Overhead
(1) Standard rate per hour	$ 4.00	$ 1.00
(2) Standard rate per gallon of output at 10 gallons per hour	.40	.10
(3) Standard cost of 92,070 gallons of output	$36,828	$ 9,207
(4) Normal input for 92,070 gallons would be 92,070 ÷ .9 = 102,300 gallons		
Standard cost of normal input (same as 3)	$36,828	$ 9,207

[1] Another way of computing this variance is to compute the difference between the standard cost of the output and the standard cost of input:

$$
\begin{array}{lll}
\text{Output:} & 92,070 \text{ gallons at } \$.90 = & \$82,863 \\
\text{Input:} & 100,000 \text{ gallons at } \$.81 = & \underline{81,000} \\
\hline
\text{Quantity variance} & & \$ \ 1,863
\end{array}
$$

Still another way is to compute the standard yield from 100,000 gallons of input, which is 90,000 gallons. The actual production exceeded the standard yield of the input by 2,070 gallons (92,070 − 90,000). At a standard material cost of $.90 per gallon, the favorable quantity (yield) variance is $1,863.

(5) Actual rate per hour—averaged	$ 4.10	$ 1.05
(6) Total actual costs	$41,000	$10,500
(7) Actual hours	10,000	10,000
(8) Standard hours allowed for 92,070 gallons of output	9,207	9,207
(9) Standard hours allowed for normal input would be the same	9,207	9,207
(10) Actual input of 100,000 gallons has a standard yield of 90,000 gallons, which should have required 9,000 standard hours	9,000	9,000

First, let us analyze our usual approach to direct labor variance analysis. Two variances, rate and usage, are computed:

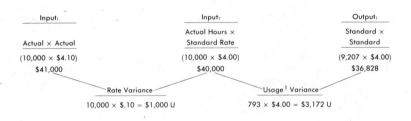

The usage variance can be further divided into a yield variance and an efficiency variance:

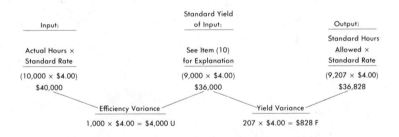

The standard yield from 100,000 gallons of input should be 90,000 gallons (100,000 × .9). The actual production of 92,070 gallons exceeded the standard yield by 2,070 gallons and produced a favorable material quantity (yield) variance of $1,863 (2,070 × $.90).

At $.40 per gallon, the favorable labor yield variance is $828 (2,070 gallons × $.40, or 207 hours × $4.00). However, the typical usage variance, as initially computed above, revealed an unfavorable variance of $3,172 and failed to disclose the favorable yield variance. The 100,000 gallons of input should have taken 9,000 hours to process into 90,000 gallons of standard yield. The actual time was 10,000 hours, so that 1,000 hours more than standard were devoted to the quantity processed.

[1] Previously, this variance has been called an efficiency variance, which is the most commonly encountered terminology.

At $4.00 per hour, these 1,000 excessive hours represent a $4,000 unfavorable efficiency variance. In summary:

Direct labor:

Efficiency variance	$4,000 U
Yield variance	828 F
Usage variance	$3,172 U

This variance analysis, like all others, is merely a first step toward directing attention to possible areas that need investigation. Many explanations are possible for these results. In many cases the failure to subdivide a usage variance into its efficiency and yield components would cloud important information. For instance, horrible inefficiency can sometimes be more than offset by an unusually favorable yield variance. Yet, in our example the $4,000 unfavorable efficiency variance was too great to be offset by the $828 yield variance. Other explanations are possible. The unfavorable efficiency variance could also have arisen because of the nature of the material, or faulty equipment, or a combination of circumstances. Moreover, the favorable yield could have been attributable to special care on the part of labor, better-quality materials, or especially efficient equipment.

The analysis of variable overhead would be similar to that used for direct labor:

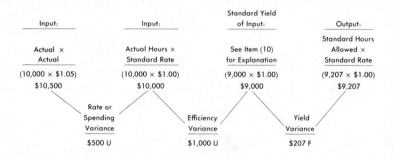

Because fixed overhead incurred in the short run is unaffected by efficiency or yield factors, such variances are not calculated for fixed costs.

SUMMARY

Variance analysis becomes more complicated when there is more than one type of product sold or where more than one material is utilized to obtain a finished product. Mix and yield variances, as well as the usual quantity and price variances, must be computed to aid management analysis.

Computations of mix variances are similar for sales-mix and material-mix situations. The objective is to hold price-cost and quantity (yield) factors constant when computing mix variances. Similarly, mix and price-cost factors are held constant when quantity (yield) variances are computed.

When yield variances exist, direct labor and variable overhead variances are separated into three major components (rate, efficiency, and yield) instead of the more typical two components (rate and usage).

PROBLEM FOR SELF-STUDY

Problem. Refer to the original budget in Example 1. Suppose that actual results show the following:

	Product X			Product Y			Total		
	Units	Price	Total	Units	Price	Total	Units	Price	Total
Sales	600	$4.00	$2,400	2,400	$1.70	$4,080	3,000	$2.16	$6,480
Variable costs	600	1.50	900	2,400	.90	2,160	3,000	1.02	3,060
Contribution margin	600	$2.50	$1,500	2,400	$ .80	$1,920	3,000	$1.14	$3,420

Prepare a complete explanation of why the contribution margin is $1,380 less than originally budgeted. Include a detailed mix, quantity, and price-cost variance analysis for each product.

Solution.

			Total	Subdivision of Variances		
	Budget	Actual	Variance	Mix	Quantity	Price-Cost
Contribution margin	$4,800	$3,420	$1,380	$120 U	$1,200 U	$60 U

Mix variance = [(Budgeted mix percentage × Actual *total* quantity) −
$$\text{Actual product quantity]} \times \text{Budgeted price}$$

$$X = [(.25 \times 3,000) - \quad 600] \times \$1.80 \ = \$270 \text{ U}$$
$$Y = [(.75 \times 3,000) - 2,400] \times \$1.00 \ = \ \underline{\quad 150 \text{ F}}$$

Total $120 U

Quantity variance = [(Budgeted mix percentage ×
Actual *total* quantity) − Budgeted product quantity] × Budgeted price

$$X = [(.25 \times 3,000) - 1,000] \times \$1.80 = \$ \ 450 \text{ U}$$
$$Y = [(.75 \times 3,000) - 3,000] \times \$1.00 = \quad \underline{750 \text{ U}}$$

Total $1,200 U

Price-cost variance = Difference in unit contribution margin ×
Actual product quantity

$$X = (\$2.50 - \$1.80) \times \quad 600 = \$420 \text{ F}$$
$$Y = (\$1.00 - \$ .80) \times 2,400 = \quad \underline{480 \text{ U}}$$

Total $ 60 U

U = Unfavorable; F = Favorable.

As the analysis shows, Y had a favorable mix variance because it represented 80 per cent of the total units sold instead of the 75 per cent originally budgeted; conversely, X had an unfavorable mix variance because its share was 20 per cent instead of the 25 per cent originally budgeted.

QUESTIONS, PROBLEMS, AND CASES

21-1. Define *sales mix.*

21-2. Define *sales mix variance.*

21-3. Define *material yield variance.*

21-4. "Material mix variances and material yield variances always tend to offset one another." Do you agree? Why?

◆ 21-5. Sales Mix, Quantity, and Price-Cost Variances. Refer to the original budget in Example 1. Suppose that actual results show the following:

	Product X			Product Y			Total		
	Units	Price	Total	Units	Price	Total	Units	Price	Total
Sales	1,400	$2.70	$3,780	2,800	$2.20	$6,160	4,200	$2.37	$9,940
Variable Costs	1,400	1.00	1,400	2,800	1.10	3,080	4,200	1.07	4,480
Contribution margin	1,400	$1.70	$2,380	2,800	$1.10	$3,080	4,200	$1.30	$5,460

Prepare a complete explanation of why the contribution margin is $660 greater than originally budgeted. Include a detailed mix, quantity, and price-cost variance analysis for each product.

21-6. Material Mix and Yield Variances. A company has the following standards:

50 pounds of Material C at	$1.40 =	$ 70.00
30 pounds of Material D at	2.00 =	60.00
20 pounds of Material E at	1.60 =	32.00
100 pounds of standard mix at	1.62 =	$162.00

100 pounds of standard mix at 1.62 = $162.00 should produce 90 pounds of finished product at a standard cost of $1.80 per pound ($162.00 ÷ 90).

No inventories of raw materials are kept. Purchases are made as needed, so that all price variances relate to materials used. Actual results showed that 50,000 pounds were used during a period.

26,000 pounds of C at actual cost of $1.20 =	$31,200
16,000 pounds of D at actual cost of 2.10 =	33,600
8,000 pounds of E at actual cost of 1.90 =	15,200
50,000	$80,000

Good output was

40,000 pounds at standard cost of $1.80	=	72,000
Total material variance to be explained	=	$ 8,000 U

What are the mix, quantity (yield), and price variances?

*21-7. **Conversion Cost Rate, Efficiency, and Yield Variances.** Suppose that in Problem 21-6 the following direct labor and variable overhead factors were combined in a single conversion cost analysis:

(1) Standard rate per hour   = $ 7.20

(2) The conversion of 10 pounds of raw material into 9 pounds of finished product should take 30 minutes, so that the standard rate per pound of output should be $7.20 ÷ 18 pounds per hour   = $ .40

(3) Standard cost of 40,000 pounds of output   = $16,000

(4) Actual rate per hour (averaged)   = $ 7.50

(5) Total actual costs   = $18,000

(6) Actual hours   =   2,400

(7) Standard hours allowed for 40,000 pounds of output (40,000 ÷ 18)   =   2,222

What are the conversion cost rate, efficiency, and yield variances?

21-8. Case on Sales-Mix Variances. Fred Putney, a bright (graduate, reported to his job on June 20 with the Hi-lite Division of Growl Although Fred was not entirely sure what his job would be, he did know would be a special assistant to the vice president in charge of the Hi-Lite John Cromwell. Cromwell was a promising young executive who had k sonally responsible for the hiring of Fred for this newly created position. taken charge of the Hi-Lite Division only eight months before; he imr instituted formal budgeting procedures to aid control.

A variable budgeting system is prepared by John's staff and fo   :d to Growler headquarters for approval. Most divisions of Growler operat   rly autonomously except that all accounting, personnel, and general admir   ion were accomplished by the headquarters staff. Thus, when the policy guidelines had been established by headquarters, it was up to the division vice presidents to set their own operating policies and operations for those costs and activities over which they had direct control. The budgets prepared by John's staff accounted only for those costs which were variable and controllable by John. However, his division's fixed costs and share of the general and administrative expense were expected to be $450,000 per quarter.

The Hi-Lite Division manufactured and marketed three basic types of light fixtures for industrial use. Competition was keen; as a result, selling and service costs were quite high. Hi-Lite was the second largest selling fixture, accounting for about 11 per cent of the market. The largest seller was Sly-Lite, Inc., which accounted for approximately 18 per cent of the market. Most firms, large and small, adopted prices similar to that charged by Sly-Lite, although in depressed times the small firms often cut prices. The Hi-Lite Division had approximately $12,000,000 in total assets. Because Growler's stated objective for all divisions was approximately 11 per cent net return after taxes for all divisions, this meant that Hi-Lite must generate a total contribution margin of $4,400,000 per year.

After Fred had spent a hectic morning shaking hands, signing forms, and getting his office arranged, he went to Cromwell to get his first assignment. After the amenities were concluded, John stated: "Fred, here are some budget data for the quarters we are just finishing. (See attached exhibits.) Although the figures are preliminary, they should be adequate for what I want you to do. If you'll notice, from Exhibits I and II our profit goal is $1,100,000 per quarter; but in the first quarter we made only $1,050,000. This quarter, however, we tightened ship a little, and the preliminary figures indicate we will have a total profit of $1,122,500. If we can maintain this profit rate, I think we can exceed headquarters' goal.

"However, there are a few things about the picture that worry me. You will notice in Exhibit III that the number of units sold decreased for two products and increased substantially for one product. Although we got a favorable turn in our selling prices, our contribution margins have deteriorated for one of our products. According to our production people, our labor and material costs should remain at the present level. Also, our sales manager feels that selling prices will probably stabilize at the present level.

"Right now, our sales manager is in the process of making up the next quarter's budget based on our sales forecast. However, before we complete the budget, I'd like to know why we made more money this quarter when we produced and sold less fixtures. I get the feeling that maybe we should modify our product mix; but before we start changing our budget procedures, I want to know the effect of product mix and volume on our profit picture. That's what I want you to do. You said you were interested in cost accounting and control, so here's a good one to start with. Go over our budget and actual (preliminary) figures and see if you can come up with some explanation for the changes in costs and profit. I'd like to have this by tomorrow afternoon so I can go over it with you before our budget conference."

Fred picked up the following highlights from Exhibit III:

	Budget	Actual
Sales (units)	380,000	370,000
Contribution Margin	$1,100,000 (30.8%)	$1,122,500 (31.4%)
Sales Mix:		
A	26.3%	23.0%
B	21.0%	25.7%
C	52.7%	51.3%

EXHIBIT I

HI-LITE DIVISION

	Quarter	Contribution Margin	Fixed, General & Admin. Expense	Estimated Income Taxes	Net Income
(Actual)	1	$1,050,000	$ 450,000	$ 300,000	$ 300,000
(Preliminary)	2	1,122,500	450,000	336,250	336,250
(Budget)	3		450,000	325,000	325,000
(Budget)	4		450,000	325,000	325,000
		$4,372,500	$1,800,000	$1,286,250	$1,286,250

EXHIBIT II

HI-LITE DIVISION
Budget Targets for the Coming Year

Total assets	$12,000,000	
Target net income	1,300,000	
Add:		
Income taxes	1,300,000	
Fixed expenses and general headquarters expenses	1,800,000	
Total contribution margin needed	$ 4,400,000	for the year,
or	$ 1,100,000	quarterly

EXHIBIT III

HI-LITE DIVISION
Contribution Margin Budget,
April 1–June 30

Product	Quantity	Variable Cost per Unit	Total Variable Cost	Selling Price per Unit	Total Sales
A	100,000	$5.60	$ 560,000	$ 8.50	$ 850,000
B	80,000	6.80	544,000	9.00	720,000
C	200,000	6.83	1,366,000	10.00	2,000,000
	380,000		$2,470,000		$3,570,000

HI-LITE DIVISION
Actual Results (Preliminary),
April 1–June 30

Product	Quantity	Variable Cost Per Unit	Total Variable Cost	Selling Price Per Unit	Total Sales
A	85,000	$6.10	$ 518,500	$ 8.80	$ 748,000
B	95,000	6.60	627,000	9.00	855,000
C	190,000	7.00	1,330,000	10.50	1,995,000
	370,000		$2,475,500		$3,598,000

REQUIRED:

Prepare a complete mix, quantity, and price-cost analysis.   Use unit contribution margins for your price-cost analysis. Comment on your analysis.

ACCOUNTING SYSTEMS

accounting systems and internal control

CHAPTER XXII

This book has already emphasized many planning and control features of accounting systems. This chapter will present a brief overview and then will concentrate on some features not previously covered, such as internal control and the impact of computers.

The accounting system is intertwined with operating management. Accounting records are kept not only because they are needed to tally performance for later appraisal and for income determination, but also because business operations would be a hopeless tangle without the paper work that is so often regarded with disdain. For example, cash receipts and disbursements must be traced, and receivables and payables must be recorded, or else confusion would ensue. The act of recording events has become as much a part of operating activities as the act of selling or buying. Even the simplest of businesses must have a minimum of records, a semblance of routine. As businesses become more complex, managers find themselves increasingly dependent on the systematic compilation of records for keeping informed and for help with planning and control.

Recent revolutionary changes in processing business data have been so extensive that a specific system is likely to be outdated by the time its description is off the press. That is why this chapter describes the general features of an effective accounting system that have wide applicability to a variety of organizations regardless of their specific systems.

The primary test of any accounting system is whether it is a help or a hindrance to management. Accounting systems should be judged by how they help promote and impel personnel toward over-all organizational goals.

AN OVERVIEW OF SYSTEMS

Focus of design must be on objectives

Ideally, an accounting system is the major business information system. It is the formal communications network that supplies dependable, useful information to help executives strive toward a mass of predetermined organizational objectives and sub-objectives. Therefore, an accounting system should be designed to provide data for (a) searching for objectives and sub-objectives together with their means of attainment (budgets, standards, and relevant costs for special decisions) and (b) appraising and investigating results (performance reports and cost analysis). The latter technique is often called *feedback*, whereby results are automatically relayed back for inspection, evaluation, and follow-up.

Because modern business seems to be in an almost constant state of change, the expert in accounting systems is perpetually concerned with shifts in objectives, in behavior, in available resources, and in organizational structures. Only in this way can an accounting system be designed to accumulate, classify, measure, and report the types of information that managerial objectives require.

An executive can easily be swamped with data if he, or the accounting systems designer, does not know how to choose items that are relevant to his problems of planning and control. Therefore, data must be carefully recorded and minutely classified. The systems designer must contend with problems such as the following: what data should be collected and in what form; where and how long it should be stored; when and by whom it should be called for; how it should be evaluated; when it should be supplemented; and so on.[1] Budgets, standards, and relevant costs have been developed in order to answer many of these *what, where, when, whom,* and *how* questions.

Types of information supplied by accounting

What information should the management accountant supply? The types of information needed have been neatly described in a study of seven large companies with geographically dispersed operations, made by H. A. Simon and his associates. Their approach would probably prove fruitful to any company:

> By observation of the actual decision-making process, specific types of data needs were identified at particular organizational levels—the vice presidential level, the level of the factory manager, and the level of the factory head [foreman], for example—

[1] See Miller and Starr, *Executive Decisions and Operations Research* (Englewood Cliffs, N.J.: Prentice-Hall, Inc. 1960), pp. 11–18, for an expanded discussion of information systems in general.

each involving quite distinct problems of communication for the accounting depart-
ment.[2]

The Simon research team found that three types of information, each serving a different purpose, often at various management levels, raise and help to answer three basic questions:

1. Scorecard questions: Am I doing well or badly?
2. Attention-directing questions: What problems should I look into?
3. Problem-solving questions: Of the several ways of doing the job, which is the best?

The scorecard and attention-directing uses of data are closely related. The same data may ser e a scorecard function for a foreman and an attention-directing function for his superior. For example, many accounting systems provide performance reports in which actual results are compared with previously determined budgets or standards. Such a performance report often helps to answer scorecard questions and attention-directing questions simultaneously. Furthermore, the actual results collected serve not only control purposes but also the traditional needs of financial accounting, which is chiefly concerned with the answering of scorecard questions. This collection, classification, and reporting of data is the task that dominates day-to-day accounting.

Problem-solving data may be used in long-range planning and in making special, nonrecurring decisions, such as whether to make or buy parts, replace equipment, add or drop a product, and so forth. These decisions often require expert advice from specialists such as industrial engineers, budgetary accountants, statisticians, and others.

In sum, the accountant's task of supplying information has three facets:

1. *Score keeping.* The accumulation of data. This aspect of accounting enables both internal and external parties to evaluate organizational performance and position.
2. *Attention directing.* The reporting and interpreting of information which helps managers to focus on operating problems, imperfections, inefficiencies, and opportunities. This aspect of accounting helps managers to concern themselves with important aspects of operations promptly enough for effective action either through perceptive planning or through astute day-to-day supervision. Attention directing is commonly associated with current planning and control and with the analysis and investigation of recurring, routine internal accounting reports.
3. *Problem solving.* This aspect of accounting involves the concise quantification of the relative merits of possible courses of action, often with

[2]H. A. Simon, *Administrative Behavior*, 2nd ed. (New York: The Macmillan Company, 1957), p. 20. For the complete study see H. A. Simon, H. Guetzkow, G. Kozmetsky, and G. Tyndall, *Centralization vs. Decentralization in Organizing The Controller's Department* (New York: Controllership Foundation, Inc., 1954). This perceptive study is much broader than its title implies.

recommendations as to the best procedure. Problem solving is commonly associated with nonrecurring decisions, situations that require special accounting analyses or reports.

The above distinctions sometimes overlap or merge. Consequently, it is often difficult to pinpoint a particular accounting task as being score keeping, attention directing, or problem solving. Nevertheless, attempts to make these distinctions provide insight into the objectives and tasks of both accountants and managers.

Management accounting and the accounting system

These three uses of data may be related to the broad purposes of the accounting system. The accounting system of the future is likely to be a single, multiple-purpose system with a highly selective reporting scheme. It will be tightly integrated and will serve three main purposes: (1) routine reporting to management, primarily for planning and controlling current operations (score keeping and attention directing); (2) special reporting to management, primarily for long-range planning and nonrecurring decisions (problem solving); and (3) routine reporting on financial results, primarily for external parties (score keeping). Although such a system can probably be designed in a self-contained, integrated manner to serve routine purposes simultaneously, its function of providing information about special problems will always entail preparing much data that will not lie within the system.

Automatic control and management control

The size of the physical handling of records is often staggering. For example, in 1965 Standard Oil Company (Indiana) processed 11 million pieces of paper monthly just to handle their credit card business. This illustrates one overwhelming feature of a total system; the physical or technical or routine control sub-parts which tend to require a minimum of human judgment and which lend themselves toward *automatic* procedures. Other examples are check handling, payroll accounting, production scheduling, inventory control, and automated manufacturing. The accountant's role in these routine situations is largely one of score keeping.

But, as Anthony[3] has stressed, *management* control systems embrace much more than the *technical* or *physical* subsystems. Human judgment plays a heavy role in such organizational activities as advertising, research, pricing, finance, and particularly the management activity of co-ordination. Attention-directing and problem-solving data become paramount, and psychological considerations appear. Automatic control systems are essentially machine systems; management control systems are man-machine systems. "Management control is essentially applied social

[3]Robert N. Anthony, "Framework for Analysis," *Management Services* (March-April, 1964), pp. 22–23.

psychology."[4]   These aspects of systems were discussed in Chapters 9 and 11.

INTERNAL CONTROL: DEFINITION

Previous chapters have covered numerous features of an effective accounting system, such as the need for the following: timely data; competent accounting personnel who encourage the respect, confidence, cooperation, and cost-consciousness of operating managers; and constant search for improvement of the accounting system. The feature of *internal control* has not yet received direct attention.

Internal control is defined by the American Institute of Certified Public Accountants as follows:

> *Internal control comprises the plan of organization and all of the coordinate methods and measures adopted within a business to safeguard its assets, check the accuracy and reliability of its accounting data, promote operational efficiency, and encourage adherence to prescribed managerial policies.*[5]

The most important clause in this definition is "promote operational efficiency." Internal control may be visualized as being much more inclusive than *internal check*,[6] which is confined to checking "the accuracy and reliability of its accounting data." Accounting is an essential instrument in maintaining and enhancing internal control. Still, internal control is a management function, not an accounting function. Another look at the definition will show it to be merely an elaboration of the broad definition of managerial *control*: attaining adherence to plans.

This book has already described the features of systems and procedures that promote efficiency (budgets, standards, responsibility accounting, and so forth). *In its broadest sense, internal control embraces all of these accounting techniques.* This chapter will highlight those aspects of internal control which minimize errors, fraud, and waste.

All good systems of internal control have certain features in common. These features may be termed a checklist of internal control. This list may be used to appraise any procedure for cash, purchases, sales, payroll, and the like. This checklist may sometimes be called *principles* or *rules*.

CHECKLIST FOR INTERNAL CONTROL

No framework for internal control is perfect in the sense that it can prevent some shrewd individual from "beating the system" either by out-

---

[4]*Ibid.*, p. 21; see also his *Planning and Control Systems* (Boston: Harvard Business School, 1965).

[5]Committee on Auditing Procedure, *Auditing Standards and Procedures* (New York: American Institute of Certified Public Accountants, 1963), p. 27.

[6]In practice, however, the words *internal control* and *internal check* are often used interchangeably, so that many accountants regard internal control narrowly as being those characteristics of an accounting system that are designed to minimize errors, fraud, and waste.

right embezzlement or by producing inaccurate records. The task is not total prevention of fraud, nor is it implementation of operating perfection; rather, the task is the designing of a tool that will help achieve efficient operations and reduce temptation. Also, the most streamlined accounting system is deficient if its prescribed procedures are not being conscientiously followed.

A checklist for a good internal control system[7] includes:

1. *Reliable Personnel.* Individuals obviously should be given duties and responsibilities commensurate with their abilities, interests, experience, and reliability. Yet many employers use low-cost talent that may prove exceedingly expensive in the long run, not only from the point of view of fraud but also from the point of view of productivity. The accounting system, no matter how elaborate, is only as good as the individuals who implement it.

2. *Separation of Powers.* Recordkeeping and physical handling of assets should not be in the hands of one person. For example, the bookkeeper should not handle cash, and the cashier should not have access to ledger accounts such as subsidiary receivable records. The general ledger bookkeeper should not have access to subsidiary records. The entire accounting function should be divorced from operating departments, so that objective, independent records may be kept either by other operating people (for example, inspectors, not machine operators, should count good pieces) or by accounting clerks (for example, stores record clerks, not storekeepers, should keep perpetual inventory counts). This point not only better insures accurate compilation of data; it also necessitates collusion of two or more persons to perpetrate a fraud.

3. *Supervision.* The typical organization chart illustrates this point. Everyone has a boss who oversees and appraises performance.

4. *Responsibility.* This means tracking actions as far down in the organization as is feasible so that results may be related to individuals. It means having salesclerks sign sales slips, inspectors initial packing slips, and workmen sign time cards and requisitions. The psychological impact of fixing responsibility promotes care and efficiency; it keeps people on their toes. Individuals tend to perform better when they must answer for inefficiencies.

The accumulation of costs by department would be impossible without some means of fixing responsibility for cost incurrence.

5. *Routine and Automatic Checks.* In a phrase, this means doing things "by the numbers." Just as manufacturing activities tend to be made more efficient by the division and specialization of repetitive activities, so can recordkeeping activities be made less costly and more accurate. Repetitive procedures may be prescribed for nonmanufacturing activities such as order-taking, order-filling, collating, and inspecting. The use of general routines permits specialization, division of duties, and automatic checks on previous steps in the routine.

[7] Also see William J. Vatter, *Managerial Accounting* (Englewood Cliffs, N.J.: Prentice-Hall, Inc., 1950), Chapter 11, for his ten principles of internal control, most of which are described here.

For example, disbursement-voucher systems are widely used in industry. The essential feature of such a system is that no checks may be signed without a disbursement voucher that so authorizes. In turn, the voucher will not be prepared unless all supporting documents, such as pertinent requisitions, purchase orders, invoices, receiving reports, and freight documents, have been reviewed. Each step in the review serves as a check on previous steps.

Forms are designed so that the absence or incorrectness of key information is automatically uncovered and corrected on the spot. For example, the absence of a receiving clerk's signature on a receiving report would halt preparation of a disbursement voucher, and the omission of a foreman's signature prevents payments of overtime pay.

6. *Document Control.* This means immediate recording, complete recording, and tamper-proof recording. This point is especially important for handling cash sales. Devices used to insure immediate recording include cash registers with loud bells and compiling tapes, private detectives, guaranteeing refunds to customers if they are not offered a receipt, and forcing clerks to make change by pricing items at $1.99, $2.99, and $3.99 rather than at $2, $3, and $4.[8]

Complete and tamper-proof recording is encouraged by having all source documents prenumbered and accounted for, by using devices such as cash registers and locked compartments in invoice-writing machines, and by designing forms for ease of recording.

7. *Bonding, Vacations, and Rotation of Duties.* Key people may be subject to excessive temptation; top executives, branch managers, and individuals who handle cash or inventories should be bonded, have understudies, and be forced to take vacations.

A facet of this idea is also illustrated by the common practice of having receivables and payables clerks periodically rotated in duties. Thus, a receivables clerk may handle accounts from A to C for three months and then be rotated to accounts M to P for three months, and so forth.

8. *Independent Check.* All phases of the system should be subjected to periodic review by outsiders (for example, by independent public accountants) and by internal auditors who do not ordinarily have contact with the operation under review.

The idea of independent check extends beyond the work performed by professional auditors. For example, bank statements should be reconciled with book balances. The bank provides an independent record of cash. Furthermore, the monthly bank reconciliations should be conducted by some clerk other than the cash, receivables, or payables clerk. Other examples of independent checks include monthly statements sent to credit customers and physical counts of inventory to check against perpetual records.

One of the main jobs of internal auditors and outside auditors is to appraise the effectiveness of internal control; such appraisal affects the

---

[8]Historically, such pricing was originally adopted to force clerks to make change as well as for its psychological impact on potential customers.

extent of the sampling of transactions needed to test validity of account balances.

9. *Physical Safeguards.* Obviously, losses of cash, inventories, and records are minimized by safes, locks, watchmen, and limited access.

10. *Cost Feasibility.* The complexity and costs of an internal control system must be compared with its benefits. Highly complex systems tend to strangle people in red tape so that the system impedes rather than promotes efficiency. Besides, there is "a cost of keeping the costs" that sometimes gets out of hand. Investments in more costly systems must be judged in the light of expected benefits. Unfortunately, such benefits are difficult to measure. It is much easier to relate new lathes or production methods to cost savings in manufacturing than a new computer to cost savings in the form of facilitating new attacks on problems of inventory control, production scheduling, and research. Yet, hard-headed efforts, as are used in appraising other business decisions, must be made to measure alternative costs of various accounting systems.

ILLUSTRATIONS

McKesson & Robbins fraud: the limitations of systems

A fraud case that had a big and lasting impact on auditing procedures was the infamous McKesson & Robbins embezzlement of the 1930's. The president engineered a complicated fraud in collusion with the assistant treasurer; the head of shipping, receiving, and warehousing; and an outside party who managed dummy companies with whom McKesson purportedly conducted business. It so happened that the partners in crime were the president's brothers. All four men did not use their real names.[9]

Essentially, the fraud involved setting up an entirely fictitious Canadian crude drug division. Pretended purchases were made from a number of Canadian vendors, who supposedly retained the merchandise in their own warehouses for the account of McKesson. Pretended sales were made by a fictitious W. W. Smith and Company, as agent for McKesson; goods were shipped directly to customers. Payment for goods purchased and collections from customers were pretended to have been made by the Montreal banking firm of Manning & Company—also for the account of McKesson. The actual cash embezzlement from the central headquarters of McKesson took the form of commissions paid to W. W. Smith and Co. All of these transactions were supported by proper-looking but false invoices, contracts, Dun and Bradstreet credit reports, and the like.

The enormity of the fraud framework can be seen from McKesson's certified balance sheet as of December 31, 1937; it showed $87 million in assets, $20 million of which were fictitious, consisting of $10 million in receivables and $10 million in inventories, and $75,000 of cash on deposit with "Manning and Company."

---

[9]For fascinating accounts of the president's exploits, see *The New Yorker*, October 22, 1955, and October 29, 1955, or *Saturday Evening Post*, February 28, 1953.

The fraud, which had been conducted over a period of twelve years, was finally uncovered by Julian Thompson, controller and treasurer, when he went to Montreal to check on inventories and found none.

The president killed himself, McKesson & Robbins was taken over by a trustee in bankruptcy, and the public accounting firms were placed in a state of shock—sending their men scurrying all over the world to make sure that their clients' inventories really existed. One major change in auditing procedure that all auditing firms adopted as an outgrowth of this case was the physical testing of inventories instead of relying on the client's word.

The Securities and Exchange Commission launched a detailed investigation of the matter. A thorough investigation of the fraud was hampered by the president's suicide, but some of the figures involved are worth repeating:

1. The costs of investigation totaled $3 million.
2. The public accounting firm that investigated the fraud had 300 accountants work a total of 146,000 man-hours. They found 91 bank accounts, 57 brokerage accounts, and 10 loan accounts that the president had used in the course of his 12 years at the helm of McKesson & Robbins. Ultimately, they found that the actual cash stolen was about $3,200,000.

The moral of this story for both managers and accountants may be best expressed by the sentence that the president underlined in a book (Morrill Goddard's *What Interests People and Why*) he had been reading shortly before committing suicide:

> *The truth, which the public has never been told, is that no practical system has ever been devised by which the complicated finances of a large institution can be thoroughly checked so that every transaction is verified, except at prohibitive time and cost.*

Using the checklist

The next illustration will show how the checklist for internal control may be used as a starting point in judging a system.

Question.[10] The *Y* Company has come to you with the following problem:

It has three clerical employees who must perform the following functions:

(1) Maintain general ledger;
(2) Maintain accounts payable ledger;
(3) Maintain accounts receivable ledger;
(4) Prepare checks for signature;
(5) Maintain disbursements journal;
(6) Issue credits on returns and allowances;

---

[10] Adapted from A.I.C.P.A. examination.

(7) Reconcile the bank account;

(8) Handle and deposit cash receipts.

Assuming that there is no problem as to the ability of any of the employees, the Company requests that you assign the above functions to the three employees in such a manner as to achieve the highest degree of internal control. It may be assumed that these employees will perform no other accounting functions than the ones listed and that any accounting functions not listed will be performed by persons other than these three employees.

a. State how you would distribute the above functions among the three employees. Assume that, with the exception of the nominal jobs of the bank reconciliation and the issuance of credits on returns and allowances, all functions require an equal amount of time.

b. List four possible unsatisfactory combinations of the above-listed functions.

Try to answer the questions before consulting the following solution.

Answer.

a. Assignment of functions:

Employee No. 1:

(1) Maintain general ledger;

(2) Reconcile bank account;

(3) Issue credits on returns and allowances.

Employee No. 2:

(1) Prepare checks for signature;

(2) Handle and deposit cash recipts;

(3) Maintain disbursements journal.

Employee No. 3:

(1) Maintain accounts payable ledger;

(2) Maintain accounts receivable ledger.

b. Undesirable combinations are as follows:

(1) Cash receipts and accounts receivable;

(2) Cash receipts and credits on returns and allowances;

(3) Cash disbursements and accounts payable;

(4) Cash receipts and bank reconciliation;

(5) General ledger and cash receipts;

(6) Accounts receivable and credits on returns and allowances.

The major feature of the suggested division of duties is the separation of powers so that *one individual does not have sole control over all recordkeeping and physical handling for any single transaction.* Not only does this limit the chances for fraud, but—probably more important—it provides for automatic checks on efficiency and accuracy.

SUMMARY

The ideal accounting system is a formal communications network that supplies dependable, useful information to help executives select and attain organizational objectives. There are three major classes of data: *score-keeping, attention-directing,* and *problem-solving.* Generally, it is better to design the accounting system primarily to provide score-keeping and attention-directing data; problem-solving data are usually collected through special studies.

A good accounting system captures the attention and holds the interest of operating managers. It is regarded as a valuable tool in day-to-day operations. It is marked by an effective system of internal control that promotes efficiency, honesty, timeliness, and accuracy; it minimizes errors, fraud, and waste.

The following general characteristics form a checklist that may be used as a starting point for judging the effectiveness of internal control:

1. Reliable personnel	7. Bonding, vacations, and rota-
2. Separation of powers	tion of duties
3. Supervision	8. Independent check
4. Responsibility	9. Physical safeguards
5. Routine and automatic checks	10. Costs and feasibility
6. Document control	

The future will bring improved accounting systems that will better meet management needs. The chiefs of such systems will be those accountants who have a grasp of all three functions—score keeping, attention directing, and problem solving.

PROBLEM FOR SELF-STUDY

Problem.[11] As a member of the controller's department, you have been asked to review the company's payroll system and procedures where all payrolls are paid in currency.

a. State what questions you would ask in your review of the system of internal control and procedures relative to payrolls.

b. Give your reasons for asking the above questions, including an explanation of how you would use the questions in deciding on the effectiveness of the control over payrolls.

Formulate your own answer before examining the solution that follows.

Answer.

a. (1) *Reliable personnel:* Who prepares payrolls? Have their past employment references been checked? What is their performance record as far as efficiency is concerned?

(2) *Separation of powers:* Are hiring and firing properly authorized and reported? Are pay rates and changes properly authorized and reported? Is payroll preparation divided among employees?

(3) *Supervision:* Who supervises payments? Are time records approved by a timekeeper or foreman?

(4) *Responsibility:* Who is in charge of each step in the payroll process? Do overtime hours require special approval? By whom?

(5) *Routine and automatic checks:* Are receipts submitted by employees? How do employees identify themselves? How is validity of signa-

---

[11] Adapted from A.I.C.P.A. examination.

tures checked? What procedures are used for review, approval, and reconciliation of payroll charges to various accounts?

(6) *Document control:* Who has control over unclaimed pay envelopes? How are envelopes claimed after regular pay dates? Are time clocks used? Are time records properly prepared and controlled?

(7) *Bonding and vacations:* Are key payroll employees bonded? Is there rotation of payroll duties?

(8) *Independent check:* Are payroll calculations independently checked before payment? Do auditors witness or perform a distribution of payroll, including control of unclaimed envelopes? Are receipts compared with payroll by somebody not engaged in payroll preparation?

(9) *Physical safeguards:* Are there physical safeguards, like alarm systems, police, safes, and the like?

(10) *Costs and feasibility:* Is the over-all system working efficiently and smoothly? Are there any glaring weaknesses? Is there any unnecessary routine or duplication of effort?

b. These questions were asked to determine that (a) hiring and separation, (b) accumulation of periodic payroll time and rate records, and (c) payouts were handled with a minimum chance of error, fraud, and waste. The above questions are designed to discover that duties are separated, that adequate personnel and payroll records are kept, and that proper authority and supervision are exercised at every step affecting payroll. The controller wants satisfactory cross-checks, physical safeguards, rotation of duties, step-by-step routines, and constant review and supervision.

APPENDIX: FACTORY LEDGERS

In this appendix we study an example of some specialized techniques for accumulating accounting data. The purpose here is not to dwell on the intricacies of a specific system. Rather it is to offer an overview of the immense task of effective systems design. Persons without accounting experience often find it difficult to visualize the avalanche of paper work that most companies face. It should be recognized that routine data collection and classification is the most time-consuming task of the controller's department. That is why the expenditure of time, care, and money on planning and shaping an accounting system is nearly always a worthwhile investment.

Classification and coding

Any sizable company finds it convenient to classify accounts in detail and to number or otherwise code the accounts accordingly. Although an outsider may not know what the code means, accounting employees become so familiar with the code that they think, talk, and write in terms of account numbers instead of account names. Thus, if Cash is account No. 1000 and Accounts Payable is account No. 7000, an outside auditor may find payments to creditors journalized as follows:

Money Columns		
#7000	125,000	
#1000		125,000

A company usually has a chart of accounts which classifies all accounts in the entire company by name and code number. Codes differ from company to company. Each coding system is usually some variation of the following example:

Geographic Location	General Ledger Account	Department	Subsidiary Classification
0	00	000	000

This classification may be used by a multi-plant company with far-flung operations. It would be too cumbersome for many companies and not detailed enough for giant companies.

Assume that a company has a central plant in Chicago and branch plants in Dallas, Pittsburgh, and San Francisco. Debits for various transactions could be coded as shown in Exhibit 22-1.

The numbers used to code debits and credits are obtained from the company chart of accounts. These numbers are originally entered or keypunched on the source documents (requisitions, vouchers, work tickets) that are the basis for ledger entries and other analyses. For example, Chicago is coded as (1), Factory Overhead Control as (91), a machining department as (011), and supplies used as (112). What would be the complete account number for indirect labor cost incurred by the finishing department in Chicago? The answer is 1-91-015-202.

Factory ledger

Many companies have branch plants sprawled all over the country and the world. Cost accumulation and analysis are most often conducted at the various geographic locations, whereas records of receivables, payables, and similar accounts may be centralized in the home office. The division of accounting between central headquarters and a branch plant calls for splitting the accounts between the two locations. At the same time, some technique must be used to ensure the dovetailing of all company accounts so that duplications, omissions, and other errors are minimized. Generally, two reciprocal accounts are introduced, one in the home office and one at the factory. An example follows.

Example of Factory Ledger. The central offices of the Homeware Company are in Chicago; but the manufacturing operations are located in Richmond, Indiana. The company uses a separate factory ledger that is maintained at Richmond for the benefit of the plant management. The

EXHIBIT 22-1

CODING OF ACCOUNTS

Transaction	General Ledger Entry	Possible Number Code for Debit				
		Geographic Location	General Ledger Account	Department	Subsidiary Classification
1. Requisition of supplies by a machining department in Chicago.	Factory overhead control Stores	1	91	011	112
2. Requisition of supplies by a finishing department in Dallas.	Factory overhead control Stores	2	91	015	112
3. Indirect labor incurred by machining department in San Francisco.	Factory overhead control Stores	4	91	011	202
4. President's salary.	Administrative expenses control Accrued payroll	1	98	060	801

factory is given credit for finished goods at cost when the goods are shipped to the central warehouses. All goods are shipped to customers from the warehouses.

The chart of general ledger accounts for the company is as follows:

Code	Home Office Accounts	Code	Factory Accounts
1	Cash in bank	A	Stores control
2	Accounts receivable control	B	Work in process control
3	Finished goods control	C	Factory overhead applied
4	Plant and equipment control	D	Factory overhead control
5	Allowance for depreciation	E	Home office ledger control
6	Accounts payable		
7	Accrued payroll		
8	Common stock		
9	Retained earnings		
10	Factory ledger control		
11	Sales		
12	Cost of goods sold		
13	Selling cost control		
14	Administrative cost control		

REQUIRED:

Below is a summary of some transactions for one month.

Indicate the accounts debited and credited in the Factory Ledger and in the Home Ledger. Show postings and endings balances in Factory Ledger Control and Home Office Ledger Control. Try to solve this problem yourself before looking at the solution.

Partial List of Transactions

1. Materials purchased on credit	$200,000
2. Direct materials requisitioned	150,000
3. Factory payroll accrued (direct labor, $130,000; other $70,000)	200,000
4. Miscellaneous factory overhead incurred*	68,000
5. Factory overhead applied	65,000
6. Cost of goods shipped to warehouse	325,000
7. Cost of goods sold	300,000
8. Sales (on credit)	450,000
9. Cash collected on account	340,000

*Credit Accounts Payable except for $5,000 depreciation.

Solution and Comments. Remember that this is only an example. The solution is shown in Exhibit 22-2. A general ledger may be split into two or more parts in any manner whatsoever, depending on practical needs. Thus, the ledger in our example could have been designed so that accounts for plant and equipment could be kept at the factory instead of at the home office. If this were done, what journal entry(s) would be changed?

EXHIBIT 22-2

SAMPLE JOURNAL ENTRIES FOR BRANCH ACCOUNTING

Transaction	Home Office Ledger		Factory Ledger		Entries That Would Be Made in a Regular, Unified Ledger	
1. Material purchases	Factory ledger control	200,000	Stores control	200,000	Stores control	200,000
	Accounts payable	200,000	Home office ledger control	200,000	Accounts payable	200,000
2. Requisitions	None.		Work in process control	150,000	Work in process control	150,000
			Stores control	150,000	Stores control	150,000
3. Factory payroll	Factory ledger control	200,000	Work in process control	130,000	Work in process control	130,000
	Accrued payroll	200,000	Factory overhead control	70,000	Factory overhead control	70,000
			Home office ledger control	200,000	Accrued payroll	200,000
4. Miscellaneous overhead	Factory ledger control	68,000	Factory overhead control	68,000	Factory overhead control	68,000
	Allowance for depreciation	5,000	Home office ledger control	68,000	Allowance for depreciation	5,000
	Accounts payable	63,000			Accounts payable	63,000
5. Overhead application	None.		Work in process control	65,000	Work in process control	65,000
			Factory overhead applied	65,000	Factory overhead applied	65,000
6. Shipments to warehouse	Finished goods control	325,000	Home office ledger control	325,000	Finished goods control	325,000
	Factory ledger control	325,000	Work in process control	325,000	Work in process control	325,000
7. Cost of goods sold	Cost of goods sold	300,000	None.		Cost of goods sold	300,000
	Finished goods control	300,000			Finished goods control	300,000
8. Sales	Accounts receivable control	450,000	None.		Accounts receivable control	450,000
	Sales	450,000			Sales	450,000
9. Collections	Cash	340,000	None.		Cash	340,000
	Accounts receivable control	340,000			Accounts receivable control	340,000

Postings:

Factory Ledger Control

(1)	200,000	(6)	325,000
(3)	200,000		
(4)	68,000		
		To bal. 143,000	
Bal. 143,000			

Home Office Ledger Control

(6)	325,000	(1)	200,000
		(3)	200,000
		(4)	68,000
To bal. 143,000			
		Bal.	143,000

Difficulties in factory ledger accounting center around lagging or otherwise faulty communications, which result in disagreement in the balances of the reciprocal accounts. Common causes for discrepancies include transfers of inventories and cash that are in transit at the trial balance cut-off date and failure to recognize nonroutine payments for factory costs by the office on behalf of the branch.

QUESTIONS, PROBLEMS, AND CASES

Note: Problems 22-20 and 22-21 are provocative. Problems 22-22 through 22-25 cover the material in the appendix.

22-1. "The designer of accounting systems must contend with a number of factors." What are some major problems that face the systems designer?

22-2. Distinguish between *attention-directing* and *problem-solving* uses of data.

22-3. "Generally, it is better to design the accounting system primarily to provide attention-directing data." Explain.

22-4. "Business operations would be a hopeless tangle without the paper work that is of often regarded with disdain." Explain.

22-5. Define *internal control*. Distinguish it from *internal check*.

22-6. "There are ten check points that I always use as a framework for judging the effectiveness of an internal control system." Name nine of the ten.

22-7. "The words *internal control* are commonly misunderstood. They are thought to refer to those facets of the accounting system that are supposed to help prevent embezzling." Do you agree? Why?

22-8. "Internal control systems have both negative and positive objectives." Do you agree? Explain.

22-9. Briefly describe how a bottler of soda water might compile data regarding control of finished product at the plant, where normal breakage can be expected.

22-10. The branch manager of a national retail grocery chain has stated: "My managers are judged more heavily on the basis of their merchandise-shrinkage control than on their over-all sales volume." Why? Explain.

22-11. Evidence of Internal Control. List six sources of evidence about a given system of internal control and state briefly how the evidence from each source can be used in evaluating the system of internal control.   [C.P.A.]

22-12. Scope of Internal Control. Internal control, in the broad sense, includes controls which may be characterized as either administrative or accounting.

REQUIRED:

1. What comprises and is generally included in (1) administrative controls and (2) accounting controls?

2. What bearing do these controls have on the work of the independent auditor?

22-13. Controlling Inventories in Supermarkets. Nearly all big food chains have "inventory teams" which make frequent surprise descents on individual stores. They then take complete physical counts of all items in the store.

REQUIRED:

Based on your general knowledge of accounting and store operations, try to formulate and describe internal control techniques for merchandise.

22-14. Describe Control Procedures for Materials and Supplies. To ensure accurate computation of costs and efficient use of resources, it is necessary to have control records. A system of procedures and methods is designed to help proper control of materials and supplies from the time production is planned until the goods are ready for sale.

REQUIRED:

1. Enumerate the general procedures which must be followed to help achieve effective materials control.

2. Apart from the books of original entry and the general ledger, list the accounting forms and records used in a system of materials control.   [S.I.C.A.]

22-15. Internal Control Over Cash and Payroll.

1. In what ways can the use of cash registers contribute to the effectiveness of internal control over receipts from cash sales? Explain.

2. The general ledger of the *XY* Manufacturing Company contains a Payroll clearing account. Debits to the account originate in the payroll section of the factory accounting office. Credits to the account originate in the cost distribution section. The company does not use standard or estimated costs. On the assumption that there is effective internal control over payrolls, you are to:

   a. State the information needed by the payroll section and indicate the source of this information.

   b. State the information needed by the cost distribution section and the source of the information.

   c. State the principal controls over the payroll in the system as you have described it.   [C.P.A.]

22-16. Appraisal of Payroll System. The Generous Loan Company has 100 branch loan offices. Each office has a manager and four or five subordinates who are employed by the manager. Branch managers prepare the weekly payroll, including their own salaries, and pay their employees from cash on hand. The employee signs the payroll sheet, signifying receipt of his salary. Hours worked by hourly personnel are inserted in the payroll sheet from time cards prepared by the employees and approved by the manager.

The weekly payroll sheets are sent to the home office along with other accounting statements and reports. The home office compiles employee earnings records and prepares all federal and state salary reports from the weekly payroll sheets.

Salaries are established by home office job-evaluation schedules. Salary adjustments, promotions, and transfers of full-time employees are approved by a home office salary committee based upon the recommendations of branch managers and area supervisors. Branch managers advise the salary committee of new full-time employees and of terminations. Part-time and temporary employees are hired without referral to the salary committee.

REQUIRED:

Based upon your review of the payroll system, how might funds per payroll be diverted?   [C.P.A.]

22-17. Verification of Work in Process Costs. A company manufactures a product called MZ which is in process for thirty days. Its ingredients are a variety of materials which are introduced into the production vats at established intervals. The resultant finished product is a liquid which at the completion of the process is drawn off into 100-gallon drums. Of the book value of the company's entire inventory, approximately 20 per cent is material, 75 per cent work in process, and 5 per cent finished product, all carried at "cost."

The company's records show that Work in Process is charged with materials put into process at cost, computed on the fifo basis, and that a flat charge per vat is made monthly to cover all other manufacturing costs, which are incurred uniformly during the production period. Finished Product is charged and Work in Process credited with the value of the liquid withdrawn at a standard cost per gallon. The company operates ninety vats, production in which is so staggered that approximately the same number of vats can be emptied each day. The company has not made any computations to support the amount as shown in the Work in Process account.

REQUIRED:

1. State what detail records you would expect the company to maintain for controlling and costing this production process.

2. Outline a procedure for verifying the book value of the work in process inventory at the close of the company's fiscal year, excluding any consideration of physical inventory taking.

3. Either prepare an illustration of a worksheet or list the worksheet headings that you would use for assembling the principal data to be obtained for your verification.

22-18. Criticism of Accounting System. The *H* Manufacturing Company is engaged in manufacturing items to fill specific orders received from its customers. Although at any given time it may have substantial inventories of work in process and finished goods, all such amounts are assignable to firm sales orders which it has received.

The company's operations, including the administrative and sales functions, are completely departmentalized. Its cost system is on a job order basis. Direct materials and direct labor are identified with jobs by the use of material issue tickets and daily time cards. Overhead costs are accumulated for each factory service, administrative, and selling department. These overhead costs, including administrative and selling expenses, are then allocated to productive departments and an overhead rate computed for each productive department. This rate is used to apply overhead to jobs on the basis of direct labor hours. The result is that all costs and expenses incurred during any month are charged to work in process accounts for the jobs.

REQUIRED:

1. You are to compare this system, as it affects inventory valuation, with the usual system for manufacturing businesses.

2. You are to criticize the system as it affects inventory valuation and income determination.

3. You are to state any justification which you see for the use of the *H* Company's system.   [C.P.A.]

22-19.   Deficiencies in Internal Control.   Discuss briefly what you regard as the more important deficiencies in the system of internal control in the following situation, and in addition include what you consider to be a proper remedy for each deficiency:

The cashier of the Easy Company intercepted customer *A*'s check payable to the company in the amount of $500 and deposited it in a bank account which was part of the company petty cash fund, of which he was custodian. He then drew a $500 check on the petty cash fund bank account payable to himself, signed it, and cashed it. At the end of the month, while processing the monthly statements to customers, he was able to change the statement to customer *A* so as to show that *A* had received credit for the $500 check that had been intercepted. Ten days later he made an entry in the cash received book which purported to record receipt of a remittance of $500 from customer *A*, thus restoring *A*'s account to its proper balance, but overstating cash in bank. He covered the overstatement by omitting from the list of oustanding checks in the bank renconcilement two checks the aggregate amount of which was $500.   [C.P.A.]

22-20.   Multiple-Choice; Discovering Irregularities.   In questions 1 through 7 you are given a well-recognized procedure of internal control. You are to identify the irregularity *which will be discovered or prevented by each procedure.* Write the numbers 1 through 7 on your answer sheet. Then place the letter of your chosen answer next to your numbers.

1. The general ledger control account and the subsidiary ledger of accounts receivable are reconciled monthly. The two bookkeepers are independent.

   a. The accounts receivable subsidiary ledger bookkeeper charges a customer with $72 instead of $74, the correct amount. The error is due to misreading the sales slip. The credit sales summary for the day has the correct amount of $74.

   b. The accounts receivable subsidiary ledger bookkeeper charges a sale to Mr. Smith instead of Mr. Smithe (that is, the wrong customer). The error is due to misreading the sales slip.

   c. The employee opening mail abstracts funds without making a record of their receipt. Customer accounts are not credited with their payments.

   d. The general ledger bookkeeper takes funds and covers the loss by charging "Miscellaneous General Expenses."

   e. When friends purchase merchandise the salesclerk allows them an employee discount by using an employee name on the sales slip and deducting the discount on the slip. This is against company policy.

2. The voucher system requires that invoices be compared with receiving reports and express bills before a voucher is prepared and approved for payment.

   a. Unrecorded checks appear in the bank statement.

   b. The treasurer takes funds by preparing a fictitious voucher charging "Miscellaneous General Expenses."

   c. An employee in the Purchasing Department sends through fictitious invoices and receives payment.

   d. A cash shortage is covered by underfooting outstanding checks on the bank reconciliation.

   e. A cash shortage is covered by omitting some of the outstanding checks from the bank reconciliation.

3. Both cash and credit customers are educated to expect a sales ticket. Tickets are serially numbered. All numbers are accounted for daily.

    a. Customers complain that their monthly bills contain items which have been paid.

    b. Some customers have the correct change for the merchandise purchased. They pay and do not wait for a sales ticket.

    c. Customers complain that they are billed for goods which they did not purchase.

    d. Customers complain that goods ordered are not received.

    e. Salesclerks destroy duplicate sales tickets for the amount of cash stolen.

4. The storekeeper should sign a receipt for goods received from the receiving and inspection room, and no payment should be made without this signature.

    a. Invoices are paid twice.

    b. Employees send through fictitious invoices and receive payment.

    c. Materials are withdrawn from the storeroom for personal use rather than for business purposes.

    d. Employees send through purchase requisitions for material for personal use. After the material is received and receiving reports are issued, employees take the merchandise for personal use.

    e. The storekeeper takes materials and charges it to company use.

5. At a movie theatre box office, all tickets are prenumbered. At the end of each day, the beginning ticket number is subtracted from the ending number to give the number of tickets sold. Cash is counted and compared with the number of tickets sold.

    a. The box office gives too much change.

    b. The ticket taker admits his friends without a ticket.

    c. The manager gives theatre passes for personal expenses. This is against company policy.

    d. A test check of customers entering the theatre does not reconcile with ticket sales.

    e. Tickets from a previous day are discovered in the ticket taker's stub box despite the fact that tickets are stamped "Good on Date of Purchase Only."

6. In Hutchinson Commons Cafeteria, the customers enter at an "IN" door and choose their meal. Before leaving the serving rail, they are billed by a "biller" for the food taken. They eat and then present their bills and make payments to a "cashier." At the end of the day, cash receipts are reconciled with billings.

    a. A friend of the "biller" and the "cashier" moves through the lines and takes a free meal without being billed or paying.

    b. A customer who has been billed goes out the "IN" entrance without paying.

    c. Meat is stolen by an employee.

    d. The biller makes an error by billing a meal at $1.15 instead of the correct amount, $1.35.

    e. A customer sneaks under the serving rail, takes an extra cup of coffee, sneaks back under the rail, and returns to his table.

7. The duties of cashier and accounts receivable bookkeeper should be separated.

    a. There are two cashiers. At the end of a certain day, there is a sizable cash shortage. Each cashier blames the other. It is impossible to fix responsibility.

    b. A cash shortage is covered by overfooting (overadding) cash in transit on the bank reconciliation.

    c. A cash shortage is covered by charging it to "Miscellaneous General Expense."

    d. Customers who paid their accounts in cash complain that they still receive statements of balances due.

    e. The accounts receivable bookkeeper charges off the accounts of friends to "Allowance for Bad Debts."

22-21. A Study in Anti-Paper Work. On January 13, 1961, *Time* magazine ran the following report concerning Marks & Spencer, Great Britain's most prosperous retail chain with 237 stores and annual sales of $420 million:

> Marks & Spencer's vendetta against paper work started one Saturday early in 1957, when Sir Simon came across two salesgirls carefully filling out long inventory-replacement cards while customers fumed for service. "What are these cards for?" he asked. The girls did not know. Sir Simon found that they were to keep track of merchandise in the stockroom, to curb employee pilfering and to tell the store manager when to reorder. Sir Simon ordered them abolished and let the sales clerks go freely into the stockrooms to get whatever they needed to sell. Pilfering not only did not increase, but the clerks sold more because they knew exactly what was in stock. Furthermore, store managers found they could tell when to reorder simply by looking to see what shelves were getting bare.
>
> From then on, war was declared. Sir Simon found that his company was riddled with ponderous forms. "I didn't understand some of them. Why, I couldn't be a sales clerk in my own organization." He told his staff to examine every form and ask, "Would our entire business collapse if we dispensed with this form?"
>
> And so, while many businessmen are installing electronic gadgets to keep their records, 72-year-old Sir Simon is taking exactly the opposite approach. He has wiped out so much record keeping that he has junked 120 tons of paper forms, saved $14 million. He was able to cut prices 5% and was rewarded with an 18% sales increase from April through September 1960. Business in the second half of his fiscal year looks even better. Some 8,000 jobs out of 28,000 have been eliminated, but no one was fired, because Sir Simon promised when he began his Marksian revolution that he would absorb everyone either through expansion or simply not refilling a job when someone left.
>
> Sir Simon also gambled that customers are as trustworthy as sales clerks, and stopped giving out sales receipts, which most stores demand before they will take merchandise back from a customer. Now, as long as an article bears the M. & S. special St. Michael brand name (commemorating his father), it is easily exchanged at any branch. He threw out time clocks, reasoning that it was silly to keep tabs on employees who were only occasionally late, just to catch the few consistently late arrivers whose habits would be known to supervisors anyway. He silenced the jangling bell in employees' canteens that announced when lunch periods were over, letting clerks decide among themselves when to eat, thus checking on each other. Thick manuals that covered what to do in any situation were tossed out, replaced by one slim book . . . .
>
> Sir Simon still spends much of his time poking about his stores, chatting with clerks to see how much more paper work can be cut out. Any operation that has been in effect over six-months—long enough for the paper work to sprout—is under suspicion.

REQUIRED:

Comment on the incidents. Do you agree with *Time's* report?

22-22. Refer to Exhibit 22-1. State the debit number code for: (a) requisition of supplies by a finishing department in San Francisco; (b) indirect labor incurred by a machining department in Dallas.

22-23. Factory Ledger Fundamentals. Refer to the chart of general ledger accounts used in the factory ledger illustration in this chapter. Indicate the proper journal entries for the following transactions. Set up your solution in a form similar to the one illustrated in Exhibit 22-2.

1. Payments made to creditors on open account	$ 50,000
2. Cash sales	3,000
3. Depreciation on factory equipment	15,000
4. Declaration of dividend	24,000
5. Payment of payroll	105,000
6. Return of materials to vendors	2,000
7. Direct materials requisitioned	40,000
8. Factory overhead applied	30,000
9. Cost of goods shipped to warehouse	50,000
10. Cost of goods sold	25,000

22-24. Factory Ledger. The *DEF* Company uses both a Factory Ledger, which includes all transactions up to Cost of Sales, and a General Ledger. It records its costs under a job cost plan.

The following transactions took place during the month of March:

1. Materials purchased and delivered directly to production order No. 305—$200.
2. Depreciation on factory buildings and equipment—$5,000.
3. Finished goods returned for credit—$2,000.
4. Cost of finished goods returned—$1,200.
5. The raw material book inventory at the end of the month amounted to $354,348. A physical inventory taken at that time showed a value of $354,148.

REQUIRED:

Prepare the journal entries necessary to record this information in the general and factory ledgers.　　　　　　　　　　　　　　　　　[S.I.C.A.]

● **22-25. Factory Ledger; Journal Entries.** The home offices of the Splitpea Company are in Chicago, but the manufacturing operations are located in Gary. The company uses a separate factory ledger which is maintained at Gary for the benefit of the plant management. The factory is given credit for finished goods when the goods are shipped to the central warehouses. All goods are shipped to customers from the warehouses.

Some transactions for the month of March, 19x6 are summarized below:

1. Miscellaneous manufacturing expenses incurred, $10,000. The invoices for $10,000 were received.
2. Materials received by the factory (proper invoice received), $75,000.
3. Sales to customers billed during March, $90,000.
4. Factory cost of goods sold, $70,000.
5. Direct materials placed into production, $50,000.

Questions 6–8 refer to certain discrepancies that were found upon auditing the reconcilement accounts. You are to select the entry (or entries) which *would correct* the general ledger accounts involved.

6. Salesmen's salaries of $2,000 were incorrectly charged to Manufacturing Expense Control.

7. Machinery of $1,200 purchased by the home office for the branch was taken up in the branch books as a Stores item.

8. The machinery in (7) had been ignored in computing depreciation for one month (rate, one per cent per month).

Code	Home Office Accounts	Code	Factory Accounts
1	Cash in Bank	A	Material Stores Control
2	Accounts Receivable	B	Work in Process Control
3	Finished Goods	C	Manufacturing Expense Control
4	Accounts Payable	D	Manufacturing Expense Applied
5	Accrued Payroll	E	Home Office Ledger Control
6	Common Stock	F	Direct Labor Control
7	Retained Earnings		
8	Factory Ledger Control		
9	Sales		
10	Factory Cost of Goods Sold		
11	Selling Cost Control		
12	Administrative Cost Control		
13	Plant and Equipment Control		
14	Allowance for Depreciation		

REQUIRED:

For each of the eight transactions, indicate by code the accounts debited and credited in the Factory Ledger and the Home Ledger. Use the account codes given. More than one account may be debited or credited for each entry.

automated and electronic data processing

This chapter surveys automated data processing and electronic data processing. Its primary purpose is to highlight the major characteristics, potentialities, and limitations of information technology. The managerial accountant is likely to be in the midst of the tasks and problems described in this chapter.

The digital computer has had a phenomenal impact on society and the individual. A complete description of its attributes is beyond the scope of this book. However, we shall consider its relation to data processing and its possible effects on organizations and systems.

Above all, do not be misled because teachers, textbooks, and many small businesses find conventional source documents, journals, and ledgers the most convenient way to visualize the data-processing function. Routine data processing is essentially file updating—bringing account balances up to date. Nelson and Woods emphasize this basic concept as follows:

> This rather elementary view of the nature of data processing holds for any level of clerical effort—manual, mechanical, tabulating, or electronic . . . the basic concept of what is done is unchanged by the nature of the personnel and equipment used to accomplish the result. Transaction [journal] files may consist of printed forms, punched cards, punched tapes, or magnetic tapes. Ledger, or balance files may consist of loose-leaf pages, card files, tape reels, or magnetic discs. In each of these cases, financial information is kept on a current basis through a system of file processing. In studying automatic digital computers, then, the distinctive characteristics do not relate to the fundamental information processing result, but rather to the speed, accuracy, and timeliness of this result.[1]

[1] O. S. Nelson and R. S. Woods, *Accounting Systems and Data Processing* (Cincinnati: South-Western Publishing Company, 1961), p. 524.

AUTOMATED DATA PROCESSING

Definition

Data processing is a generic term that refers to the accumulation, classification, analysis, and reporting of large quantities of information. Pen-and-ink bookkeeping is one form of data processing. Among systems specialists, *automated data processing* (ADP) refers to a unified system which captures input data in a form suitable for subsequent manipulation with no human copying to satisfy the requirements of all end uses of the data. ADP tries to combine all phases of data processing, such as cost accounting, payroll, purchasing, inventory control, and production control, into one information-processing system that speeds and smoothes communications between all parts of a company, helps maximize over-all efficiency, and avoids duplication of effort.

The ADP system centers about mechanical or electronic office equipment rather than human beings as the major processors of information. This implies using human effort only at the outset in recording source information. The original writing is reproduced by carbon or other means. Automatic equipment then takes over and performs remaining chores with greater speed and accuracy than human labor can provide. For example, Uni-Tote is an automated retail accounting and control system. The salesgirl activates the point-of-purchase keyboard units, which is connected by wires to the central control unit. This records all sales, prints a complete sales journal, checks charge sales, and produces a punched card that acts as a key to automatic billing and inventory control.

Mechanical equipment: punched-card accounting

Companies that have substantial paper work usually find it economical to use electromechanical equipment for a variety of accounting tasks. Accurate numerical coding of accounts becomes an essential ingredient of mechanical data-processing systems that rely on punched cards, paper tape, or magnetic tape as the source document. For example, consider the use of punched-card accounting. Three phases take place in every data-processing cycle: recording, classifying, and summarizing (reporting).

The original record (a sale, or a work ticket) may be written on a card (see Exhibit 23-1). This source information is coded and is represented by holes that are punched into the card via a machine called a *key punch*. From this point on, electrical-mechanical devices take over. This punching stage is crucial because improper coding will result in a mountain of subsequent trouble and useless reports. Consequently, some type of *verifier* is used to make sure that the card agrees with the original source writing. In many systems, after a card has been punched, it is taken to a verifier, where an operator enters the original source writing in the keyboard. The machine makes no response unless something different is put into the keyboard from what is on the card. If this happens, the machine locks and thus signals an error.

Classification is accomplished by sorting machines that "read" the holes and thereby shuffle the cards into groups (pockets at the bottom of the machine) needed for various reports. *Sorters* can also *select* (pulling certain cards) and *merge* (combining two sets of cards into a given sequence). *Collators* are auxiliary machines that select and merge more efficiently and that can also *match* (two sequentially arranged decks of cards are processed simultaneously so that matching cards fall together in one pocket and unmatched cards are stacked in separate pockets).

EXHIBIT 23-1

PUNCHED CARD

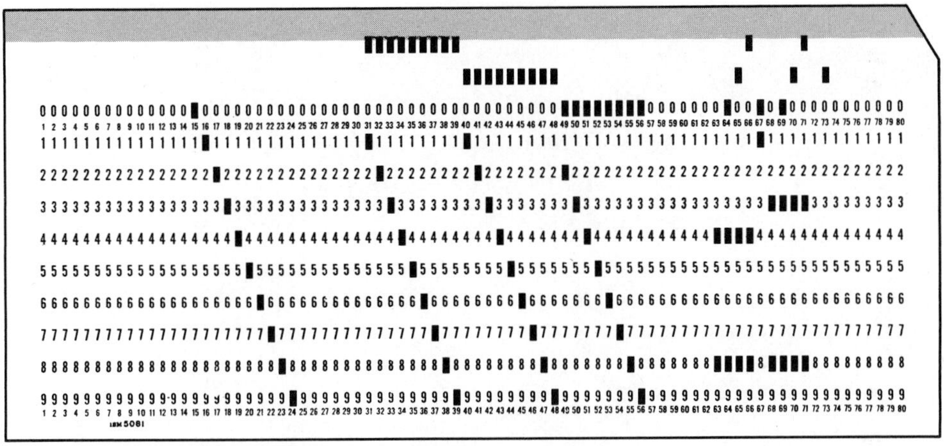

Summarizing is performed by special machines that print in legible form the data from individual cards. These machines can also accumulate and print totals from desired groups of cards. These machines are called *punched-card accounting machines, tabulators,* or *tabulating machines.* As cards are fed into these machines, brushes "read" the holes via electrical contact and thereby actuate the printing mechanism. These machines either *list* (print out in report form all or a portion of the data from the cards) or *accumulate* (the machine contains adding machines that accumulate desired subtotals and totals, which are automatically printed on report forms) or do both simultaneously.

The versatility of these machines has resulted in their replacing manual recordkeeping where the volume of transactions warrants it. Thus, the source documents and journal entries are transferred to punched cards. The machines classify, summarize, and print account balances for financial statements, ledgers, and special reports.

Machine accounting provides fast, flexible reports and can accommodate a variety of detailed analytical work such as sales analyses, payroll analyses and preparation, and perpetual inventory records. For example, as shown in Exhibit 23-2, each sales invoice can be coded; its data may be transferred to a single punched card that is the basis for not only accumulating total sales but for sales analyses by product line, salesman, geographic location, division, and customer classification. If sales by product line for each salesman is desired, a sort (tabulation) may be run first by salesman and then by product line for each salesman. These summaries can be prepared much faster and more accurately by machines than by manual analysis, because a single accurate punched card is all that is needed as input.

EXHIBIT 23-2

FLOW CHART FOR ANALYSIS OF SALES

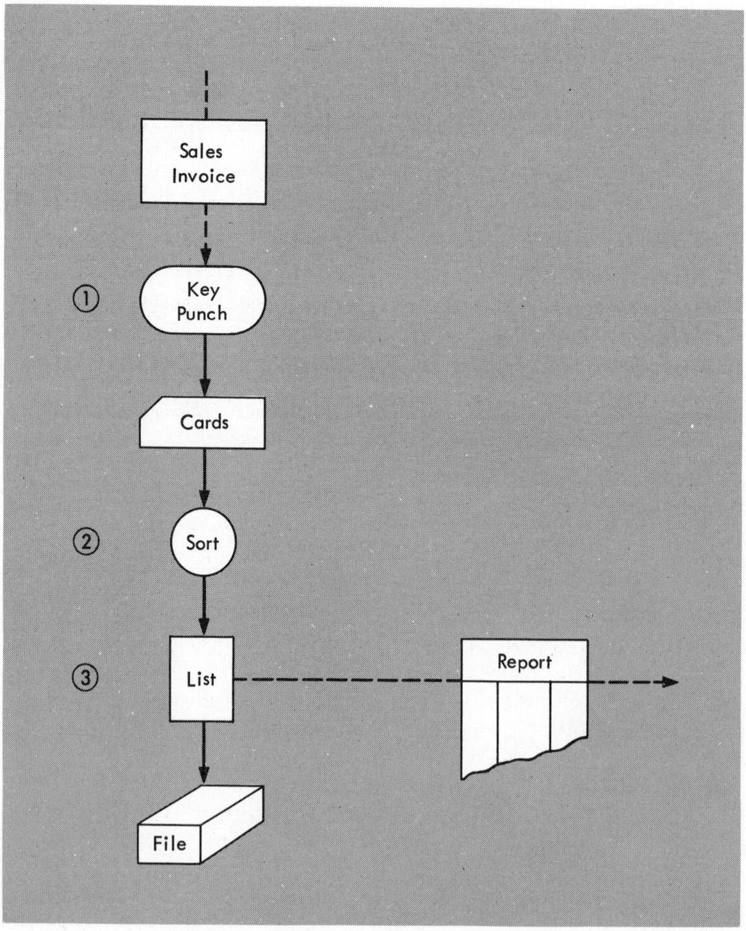

This introduction to machine accounting has necessarily been sketchy, because a thorough presentation is beyond the scope of this book. The reader who is interested in studying machine accounting further might contact a local representative of one of the manufacturers of office equipment. These men are usually eager to provide descriptive literature on the wonders of their machines. A suggested reading list is at the end of this chapter.

ELECTRONIC DATA PROCESSING

Computer is major feature of EDP

Electronic data processing (EDP) is a highly developed form of automated data processing. EDP is "a machine system capable of receiving, storing, operating on, and recording data without the intermediate use of tabulating cards. The system is also able to store internally at least some instructions for data-processing operations, and to locate and control access to data stores internally."[2] In EDP, the major processing work is performed by electronic digital computers rather than by punched-card machines. Of course, these computers can be fed data from mechanical equipment and can also supply data to mechanical equipment as long as a common medium, such as punched cards, punched paper tape, or magnetic tape, is used. This mechanical equipment surrounding the computer is often called *peripheral* equipment.

Although the term "automated data processing" is well chosen, the term "electronic data processing" is relatively poor, because the electronic computer's capabilities extend far beyond routine data processing. The computer has facilitated the use of mathematical and statistical methods for planning and control decisions. This is the feature of the computer which has led many individuals to predict far-reaching impacts on management organization and, in fact, on civilization itself.

Thus, ADP can be characterized by mechanical accounting machines or punched-card machines which have narrow applications, or it can be characterized by the electronic computer, which can be applied to a vast area of problems. A comparison of ADP using punched cards and ADP using computers is given in Exhibit 23-3.

Operating characteristics of the computer

An electronic digital computer is a device that can accept representations of real numbers, or other numerically coded characters, can apply prescribed processes to them, and can produce the results of the processes. Most digital computers contain internally stored instructions. Such computers typically can also operate upon the instructions them-

[2]Robert H. Gregory and Richard L. Van Horn, *Automatic Data-Processing Systems* (2nd. ed., San Francisco: Wadsworth Publishing Company, Inc., 1963), p. 756.

EXHIBIT 23-3

AUTOMATED DATA PROCESSING: COMPARISON OF PUNCHED-CARD AND ELECTRONIC DATA-PROCESSOR EQUIPMENT[3]

Characteristics	Punched-Card Processor	Electronic-Computer Data Processor
Bulk storage of data	Stores data on punched cards.	Stores data on magnetic-tape drums or disks.
Manual handling of data after preparation	Requires people to handle cards frequently—at each minor and major stage in processing.	Requires people to handle magnetic tape at major stages of processing only.
Data input and output rate	Handles 100 to 1,000 cards a minute for a maximum rate of 1,300 characters a second.	Handles input and output at rates of 10,000 to 100,000 and more characters a second.
Computation speed	Performs a few operations a second.	Performs thousands of arithmetical and logical operations a second.
Number of operations on each pass of data	Performs one or a few operations.	Performs a long sequence of operations.
Access to data for computations	At any one time, can refer to data on one or a few cards.	Can select one item of data out of hundreds or thousands.
Versatility	Follows a limited preset pattern of operations on each pass of data.	Changes pattern of operations, within broad limits, depending on data received or results produced.

selves, and change the order of instructions in accordance with results already computed.

The computer itself has three major operating characteristics, which are diagrammed in Exhibit 23-4:

1. *Storage.* Computers contain *memory units* that hold data readily available for future operations. What is memory? It is the ability to store and retrieve information about an experience without repeating all the conditions under which it first took place. An analogy here may be clarifying. Daystrom, Incorporated, discussed memory in an advertisement as follows:

> A piano has a stored memory consisting of 88 tones. Each string is a *memory location.* The pianist can trigger any one at will. Through the keyboard, he gives instruction to the mechanism in much the same way as the operator of a *digital computer.* The piano can even perform simple mathematical operations. When two or more keys are struck simultaneously, it delivers quantities of true *digital information* to a totalizer (the human ear) and instructs this device to add them up. What we hear as a chord is the sum of these "remembered" quantities.
>
> The analogy goes even further. The music the pianist reads is no less than a *program*—a meaningful sequence of instructions to the mecha-

[3] Adapted from Gregory and Van Horn, *op. cit.*, p. 17.

EXHIBIT 23-4

BLOCK DIAGRAM OF DIGITAL COMPUTER

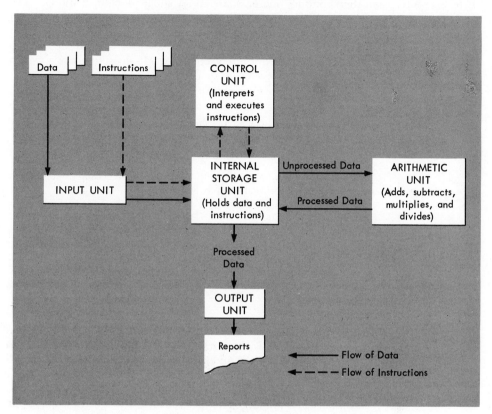

nism. A player piano—in the true fashion of automation—dispenses with human intervention and reads the program itself, from the same kind of coded tape many computers use . . . .

The discovery that *all* information can be reduced into very simple terms is responsible for the great versatility of many advanced computers. It enables us to store great quantities of data in compact form . . . and in such form that any item of information can be located almost instantly when wanted . . . or replaced with another.

Today's computers—even the biggest—can't compare with the human brain in memory capacity . . . but they far surpass it in the accuracy and speed of their recall. And this is just the beginning.

2. *Arithmetic.* Computers can perform all arithmetic functions at amazing speeds. Their electronic circuits operate at the speed of light. This characteristic not only speeds data processing; it permits complex business problems to be attacked with mathematical tools that could not be used previously because it was either impractical or impossible to manipulate the pertinent mathematical models. The computer has been instrumental in the growth of operations research.

3. *Control.*   Computers can compare two items for algebraic sign, equality, or size. Depending on the results of such observations, computers can then conduct one or a variety of subsequent operations. This feature of control distinguishes electronic methods from all other data-processing techniques. A computer can guide itself through lists of instructions (called a *program*) governing the work it has to do, which, within wide limits, may be infinitely complex. It does this via a system of electronic circuits usually referred to as a *control unit.*

The function of control is executed as follows:

(1) The planners of a particular application formulate the steps required to accomplish a procedure.

(2) These steps are documented in great detail and with the utmost precision.

(3) The steps are converted into a series of instructions taken from a standard list appropriated to a particular machine.

(4) The instructions are coded in the language recognized by the computer.

(5) The coded instructions are inserted into the computer (via input equipment) and held for the duration of a particular processing run in the internal storage area.

(6) The control unit executes each instruction, and from the instructions themselves and/or the results of their execution, determines which command it should execute next.[4]

In summary, computers gather raw data in the internal storage unit. Under the control of a program of instructions, these data are transmitted electronically to the internal arithmetic unit. Here adding, subtracting, multiplying, and dividing are performed; for example, a credit is added to accounts payable, a customer payment is subtracted from accounts receivable, a withholding is deducted from an employee's gross pay, a unit price is multiplied by a quantity. The arithmetic unit also performs logical operations, such as deciding whether an employee's gross pay is still subject to Social Security withholding taxes and whether an inventory balance has fallen below the reorder point. The computer accomplishes this typically by comparing two numbers. Is number A equal to number B? If equal, do process C; if not equal, do process D. The results are then returned electronically to the storage unit, which holds the processed data until wanted. Then the processed data are electronically routed to the output unit, which produces the desired reports.

Thus, computers seize raw information, submit it to arithmetic operations, reach logical decisions with respect to it, and issue processed data. All this is accomplished with electronic swiftness, limited only by the mechanical abilities of input and output devices.

[4] Felix Kaufman, *Electronic Data Processing and Auditing* (New York: The Ronald Press Company, 1960), p. 15.

Impact of EDP on the accounting process

The impact of EDP on the conventional accounting process has the following highlights:[5]

1. Emphasis on high-volume subsidiary records as the central elements in primary processing operations.

2. Journals (transaction listings) as by-products of processing instead of as elements in the main processing stream.

3. Accounting files containing much data appropriate to a variety of purposes, including planning, control, product costing, and special decisions.

4. Major files in machine-sensible form; not likely also to exist continuously in the language of the outside world.

5. Ideally, source data enter the computer system once, all files are affected more or less simultaneously, and final reports are produced.

Advantages of computers

What does EDP offer that non-EDP systems cannot provide? Depending on the individual case, EDP offers savings in clerical costs, timelier data, and new and better data not formerly available. Previously, accountants were limited in their ability to provide useful data because of the inflexibility of the ledger design, the time-consuming nature of data processing, and the sheer clerical costs involved. As long as the computer is instructed properly and is given correct source data, it can rapidly perform a bewildering variety of analyses based on a single source document. A new era of data processing has just begun, where costs of getting wanted data will no longer be staggering.

As far as ordinary clerical tasks alone are concerned, computers are the quickest processing device, and they are steadily becoming more economical when compared to modern mechanical tabulating equipment. Utilities and insurance companies were among the first to find computers to be more economic than mechanical equipment for monthly or daily manipulation of countless figures for vast numbers of accounts. Every day electronic computers handle millions of pay checks, bank accounts, insurance premiums, and utility bills. EDP is used to perform the largest single bookkeeping task in the world—maintaining master records on the 150 million people covered by Social Security. The computers use earnings reports submitted by employers to update all records quarterly.

However, computers can do more than grade-school arithmetic: they can read, write, compare, make yes-or-no choices, and transfer information from one location to another. They become valuable tools for solving all sorts of planning and control problems: for example, electronic

---

[5] These are essentially the conclusions reached by Felix Kaufman, *op. cit.*, pp. 81–82.

inventory control systems embracing perpetual records and reordering, designing products, routing freight cars, determining product mix, forecasting sales, and scheduling production.

The speed of the computer generally helps to collapse the business-planning period so that the interval between an event and an adjustment in behavior will decrease. For example, production schedules and budgets usually are primarily based on future sales estimates. The integration of production, inventories, and sales functions, coupled with the speed of the computer, allows a company to readjust estimates quickly and frequently, so that no single estimate needs to speculate very far into the future. This results in lower inventory levels and in increased flexibility in adapting to surprises.[6]

Shultz and Whisler predict that the decision process will be improved by using computers because "(a) more data can be considered, (b) greater speed of analysis is possible, (c) a greater range of alternatives can be explored, and (d) a more comprehensive view of a given decision's impact within the organization is possible."[7]

Other examples of computer applications

The following short descriptions demonstrate the versatility of the computer.

1. *Blending Raw Materials.* Braun Brothers Packing Co., of Troy, Ohio, pitted the experience and know-how of their top executives against a computer once a week for four months. The problem was to find the optimum blend of ingredients for making tasty bologna. There are always thousands of combinations to consider among the available beef, beef cheeks, beef plate, neckbone meat, picnics, neck trimmings, trim conversion, and rework from previous batches. The computer took an average of thirty-six minutes to produce a faster, surer, and cheaper answer than the answer of the human sausage experts. Braun Brothers now mixes all its sausage by order of the computer.

To be sure, the computer does not perform its sausage-mixing chore by exercising innate brainpower. The human sausage expert had taught the computer all the tricks he knew. The computer applies this knowledge, which is reflected in an instructional program, to what meat cuts are on hand and their current prices and automatically reports the shrewdest mix.

2. *Inventory Control.* Computers keep up-to-date records of goods on hand and print out orders for new stock as needed. A large shoe manufacturer pastes a punched card on every box. When the card is returned to the factory, the computer uses it and times reorders automatically. Lerner's, a clothing store chain, relies on its computer to keep count of store-to-store demand for colors and styles so that the company

---

[6]Shultz and Whisler (ed.), *Management Organization and the Computer* (Glencoe, Illinois: The Free Press, 1960), p. 158.

[7]*Ibid.*, p. 18.

can react swiftly to changes in demand. Standard Oil Company (N.J.) has a material and stores data-processing system for over 39,000 supply items that provides maximum automatic stock-level control records, automatic purchase-order preparation and follow-up, automatic invoice verification, and preparation of accounts payable checks.

3. *Miscellaneous Uses.* A computer informs a national shirt manufacturer which collar styles to continue and which to abandon; another does the same for handbag styles in a St. Louis store; others analyze stock market portfolios for brokers' larger customers. Computers also are key control mechanisms in manufacturing ammonia, vinyl plastic, and gasoline. Computers are also essential in directing automated machine tools.

In a day's time, a computer has assembled 16,000 alternative designs for a chemical plant and has selected the most efficient one at a saving of half a million dollars in construction costs.

One of the computer's most striking applications has been the use of a central computer to process data gathered at remote points. Within a few hours it can receive and process sales orders, schedule production, and update inventory records. Airlines use computer-based communications systems to control millions of reservations every year.

For a comparison of payroll accounting under EDP and punched-card systems, see Exhibit 24-3 in the next chapter. Note there how EDP tends to break down departmental walls.

Future of computers

Most accountants and managers tend to view computers as magnificent but dumb animals which must be given a detailed program before performing tasks. On the other hand, some individuals think the computer will have a revolutionary effect on business and scientific practice. Simon and Newell have observed:

> Here is the practical reply to the argument stated earlier, that a computer can do only what it has been programed to do. If a computer can be programed to solve problems, it can also be programed to learn to solve problems—i.e., to modify its problem-solving techniques in application to particular subject matter areas. Presumably it will do this in the same way that human beings do: it will be exposed to a variety of situations, will tackle them with its (inefficient) general pattern-recognizing and problem-solving programs, and will analyze its experiences to devise special-purpose methods for particular subject matter and to acquire the facts it needs to deal with that subject matter.
>
> Again we are not spinning out pure fancies. A number of programs have been written that allow computers to learn from experience. For example, the program that solves problems by means-end analysis has the capacities also to remember theorems it has proved, to remember how it proved them, (both of these are matters of "pure" memorization), and to remember that certain special methods have been effective in certain contexts. The last-named capacity begins to approach the kind of learning a good student does when he solves problems. A computer with this capacity can gradually, from its experience, acquire a problem-solving program far more powerful than the one initially programed into it—and more powerful, indeed, than the one its programer possesses.

... We have computers which are performing certain kinds of problem-solving tasks in the area of mathematics sufficiently well to earn them passing grades at the college sophomore level.

... Once we have succeeded in getting a program for intelligent thinking inside a computer, we can reproduce the program without the arduous and uncertain twenty-year training which is necessary in the case of human beings .... This suggests to me the possibility that perhaps the area of ultimate greatest comparative advantage for the computer is the area of creative thinking, in which it is extremely difficult for one person to tell another how he thinks. The computer may turn out to be more competitive, economically, with scientists than with executives; and more competitive with executives than with clerks.[8]

Installing the computer

The appraisal of an existing non-EDP system is the first step in switching to EDP. The non-EDP system itself is culled and streamlined. Some managers feel that this self-scrutiny is worth while even if the EDP system is never installed.

Although they can easily outperform human beings on a variety of tasks, computers must be given a *detailed* set of instructions, more carefully thought out than any set in systems history. As one controller told this writer, "If you ever talk to anybody who is going to install a computer, tell him to postpone delivery for two years. It will take that long to prepare for the invasion of the monster." It takes considerable time to study an existing system and to decide how the system may best be revamped to work with a computer. Besides, the documenting and flow-charting of the system to fit both general and exceptional conditions is meticulous, time-consuming work. Many consultants recommend starting afresh by designing a brand-new system instead of trying to fit a computer into an existing system.

The biggest contrast between EDP systems and other systems is that an extensive data-processing activity becomes self-contained instead of being dependent on human beings at various stages of the system for successful execution. This highlights the importance of careful planning on the part of the programers.

EDP and internal control

The source documents are the heart of any accurate accounting system, whether it be pen-and-ink bookkeeping, punched-card accounting, or EDP. Once prepared, the source document is more likely to transmit correct information if it is not recopied or passed from one human being to another or from one department to another. Well-planned EDP systems maximize the efficiency and effectiveness of an information system. A well-planned EDP system is superior to systems dependent on human

[8]Herbert A. Simon and Allen Newell, "What Have Computers to Do with Management?" in Shultz and Whisler (ed.), *op. cit.*, pp. 58, 65.

beings for execution because the EDP system cannot depart from its instructions, whereas people can and do ignore or overlook standard operating procedures.

The computer is the center of internal check. The insertion of internal-control checks and balances in the computer will assure automatic conforming to prescribed procedures. In contrast, non-EDP systems can show an ideal internal-control design; but how well the design is working from day to day is dependent on the reliability of a number of key people.

The program is the central point for generating errors, fraud, and waste in an EDP system. The individuals who create and maintain programs can manipulate them for undesirable ends. The focus for internal control must be on the techniques and procedures used to formulate and alter programs. In other words, EDP systems cut across organizational lines and concentrate control. Top management and auditors need to be sure that this power is handled properly.

Computers and organizations

As one can imagine, the installation of EDP can have a tremendous impact on all managerial levels. The reactions to change will differ, depending on the personalities and environment involved.

Non-EDP systems usually are highly departmentalized. For example, credit and purchasing departments normally have more manpower devoted to recordkeeping than to their primary functions. EDP systems tend to seize data-processing functions from departments, to take information from department files and store it on reels of magnetic tape, and to jar long-standing organizational structures.

For example, the head of most purchasing departments is concerned with statistical processing work. He devotes much time to recordkeeping and to supervising large clerical staffs. The computer tends to take the work away completely and leave him only with the task of selecting suppliers—the essence of his managerial job. In other words, the computer tends to remove much of the drudgery from the middle manager's job, leaving him with fewer people to oversee and with more time to devote to his major duty. However, many managers are likely to resent and resist these changes.

International Shoe Company has used a computer to facilitate centralization of planning and control. The computer was not applied to a single problem, such as payroll or accounts receivable; instead it was used for relating sales to inventories of finished goods, for converting basic sales estimates into estimates of raw materials and estimates of labor requirements by operations by machine, and so forth. In brief, estimates are processed so that production, merchandising, and procurement no longer function as semi-independent entities. Constant recalculation of sales against materials and against production capacity automatically helps foresee trouble in time to take preventive action. Leonard F. Vogt, General Manager, Methods and Procedures, International Shoe Company, observed:

The information system has tied these units together so that, functionally, they are now one unit, since the planning and estimating system that we use is so pervasive and has behind it such full administrative control that we believe it unrealistic to think of it as a staff function. Information technologists who build information systems of this sort are, in large measure, clearly indicating the decisions which other individuals in all departments must make.

. . . Today we have a vice president of merchandising and production, *whereas up until recently these had been separate functions. Our new information system has pointed up the very close relationship of these two functions.*[9]

On-line, real-time systems. The more advanced of today's computer systems provide better planning and control information than ever before, because relevant facts are being supplied "on-line" and in "real time." *On-line* means compiling information instantaneously, as events occur. *Real-time* means supplying the relevant information rapidly enough so that interested managers or other parts of the system may exert control. An "on-line, real-time" system is often abbreviated as an OLRT system.

An OLRT system has a central data-processing center consisting of computers, communications equipment, storage equipment, and input-output devices such as punched-card or punched-tape readers and punches and high-speed printers. Point of origin devices (POD) are physically located where the needed information originates or where it is required for operating decisions. POD devices are directly connected to the central processing center in a two-way communication pattern.

Among the users of OLRT systems are the federal, state, and local governments, banks, radio and television companies, telephone companies, stock brokerage firms, and airlines. Almost all the major American air carriers have an OLRT reservations system installed, or one on order. For instance, with American Airlines' $30-million SABRE system, a reservations clerk asks for space on a particular flight by punching a few buttons on a special console typewriter. If a certain light flashes, the agent knows that space is available and that, as of that instant, he has priority for that space over anyone else asking for the flight through any of the other thirty-five centers on line. There are many other features of SABRE which are too detailed to describe here. Computer pundits claim that, by the early 1970's, nearly all data-processing systems will be OLRT.

Implications for information systems: how can they be integrated? As operations research techniques and computers become more widely understood and more useful, information systems in organizations will be redesigned to take advantage of their powerful features for helping management to plan and control. Advanced business systems tend to break down traditional department walls and tend to redefine managers' duties—freeing them for more attention directing and problem solving.

Somebody has to coordinate the over-all business information system. The accountant, who has long dominated quantitative information systems, is the logical candidate for the job. But now he must know how to blend operations research techniques, computer technology, and mod-

---

[9]Shultz and Whisler (ed.), *op. cit.*, pp. 150–151 and p. 160.

ern accounting for management control so that the quality of management becomes better than ever. In short, such a person must be an astute combination score keeper, attention director, and problem solver—with a breadth of knowledge that extends beyond the traditional boundaries of accounting and into the fields of mathematics, statistics, and the behavioral sciences.

The digital computer has prompted many persons to visualize totally integrated information systems for big organizations, systems that weld all information together into one enormous whole headed by a director of information systems.

On the surface, this may have appeal. But Dearden[10] raises some provocative questions about how to achieve this total-systems goal. He maintains that there are three major information systems in a typical company: financial information, personnel data, and physical or logistics information. He believes that the need to coordinate these systems does not justify the combination of unlike activities and differing levels of responsibility into a single group responsible for all information systems. Dearden thinks that the operating (line) manager, the user, should be instrumental in specifying what information should be provided. Then the data processor takes over, and centralization of the *technical* aspects of processing becomes attractive.

The important point is that the person responsible for data processing should not be responsible for deciding what kind of information should be generated by the system. In short, the complexity of the task prevents attainment of the dream of a fully integrated system. Moreover, the role of any head of a total-information system should be limited to coordination; the design of the important subsystems, such as budgeting, production control, or distribution, should primarily rest with the users of those systems.

SUMMARY

Automated data processing (ADP) is a unified information system which captures input data in a form suitable for subsequent manipulation, with no human copying, to satisfy the requirements of all end uses of the data. ADP is usually accomplished by the use of electromechanical or electronic equipment.

Electronic data processing (EDP) is a highly developed form of ADP. EDP uses a computer as the central processor of masses of data. The term *electronic data processing* was ill chosen, because the computer's capabilities extend far beyond mere data processing. The computer has facilitated the use of mathematical and statistical methods for planning and control decisions.

The computer's speed, memory, and arithmetic operations free

[10] John Dearden, "How to Organize Information Systems," *Harvard Business Review*, (March–April, 1965), pp. 65–73.

middle managers from preoccupation with data processing. The computer centralizes data processing, planning, and control and forces integration of various business functions.

The computer has brought a revolutionary impact upon business in general and upon accounting systems in particular. The varied high-speed talents of the computer should enable accounting to serve the management of complex enterprises better than ever before. The future is sure to bring improved, tightly knit information systems that will better meet management needs. The chiefs of such information systems will be those accountants who have a wide viewpoint and an understanding of the capabilities of digital computers.

SUGGESTED READINGS

Chapin, N., *An Introduction to Automatic Computers* (2nd ed., Princeton, N.J.: D. Van Nostrand Co., Inc., 1963).

Davis, G., *Electronic Data Processing* (New York: McGraw-Hill Book Company, Inc., 1965).

Dearden, J., and F. W. McFarlan, *Management Information Systems* (Homewood, Ill.: Richard D. Irwin, Inc., 1966).

Elliott, C. O., and R. Wasley, *Business Information Processing Systems* (Homewood, Ill.: Richard D. Irwin, Inc., 1965).

Gillespie, C., *Accounting Systems: Procedures and Methods* (2nd ed., Englewood Cliffs, N.J.: Prentice-Hall, Inc., 1961).

Gregory, R. H., and R. L. Van Horn, *Automatic Data-Processing Systems* (2nd ed., Belmont, Calif.: Wadsworth Publishing Company, Inc., 1960).

Hein, L., *An Introduction to Electronic Data Processing in Business* (Princeton, N.J.: D. Van Nostrand Co., Inc., 1961).

Kaufman, F., *Electronic Data Processing and Auditing* (New York: The Ronald Press Company, 1961).

Nelson, O. S., and R. S. Woods, *Accounting Systems and Data Processing* (Cincinnati: South-Western Publishing Company, 1961).

Prince, T., *Business Information Systems* (New York: McGraw-Hill Book Company, Inc., 1966).

Shultz, G. P., and T. L. Whisler, *Management Organization and The Computer* (Glencoe, Ill.: The Free Press, 1960).

QUESTIONS, PROBLEMS, AND CASES

Note: Problems 23-15 through 23-17 are recommended.

23-1. What is the difference between ADP and EDP?

23-2. Describe the functions of the following:

    a. Key punch
    b. Verifier
    c. Sorter
    d. Collator
    e. Tabulator
    f. Peripheral equipment

23-3. What is the basic function of the electronic digital computer?

23-4. Describe the three major operating characteristics of a computer.

23-5. What are the major advantages of computers?

23-6. Simon and Newell have said: "The computer may turn out to be more competitive, economically, with scientists than with executives; and more competitive with executives than with clerks." Do you agree? What led Simon and Newell to this conclusion?

23-7. What is a computer program?

23-8. What impact will EDP have on internal control?

23-9. What will be the probable impact of the computer on a company organization? Will computers lead to more centralization? Why?

23-10. "The computer performs logical operations." Explain.

23-11. Summarize the impact of EDP on the conventional accounting process.

23-12. Give four examples of electronic computer applications other than routine data processing.

23-13. Complexities of Electronic Computers. A controller remarked: "Things in business are moving much too fast for me these days. I understood the mechanics of pen-and-ink systems, the desk calculator systems, and even the electromechanical systems. But these electronic computers are too complex for me to understand unless I go back to college for a couple years of courses."

REQUIRED:

Appraise the remarks of the controller.

23-14. Feasibility Studies for EDP. The "feasibility study" is a planning and evaluation of a proposed data-processing system. What factors are probably of key importance in evaluating a change in a system?

23-15. Value of a Systems Survey and EDP. It has often been stated that a thorough survey of an accounting system in connection with a contemplated purchase of a computer is worthwhile even if the EDP system is never installed.

REQUIRED:

Why does the possibility of acquiring an electronic computer often help modernization of accounting systems even if the computer is not acquired?

23-16. Systems Design for Sales: Impact of EDP. A medium-sized manufacturing organization has five officers at the vice-presidential level: (1) sales, (2) secretary-treasurer, (3) controller, (4) industrial relations, and (5) manufacturing. Its accounting procedures for sales orders are as shown on page 741.[11]

REQUIRED:

1. After studying the chart on page 741, sketch how EDP might have an impact on the organization and on data-processing functions. For an example of what is wanted, see the bottom of Exhibit 24-3.

[11] American Institute of Accountants, *Internal Control* (New York: American Institute Publishing Co., 1949).

2. Comment on the major feature of the possible impact of EDP on sales procedures and on inventory control.

23-17. Computers, Planning, and the Critical Path Method.* King Construction Company is a relatively young firm located in Louisville, Kentucky. The company has enjoyed rapid growth and after only ten years of operation has qualified to operate in 41 states, with its 1964 business exceeding $25 million. Projects consist primarily of motels, apartment buildings, shopping centers, and industrial buildings, ranging in cost from three-quarters of a million to three million dollars.

About five years ago, at the beginning of its expansion period, the company developed an interest in electronic data processing and installed punched-card equipment to process payrolls, cost reporting, accounts payable, and other administrative data.

All of the firm's business is procured through negotiation rather than by competitive bidding. In order effectively to negotiate for a project, the company must submit its proposal as soon as possible, while the prospect's interest in the project is still high. In 1960, the firm began considering a computer to expedite the preparation of proposals. At the same time it learned of the project-planning method known as CPM—the Critical Path Method. Using this method, all jobs on a given project are charted to show the sequence that must be followed to achieve the shortest construction time and the lowest cost. A "critical" job is one that if delayed will delay the whole project. The "critical path" is the specific sequence of critical jobs.

Recognizing both the growing need for a quicker way to produce estimates and the advantages of the Critical Path Method of scheduling, King Construction installed a computer in its headquarters in 1963. The computer is equipped with random access storage. All construction job items have been catalogued, costed, and stored in the computer for use in estimating. The estimator assigns a code to each item. This code details the specifications and the construction method to be used. For example, concrete floor slabs are coded by type, reinforcing, and other specifications and by the method of pouring and finishing. A batch of punched cards is prepared from the estimator's decisions— about 500 cards for the basic jobs on a million-dollar project. From these cards the computer generates some 5,000 cards to carry the complete information on all related operations. In this manner the computer dictates all of the tasks associated with a particular job, making it virtually impossible to overlook a single item. With this method, a firm proposal can be submitted to the prospect within forty-eight hours of the initial discussion. The same information, after being entered into cards, is used to produce the Critical Path Schedule.

King Construction is among the first construction firms in the country to use a computer for both estimating and scheduling.

For the Critical Path Method of scheduling to be fully effective, the Critical Path Schedule must be regularly updated as work on a project progresses. In order to accomplish this updating, a data communications system had to be developed that would be able rapidly to collect at the computer center in Louisville the necessary progress information from the company's many far-flung construction sites. A system was designed using card readers equipped with keyboards to transmit work progress information over regular long-distance telephone service from the construction sites to Louisville.

On Friday afternoon each project superintendent reports the information

---

*From Edgar C. Gentle, Jr. (ed.), *Data Communications in Business* (New York: ©American Telephone and Telegraph Co., 1965), pp. 96–98.

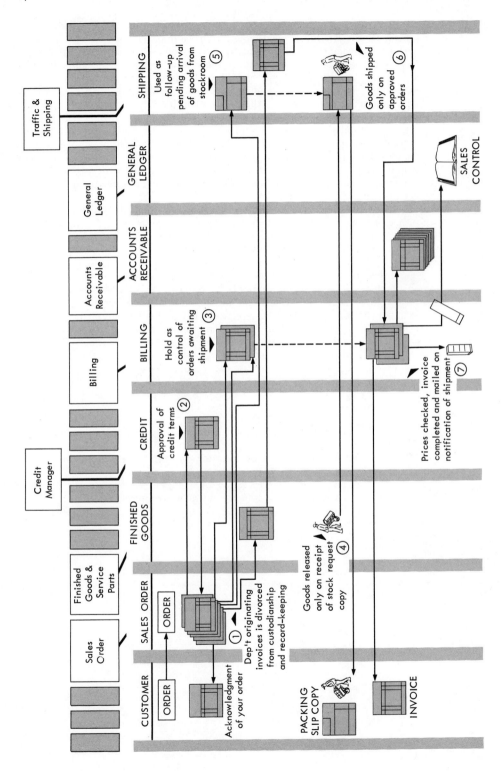

necessary to update the schedule for his project to the home office. He has pre-punched cards containing identifying information for each job on which work was performed during the week. On each card he notes his estimate of the time, in days and tenths of days, that will be required to complete the job. He places a regular long-distance telephone call to Louisville and uses his card reader to transmit the report. This is done by placing each job card in the card reader, which automatically transmits the prepunched identifying information to a card punch in Louisville. He then enters from the keyboard on his card reader the estimated number of days to completion as previously noted on the card. Any special explanations and discussion can be handled by throwing a switch that enables the superintendent to talk with the home office. He needs no clerical help to prepare the twenty cards that are normally involved in one week's work. All project reports are thus received by the home office before the end of the day each Friday.

On Saturday morning the data are electronically processed and each project is completely rescheduled—all the way to the estimated completion date. The revised schedules are airmailed to the construction sites Saturday afternoon so as to reach the superintendents by Monday morning.

The computer figures the costs of each project to date and, based on up-dated schedule information, predicts the final costs and profits. It also gives the current over-all financial position of the company. At the Louisville headquarters there is a control room where all project information is displayed: architect's sketches, progress photographs, updated Critical Path Charts, and the current cost and profit picture. Each Monday morning top management meets in the control room and reviews each project and the company as a whole. If a project's time, cost, and profit figures are significantly above or below the estimates, an investigation is made to determine the cause and a course of action.

REQUIRED:

1. What problem did the data communications system solve? How was it solved?

2. When did the progress information have to be at the computer site? Why was this schedule critical?

3. What advantage does it give the company to have weekly information on the progress of its jobs? How much is it worth in terms of dollars?

accounting for payroll

CHAPTER XXIV

Withholding, fringe benefits, and governmental requirements complicate the tasks of accounting for payroll. There are three major problems: (a) distributing labor costs to functions, departments, and products; (b) accurately computing and promptly paying individual employees; and (c) computing and remitting withholdings and fringe benefits. Many of the aspects of classifying and controlling labor costs (point (a) above) have been covered previously (Chapters 4 and 6). This chapter will concentrate on other facets of payroll.

Individuals who are responsible for payroll accounting agree that pinpoint accuracy is a foremost criterion for judging the merits of any payroll system. Whatever their educational level, be it twenty years of schooling or two, employees are excellent auditors of their own pay checks. Employees demand prompt and accurate payment, and they voice their dissatisfaction with vigor.

Incidentally, where pay scales vary and are subject to individual bargaining, such as in many office jobs, data should be kept secret. People tend to overvalue their own services and undervalue their neighbor's. There have been many cases where morale has been wrecked by open knowledge of pay scales.

GOVERNMENTAL IMPACT

Complexity of payroll accounting

Many years ago an employee who earned $60 per week received $60 in cash on payday. The bookkeeping problems for payroll were

743

relatively simple. Only two parties were involved in the employer-employee relationship.

Nowadays the data-processing problems of accounting for payroll are staggering, and the clerical expenses for payroll accounting have soared accordingly. The rash of withholdings, fringe benefits, and incentive pay schemes requires an intricate network of accounts and supporting documents. Accounting for payroll has become so voluminous that new machine or computer installations invariably handle payroll as one of their first routine tasks.

Governmental requirements regarding payroll records play a big role in systems and forms design. Exhibits 24-1 and 24-2 show some of the governmental impact on payroll accounting. The government has at least two major influences on payroll accounting: (1) it requires the employer to be its collecting *agent* for income taxes from employees and (2) it levies special payroll taxes on the employer.

Withholding taxes

The employer must withhold ordinary income taxes plus a special income tax, commonly called the *Social Security tax*. Other terms for the Social Security taxes are *federal insurance contributions act tax* (F.I.C.A. tax) and *federal old-age benefits tax* (F.O.A.B. tax). The timing of these tax payments to the government is shown in Exhibits 24-1 and 24-2. The basic journal entry pattern is as follows:

Work in process control	120,000	
Factory overhead control	30,000	
Selling expense control	40,000	
Administrative expense control	10,000	
Accrued payroll (gross)		200,000
Accrued payroll	35,000	
Withheld income taxes payable		29,000
Withheld F.I.C.A. taxes payable		6,000
Withheld income taxes payable	29,000	
Withheld F.I.C.A. taxes payable	6,000	
Cash (or some similar credit that has this ultimate effect on cash)		35,000

The above entries show that the *gross* payroll cost is the measure of the various basic labor costs incurred by the employer. The taxes *on employees* are withheld and remitted (usually monthly) to the government. Somehow this practice tends to make the pain of the tax bite seem less severe to the employee. Thus, the employer does not regard withheld taxes

EXHIBIT 24-1

U.S.A. PAYROLLS AND TAXES

Tax	Rate	Basis for Computation	Date of Filing Form	Period Covered	Payment Date
Federal income tax on employees	Depends on gross earnings and dependents.	Gross earnings paid.	On or before end of month following close of calendar quarter.	Calendar quarters supplemented by a reconciliation at year end.	If these three taxes are $100 or less per month, payment is made on due date for filing. If they exceed $100, each monthly total for the first two months of the calendar quarter must be deposited by the fifteenth of the following month in a bank acting as a collection agent for the government.[3] A deposit for the third month is optional. The third month's payment can accompany the filing of the quarterly return. Depository receipts for the first two months' deposits are attached to the return.
F.I.C.A. tax on employees	1967–68: 4.4% 1969–72: 4.9% 1973–1975: 5.4%	First $6,600 of gross earnings paid to each employee.	Same as above. Form 941.	Calendar quarters.	
F.I.C.A. tax on employers	Same as above	First $6,600 of gross earnings paid to each employee.	Same as above. Form 941.	Calendar quarters.	
State Unemployment Insurance Tax on employers[1]	Generally 2.7%, but may vary from .2% to 4%, depending on various state merit rating systems for employer's labor turnover experience.	First $3,000 of gross earnings paid to each employee.[2]	Same as above. Special state form.	Calendar quarters.	Same as for filing.
Federal Unemployment Insurance Tax on employer	Generally, effective rate is .4% (3.1% nominal rate less 2.7% rate credit for State unemployment tax payments).	Same as above.[2]	January 31. Form 940.	Previous calendar year.	Same as for filing.
State Workmen's Compensation Insurance (or Tax) on employers.	Varies for different occupational classifications.	Gross earnings paid.	If insured by private company, annual premium is usually paid in advance. If taxed by state, same due-date provisions apply as for state unemployment tax.		

[1] A few states also have an employee unemployment tax.
[2] Employers are not subject to tax unless they have four or more employees for at least one day a week for 20 weeks in a calendar year.
[3] Beginning in late 1967, these payments will have to be deposited twice monthly.

as an employer tax; instead, the employer performs a collection-agent service for the government.[1]

EXHIBIT 24-2

CALENDAR OF EMPLOYER'S OBLIGATIONS UNDER U.S.A. FEDERAL LAW

	Form
When Hiring	
Get withholding exemption certificate	W-4
Get Social Security number. If employee has no account number, he should file application on	SS-5
When Paying	
Withhold both income taxes and F.I.C.A. taxes.	
By 15th Day of Every Month	
Deposit prior month's withholdings in a bank which acts as a federal depository. For details, see Exhibit 24-1. Obtain depository receipt	450
By End of April, July, October, and January	
File combined return for all F.I.C.A. taxes and withheld income taxes covering the quarter ending with the prior month. For example, the first calendar quarter's return must be filed by April 30. Payment would be made by submitting two form 450's (the depository receipts for January and February) plus a cash payment for March	941
By January 31 and at Termination of Employment	
Give each employee a withholding statement in duplicate showing F.I.C.A. earnings and withholdings and total earnings subject to income tax withholdings and income tax withheld.	W-2
By January 31	
File Reconciliation of Quarterly Returns	W-3
plus Collector's Copy of all individual W-2's given to employees for prior year	W-2a
File annual return and pay unemployment tax	940

Other withholdings

A flock of other withholdings from employees also exist. Withholdings as such are not employer costs. They are merely slices of the em-

[1] Employees who have held jobs with two or more employers during a single year are entitled to a refund if excess F.I.C.A. taxes were withheld. For example, if the F.I.C.A. withholding rate is five per cent and an employee earned $7,000 from one employer and $4,000 from another, each employer would legally have to withhold five per cent of the first $6,600 paid. Therefore, this employee would be entitled to a refund as follows:

Employer 1	.05 × $6,600 =	$330
Employer 2	.05 × $4,000 =	200
Total withheld		$530
Taxable limit for individual:	.05 × $6,600 =	330
Excess F.I.C.A. tax withheld		$200

His claim would be filed on his own individual income tax return. His forms W-2 would be evidence in support of his claim.

The employer is not entitled to any refund.

ployee's gross earnings that are being funneled via the employer to third parties, primarily for the employee's convenience. Examples include employee contributions to group life insurance plans, hospitalization insurance, pension funds, employee savings plans, donations, and union dues.

FRINGE BENEFITS

Large size of fringe benefits

The gross earnings of employees are only nominal measures of the payroll costs really borne. The employer not only must pay payroll taxes like old-age and unemployment levies; he also must incur many more fringe costs. The following breakdown of payroll costs illustrates the general pattern:

Gross earnings of employee (Assume $9,000)	100.00%
Federal old-age tax on employers (Rate based on average employee earnings of $9,000. Tax would be, say, 5% of $6,600, or $330. Divide $330 by $9,000)	3.67
Federal unemployment tax (.4% of $3,000, or $12. (Divide $12 by $9,000.)	.13
State unemployment tax (2.7% of $3,000, or $81. Divide $81 by $9,000.)	.90
Workmen's compensation tax (Rates vary with hazards; average rate shown.)	1.50
Vacations and paid holidays (10 days' vacation and 7 holidays. Divide 17 by 260 days' pay.)	6.20
Minimum total for most employers	112.40%
Add:	
Employer contributions to pension funds (average rate)	5.00
Employer contributions to health, life, and other insurance, etc. (average rate)	3.00
Employer contributions to guaranteed annual wage funds (average rate)	2.50
Total cost incurred by many employers	122.90%

These figures demonstrate that fringe costs are no longer a little dribble; their waterfall proportions have caused an increasing number of companies to recast their account classifications. Instead of treating all fringe costs as overhead, some companies add an average (that is, "equalized" or "leveled") fringe rate to the basic direct labor rate to bring into focus a better measure of direct labor costs. This leveled rate is computed as shown in the above table. However, perhaps because of inertia, most companies continue to treat fringe costs as a part of overhead.

Timing of cost recognition

As in many other phases of accounting, there is often a time lag between incurrence and payment of various payroll fringe costs. For example, the liability for vacation payments really accrues from week to week as each employee accumulates his claim to vacation pay. Thus, many companies use an estimate to spread total vacation costs over a year instead of recognizing such costs as payments are made:

Work in process control (direct labor)	19,000	
Factory overhead control (indirect labor plus $1,000 vacation pay)	7,000	
Estimated liability for vacation pay		1,000
Accrued payroll		25,000

To accrue vacation pay throughout the year because it is related to work done throughout the year. Leveled rate is 4% of Accrued Payroll. Entry here is, say, for January

Accrued payroll	25,000	
Estimated liability for vacation pay	300	
Cash		22,000
Withholdings payable (various)		3,300

The accrued vacation pay is debited as vacation payments are made.

Similar treatment can be given to bonus plans, holiday pay, and contributions to pension funds and to guaranteed annual wage funds. The decision to adopt such leveling arrangements in accounting for fringe costs largely depends on the significance of the amounts involved and on the distortion of month-to-month costs that may arise from failure to spread charges over the year.

EMPLOYER PAYROLL TAXES: THEORY AND PRACTICE

At this writing, employers must pay old-age taxes on the first $6,600, and unemployment taxes on the first $3,000, paid to each employee every calendar year. In most cases, this means that heavier tax outlays will be made in the earlier months of the year than in the later months, because the employer liability diminishes as wage payments to an increasing number of employees gradually reach and pass the yearly statutory taxable wage limit.

The problem of timing charges for employer payroll taxes raises some special theoretical questions. The employer's legal liability is ordinarily a function of wages *paid* rather than of wages *accrued*. Yet in practice, employer payroll taxes usually are accrued as wages are *earned*. Furthermore, such payroll tax accrual diminishes as months pass because more and more employees' earnings gradually surpass the maximum taxable limit.[2]

To illustrate, assume that a company has a gross payroll of $25,000 per month, $16,000 of which is direct labor. Assume that the tax

[2]Conceivably, in some companies, if no new workers are hired in November or December, the employer may show no payroll tax costs for these months.

rate on employers is .4 per cent for federal unemployment, 2.7 per cent for state unemployment, and 4.9 per cent for old-age benefits, a total payroll tax rate of 8 per cent.

Early months:	Work in process control	16,000	
	Factory overhead control		
	($9,000 plus $2,000)	11,000	
	Accrued payroll		25,000
	Employer's payroll taxes payable		2,000
	Payroll tax is .08 × $25,000 = $2,000.		
Late months:	Work in process control	16,000	
	Factory overhead control	9,000	
	Accrued payroll		25,000
	Payroll is not subject to payroll tax because every employee's salary has passed the maximum taxable limits.		

In theory, employer payroll taxes (a) should be accrued as wages are earned (this practice is widely followed) and (b) should be spread over the year, using a leveled rate. Thus, payroll taxes would be handled in a fashion similar to the previous illustration on vacation pay. The reasoning in support of spreading payroll taxes over the year is that, for a going concern, the commitment to hire employees is made for a year; the payroll tax is an annual tax that is related to the year as a whole. Because it benefits the entire year's operations, such a tax should not be loaded on the early months of the year. In practice, the additional clerical costs and complications often outweigh any informational advantages of this more refined approach. Therefore, early months bear the brunt of payroll tax charges.

ILLUSTRATION OF PAYROLL ACCOUNTING

The Stengal Company has a gross payroll of $1,000 per day, based on a five-day, forty-hour, Monday-through-Friday work week. Withholdings for income taxes amount to $100 per day. Payrolls for each week are paid on the following Tuesday.

Gross payrolls consist of $600 direct labor, $200 indirect labor, $140 selling expense, and $60 administrative expenses each day. The general ledger entry to record the total of the payroll cost incurred (including accrued employer payroll fringe costs) is made on the last day of each month. Fringe costs borne by the employer include:

	Per Cent of Gross Payroll
Vacation pay	4.0%
F.I.C.A. tax (old-age benefits)	4.9%
Federal unemployment tax	0.4%
State unemployment tax	2.7%

For our purposes, assume that the company starts business on March 3.

			MARCH								APRIL			
S	M	T	W	T	F	S		S	M	T	W	T	F	S
						1				1	2	3	4	5
2	3	4	5	6	7	8		6	7	8	9	10	11	12
9	10	11	12	13	14	15		13	14	15	16	17	18	19
16	17	18	19	20	21	22		20	21	22	23	24	25	26
23	24	25	26	27	28	29		27	28	29	30			
30	31													

REQUIRED:

Try to solve by yourself before examining the solution. (Exhibit 24-1 contains some helpful information.)

(a) All general journal payroll entries for March 11, 18, 25, and 31, April 1, 8, 15, 22, 29, and 30.

(b) All postings to Accrued Payroll, Employees' Income Taxes Payable, Employees' F.I.C.A. Taxes Payable, and Employer's F.I.C.A. Taxes Payable.

Solution.

(a) Journal entries follow:

March 11	Accrued payroll (5 × $1,000)	5,000.00	
	Cash		4,255.00
	Employees' income taxes payable (assume 5 × $100)		500.00
	Employees' F.I.C.A. taxes payable (.049 × $5,000)		245.00
	To pay payroll.		

The identical entry would be repeated every Tuesday, March 18 through April 29. Note that payroll settlements are made every *payday*, regardless of when payroll costs are recognized as being incurred.

March 31	Work in process control (21 days × $600)	12,600.00	
	Factory overhead control (21 × $200) + .12(21 × $200) + .12($12,600)	6,216.00	
	Selling expense control (21 × $140) + .12(21 × $140)	3,292.80	
	Administrative expense control (21 × $60) + .12(21 × $60)	1,411.20	
	Accrued payroll (21 days × $1,000)		21,000.00
	Estimated liability for vacation pay (.04 × $21,000)		840.00

Employer's F.I.C.A. taxes payable
(.049 × $21,000)   1,029.00

Federal unemployment taxes payable
(.004 × $21,000)   84.00

State unemployment taxes payable
(.027 × $21,000)   567.00

This entry is made and posted monthly. If desired, it could be made weekly, bi-weekly, or at any other interval. As contrasted with the previous entry, this entry recognizes cost incurrence rather than payment. Its measurements depend on the number of work days in a calendar month.

(Note that the entries on *paydays* are the same for April as for March.)

April 30   Work in process (22 × $600)   13,200.00

Factory overhead control
(22 × $200) + .12(22 × $200) + .12($13,200)   6,512.00

Selling expense control
(22 × $140) + .12(22 × $140)   3,449.60

Administrative expense control
(22 × $60) + .12(22 × $60)   1,478.40

Accrued payroll (22 × $1,000)   22,000.00

Estimated liability for vacation pay
(.04 × $22,000)   880.00

Employer's F.I.C.A. taxes payable
(.049 × $22,000)   1,078.00

Federal unemployment taxes payable
(.004 × $22,000)   88.00

State unemployment taxes payable
(.027 × $22,000)   594.00

The above entry is based on 22 days of work done in April.

April 30   Employees' income taxes payable
(3 paydays × $500)   1,500.00

Employees' F.I.C.A. taxes payable
(3 × $245)   735.00

Employer's F.I.C.A. taxes payable
(3 × $245)   735.00

Cash   2,970.00

Payment of taxes withheld on *paydays* in
March plus employer's matching of F.I.C.A.
taxes withheld.

These taxes are detailed on Form 941, a quarterly return. Legal liability arises as payroll is paid during a calendar quarter rather than as payroll is accrued. Compare, for example, the employer's F.I.C.A. taxes accrued as of March 31 ($1,029) with the amount remitted with this return ($735). This difference represents six days' cost in March that was not paid with this quarterly return. It will be paid during a subsequent period.

April 30   State unemployment taxes payable
(.027 × $5,000 × 3 paydays in March)   405.00

Cash   405.00

Payment to state for legal liability for
first calendar quarter.

(b) Postings to certain accounts for March and April follow:

ACCRUED PAYROLL

March 11	5,000			
March 18	5,000			
March 25	5,000			
To balance	6,000	March 31	21,000	
		March 31 balance, six days' gross earnings	6,000	
April 1	5,000			
April 8	5,000			
April 15	5,000			
April 22	5,000			
April 29	5,000	April 30	22,000	
To balance	3,000			
		April 30 balance, three days' gross earnings	3,000	

Employees' Income Taxes Payable			Employees' F.I.C.A. Taxes Payable	
	March 11,18,25	1,500		March 11,18,25	735
	April 22,29	2,500		April 1,8, 15,22,29	1,225
April 30	1,500			April 30	735	

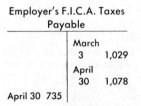

Employer's F.I.C.A. Taxes Payable

	March 3	1,029	
	April 30	1,078	
April 30	735		

A study of the above T-accounts shows the following:

(1) The Accrued Payroll balance at the close of business on March 31 represents the unpaid amount of *gross* earnings of employees applicable to the last six days worked in March.

(2) The timing of recognition of liability for employees' and employer's F.I.C.A. taxes differs. Legally, both liabilities arise when payroll is paid. But the employer accrues his liability when he recognizes regular labor cost incurrence, because such payroll taxes are basically related to time of *earnings* rather than to time of *payout*.

INCENTIVE PLANS

Objective of incentives

Most employees are paid a flat salary or a flat rate per hour, but wage incentive systems are widespread. Incentive plans provide extra compensation for performance that is superior to some predetermined goal or standard. The wide variety of factory incentive systems have a common objective: minimization of total costs for a given volume of production. In other words, the sweetening of the pay envelope must at least be balanced by reductions in other cost factors or by reductions in labor cost per unit. For example, assume that a worker is paid $2.00 an hour and produces 10 units in that time. He is placed on a strict piece-rate system at a rate of 18¢ per piece. His productivity may increase to 12 units per hour. His earnings would then be $2.16 per hour (12 × 18¢): higher pay per worker and yet less cost per unit for the employer. A piece rate of 21¢ or more may even be desirable for the employer, if savings in other costs like materials, power, repairs, or other variable overhead items can offset increased labor costs.

Incentive plans are not panaceas for problems of cost control. They add to clerical costs and spoilage costs and tend to lessen quality. Yet many companies have been pleased with over-all results. In any event, no incentive plan will be able to substitute for adequate management as the most effective means of controlling labor costs.

Accounting for incentive plans

Incentive plans vary widely in their details and application. The Gantt Task and Bonus Plan awards a higher piece rate, or bonus, for all production in excess of standard. The Taylor Differential Piece-Rate System applies a higher piece rate for *all* production per hour or day as long as the hourly or daily production standard is met. Incentive plans may be arranged to reward individual performance, group performance, assembly-line performance, and even plant-wide performance.

A common incentive plan is piecework coupled with a guaranteed minimum hourly rate. Thus, if the standard number of pieces per hour is not produced, pay is provided to "make up" the difference between the guaranteed rate and the piecework earnings. An example of computations follows:

DAILY EARNINGS SUMMARY*

Clock Number	Name	Department	Operation	Units Produced	Piece Rate	Piecework Earnings	Make-up	Total Earnings
414	Atwood	4	1004	500	$.04	$20.00	$ —	$20.00
445	Barnes	4	1004	330	.04	13.20	2.80	16.00
446	Charnes	4	1004	400	.04	16.00	—	16.00

*Guaranteed rate is $2.00 per hour or $16.00 per day.

Make-up pay would be charged to the department as an overhead item and would be part of the department's overhead budget. The standard labor cost for the operation would be four cents per unit.

PAYROLL BANK ACCOUNT

Companies with many employees usually use a separate checking account to keep payroll checks apart from checks for other disbursements. This facilitates control, preparation, and reconciliation of vast numbers of payroll checks. The general working of a payroll bank account is as follows:

Accrued payroll	10,000	
Withholdings payable		1,500
Cash (in regular checking account)		8,500

A single $8,500 check is drawn against the company's general bank account to cover the net payroll. The bank would transfer $8,500 from the general deposit account to a special payroll account. Assume that there are 100 employees. One hundred payroll checks totaling $8,500 would be prepared and issued. The size, color, and numerical sequence of these checks would differ from those of the general checks. Note that, as far as this company is concerned, its payroll bank account will always have a zero balance. Any balance in the payroll account as shown by the bank represents outstanding payroll checks.[3]

PAYROLL PROCEDURES

The top half of Exhibit 24-3 shows how payroll data are accumulated, classified, and summarized for reports using punched cards and semi-automatic office equipment. The bottom part of the exhibit shows how the introduction of an electronic data-processing (EDP) system would affect payroll procedures. An EDP system cuts across conventional organizational lines and:

1. As part of its primary task of preparing a payroll, EDP could process all types of events affecting the master payroll records by using those files but once.

2. It would perform certain timekeeping activities.

3. It would reconcile dual time-reporting arrangements.

4. It could develop labor cost distribution data as it performs the basic payroll operation and distribute these data without requiring intervening nonelectronic operations.

5. In a highly integrated system, it can handle many personnel data-processing functions simultaneously with the payroll processes.[4]

[3] The use of special bank accounts is not confined to payrolls. They can also be used for dividends, commissions, royalties, and so forth.
[4] Felix Kaufman, *Electronic Data Processing and Auditing* (New York: The Ronald Press Company, 1961), pp. 41 and 44–45.

PROCEDURAL FLOW CHART FOR PAYROLL FOR MEDIUM-SIZED MANUFACTURING COMPANY

Handled By Punched Cards and Semi-Automatic Office Equipment

Impact Change to Electronic Data Processing (EDP)

ACCOUNTING DEPARTMENT

BANK	TREASURER	TIMEKEEPING	COST DISTRIBUTION	PAYROLL	ACCOUNTS PAYABLE	GENERAL LEDGER	INTERNAL AUDITORS	EMPLOYMENT	FACTORY DEPARTMENTS

Work Tickets

Hiring and Rate Notice

Withholding Authorization

Work Tickets

These must agree

Clock Cards

Used for postings to subsidiary ledgers

Summary postings to Accrued Payroll

These must agree

Master Payroll

Voucher

Occasional Payoffs Made by Auditors

Hiring and Rate Notice

Withholding Authorization

Work Tickets

Voucher

Check

for master payroll

Paychecks

EDP Center

Quarterly and Annual Payroll Data

Labor Distribution Data

Deposited In special Payroll Account. Individual paychecks clear against this account

Clock Cards

Paychecks

Voucher

Time Card Irregularities

Labor Variances

SUMMARY

Payroll accounting is overwhelmed with detail, much of which is kept because of legal requirements rather than because of managerial needs.

The data-processing function is often divided between cost distribution and payouts to employees. Although electronic data processing increasingly accomplishes these objectives simultaneously, most companies distribute costs on one time basis (for example, monthly in the general ledger, daily in subsidiary records) and account for payouts on another time basis (for example, weekly).

PROBLEM FOR SELF-STUDY

Review the problem used as an illustration in the chapter.

QUESTIONS, PROBLEMS, AND CASES

Note: Problem 24-24 is particularly recommended.

24-1. "Accounting for payroll embraces plenty of big problems." Name three.

24-2. "The need for accuracy in payroll accounting is paramount." Explain.

24-3. "The government has at least two major influences on payroll accounting." What are they?

24-4. Name the major taxes associated with payrolls.

24-5. George Ripon worked for three employers during a year. His gross earnings were $1,000, $7,800, and $1,500—a total of $10,300.

    (a) How much of the earnings should each employer regard as subject to F.I.C.A. taxes?

    (b) How much of Ripon's earnings should he regard as subject to F.I.C.A. taxes?

24-6. "The Federal Unemployment Insurance Tax rate is 0.4%." Do you agree? Why?

24-7. Identify the following forms: W-4, 941, W-2, W-3, 940.

24-8. "Withheld taxes are taxes on employers." Do you agree? Why?

24-9. Name four common withholdings other than taxes.

24-10. "Payroll fringe costs are large enough these days to justify adding an average fringe rate to the basic direct labor rate." Do you agree? Why?

24-11. "Leveling or averaging of vacation costs and holiday pay is used to relate them to work done throughout the year." What criteria should affect the decision to adopt such leveling arrangements?

24-12. "Conceivably, in some companies an employer may show no payroll tax costs for the last quarter of the year." Why? Explain.

24-13. Contrast the theoretical and practical accounting treatments of employer payroll taxes.

24-14. If all bookkeeping is up to date, what does the balance in Accrued Payroll represent?

24-15. "The timing of recognition of liability for employees' and employer's F.I.C.A. taxes differs." Explain.

24-16. What are incentive plans? What is their objective?

24-17. What is "make-up"? How is it accounted for?

24-18. A company uses a separate payroll bank account. Weekly wage payments are $10,000. A $1,000 minimum balance is kept to provide for salary advances, separation payments, and so forth. What cash balance should ordinarily be shown on the company balance sheets?

24-19. Briefly describe how EDP can affect conventional payroll procedures.

24-20. Unemployment Compensation Taxes. The cost of unemployment compensation taxes to an employer is sometimes reduced as a result of a "good" experience rating. A manufacturer negotiated with the Federal Government a contract which necessitated the construction of a specific plant and related facilities for the sole purpose of producing the goods called for in the contract. Because the goods were required to meet emergency needs of the government, it was possible that after the plant facilities were constructed, the employees hired, and work on the order begun, the contract would be cancelled. The ensuing termination of services of employees hired for this specific job would make the employer's experience rating worse, which in turn would increase the cost of his unemployment compensation taxes. This "possible" cost was recognized as a cost in negotiating the contract.

Describe in order of preference three alternate methods of recording in accounts and/or disclosing on the financial statements the "possible" cost during the course of operations of this emergency plant under the contract. State your reasons.   [C.P.A.]

24-21. Accounting for Idle Time.* The labor distribution of the Dunne Desk Company is made from its payroll, all the wages of its twenty shop employees, except the foreman's, being treated as direct labor. The company pays for idle time of workmen caused by material shortages, and this amounts to a substantial portion of the payroll.

For the year 19x1, the direct labor, according to the ledger, was $20,000 and the overhead $16,000. Accordingly, an overhead rate of 80 per cent was used in 19x2 for the purpose of estimating costs of new products. The manager thinks that the estimates are wrong, for his income statement shows a gross margin of only $1 a desk, whereas his selling prices are at least $5 a desk above the estimated costs. He suspects that the idle-time factor is not being included in the cost estimates, and he asks you to investigate the situation.

1. How would you proceed to determine whether the manager's suspicions are correct?

2. Recompute the overhead rate for 19x1 on the assumption that $2,000 was paid for idle time which should be treated as overhead instead of as direct labor.

3. Suggest a change in the method of labor-cost allocation that would result in a more accurate accounting for idle time.

24-22. Incentives: Compute Labor Bonus. There are ten men working as a group on a particular manufacturing project. When the weekly production of the group exceeds a standard number of pieces per hour, each man in the group is paid a bonus for the excess production in addition to his wages at hourly rates. The amount of the bonus is computed by first determining the per-

*Adapted from a problem originated by Professor James H. March.

centage by which the group's production exceeds the standard. One-half of this percentage is then applied to a wage rate of $1.25 to determine an hourly bonus rate. Each man in the group is paid, as a bonus, this bonus rate applied to his total hours worked during the week. The standard rate of production before a bonus can be earned is 200 pieces per hour.

On the basis of the production record stated below, compute:

1. The rate and amount of bonus for the week.

2. The total wages of Allen, who worked 40 hours at a base rate of $1.00 per hour, and of Knoll, who worked $39\frac{1}{2}$ hours at a base rate of $1.50 per hour.

Production Record

	Hours Worked	Production
Monday	72	17,680
Tuesday	72	17,348
Wednesday	72	18,000
Thursday	72	18,560
Friday	71.5	17,888
Saturday	40	9,600
	399.5	99,076

[C.P.A.]

24-23. Incentive Wage Plans. During your audit of the accounts of the Gelard Manufacturing Corporation, your assistant tells you that he has found errors in the computation of the wages of factory workers and he wants you to verify his work.

Your assistant has extracted from the union contract the following description of the systems for computing wages in various departments of the Company. The contract provides that the minimum wage for a worker is his base rate, which is also paid for any "down time"—time when the worker's machine is under repair or he is without work. The standard work week is 40 hours. The union contract also provides that workers be paid 150 per cent of base rates for overtime production. The Company is engaged in interstate commerce.

1. *Straight piecework.* The worker is paid at the rate of $.20 per piece produced.

2. *Percentage bonus plan.* Standard quantities of production per hour are established by the engineering department. The worker's average hourly production, determined from his total hours worked and his production, is divided by the standard quantity of production to determine his efficiency ratio. The efficiency ratio is then applied to his base rate to determine his hourly earnings for the period.

3. *Emerson Efficiency System.* A minimum wage is paid for production up to $66\frac{2}{3}$ per cent of standard output or "efficiency." When the worker's production exceeds $66\frac{2}{3}$ per cent of the standard output, he is paid at a bonus rate. The bonus rate is determined from the following table:

Efficiency	Bonus
Up to $66\frac{2}{3}$ %	0%
$66\frac{2}{3}$ % –79%	10%
80% –99%	20%
100%–125%	45%

Your assistant has prepared the following schedule of information pertaining to certain workers for a weekly payroll selected for examination:

Worker	Wage Incentive Plan	Total Hours	Down Time Hours	Units Produced	Standard Units	Base Rate	Gross Wages Per Books
Long	Straight piecework	40	5	400	—	$1.80	$ 82.00
Loro	Straight piecework	46	—	455(1)	—	1.80	91.00
Huck	Straight piecework	44	4	420(2)	—	1.80	84.00
Nini	Percentage bonus plan	40	—	250	200	2.20	120.00
Boro	Percentage bonus plan	40	—	180	200	1.90	67.00
Wiss	Emerson	40	—	240	300	2.10	92.00
Alan	Emerson	40	2	590	600(3)	2.00	118.00

(1) Includes 45 pieces produced during the 6 overtime hours.
(2) Includes 50 pieces produced during the 4 overtime hours. The overtime, which was brought about by the "down time," was necessary to meet a production deadline.
(3) Standard units for 40 hours' production.

REQUIRED:

Prepare a schedule comparing each individual's gross wages per books and his gross wages per your calculation. Computations of workers' wages should be in good form and labeled with the workers' names.   [C.P.A. Adapted.]

24-24. Journal Entries for Payroll. The Stable Company operates the year around with a gross payroll of $500 a day. Withholdings for Social Security taxes and federal income taxes amount to $100 a day. The concern works five days a week, and the payroll period covers Monday to Friday, both inclusive. Payrolls for the week are paid on the following Tuesday.

Gross payrolls consist of $300 direct labor, $100 indirect labor, $70 selling expense, and $30 general and administrative expense each day. The general ledger entry to record the total of the payroll cost incurred each month is made on the last day of the month. These totals are obtained by summarizing the Payroll Cost Recapitulation sheets. This firm uses a "leveled" percentage of 4 per cent to estimate its own contribution to Social Security.

APRIL

S	M	Tu	W	Th	F	Sat
		1	2	3	4	5
6	7	8	9	10	11	12
13	14	15	16	17	18	19
20	21	22	23	24	25	26
27	28	29	30			

Using the above calendar as a guide, answer the following questions:
1. What is the balance in Accrued Payroll as of the close of business on March 31?

What journal entries should be made on:

2. April 1?

3. April 29?

4. April 30?

5. What is the ending balance in Accrued Payroll as of the close of business on April 30?

24-25. Journal Entries for Payroll.* The balance of the Accrued Wages of Kem Industries, Inc., was $12,120 on October 31, 19x1. The company has a job order cost system. The cost accounts are in the general ledger. Time tickets for pay periods falling wholly or partly in November are summarized as follows:

Pay Period	Direct Labor	Factory Overhead	Total
Nov. 1–7	$8,250	$4,510	$12,760
Nov. 8–14	8,450	4,490	12,940
Nov. 15–21	8,570	4,570	13,140
Nov. 22–28	7,920	4,060	11,980
Nov. 29–Dec. 5	8,430	4,470	12,900

Of the wages earned in the pay period ending December 5, one-third is applicable to November.

Payrolls for pay periods ending in November are summarized as follows:

Pay Period Ending	Gross Earnings	Deductions F.I.C.A.	Income Tax	Net Pay
Oct. 31	$12,120	$110	$1,200	$10,810
Nov. 7	12,760	108	1,250	11,402
Nov. 14	12,940	112	1,280	11,548
Nov. 21	13,140	102	1,300	11,738
Nov. 28	11,980	95	1,200	10,685

The payroll for the period ending November 28 was paid December 2.

REQUIRED:

1. Journal entry for labor cost allocation.

2. Journal entry for payrolls paid in November.

3. Postings in the Accrued Wages account.

4. Journal entry for accrual of employers' payroll taxes for the month of November at a leveled rate of 4 per cent of gross earnings.

5. Answer the following questions:

    a. Theoretically, should the accrual of employers' payroll taxes be based on wages earned or on wages paid during the month?

    b. Why is the amount of F.I.C.A. deductions less than 1 per cent of the gross earnings?

    c. What does the balance of Accrued Wages represent?

Journal explanations in all cases should state clearly how you arrived at your amounts.

*Adapted from a problem originated by Professor James H. March.

A REAPPRAISAL

SECTION

cost accounting in the C.P.A. examination

CHAPTER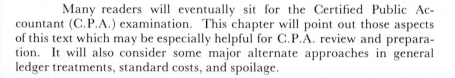

Many readers will eventually sit for the Certified Public Accountant (C.P.A.) examination. This chapter will point out those aspects of this text which may be especially helpful for C.P.A. review and preparation. It will also consider some major alternate approaches in general ledger treatments, standard costs, and spoilage.

COST TOPICS IN THE C.P.A. EXAMINATION

A fifteen-year tabulation of C.P.A. examination problems has shown the following frequency:

	Number of Problems in C.P.A. Examination in Accounting Practice			
	1951–1955	1956–1960	1961–1965	Total
Process costs, including five problems on joint costs	4	6	6*	16
Standard costs, flexible budgets, and analysis of variances	2	4	4	10
Cost-volume-profit analysis, including direct costing	2	3	5	10
General knowledge of manufacturing accounts and overhead application	4	1	1	6
Over-all cash and income statement budgeting	1	4	2	7
Relevant costs for special decisions; one optional discounted cash-flow problem was included in November, 1964.	—	3	5	8
	13	21	23	57

*Three of these were joint-cost problems.

A detailed analysis of the relative importance of cost accounting will be found in the Appendix to this chapter. In short, cost accounting is now more than ever the most important single topic in the Theory and Accounting Practice sections.

The above statistics concerning 1961–1965 reveal that process costing is still the favorite cost topic. But its dominance is waning. A relevant-cost problem has appeared regularly in recent years, and standard costs and cost-volume-profit analysis also are getting more attention than in previous years. These changes reflect the increasing general emphasis on management uses of accounting.

This book includes numerous questions and problems extracted from past C.P.A. examinations. The Appendix to this chapter contains a chapter-by-chapter tabulation of the C.P.A. problems for 1961–1965 used in this text.

C.P.A. REVIEW

The C.P.A. candidate faces an imposing task of review. In addition to preparing for likely cost accounting topics, he must recognize two special characteristics of a national examination. First, accounting terminology is not uniform. Second, alternative solutions are possible for many accounting problems.

Divergent terminology

Variations in terminology will inevitably appear in a national examination which is drawn from many sources. Likely questions and problems are contributed by individual accounting practitioners, public accountants, accounting teachers, and employees of the A.I.C.P.A. (American Institute of Certified Public Accountants). They are stockpiled by the A.I.C.P.A. and used as needed.

Thus, the candidate should be familiar with the variety and interchangeability of many cost terms.[1] For example, *factory overhead* is usually interchangeable with the following terms: *indirect manufacturing costs, manufacturing expenses, factory burden,* and *manufacturing overhead.*

Alternative solutions

Alternative solutions can arise because (a) there are slight variations in practical accounting procedures or techniques and (b) there are different schools of thought on certain cost matters, such as ledger designs, analysis of variances, and accounting for spoilage. Thus, the candidate must anticipate problem situations that do not exactly coincide with either

---

[1] Eric Kohler, *Dictionary for Accountants* (3rd ed.; Englewood Cliffs, N.J.: Prentice-Hall, Inc., 1963) is a helpful reference.

the text treatments which he knows or the cases in practice which he has encountered.

The American Institute of Certified Public Accountants takes elaborate steps to insure equitable grading of C.P.A. examinations. The A.I.C.P.A. graders recognize and give full credit to all alternative solutions that are reasonable. Therefore, the C.P.A. candidate should not be discouraged if in the course of his review he finds published C.P.A. solutions[2] that do not precisely agree with his favorite approach or the approach that he learned when he took a cost accounting course. The A.I.C.P.A. has found it impracticable to publish a large collection of alternative solutions, so it usually confines its "unofficial answers" to one widely accepted approach.

C.P.A. problems are designed to be straightforward. Requirements should be taken at face value. Special assumptions are rarely necessary. Sometimes a candidate still feels that an assumption must be made. If so, the assumption should be stated, together with the reasons therefor. *Such reasons should include a statement as to why a possible alternate assumption is being rejected.*

In summary, although the candidate does not have to worry about the acceptability of alternate solutions to a given C.P.A. problem, he should have an awareness of divergencies in accounting practice and terminology. As a minimum, his terminology should coincide with that given in the problem. He should also know what areas of cost accounting tend to have alternative treatments. In these areas especially, he should take particular pains with his answer so that it will be clear to all graders.[3] We shall examine these areas in the remainder of this chapter.

ALTERNATE GENERAL LEDGER TREATMENTS

The text has generally shown one technique for cost accumulation in the general ledger. Obviously, there are alternative methods, some of which have been briefly described (Chapters 4 and 6). Comparisons of a few alternative techniques are shown in Exhibit 25-1. The first and third columns show the methods used throughout this book; the second and fourth columns show alternate techniques which are preferred by many accountants for reasons of convenience or feasibility. For example, consider the problem of when to isolate a materials usage variance. In concept, it should be isolated as quickly as possible for control purposes

---

[2]Divergencies in practice and terminology not only creep into the examination but also into the "unofficial answers" which are published by the A.I.C.P.A. subsequent to the examination dates. These published answers are neither official nor necessarily the only acceptable solutions. Yet many students and teachers have the mistaken belief that the A.I.C.P.A. published solutions are *the* only acceptable answers.

[3]The candidate can be confident that the *proper* use of the specific techniques he has learned will be given full credit. However, in some instances, he can strengthen his solution by pointing out important aspects that might receive alternative treatment.

EXHIBIT 25-1

ALTERNATIVE GENERAL LEDGER DESIGNS

Transaction	Nonstandard Cost Accounting		Standard Cost Accounting	
	Col. (1)	Col. (2)	Col. (3)	Col. (4)
Direct material usage	Work in process xx 　Stores xx	Direct material used xx 　Stores xx Work in process xx 　Direct material used xx	Work in process xx Usage variance xx 　Stores xx	Work in process xx 　Stores xx Finished goods xx Usage variance xx 　Work in process xx
Payroll accounting	Work in process xx Department overhead xx 　Accrued payroll xx	Direct labor xx Department overhead xx 　Accrued payroll xx Work in process xx 　Direct labor xx	Work in process xx Direct labor rate variance xx Direct labor efficiency variance xx Department overhead xx 　Accrued payroll xx	Direct labor xx Department overhead xx Direct labor rate variance xx 　Accrued payroll xx Work in process xx 　Direct labor xx Finished goods xx Direct labor efficiency variance xx 　Work in process xx
Overhead accounting	Department overhead xx 　Various accounts xx or (a) Depreciation xx 　Repairs xx 　Supplies used xx 　Various accounts xx (b) Department overhead xx 　Depreciation xx 　Repairs xx 　Supplies used xx	(Similar methods to those shown at the left.)		

(see column 3). Yet often the usage variance is impossible to calculate until the work is completed. Consequently, in these cases, the method shown in the fourth column is used.

STANDARD COSTS

Standard costs may be integrated into the general ledger in a number of ways, depending on the preferences of the person who is setting up the standard cost system. The candidate should be familiar with alternative methods, because the ledger procedure described in a given problem will influence a solution. No computations or entries should be prepared until the given general ledger procedure (and specific types of variance analysis called for, if any) is fully comprehended. Problems on standard costs usually emphasize general ledger entries and variance analysis. A key account, Work in Process, could appear in any one of three alternative ways, depending upon the system employed:

(Alternative 1)	Work In Process
Actual quantities × Actual prices	Standard quantities × Standard prices

(Alternative 2)	Work In Process
Actual quantities × Standard prices	Standard quantities × Standard prices

(Alternative 3)	Work In Process
Standard quantities × Standard prices	Standard quantities × Standard prices

As explained in Chapter 6, the timing of the isolation of material, labor, and overhead variances will be influenced by the specific system employed.

Although the computations of material and labor variances are usually the same regardless of the standard cost system used, the computations of overhead variances are by no means uniform in practice. The methodology described in Chapter 8 is generally superior to other methods, but published solutions to C.P.A. problems have shown a number of alternative approaches. Moreover, a single overhead application rate, composed of both variable and fixed elements as described in the Appendix to Chapter 8, is often used. These alternative solutions are described below, using the following basic data:

Budget formula for monthly overhead: $100,000 fixed overhead + ($1.00 × direct labor hours)

Normal or standard volume: 400,000 hours

Combined overhead rate for product costing: $\dfrac{\$100,000 + (400,000 \times \$1.00)}{400,000} = \$1.25$

Month of August:

Actual direct hours	450,000
Standard direct hours allowed for work done	430,000
Actual overhead, including $103,000 of fixed costs	$570,000
Applied overhead, 430,000 × $1.25	$537,500
Total variance, $570,000 less $537,500	$ 32,500

Alternative 1. The recommended approach as described in Chapter 8. Budget based on standard hours allowed.

	Actual	Budget-Actual Hours	Budget— Standard Hours .	Applied
		$100,000 + $1(450,000)	$100,000 + $1(430,000)	
V	$467,000	$450,000	$430,000	$430,000
F	103,000	100,000	100,000	107,500
	$570,000	$550,000	$530,000	$537,500

Spending Variance,   Efficiency Variance,   Volume Variance,
    $20,000 U $20,000 U $7,500 F
                   ($1.00 × 20,000 hours)($.25 × 30,000 hours)

Budget Variance, $40,000 U

Alternative 2. The pertinent budget level for measuring volume variance is considered to be actual hours rather than standard hours as in Alternative 1. Also, fixed factory overhead shows an efficiency variance (sometimes called an *effectiveness variance*), measured like other efficiency variances. This supposedly gives a measure of the efficient or inefficient utilization of facilities.

	Actual	Budget—Actual Hours	Actual Hours × Overhead Rate	Applied
V	$467,000	$450,000	$450,000	$430,000
F	103,000	100,000	112,500	107,500
	$570,000	$550,000	$562,500	$537,500

Budget Variance,   Volume Variance,   Efficiency Variance:
    $20,000 U $12,500 F   Variable $20,000 U
                   (450,000 − 400,000)   Fixed   5,000 U
                        × $.25 $25,000 U

Comparison of Alternatives 1 and 2: Efficiency Variance for Fixed Overhead?   Note that the efficiency variance is a sub-part of the budget variance under Alternative 1, whereas it could be considered a sub-part of the volume variance under Alternative 2. Let us compare these two alternatives more closely.

Alternative 1: Budget variance consists of both spending and efficiency variance.

Alternative 2: Budget variance is the same as the "spending" variance under Alternative 1.

The efficiency variance for variable overhead is the same under both alternatives.

Under Alternative 2, the fixed overhead analysis differs considerably from Alternative 1. Basically, however, all that is done is to take the volume variance of $7,500 computed in Alternative 1 and subdivide it further as follows:

Volume variance in Alternative 1		$7,500 F
Breakdown in Alternative 2:		
Fixed overhead efficiency variance, $.25 × 20,000 hours	$ 5,000 U	
True "volume" variance (actual hours worked minus normal hours) × rate, 50,000 hours × $.25	12,500 F	7,500 F

The efficiency variance for fixed overhead is a misnomer; it would be better to call it an effectiveness variance. It should be distinguished sharply from the efficiency variances for material, labor, and variable overhead, because efficient usage of these three factors can affect actual cost incurrence, whereas short-run fixed overhead cost incurrence is not affected by efficiency. Thus, a better label for the fixed overhead "efficiency" variance would be an "effectiveness" variance, a sort of rough-and-ready measure that may have some psychological value as a reminder to the department head that his efficiency has an impact on effective utilization of facilities.

This writer sees little merit in this computation except where ineffective utilization of facilities means a loss of sales. For instance, if maximum capacity is 500,000 standard hours, and the sales department can obtain orders in excess of 500,000-hour capacity, the inefficient use of facilities involves an opportunity cost which is properly chargeable to the foreman. The best measure of this cost would be the lost contribution margins on the orders not filled. In lieu of this measure, the use of the effectiveness variance could be a crude attempt to quantify the foreman's performance. Hence, if an efficiency or effectiveness variance is employed, its weakness should be recognized.

Thus, the volume variance in Alternative 1 would be chargeable to someone other than the foreman. It might be traceable to the sales manager, to the head of production control, or to random outside influences. Under Alternative 1, the foreman would not ordinarily be considered explicitly responsible for efficient use of facilities.

Alternative 3. This is a hybrid of Alternatives 1 and 2. It demonstrates that overhead variance analysis can be conducted in a great number of ways. Here the budget is based on standard hours, but the efficiency variance is computed by using a combined $1.25 rate rather than attributing efficiency to variable overhead control only.

Actual	Budget—Standard Hours	Applied
$570,000	$530,000	$537,500

Budget Variance, $40,000 U   Volume Variance, $7,500 F

Subdivide the budget variance as follows:

Efficiency variance is $1.25 × 20,000 hours	$25,000	U
Remainder is spending variance	15,000	U
Budget variance	$40,000	U

Alternative 4.   This is the most miserable alternative of all, because the flexible budget concept is not employed. Instead, the appropriate budget is considered to be the one based on the planned activity level used to set the overhead rate for product costing (normal or standard volume), regardless of the actual level of activity that ensues. The resulting variance analysis seems more confusing than it is worth; yet it is shown here because several C.P.A. solutions through the years have presented this approach.

Actual	Budget— Normal Activity	Actual Hours × Overhead Rate	Applied
$570,000	$500,000	$562,500	$537,500

*Budget Variance,   †Volume Variance,   Efficiency Variance,
$70,000 U $62,500 F $25,000 U

*Note that this compares actual cost incurrence with a budget based on activity entirely different from the actual activity level.

†The volume variance's main weakness is the use of a combined rate rather than the fixed overhead rate, which is pertinent to the measure of a volume variance.

SPOILAGE

The alternate ways of accounting for spoilage in process costing were discussed in Chapter 20. Many published C.P.A. solutions ignore the computations of equivalent units for spoilage, shrinkage, or waste. The reason cited in favor of this short-cut technique is that it automatically spreads spoilage costs over good units through the use of higher equivalent unit costs. However, the results of this short cut are questionable in many cases, as was shown in Chapter 20. If the candidate faces a spoilage problem, he should solve it in the conceptually correct manner but make a special note to describe his approach and to state that alternative approaches ignore computations of equivalent units for spoilage, shrinkage, and waste.

S U M M A R Y

The C.P.A. candidate needs to be aware of which cost accounting topics are most likely to appear on the C.P.A. examination. These include process costs and joint costs; standard costs and analysis of variances; cost-volume-profit relationships; budgeting in general; and relevant costs. He also should have a general knowledge of what areas in cost accounting are marked by divergent accounting terminology and techniques. These include general ledger design, analysis of overhead variances, and accounting for spoilage.

Careful study of appropriate topics in this book will fortify the C.P.A. candidate with sufficient background for success in the cost accounting phases of the C.P.A. examination.

SUGGESTED READINGS

Charles T. Horngren and J. Arthur Leer, *CPA Problems and Approaches to Solutions.* (2nd ed., Englewood Cliffs, N.J.: Prentice-Hall, Inc., 1964).

Herbert E. Miller (ed.), *CPA Review Manual.* (3rd ed., Englewood Cliffs, N.J.: Prentice-Hall, Inc., 1966).

APPENDIX A:
IMPORTANCE OF COST ACCOUNTING IN THE C.P.A. EXAMINATION

The C.P.A. examination has four parts: Auditing, Law, Theory, and Practice. The latter usually requires the greatest preparation and contains problems on a variety of topics, such as consolidations, income taxes, statement of sources and applications of funds, and many others. Cost accounting is a very prominent topic in the Theory and Practice sections of the C.P.A. examination;[4] it is of minor importance in the Auditing and Law sections.

It is sometimes difficult to classify a given question into a clear-cut category. However, various tabulations of the relative importance of cost accounting lead to the following general conclusions:

1. The Theory section was commenced in May, 1943. Tabulations since that time show that fixed assets and cost accounting are the two most frequently covered topics. Roughly one-eighth of all theory questions have been on cost accounting. Questions on various methods of overhead application are special favorites.

2. The Practice section emphasizes cost accounting more than any other single topic. Exhibit 25-2 is a five-year analysis of cost accounting problems in the Practice section of the C.P.A. examinations for 1961–1965. Those included in this book are cross-referenced to show in what chapter they appear. This exhibit shows that for 1961–1965, 21.5 per cent (23 out of 107 problems) of the number of problems were on cost accounting and related areas. These represented 23.9 per cent of the total point weight (239 out of 1,000 points for 10 examinations). The relative frequency of individual cost accounting topics on the examinations for 1951–1965 was analyzed at the beginning of this chapter.

---

[4]For a thorough analysis see Milton F. Usry, "Cost Accounting on the C.P.A. Examination," *Accounting Review* (October, 1966) pp. 754–762.

EXHIBIT 25-2

ANALYSIS OF COST ACCOUNTING PROBLEMS IN THE PRACTICE SECTION
OF THE C.P.A. EXAMINATION, 1961–1965

	Total Number of Problems Included	Relative Importance of Cost Accounting				Problem Number in This Book	Description of Problem
Exam		Number of Problems Included	Point Weight Out of Possible 100	Individual Point Weights*	Estimated Time Allowed		
M 61	10	1	11	11	50	25-4	Standard costs; analysis of variances.
N 61	10	3	26	6	27	—	Analysis of changes in revenue.
				8	35	—	Cost-volume-profit relationships.
				12	55	20-22	Process costs; lost units.
M 62	10	2	24	13	60	—	Computation of inventory stolen from manufacturer.
				11	50	10-15	Direct costing and cost-volume-profit relationships.
N 62	11	2	22	9	45	—	Joint costs, by-product, lower of cost or market.
				13	60	—	Budgets of income and cash flow.
M 63	11	2	20	9	45	8-19	Standard costs; analysis of variances.
				11	55	13-11	Relevant cost analysis, make- or-buy decision.
N 63	11	2	22	11	55	13-16	Contribution to profit; product mix.
				11	55	18-21	Process costs; joint costs, by-product.
M 64	12	2	22	11	55	18-23	Joint costs; calculation of maximum price to pay for materials.
				11	55	20-16	Process costs.
				11	55	5-13	Cash budget.
N 64	11	3	33	11	55	6-26	Standard costs; proration of variances.
				11	55	15-19	Discounted cash flow; purchase decision.
M 65	10	3	30	11	55	19-8	Flexible budgets and process costs.
				8	37	—	Analysis of change in gross profit.
				11	55	13-17	Relevant cost analysis and pricing.
N 65	11	3	29	9	45	7-13	Cost-volume-profit analysis.
				11	55	19-20	Fifo process costing.
				9	45	4-22	Government fixed-price incentive contracts.
	107	23	239				Note that 21.5% (23 out of 107 problems) of the number of problems for 1961–1965 represented 23.9% of the point weight (239 out of 1,000 points for ten examinations).
	100%	21.5%					

*Estimates of point weights are based on relative times allowed.

Incidentally, because the content changes through the years, the candidate should not analyze topical frequency for a span longer than five to ten years prior to the most recent examination. Primary attention should be devoted to the most recent five-year span.

APPENDIX B: CANADIAN COST ACCOUNTING PROBLEMS

The Society of Industrial and Cost Accountants of Canada administers a set of annual examinations on accounting. There are various sections with graduated levels of difficulty. The problems with footnotes "[S.I.C.A.]" in this book have been taken with permission from the Society's examinations. Some of these problems have been adapted to bring out particular points in the chapter for which they were chosen.

Several additional problems have been taken from the examinations of the Certified General Accountants Association of Canada (C.G.A.A.).

QUESTIONS, PROBLEMS, AND CASES

25-1. What are two special characteristics of the national C.P.A. examination that the candidate must recognize?

25-2. "We should be careful to review the A.I.C.P.A. solutions to past C.P.A. questions so that we learn the official answers." Do you agree? Why?

25-3. Four Methods of Analyzing Overhead Variances. The Signe Company uses a combined overhead rate of $4.00 per hour for product costing under a standard cost system. Normal activity is 10,000 hours, or 5,000 finished units. At that level the overhead budget is: variable, $30,000; fixed, $10,000.

Actual level of activity: 8,700 hours and 4,400 units produced.
Actual overhead incurred: variable, $28,000; fixed, $9,700.

REQUIRED:

Show at least four different methods of analyzing overhead variances. Include one method where the appropriate budget is considered to be one based on normal activity regardless of the actual activity that ensues; that is, assume that the flexible-budget concept is not employed.

25-4. Standard Costs, Alternate Analysis of Variances. The Dearborn Company manufactures product X in standard batches of 100 units. A standard cost system is in use. The standard costs for a batch are as follows:

Raw materials	60 lbs. @ $ .45 per lb.	$ 27.00
Direct labor	36 hrs. @ $2.15 per hr.	77.40
Overhead	36 hrs. @ $2.75 per hr.	99.00
		$203.40

Production for April, 19x0, amounted to 210 batches. The relevant statistics follow:

Standard output per month	24,000 units
Raw materials used	13,000 lbs.
Cost of raw materials used	$ 6,110.00
Direct labor cost	$16,790.40
Overhead cost	$20,592.00
Average overhead rate per hour	$2.60

The management has noted that actual costs per batch deviate somewhat from standard costs per batch.

REQUIRED:

Prepare a statement which will contain a detailed explanation of the difference between actual costs and standard costs. [C.P.A.]

decision making: uncertainty, subjective probabilities, and the accountant

CHAPTER XXVI

This chapter stresses the uncertainty that underlies decision making and the usefulness of a systematic approach to decisions. The major objective is to point out that many figures which accountants scrupulously manipulate are far from precise; decision making is put in focus so that the accounting techniques which have been examined closely throughout this book may be viewed in perspective. Many readers will object that the subject matter here is not accounting. The validity of such an objection depends on how "accounting" is defined. The collection of figures for decision making may be described by several different terms, including the following: operations research, statistics, application of probability theory, and engineering economy. The point is that the accountant who works in the area of special decision making (or any area of planning and control, for that matter) should recognize the applicability and worth of related quantitative techniques. Whether he acquires this awareness by reading accounting books, statistics books, or general management books does not really matter.

The accountant needs to be familiar with the entire decision making process if he is going to be of maximum service to line management. This chapter will consider the nature of decision making, a case illustration of a systematic approach to decision making and uncertainty, and accounting and subjective probabilities.

NATURE OF DECISION MAKING

Decision making is the essence of this thing called "management." Decision making is really *choosing*. A selection must be made between

775

alternate courses of action. Each available course of action has future outcomes which are usually marked by uncertainty because the future seldom can be predicted with precision.

Future

Every decision deals with the future—whether it be ten seconds ahead (the decision to have dessert or not) or 80 years ahead (the decision of plant location). A decision always involves a forecast or prediction of what is going to occur. If the future could be foreseen, decisions would not be the hand-wringing, tortuous events they so often are—the decision would automatically become the one that garners the most future benefits.

Uncertainty and materiality

Managers are faced with countless decisions. Some are routine and far from terrifying, because either there is little uncertainty or the cost is minor. For example, the decision as to what type of eraser to buy may hardly be described as earth-shaking for two reasons. There is a certainty that some kind of eraser must be used for some clerical tasks. Further, the cost is relatively small. Other decisions are serious and difficult because the uncertainty is great and the dollar amounts involved are large—for example, the adding of a new product line, make or buy, and rent or buy.

Influencing aspects

Nobody really knows what exact mental processes are used to make a final decision. Every decision, in the last analysis, is a result of some combination of intellect and will. The managerial intellect, if functioning properly, chooses the most "beneficial" alternative. But life is marked by seemingly irrational decisions. The ultimate choice is influenced by the interplay of the intellect, the will, the emotions, time limitations, hunches, feelings, ramblings, and preoccupation with irrelevancies. The final decision depends on how the individual weighs all these influencing aspects.

Need for information and for logic

In order for a businessman to make a high percentage of successful decisions, he must be well informed. It is also important that he follow some sort of logical mental process in arriving at his decisions, rather than arrive at them only on the basis of his whims, fancies, or emotions. Given the same set of facts, he should be able to arrive at the same decision on Monday or Friday. Often experienced managers, who profess the use of a "seat of the pants" decision making process, unconsciously follow some logical thought pattern without realizing that they are using scientific methodology. Initially, however, and for decisions of signal importance, it is wise to follow consciously a logical pattern.

Seven steps

One rational approach to making decisions consists of the following steps, which will be discussed in the subsequent case illustration:

1. Determine the problem and what specific objectives are desired by management.
2. Determine the alternative courses of action.
3. Determine the consequences of each alternative and who will implement each.
4. Attempt to compute the costs and revenues under each alternative— measuring uncertainty.
5. Select an alternative.
6. Transform the decision into action.
7. Appraise the results.

Case Illustration of Decision Making and Uncertainty. As an example of the process of rational decision making, consider the case of the executive vice president of the United Sound Company (USCO). USCO is a medium-sized consumer-electronics manufacturer. It markets a substantial portion of its output through a major mail-order house. The company is a sole supplier to the mail-order house for radios, phonographs, and television sets. Over the years, USCO has prospered as the mail-order house grew. USCO has acquired a reputation for reliability, product quality, and prompt delivery. Thus, the company has enjoyed a favored position in its customer's purchasing department, but USCO has never had any long-run contract with the mail-order house.

Foreign manufacturers of radios and television sets have recently started to invade the American market. Because of ingenious, novel engineering and low labor rates, these companies are able to produce products which offer domestic manufacturers severe competition in quality and price. One of these foreign firms has offered to sell a high-quality transistorized portable FM-AM radio to USCO's customers for $15.95 each, in lots of 1,000, f.o.b. Chicago.

This radio is an eight-transistor portable, packaged the size of a king-sized pack of cigarettes. Its characteristics, except sound quality, are comparable to those of a hard-tube portable that USCO has been selling to its customers for $27.50 each in lots of 1,000. Because the foreign model is half as large as the USCO model in all dimensions, the mail-order house is not concerned about some loss of tone.

To meet competition, the mail-order house has decided to market the foreign portable next year unless USCO can offer a similar device at a similar price. The USCO board members have decided to proceed with the development of a transistor radio. They believe that their whole company's sales are endangered if the foreign concern manages to get a foothold in their customer's purchasing department. USCO must have this device developed and ready for production in six months.

Mr. McAdoo, the executive vice president, has received the following from the President:

TO: Mr. McAdoo

FROM: The President—USCO

       Subject: Transistorized portable radio

Please proceed with plans to have an eight-transistor portable radio in production in six months. This radio should be no larger than a pack of "king-size" cigarettes and should be designed to yield a ,profit at our selling price of $15.95 or less in lots of 1,000.

               Signed: A. Baxter

                    President

1. Determine the problem. The problem itself is often obvious; it is deliberately made obvious in the illustrations in this book. But frequently the chief difficulty in a real business situation is isolating and defining the problem; attention is erroneously devoted to side issues, symptoms, or sub-phases of the central problem. The ability to find and formulate the central problem is a prized talent in business and in other occupations.

Essentially the problem *facing Mr. McAdoo* is to develop a portable radio which:

    a. Is the size of a pack of king-sized cigarettes;

    b. Has eight transistors;

    c. Can be manufactured as cheaply as possible and sold at a profit by USCO for $15.95;

    d. Can be in production in six months.

Obviously, each of these statements leaves something to be answered before such a radio can actually be made. Each will elicit further questions before the device can even be developed.

Under point (a) above:

Is there to be an outer carrying case with this portable, and, if so, are its inside or outside dimensions to be the size of the cigarette package?

If there is to be such a case, is it to be made of split leather or leather-ette or some other substance?

Under point (b) above:

Can the radio have less than eight transistors if simpler design can be developed? Will the mail-order house accept a four-transistor radio if it has the same qualities as the foreign model? Or will the mail-order house insist on eight transistors because the public judges a radio's quality by the number of transistors it contains? What minimum signal strength should the portable be capable of receiving?

Under point (c) above:

What is the maximum manufacturing cost for lots of 1,000?

Many more questions can be raised, all of which must be investigated before a product design and development program is launched.

Mr. McAdoo's first task is to write a complete set of target specifications for the new product. The reduction of detailed specifications to written form, however, is not Mr. McAdoo's major difficulty. It is a chore which he and his assistants should easily accomplish. The central problem is to devise a program for designing the radio which will have the lowest long-run cost to the United Sound Company.

2. Determine the alternative courses of action. Once Mr. McAdoo has successfully isolated his problem, he is faced with the question of determining alternative courses of action. After some careful consideration of the project, he is able to list three possibilities which deserve close attention:[1]

a. Purchase one of the foreign models on the market and let an USCO draftsman copy it. This would save a great deal of time and money. It certainly deserves consideration.

b. All of the development and drafting can be done in USCO's own engineering department. This is an obvious solution. Although this company is primarily a manufacturing concern, it retains a small engineering department to develop new equipment and improve old products. The engineering staff is definitely capable of handling the project. The staff situation is such that either the appropriate engineering people will be used for developing the transistor portable or they will be laid off.

c. Subcontract the development and drafting to some outside consulting engineering firm which specializes in electronics. This is also definitely worth investigating.

3. Determine the consequence of each alternative and who will implement each. It is entirely possible that copying a foreign device would complicate the parts and tooling situation. The specifications of the foreign parts might not be exactly the same as those of easily obtainable American parts. Because the foreign portables are made in a factory with much lower labor costs than USCO's, they probably contain hand-made portions that USCO would have to redesign for machine manufacture. Copying a device already on the market would also increase the danger of patent infringement, with the possible additional cost of a lawsuit.

The second alternative can be handled within USCO. The talent is available, and there would be an unmeasurable long-run benefit, because the company engineers would develop an intimate comprehension of the design and workings of the product. This knowledge would undoubtedly be helpful in tackling future production difficulties.

Sending the design out to an engineering consultant has the advantage of a firm price and assurance of completion within the six-month time limit. Presumably top-grade outside engineering talent might furnish a simpler, more economical design than the USCO engineers could supply.

4. Attempt to compute the costs under each alternative; measuring uncertainty. This phase of the decision-making process is not always so simple; the accountant is usually embroiled here along with other executives. Mr. McAdoo is able to get engineering department estimates of $10,000 for

[1] Time pressure frequently prevents discovery of alternatives. Many executives are so harried with their daily operating chores that they, as many baseball managers say, "play each game one at a time."

USCO's copying an existing model and of about $29,500 for the complete development of the radio by USCO. There is a firm outside quotation from a competent engineering company of $30,000 for complete drawings of a radio to conform with Mr. McAdoo's specifications.

Although the third figure can be considered precise, assuming that an ironclad contract can be negotiated, the first two are not. They are *estimates*, and only time will prove their degree of accuracy. Before Mr. McAdoo can consider which method is least expensive, he must consider the probable precision of the first two figures.

Uncertainty plagues the prediction of future figures. The reliability of single-figured estimates, such as $10,000 for the copying of the foreign model and the $29,500 for complete internal development, is marked by various degrees of *uncertainty*. As Spencer and Siegelman state:

> Uncertainty is a subjective phenomenon; no two individuals will view an event and necessarily formulate the same quantitative opinion. This is due to a lack of sufficient historical data on which to base a probability estimate . . . . The parameters of the probability distribution [the range and likelihood of various outcomes] cannot be established empirically, because all predictions are subjective and within the framework of each manager's own anticipations of the future. At best, subjective probabilities can be assigned to these anticipated outcomes, but the distribution of expectations resulting therefrom cannot be established with objective certainty.[2]

USCO engineers have previously dealt with a number of assorted development projects which have required cost predictions. After many frustrating, haphazard approaches to the problems, the engineers have developed a satisfactory, systematic means of reconciling divergent views and formulating group opinion. This rational approach will be illustrated for both the $10,000 estimate and the $29,500 estimate.

In estimating costs of copying a foreign model, the engineers pooled their judgment and experience in group study and discussions. They agreed that the probable range of development costs would be from

[2]Spencer and Siegelman, *Managerial Economics* (Homewood, Illinois: Richard D. Irwin, Inc. 1964), p. 8. *Risk*, in contrast with uncertainty, is objective in nature. Risk can be expressed as the quantitative measure of the probability of an outcome. Thus, the probability of getting a head in the toss of a symmetrical coin is .5; that of drawing a particular playing card from a well-shuffled deck, $\frac{1}{52}$. Many writers also classify some decisions as being under *certainty*, where all the relevant facts are accurately known. The decision under certainty merely consists of choosing the one alternative that promises the greatest benefit. However, decisions under certainty are not always obvious. There are often countless alternatives, all of which may offer specific outcomes. The problem then is *finding* the best one. For example, the problem of allocating 100 job orders to 50 different machines, any one of which could do the job, can literally involve *billions* of different combinations. For an example of decision-making under certainty, see the example of linear programming in the last chapter of this book. Also see Miller and Starr, *Executive Decisions and Operations Research* (Englewood Cliffs, N.J.: Prentice-Hall, Inc., 1960), pp. 80–81.

a minimum of $8,500 to a maximum of $11,500. Note that they are almost 100 per cent *certain* about the *range* of outcomes, but they are uncertain about the exact figure. In order to submit a single figure, the engineers assign subjective probabilities to various figures, as shown at the top of Exhibit 26-1.

EXHIBIT 26-1

ESTIMATED DEVELOPMENT COSTS—COPYING FOREIGN MODEL

Expected Costs	Percentage Chance of Occurrence	Probability
$ 8,500	5%	.05
9,000	10%	.10
9,500	15%	.15
10,000	40%	.40
10,500	15%	.15
11,000	10%	.10
11,500	5%	.05
	100%	1.00

The above figures can be graphed as follows:

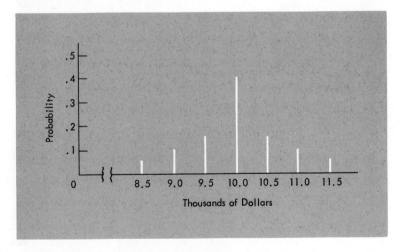

As shown in Exhibit 26-1, the group agreed that chances are four out of ten that costs will be $10,000; seven out of ten that costs will be between $9,500 and $10,500; nine out of ten that costs will be between $9,000 and $11,000; and ten out of ten that costs will be between $8,500

and \$11,500.[3] Note carefully that these are *subjective* probabilities; they are not objectively determined like odds in games of chance such as coin-tossing or roulette. Yet this method represents an attempt at a systematic, rational approach to the difficult prediction problem. The table and graph are the result of rigorous, balanced analysis on the part of those who know the most about the problem at hand. The engineers agreed that \$10,000 (the mean, median, and mode) was the best single-figure estimate of probable costs, but they realized that their forecast was subject to error. The subjective measure of that probable error is portrayed graphically as a symmetrical distribution about the \$10,000 best guess.

Schlaifer[4] and others have expressed the relationships just discussed in the form of an *expected-value table* that takes the following format:

Event	W Probability	X Value Conditional	WX Value Expected
A	.05	\$ 8,500	\$ 425
B	.10	9,000	900
C	.15	9,500	1,425
D	.40	10,000	4,000
E	.15	10,500	1,575
F	.10	11,000	1,100
G	.05	11,500	575
	1.00		

Expected value (arithmetic mean), $\Sigma WX = \bar{X} = \$10,000$

Note the steps:

1. List every possible event in column 1.
2. Enter the probability of each event in column 2.
3. Enter the conditional value of each event in column 3.

[3] The outside firm quote of \$30,000 in alternative (c) could be graphed for comparison with the graph in Exhibit 26-1:

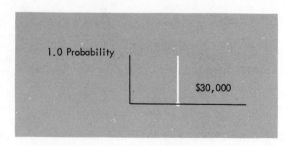

In this case, it is a single point with no dispersion on either side, because there is *certainty* instead of uncertainty.

[4] Robert Schlaifer, *Probability and Statistics for Business Decisions* (New York: McGraw-Hill Book Co., Inc., 1959), p. 25.

4. For each event, multiply probability times conditional value and enter the product in column 4, taking care to preserve the algebraic sign.
5. Add the products in column 4, with due regard to algebraic sign.

The question of alternative (b) is more complex. All agree that complete internal development of the radio will necessitate certain minimum costs for parts, shop, drafting, engineering labor, and the like. The engineering group is able to agree that this bare minimum is $23,500.

After a great deal of study, the group is able to see a number of possible hitches in the project which could boost costs immensely. The engineers recognize that they have not had a great deal of experience with transistors, and that they may eventually find that they do not know as much as they had hoped. When they actually get into designing such a radio, costs may start to soar. This portable is going to require a very small, oval speaker, which the subcontractor who supplies USCO's speakers has never made. This may be much more costly to develop than anyone anticipates. USCO has never worked on any miniature equipment where tiny components must be actually packed into their case. All in all, the cost of developing the radio may be *much higher* than they expect. If everything goes wrong, costs might reach as high as $55,000.

The engineers' considered judgment of what development costs would probably be is shown in Exhibit 26-2.

EXHIBIT 26-2

ESTIMATED DEVELOPMENT COSTS—COMPLETELY
NEW MODEL

Event	Probability	Value Conditional	Value Expected
A	.18	$23,500	$ 4,230
B	.30	25,000	7,500
C	.15	26,500	3,975
D	.12	30,000	3,600
E	.10	35,000	3,500
F	.08	40,000	3,200
G	.05	47,500	2,375
H	.02	55,000	1,100
	1.00		

Expected value (arithmetic mean), $\Sigma WX = \overline{X} = $29,480$
rounded to $29,500$

The situation here differs substantially from the previous alternative. The engineers agreed that $25,000 was the most likely (modal) single-figure estimate, but the distribution about this figure is far from symmetrical. The graph tails off (is skewed) to the right, reflecting the probabilities of upward cost thrusts that would make $25,000 look like a wild guess.

The above figures can be graphed as follows:

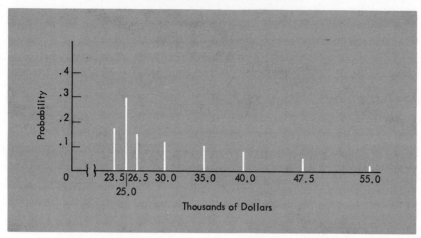

Limitations of data

Note that merely to compare $10,000, $29,500, and $30,000 is oversimplification. These three single figures are not strictly comparable, because one represents certainty whereas the other two represent the expected values within their respective ranges. The decision maker must explicitly or implicitly (by "feel" or hunch) recognize that he is comparing figures that have varying degrees of uncertainty (spread, dispersion), as portrayed by the graphs in Exhibits 26-1 and 26-2.

The degree of uncertainty is a measure of the dispersion (or spread) of possible outcomes on either side of the single figure (the mean, the expected value).[5] In Exhibit 26-1, there is an even chance that a deviation from the expected value will fall above or below $10,000. In Exhibit 26-2, a deviation from the $29,500 expected value may easily be in the direction of higher costs.

Our concern here is not to investigate statistical techniques as an objective in itself. Rather, it is to highlight the problems of uncertainty that taint the decision maker's computations and to suggest that a method-

---

[5]The arithmetic mean has been used in these illustrations. A minority of economists and statisticians maintain that the mode would be better because it is the most likely *single* outcome. Yet, in cases where the range of outcomes under consideration is badly dispersed or highly skewed, the mean is advantageous because it is affected by extreme observations in proportion to their frequency, whereas the mode is relatively unaffected. Thus, the mean and mode coincide in alternative (a), but the mode is $25,000 and the mean is $29,500 in alternative (b). In such a situation as alternative (b), the decision maker may easily regard the mean as being more helpful for comparison than the mode. The mean of $29,500 is much closer to the $30,000 outside quotation than the $25,000 mode because the mean reflects the influence of high-cost extreme observations. In short, the mean is usually better than the mode as a single-figured estimate; but the whole distribution should be examined before reaching a decision.

ical approach to dealing with uncertainty is better than a haphazard, blindman's-bluff approach.

    5. Select an alternative. In comparing Exhibits 26-1 and 26-2 with the firm outside quote of $30,000, Mr. McAdoo is able to conclude that it is certainly cheaper to copy a foreign device, and that it does not make much difference, from a cost standpoint, which of the other alternatives is followed. Although Exhibit 26-2 shows $29,500 as the most probable cost, the costs of this method could easily be much higher.

    After weighing all of the relative merits of each alternative, Mr. McAdoo discards copying another product because of the possible danger of legal trouble and the danger of arriving at a design which would not be suited for USCO's manufacturing facilities, even though the initial development costs are a good deal lower.

    In weighing the relative merits of alternatives (b) and (c), he decides on (c). The case here is not at all clear-cut to him. Each seems to have minor advantages and disadvantages. He is able to justify his decision in favor of farming the whole job out by arguing that the engineering consulting firm's experience will help meet the timetable and may easily cost far less in case USCO's engineering staff runs into trouble. In effect, he decides that the value of the possible long-run future benefits in the form of better technical product knowledge is not worth the extra costs (the excess over $30,000) that may be incurred by developing the product internally.

    6. Transform the decision into action. This is not so easy in the case of all decisions, but Mr. McAdoo merely routes the project to the consulting firm.[6]

    7. Appraise the results. It is Mr. McAdoo's responsibility to see that the project is done in the required time, but this is not truly an appraisal of the results of his decision. His basic decision dealt with determining the lowest long-run cost of development of this radio. There is no way of being sure in this case (and in most cases) that he has found the lowest-cost method. Because neither of the others was tried, there is no way of saying for certain that one of them would not have been better. Furthermore, it is possible that there is another method, not considered by Mr. McAdoo, which would have been still cheaper. Perhaps USCO should not have developed a radio at all, but should simply have purchased them from some foreign firm and resold them to customers.

    If the radio is completed within the requisite time and budget limits, and if it becomes profitable for Mr. McAdoo's company, his work will be judged successful. Success in business, however, is a relative thing. Mr. McAdoo's decision will be acceptable if the device is ready in six months at a cost of $30,000 as anticipated, but he will probably never be sure that his decision was the best one possible.[7]

    [6]A well-thought-out decision is not enough to reach objectives. If the decision is to be implemented within the company, there is usually a key executive who will be the activating force. His performance will determine whether objectives are attained.

    [7]Under uncertainty, the conformity of the actual outcome with the predicted outcome is purely random.

ACCOUNTING AND SUBJECTIVE PROBABILITIES

Practicality of approach

Many accounting practitioners and businessmen shudder at the notion of using subjective probabilities to quantify things that are supposedly "intangible" or "unmeasurable" or "qualitative" or "unquantifiable." However, their position is weak simply because decisions *do* have to be made. The attempts by statisticians, mathematicians, and modern accountants to measure the unmeasurable is an old and natural chore that scientists have performed for centuries. The use of subjective probabilities merely formalizes the intuitive judgments and hunches that businessmen so often use. It forces the decision maker to expose and evaluate what he may have done unconsciously for years. This is essentially the same point that was illustrated when pricing was discussed in Chapter 13.

How can accountants make use of probability theory in practical situations? They can explicitly indicate the degree of uncertainty accompanying the budget or relevant-cost figures which they submit to management. The following four examples show how the accountant can formally inject the judgment of management into his analytical reports.

Example 1: **Vending Machine.** The figures used in many examples in previous chapters were subject to uncertainty. For simplicity, however, the future dollar amounts of sales, direct material, direct labor, and other operating costs were given as if they represented errorless predictions. Consider a new vending machine which "promises annual operating income of $1,600 before depreciation." Now this $1,600 prediction may be the wild guess of the hopeful vending-machine salesman. However, let us hope that some careful thought influenced the forecast. One technique for arriving at the $1,600 figure could be as follows:

COMPUTATION OF EXPECTED OPERATING INCOME
BEFORE DEPRECIATION

Event	Probability	Value Conditional	Value Expected
Optimistic	.3	2,100	$ 630
Most likely	.5	1,500	750
Pessimistic	.2	1,100	220
	1.0		
Weighted average (Expected value)			$1,600

The report for guiding management in this decision may, as accountants tend to visualize, show only the $1,600 figure. But managerial accountants need not restrict themselves to reporting the single figure. They may find the following more detailed report more effective:

Assumption	Operating Income Before Depreciation	Weighting By Percentage Chance of Incurrence	Computation of Weighted Average
Optimistic events	$2,100	30%	$ 630
Most likely events	1,500	50%	750
Pessimistic events	1,100	20%	220
Expected value to be used for decision			$1,600

The specific type of reporting used may take many forms. The important point is that this approach spells out explicitly what managers have always done implicitly whether they realized it or not.

Example 2: Buying Equipment.

Problem: The board of directors is faced with a decision on buying special equipment for a new product. The wisdom of the decision is ultimately dependent on total sales volume. Labor and associated variable costs per unit will be much less with the more elaborate equipment. Assume zero disposal values for the equipment:

Equipment	Total Original Cost	Variable Costs Per Unit of Product
M-1	$40,000	$4.00
M-2	95,000	3.00

Marketing executives believe that this highly specialized product will be salable only over the next year. They are highly uncertain about sales prospects, but their best judgment of sales potential at $5.00 per unit is as follows:

Total Units	Total Sales	Probability
30,000	$150,000	.2
50,000	250,000	.4
60,000	300,000	.2
70 000	350,000	.2

REQUIRED:

Prepare an analysis to guide the board's action. Prepare your own solution before examining the one that follows.

Solution.

COMPUTATION OF EXPECTED SALES IN UNITS

Event	Probability	Value (in Units)	
		Conditional	Expected
A	.2	$30,000	$ 6,000
B	.4	50,000	20,000
C	.2	60,000	12,000
D	.2	70,000	14,000
			$52,000

Costs at $260,000 sales volume (52,000 units):

$$\text{M-1: } \$40,000 + \$4.00\,(52,000) = \$248,000$$
$$\text{M-2: } \$95,000 + \$3.00\,(52,000) = \$251,000$$

Profits:

$$\text{M-1: } \$260,000 - \$248,000 = \$12,000$$
$$\text{M-2: } \$260,000 - \$251,000 = \$ 9,000$$

Therefore, buy M-1.

Example 3: Inspection or Maintenance.

Problem:[8] An automatic machine has just been readjusted by an operator. A production run of 500 parts has been scheduled. For simplicity, only four events are assumed possible:

Event	Probability
5 rejects	.7
25 rejects	.1
75 rejects	.1
125 rejects	.1
	1.0

The incremental cost of reworking a defective part is 40 cents. An expert mechanic can check the setting; he can, without fail, bring the rejects down to 5. The use of the mechanic costs $6 per setting. Should the setting be checked? Try to solve before consulting the solution.

---

[8] Adapted from an example in Schlaifer, *op. cit.*, Chapter 22.

Solution.

Do Not Check Setting

Event	Probability	Value Conditional*	Expected
A (5 rejects)	.7	$ 2.00	$ 1.40
B (25 rejects)	.1	10.00	1.00
C (75 rejects)	.1	30.00	3.00
D (125 rejects)	.1	50.00	5.00
			$10.40

*Number of rejects times $.40.

Check Setting

Event	Probability	Value Conditional	Expected
5 rejects	1.00	$ 8.00*	$ 8.00

*$6.00 for mechanic plus ($.40 times 5 rejects).

In this case, there is a $2.40 advantage in using the mechanic.[9]

Example 4: Size of Inventory.

Problem: Once a day a retailer stocks bunches of fresh-cut flowers which cost 40 cents and sell for $1.00 each. The retailer never cuts his price; leftovers are given to a nearby church. He estimates demand characteristics as follows:

Demand	Probability
0	.05
1	.20
2	.40
3	.25
4	.10
5 or more	.00
	1.00

He wants to know how many units he should stock in order to maximize profits. Try to solve before consulting the solution that follows.

---

[9]This case is expanded by Harry V. Roberts, "The New Business Statistics," *Journal of Business* (January, 1960), pp. 21–30. The article shows how the original probabilities in this situation may be modified by taking a sample of ten parts from the machine. There is also a good summary discussion of the cost and applicability of samples in decision making.

Solution. The profit, per unit sold, is $.60; the loss, per unit unsold, is $.40. All of the alternatives may be assessed in the following *payoff table.*[10]

Event: Demand	Probability of Event	Act: Units Purchased									
		0		1		2		3		4	
		C.V.*	E.V.†	C.V.	E.V.	C.V.	E.V.	C.V.	E.V.	C.V.	E.V.
0	.05	0	0	$−.40	$−.02	$− .80	$−.04	$−1.20	$−.06	$−1.60	$−.08
1	.20	0	0	.60	.12	.20	.04	− .20	−.04	− .60	−.12
2	.40	0	0	.60	.24	1.20	.48	.80	.32	.40	.16
3	.25	0	0	.60	.15	1.20	.30	1.80	.45	1.40	.35
4	.10	0	0	.60	.06	1.20	.12	1.80	.18	2.40	.24
			$0		$ .55		$ .90		$ .85		$ .55

*Conditional value.
†Expected value.

The expected value (E.V.) of any act is computed by taking a weighted average of the appropriate conditional value (C.V.) of each act. The probabilities in column 2 are used as the weighting factors. To maximize expected profit, the retailer should stock two units (E.V. = $.90).

Obtaining additional information

Sometimes the executive is hesitant about making a decision. He would like to obtain more information before making a final choice. Some additional information is nearly always obtainable—at a price. Schlaifer has suggested a technique for computing the maximum amount that should be paid for such additional information. The general idea is to compute the expected value, under ideal circumstances—that is, circumstances which would permit the retailer to predict, with absolute certainty, the number of units to be sold on any given day. A payoff table *with perfect information* would appear as follows:

Event: Demand	Probability of Event	Perfect Information	
		Conditional Value	Expected Value
0	.05	$0	$0
1	.20	.60	.12
2	.40	1.20	.48
3	.25	1.80	.45
4	.10	2.40	.24
			$1.29

[10] Schlaifer, *op. cit.*

In this table, it is assumed that the retailer will never err in his forecasts and that demand will fluctuate from zero to four exactly as indicated by the probabilities. The maximum day-in, day-out profit is $1.29. Consequently, the most he should be willing to pay for perfect advance information would be the difference between the expected value with perfect information and the expected value with existing information, $1.29 − the $.90 E.V. computed in the previous example, or 39¢. Schlaifer calls the latter the expected value of perfect information, the top price the retailer should pay for additional knowledge.

In the real world, of course, the retailer would not pay 39¢, because no amount of additional information is likely to provide perfect knowledge. But businesses often obtain additional knowledge through sampling, and sampling costs money. The executive needs a method, such as the one described at length by Schlaifer (a) of assessing the probable benefits, in relation to its cost, of additional information from sampling and (b) of determining the best sample size. In the present example, no sampling technique would be attractive if its cost, allocated to each day's operations, exceeded 39¢.

Other examples which may involve the accountant

The above examples demonstrated the basic approach to uncertainty that the accountant may take. Although professional statistical and mathematical help may be needed in complex situations, the accountant's formal recognition of uncertainty and probability theory will improve the usefulness of his reports for decision making and will strengthen his ability to interpret his everyday accounting figures. The use of probability theory is no longer fanciful conjecture. It is being used in auditing, in planning marketing strategies, in computing optimum production order-sizes where scrap is expected, in laying out repair and maintenance policies, and in countless forecasting techniques. We can expect probability theory to be used more frequently in budgeting specific costs, in computing cash flows in capital budgeting, and in a variety of other decisions.

Expected monetary value and utility

In most business cases, expected monetary value is a useful guide to action; that is, the manager chooses the act that he expects will bring the greatest financial advantage. However, there are instances where expected monetary profit will not be governing. For psychological reasons— perhaps fear of bankruptcy—managers may have *personal* evaluations that do not coincide with monetary evaluations.

For example, two businessmen may have very different attitudes toward the same situation. Suppose that they both have an opportunity to prepare a proposal at a cost of $10,000. There is a 50–50 chance that the proposal will be accepted, in which case a $25,000 net profit is sure. The expected monetary value is $7,500, computed as follows:

Event	Probability	Monetary Value	
		Conditional	Expected
Get contract	.5	$25,000	$12,500
Do not get contract	.5	−10,000	−5,000
	1.0		
		Expected monetary value	$ 7,500

The expected monetary value of not making the proposal is zero. Schlaifer comments on this situation as follows:

> *If one of them is extremely hard pressed for cash and could easily be bankrupted by the loss of $10,000, he may well decide to let this opportunity go; if the other man has adequate working capital he may with equally good reason decide to make the proposal.*
>
> *... What must be decided is simply whether it is worth taking a loss of $10,000 in order to have an even chance of a $25,000 profit, and there is* no conceivable *computation or method of analysis which will be of the least help to anyone in making such a decision—it* must *turn* entirely *on a direct expression of personal preference.*[11]

Thus, where amounts at stake are large, a dollar may not be worth a dollar to the businessman; that is, a dollar may have a *utility* value of only 70 cents (a direct expression of personal preference). Strict money value then will not be a valid guide to action. The *approach* to the decision will be the same; but in these special cases, dollar values will no longer coincide with *utility values.* So the latter will replace dollar values in the evaluation.

SUMMARY

Decisions are really choosing between alternative courses of action that have *future* outcomes which are usually uncertain. The adverse effects of this uncertainty can be minimized by becoming well informed on the subject with which the decision is concerned. The more relevant information which can be accumulated about the subject of a decision, the clearer a "correct" course of action becomes.

For new or important decisions, it is best to follow consciously a systematic pattern for decision making such as the one described in this chapter. Actual attainment of these decision steps is not often easy. Examples used in this text are simplified because the key points are isolated for study, but this is seldom so in real cases. The manager has to decide for himself what the problem is. Often the problem presented to the

[11] Schlaifer, *op. cit.,* pp. 26–27. Schlaifer discusses utility value at length (pp. 26–48). When the businessman assigns utilities (p. 48), in his judgment his *long-run* expected profit is increased by playing it safe until he has built up greater financial strength.

manager is not the real problem at all, but merely a symptom. The manager must diagnose the true difficulty before he can begin to solve it. It is often easy to think of a number of alternative courses of action in a given situation, but it is not so easy to conceive the new imaginative ones which set a brilliant manager apart from the ordinary businessman. Equally difficult is the task of predicting all the consequences, both good and bad, of a radically new course of action.

Businessmen are often prone to regard quantitative forecasts as fact just because there are accurate-looking numbers associated with them. The presence of uncertainty should influence cost comparisons. *The case illustration showed that comparisons of $10,000, $29,500, and $30,000 costs by themselves were not enough.* The $10,000 estimate was the mean and mode of a symmetrical distribution; the $29,500 estimate was the mean of a badly skewed distribution; the $30,000 estimate was a virtual certainty. Cognizance of varying probabilities is essential in the decision-making process.

The use of probability theory in business problem solving is becoming widespread. The managerial accountant will find it directly applicable for planning, control, and special decisions.

SUGGESTED READINGS

Bierman, H., *Topics in Cost Accounting and Decisions* (New York: McGraw-Hill Book Company, Inc., 1963).

Bierman, H., C. P. Bonini, L. E. Fouraker, and R. Jaedicke, *Quantitative Analysis for Business Decisions*, Rev. Ed. (Homewood, Ill.: Richard D. Irwin, Inc., 1965).

Bross, Irwin D. J., *Design for Decision* (New York: The Macmillan Company, 1953).

Chernoff, Herman, and Lincoln E. Moses, *Elementary Decision Theory* (New York: John Wiley and Sons, 1959).

Roberts, Harry, "The New Business Statistics," *Journal of Business* (January, 1960), pp. 21–30.

Schlaifer, Robert, *Probability and Statistics for Business Decisions* (New York: McGraw-Hill Book Co., Inc., 1959). Chapter 7 should be of special interest to accountants because it distinguishes between the total-cost (or profit) approach and the incremental-cost (or profit) approach. The *cost of uncertainty* is defined and demonstrated.

PROBLEMS FOR SELF-STUDY

Review the five examples by trying to compute your own solutions.

QUESTIONS, PROBLEMS, AND CASES

Note: Problems 26-16, 26-21, 26-23, 26-24, and 26-26 are particularly recommended.

26-1. Define *decision making*.

26-2. List seven steps for making decisions.

26-3. "Determining the problem is the key to successful decision making." Comment.

26-4. A fire has destroyed a factory. As the company manager, list as many possible alternative solutions as you can formulate.

26-5. "Taking no action always must be listed among alternative courses of action." Discuss.

26-6. "The management consultant is happy when he finds that his client has wholeheartedly accepted a beautiful decision program, the consultant's brainchild and product of weeks of analysis." Later the consultant's joy often becomes sadness when he finds that the decisions were never transformed into action. What is the principal reason for the apparent failure of the consultant's plans?

26-7. "The wisdom of a decision can never really be measured until the future becomes the past." What are the merits and weaknesses of a post-decision audit?

26-8. Distinguish between *risk, certainty,* and *uncertainty.*

26-9. Define *expected value.*

26-10. What steps should be taken in computing expected value?

26-11. Should the mode or mean be used as the best single quantification of an expected outcome?

26-12. Many businessmen refuse to accept marginal business at cut prices under any circumstances. They say that acceptance of such orders will hurt the industry price structure and thus boomerang to the detriment of "unmeasurable" future profits. Does the businessman base such decisions on qualitative tangible factors? Explain.

26-13. What is the major benefit of using subjective probabilities in forecasting?

26-14. What is *utility value?*

26-15. Assessment of Subjective Probabilities. Sears and Montgomery Ward faced the same general economic conditions in the decade after World War II. Ward's policy was to keep a relatively large proportion of its assets in liquid form, whereas Sears invested heavily in expansion of operations.

REQUIRED:

Comment on the influence of subjective probabilities on the chief executives.

26-16. Role of Uncertainty in Forecasts. Refer to Problem 13-10. The forecast of $150,000 of sales per year was arrived at by the owner and his brother-in-law, who runs a car-washing palace on the opposite side of town. They had made a thorough study of the market potential and had arrived at the following estimates:

Sales	Probability
$100,000	.1
130,000	.2
160,000	.5
180,000	.2
	1.0

REQUIRED:

Show how the $150,000 forecast was decided upon.

26-17. Selection of Production Plan.* Assume that the XYZ Company manufactures the Gadget, in which a Gismo is installed. The Gismo costs $10, but if and when a Gadget is returned because of a defective Gismo, the replacement cost of such will be $25 because of special handling and the necessary dismantling of the Gadget. Prior to the installation of such Gismo, these alternatives are available to management:

(1) If the Gismos are tested by random sampling, it is believed that quality can be controlled so that only 3 per cent of the installed Gismos will be defective. The average cost of such sampling, per Gadget, is $.10.

(2) All Gismos can be tested and no replacements will be necessary. The average cost is $1.50.

(3) The manufacturer of the Gismo will guarantee that 92 per cent will be good. The cost of replacing Gismos in excess of this 8 per cent level will be borne by such manufacturer. However, the price per Gismo will be $10.25.

REQUIRED:

Assume that annual production is 100,000 units. Select an alternative. Show computations.

26-18. Marketing a New Product; Selection of Equipment. The Ardo Company makes specialty items that are sold through novelty stores. The demand for specific items is difficult to predict. Yet long experience is helpful in predicting the probable range of sales volumes for most items.

The president must decide on whether to manufacture and market a new item which will sell for $2.00 per unit. If the item is produced, one of the following types of special equipment will be used. The equipment will be scrapped after the selling season is over:

	Special Equipment	
	A	B
Cost of equipment	$50,000	$100,000
Variable production cost per unit	$1.39	$.90

No matter which equipment is chosen, batches of production may be closely geared to demand so that no unsold units will be left after the season is over.

The president and other executives have assigned the following probabilities to the range of anticipated sales volumes:

Sales Volume in Units	Probability
50,000	.30
100,000	.40
150,000	.20
200,000	.10
	1.00

*Adapted from Malcom Pye, "Reasons, Probabilities, and Accounting Principles," *Accounting Review* (July, 1960), pp. 440–441.

REQUIRED (Show computations):

1. Assuming that profit maximization is the sole objective, which course of action should be taken?
2. What sales volume in units would show identical profits regardless of the choice of machine?

26-19. Competitive Bidding. A road-building company gets contracts by competitive bidding. It has estimated that its costs on a particular project will be $100,000. Based on past experience, the president anticipates the following probabilities of bids:

Bid*	Probability of Bid
$ 90,000	.05
100,000	.10
110,000	.20
120,000	.30
130,000	.25
140,000	.10
150,000	.00
	1.00

*For simplicity, assume that bids must be in $10,000 units.

REQUIRED:

The company's objective is to maximize expected profit. What bid should be made? Show computations.

26-20. Setting Prices and Uncertainty. Assume that the unit cost of a product is known with certainty to be $1.60 each. The top executives are trying to decide whether to set a selling price of $2.00 or of $2.20. The top price has been $2.00 for the past 30 months. Average monthly sales are forecasted as follows:

At a Price of $2.00	
Units	Probability
1,050	.05
1,000	.90
950	.05

At a Price of $2.20	
Units	Probability
800	.10
750	.60
700	.30

REQUIRED:

Which is the optimal price? Show computations.

26-21. Uncertainty and Cost-Volume-Profit Analysis.* The Jaedicke and Robichek Company is considering two new products to introduce. Either can be produced by using present facilities. Each product requires an increase in annual fixed expenses of $400,000. Each product has the same selling price and variable cost per unit, $10 and $8, respectively.

Management, after studying past experience with similar products, has prepared the following subjective probability distribution:

Events (Units Demanded)	Probability— Product A	Probability— Product B
50,000	—	.1
100,000	.1	.1
200,000	.2	.1
300,000	.4	.2
400,000	.2	.4
500,000	.1	.1
	1.00	1.00

REQUIRED:

1. What is the breakeven point for each product?
2. Which product should be chosen? Why? Show computations.
3. Suppose that management was absolutely certain that 300,000 units of Product B would be sold. Which product should be chosen? Why? What benefits are available to management from the provision of the complete probability distribution instead of just a lone expected value?

26-22. Expected Value Tables. As an appliance dealer, you may be deciding on how to service your one-year warranty on the 1,000 color television sets that you have just sold to a large local hotel. You have three alternatives:

1. A reputable service firm has offered to service the sets, including all parts and labor, for a flat fee of $18,000.
2. For $15,000, another reputable service firm would furnish all necessary parts and provide up to 1,000 service calls at no charge. Service calls in excess of that number would be $4 each. The number of calls are likely to be:

Event	Chance of Occurrence	Probability of Occurrence	Total Cost
A: 1,000 calls or less	50%	.5	$15,000
B: 1,500 calls	20	.2	17,000
C: 2,000 calls	20	.2	19,000
D: 2,500 calls	10	.1	21,000
	100%	1.0	

*Adapted from Robert K. Jaedicke and Alexander A. Robichek, "Cost-Volume-Profit Analysis under Conditions of Uncertainty," *The Accounting Review* (October, 1964), pp. 917–926.

3. You can hire your own labor and buy your own parts. Your past experience with similar work has helped you to formulate the following probabilities and costs:

Event	Chance of Occurrence	Probability of Occurrence	Total Cost
A: Little trouble	10%	.1	$ 8,000
B: Medium trouble	70	.7	10,000
C: Much trouble	20	.2	30,000
	100%	1.0	

REQUIRED:

Using expected value tables, compare the three alternatives. Which plan do you favor? Why?

26-23. Inventory Levels and Sales Forecasting. The owner of a small bakery must decide on how many dozens of a new kind of petite sweet roll to bake each day. He estimates it will cost him 15¢ per dozen to bake the new roll, which can then be sold for 35¢ per dozen. However, if the rolls are not sold during the day on which they are baked, the baker is certain that any unsold can be sold the next day for 10¢ per dozen. Though he has never sold this type of roll before, his experience leads him to assess probable demand as follows:

1st Month:

Demand (dozen per day)	Probability
Less than 3	.00
3	.10
4	.25
5	.45
6	.20
7 or more	.00

2nd Month and thereafter:

Demand (dozen per day)	Probability
Less than 3	.00
3	.00
4	.15
5	.35
6	.40
7	.10
8 or more	.00

How many dozen rolls should he bake each day for the first month? The second month?

26-24. Value of Perfect Information. In the previous problem, assume that the local witch goes into a trance every night, during which she forecasts the exact demand for sweet rolls for the next day. What would be the baker's expected profit per day? How much would the baker be willing to pay the witch for this information? Do this for both time periods referred to above.

26-25. Probabilities and a New Product. James Doyle is trying to assess the profit potential for a new novelty product, a Batman toy auto. Doyle is experienced in the novelty market and is well qualified to assess the auto's chances for success. He is certain that sales will not be less than 25,000 units. Plant capacity limits total sales to a maximum of 80,000 units during the auto's brief life. Doyle thinks that there are two chances in five for a sales volume of 50,000 units. The probability that sales will exceed 50,000 units is four times the probability that they will be less than 50,000.

If sales are less than 50,000, he feels quite certain that they will be 25,000 units. If sales exceed 50,000, unit volumes of 60,000 and 80,000 are equally likely. A 70,000-unit volume is four times as likely as either.

Variable production costs are $3 per unit, selling price is $5, and the special manufacturing equipment (which has no salvage value or alternate use) and promotional outlays will cost $125,000. Assume, for simplicity, that the above-mentioned are the only possible sales volumes.

Should the Batman toy auto be produced? Show detailed computations.

26-26. Relevant Costs, Probabilities, Discounted Cash Flow, and Pricing. The Vang Construction Company is bidding on a construction contract. If the bid is accepted, work will begin in a few days, on January 1, 19x1. Ten thousand units of material X will be needed at that date. The company currently has 10,000 units, originally costing a total of $10,000, of this material in stock. The current purchase cost of material X is $1.20 per unit. The company could sell material X now for $.80 per unit after all selling costs.

If this current contract is not landed, material X could be used on another job to begin in one year, on January 1, 19x2. Then the company would not need to buy a substitute material at $1.02 per unit.

If it is not used in either of these ways, material X would be of no use to the company and would be sold a year hence, probably for $.80 per unit, net. The president estimates that the probability of using material X on the other job is .70.

The president of the construction company is puzzled about the appropriate total cost of material X to be used in bidding on the current contract. That is, he has assembled the following data:

	Total Costs
Miscellaneous materials	$ 40,000
Material X, 10,000 units	?
Direct labor	60,000
Relevant overhead	30,000
	$xxx,xxx

Competition is intense and mark-ups are thin. He asks you to suggest the appropriate total cost figure for material X. Show all computations, carefully labeled, and state all assumptions made. The minimum desired rate of return is 10 per cent per annum; assume that the present value at 10 per cent of $1.00 to be received one year hence is .900.

cost accounting and statistical methods

CHAPTER XXVII

The accountant is no longer the only individual who offers practical quantitative techniques to aid the administrator. Applications of statistics and mathematics to business problems are becoming widespread. The remaining two chapters in this text will survey the roles of statistics and mathematics in modern business. As a minimum, accountants need to be aware of the existence of the statistical and mathematical tools that promise to have a lasting impact on future accounting practice.

WHAT STATISTICS OFFERS

Sampling applications

Statistics is a body of methods for making optimum decisions in the face of uncertainty. The most powerful statistical tools are sampling techniques. A *sample* is a portion of a group (population or universe) chosen to estimate some characteristic of the entire group without complete examination of all the items constituting the group. *Proper* use of sampling theory can improve accounting practice, lessen the reliance on purely subjective judgment, and reduce the ever-mounting "costs of keeping track of costs." In other words, prudent use of statistical tools can lead to better planning and control at less administrative cost.

For example, certain airlines use samples to settle interline debts. Vance describes the approach as follows:

> *The problem of interline revenue settlements is a substantial one and is growing larger. For example, United Air Lines picks up over 100,000 coupons per month from*

tickets sold by other airlines. Furthermore, there are more than 60 possible fares for a trip from Chicago to New York to take a single case.... A stratified sample of the coupons is taken, the strata being first class, coach, military, and others. The sample is selected by taking a number from 1 to 10 at random and picking the coupons that have this number as the last digit in the ticket number.... Then the tickets selected for the sample are priced in the usual way. This total is then multiplied by the ratio of the sample size to the total lot size and this estimate of the total amount due on the whole batch of tickets is billed to the airline that sold the tickets.... A representative of United estimates that in a year's billing of $7,000,000 the error will be plus or minus $3,400. In United's case the yearly cost of billing one carrier on the old basis is $15,000, so the saving is substantial.[1]

Sampling has also been used for estimating spoilage, determining product costs, test-checking vouchers and other business documents for clerical accuracy, estimating complete physical inventories, confirming accounts receivable, aging accounts receivable, detecting weaknesses in internal control, costing sales where there are many low-cost products, and a variety of inspection procedures.

Sampling techniques are especially useful in inspection procedures. The idea is to decide on the quality of an entire lot (universe) on the basis of a sample. Statistical techniques are used to determine the proper size of the sample, which is dependent on the reliability and precision desired by management.

Clearly, sampling techniques offer opportunities to get useful information more quickly and at less cost than by processing great masses of accounting data. The increasing business use of sampling techniques is bound to continue, because their usefulness is being more widely understood and their cost advantages are often impressive.

Validity of samples

Many people have a natural aversion to jumping to conclusions about a universe on the basis of a sample. They cherish the notion that only a 100 per cent inspection or a 100 per cent collection of machine times will yield perfection or will give the real story on performance. Statistically, this viewpoint is valid, but in practice it is not only impractical but psychologically invalid. Human beings do the inspecting and collecting of data; weariness and human errors will prevent attaining perfection in a 100 per cent inspection.

Statistical sampling can get equivalent or better accuracy than a 100 per cent count:

...the greater accuracy is possible because sample surveys can often be more carefully designed, personnel can be better trained and supervised, and special problems can be followed up more easily with a sample survey than with a census.[2]

[1] Lawrence L. Vance, "A Review of Developments in Statistical Sampling for Accountants," *Accounting Review* (January, 1960), pp. 24–25.

[2] Vance and Neter, *Statistical Sampling for Auditors and Accountants* (New York: John Wiley & Sons, Inc., 1956), p. 12.

The most widely used statistical sampling application in business is known as *statistical quality control* (SQC). We shall now see how the objectives of SQC closely parallel the objectives of standard cost accounting.

STATISTICAL QUALITY CONTROL AND STANDARD COSTS

Difficulties in analysis of variances

The heart of managerial use of standard costs is the analysis of variances.[3] Variances signal the need for managerial investigation so that control may be kept effective and better ways of doing things may be discovered. But there is a danger here. Which variances are significant enough to warrant investigation? Are significant variances overlooked because they offset one another to show an apparently satisfactory condition?

Management tends to use judgment in deciding whether or not a variance on a given item deserves investigation. For some items, any tiny variance from standard may spark scrutiny. For other items, 5, 10, or 25 per cent variances from standard may be necessary to spur follow-ups. These judgments generally grow from the experience and know-how of the executives involved. Guesses or hunches are fundamental parts of managerial behavior; yet these subjective methods often engender management disagreements and barren investigations.

Another difficulty is that the accounting system often compiles variances for a period of time. A cost-conscious management will follow up variances quickly—sometimes daily or even hourly. But delayed reports and everyday busy work often allow variances to accumulate so that it becomes too late to find out what caused the variances. Further, favorable and unfavorable variances are frequently combined, so that significant variances may be offset in accounts and in management reports. Each overtime authorization, for example, is an incremental decision and should not be related to average rates of overtime allowances. This combination of delayed reporting and cost accumulations that represent a conglomeration of different operations makes it difficult to find causes for variances and to trace causes for them below the foreman level to individual machines, men, and materials.

In summary, the accountant often grinds out variances without any indication of their significance. When should management be concerned about a given variance? Frequently the answer to such a question is based on subjective judgments, guesses, or hunches. The field of statistics offers tools to help reduce these subjective features of variance analysis.

---

[3] *Variance* is used throughout this book to denote a deviation between a planned cost and an "actual" cost. In statistics, *variance* is defined as the square of the standard deviation.

Standard as a band rather than a single measure

The standard cost accounting system is built upon a set of standards. Standards, in their purest sense, are measures of performance expressed in physical terms—gallons, pounds, labor time taken, dimensions, color, hardness. The "right" standard is generally defined as very efficient performance under a given set of operating methods, working conditions, and skills. The conversion of physical standards into dollar standards is achieved by applying appropriate price tags to the operation under review. Note especially that the accountant's system views a standard as a *single* acceptable measure.

Practically, the accountant and everybody else realizes that the standard is a *band* or *range* of possible acceptable outcomes. In other words, the performance (and costs) ought to be generated by a well-behaved underlying process. If the process is not behaving, it may be economical to intervene to make it behave better. For example, a foreman may expect a machine operator to produce an average of 100 bearing brackets per hour. If he notices that 105 are being turned out the first hour; 98 the second; 103 the third; and 95 the fourth, he may consider such a variation in performance to be *normal*. However, if the performance falls to 85 and then jumps to 120, he may consider the performance *abnormal* and worth investigating. Statistical quality control offers techniques for distinguishing between normal and abnormal variances. The *control chart*, originated in the 1920's by Dr. Walter A. Shewhart, of the Bell Telephone Laboratories, is the major device for communicating these distinctions.

Purpose of control charts

The statistical control chart has been developed in the field of statistical quality control. The problems attacked by quality control procedures are broader than the word *quality* suggests. For example, SQC techniques may deal with the time per labor operation or the quantity of material used in a product.

Control charts use samples as a way of isolating operating situations that need managerial investigation. These charts help sharpen managerial control by disclosing current situations—not situations too old for fruitful scrutiny. The programmed taking of samples detects variances which otherwise go unnoticed.

A control chart looks like the chart in Exhibit 27-1. Assume that average performance for assembling a finished unit is 10.5 minutes, that the upper control limit is 13 minutes, and that the lower control limit is 8 minutes.

The accountant who has a statistical approach to variance analysis thinks along the following lines:

> *Measured quality of manufactured product is always subject to a certain amount of variation as a result of chance. Some stable "system of chance causes" is inherent*

in any particular scheme of production and inspection. Variation within this stable pattern is inevitable. The reasons for variation outside this stable pattern may be discovered and corrected.[4]

The control chart is a way of looking at a process to see how it is behaving. The chart helps distinguish chance variances (also called *random causes*) from variances that need investigation (often called *assignable causes*). The analysis of the latter helps to obtain improvements in products and processes. The identification of chance variances avoids unnecessary investigations of variances and eliminates frequent changes (for example, machine settings) that may tend to increase rather than to decrease the variability of the process.

EXHIBIT 27-1

CONTROL CHART

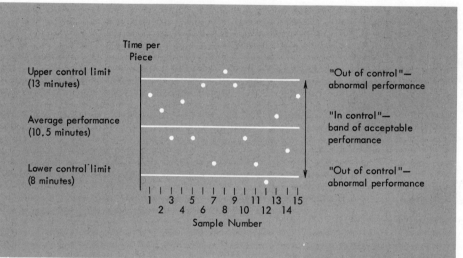

Statistical control charts are applicable to any repetitive manufacturing or nonmanufacturing operation. Examples include billing errors, filling containers, boring, turning, stamping, using materials and supplies, printing errors, customer complaints, sales returns, orders received, travel expenses, and the like.

State of statistical control

The control chart helps to decide whether a process (operation) is in a *state of statistical control. A process is said to be in the state of statistical*

---

[4] Eugene Grant, *Statistical Quality Control*, 3rd ed., (New York: McGraw-Hill Book Company, Inc., 1964), p. 3. This is a lucid book-length treatment of the entire field.

control if the variation is such as would occur in random sampling from some stable population. If this is the case, the variation among the items, is attributable to chance—is inherent in the nature of the process. There is no point in seeking special causes for individual cases, because random variations are beyond management's ability to regulate or eliminate. With a given process and a given state of knowledge about the process, this chance variation is either impossible or impracticable to reduce. If the performance of a process is considered to be unsatisfactory even though it is statistically in control, the only remedy is some change in the process.[5]

The probability is small that a point will fall outside the control limits from chance causes alone; so it is concluded that the process is out of control when this occurs. When the process is out of control, it is often possible to locate specific causes for the variation. Removal of these causes improves the future performance of the process.

This statistical approach saves effort in the investigation of variances which are chance occurrences. On the other hand, this tool offers a practical method of determining which variances are significant.

Wallis and Roberts point out:[6]

> *When the process is in control, one may predict future performance on the basis of past performance. Note that statistical control does not judge whether the process (operation) is satisfactory; it only judges whether it is in a state of statistical control and hence predictable.*

Illustration of control chart

The Basic Data. Consider the following example. Assume that a sample study is made of hand-assembly operation on a transistor radio. Samples of the time spent to assemble one unit are taken twice a day, in mid-morning and mid-afternoon. Four units are included in each sample. Observations are continued for two weeks, so that 20 samples are collected. The results are shown in Exhibit 27-2. Each figure in a sample is the actual time taken to assemble one unit.

Two key figures are computed for each sample, the arithmetic mean ($\bar{X}$, called "X bar") and the range (R). The calculations for Sample (1) are as follows:

$$\bar{X} = 12 + 11 + 10 + 9 \text{ divided by } 4$$
$$\bar{X} = 42 \div 4 = 10.50$$
$$R = \text{largest figure in sample minus smallest figure}$$
$$R = 12 - 9 = 3$$

Similar calculations are made for each of the 20 samples.

The next steps are (a) to average the averages, that is, to obtain the grand mean ($\bar{\bar{X}}$) of the means ($\bar{X}$), and (b) to obtain the average ($\bar{R}$) of

---

[5] Wallis and Roberts, *Statistics: A New Approach* (Glencoe, Ill.: The Free Press, 1956), p. 495.

[6] *Ibid.*, p. 496.

EXHIBIT 27-2

MEASUREMENT OF TIME SPENT PER UNIT
Two Samples Taken Daily for 10 Days

Sample Number	Time spent on each of four items within samples				Arithmetic Mean $\overline{X}$	Range R
1	12	11	10	9	10.50	3
2	10	10	9	11	10.00	2
3	13	11	10	9	10.75	4
4	10	9	8	11	9.50	3
5	12	11	10	10	10.75	2
6	11	11	14	9	11.25	5
7	10	9	12	10	10.25	3
8	11	12	10	11	11.00	2
9	13	9	10	10	10.50	4
10	11	9	10	10	10.00	2
11	11	11	11	10	10.75	1
12	8	14	10	10	10.50	6
13	10	11	9	11	10.25	2
14	12	10	9	10	10.25	3
15	8	10	10	12	10.00	4
16	11	10	10	9	10.00	2
17	13	10	9	11	10.75	4
18	11	8	10	13	10.50	5
19	10	9	13	12	11.00	4
20	13	12	8	13	11.50	5
				Totals	210.00	66
				Grand arithmetic mean	10.50 $(\overline{\overline{X}})$	3.3 $(\overline{R})$

the ranges. These calculations follow:

$$\overline{\overline{X}} = \text{Sum of } \overline{X}\text{'s divided by number of samples}$$
$$\overline{\overline{X}} = 210.00 \div 20 = 10.50$$
$$\overline{R} = \text{Sum of } R\text{'s divided by number of samples}$$
$$\overline{R} = 66 \div 20 = 3.3$$

Standard deviation

The standard deviation[7] is an integral part of the theory underlying the setting of control limits. The standard deviation is the most
widely used measure of dispersion around the mean. Statisticians use the
Greek letter *sigma*, σ, to denote a standard deviation.

[7] Standard deviation is the square root of the mean of the squared deviations. A
deviation is the difference between an individual observation and the mean of the
data.

The purpose here is to show how the standard deviation can be a central part of the control-chart concept rather than to dwell on the theoretical justification for its use. Any basic book on statistics will show detailed explanations of the calculation and concept of standard deviation.

Theory of control chart

Trueblood and Cyert state:

> *The theory of the control chart is based on the behavior of the sample means. As long as the universe can be reasonably approximated by a normal distribution, it can be safely assumed that the distribution of arithmetic means will be normally distributed. Even where the universe is abnormal, the distribution of the sample means will usually approach a normal distribution if the sample is sufficiently large.*[8]

In practice the means (averages) of small samples—samples of four are widely used—are plotted successively on a control chart. These means will approach a normal (bell-shaped) distribution. Statistical tables of the normal distribution will show what proportions of the observations ($\overline{X}$) will be within a given distance of $\overline{\overline{X}}$, measuring the distance as multiples of sigma ($\sigma_{\overline{x}}$). To be specific, 68.27 per cent of the observations will be in the interval $\overline{\overline{X}} \pm 1$ sigma, 95.45 per cent in the interval $\overline{\overline{X}} \pm 2$ sigmas, and 99.73 per cent in the interval $\overline{\overline{X}} \pm 3$ sigmas.

As shown in Exhibit 27-3, the control chart often uses $\overline{\overline{X}} \pm 3$ sigmas as *upper and lower control limits*. Each successive $\overline{X}$ is plotted, and, if they are normally distributed, only about three in a thousand will fall outside the control limits as long as the universe does not change.

Setting the limits

Statistical tables are available for setting control limits when $\overline{\overline{X}}$, $\overline{R}$, and the sample size are known. The detailed work is really finished, because we need not bother calculating the standard deviation (this is often a laborious task). The table to be used is called "Factors for Determining from $\overline{R}$ the 3-Sigma Control Limits for $\overline{X}$ and R Charts." Do not let the imposing title scare you. Refer to Exhibit 27-4 and find the line for $n = 4$ as you study the following computations of control limits:

For $\overline{X}$:

$$\text{Control limits} = \overline{\overline{X}} \pm A_2\overline{R}$$
$$= 10.5 \pm .73\,(3.3)$$
$$= 10.50 \pm 2.41$$

$$\text{Upper control limit,} \quad UCL_{\overline{x}} = 12.91$$
$$\text{Lower control limit,} \quad LCL_{\overline{x}} = 8.09$$

[8] Robert M. Trueblood and Richard M. Cyert, *Sampling Techniques in Accounting* (Englewood Cliffs, N.J.: Prentice-Hall, Inc., 1957), p. 145.

EXHIBIT 27-3

RELATIONSHIP BETWEEN NORMAL DISTRIBUTION AND CONTROL CHART

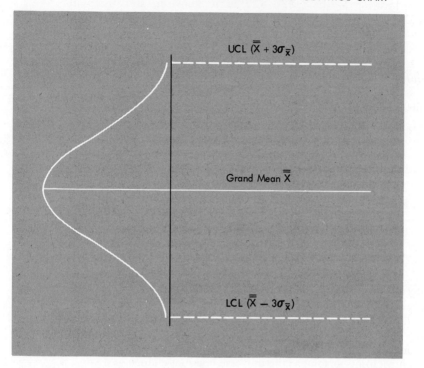

UCL $(\bar{\bar{X}} + 3\sigma_{\bar{x}})$

Grand Mean $\bar{\bar{X}}$

LCL $(\bar{\bar{X}} - 3\sigma_{\bar{x}})$

For R:

$$
\begin{aligned}
\text{Upper control} \qquad &= D_4\bar{R} \\
UCL_r &= 2.28\,(3.3) \\
UCL_r &= 7.524 \\
\text{Lower control limit} \qquad &= D_3\bar{R} \\
LCL_r &= 0\,(3.3) \\
LCL_r &= 0
\end{aligned}
$$

Note that factors A_2, D_3, and D_4 are contained in the statistical table of Exhibit 27-4. They are based on the concept of standard deviation. Such tables are widely used in practice.

$$
\begin{aligned}
\text{Upper control limit for } \bar{X} &= UCL_{\bar{x}} = \bar{\bar{X}} + A_2\bar{R} \\
\text{Lower control limit for } \bar{X} &= LCL_{\bar{x}} = \bar{\bar{X}} - A_2\bar{R}
\end{aligned}
$$

(If aimed-at or standard value $\bar{X}'$ is used rather than $\bar{\bar{X}}$ as the central line on the control chart, $\bar{X}'$ should be substituted for $\bar{\bar{X}}$ in the preceding formulas.)

EXHIBIT 27-4[9]

FACTORS FOR DETERMINING FROM $\bar{R}$ THE
3-SIGMA CONTROL LIMITS FOR $\bar{X}$ AND R CHARTS

Number of Observations in Subgroup n	Factor for $\bar{X}$ Chart A_2	Factors for R Chart	
		Lower Control Limit D_3	Upper Control Limit D_4
2	1.88	0	3.27
3	1.02	0	2.57
4	0.73	0	2.28
5	0.58	0	2.11
6	0.48	0	2.00
7	0.42	0.08	1.92
8	0.37	0.14	1.86
9	0.34	0.18	1.82
10	0.31	0.22	1.78
11	0.29	0.26	1.74
12	0.27	0.28	1.72
13	0.25	0.31	1.69
14	0.24	0.33	1.67
15	0.22	0.35	1.65
16	0.21	0.36	1.64
17	0.20	0.38	1.62
18	0.19	0.39	1.61
19	0.19	0.40	1.60
20	0.18	0.41	1.59

Upper control limit for $R \; = \; UCL_R \; = \; D_4\bar{R}$
Lower control limit for $R \; = \; LCL_R \; = \; D_3\bar{R}$

All factors above are based on the normal distribution.

Plotting

All the data are now ready for preparation of a control chart. The $\bar{X}$ chart is shown in Exhibit 27-5. Sample numbers appear on the horizontal scale, while the $\bar{X}$'s are measured on the vertical scale. First, lines for $\bar{\bar{X}}$ and the control limits are plotted. Then $\bar{X}$ for each sample is plotted. No observations are outside the control limits, so the process is apparently in control as far as the sample means are concerned. If any observations were outside the control limits, they would signal the need for investigation.

[9] Grant, *op. cit.*, p. 563.

EXHIBIT 27-5

CONTROL CHART FOR X̄

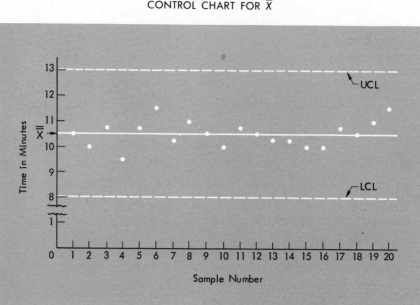

The *R* Chart is shown in Exhibit 27-6. Sample numbers appear on the horizontal scale, while *R*'s of each sample are measured on the vertical scale. The process also seems to be in control as far as the range is concerned.

Caution is needed here. Given certain men, materials, machines, and methods, the process or operation may be statistically in control. However, this does not mean that the process or operation is beyond change or improvement. All it means is that variations from an average or standard have been measured, and that these variations are apparently due to random causes.

Observations out of control

A sample mean that falls outside the control limits or a "run" of observations that fall on one side of X̄ are signals for managerial investigation. Samples may be taken hourly, daily, upon completion of a run, or at any other suitable time. Consider the following samples that are out of control (plot them on their respective charts to see for yourself):

Sample Number	Time Spent on Each of Four Items Within Samples				Arithmetic Mean X̄	Range R
21	13	15	12	15	13.75	3
22	7	10	15	11	10.75	8

EXHIBIT 27-6

CONTROL CHART FOR R

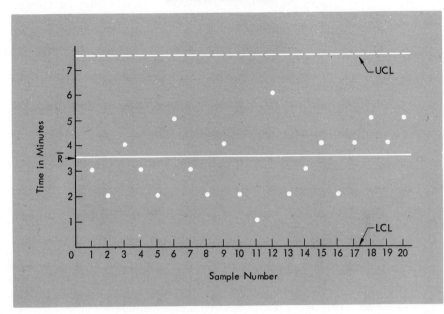

Sample Number

Sample 21 indicates a marked upward shift in average time spent per unit, although the range is in control. There may be several reasons for this. Perhaps the sample was taken very late on a Friday afternoon or very early on a Monday morning, or the weather was oppressive, or the worker(s) was just learning. Remedial action would be taken as soon as causes for the out-of-control situation were discovered. The conventional accounting system may easily bury such information in a mass of other detail, or the information may be found too late for management either to discover the cause or to take corrective action. The chief drawback of many accounting systems is their failure to pick out key numbers that require quick action.

Sample 22 has a mean in control but a range that is out of control. The investigation of such a marked dispersion in performance often finds new and better ways of doing things—methods, motions, machine settings, and the like.

The R chart is not used in industry nearly as much as the $\overline{X}$ chart is used. R rarely goes out of control, while $\overline{X}$ frequently does. Thus, the clerical costs of keeping R charts sometimes may be avoided without much loss in useful data.[10]

---

[10] Edwin Gaynor, "Use of Control Charts in Cost Control," *N.A.A. Bulletin* (June, 1954).

STATISTICAL MEAN AND STANDARDS

How can the managerial notion of standards be reconciled with the statistical mean used on control charts? There are two situations. The first is the setting of tight standards as incentives, a situation in which management normally expects unfavorable variances. In these cases, the statistical mean and the standard will not coincide.

In the second situation, where management desires the standard to be currently attainable, the control-chart mean and the standard may coincide. Properly used, the control chart helps in the setting of currently attainable standards and in the signalling that either the standards are unrealistic or that the operation is no longer in control *in terms of its physical "natural" standard*.

The control chart can be helpful in setting standards because it indicates the random variability of the results and gives an indication of how tight an attainable standard may be.

The control chart's spotlighting of assignable favorable or unfavorable variances leads to the study of operations that are *worth* investigating. It is designed to strike an economical balance between (a) the costs of barren, costly chasing-down of variances that are really random and (b) the cost of ignoring important changes in the behavior of the process.

In other words, well-conceived attainable standards explicitly or implicitly will automatically consider average (statistical-mean) performance. This performance is based on observations of an efficient operation. Thus, the control-chart mean and the physical standard go hand in hand; ideally, the control-chart mean *is* the standard, where the standard is supposed to be currently attainable.

All manufacturing processes have some natural variability, depending on the characteristics of elements of the process—machines, men, materials, and methods. The control chart helps determine the amount of this random variability and thus helps determine the reasonableness of the standards. Thus, if standard labor time for performing a drilling operation is four minutes, and control charts reveal a large random variability so that many drill operations will be outside the standard time limits, at least one of two things may happen. Standards may be revised, or the operation itself may be studied for possible carelessness of the operators or faulty machine settings.

Control limits not only spotlight assignable causes (those that deserve investigation) but also indicate when *not* to take detective action regarding variances. Sometimes operators or managers waste too much time on setups or machine settings and thus cause an observation to be outside the control limits. Investigation of such an observation points out this fault.

The chart and the individual

Many companies favor exhibiting multi-color quality-control charts near individual machines or processes. The operator may then examine his own performance, which is posted as each sample is taken. This public scorecard spurs people toward improved performance in most cases, although there is some controversy as to whether or not this psychological technique is effective in all cases.

Engineering tolerance limits

It is often fruitful to compare the statistical control patterns of a process against the specification limits as determined by engineers or draftsmen as "engineered standards or tolerances."[11]

> **Example.** The diameter of a special machine bolt had specifications of .250 ± .002 inches. There was much production trouble in attaining this tolerance and a high rejection rate upon inspection. The foreman insisted that a ±.002-inch tolerance could not be attained with existing equipment. The experienced engineer who had specified the tolerance insisted that it could be attained.
>
> To resolve the dispute, painstaking statistical sample studies were made on a typical week's production. Both foreman and engineer agreed that the equipment, tools, jigs, and other requirements were satisfactory.
>
> The pattern of results is shown in Exhibit 27-7. The "natural" statistical control limits were ±.005 inches, so all agreed that the ±.002-inch tolerance could not be normally met with the existing process.

Four alternatives are usually available in these situations:

1. Widen the tolerance. This is often feasible and an obvious solution.

2. Buy new equipment.

3. Continue to produce the bolts to this tolerance using existing equipment and expecting a high rate of rejects. This solution is frequently the one found where better productive equipment is unavailable and where narrow tolerances are absolutely necessary because of safety requirements or the economic importance of the final finished product. Examples would be aircraft parts or missile components.

4. Completely re-examine and redesign the process. This involves reviewing such aspects as materials, skills, machines, specifications, and methods.

This case showed that control charts may reveal performance within statistical control but well outside the engineering tolerance limits. This would give the production manager or foreman valid evidence of the unreasonableness of the tolerance limits. In this case, chance variation was the reason for inability to meet tolerances. So again control charts often tell management what *not* to do; it would be fruitless to exert managerial pressure for improvement in performance under the given conditions.

On the other hand, control charts may reveal processes which perform well within the tolerance limits. In these cases, lower-cost alter-

---

[11] See A. V. Feigenbaum, *Quality Control* (New York: McGraw-Hill Book Company, Inc., 1951), for a discussion, comparison, and many examples.

natives may not be available. But perhaps either full advantage is not being taken of the precision or capabilities of process facilities, or too high-cost men, materials, or equipment are being used in relation to the product needs.

EXHIBIT 27-7

CHART OF RELATIONSHIPS BETWEEN SPECIFICATION LIMITS AND STATISTICAL CONTROL LIMITS

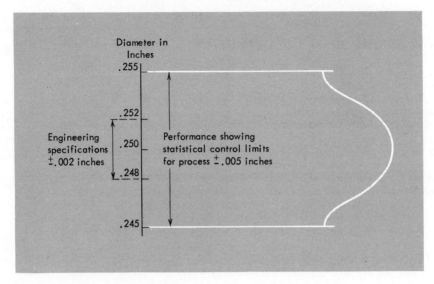

SETTING CONTROL LIMITS

Statistical control limits, as usually calculated, are based on the proven concept that a population of means of repeated random samples from a fixed universe will vary in a foreseeable manner (the normal curve). The control chart implements carefully developed, tested principles. It circumvents the arbitrary, inconsistent features of fitful analysis of variances.

Although control limits should ideally be tailored to the case at hand, limits at $X \pm 3$ sigmas are used most often in practice. Sometimes two-sigma limits are used, but this increases the frequency of false alarms —the appearance of "assignable" variations that are often really random.

The accountant or statistician will get into more personal trouble by sounding false alarms than by occasionally overlooking real assignable causes. Of course, if he drew the control limits at 10 sigmas, he would never sound any false alarm; on the other hand, he would almost never detect assignable causes of even a gross sort.[12]

[12] Wallis and Roberts, *op. cit.*, p. 508.

The appropriate basis for setting control limits is a comparison of the costs of the two types of errors in a given case. One type of error is sounding an alarm on an observation that is really random (setting the control limits too narrow). The other type is failure to detect assignable causes (setting the control limits too wide).[13] However, three-sigma limits are used most widely as a workable rule of thumb instead of tailoring limits to each case. Grant points out:

> The real basis for the use of 3-sigma limits ... is experience that when closer limits, such as 2-sigma, are used, the control chart often gives indication of assignable causes of variation that simply cannot be found, whereas when 3-sigma limits are used and points fall out of control, a diligent search will usually disclose the assignable causes of variation.[14]

Although three-sigma limits are widely used, some highly re-spected statisticians favor an approach which has two unconventional aspects. First, one plots the chart without control limits and makes up one's mind intuitively as to what action is indicated. Cycles, trends, sharp drops, and so forth, may give clues for investigation. Second, one plots each observation instead of the means of small samples, because the latter tend to be normally distributed even when the original process is not. Knowing what the original process is like is often very important.[15]

OTHER APPLICATIONS OF STATISTICS

Statistical tools such as sampling and control charts can be helpful in approaching a wide variety of problems, such as (a) providing more economical inspection procedures via sampling; (b) discovering in a drift of the process away from the desired level predictions of approaching troubles; (c) analyzing relationships between scrap, spoilage, and good output so that accurate forecasts of cost behavior and product costs can be formulated; and (d) appraising budget forecasts and subsequent devia-tions in terms of the normal curve and the standard deviation.

---

[13] Certain statistical tools are used to make this comparison. But a discussion of these techniques is beyond the scope of this text. Essentially, it is a matter of finding the limits that will minimize the total costs of both types of errors. Limits at two sigmas or less are often found in chemical industries because the cost of making adjustments in the process is negligible.

[14] Grant, *op. cit.*, p. 104.

[15] Feng-shyang Luh, *Controlled Cost: An Operational Concept and Statistical Approach to Standard Costing* (Unpublished Ph. D. Dissertation, The Ohio State University, 1965), objects to the notion of standard cost as being a range of cost with firm upper and lower bounds, because (p. 63) "such a definition fails to reflect the pattern of variation within the range and does not identify occasional variations falling outside the range because of chance causes." His proposed controlled cost system (p. 64) "specifies the level of cost that should be attained under an efficient operation in terms of the probability distribution of cost. Thus, the variability of cost is properly reflected in the system. Occasional extreme fluctuations due to chance causes are also an integral part of the controlled cost system."

SUMMARY

Statistical sampling is a useful technique that is applicable to many cost-control situations, especially that of the analysis of variances and that of inspection procedures. In many companies a huge amount of unnecessary time is wasted running down random variances for an arbitrary and ill-informed management. Quality-control charts are helpful in discriminating between chance variances and the assignable variances that deserve investigation. Control charts save time and costs and secure accurate results.

Formal statistical techniques can aid the accountant in improving his services to management. The accountant need not be an expert in the field of statistics to recognize the applicability of certain statistical tools to managerial problems. Nearly every business of any size has at least one accountant; only large businesses employ full-time statisticians. Even where companies employ professional statisticians in quality-control departments, a barrier exists between the accountants and statisticians because often neither group knows what the other group is talking about. Cost accountants need to remove their blinders when tussling with some of their vexing quantitative problems. Statistics offer a rich source of almost untapped help. The modern cost accountant needs some statistical techniques as an instrument in his toolbag. At the same time, the accountant who uses statistics should know when to call upon help from the professional statistician.

PROBLEM FOR SELF-STUDY

Using the basic data in the illustration of the control chart, compute $\bar{X}$ and $\bar{R}$. Also compute the upper and lower control limits. Then re-examine the control charts for $\bar{X}$ and R.

QUESTIONS, PROBLEMS, AND CASES

Note: Problems 27-19 and 27-20 are especially recommended.

27-1. Define a *sample*. Is sampling more accurate than a 100 per cent count? Why?

27-2. Name five statistical applications to business situations.

27-3. What are some common difficulties in the analysis of variances?

27-4. Contrast the accountant's and the statistician's concept of the word *standard*.

27-5. Describe the basic approach of statistical quality control.

27-6. What does the word *quality* mean as it is used in *statistical quality control*?

27-7. What is the *state of statistical control*?

27-8. "When a process is in control, it is beyond change or improvement." Comment.

27-9. Can the managerial notion of standards be reconciled with the statistical mean used on control charts?

27-10. "If statistical control patterns do not coincide with engineering tolerances, you may as well alter the latter or else buy new equipment." Do you agree? Why?

27-11. What is the appropriate basis for setting control limits in a given case?

27-12. Why are three-sigma control limits used most widely in practice?

27-13. "This statistics stuff is O.K., I guess, but my company has a separate SQC department; so, as the company controller, I don't have to worry about it." Comment.

27-14. "The procedure included isolating the important areas of better-than-budget and worse-than-budget performance. By mutual agreement, it was decided previously that any variance over $2,000 should be disclosed, as well as any excess cost of two per cent or more." Comment.

27-15. Some critics of conventional SQC techniques maintain that all the original data in a sample should be plotted rather than just the $\overline{X}$. Why?

27-16. SQC and Investigation of Variances. Dick Cleaver is an observant cost accountant for a large tool manufacturer. One month he noted that the cost for a particular machined part increased to 13.5 cents from about 11 cents, where it had been running in recent months. Cleaver investigated the cost distribution for the part and found that it had a material cost of one cent and that the rest was direct labor and overhead, which was applied at the rate of $6.00 per hour. He checked the time cards and found that a new man had been put on the job, but he did not believe that a new operator should increase costs that much.

A time-study engineer unobtrusively observed the worker twice a day for ten successive days and checked with a stopwatch the time required to make six parts. The times were as follows:

			Time per Piece (minutes)					
Trial	1	2	3	4	5	6	$\overline{X}$	R
1.	1.2	1.1	1.3	1.1	1.0	1.1	1.13	.3
2.	.8	.9	.8	.7	.8	.7	.78	.2
3.	.7	.9	1.0	.9	.8	.9	.87	.3
4.	1.0	1.1	.9	1.0	.9	.9	.97	.2
5.	.7	1.0	1.3	1.0	.9	1.1	.83	.6
6.	1.3	1.2	1.5	1.3	1.1	1.2	1.27	.4
7.	1.1	1.2	1.1	1.4	1.0	.9	1.12	.5
8.	1.7	1.5	1.5	1.4	1.3	1.5	1.48	.3
9.	1.0	1.1	1.1	.9	.9	.8	.97	.3
10.	1.1	1.3	1.1	1.0	1.1	1.0	1.10	.3
11.	.9	.9	.8	.7	.8	1.0	.85	.3
12.	.8	.7	.7	.7	.8	.9	.77	.2
13.	1.0	1.2	1.3	1.1	1.1	1.0	1.12	.3
14.	1.1	1.3	.9	.9	.9	.9	1.00	.4
15.	1.2	1.1	1.1	1.0	.9	.8	1.18	.4
16.	.9	.9	1.0	1.1	1.0	.9	.97	.2
17.	.8	.9	1.0	1.0	1.1	1.2	1.00	.4
18.	1.3	1.2	1.2	1.1	1.3	1.5	1.26	.4
19.	.7	.8	.8	.9	1.0	1.1	.88	.4
20.	1.1	1.0	1.2	1.3	1.1	1.0	1.12	.3
						Totals	20.67	6.7

REQUIRED:

1. Assuming that the material cost was one cent per unit and that the total of conversion costs was applied at $6.00 per hour, compute $\overline{X}$, $\overline{R}$, and the upper and lower control limits for each in dollars and cents.

2. Draw a control chart for $\overline{X}$ and R, with the centers on $\overline{\overline{X}}$ and $\overline{R}$, respectively. Show the control limits and the twenty values for $\overline{X}$ and R.

3. On the basis of your analysis of Cleaver's data, do you think that the operator has been loafing?

27-17. SQC and Control of Materials.* The A.B.C. Wastebasket Company manufactures six different varieties of wastebaskets, each of which is available in six different colors. The baskets are similar in size on the inside, and a standard-size liner will fit any one of the six styles. The company employs nine people to handle these lining duties. Based on studies of the lining process, the following standard costs were developed:

STANDARD COST

Description	Quantity	Unit Cost	Total Cost
Pressboard side-liner	1	$.20	$.20
Bottom liner	1	.05	.05
Heavy-duty staples	6	.005	.03
Glue	1 oz.	.01	.01
Labels	1	.02	.02
Total standard cost			$.31

The lining supervisor requisitions all material, keeps a daily record of wastebaskets lined by style and color, checks the previous day's fabrication schedule to determine what will be coming in for lining the following day, and prepares wastage reports for cost accounting.

Because the supervisor finds it more and more difficult to account for the variance between actual weekly costs and the standard cost in the time allotted to him, he seeks assistance from the accountant. The accountant tackles the job of finding a method by which the variance will be quickly explained and which will indicate the exact cause of this variance.

The actual materials cost of the wastebaskets being lined was sampled as follows:

ACTUAL LINING MATERIALS COST

Days	1	2	3	4	5	6	7	8	9	10	Cost Average $\overline{X}$	Cost Range "R"
1	.29	.28	.28	.29	.27	.28	.30	.29	.31	.32	.291	.05
2	.36	.32	.33	.32	.31	.31	.30	.32	.31	.31	.319	.06
3	.32	.31	.29	.28	.29	.29	.27	.26	.28	.29	.288	.06
4	.25	.27	.26	.30	.31	.30	.29	.28	.28	.29	.283	.06
5	.35	.30	.33	.29	.27	.39	.33	.29	.25	.26	.306	.03
6	.35	.30	.33	.29	.27	.39	.33	.29	.25	.26	.306	.14
7	.28	.27	.28	.29	.30	.30	.29	.29	.30	.30	.290	.03
8	.31	.30	.31	.31	.28	.27	.27	.28	.30	.29	.292	.04
9	.23	.35	.32	.31	.30	.31	.30	.29	.25	.27	.293	.12
10	.27	.28	.28	.30	.29	.27	.29	.31	.27	.27	.283	.04
Grand averages											$.2933	$.063

*Adapted from Dewey W. Neal, "Cost Control Charts—An Application of Statistical Techniques," *N.A.A. Bulletin* (May, 1961), pp. 73–78.

REQUIRED:

1. Assuming 3-sigma limits, compute the control limits for $\bar{X}$ and R.
2. Prepare control charts.
3. Are any samples out of control? What are possible explanations for out-of-control performance? What are the advantages of approaching control of material usage through sampling?

27-18. Samples versus Individual Measurements as a Basis for Control. An SQC program is being used to help control material usage on a stamping operation. Samples of four units each are taken hourly. The following three samples are typical of a pattern which has been in effect for quite some time:

Sample Number	Cost for Each of Four Items Within Samples				Arithmetic Mean
1	$94	$87	$85	$94	$90
2	82	94	94	78	87
3	94	90	94	86	91

The control limits for $\bar{X}$ are $88 \pm \$6$.

REQUIRED:

1. Prepare two control charts, using the control limits designated. First, prepare a $\bar{X}$ chart for the three samples. Second, on another chart plot the individual measurements.
2. Comment on the charts. Does the second chart reveal anything that the first chart did not?

27-19. Case Study of Cost-Plus Contract and Allocation of Joint Costs. The president of the Quartz Crystal Company has asked for your help with a joint-cost problem. His company makes radio crystals, many of which are used in precision communications equipment. The process entails cutting quartz into octagon shape, culling, grinding, and sorting by thicknesses called *degrees of arc*. Up to this point, each crystal has received exactly the same amount of processing. Traditionally, the company has assigned costs by merely dividing the total material and joint processing costs by the number of crystals produced to obtain a unit cost per crystal.

The company is currently negotiating a "cost-plus" contract with the Federal Government for some crystals which have extremely rigid specifications and which are to be culled out of regular production runs. The government representative is insisting that the traditional company costing procedure be used in the allocation of costs. The president insists that such a procedure is "unfair." He wants you to examine their process and to formulate a convincing method of joint-cost allocation that will load more costs on the government crystals.

You have made a study of the process and have discovered the following information.

A critical part of the joint process is *sawing*. For example, a saw set at a given angle or thickness for a specific crystal will produce a spread of quantities both above and below a desired thickness. The normally expected quantities per month from the saws set at 36 degrees are shown as follows:

Thickness or Degrees of Arc	Quantity
44	100
43	200
42	500
41	1,000
40	2,500
39	6,500
38	8,500
37	9,500
36	10,000
35	9,500
34	8,500
33	6,500
32	2,500
31	1,000
30	500
29	200
28	100
	67,600

The tolerance (spread) allowed under the government contract is 36 degrees plus or minus one degree. The normal total processing costs per month are $118,455.

REQUIRED:

Based on the information given, prepare a report to the president showing how joint costs can be allocated for purposes of negotiating the government contract. Include an explanation that will be convincing to the government.

27-20. Case Study of Statistical Quality Control.*   In the kit of tools provided by statistical quality control, the most potent tool for the diagnosis of production problems is the Shewhart control chart for variables. A course in Statistical Quality Control often starts with a brief introduction of this control chart. This chart was the topic for discussion in the third two-hour lecture in an evening course given in the subject.

One of the members of the class was a production foreman in a small department in a plant which had never before used any statistical quality-control methods. After hearing the two-hour lecture, this foreman, in order to familiarize himself with the control chart, made an experimental application to one of the operations in his department.

This operation consisted in thread-grinding a fitting for an aircraft hydraulic system. The pitch diameter of the threads was specified as 0.4037 ± 0.0013 inches. All these fittings were later subject to inspection of this dimension by

---

*Adapted from Eugene L. Grant, *Statistical Quality Control* (3rd ed., New York: McGraw-Hill Book Company, Inc., 1964), pp. 14–15.

go and not-go thread-ring gages. This inspection usually took place several days after production. In order to minimize gage wear in this inspection operation, it was the practice of the production department to aim at an average value a little below the nominal dimension of 0.4037 inches.

To make actual measurements of pitch diameter to the nearest ten-thousandth of an inch, the foreman borrowed a visual comparator that had been used for other purposes. Approximately once every hour he measured the pitch diameter of five fittings that had just been produced. For each sample of five he computed the average and the range (largest value in sample minus smallest value). The figures he obtained are shown in Table 1.

REQUIRED:

1. Prepare an $\bar{X}$ chart based on the average value of the observations.
2. Prepare an R chart.
3. What conclusions do you derive from studying the charts?

TABLE 1

MEASUREMENTS OF PITCH DIAMETER OF THREADS ON AIRCRAFT FITTINGS
(Values are expressed in units of 0.0001 in. in excess of 0.4000 in.
Dimension is specified as 0.4037 ± 0.0013 in.)

Sample Number	Measurement on Each Item of Five Items Per Hour					Average $\bar{X}$	Range R
1	36	35	34	33	32	34.0	4
2	31	31	34	32	30	31.6	4
3	30	30	32	30	32	30.8	2
4	32	33	33	32	35	33.0	3
5	32	34	37	37	35	35.0	5
6	32	32	31	33	33	32.2	2
7	33	33	36	32	31	33.0	5
8	23	33	36	35	36	32.6	13
9	43	36	35	24	31	33.8	19
10	36	35	36	41	41	37.8	6
11	34	38	35	34	38	35.8	4
12	36	38	39	39	40	38.4	4
13	36	40	35	26	33	34.0	14
14	36	35	37	34	33	35.0	4
15	30	37	33	34	35	33.8	7
16	28	31	33	33	33	31.6	5
17	33	30	34	33	35	33.0	5
18	27	28	29	27	30	28.2	3
19	35	36	29	27	32	31.8	9
20	33	35	35	39	36	35.6	6
Totals						671.0	124

cost accounting and operations research

CHAPTER XXVIII

Now we shall briefly re-examine modern cost accounting. Then we shall relate management cost accounting to the branch of quantitative methods called *operations research*. This chapter is a survey. Technical competence in operations research can be achieved only by specialized study.

MODERN COST ACCOUNTING

Cost accounting is a quantitative method that accumulates, classifies, summarizes, and interprets information for three major purposes: (1) operational planning and control, (2) special decisions, and (3) product-costing. The importance and usefulness of cost accounting are dependent on how well it can help managers achieve these three broad and demanding purposes. If cost accounting is preoccupied with the product-costing purpose (important as it is), the other two purposes probably will be unfulfilled.

If all three purposes are recognized by the practicing cost accountant, his motivations and actions are bound to strengthen the role of cost accounting in the future of business. This means that we can expect an increasing use of managerial accounting tools, such as budgeting, standard costing, responsibility accounting, the contribution approach, and tailor-making relevant data for special decisions. Note that these tools embrace far more than double-entry bookkeeping and preparing conventional financial statements. As the limiting impact of a single important purpose (product-costing) is replaced by the challenging impact of three important purposes, the cost accountant will find his scope enlarging accordingly. He will become aware that cost accounting methodology has a vital interrelationship with other areas, such as engineering, statistics, mathematics, economics, organization theory, decision theory, and social psychology.

This awareness does not imply that the cost accountant must be a master in all fields. But it does mean that he should be broad-minded enough to recognize that other fields contain approaches and techniques which may be pertinent to some of his problems. Earlier chapters offer examples of interrelationships among business fields: industrial engineering and setting standards; analysis of variances and statistical quality control; budgets, motivation, and psychology; theory of probability and estimating future data; integrated data-processing, digital computers, and problems of organization; controllership and operating management.

Some accountants rigidly maintain that these interrelationships are "not accounting" and therefore are of little concern to the cost accountant. This unrealistic view implies that accounting is an art that should be practiced for its own sake and that business operations are heavily compartmentalized with practically no interaction between functions. The point is that the cost accountant is most effective when he is highly conscious of these interrelationships. Whether he becomes aware of them through management books, accounting books, engineering books, or on-the-job training does not really matter.

The remainder of this chapter will discuss a relatively new field, *operations research*, in relation to cost accounting.

OPERATIONS RESEARCH

Definition

Operations research (abbreviated hereafter as *OR*) is a diffused collection of mathematical and statistical models which are applied to decision making.[1] It is marked by a scientific method, an over-all approach, mixed teams of engineers, statisticians, mathematicians, and, to a lesser extent, accountants, and the use of mathematical and statistical models as a framework for analysis. OR is primarily a tool for *planning* rather than *controlling*; that is, it is a rigorous means for discovering feasible alternatives, evaluating them, and choosing the best alternative. Operations researchers stress the fact that careful planning is the key to business success.

[1] Operations research is sometimes referred to as *management science*. The distinction between the two is fuzzy. Management science is a broader concept in the sense that it embraces computer technology as a science plus operations research. For example, the management science division of one large public accounting firm has two major departments: "operations research" and "computers." Operations research techniques were developed initially in England during World War II. Groups of physicists, chemists, statisticians, mathematicians, and military commanders combined their talents to solve complex problems. Examples include problems of optimal bombing-group sizes, convoy sizes and patterns, and schedules for repairing aircraft engines.

In many instances the crucial managerial task is determining objectives and marshalling the most effective resources for their attainment. Control is secondary in the sense that even poor decisions can be implemented in an efficient way. For example, faultless control may be exercised in the production of a hopelessly inferior product which should have been abandoned years ago.

Scientific method

Scientific method is intelligent problem solving. It consists of four steps:

(1) *Observation and Analysis.* The scientist examines a real situation to discover and gather relevant facts and relationships. It implies searching for and explicitly stating the nature of the problem. The isolation of the central problem is a crucial task.

(2) *Hypothesis.* The observations in (1) lead him to formulate a hypothesis, or theory, or *model*, which expresses the important patterns or weighted interrelationships of all relevant factors in the real situation.

(3) *Prediction.* From the hypothesis, or model, he makes predictions of what will occur.

(4) *Verification.* He collects new facts to see if his predictions are borne out by experiment or experience.

He goes through the observation, hypothesis, prediction, verification cycle over and over again, with the result of either extending, revising, or discarding his theory.

In practical applications of the scientific method, these steps often overlap and are sometimes difficult to separate. For example, steps (1) and (2) may occur simultaneously in the sense that gathering relevant facts naturally presupposes some hypothesis about which facts are pertinent. In turn, such a hypothesis must have been based on some factual knowledge.

Science and the scientific method are not the same thing. A science is a body of systematic, ordered knowledge, whereas the scientific method is the process of locating, defining, and solving problems. Despite the common belief that the existence of most problems is obvious, seeing problems is often the most difficult phase of the scientific method. It involves searching, sifting, classifying, comparing, clinging to the relevant, and discarding the irrelevant.

Mathematical models: nucleus of OR

The nucleus of operations research is the formulation of a *model*, a structure of the interrelationships among the recognized factors in the real situation. It spotlights the important interrelationships and de-emphasizes unimportant factors. A model may take many forms. We are all familiar with model airplanes or ships. Accountants work with models constantly; accounting systems and financial reports are types of models. Mathematical equations and inequations are the favorite models of operations researchers.

Models are useful because they facilitate conceptions of realities and ease the anticipation and measurement of the effects of alternative actions. Thus, models *which portray real situations* are immensely practical simply because they help executives foresee the consequences of various alternatives without having to discover them through exhaustive and costly actual experience.

Models replace hunches, guesses, and intuition with an explicit assembly and evaluation of a *vast number* of relevant factors. Thus, regardless of the enormous number of constraints or alternatives, the problem may be expressed in mathematical form (for example, a set of equations with many unknowns). Once the equations are formulated, the digital computer can solve them. The growing importance of OR would be impossible without the computer, which permits the solution of complex mathematical models that formerly defied any practical solution.

Limitations of models

The accountant's conventional financial statements are models for pointing toward problems that need the executive's attention: increases in payroll costs, decreases in sales, and build-ups in payables or inventories, to name a few. But models must conform to reality in two major respects:

1. The model must reflect reality. Thus, an impressive income statement that is fraught with erroneous figures is not only useless but may be misleading. This may seem obvious; yet many enthusiasts of OR construct elaborate models that may be interesting in concept but are downright impractical because the needed data cannot be isolated to test the model. For instance, there is some tendency to use unit costs, which may be inappropriate if they are conglomerations of variable, fixed, and joint costs.

2. A model depicting one type of reality is used in a situation for which it was not designed. Operations researchers are seldom guilty of this error, but accountants must stand up and be counted in this regard. For example, the costs that may be appropriate for an income statement may not be pertinent for other problem situations. Chapters 13 and 14 emphasized this point. For instance, historical depreciation costs, although relevant in income determination, are irrelevant in equipment-replacement problems. Opportunity costs, such as lost contribution margins on missed sales, are often crucial but are usually ignored in the formal accounting system.

In summary, models used to guide decisions must be realistic in the sense that they highlight and properly measure the relevant aspects of the problem. Accountants and operations researchers are both guilty on this score. Accountants occasionally misapply a model designed for one purpose to the wrong situation, whereas the OR men sometimes tend to study a situation, construct a fancy model, and stop there without testing to see if their model is realistic.

OR techniques

Mathematical and statistical techniques are the principal tools used by OR men for constructing and testing their models. These techniques include *linear programming, correlation,* and an extensive batch of *probabilistic models.* Linear programming is the most widely used OR technique; it is discussed in a later section of this chapter. Correlation techniques are used to discover and evaluate possible cause-and-effect relationships. These techniques have been used most widely in trying to solve problems of utilizing advertising and selling efforts. In many cases, arbitrary methods of setting advertising and sales promotion budgets as fixed percentages of sales are being replaced by tested formulas based on mathematical equations containing many variables.

Most of the analytical techniques used in OR make heavy use of statistical probability theory to deal explicitly with the uncertainty that plagues management. The models so developed are often called *probabilistic models.* Applications include the inventory-control and statistical quality-control problems which were discussed in Chapters 16, 26, and 27. For example, complex problems of how much inventory to stock, where to stock, and when to stock have been successfully solved by OR specialists.

Another example of probabilistic models is *waiting-line* or queuing theory, which deals with the problem of supplying sufficient facilities to meet the needs of things or individuals that demand service in uneven spurts: cars at a toll booth, boats at landing docks, machines awaiting a limited number of repairmen. There are a vast number of variables in these problems, each combination of which requires separate mathematical analysis. These variables include different probability distributions for arrivals and for service times, number of facilities, servicing order, priorities, and others.

One of the ingredients of the decision is computing the waiting-time costs. Although the cost of operating extra facilities (having an extra repairman or bank teller) may be obtainable from regular accounting data, the cost of waiting may not be so easy to obtain. Measuring the dollar loss if prospective customers leave or never appear is difficult and often nearly impossible. Once again, waiting-line models are useful only if they reflect reality. OR men will maintain that waiting-line analysis will be more likely to yield optimum results than mere haphazard selection of required facilities.

Another interesting OR model is the *competitive model* that may be useful in competitive-bidding situations. This model is an application of managerial economics which uses probability theory in dealing with such relevant variables as a company's own costs, competitors' costs, and competitors' bids. The objective of this application of probability theory is to help management follow an optimal pricing policy.[2]

PERT (Program Evaluation and Review Technique) is a formal, probabilistic diagram of the interrelationships of a complex time series of

---

[2] For an excellent description, see Miller and Starr, *Executive Decisions and Operations Research* (Englewood Cliffs, N.J.: Prentice-Hall, Inc., 1960), pp. 223–238.

activities. Its objective is to discover potential bottlenecks and to chart progress. PERT was initially used in missile research and development, where time estimates are considered crucial. Many military contracts now specify that PERT must be used. PERT also is very popular in the construction industry. When PERT is combined with costs to determine optimum trade-offs between time and costs, it is called PERT-COST. See Problem 23-17 for an example of PERT.

Simulation is the formulation of a detailed model of a system or process. It is valuable because it permits experimentation with different alternatives before a final course of action is selected.

Normal and Poisson distributions are widely used in model building by statisticians. The data may then be tested repeatedly on a digital computer and average expected results obtained.

However, because normal and Poisson distributions often do not adequately describe the distribution of demand met in practice, a simulation is not necessarily repeated over and over and then averaged. In inventory control models, for example, a company's historical demand data may be fed into a simulation; the ingredients (combinations of various stock levels, purchase-order sizes, and sales) of the model may then be manipulated until the best (optimal) set is discovered. The solution can then be tested on a separate set of historical demand data, preferably from a different year.

Dynamic programming is a technique for optimizing the over-all effect of a time sequence of interrelated decisions, basically by working backward from the last point to the first point in a complex network of decisions.

The accountant and OR

Although operations researchers like to think otherwise, many facets of OR are not new. Intelligent accountants and managers have been using the scientific method, an over-all approach, and mixed teams for years. The sole distinguishing characteristic of OR is the heavy use of mathematical and statistical models as a framework for analysis. However, the rise of OR as a distinct field is an indication that not enough practicing accountants have the broad-gauged approach that is so necessary for tackling business problems.

The modern cost accountant has many traits of the OR practitioner. He recognizes that different costs are applicable for different purposes, that probability theory and statistical tools may be helpful with certain problems, and that an over-all, formalized, "scientific" approach to business problems is extremely helpful. In other words, the modern managerial accountant already has the OR approach and, in fact, may hold the key to OR's ultimate success or failure. Why? Because OR models and solutions, despite awesome matrices, equations, inequations, payoff tables, and utility measures, are dependent on the reliability of the data used. Much of this information is furnished by the accountant. In cases where the accounting system cannot be the cornerstone for supplying data, the OR specialist often will be constructing a less reliable and hence less useful model.

LINEAR PROGRAMMING

Definition

Linear programming is a powerful mathematical method for selecting an optimum plan; it is an efficient search procedure for computing the best solution to certain business problems which contain many interacting variables and which essentially involve selecting the combination of resources that maximizes profits or minimizes costs.[3] In many cases of linear programming, the goal is to maximize the total profit for a given total of scarce resources. There are nearly always scarce resources which are constraints (also called *restraints* or *restrictions*) on available alternatives. Examples of linear-programming applications include: determining optimum product mixes, material mixes, machine and manpower combinations, utilizing storage or shipping facilities, and, in general, combining manpower, materials, and facilities to best advantage when all the relationships are approximately linear and many combinations are possible. More specifically, practical applications have been successfully applied as follows: designing transformers, scheduling flight crews, blending gasoline, formulating shipping schedules, routing production, and selecting transportation routes.

In practical situations, most linear-programming problems are solved by digital computers because the number of variables is vastly greater than is used in the example we shall consider.

The techniques, the accountant, and the manager

All of us are more or less familiar with linear equations (for example, $X + 3 = 9$). We also know that simultaneous linear equations with two or three unknowns become progressively more difficult to solve with pencil and paper. Linear programming essentially involves: (1) constructing a set of simultaneous linear equations, which represent the model of the problem and which include many variables; and (2) solving the equations with the help of the digital computer.

The formulation of the equations—that is, the building of the model—is far more challenging than the mechanics of the solution. The model must be a valid and accurate portrayal of the problem. Computer programmers can then take the equations and process the solution.

As a minimum, accountants and executives should be able to recognize those types of problems in their organizations that are most

---

[3]The desired objective in a specific case may be one of a number of possibilities: sales maximization, minimization of idle time, maximum utilization of a particular machine, and so on.

susceptible to analysis by linear programming. Hopefully, the managers and accountants should be able to help in the construction of the model— that is, in specifying the objectives, the constraints, and the variables. Ideally, they should understand the mathematics and should be able to talk comfortably with the operations researchers who are attempting to express their problem mathematically. However, the position taken here is that the accountant and the manager should concentrate on the formulation of the model and not worry too much about the technical intricacies of the solution. The latter may be delegated to the mathematicians; the ability to delegate the former is highly doubtful.

Example of Linear Programming. Consider a company which has two departments, machining and finishing. This plant makes two products, each of which requires processing in each of the two departments. Relevant data are summarized as follows:

| | Capacities (Per Day) in Units | | Contribution |
| | Dept. 1 | Dept. 2 | Margin Per |
Products	Machining	Finishing	Unit
A	200	120	$2.00
or			
B	100	200	$2.50

Severe material shortages for Product B will limit its production to a maximum of 90 per day. How many units of each product should be produced to obtain the maximum profit?

Two underlying assumptions are necessary for using linear-programming techniques. First, all relationships between capacity and the amounts produced are linear; that is, these relationships can be demonstrated graphically by straight lines rather than by curves. Second, all stated factors and relationships are known with certainty; in other words, all ingredients of the situation are exactly known rather than uncertain or probable.[4]

The linear-programming approach has the following basic pattern, although variations and short cuts are available in unique situations:

1. Determine objectives. Usually this takes some form of either maximization of profit or minimization of cost. Technically, this objective is called an *objective function*, a figure of merit, or a measure of effectiveness.
2. Determine basic relationships in the situation, especially the constraints.
3. Determine available *feasible* alternatives.
4. Compute the optimum solution. Techniques may vary here. In uncomplicated situations, the graphic approach is easiest to see. However, algebraic approaches are more widely used in practice.

---

[4] However, probabilities may be used to forecast the specific data used in the construction of the linear-programming model.

Using our example, let's apply these steps.

1. *Determine objectives.* The objective here will be to find the product combination that maximizes *total* contribution margin. This can be expressed in equation form as follows: $2.00A + $2.50B = Total contribution margin. We want to maximize this objective function.
2. *Determine basic relationships.* The relationships here can be depicted by inequalities as follows:

Department 1: $A + 2B \leq 200$
Department 2: $A + .6B \leq 120$
Material shortage for Product B: $B \leq 90$
Because negative production
   is impossible. $B \geq 0$ and $A \geq 0$

The three solid lines on the graph in Exhibit 28-1 will aid visualization of the existing constraints for Departments 1 and 2, and the material shortage.

EXHIBIT 28-1

LINEAR PROGRAMMING—GRAPHIC SOLUTION

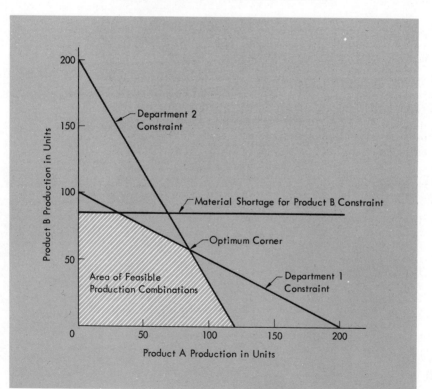

3. *Determine available feasible alternatives.* The feasible alternatives are those that are technically possible. We do not want to bother with useless computations for impossible alternatives. The shaded area in Exhibit 28-1 shows the boundaries of those product combinations that are feasible.
4. *Compute optimum solution.* In steps (2) and (3) we have concentrated on physical relationships alone. Now we return to the economic relationships expressed as the objective in step (1). We test various feasible product combinations to see which one maximizes the total contribution margin.

In the graphic solution, we are fortunate because the optimal solution must lie on one of the corners of the Area of Feasible Product Combinations. Methods exist for moving from one corner to another to see if the total contribution is improved. This procedure is continued until the optimal solution is found. In this case, the optimum corner shows that the best combination is 86 units of A plus 57 units of B.

The same result can be accomplished algebraically, usually by working with the corners of the polygon. The steps are simple:

a. Start with a possible combination.
b. Compute the profit.
c. Move to another possible combination to see if it will improve the result in (b). Keep moving from corner to corner until no further improvement is possible.[5]

These computations, corner by corner, are summarized as follows:

Trial	Corner	Combination		Total Contribution Margin			
		Product A	Product B				
1	0,0	0	0	$2.00 (0)	+ $2.50 (0)	=	$ 0
2	0,90	0	90	2.00 (0)	+ 2.50 (90)	=	225.00
3	20,90	20	90	2.00 (20)	+ 2.50 (90)	=	265.00
4	86,57	86	57	2.00 (86)	+ 2.50 (57)	=	314.50*
5	120,0	120	0	2.00 (120)	+ 2.50 (0)	=	240.00

*Optimum.

Why must the best solution lie on a corner? Consider all possible combinations that will produce a total contribution margin of $1 ($2.00 A + $2.50 B = $1). This is a straight line through (.5,0) and (0,.4). Other total contribution margins are represented by lines parallel to this one. Their associated total contribution margins increase the further the lines get from the origin. The optimum line is the one furthest from the origin which has a feasible point on it; intuitively, we know that this happens at a corner (86,57). Furthermore, if you put a ruler on the graph and move it parallel with the $1 line, the optimum corner will become apparent.

At the outset of this example, the reader may have jumped to the conclusion that production of Product B, which promises the most margin

[5] This is a simplified version of the *simplex* method, which is described later in this section.

per unit, should be maximized. Then any remaining productive capacity should be devoted to Product A. This is fallacious reasoning, because the scarce factor is productive capacity. The key to the optimal solution rests in the relative rates of substitution and profitability per unit (hour or day) of *productive capacity*. This point becomes clearer if we examine the graph. Moving from corner (20,90) to corner (86,57) implies that the company is transferring the scarce resource (productive capacity) between the products. In Department 1, each productive hour devoted to one unit of Product B may be given (sacrificed or traded) for two units of Product A. Will this exchange add to profitability? Yes, as shown below:

Total contribution margin at Corner (20,90)		$265.00
Added contribution margin from Product A:		
66 units @ $2.00	$132.00	
Lost contribution margin, Product B:		
33 units @ $2.50	82.50	
Net additional contribution		49.50
Total contribution margin at Corner (86,57)		$314.50

As we move from corner (86,57) to corner (120,0), we face the Department 2 constraint rather than the Department 1 constraint. The rate of substitution may be stated as follows: each productive hour devoted to one unit of Product B may be devoted to .6 of a unit of Product A. This would entail giving up $2.50 contribution margin in exchange for .6($2.00) or $1.20 contribution margin, a decrease of the total contribution margin of $1.30 for each unit of Product B given up. Therefore, corner (86,57) is the optimum solution.

Note that the heart of the substitutions discussed above is a matter of swapping a given contribution margin per unit of scarce resource for some other contribution margin per unit of scarce resource; it is not simply a matter of comparing margins per unit of *product*.

Simplex method

The fundamental problem of linear programming is to discover the specific set of variables that satisfies all constraints and maximizes (or minimizes) the objective sought. Although graphical methods aid visualization and are useful for two or possibly three variables, they are impractical where many variables exist. The simplex method is a general technique for solving any linear-programming problem. However, it is much too detailed to be described here. Briefly, the *simplex method* is an iterative (that is, step-by-step) process that is very effective, especially when a digital computer performs the calculations. Essentially, it starts with a specific feasible alternative and algebraically tests it by substitution to see if the solution can be improved. These substitutions continue until no further improvement is possible. The optimum solution is therefore achieved.

Reliability of cost data

Cost accountants who are skeptical of linear programming because imprecise data may be used should consider Miller and Starr's remarks:

> ...*even if the cost figures are not really reliable, the linear programming procedure will still be based on the same data that management would use if it selected a strategy by some other means. Therefore, the use of linear programming will at least ensure the selection of the optimal strategy on the basis of the data management would use anyhow.*[6]

SUMMARY

The main point of this chapter is that the alert cost accountant should seize those contributions of allied fields which will strengthen and enrich his role as the major advisor to operating management. After all, few companies can afford the full-time services of a mathematician, a statistician, or some variation thereof. The accountant will undoubtedly remain entrenched as the top figure man in most organizations. However, this position will be endangered if the accountant does not broaden his horizons to recognize the following:

> ...*the accounting method has no monopoly on data collection and analysis. Despite its long period of service, and its constant change to meet new conditions and problems, accounting is still capable of further development and growth. One direction in which such growth and added effectiveness may be achieved is to recognize that no one method of data collection and processing is a complete answer to the problems of management. Accounting should be combined with other techniques, to build a more efficient and more clearly integrated approach to the collection and processing of quantitative data. To this end, various groups interested in special techniques should combine their efforts to achieve better results. Accountants should use sampling and other statistical techniques more widely; data should be collected by combinations of techniques that will provide optimum service in meeting managerial needs. Those who are interested in data-processing and interpretation should work with accountants to improve the overall impact of quantitative methods in business. The combination of techniques and viewpoints can do much to assist management in meeting the ever-mounting difficulties of the business world.*[7]

SUGGESTED READINGS

Bierman, H., C. P. Bonini, L. E. Fouraker, and R. K. Jaedicke, *Quantitative Analysis for Business Decisions*, Rev. Ed. (Homewood, Ill.: Richard D. Irwin, Inc., 1965).

Bowman, Edward H., and Robert B. Fetter, *Analysis for Production Management* (Homewood, Ill.: Richard D. Irwin, Inc., 1957).

Charnes, A., and W. W. Cooper, *Management Models and Industrial Applications of Linear Programming*, two vols. (New York: John Wiley & Sons, Inc., 1961).

[6] Miller and Starr, *Executive Decisions and Operations Research, op. cit.*, p. 405.
[7] William J. Vatter, "Contributions of Accounting to Measurement in Management," *Management Science* (October, 1958), p. 37.

Churchman, C. W., R. A. Ackoff, and E. L. Arnoff, *Introduction to Operations Research* (New York: John Wiley & Sons, Inc., 1957).

Ferguson, Robert O., and Lauren F. Sargent, *Linear Programming: Fundamentals and Applications* (New York: McGraw-Hill Book Company, Inc., 1958).

Gass, Saul I., *Linear Programming: Methods and Applications* (New York: McGraw-Hill Book Company, Inc., 1958).

Goetz, Billy E., *Quantitative Methods: A Survey and Guide for Managers* (New York: McGraw-Hill Book Company, Inc., 1965).

Miller, D. W., and M. K. Starr, *Executive Decisions and Operations Research* (Englewood Cliffs, N. J.: Prentice-Hall, Inc., 1960).

Stockton, R. Stansbury, *Introduction to Linear Programming*, 2nd ed. (Boston: Allyn and Bacon, Inc., 1964). This is an excellent book for beginners who especially dread mathematics.

Vajda, Steven, *Readings in Linear Programming* (New York: John Wiley & Sons, Inc., 1958).

PROBLEM FOR SELF-STUDY

Review the example of linear programming. In particular, express the objectives and constraints in mathematical form. Superimpose a ruler on the graph as directed in the text's explanation of why the best solution must lie on a corner.

QUESTIONS, PROBLEMS, AND CASES

Note: Problem 28-12 is a basic introduction to linear programming.

28-1. Define *operations research*. What are its two most prominent characteristics?

28-2. Distinguish between *science* and *scientific method*.

28-3. What is a *model?*

28-4. Name and briefly describe some OR techniques.

28-5. Compare and contrast the work of the modern cost accountant with that of the operations researcher.

28-6. Define *linear programming*.

28-7. Give five examples of business applications of linear programming.

28-8. Define *cost accounting*.

28-9. What is an *objective function?* A *feasible* alternative?

28-10. What are the four basic steps in linear programming?

28-11. Linear Programming; Graphic Solution.* A firm produces and sells two products, A and B. Selling price and cost data are as follows:

	Product A	Product B
Selling price	$10	$8
Variable costs of production and selling	5	6
Hours of production time per unit	4	1
Total fixed costs, $200,000.		

*Adapted from Robert K. Jaedicke, "Improving B-E Analysis by Linear Programming Technique," *N.A.A. Bulletin* (March, 1961), pp. 5–12.

The maximum number of units of B that can be sold is 300,000. The total production hours available is 400,000.

REQUIRED:

Express the basic relationships in mathematical form. Graph the relationships. Which product combination is optimal?

28-12. Allocation of Machine Time. Machine 1 has 24 hours available time and Machine 2 has 20 hours for processing of two products. Product x yields a contribution margin of $2 per unit; product y, $1 per unit. These products must be sold in proportions such that the quantity of x will be equal to or less than the quantity of y. x requires 6 hours' time on Machine 1 and 10 hours' time on Machine 2. Product y requires 4 hours' time on Machine 1 only.

REQUIRED:

Using graphic techniques, determine which product combination will maximize profit. Express the relationships in mathematical form.

28-13. Finding Optimal Mixture for Box of Chocolates.* A candy manufacturer is attempting to find the optimal mixture for a box of chocolates. There are two kinds of candy that he wants in the box, C_1 and C_2. The following are the characteristics of the candy and the box:

	C_1	C_2	Box
Number of pieces	x	y	35 or greater
Weight per piece (oz.)	1.6	0.8	32 or greater
Space per piece (sq. in.)	2.0	1.0	65*
Cost per piece	$0.02	$0.01	$0.60 maximum

*Maximum. By the use of fillers, the box can range from 40 square inches to 65 square inches.

REQUIRED:

Find the optimal mixture by graphic means.

28-14. Adding Another Constraint. Assume the same facts and requirements as in 28-14 except that at least 10 pieces of C_1 must be in the mixture.

28-15. Linear Programming and Minimum Cost. The local agricultural center has advised Sam Bowers to spread at least 4,800 pounds of a special nitrogen fertilizer ingredient and at least 5,000 pounds of a special phosphate fertilizer ingredient in order to increase his crops. Neither ingredient is available in pure form.

A dealer has offered 100-pound bags of VIM @ $1 each. VIM contains the equivalent of 20 pounds of nitrogen and 80 pounds of phosphate. VOOM is also available in 100-pound bags, @ $3 each; it contains the equivalent of 75 pounds of nitrogen and 25 pounds of phosphate.

Express the relationships as inequalities. How many bags of VIM and VOOM should Bowers buy in order to obtain the required fertilizer at minimum cost? Solve graphically.

*Adapted from Miller and Starr, *Executive Decisions and Operations Research* (Englewood Cliffs, N.J.: Prentice-Hall, Inc., 1960), pp. 158–161.

28-16. Case Study in Administration of Sales Effort and Scheduling Production for Maximum Profit.

Description of the Company

Products: Riegel Paper Corporation is an integrated pulp-and-paper manufacturer and paper converter of glassine and greaseproof packaging papers made to customer specifications. These are plain, printed, waxed, laminated, or lacquer-coated. Specialty papers, such as bristol board and filter paper, are also produced.

In all, approximately 600 different papers are produced. Minor variations of color, weight, and finish within these papers produce a total of approximately 2,500 individual product specifications. Sales volume is $75 million per year. There are 2,600 employees.

Facilities: Pulp mill and one paper machine at Acme, N.C. Seven paper machines at Milford, N.J.; two at Warren, N.J.; one at Hughesville, N.J.; one at Riegelsville, N.J. Major converting facilities at Milford, N.J., and Edinburgh, Indiana. Central sales and corporate administrative offices in New York City.

Approximately one-half of the company's 2,600 employees are located at Milford, N.J.

Cost Accounting and Control

The company has a standard budget covering all operating costs, including those of sales and administration. These operating costs are then distributed as machine rates—that is, the "full cost" per hour to operate each paper machine and converting machine. The costing system is unusual in that no line is drawn between costs at the mill and costs for sales and administration—*all* costs are assigned to the machine rates. Cost distribution for each item of expense is made according to the most "equitable" index available. For example, standard expense for the customer order and traffic departments is distributed to various mills in proportion to the number of orders accepted for production at each mill over the previous year. Distribution to each paper machine within a mill is made proportional to the production capacity of the machine.

The standard machine rate is then used to develop standard costs and profit for each product. Although the term "standard" cost is used, a more accurate descriptive term would be "expected actual." That is, if the paper machines were running at only 80 per cent of efficiency (based on industrial engineering time standards), the cost entered in the budget and in the product costs would be that incurred at 80 per cent, rather than 100 per cent, efficiency.

Actual costs of producing products are not compiled. Prior to 1950 this was done, but the clerical costs were excessive and there were many inaccuracies in time-keeping procedures. Therefore, it was discontinued, on the assumption that the cost of compiling such data could not be justified even if it were feasible to improve the system to produce acceptable accuracy. Rather, a system of departmental performance standards was introduced. Standard production times are compiled for products produced each day, and the resulting efficiencies are reported daily to department managers.

The only other cost control is to compare the operating expense budget with actual expense for each accounting period (four weeks), and to investigate any significant variances. As budgeted and actual production generally agree very closely, very little variance due to production volume is encountered.

The "standard" product costs, then, serve only to guide the Sales Department in their allocation of sales effort.

Directing Sales Effort and Scheduling Paper Machines at the Milford Mill

Scheduling paper machines at mills other than those at Milford presents little difficulty, because, in general, the grades of paper that they produce can be made on only one machine. However, there are seven paper machines at Milford which produce glassine, greaseproof, and other packaging papers. These grades can usually be produced on four or five machines out of the seven. Two of the machines are exactly alike; therefore there are actually six different machines among which there are variations of width and standard operating speeds. The following table shows these variations, using two grades of paper as examples:

| Paper | | | Running Speeds | |
Machine	Width	Hourly Rate	Grade x	Grade y
1	88 in.	$107	385 ft. per min.	
2	128	210		500 ft. per min.
3	72	93	340	
4	72	93	340	
5	98	164		525
6	98	115	375	
7	88	139		525

Standard cost and profit are computed for each machine on which each product can be run, and full use of the machine's width is assumed. Thus, there is a twofold problem in maximizing profit from paper produced on these machines: (1) directing sales effort to the most profitable grades, and (2) using the capacity of the machines to produce these grades at lowest cost.

Comparison of costs on two grades which can be made on the same three machines will serve to illustrate all aspects of the problem in practice (All prices and costs are expressed per hundredweight):

| | (1) | (2) | (3) | (4) | (5) | |
| | | | | | Machine No. 1 | |
Grade	Sales Price	Material Cost	Gross Margin* (1) − (2)	Manufacturing Costs	Net Profit (3) − (4)	Production Hrs. Per Cwt.
"A"	$26.48	$8.86	$17.62	$12.85	$4.77	.1200
"B"	$23.51	$8.73	$15.38	$11.61	$3.77	.1086
					Machine No. 3	
"A"			$17.62	$15.40	$2.22	.1655
"B"			$15.38	$12.23	$3.15	.1320
					Machine No. 6	
"A"			$17.62	$12.72	$4.90	.1107
"B"			$15.38	$11.21	$4.17	.0976

*Note that "gross margin" as used by this company is sales less material costs.

Examination of the above data shows that production of Grade "A" on machine No. 6 will yield the greatest "net profit." However, if this grade is produced on machine No. 3, it yields a lower "net profit" than Grade "B". Further, the particular order for Grade "A" may be for 18-inch rolls, which means that only 90 inches of 98-inch width of machine No. 6 could be used, whereas the entire 72 inches of machine No. 3 could be used.

REQUIRED:

Does the "standard net profit" provide a suitable index for the administration of sales effort and for efficient scheduling of paper machines, or are some revisions advisable? Show and explain your computations. Can you relate any techniques of operations research to this case?

APPENDIXES

SECTION 7

list of N.A.A. research publications

Accounting Research Reports*

No.

11-15
(Combined). "How Standards Costs Are Being Used Currently." (1948)

16-18
(Combined). "The Analysis of Cost-Volume-Profit Relationships." (1949–1950)

19–21
(Combined). "The Analysis of Non-Manufacturing Costs for Managerial Decisions." (1951)

22. "The Analysis of Manufacturing Cost Variances." (August, 1952)

23. "Direct Costing." (April, 1953)

24. "Product Costs for Pricing Purposes." (August, 1953)

25–27
(Combined). "Cost Control for Marketing Operations." (1954)

28. "Presenting Accounting Information to Management." (December, 1954)

*National Association of Accountants.

841

29. "Accounting for Research and Development Costs." (June, 1955)

30. "Accounting for Intra-Company Transfers." (June, 1956)

31. "Costing Joint Products." (April, 1957)

32. "Accounting for Labor Costs and Labor-Related Costs." (November, 1957)

33. "Current Practice in Accounting for Depreciation." (April, 1958)

34. "Classification and Coding Techniques to Facilitate Accounting Operations." (April, 1959)

35. "Return on Capital as a Guide to Managerial Decisions." (December, 1959)

36. "Management Accounting Problems in Foreign Operations." (March, 1960)

37. "Current Applications of Direct Costing." (January, 1961)

38. "Cash Flow Analysis for Managerial Control." (October, 1961)

39. "Accounting for Costs of Capacity." (May, 1963)

40. "Techniques in Inventory Management." (February, 1964)

41. "Control of Maintenance Cost." (May, 1964)

42. "Long-Range Profit Planning." (December, 1964)

(Also of interest is Walter B. McFarland, *Concepts for Management Accounting* (New York: National Association of Accountants, 1966). The aim of this book is "to unify the association's research findings from previous studies into ordered patterns.")

Accounting Practice Reports†

No.

1. "Controlling and Accounting for Supplies." (June, 1955)
2. "Planning, Controlling, and Accounting for Maintenance." (November, 1955)
3. "Modifying the Calendar to Meet Business Needs." (June, 1956)
4. "Accounting for Returnable Containers." (January, 1957)
5. "Speeding Up Interim Closings and Reports." (March, 1958)
6. "Serving Sales Through Planning of Production and Inventory." (January, 1959)
7. "The Capital Expenditure Control Program." (March, 1959)
8. "Cost Improvement for Profit Improvement." (October, 1959)
9. "Reports Which Managements Find Most Useful." (February, 1960)
10. "Separating and Using Costs as Fixed and Variable." (June, 1960)
11. "Applying Accruals and Deferrals to Interim Closings." (April, 1961)
12. "Cost Control of Spoiled Work." (June, 1961)
13. "Use of Graphs in Internal Reporting." (October, 1961)
14. "Experience with Return on Capital to Appraise Management Performance." (February, 1962)
15. "Development and Reporting of Variances." (July, 1962)
16. "Departures in Communicating Accounting Data to Foremen." (January, 1963).

†Research publications of the National Association of Accountants, 505 Park Avenue, New York City. These were issued as separate third sections of the association's monthly *N.A.A. Bulletin*, now called *Management Accounting*.

glossary

 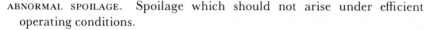

ABNORMAL SPOILAGE. Spoilage which should not arise under efficient operating conditions.

ABSORPTION COSTING. That type of product costing which assigns fixed manufacturing overhead to the units produced as a product cost. Contrasts with direct costing.

ACCOUNTING METHOD. *See* Unadjusted rate of return.

ACCOUNTING SYSTEM. A formal communications network that supplies relevant information for planning, control, decision making, and evaluation. Accounting systems are judged by how they help promote and impel personnel toward organizational goals.

ACTIVITY ACCOUNTING. *See* Responsibility accounting.

ALLOCATION. Assigning one or more items of cost or revenue to one or more segments of an organization according to benefits received, responsibilities, or other logical measures of use.

APPROPRIATION. An authorization to spend up to a specified dollar amount.

ASSET TURNOVER. The ratio of sales to total assets available.

ATTENTION DIRECTING. That function of the accountant's information-supplying task which focuses problems in the operation of the firm or which points out imperfections or inefficiencies in certain areas of the firm's operation.

844

BILL OF MATERIALS.   A specification of the quantities of direct materials allowed for manufacturing a given quantity of output.

BOOK VALUE METHOD.   *See* Unadjusted rate of return.

BREAKEVEN POINT.   That level of operations where total costs equal total revenue.

BUDGET.   A plan of action expressed in figures.

BUDGET VARIANCE (SPENDING VARIANCE).   The difference between the amount incurred and the budget figure.

BY-PRODUCTS.   Joint products that have minor sales value as compared with that of the major or chief product(s).

CAPACITY COSTS.   An alternate term for *fixed costs*, emphasizing the fact that fixed costs are needed in order to provide operating facilities and an organization ready to produce and sell at a planned volume of activity.

CAPITAL BUDGETING.   Long-term planning for proposed capital outlays and their financing.

CASH BUDGET.   A schedule of expected cash receipts and disbursements.

CASH FLOW.   The net effect of cash receipts and disbursements for a specified period.

COMMITTED COSTS.   Those fixed costs arising from the possession of plant and equipment and a basic organization and, thus, affected primarily by long-run decisions as to the desired level of capacity.

COMMON COST.   *See* Joint cost.

COMPTROLLER.   *See* Controller.

CONTINUOUS BUDGET.   A budget which perpetually adds a month or quarter in the future as the month or quarter just ended is dropped.

CONTRIBUTION APPROACH.   A method of preparing income statements which separates variable costs from fixed costs in order to emphasize the importance of cost behavior patterns for purposes of planning and control.

CONTRIBUTION MARGIN.   Excess of sales price over variable expenses. Also called *marginal income*. May be expressed as a total, a ratio, or on a per-unit basis.

CONTROL CHART.   A scatter diagram that helps to distinguish chance variances from variances that need investigation. Used in statistical quality control situations.

CONTROLLABLE COST.   A cost which may be directly regulated at a given level of managerial authority, either in the short run or in the long run.

CONTROLLER. The chief management accounting executive. Also spelled *comptroller*.

CONTROLLING. Obtaining conformity to plans through action and evaluation.

CONVERSION COST. The sum of direct labor and factory overhead.

COST ACCOUNTING. A quantitative method that accumulates, classifies, summarizes, and interprets information for three major purposes: (1) operational planning and control, (2) special decisions, and (3) product costing.

COST CENTER. The smallest unit of activity or area of responsibility for which costs are accumulated.

COST OF GOODS SOLD. Inventoriable costs released to the current period (an expense) as a result of the sale of goods.

COSTS OF CARRYING. The unavoidable costs of carrying inventory. They are primarily interest on investment, obsolescence write-offs, and space costs. Overstocking may raise these costs to dangerous levels.

COSTS OF NOT CARRYING. These include expensive expediting, loss of sales, and loss of customer goodwill associated with carrying too little inventory. They are more difficult to measure than costs of carrying, and they are potentially more harmful.

CURRENTLY ATTAINABLE STANDARDS. Standards expressing a level of economic efficiency which can be reached with skilled, diligent, superior effort.

DATA PROCESSING. The accumulation, classification, analysis, and reporting of large quantities of information. Mechanical equipment rather than human beings are the major processors of this information.

DECISION MAKING. Choosing between alternate courses of action.

DIFFERENTIAL COST. *See* Incremental cost.

DIRECT COSTING. That type of product costing which charges fixed manufacturing overhead immediately against the revenue of the period in which it was incurred, without assigning it to specific units produced. Also called *variable costing* and *marginal costing*.

DIRECT LABOR. All labor which is obviously related and specifically and conveniently traceable to specific products.

DIRECT MATERIAL. All raw material which becomes an integral part of the finished good and which can be conveniently assigned to specific physical units.

DISCRETIONARY COSTS. Those fixed costs that arise from periodic, usually yearly, appropriation decisions that directly reflect top-management policies. Also called *managed costs* and *programmed* costs.

DISTRIBUTION COSTS. Nonmanufacturing costs of marketing, shipping, warehousing, billing, financing, and so forth.

ECONOMIC ORDER QUANTITY. The amount of inventory which should be ordered at one time in order to minimize the associated annual costs of the inventory.

EFFICIENCY VARIANCE. Quantity variance applied to labor and variable overhead.

EQUIVALENT UNITS. The number of full doses of work applied to units of product. For example, if 1,000 units are ¾ complete in terms of direct labor, then 750 equivalent units of direct labor exist.

EXCESS MATERIAL REQUISITIONS. A form to be filled out by the production staff to secure any materials needed in excess of the standard amount allotted for output.

EXPECTED ANNUAL ACTIVITY. A widely used basis for determining a fixed overhead rate.

EXPECTED VALUE. A weighted average of all the conditional values of an act. Each conditional value is weighted by its probability.

EXPIRED COST. A cost which should be released to the current period as an expense or loss.

FACTORY BURDEN. *See* Factory overhead.

FACTORY OVERHEAD. All factory costs other than direct labor and direct material. Also called *factory burden, indirect manufacturing costs, manufacturing overhead*, and *manufacturing expense* (the latter is a misnomer).

FEEDBACK. The data (performance reports and cost analyses) supplied by an accounting system for purposes of investigation, evaluation, and follow-up.

FINISHED GOODS INVENTORY. The cost of a manufacturer's completed product which is being held for sale.

FIXED COST. A cost which, for a given period of time and range of activity called the relevant range, does not change in total but becomes progressively smaller on a per-unit basis as volume increases.

FLEXIBLE BUDGET. A budget, usually referring to overhead costs only, which is prepared for a range, rather than for a single level of activity; one which can be automatically geared to changes in the level of volume. Also called *variable budget*. Direct materials and direct labor are sometimes included in the flexible budget.

FORECAST. In budgeting, a projection of what costs and revenues should be.

FUNCTIONAL AUTHORITY. The right to command action laterally and downward with regard to a specific function or specialty.

FUNCTIONAL COSTING.   Classifying costs by allocating them to the various functions performed, such as warehousing, delivery, billing, and so forth.

HISTORICAL COST.   *See* Sunk cost.

IDEAL CAPACITY.   The absolute maximum number of units that could be produced in a given operating situation, with no allowance for work stoppages or repairs. Also called *theoretical capacity*.

IDLE TIME.   A classification of indirect labor which constitutes wages paid for unproductive time due to circumstances beyond the worker's control.

IMPUTED COST.   A cost that does not appear in conventional accounting records and does not entail dollar outlays. A common example is the inclusion of "interest" on ownership equity as a part of operating expenses.

INCREMENTAL APPROACH.   In capital budgeting, a method of determining which of two alternative courses of action is preferable by calculating the present value of the difference in net cash inflow between one alternative and the other.

INCREMENTAL COST.   The difference in total cost between two alternatives. Also called *differential cost* and *relevant cost*.

INDIRECT LABOR.   All labor which is not specifically associated with or cannot be practically traced to specific units of output.

INDIRECT MANUFACTURING COSTS.   *See* Factory overhead.

INTERNAL CHECK.   The coordinated methods and measures in an organization designed to check the accuracy and validity of organization data and to safeguard assets. This definition represents parts (c) and (d) of the definition of *internal control*, a more inclusive concept.

INTERNAL CONTROL.   The coordinated methods and measures in an organization designed to: (a) promote efficiency; (b) encourage adherence to prescribed management plans and policies; (c) check the accuracy and validity of organization data; and (d) safeguard assets.

INVENTORIABLE COST.   A cost associated with units produced; a cost which may be looked upon as "attaching" or "clinging" to units produced.

JOB COST SHEET.   *See* Job order.

JOB ORDER.   The basic record for the accumulation of job costs. Also called *job cost sheet*.

JOB ORDER COSTING.   A system of applying manufacturing costs to specific jobs or batches of specialized or unique production in proportion to the amounts of materials, attention, and effort used to produce each unit or group of units.

JOINT COST.   A cost which is common to all the segments in question and which is not clearly or practically allocable except by some questionable allocation base. Also called *common cost*.

JOINT PRODUCT COSTS.   Costs of two or more manufactured goods, of significant sales values, that are produced by a single process and that are not identifiable as individual products up to a certain stage of production known as the *split-off point*.

LEAD TIME.   The time interval between placing an order and receiving delivery.

LINEAR PROGRAMMING.   A mathematical approach to a group of business problems which contain many interacting variables and which basically involve combining limited resources to maximize profits or minimize costs.

LINE AUTHORITY.   Authority which is exerted downward over subordinates.

MANAGED COSTS.   *See* Discretionary costs.

MANAGEMENT BY EXCEPTION.   The practice, by the executive, of focusing his attention mainly on significant deviations from expected results. It might also be called *management by variance*.

MANAGEMENT SCIENCE.   The formulation of mathematical and statistical models applied to decision making and the practical application of these models through the use of digital computers.

MANUFACTURING EXPENSES.   *See* Factory overhead.

MANUFACTURING OVERHEAD.   *See* Factory overhead.

MARGINAL COSTING.   *See* Direct costing.

MARGINAL INCOME.   *See* Contribution margin.

MARGIN ON SALES.   The ratio of net income to sales.

MASTER BUDGET.   The budget which consolidates the organization's overall plans.

MERCHANDISE INVENTORY.   The inventory held by a retailer or wholesaler which is intended solely for resale.

MIXED COST.   A cost that has both fixed and variable elements.

NEGOTIATED MARKET PRICE.   A transfer price negotiated by the buying and selling segments when there is no market mechanism to fix a price clearly relevant to the situation.

NET PRESENT VALUE METHOD.   A method of calculating the expected utility of a given project by discounting all expected future cash flows to the present, using some predetermined minimum desired rate of return.

NORMAL ACTIVITY (NORMAL VOLUME, STANDARD VOLUME, OR STANDARD ACTIVITY). The level of production that will satisfy average consumer demand over a span of time which includes seasonal, cyclical, and trend factors.

NORMAL CAPACITY. *See* Normal activity.

NORMAL COSTING. A type of product costing which applies to units produced, as costs of production, the actual direct materials consumed, the actual direct labor used, and an estimated, predetermined portion of overhead calculated on the basis of a normal or average schedule of production.

NORMAL SPOILAGE. Spoilage expected during a production run under efficient operating conditions.

ON-LINE, REAL-TIME. Computer compilation of information as events occur (on-line) and supplying the relevant information rapidly enough so that interested managers may exert needed control (real-time).

OPERATIONS RESEARCH (OR). A diffused collection of mathematical and statistical models applied to decision making.

OPPORTUNITY COST. The maximum alternative earning that might have been obtained if the productive good, service, or capacity had been applied to some alternative use.

ORDER-FILLING COST. A marketing cost incurred in the storing, packing, shipping, billing, credit and collection, and other similar aspects of selling merchandise.

ORDER-GETTING COST. A marketing cost incurred in the effort to attain a desired sales volume and mix.

ORDER POINT. That level of inventory which should trigger a reorder of goods. It is usually measured by the safety stock plus average usage during lead time.

ORGANIZATION CHART. A drawing of the lines of authority and responsibility in an organization.

OUT-OF-POCKET COSTS. Costs which entail current or near-future outlays for the decision at hand.

OVERABSORBED OVERHEAD. *See* Overapplied overhead.

OVERAPPLIED OVERHEAD. The excess of amount of overhead cost applied to product over the amount of overhead cost incurred. Also called *overabsorbed overhead*.

OVERTIME PREMIUM. A classification of *indirect labor costs*, consisting of the extra wages paid to *all* factory workers for overtime work.

PAYBACK. The measure of the time needed to recoup, in the form of cash inflow from operations, the initial dollars invested. Also called *payout* and *payoff*.

PAYBACK RECIPROCAL.   This approximates the true rate of return when the life of the project is at least twice the payback period and when cash inflows are uniform.

PAYOFF TABLE.   A convenient technique for showing the total expected value of each of a number of contemplated acts in the light of the varying probabilities of the events which may take place and the varying values of each act under each of the events.

PAYOUT.   *See* Payback.

PERFORMANCE REPORT.   The comparison of actual results with budgeted allowances.

PERIOD COST.   *See* Expired cost.

PERIODIC INVENTORY METHOD.   An inventory accounting system which requires a physical count of inventory to determine the ending amounts of raw materials, work in process, and finished goods, and hence also the cost of goods sold.

PERPETUAL INVENTORY METHOD.   An inventory accounting system whereby a continuous record is kept which tracks raw materials, work in process, finished goods, and cost of goods sold on a day-to-day basis.

PERT.   (Program Evaluation and Review Technique).   A formal probabilistic diagram of the temporal interrelationships of a complex series of activities.

PLANNING.   Selecting objectives and the means for their attainment.

POPULATION (universe).   A group of items or individuals from which a sample is drawn.

PRACTICAL ATTAINABLE CAPACITY.   *See* Practical capacity.

PRACTICAL CAPACITY.   The maximum level at which the plant or department can realistically operate most efficiently, that is, ideal capacity less allowances for unavoidable operating interruptions.   Also called *practical attainable capacity*.

PRICE VARIANCE.   The difference between the actual price and the standard price, multiplied by the total number of items acquired.   The term "price variance" is usually linked with direct materials; the term "rate variance," which is conceptually similar to the price variance, is usually linked with direct labor.

PRIME COST.   The sum of direct material and direct labor.

PROBLEM SOLVING.   That function of the accountant's information-supplying task which expresses in concise, quantified terms the relative advantages and disadvantages to the firm of pursuing a possible future course of action, or the relative advantages of any one of several alternative methods of operation.

PROCESS COSTING. A method of costing products with average costs computed on the basis of total costs divided by equivalent units of work performed. Usually used in high-volume, similar-product situations.

PRODUCT COST. *See* Inventoriable cost.

PROFITABILITY ACCOUNTING. *See* Responsibility accounting.

PROFIT CENTER. A segment of a business that is responsible for both revenue and expense.

PRO-FORMA STATEMENTS. Forecasted financial statements.

PROGRAM. A list of instructions which indicates to a computer the nature and sequence of operations it is to perform.

PROGRAMMED COSTS. *See* Discretionary costs.

PROJECT SELECTION. *See* Capital budgeting.

QUALITATIVE FACTOR. A factor which is of consequence but which cannot be measured precisely and easily in dollars.

QUALITY CONTROL. A statistical sampling application which spotlights controllable variances.

QUANTITY DISCOUNT. A reduction in unit price inversely proportional to the size of the order. Usually constrained by the Robinson-Patman Act.

QUANTITY VARIANCE. The standard price for a given resource, multiplied by the difference between the actual quantity used and the total standard quantity allowed for the number of good units produced.

QUOTE SHEET. An analysis of costs used as a basis for determining selling prices.

RATE VARIANCE. The difference between actual wages paid and the standard wage rate, multiplied by the total actual hours of direct labor used. *See* Price variance.

REAPPORTIONMENT. Allocation of the costs of operating the service departments to the various production departments in proportion to the relative benefits or services received by each production department.

RELATIVE SALES VALUE METHOD. A method of joint-cost assignment which assigns costs in proportion to a product's ability to absorb the costs.

RELEVANT COST. *See* Incremental cost.

RELEVANT DATA FOR DECISION MAKING. Expected future data which will differ as between alternatives.

RELEVANT RANGE. The band of activity in which budgeted sales and expense relationships will be valid.

RESPONSIBILITY ACCOUNTING. A system of accounting which recognizes various responsibility centers throughout the organization and which reflects the plans and actions of each of these centers by allocating particular revenues and costs to the one having the pertinent responsibility. Also called *profitability accounting* and *activity accounting*.

RETURN ON INVESTMENT (rate of return). The most widely used single measure of a firm's operating efficiency. It is the ratio of net income to invested capital or asset turnover times margin on sales.

SAFETY STOCK. A minimum inventory that provides a cushion against reasonably expected maximum demand and against variations in lead time.

SALES MIX. The relative combination of the quantities of a variety of company products that compose total sales.

SAMPLE. A portion of a group (population or universe) chosen to estimate some characteristic of the entire group without complete examination of all the items constituting the group.

SCORE KEEPING. That data-accumulation function of the accountant's information-supplying task which enables both internal and external parties to evaluate the financial performance of the firm.

SCRAP. Residue from manufacturing operations that has measurable but relatively minor recovery value.

SEGMENT. Any line of activity or part of an organization for which separate determination of costs and/or sales is wanted.

SEGMENT MARGIN. The contribution margin for each segment less all separable fixed costs, both discretionary and committed. A measure of long-run profitability.

SEPARABLE COST. A cost directly identifiable with a particular segment.

SERVICE DEPARTMENTS. Those departments that exist solely to aid the production departments by rendering specialized assistance with certain phases of the work.

SHORT-RUN PERFORMANCE MARGIN. The contribution margin for each segment, less separable discretionary costs.

SHUTDOWN COST. A fixed cost which continues to be incurred even when there is no activity (production).

SOURCE DOCUMENT. The original record of any transaction, internal or external, which occurs in the firm's operation.

SPENDING VARIANCE. Basically, a price variance applied to variable overhead. However, other factors besides prices may influence the amount of the variance.

SPLIT-OFF POINT. That point in a production process where goods with joint costs are separated.

STAFF AUTHORITY. The authority to *advise* but not to command; may be exerted laterally or upward.

STANDARD ABSORPTION COSTING. That type of product costing in which the cost of the finished unit is calculated as the sum of the costs of the standard allowances for the factors of production, without reference to the costs actually incurred.

STANDARD COST. A carefully predetermined cost that should be attained. Usually expressed per unit.

STANDARD DIRECT COSTING. That type of product costing in which the cost of the finished unit is calculated as the sum of the costs of the *standard allowances* for the factors of production, *excluding* fixed factory overhead, which is treated as a period cost, and without reference to the costs actually incurred.

STANDARD HOURS ALLOWED (earned or worked). The number of standard hours that are chargeable to production for the actual goods produced.

STATIC BUDGET. A budget prepared for only one level of activity and, consequently, one which does not adjust automatically to changes in the level of volume.

STEP-VARIABLE COSTS. Those variable costs which change abruptly at intervals of activity because their acquisition comes in indivisible chunks.

SUNK COST. A cost which has already been incurred and which, therefore, is irrelevant to the decision-making process. Also called *historical cost*.

TAX SHIELD. The amount of depreciation charged against income, thus protecting that amount from tax.

THEORETICAL CAPACITY. *See* Ideal capacity.

TIME-ADJUSTED RATE OF RETURN. The rate of interest at which the present value of expected cash inflow from a particular project equals the present value of expected cash outflow of that same project.

TOTAL PROJECT APPROACH. A method of comparing two or more alternative courses of action by computing the total expected cash inflows and outflows of each alternative and then converting these flows to their present value by applying some predetermined minimum rate of return.

TRANSFER PRICE. The price charged by one segment of an organization for a product or service which it supplies to another segment of the same organization.

TREASURER. The custodian of cash in a business organization.

UNADJUSTED RATE OF RETURN. An expression of the utility of a given project as the ratio of the increase in future average annual net income to the initial increase in required investment. Also called *book value method* and *accounting method*.

UNDERABSORBED OVERHEAD.   *See* Underapplied overhead.

UNDERAPPLIED OVERHEAD.   The excess of the amount of overhead cost incurred over the amount of overhead cost applied. Also called *underabsorbed overhead*.

UNEXPIRED COST.   A cost which may be properly carried forward to future periods as an asset measure.

UNIT COST.   A total cost divided by some related base, such as labor hours, machine-hours, or units of product.

USAGE VARIANCE.   *See* Quantity variance.

VARIABLE BUDGET.   *See* Flexible budget.

VARIABLE COST.   A cost which is uniform *per unit*, but which fluctuates *in total* in direct proportion to changes in the related total activity or volume.

VARIABLE COSTING.   *See* Direct costing.

VARIANCE.   The deviation of actual results from the expected or budgeted result.

WORK IN PROCESS INVENTORY.   The cost of uncompleted goods still on the production line.

index

Note: See also the glossary,
pages 844–855.

ABC METHOD, INVENTORY CLASSI-
FICATION, 533–534

ABSORPTION COSTING:
compared with direct costing,
305–309
definition, 305–306
income statement, illustrated,
307, 310
relevant costing, 323–325

ACCOUNTANT:
future, 12
operations research, 822–823
communications, 275
role, 8–9, 277, 405–406, 701–702
staff position, 8
statistics, 800
view of variable costs, 195–196

ACCOUNTING:
data processing, 723–737
function, 3–5
management cycle, 5
planning and control, 5

ACCOUNTING METHOD OF RATE-OF-
RETURN:
compared with other methods,
465–468
equation, 463
investment base, 463–465
post audit, 467

ACCOUNTING RECORDS, MOTIVATION
DEVICE, 284–285

ACCOUNTING SYSTEM, 699–715, 723–
737:
classification of accounts, 710–
711
control function, 702–706
criteria for design, 700
data processing, 723–737
factory ledger, 710–713
function, 700

857

J

L

P

W